Market Risk Analysis
Volume II

Practical Financial Econometrics

Market Risk Analysis
Volume II

Practical Financial Econometrics

Carol Alexander

John Wiley & Sons, Ltd

Published in 2008 by   John Wiley & Sons Ltd, The Atrium, Southern Gate, Chichester,
West Sussex PO19 8SQ, England

Telephone   (+44) 1243 779777

Email (for orders and customer service enquiries): cs-books@wiley.co.uk
Visit our Home Page on www.wiley.com

Other Wiley Editorial Offices

John Wiley & Sons Inc., 111 River Street, Hoboken, NJ 07030, USA

Jossey-Bass, 989 Market Street, San Francisco, CA 94103-1741, USA

Wiley-VCH Verlag GmbH, Boschstr. 12, D-69469 Weinheim, Germany

John Wiley & Sons Australia Ltd, 42 McDougall Street, Milton, Queensland 4064, Australia

John Wiley & Sons (Asia) Pte Ltd, 2 Clementi Loop #02-01, Jin Xing Distripark, Singapore 129809

John Wiley & Sons Canada Ltd, 6045 Freemont Blvd, Mississauga, Ontario, Canada L5R 4J3

Wiley also publishes its books in a variety of electronic formats. Some content that appears in print may
not be available in electronic books.

British Library Cataloguing in Publication Data

A catalogue record for this book is available from the British Library

ISBN 978-0-470-99801-4 (H/B)

Typeset in 10/12pt Times by Integra Software Services Pvt. Ltd, Pondicherry, India
Printed and bound in Great Britain by CPI Group (UK) Ltd, Croydon, CR0 4YY

To Rick van der Ploeg

Contents

List of Figures

List of Tables

List of Examples

Foreword

How many children dream of one day becoming risk managers? I very much doubt little Carol Jenkins, as she was called then, did. She dreamt about being a wild white horse, or a mermaid swimming with dolphins, as any normal little girl does. As I start crunching into two kilos of Toblerone that Carol Alexander-Pézier gave me for Valentine's day (perhaps to coax me into writing this foreword), I see the distinctive silhouette of the Matterhorn on the yellow package and I am reminded of my own dreams of climbing mountains and travelling to distant planets. Yes, adventure and danger! That is the stuff of happiness, especially when you daydream as a child with a warm cup of cocoa in your hands.

As we grow up, dreams lose their naivety but not necessarily their power. Knowledge makes us discover new possibilities and raises new questions. We grow to understand better the consequences of our actions, yet the world remains full of surprises. We taste the sweetness of success and the bitterness of failure. We grow to be responsible members of society and to care for the welfare of others. We discover purpose, confidence and a role to fulfil; but we also find that we continuously have to deal with risks.

Leafing through the hundreds of pages of this four-volume series you will discover one of the goals that Carol gave herself in life: to set the standards for a new profession, that of market risk manager, and to provide the means of achieving those standards. Why is market risk management so important? Because in our modern economies, market prices balance the supply and demand of most goods and services that fulfil our needs and desires. We can hardly take a decision, such as buying a house or saving for a later day, without taking some market risks. Financial firms, be they in banking, insurance or asset management, manage these risks on a grand scale. Capital markets and derivative products offer endless ways to transfer these risks among economic agents.

But should market risk management be regarded as a professional activity? Sampling the material in these four volumes will convince you, if need be, of the vast amount of knowledge and skills required. A good market risk manager should master the basics of calculus, linear algebra, probability – including stochastic calculus – statistics and econometrics. He should be an astute student of the markets, familiar with the vast array of modern financial instruments and market mechanisms, and of the econometric properties of prices and returns in these markets. If he works in the financial industry, he should also be well versed in regulations and understand how they affect his firm. That sets the academic syllabus for the profession.

Carol takes the reader step by step through all these topics, from basic definitions and principles to advanced problems and solution methods. She uses a clear language, realistic illustrations with recent market data, consistent notation throughout all chapters, and provides a huge range of worked-out exercises on Excel spreadsheets, some of which demonstrate analytical tools only available in the best commercial software packages. Many chapters on advanced subjects such as GARCH models, copulas, quantile regressions, portfolio theory, options and volatility surfaces are as informative as and easier to understand than entire books devoted to these subjects. Indeed, this is the first series of books entirely dedicated to the discipline of market risk analysis written by one person, and a very good teacher at that.

A profession, however, is more than an academic discipline; it is an activity that fulfils some societal needs, that provides solutions in the face of evolving challenges, that calls for a special code of conduct; it is something one can aspire to. Does market risk management face such challenges? Can it achieve significant economic benefits?

As market economies grow, more ordinary people of all ages with different needs and risk appetites have financial assets to manage and borrowings to control. What kind of mortgages should they take? What provisions should they make for their pensions? The range of investment products offered to them has widened far beyond the traditional cash, bond and equity classes to include actively managed funds (traditional or hedge funds), private equity, real estate investment trusts, structured products and derivative products facilitating the trading of more exotic risks – commodities, credit risks, volatilities and correlations, weather, carbon emissions, etc. – and offering markedly different return characteristics from those of traditional asset classes. Managing personal finances is largely about managing market risks. How well educated are we to do that?

Corporates have also become more exposed to market risks. Beyond the traditional exposure to interest rate fluctuations, most corporates are now exposed to foreign exchange risks and commodity risks because of globalization. A company may produce and sell exclusively in its domestic market and yet be exposed to currency fluctuations because of foreign competition. Risks that can be hedged effectively by shareholders, if they wish, do not have to be hedged in-house. But hedging some risks in-house may bring benefits (e.g. reduction of tax burden, smoothing of returns, easier planning) that are not directly attainable by the shareholder.

Financial firms, of course, should be the experts at managing market risks; it is their métier. Indeed, over the last generation, there has been a marked increase in the size of market risks handled by banks in comparison to a reduction in the size of their credit risks. Since the 1980s, banks have provided products (e.g. interest rate swaps, currency protection, index linked loans, capital guaranteed investments) to facilitate the risk management of their customers. They have also built up arbitrage and proprietary trading books to profit from perceived market anomalies and take advantage of their market views. More recently, banks have started to manage credit risks actively by transferring them to the capital markets instead of warehousing them. Bonds are replacing loans, mortgages and other loans are securitized, and many of the remaining credit risks can now be covered with credit default swaps. Thus credit risks are being converted into market risks.

The rapid development of capital markets and, in particular, of derivative products bears witness to these changes. At the time of writing this foreword, the total notional size of all derivative products exceeds $500 trillion whereas, in rough figures, the bond and money markets stand at about $80 trillion, the equity markets half that and loans half that again. Credit derivatives by themselves are climbing through the $30 trillion mark. These derivative markets are zero-sum games; they are all about market risk management – hedging, arbitrage and speculation.

This does not mean, however, that all market risk management problems have been resolved. We may have developed the means and the techniques, but we do not necessarily understand how to address the problems. Regulators and other experts setting standards and policies are particularly concerned with several fundamental issues. To name a few:

1. How do we decide what market risks should be assessed and over what time horizons? For example, should the loan books of banks or long-term liabilities of pension funds be marked to market, or should we not be concerned with pricing things that will not be traded in the near future? We think there is no general answer to this question about the most appropriate description of risks. The descriptions must be adapted to specific management problems.

2. In what contexts should market risks be assessed? Thus, what is more risky, fixed or floating rate financing? Answers to such questions are often dictated by accounting standards or other conventions that must be followed and therefore take on economic significance. But the adequacy of standards must be regularly reassessed. To wit, the development of International Accounting Standards favouring mark-to-market and hedge accounting where possible (whereby offsetting risks can be reported together).

3. To what extent should risk assessments be 'objective'? Modern regulations of financial firms (Basel II Amendment, 1996) have been a major driver in the development of risk assessment methods. Regulators naturally want a 'level playing field' and objective rules. This reinforces a natural tendency to assess risks purely on the basis of statistical evidence and to neglect personal, forward-looking views. Thus one speaks too often about risk 'measurements' as if risks were physical objects instead of risk 'assessments' indicating that risks are potentialities that can only be guessed by making a number of assumptions (i.e. by using models). Regulators try to compensate for this tendency by asking risk managers to draw scenarios and to stress-test their models.

There are many other fundamental issues to be debated, such as the natural tendency to focus on micro risk management – because it is easy – rather than to integrate all significant risks and to consider their global effect – because that is more difficult. In particular, the assessment and control of systemic risks by supervisory authorities is still in its infancy. But I would like to conclude by calling attention to a particular danger faced by a nascent market risk management profession, that of separating risks from returns and focusing on downside-risk limits.

It is central to the ethics of risk managers to be independent and to act with integrity. Thus risk managers should not be under the direct control of line managers of profit centres and they should be well remunerated independently of company results. But in some firms this is also understood as denying risk managers access to profit information. I remember a risk commission that had to approve or reject projects but, for internal political reasons, could not have any information about their expected profitability. For decades, credit officers in most banks operated under such constraints: they were supposed to accept or reject deals a priori, without knowledge of their pricing. Times have changed. We understand now, at least in principle, that the essence of risk management is not simply to reduce or control risks but to achieve an optimal balance between risks and returns.

Yet, whether for organizational reasons or out of ignorance, risk management is often confined to setting and enforcing risk limits. Most firms, especially financial firms, claim to have well-thought-out risk management policies, but few actually state trade-offs between risks and returns. Attention to risk limits may be unwittingly reinforced by regulators. Of course it is not the role of the supervisory authorities to suggest risk–return trade-offs; so supervisors impose risk limits, such as value at risk relative to capital, to ensure safety and fair competition in the financial industry. But a regulatory limit implies severe penalties if breached, and thus a probabilistic constraint acquires an economic value. Banks must therefore pay attention to the uncertainty in their value-at-risk estimates. The effect would be rather perverse if banks ended up paying more attention to the probability of a probability than to their entire return distribution.

With *Market Risk Analysis* readers will learn to understand these long-term problems in a realistic context. Carol is an academic with a strong applied interest. She has helped to design the curriculum for the Professional Risk Managers' International Association (PRMIA) qualifications, to set the standards for their professional qualifications, and she maintains numerous contacts with the financial industry through consulting and seminars. In *Market Risk Analysis* theoretical developments may be more rigorous and reach a more advanced level than in many other books, but they always lead to practical applications with numerous examples in interactive Excel spreadsheets. For example, unlike 90% of the finance literature on hedging that is of no use to practitioners, if not misleading at times, her concise expositions on this subject give solutions to real problems.

In summary, if there is any good reason for not treating market risk management as a separate discipline, it is that market risk management should be the business of *all* decision makers involved in finance, with primary responsibilities on the shoulders of the most senior managers and board members. However, there is so much to be learnt and so much to be further researched on this subject that it is proper for professional people to specialize in it. These four volumes will fulfil most of their needs. They only have to remember that, to be effective, they have to be good communicators and ensure that their assessments are properly integrated in their firm's decision-making process.

Jacques Pézier

Preface to Volume II

For well over a decade, econometrics has been one of the major routes into finance. I took this route myself several years ago. Starting an academic career as an algebraist, I then had a brief encounter with game theory before discovering that the skills of an econometrician were in greater demand. I would have found econometrics much more boring than algebra or game theory had it not been for the inspiration of some great teachers at the London School of Economics, and of Professor Robert Engle who introduced me to GARCH models some twenty years ago.

At that time finance was one of the newest areas of applied econometrics and it was relatively easy to find interesting problems that were also useful to practitioners. And this was how my reputation grew, such as it is. I was building GARCH models for banks well before they became standard procedures in statistical packages, applying cointegration to construct arbitrage strategies for fund managers and introducing models for forecasting very large covariance matrices. In the end the appreciation of this work was much greater than the appreciation I received as an academic so I moved, briefly, to the City. Then, almost a decade ago, I returned to academic life as a professor of financial risk management. In fact, I believe I was the first professor to have this title in the UK, financial risk management being such a new profession at that time. It was the late 1990s, and by then numerous econometricians were taking the same route into finance that I had. Some of the top finance journals were populating many of their pages with applied financial econometrics, and theoretical econometric journals were becoming increasingly focused on financial problems. Of course I wanted to read and learn all about this so that I could publish the academic papers that are so important to our profession. But I was disappointed and a little dismayed by what I read. Too few of the papers were written by authors who seemed to have a proper grasp of the important practical problems in finance. And too much journal space was devoted to topics that are at best marginal and at worst completely irrelevant to financial practitioners.

Econometrics has now become a veritable motorway into finance where, for many, prospects are presently more lucrative than those for standard macro- or micro-economists. The industry has enormous demand for properly trained financial econometricians, and this demand will increase. But few econometricians enter the industry with an adequate knowledge of how their skills can be employed to the best advantage of their firm and its clients, and many financial econometricians would benefit from improving their understanding of what constitutes an important problem.

AIMS AND SCOPE

This book introduces the econometric techniques that are commonly applied to finance, and particularly to resolve problems in market risk analysis. It aims to fill a gap in the market by offering a critical text on econometrics that discuss what is and what is not important to financial practitioners. The book covers material for a one-semester graduate course in applied financial econometrics in a very pedagogical fashion. Each time a concept is introduced, an empirical example is given, and whenever possible this is illustrated with an Excel spreadsheet.

In comparison with Greene (2007), which has become a standard graduate econometrics text and which contains more than enough material for a one-year course, I have been very selective in the topics covered. The main focus is on models that use time series data, and relatively few formal proofs are given. However, every chapter has numerous empirical examples that are implemented in Excel spreadsheets, many of which are interactive. And when the practical illustration of the model requires a more detailed exposition, case studies are included. More details are given in the section about the CD-ROM below.

Econometrics is a broad discipline that draws on basic techniques in calculus, linear algebra, probability, statistics and numerical methods. Readers should also have a rudimentary knowledge of regression analysis and the first chapter, which is on factor model, refers to the capital asset pricing model and other models derived from the theory of asset pricing. All the prerequisite material is covered *Market Risk Analysis* Volume I: *Quantitative Methods in Finance*. However, there is only one chapter on basic regression in Volume I. A very comprehensive introductory text, written at a more elementary level than this but also aimed towards the finance student market, is Brooks (2008). For many years Professor Chris Brooks has been a close colleague at the ICMA Centre.

The other volumes in *Market Risk Analysis* are Volume III: *Pricing, Hedging and Trading Financial Instruments* and Volume IV: *Value at Risk Models*. Although the four volumes of *Market Risk Analysis* are very much interlinked, each book is self-contained. This book could easily be adopted as a stand-alone course text in applied financial econometrics, leaving students to follow up cross-references to other volumes only if they wish.

OUTLINE OF VOLUME II

Chapter 1, *Factor Models*, describes the models that are applied by portfolio managers to analyse the potential returns on a portfolio of risky assets, to determine the allocation of their funds to different assets and to measure portfolio risk. The chapter deals with models having fundamental factors and which are normally estimated by regression. We focus on the Barra model, giving a detailed description of its construction, and emphasizing the dangers of using tracking error as a risk metric for actively managed portfolios.

Chapter 2, *Principal Component Analysis*, covers statistical factor models, which are also used for portfolio management and risk management, but they are most successful when applied to a highly correlated system such as a term structure of interest rates, of futures prices or of volatility. Since it is not easy to find a complete treatment of principal component analysis in a finance-oriented text, we provide full details of the mathematics but, as usual, we focus on the applications. Empirical examples include bond portfolio immunization, asset–liability management and portfolio risk assessment.

Chapter 3, *Classical Models of Volatility and Correlation*, provides a critical review of the time series models that became popular in the industry during the 1990s, making readers aware of the pitfalls of using simple moving averages for estimating and forecasting portfolio risk. These are based on the assumption that returns are independent and identically distributed so the volatility and correlation forecasts from these models are equal to the current estimates. The sample estimates vary over time, but this is only due to sampling error. There is nothing in the model to capture the volatility and correlation clustering that is commonly observed in financial asset returns.

Chapter 4, *Introduction to GARCH Models*, provides a complete and up-to-date treatment of the generalized autoregressive conditional heteroscedasticity models that were introduced by Engle (1982) and Bollerslev (1986). We explain how to: estimate the model parameters by maximizing a likelihood function; use the model to forecast term structures for volatility and correlation; target the long term volatility or correlation and use the GARCH model to forecast volatility and correlation over the short and medium term; and extend the model to capture non-normal conditional returns distributions and regime-switching volatility behaviour. There are so many approaches to modelling multivariate distributions with time varying volatility and correlation that I have been very prescriptive in my treatment of multivariate GARCH models, recommending specific approaches for different financial problems. Throughout this long chapter we illustrate the GARCH model optimization with simple Excel spreadsheets, employing the Excel Solver whenever possible. Excel parameter estimates for GARCH are not recommended, so the estimates are compared with those obtained using GARCH procedures in the Matlab and EViews software. The section on simulation is enlightening, since it demonstrates that only regime-switching GARCH models can properly capture the observed behaviour of financial asset returns. The final section covers the numerous applications of GARCH models to finance, including option pricing, risk measurement and portfolio optimization.

Chapter 5 is on *Time Series Models and Cointegration*. Building on the introduction to stochastic processes given in Chapter I.3, this begins with a mathematical introduction to stationary and integrated processes, multivariate vector autoregressions and unit root tests. Then we provide an intuitive definition of cointegration and review the huge literature on applications of cointegration in financial markets. A case study focuses on the benchmark tracking and statistical arbitrage applications that I developed more than a decade ago, and which are now used by major fund managers. The final section provides a didactic approach to modelling short term dynamics using error correction models, focusing on the response of cointegrated asset prices to market shocks and the time taken for a spread to mean-revert. Another case study examines pairs trading volatility indices.

Chapter 6, *Introduction to Copulas*, took much longer to write than the other chapters. I was less familiar with copulas than with the other topics in this book, and found the available literature a little obscure and off-putting. However, copulas are of crucial importance to the development of our subject and no reputable financial econometrician can afford to ignore them. So it became quite a challenge to present this material in the pedagogical style of the rest of the book. I have programmed several copulas, including the normal, normal mixture, Student's t, Clayton and Gumbel copulas, in interactive Excel spreadsheets, so that you can see how the shape of the copula alters on changing its parameters. The quantile curves of conditional copulas play a crucial role in financial applications – for instance, in quantile regression – so these have been derived mathematically and also encoded into Excel. Many other applications such as value-at-risk measurement, portfolio optimization and risk aggregation, which are discussed in the last section of the chapter, are based on simulation with copulas. Two simulation algorithms are described and spreadsheets generate simulations based on different copulas.

Chapter 7 covers the *Advanced Econometric Models* that have important applications to finance. A significant portion of this chapter provides a tutorial on quantile regression, and contains two case studies in Excel. The first implements linear and non-linear quantile regressions to examine the relationship between an equity index and its volatility, and the second demonstrates how non-linear quantile regression using copulas can be applied to hedge a portfolio with futures. A relatively brief treatment of other non-linear models is restricted to polynomial regression and discrete choice models, the latter being illustrated with an application to credit scoring models. What I hope is an accessible specification of Markov switching models is followed with a short review of their applications and the software that can be used for estimation, and the chapter concludes by describing the main high frequency data sets and two of the most important financial problems in high frequency data analysis. First, for capturing the clustering of the times between trades we describe the autoregressive conditional duration model. Then we review the large and growing literature on using high frequency data to forecast realized variance and covariance, this being important for pricing the variance swaps and covariance swaps that are actively traded in over-the-counter markets.

The last chapter, Chapter 8 on *Forecasting and Model Evaluation*, describes how to select the best model when several models are available. The model specification and evaluation criteria and tests described here include goodness-of-fit criteria and tests, which measure the success of a model to capture the empirical characteristics of the estimation sample, and post-sample prediction criteria and tests, which judge the ability of the model to provide accurate forecasts. Models for the conditional expectation, volatility and correlation of financial asset returns that were introduced in earlier chapters are considered here, and we explain how to apply both statistical and operational criteria and tests to these models. Amongst the statistical tests, we emphasize the Kolmogorov–Smirnoff and related tests for the proximity of two distributions and the coverage tests that are applied to evaluate models for predicting quantiles of conditional distributions. We also explain how to simulate the critical values of non-standard test statistics. A long section on operational evaluation first outlines the model backtesting procedure in general terms, and then explains how backtests are applied in specific contexts, including tests of: factor models used in portfolio management; covariance matrices used for portfolio optimization and value-at-risk estimation; and models that are used for short term hedging with futures, trading implied volatility, trading variance swaps and hedging options

ABOUT THE CD-ROM

Whenever possible the econometric models, tests and criteria that are introduced in this book are illustrated in an Excel spreadsheet. The Excel workbooks for each chapter may be found on the accompanying CD-ROM. Many of the spreadsheets are interactive, so readers may change any parameters of the problem (the parameters are indicated in *red*) and see the new solution (the output is indicated in *blue*). Rather than using VBA code, which will be obscure to many readers, I have encoded the formulae directly into the spreadsheet. Thus the reader need only click on a cell to read the formula. Whenever a data analysis tool such as regression or a numerical tool such as Solver is used, clear instructions are given in the text, and/or using comments and screenshots in the spreadsheet. Hence, the spreadsheets are designed to offer tutors the possibility to set, as exercises for their courses, an unlimited number of variations on the examples in the text.

Excel is not always an adequate program for estimating econometric models, and I have been particularly emphatic on this point for the spreadsheets that estimate GARCH model parameters. Excel has its limits in other respects, too, and so references to and recommendations of proper econometric programs are given where necessary. For instance, the CD-ROM includes the EViews code for Markov switching models that was written by my PhD student Andreas Kaeck.

Several case studies, based on complete and up-to-date financial data, and all graphs and tables in the text are also contained in the Excel workbooks on the CD-ROM. The case study data can be used by tutors or researchers since they were obtained from free internet sources, and references for updating the data are provided. Also the graphs and tables can be modified if required, and copied and pasted as enhanced metafiles into lecture notes based on this book.

ACKNOWLEDGEMENTS

I would like to express my sincere gratitude to all the past and present PhD students who have worked with me on financial econometrics. They are my motivation and very often my inspiration. These include two very talented current students, Andreas Kaeck and Stamatis Leontsinis, and a truly remarkable team of women: Dr Anca Dimitriu, now at Goldman Sachs; Dr Andreza Barbosa, now at JP Morgan-Chase; Dr Emese Lazar, now a much-valued colleague at the ICMA Centre; and Silvia Stanescu, who is still studying for her PhD. Particular thanks are due to Emese, Silvia and Andreas, who provided very useful comments on earlier drafts of several chapters, and to Joydeep Lahiri, who provided the Matlab figures of copulas densities.

Thanks to Sam Whittaker, Viv Wickham, Caitlin Cornish, Louise Holden and all the staff at Wiley, and to Richard Leigh, copy editor extraordinaire, for his extremely careful work. The Bank of England, the US Federal Reserve, Yahoo! Finance, the British Bankers' Association, European Central Bank and all the other sources of free financial data used in this book should be acknowledged. I have made considerable use of these websites and without them it would be impossible to provide such a complete set of free learning tools. Thanks also to Professor Robert Engle, of the Stern School New York, for introducing me to this subject in such an inspiring way and for his continued support.

But most of all, thanks to Ronnie Barnes and Philippe Derome. We first 'met' when they, independently, contacted me regarding errors in the first printing of Volume I. Ever since they have been working tirelessly to help find typos, and to improve clarity, in all four books in this series. Ronnie is a highly trained mathematician with an eagle's eye and Philippe accepts nothing without rigorous examination. Entirely thanks to Ronnie and Philippe, the reprints of Volume II now have an extremely high standard of presentation.

Discussion forums and other resources for the Market Risk Analysis series are available at **www.marketriskanalysis.com**

II.1
Factor Models

II.1.1 INTRODUCTION

This chapter describes the factor models that are applied by portfolio managers to analyse the potential returns on a portfolio of risky assets, to choose the optimal allocation of their funds to different assets and to measure portfolio risk. The theory of linear regression-based factor models applies to most portfolios of risky assets, excluding options portfolios but including alternative investments such as real estate, hedge funds and volatility, as well as traditional assets such as commodities, stocks and bonds. Stocks and bonds are the major categories of risky assets, and whilst bond portfolios could be analysed using regression-based factor models a much more powerful factor analysis for bond portfolios is based on principal component analysis (see Chapter II.2).

An understanding of both multiple linear regression and matrix algebra is necessary for the analysis of multi-factor models. Therefore, we assume that readers are already familiar with matrix theory from Chapter I.2 and the theory of linear regression from Chapter I.4. We also assume that readers are familiar with the theory of asset pricing and the optimal capital allocation techniques that were introduced in Chapter I.6.

Regression-based factor models are used to forecast the expected return and the risk of a portfolio. The expected return on each asset in the portfolio is approximated as a weighted sum of the expected returns to several market risk factors. The weights are called *factor sensitivities* or, more specifically, *factor betas* and are estimated by regression. If the portfolio only has cash positions on securities in the same country then market risk factors could include broad market indices, industry factors, style factors (e.g. value, growth, momentum, size), economic factors (e.g. interest rates, inflation) or statistical factors (e.g. principal components).[1] By inputting scenarios and stress tests on the expected returns and the volatilities and correlations of these risk factors, the factor model representation allows the portfolio manager to examine expected returns under different market scenarios.

Factor models also allow the market risk manager to quantify the systematic and specific risk of the portfolio:

- The market risk management of portfolios has traditionally focused only on the *undiversifiable risk* of a portfolio. This is the risk that cannot be reduced to zero by holding a large and diversified portfolio. In the context of a factor model, which aims to relate the distribution of a portfolio's return to the distributions of its risk factor returns, we also call the undiversifiable risk the *systematic risk*. A multi-factor model, i.e. a factor model with more than one risk factor, would normally be estimated using a multiple linear regression where the dependent variable is the return on an individual asset and the

---

[1] But for international portfolios exchange rates also affect the returns, with a beta of one. And if the portfolio contains futures then zero coupon rates should also be included in the market risk factors.

independent variables are the returns on different risk factors. Then the systematic risk is identified with the risk of the factor returns and the net portfolio sensitivities to each risk factor.

- The *specific risk*, also called the *idiosyncratic risk* or *residual risk*, is the risk that is not associated with the risk factor returns. In a linear regression model of the asset return on risk factor returns, it is the risk arising from the variance of the residuals. The specific risk on an individual asset may be high, especially when the model has only a few factors to explain the asset's returns. But in a sufficiently large and diversified portfolio the specific risk may be reduced to almost zero, since the specific risks on a large number of assets in different sectors of the economy, or in different countries, tend to cancel each other out.

The outline of the chapter is as follows. Section II.1.2 explains how a single-factor model is estimated. We compare two methods for estimating factor betas and show how the total risk of the portfolio can be decomposed into the systematic risk due to risk of the factors, and the specific risk that may be diversified away by holding a sufficiently large portfolio. Section II.1.3 describes the general theory of multi-factor models and explains how they are used in style attribution analysis. We explain how multi-factor models may be applied to different types of portfolios and to decompose the total risk into components related to broad classes of risk factors. Then in Section II.1.4 we present an empirical example which shows how to estimate a fundamental factor model using time series data on the portfolio returns and the risk factor returns. We suggest a remedy for the problem of multicollinearity that arises here and indeed plagues the estimation of most fundamental factor models in practice.

Then Section II.1.5 analyses the Barra model, which is a specific multi-factor model that is widely used in portfolio management. Following on from the Barra model, we analyse the way some portfolio managers use factor models to quantify *active risk,* i.e. the risk of a fund relative to its benchmark. The focus here is to explain why it is a mistake to use *tracking error*, i.e. the volatility of the active returns, as a measure of active risk. Tracking error is a metric for active risk only when the portfolio is tracking the benchmark. Otherwise, an increase in tracking error does not indicate that active risk is increased and a decrease in tracking error does not indicate that active risk has been reduced. The active risk of actively managed funds which by design do not track a benchmark cannot be measured by tracking error. However, we show how it is possible to adjust the tracking error into a correct, but basic active risk metric. Section II.1.6 summarizes and concludes.

II.1.2   SINGLE FACTOR MODELS

This section describes how single factor models are applied to analyse the expected return on an asset, to find a portfolio of assets to suit the investor's requirements, and to measure the risk of an existing portfolio. We also interpret the meaning of a factor beta and derive a fundamental result on portfolio risk decomposition.

II.1.2.1   Single Index Model

The capital asset pricing model (CAPM) was introduced in Section I.6.4. It hypothesizes the following relationship between the expected excess return on any single risky asset and the expected excess return on the market portfolio:

$$E(R_i) - R_f = \beta_i(E(R_M) - R_f),$$

where R_i is the return on the ith risky asset, R_f is the return on the *risk free* asset, R_M is the return on the *market portfolio* and β_i is the beta of the ith risky asset. The CAPM implies the following linear model for the relationship between ordinary returns rather than excess returns:

$$E(R_i) = \alpha_i + \beta_i E(R_M), \qquad \text{(II.1.1)}$$

where $\alpha_i \neq 0$ unless $\beta_i = 1$.

The single index model is based on the expected return relationship (II.1.1) where the return X on a factor such as a broad market index is used as a proxy for the market portfolio return R_M. Thus the single index model allows one to investigate the risk and return characteristics of assets *relative* to the broad market index. More generally, if the performance of a portfolio is measured relative to a benchmark other than a broad market index, then the benchmark return is used for the factor return X.

We can express the single index model in the form

$$R_{it} = \alpha_i + \beta_i X_t + \varepsilon_{it}, \qquad \varepsilon_{it} \sim \text{i.i.d.}(0, \sigma_i^2). \qquad \text{(II.1.2)}$$

Here α_i measures the asset's expected return relative to the benchmark or index (a positive value indicates an expected outperformance and a negative value indicates an expected underperformance); β_i is the *risk factor sensitivity* of the asset; $\beta_i \sigma_X$ is the *systematic volatility* of the asset, σ_X being the volatility of the index returns; and σ_i is the *specific volatility* of the asset.

Consider a portfolio containing m risky assets with portfolio weights $\mathbf{w} = (w_1, w_2, \dots, w_m)'$, and suppose that each asset has a returns representation (II.1.2). Then the portfolio return may be written

$$Y_t = \alpha + \beta X_t + \varepsilon_t \quad t = 1, \dots, T, \qquad \text{(II.1.3)}$$

where each characteristic of the portfolio (i.e. its alpha and beta and its specific return) is a weighted sum of the individual assets' characteristics, i.e.

$$\alpha = \sum_{i=1}^{m} w_i \alpha_i, \quad \beta = \sum_{i=1}^{m} w_i \beta_i, \quad \varepsilon_t = \sum_{i=1}^{m} w_i \varepsilon_{it}. \qquad \text{(II.1.4)}$$

Now the portfolio's characteristics can be estimated in two different ways:

- Assume some portfolio weights $\mathbf{w}$ and use estimates of the alpha, beta and residuals for each asset in (II.1.4) to infer the characteristics of this hypothetical portfolio. This way an *asset manager* can compare many different portfolios for recommendation to his investors.

- A *risk manager*, on the other hand, will apply the weights $\mathbf{w}$ of an existing portfolio that is held by an investor to construct a constant weighted artificial returns history for the portfolio. This series is used for Y_t in (II.1.3) to assess the relative performance, the systematic risk and the specific risk of an existing portfolio.[2]

Thus risk managers and asset managers apply the same factor model in different ways, because they have different objectives. Asset managers need estimates of (II.1.2) for every

---

[2] The reconstructed 'constant weight' series for the portfolio returns will not be the same as the actual historical returns series for the portfolio, unless the portfolio was rebalanced continually so as to maintain the weights constant. The reason for using current weights is that the risk manager needs to represent the portfolio as it is now, not as it was last week or last year, and to use this representation to forecast its risk over a future risk horizon of a few days, weeks or months.

asset in the investor's universe in order to forecast the performance of many different portfolios and hence construct an optimal portfolio; by contrast, a risk manager takes an existing portfolio and uses (II.1.3) to forecast its risk characteristics. The next section explains how risk managers and asset managers also use different data and different statistical techniques to estimate the factor models that they use.

II.1.2.2   Estimating Portfolio Characteristics using OLS

The main lesson to learn from this section is that risk managers and asset managers require quite different techniques to estimate the parameters of factor models because they have different objectives:

- When asset managers employ a factor model of the form (II.1.2) they commonly use long histories of asset prices and benchmark values, measuring returns at a weekly or monthly frequency and assuming that the true parameters are constant. In this case, the *ordinary least squares* (OLS) estimation technique is appropriate and the more data used to estimate them the better, as the sampling error will be smaller. Three to five years of monthly or weekly data is typical.
- When risk managers employ a factor model of the form (II.1.3) they commonly use shorter histories of portfolio and benchmark values than the asset manager, measuring returns daily and not assuming that the true values of the parameters are constant. In this case, a time varying estimation technique such as exponentially weighted moving averages or generalized autoregressive conditional heteroscedasticity is appropriate.

We shall now describe how to estimate (II.1.2) and (II.1.3) using the techniques that are appropriate for their different applications. For model (II.1.2) the OLS parameter estimates based on a sample of size T are given by the formulae[3]

$$\hat{\beta}_i = \frac{\sum_{t=1}^{T} \left(X_t - \overline{X}\right)\left(R_{it} - \overline{R}_i\right)}{\sum_{t=1}^{T} \left(X_t - \overline{X}\right)^2} \quad \text{and} \quad \hat{\alpha}_i = \overline{R}_i - \hat{\beta}_i \overline{X}, \tag{II.1.5}$$

where $\overline{X}$ denotes the sample mean of the factor returns and $\overline{R}_i$ denotes the sample mean of the ith asset returns. The OLS estimate of the specific risk of the ith asset is the estimated standard error of the model, given by

$$s_i = \sqrt{\frac{RSS_i}{T-2}}, \tag{II.1.6}$$

where RSS_i is the residual sum of squares in the ith regression. See Section I.4.2 for further details. The following example illustrates the use of these formulae to estimate model (II.1.2) for two US stocks, using the S&P 500 index as the risk factor.

EXAMPLE II.1.1: OLS ESTIMATES OF ALPHA AND BETA FOR TWO STOCKS

Use weekly data from 3 January 2000 until 27 August 2007 to estimate a single factor model for the Microsoft Corporation (MSFT) stock and the National Western Life Insurance Company (NWL) stock using the S&P 500 index as the risk factor.[4]

---

[3] See Section I.4.2.2.
[4] Dividend adjusted data were downloaded from Yahoo! Finance.

(a) What do you conclude about the stocks' characteristics?

(b) Assuming the stocks' specific returns are uncorrelated, what are the characteristics of a portfolio with 70% of its funds invested in NWL and 30% invested in MSFT?

SOLUTION   The spreadsheet for this example computes the weekly returns on the index and on each of the stocks and then uses the Excel regression data analysis tool as explained in Section I.4.2.7. The results are

$$R_{\mathrm{NWL}} = \underset{(2.224)}{0.00358} + \underset{(7.129)}{0.50596}\,R_{\mathrm{SPX}}, \quad s_{\mathrm{NWL}} = 0.03212,$$

$$R_{\mathrm{MSFT}} = \underset{(-0.3699)}{-0.00066} + \underset{(14.002)}{1.10421}\,R_{\mathrm{SPX}}, \quad s_{\mathrm{MSFT}} = 0.03569,$$ (II.1.7)

where the figures in parentheses are the t ratios. We conclude the following:

- Since $\hat{\alpha}_{\mathrm{NWL}} = 0.00358$ and this is equivalent to an average outperformance of 18.6% per annum, NWL is a stock with a significant alpha. It also has a low systematic risk because $\hat{\beta}_{\mathrm{NWL}} = 0.50596$, which is much less than 1. Its specific risk, expressed as an annual volatility, is $0.03212 \times \sqrt{52} = 23.17\%$.

- Since the t ratio on $\hat{\alpha}_{\mathrm{MSFT}}$ is very small, MSFT has no significant outperformance or underperformance of the index. It also has a high systematic risk because the beta is slightly greater than 1 and a specific risk of $0.03569 \times \sqrt{52} = 25.74\%$, which is greater than the specific risk of NWL.

Now applying (II.1.4) gives a portfolio with the following characteristics:

$$\hat{\alpha} = 0.7 \times 0.00358 - 0.3 \times 0.00066 = 0.00231,$$
$$\hat{\beta} = 0.7 \times 0.50596 + 0.3 \times 1.10421 = 0.68543,$$

and assuming the specific returns are uncorrelated implies that we can estimate the specific risk of the portfolio as

$$s = \sqrt{0.7^2 \times 23.17^2 + 0.3^2 \times 25.74^2} = 17.96\%.$$

The next example shows that it makes no difference to the portfolio alpha and beta estimates whether we estimate them:

- from the OLS regressions for the stocks, applying the portfolio weights to the stocks alphas and betas using (II.1.4) as we did above;
- by using an OLS regression of the form (II.1.3) on the constant weighted portfolio returns.

However, it does make a difference to our estimate of the specific risk on the portfolio!

EXAMPLE II.1.2: OLS ESTIMATES OF PORTFOLIO ALPHA AND BETA

A portfolio has 60% invested in American Express (AXP) stock and 40% invested in Cisco Systems (CSCO). Use daily data from 3 January 2000 to 31 December 2007 on the prices of these stocks and on the S&P 100 index (OEX) to estimate the portfolio's characteristics by:[5]

---

[5] Data were downloaded from Yahoo! Finance. The reason we use log returns in this example is explained in Section I.1.4.4.

(a) applying the same method as in Example II.1.1;
(b) regressing the constant weighted returns series $\{0.6 \times \text{Amex Return} + 0.4 \times \text{Cisco Return}\}$ on the index returns.

SOLUTION   The results are computed using an OLS regression of each stock return and of the constant weighted portfolio returns, and the alpha and beta estimates are summarized in Table II.1.1. Note that for the first two rows the last column is a weighted sum of the first two. That is, the portfolio's alpha could equally well have been calculated by just taking the weighted sum of the stocks' alphas, and similarly for the beta. However, if we compute the specific risk of the portfolio using the two methods we obtain, using method (a),

$$s_P = \sqrt{0.6^2 \times 0.01416^2 + 0.4^2 \times 0.02337^2} \times \sqrt{250} = 19.98\%.$$

But using method (b), we have

$$s_P = 0.01150 \times \sqrt{250} = 18.19\%.$$

The problem is that the specific risks are *not* uncorrelated, even though we made this assumption when we applied method (a).

Table II.1.1   OLS alpha, beta and specific risk for two stocks and a 60:40 portfolio

	Amex	Cisco	Portfolio
Alpha	0.00018	−0.00022	0.00002
Beta	1.24001	1.76155	1.44863
Regression standard error	0.01416	0.02337	0.01150
Specific risk	22.39 %	36.96 %	18.19 %

We conclude that to estimate the specific risk of a portfolio we need to apply method (b). That is, we need to reconstruct a constant weighted portfolio series and calculate the specific risk from that regression. Alternatively and equivalently, we can save the residuals from the OLS regressions for each stock return and calculate the covariance matrix of these residuals. More details are given in Section II.1.3.3 below.

II.1.2.3   Estimating Portfolio Risk using EWMA

Whilst OLS may be adequate for asset managers, it is not appropriate to use a long price history of monthly or weekly data for the risk management of portfolios. Market risks require monitoring on a frequent basis – daily and even intra-daily – and the parameter estimates given by OLS will not reflect current market conditions. They merely represent an *average* value over the time period covered by the sample used in the regression model.

So, for the purpose of mapping a portfolio and assessing its risks, higher frequency data (e.g. daily) could be used to estimate a time varying portfolio beta for the model

$$Y_t = \alpha_t + \beta_t X_t + \varepsilon_t, \tag{II.1.8}$$

where X_t and Y_t denote the returns on the market factor and on the stock (or portfolio), respectively, at time t. In this model the systematic and specific risks are no longer assumed constant over time. The time varying beta estimates in (II.1.8) better reflect the current risk factor sensitivity for daily risk management purposes. To estimate time varying betas we cannot apply OLS so that it covers only the recent past. This approach will lead to very significant problems, as demonstrated in Section II.3.6. Instead, a simple time varying model for the covariance and variance may be applied to estimate the parameters of (II.1.8). The simplest possible time varying parameter estimates are based on an *exponentially weighted moving average* (EWMA) model. However the EWMA model is based on a very simple assumption, that returns are i.i.d. The EWMA beta estimates vary over time, even though the model specifies only a constant, unconditional covariance and variance. More advanced techniques include the class of *generalized autoregressive conditional heteroscedasticity* (GARCH) models, where we model the *conditional* covariance and variance and so the true parameters as well as the parameter estimates change over time.[6]

A time varying beta is estimated as the covariance of the asset and factor returns divided by the variance of the factor returns. Denoting the EWMA smoothing constant by λ, the EWMA estimate of beta that is made at time t is

$$\hat{\beta}_t^\lambda = \frac{\mathrm{Cov}_\lambda(X_t, Y_t)}{V_\lambda(X_t)}. \qquad \text{(II.1.9)}$$

That is, the EWMA beta estimate is the ratio of the EWMA covariance estimate to the EWMA variance estimate with the *same* smoothing constant. The modeller must choose a value for λ between 0 and 1, and values are normally in the region of 0.9–0.975. The decision about the value of λ is discussed in Section II.3.7.2.

We now provide an example of calculating the time varying EWMA betas for the portfolio in Example II.1.2. Later on, in Section II.4.8.3 we shall compare this beta with the beta that is obtained using a simple bivariate GARCH model. We assume $\lambda = 0.95$, which corresponds to a half-life of approximately 14 days (or about 3 weeks, in trading days) and compare the EWMA betas with the OLS beta of the portfolio that was derived in Example II.1.2. These are shown in Figure II.1.1, with the OLS beta of 1.448 indicated by a horizontal grey line. The EWMA beta, measured on the left-hand scale, is the time varying black line. The OLS beta is the average of the EWMA betas over the sample. Also shown in the figure is the EWMA estimate of the systematic risk of the portfolio, given by

$$\text{Systematic Risk} = \hat{\beta}_t^\lambda \sqrt{V_\lambda(X_t)} \times \sqrt{h}, \qquad \text{(II.1.10)}$$

where h denotes the number of returns per year, assumed to be 250 in this example.

During 2001 the portfolio had a beta much greater than 1.448, and sometimes greater than 2. The opposite is the case during the latter part of the sample. But note that this remark does depend on the choice of λ: the greater the value of λ the smoother the resulting series, and when $\lambda = 1$ the EWMA estimate coincides with the OLS estimate. However, when $\lambda < 1$ the single value of beta, equal to 1.448, that is obtained using OLS does not reflect the day-to-day variation in the portfolio's beta as measured by the EWMA estimate.

A time varying estimate of the systematic risk is also shown in Figure II.1.1. The portfolio's systematic risk is depicted in the figure as an annualized percentage, measured on the right-hand scale. There are two components of the systematic risk, the beta and the volatility of the market factor, and the systematic risk is the *product* of these. Hence the systematic risk was relatively low, at around 10% for most of the latter part of the sample even though the

---

[6] EWMA and GARCH models are explained in detail in Chapters II.3 and II.4.

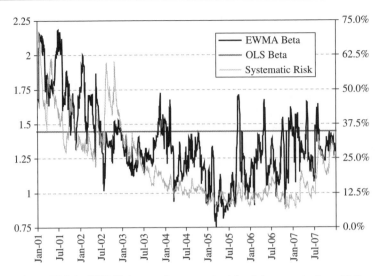

Figure II.1.1   EWMA beta and systematic risk of the two-stock portfolio

portfolio's beta was greater than 1, because the S&P 100 index had a very low volatility
during this period. On the other hand, in August and October 2002 the portfolio had a
high systematic risk, not because it had a high beta but because the market was particularly
volatile then. By contrast, the OLS estimate of systematic risk is unable to reflect such time
variation. The average volatility of the S&P 100 over the entire sample was 18.3% and so
OLS produces the single estimate of 18.3% × 1.448 = 26.6% for systematic risk. This figure
represents only an average of the systematic risk over the sample period.

II.1.2.4   Relationship between Beta, Correlation and Relative Volatility

In the single index model the beta, market correlation and relative volatility of an asset or a
portfolio with return Y when the market return is X are defined as

$$\beta = \frac{\text{Cov}(X, Y)}{V(X)}, \quad \varrho = \frac{\text{Cov}(X, Y)}{\sqrt{V(X)V(Y)}}, \quad v = \sqrt{\frac{V(Y)}{V(X)}} \qquad \text{(II.1.11)}$$

Hence,

$$\beta = \varrho v, \qquad \text{(II.1.12)}$$

i.e. the *equity beta* is the product of the *market correlation* ϱ and the *relative volatility* v of
the portfolio with respect to the index or benchmark.

The correlation is bounded above and below by $+1$ and -1 and the relative volatility
is always positive. So the portfolio beta can be very large and negative if the portfolio is
negatively correlated with the market, which happens especially when short positions are
held. On the other hand, very high values of beta can be experienced for portfolios containing
many risky stocks that are also highly correlated with the market.

In Figures II.1.2 and II.1.3 we show the daily EWMA estimates of beta, relative volatility and correlation (on the right-hand scale) of the Amex and Cisco stocks between

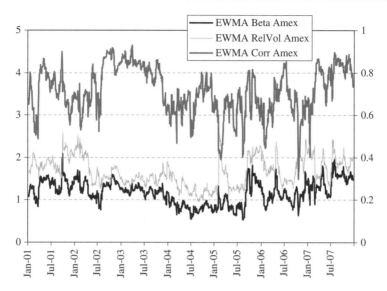

Figure II.1.2   EWMA beta, relative volatility and correlation of Amex ($\lambda = 0.95$)

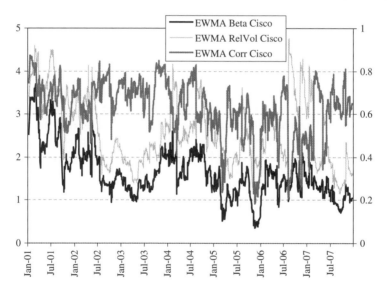

Figure II.1.3   EWMA beta, relative volatility and correlation of Cisco ($\lambda = 0.95$)

January 2001 and December 2007.[7] The same scales are used in both graphs, and it is clear that Cisco has a greater systematic risk than Amex. The average market correlation of both stocks is higher for Amex (0.713 for Amex and 0.658 for Cisco) but Cisco is much more volatile than Amex, relative to the market. Hence, EWMA correlation is more unstable and its EWMA beta is usually considerably higher than the beta on Amex.

---

[7] As before, $\lambda = 0.95$.

II.1.2.5   Risk Decomposition in a Single Factor Model

The principle of portfolio diversification implies that asset managers can reduce the specific risk of their portfolio by diversifying their investments into a large number of assets that have low correlation – and/or by holding long and short positions on highly correlated assets. This way the portfolio's specific risk can become insignificant. *Passive managers*, traditionally seeking only to track the market index, should aim for a net $\alpha = 0$ and a net portfolio $\beta = 1$ whilst simultaneously reducing the portfolio's specific risk as much as possible. *Active managers*, on the other hand, may have betas that are somewhat greater than 1 if they are willing to accept an increased systematic risk for an incremental return above the index.

Taking the expectation and variance of (II.1.3) gives

$$E(Y) = \alpha + \beta E(X). \tag{II.1.13}$$

If we assume $\mathrm{Cov}(X, \varepsilon) = 0$,

$$V(Y) = \beta^2 V(X) + V(\varepsilon). \tag{II.1.14}$$

It is very important to recognize that the total portfolio variance (II.1.14) represents the variance of portfolio returns around the expected return (II.1.13). It does not represent the variance about any other value! This is a common mistake and so I stress it here: it is statistical nonsense to measure the portfolio variance using a factor model and then to assume this figure represents the dispersion of portfolio returns around a mean that is anything other than (II.1.13). For example, the variance of a portfolio that is estimated from a factor model does *not* represent the variance about the target returns, except in the unlikely case that the expected return that is estimated by the model is equal to this target return.

The first term in (II.1.14) represents the systematic risk of the portfolio and the second represents the specific risk. When risk is measured as standard deviation the systematic risk component is $\beta\sqrt{V(X)}$ and the specific risk component is $\sqrt{V(\varepsilon)}$. These are normally quoted as an annualized percentage, as in the estimates given in the examples above.

From (II.1.14) we see that the volatility of the portfolio return – about the expected return given by the factor model – can be decomposed into three sources:

- the sensitivity to the market factor beta,
- the volatility of the market factor, and
- the specific risk.

One of the limitations of the equity beta as a risk measure is that it ignores the other two sources of risk: it says nothing about the risk of the market factor itself or about the specific risk of the portfolio.

We may express (II.1.14) in words as

$$\text{Total Variance} = \text{Systematic Variance} + \text{Specific Variance} \tag{II.1.15}$$

or, since risk is normally identified with standard deviation (or annualized standard deviation, i.e. volatility),

$$\text{Total Risk} = (\text{Systematic Risk}^2 + \text{Specific Risk}^2)^{1/2}. \tag{II.1.16}$$

Thus the components of risk are *not* additive. Only variance is additive, and then only under the assumption that the covariance between each risk factor's return and the specific return is 0.

II.1.3   MULTI-FACTOR MODELS

The risk decomposition (II.1.14) rests on an assumption that the benchmark or index is uncorrelated with the specific returns on a portfolio. That is, we assumed in the above that $\mathrm{Cov}(X, \varepsilon) = 0$. But this is a very strong assumption that would not hold if there were important risk factors for the portfolio, other than the benchmark or index, that have some correlation with the benchmark or index. For this reason single factor models are usually generalized to include more than one risk factor, as assumed in the *arbitrage pricing theory* developed by Ross (1976). By generalizing the single factor model to include many risk factors, it becomes more reasonable to assume that the specific return is not correlated with the risk factors and hence the risk decomposition (II.1.16) is more likely to hold.

The success of multi-factor models in predicting returns in financial asset markets and analysing risk depends on both the choice of risk factors and the method for estimating factor sensitivities. Factors may be chosen according to fundamentals (price–earning ratios, dividend yields, style factors, etc.), economics (interest rates, inflation, gross domestic product, etc.), finance (such as market indices, yield curves and exchange rates) or statistics (e.g. principal component analysis or factor analysis). The factor sensitivity estimates for fundamental factor models are sometimes based on cross-sectional regression; economic or financial factor model betas are usually estimated via time series regression; and statistical factor betas are estimated using statistical techniques based on the analysis of the eigenvectors and eigenvalues of the asset returns covariance or correlation matrix. These specific types of multi-factor models are discussed in Sections II.1.4–II.1.6 below. In this section we present the general theory of multi-factor models and provide several empirical examples.

II.1.3.1   Multi-factor Models of Asset or Portfolio Returns

Consider a set of k risk factors with returns $X_1, \ldots, X_k$ and let us express the systematic return of the asset or the portfolio as a weighted sum of these. In a multi-factor model for an asset return or a portfolio return, the return Y is expressed as a sum of the systematic component and an idiosyncratic or specific component ε that is not captured by the risk factors. In other words, a multi-factor model is a multiple regression model of the form[8]

$$Y_t = \alpha + \beta_1 X_{1t} + \ldots + \beta_k X_{kt} + \varepsilon_t. \tag{II.1.17}$$

In the above we have used a subscript t to denote the time at which an observation is made. However, some multi-factor models are estimated using cross-sectional data, in which case the subscript i would be used instead.

Matrix Form

It is convenient to express (II.1.17) using matrix notation, but here we use a slightly different notation from that which we introduced for multivariate regression in Section I.4.4.2. For reasons that will become clear later, and in particular when we analyse the Barra model, it helps to isolate the constant term alpha in the matrix notation. Thus we write

$$\mathbf{y} = \boldsymbol{\alpha} + \mathbf{X}\boldsymbol{\beta} + \boldsymbol{\varepsilon}, \quad \varepsilon_t \sim \mathrm{i.i.d.}(0, \sigma^2), \tag{II.1.18}$$

---

[8] In this chapter, since we are dealing with *alpha models*, it is convenient to separate the constant term alpha from the other coefficients. Hence we depart from the notation used for multiple regression models in Chapter I.4. There the total number of coefficients including the constant is denoted k, but here we have $k + 1$ coefficients in the model.

where the data may be cross-sectional or time series, $\mathbf{y}$ is the column of data on the asset or portfolio return, $\mathbf{X}$ is a matrix containing the data on the risk factor returns, $\boldsymbol{\alpha}$ is the vector $\alpha \mathbf{1}$, where $\mathbf{1} = (1, \ldots, 1)'$, $\boldsymbol{\beta}$ is the vector $(\beta_1, \ldots, \beta_k)'$ of the asset or portfolio betas with respect to each risk factor, and $\boldsymbol{\varepsilon}$ is the vector of the asset's or portfolio's specific returns.

OLS Estimation

We remark that (II.1.18) is equivalent to

$$\mathbf{y} = \tilde{\mathbf{X}}\tilde{\boldsymbol{\beta}} + \boldsymbol{\varepsilon}, \quad \boldsymbol{\varepsilon} \sim \text{i.i.d.} \left(0, \sigma^2 \mathbf{I}\right), \tag{II.1.19}$$

where $\mathbf{I}$ is the identity matrix and

$$\tilde{\mathbf{X}} = \begin{pmatrix} \mathbf{1} & \mathbf{X} \end{pmatrix} \quad \text{and} \quad \tilde{\boldsymbol{\beta}} = \begin{pmatrix} \alpha \\ \boldsymbol{\beta} \end{pmatrix}.$$

To write down an expression for the OLS estimates of the portfolio alpha and betas, it is easier to use (II.1.19) than (II.1.18). Since (II.1.19) is the same matrix form as in Section I.4.4.2, the OLS estimator formula is

$$\hat{\tilde{\boldsymbol{\beta}}} = \left(\tilde{\mathbf{X}}'\tilde{\mathbf{X}}\right)^{-1}\tilde{\mathbf{X}}'\mathbf{y}. \tag{II.1.20}$$

Expected Return and Variance Decomposition

Applying the expectation and variance operators to (II.1.18) and assuming that the idiosyncratic return is uncorrelated with each of the risk factor returns, we have

$$E(Y) = \alpha + \boldsymbol{\beta}'E(\mathbf{X}) \tag{II.1.21}$$

and

$$V(Y) = \boldsymbol{\beta}'\boldsymbol{\Omega}\boldsymbol{\beta} + V(\varepsilon), \tag{II.1.22}$$

where $E(\mathbf{X})$ is the vector of expected returns to each risk factor and $\boldsymbol{\Omega}$ is the covariance matrix of the risk factor returns. When OLS is used to estimate α and $\boldsymbol{\beta}$, then $E(\mathbf{X})$ is the vector of sample averages of each of the risk factor returns, and $\boldsymbol{\Omega}$ is the equally weighted covariance matrix.

Again I stress that the portfolio variance (II.1.22) represents the dispersion of asset or portfolio returns *about the expected return* (II.1.21); it does not represent dispersion about any other centre for the distribution.

EXAMPLE II.1.3: SYSTEMATIC AND SPECIFIC RISK

Suppose the total volatility of returns on a stock is 25%. A linear model with two risk factors indicates that the stock has betas of 0.8 and 1.2 on the two risk factors. The factors have volatility 15% and 20% respectively and a correlation of -0.5. How much of the stock's volatility can be attributed to the risk factors, and how large is the stock's specific risk?

SOLUTION   The risk factor's annual covariance matrix is

$$\boldsymbol{\Omega} = \begin{pmatrix} 0.0225 & -0.015 \\ -0.015 & 0.04 \end{pmatrix},$$

and the stock's variance due to the risk factors is

$$\boldsymbol{\beta}'\boldsymbol{\Omega}\boldsymbol{\beta} = \begin{pmatrix} 0.8 & 1.2 \end{pmatrix} \begin{pmatrix} 0.0225 & -0.015 \\ -0.015 & 0.04 \end{pmatrix} \begin{pmatrix} 0.8 \\ 1.2 \end{pmatrix} = 0.0432.$$

The volatility due to the risk factors is the square root of 0.0432, i.e. 20.78%. Now assuming that the covariance between the specific return and the systematic return is 0 and applying (II.1.15), we decompose the total variance of $0.25^2 = 0.0625$ as

$$0.0625 = 0.0432 + 0.0193.$$

Hence, the specific volatility of the stock is $\sqrt{0.0193} = 13.89\%$.

In summary, the stock's volatility of 25% can be decomposed into two portions, 20.78% due to the risk factors and 13.89% of idiosyncratic volatility (specific risk). Note that

$$25\% = (20.78\%^2 + 13.89\%^2)^{1/2},$$

in accordance with (II.1.16).

The example above illustrates some important facts:

- When the correlation between the specific return and the systematic return is zero, the variances are additive, not the volatilities.
- When the correlation between the specific return and the systematic return is non-zero, not even the variances are additive.
- The asset or portfolio's alpha does *not* affect the risk decomposition. The alpha does, however, have an important effect on the asset or portfolio's expected return.

II.1.3.2 Style Attribution Analysis

In 1988 the Nobel Prize winner William F. Sharpe introduced a multi-factor regression of a portfolio's returns on the returns to standard factors as a method for attributing fund managers' investment decisions to different styles.[9] For equity portfolios these standard factors, which are called *style factors*, are constructed to reflect value stocks and growth stocks, and are further divided into large, small or medium cap stocks.[10]

- A *value stock* is one that trades at a lower price than the firm's financial situation would merit. That is, the asset value per share is high relative to the stock price and the *price–earnings ratio* of the stock will be lower than the market average. Value stocks are attractive investments because they appear to be undervalued according to traditional equity analysis.[11]
- A *growth stock* is one with a lower than average *price–earnings–growth ratio*, i.e. the rate of growth of the firm's earnings is high relative to its price–earnings ratio. Hence growth stocks appear attractive due to potential growth in the firm assets.

The aim of style analysis is to identify the styles that can be associated with the major risk factors in a portfolio. This allows the market risk analyst to determine whether a fund manager's performance is attributed to investing in a certain asset class, and within this class

---

[9] See Sharpe (1988, 1992).
[10] Cap is short for *capitalization* of the stock, being the total value of the firm's equity that is issued to the public. It is the market value of all outstanding shares and is computed by multiplying the market price per share by the number of shares outstanding.
[11] The price–earnings ratio is the ratio of the stock's price to the firm's annual earnings per share.

investing in the best performing style, or whether his success or failure was mainly due to market timing or stock picking. It also allows the analyst to select an appropriate benchmark against which to assess the fund manager's performance. Furthermore, investors seeking a fully diversified portfolio can use style analysis to ensure their investments are spread over both growth and value investments in both large and small cap funds.

Style Indices

A large number of value and growth style indices based on stocks of different market caps are available, including the value and growth indices from the S&P 500, Russell 1000, Russell 2000 and Wilshire 5000 indices. As the number of stocks in the index increases, their average market cap decreases. Hence, the S&P 500 value index contains value stocks with an average market cap that is much larger then the average market cap of the stock in the Wilshire 5000 value index. The criterion used to select the stocks in any index depends on their performance according to certain value and growth indicators. Value indicators may include the *book-to-price ratio* and the *dividend yield*, and growth indicators may include the *growth in earnings per share* and the *return on equity*.[12]

Who Needs Style Analysis?

Whilst style analysis can be applied to any portfolio, hedge funds are a main candidate for this analysis because their investment styles may be obscure. Information about hedge funds is often hard to come by and difficult to evaluate. Because of the diverse investment strategies used by hedge funds, style indices for hedge funds include factors such as option prices, volatility, credit spreads, or indices of hedge funds in a particular category or strategy.

How to Attribute Investment Styles to a Portfolio

Denote by $\mathbf{y}$ the vector of historical returns on the fund being analysed, and denote by $\mathbf{X}$ the matrix of historical data on the returns to the style factors that have been chosen. The selection of the set of style indices used in the analysis is very important. We should include enough indices to represent the basic asset classes which are relevant to the portfolio being analysed and are of interest to the investor; otherwise the results will be misleading. However, the risk–return characteristics for the selected indices should be significantly different, because including too many indices often results in severe multicollinearity.[13]

Style attribution analysis is based on a multiple regression of the form (II.1.18), but with some important constraints imposed. If we are to *fully* attribute the fund's returns to the styles then the constant α must be 0, and the regression coefficients β must be non-negative and sum to 1. Assuming the residuals are i.i.d., the usual OLS regression objective applies, and we may express the estimation procedure in the form of the following *constrained least squares* problem:

$$\min_{\beta}(\mathbf{y} - \mathbf{X}\beta)^2 \text{ such that } \sum_{i=1}^{k} \beta_i = 1 \text{ and } \beta_i \geq 0, i = 1, \ldots, k. \qquad \text{(II.1.23)}$$

---

[12] Up-to-date data on a large number of style indices are free to download from Kenneth French's homepage on http://mba. tuck.dartmouth.edu/pages/faculty/Ken.french/data_library.html. Daily returns since the 1960's and monthly and annual returns since the 1920's are available on nearly 30 US benchmark portfolios.
[13] Multicollinearity was introduced in Section I.4.4.8 and discussed further in Section II.1.3.6.

This is a quadratic programming problem that can be solved using specialist software.

For illustrative purposes *only* we now implement a style analysis using the Excel Solver. However, it should be emphasized that the optimizer for (II.1.23) should be carefully designed and using the Solver is not recommended in practice. See the excellent paper by Kim et al. (2005) for further details on estimating style attribution models.

EXAMPLE II.1.4: STYLE ATTRIBUTION

Perform a style analysis on the following mutual funds:

- VIT – the Vanguard Index Trust 500 Index;
- FAA – the Fidelity Advisor Aggressive Fund;
- FID – the Fidelity Main Mutual Fund.

Use the following style factors:[14]

- Russell 1000 value: mid cap, value factor;
- Russell 1000 growth: mid cap, growth factor;
- Russell 2000 value: small cap, value factor;
- Russell 2000 growth: small cap, growth factor.

SOLUTION   Daily price data adjusted for dividends are downloaded from Yahoo! Finance from January 2003 to December 2006, and the results of the Excel Solver's optimization on (II.1.23) are reported in Table II.1.2, first for 2003–2004 and then for 2005–2006. This methodology allows one to compare the style differences between funds and to assess how the styles of a given fund evolve through time.

Table II.1.2   Results of style analysis for Vanguard and Fidelity mutual funds

2003–2004	R1000V	R1000G	R2000V	R2000G
VIT	92.2%	0.0%	0.0%	7.8%
FAA	43.7%	5.0%	0.0%	51.3%
FID	94.1%	0.0%	0.0%	5.9%
2005–2006	R1000V	R1000G	R2000V	R2000G
VIT	90.7%	1.7%	0.0%	7.6%
FAA	22.5%	7.0%	0.0%	70.5%
FID	76.8%	3.9%	0.0%	19.3%

For example, during the period 2003–2004 the FAA appears to be a fairly balanced fund between value and growth and small and mid cap stocks. Its returns could be attributed 43.7% to mid cap value stocks, 5% to mid cap growth stocks and 51.3% to small cap growth stocks. However, during the period 2005–2006 the balance shifted significantly toward small cap growth stocks, because only 22.5% of its returns were attributed to mid cap value stocks, and 7% to mid cap growth stocks, whereas 70.5% of its returns were attributed to small cap growth stocks.

---

[14] To reflect cash positions in the portfolio Treasury bills should be added to the list of style factors, but since our aim is simply to illustrate the methodology, we have omitted them.

II.1.3.3 General Formulation of Multi-factor Model

We start with the assumption of a multi-factor model of the form (II.1.18) for each asset in the investment universe. Each asset is assumed to have the same set of risk factors in the theoretical model, although in the estimated models it is typical that only a few of the risk factors will be significant for any single asset. Thus we have a linear factor model,

$$Y_{jt} = \alpha_j + \beta_{j1}X_{1t} + \ldots + \beta_{jk}X_{kt} + \varepsilon_{jt}, \quad \varepsilon_{jt} \sim \text{i.i.d.}(0, \sigma_j^2), \qquad (\text{II.1.24})$$

for each asset $j = 1, \ldots, m$. The equivalent matrix form of (II.1.24) is

$$\mathbf{y}_j = \boldsymbol{\alpha}_j + \mathbf{X}\boldsymbol{\beta}_j + \boldsymbol{\varepsilon}_j, \quad \boldsymbol{\varepsilon}_j \sim \text{i.i.d.}(0, \sigma_j^2 \mathbf{I}), \qquad (\text{II.1.25})$$

where T is the number of observations in the estimation sample; $\mathbf{y}_j$ is the $T \times 1$ vector of data on the asset returns; $\mathbf{X}$ is the same as in (II.1.18), i.e. a $T \times k$ matrix containing the data on the risk factor returns; $\boldsymbol{\alpha}_j$ is the $T \times 1$ vector $(\alpha_j, \ldots, \alpha_j)'$; $\boldsymbol{\beta}_j$ is the $k \times 1$ vector $(\beta_{j1}, \ldots, \beta_{jk})'$ of the asset's betas with respect to each risk factor; and $\boldsymbol{\varepsilon}_j$ is the vector of the asset's specific returns.

We can even put all the models (II.1.25) into one big matrix model, although some care is needed with notation here so that we do not lose track![15] Placing the stock returns into a $T \times m$ matrix $\mathbf{Y}$, where each column represents data on one stock return, we can write

$$\mathbf{Y} = \mathbf{A} + \mathbf{X}\mathbf{B} + \boldsymbol{\Psi}, \quad \boldsymbol{\Psi} \sim (\mathbf{0}, \boldsymbol{\Sigma}), \qquad (\text{II.1.26})$$

where $\mathbf{X}$ is the same as above, $\mathbf{A}$ is the $T \times m$ matrix whose jth column is the vector $\boldsymbol{\alpha}_j$, and $\mathbf{B}$ is the $k \times m$ matrix whose jth column is the vector $\boldsymbol{\beta}_j$. In other words, $\mathbf{B}$ is the matrix whose i, jth element is the sensitivity of the jth asset to the ith risk factor, $\boldsymbol{\Psi}$ is the $T \times m$ matrix of errors whose jth column is the vector $\boldsymbol{\varepsilon}_j$, and $\boldsymbol{\Sigma}$ is the covariance matrix of the errors, i.e.

$$V(\boldsymbol{\Psi}) = \boldsymbol{\Sigma} = \begin{pmatrix} \sigma_1^2 & \sigma_{12} \cdots & \sigma_{1m} \\ \vdots & \vdots \ \vdots & \vdots \\ \sigma_{m1} & \sigma_{m2} \cdots & \sigma_m^2 \end{pmatrix},$$

where σ_{ij} denotes the covariance between ε_i and ε_j.

Now consider a portfolio with $m \times 1$ weights vector $\mathbf{w} = (w_1, \ldots, w_m)'$. The portfolio return at time t as a weighted sum of asset returns, i.e.

$$Y_t = \sum_{j=1}^{m} w_j Y_{jt}.$$

In other words, the $T \times 1$ vector of data on the 'current weighted' portfolio returns is

$$\mathbf{y} = \mathbf{Y}\mathbf{w}.$$

Hence, by (II.1.26),

$$\mathbf{y} = \mathbf{A}\mathbf{w} + \mathbf{X}\mathbf{B}\mathbf{w} + \boldsymbol{\Psi}\mathbf{w}. \qquad (\text{II.1.27})$$

---

[15] We only provide an intuitive representation here. The correct approach uses stacked variables and derives the covariance matrix of the errors as a Kronecker product of $\boldsymbol{\Sigma}$ with the $T \times T$ identity matrix. See, for example, Greene (2007) or Gross (2003) for further details.

But, of course, (II.1.27) must be identical to the model (II.1.18). Thus:

- the portfolio alpha vector is $\boldsymbol{\alpha} = \mathbf{Aw}$;
- the beta on the jth risk factor is the weighted sum of the asset betas on that risk factor, i.e. the portfolio beta vector is $\boldsymbol{\beta} = \mathbf{Bw}$;
- the portfolio's specific returns are $\boldsymbol{\varepsilon} = \boldsymbol{\Psi}\mathbf{w}$, i.e. the specific return at time t is the weighted sum of the assets' specific returns at time t.

We remark that the expression of the portfolio's specific return in the form $\boldsymbol{\Psi}\mathbf{w}$ makes it clear that we must account for the correlation between asset specific returns when estimating the specific risk of the portfolio.

The above shows that, theoretically, we can estimate the portfolio's characteristics (alpha and beta and specific return) in two equivalent ways:

- find the portfolio weighted sum of the characteristics of each asset, or
- estimate the portfolio characteristics directly using the model (II.1.18).

However, whilst this is true for the theoretical model it will *not* be true for the estimated model unless there is only one factor. The reason is that because of the sampling error, weighting and summing the estimated asset characteristics as in (II.1.27) gives different results from those obtained by forming a current weighted historical series for the portfolio return and estimating the model (II.1.18).

Applying the variance operator to (II.1.27) and assuming that each asset's specific return is uncorrelated with each risk factor, gives an alternative to (II.1.22) in a form that makes the portfolio weights explicit, viz.

$$V(Y) = \boldsymbol{\beta}'\boldsymbol{\Omega}\boldsymbol{\beta} + \mathbf{w}'\boldsymbol{\Sigma}\mathbf{w}, \tag{II.1.28}$$

where $\boldsymbol{\Sigma}$ is the covariance matrix of the assets' specific returns. So as in (II.1.14) one can again distinguish three sources of risk:

- the risks that are represented by the portfolio's factor sensitivities $\boldsymbol{\beta}$;
- the risks of the factors themselves, represented by the risk factor covariance matrix $\boldsymbol{\Omega}$;
- the idiosyncratic risks of the assets in the portfolio, represented by the variance of residual returns, $\mathbf{w}'\boldsymbol{\Sigma}\mathbf{w}$.

EXAMPLE II.1.5: SYSTEMATIC RISK AT THE PORTFOLIO LEVEL

Suppose a portfolio is invested in only three assets, with weights -0.25, 0.75 and 0.5, respectively. Each asset has a factor model representation with the same two risk factors as in Example II.1.3 and the betas are: for asset 1, 0.2 for the first risk factor and 1.2 for the second risk factor; for asset 2, 0.9 for the first risk factor and 0.2 for the second risk factor; and for asset 3, 1.3 for the first risk factor and 0.7 for the second risk factor. What is the volatility due to the risk factors (i.e. the systematic risk) for this portfolio?

SOLUTION   The net portfolio beta on each factor is given by the product $\mathbf{Bw}$. We have

$$\mathbf{B} = \begin{pmatrix} 0.2 & 0.9 & 1.3 \\ 1.2 & 0.2 & 0.7 \end{pmatrix} \quad \text{and} \quad \mathbf{w} = \begin{pmatrix} -0.25 \\ 0.75 \\ 0.5 \end{pmatrix}, \quad \text{so} \quad \boldsymbol{\beta} = \begin{pmatrix} 1.275 \\ 0.2 \end{pmatrix}.$$

With the same risk factor covariance matrix as in the previous example,

$$\boldsymbol{\beta}'\boldsymbol{\Omega}\boldsymbol{\beta} = \begin{pmatrix} 1.275 & 0.2 \end{pmatrix} \begin{pmatrix} 0.0225 & -0.015 \\ -0.015 & 0.04 \end{pmatrix} \begin{pmatrix} 1.275 \\ 0.2 \end{pmatrix} = 0.0305,$$

so the portfolio volatility due to the risk factors is $\sqrt{0.0305} = 17.47\%$.

II.1.3.4   Multi-factor Models of International Portfolios

In this text we always use the term *foreign exchange rate* (or *forex rate*) for the domestic value of a foreign unit of currency. International portfolios have an equivalent exposure to foreign exchange rates; for each nominal amount invested in a foreign security the same amount of foreign currency must be purchased. Put another way, for each country of investment the foreign exchange rate is a risk factor and the portfolio's sensitivity to the exchange rate risk factor is one. In addition to the exchange rate, for each country of exposure we have the usual (fundamental or statistical) market risk factors.

Consider an investment in a single foreign asset. The price of a foreign asset in domestic currency is the asset price in foreign currency multiplied by the foreign exchange rate. Hence the log return on a foreign asset in domestic currency terms is

$$R_D = R_F + X,$$

where R_F is the asset return in foreign currency and X is the forex return. We suppose the systematic return on the asset in foreign currency is related to a single *foreign market risk factor*, such as a broad market index, with return R and factor beta β. Then the systematic return on the asset in domestic currency is $\beta R + X$. Hence, there are two risk factors affecting the return on the asset:

- the exchange rate (with a beta of 1); and
- the foreign market index (with a beta of β).

Thus the systematic variance of the asset return in domestic currency can be decomposed into three different components:

$$\text{Systematic Variance} = V(\beta R + X) = \beta^2 V(R) + V(X) + 2\beta \text{Cov}(R, X). \qquad \text{(II.1.29)}$$

For instance, if the asset is a stock, there are three components for systematic variance which are labelled:

- the *equity variance*, $\beta^2 V(R)$;
- the *forex variance*, $V(X)$;
- the *equity–forex covariance*, $2\beta \text{Cov}(R, X)$.

A portfolio of foreign assets in the same asset class with a single foreign market risk factor having return R has the same variance decomposition as (II.1.29), but now β denotes the *net* portfolio beta with respect to the market index, i.e. $\beta = \mathbf{w}'\boldsymbol{\beta}$, where $\mathbf{w}$ is the vector of portfolio weights and $\boldsymbol{\beta}$ is the vector of each asset's market beta.

We can generalize (II.1.29) to a large international portfolio with exposures in k different countries. For simplicity we assume that there is a single market risk factor in each foreign market. Denote by $R_1, R_2, \ldots, R_k$ the returns on the market factors, by $\beta_1, \beta_2, \ldots, \beta_k$ the portfolio betas with respect to each market factor and by $X_1, X_2, \ldots, X_k$ the returns on the foreign exchange rates. Assuming R_1 is the domestic market factor, then $X_1 = 1$ and there are k equity risk factors but only $k - 1$ foreign exchange risk factors. Let $\mathbf{w} = (w_1, w_2, \ldots, w_k)'$ be the country portfolio weights, i.e. w_i is the proportion of the portfolio's value that is invested in country i. Then the systematic return on the portfolio may be written as

$$w_1 \beta_1 R_1 + w_2(\beta_2 R_2 + X_2) + \ldots + w_k(\beta_k R_k + X_k) = (\mathbf{Bw})'\mathbf{x} \qquad \text{(II.1.30)}$$

where $\mathbf{x}$ is the $2k - 1 \times 1$ vector of equity and forex risk factor returns and $\mathbf{B}$ is the $(2k - 1) \times k$ matrix of risk factor betas, i.e.

$$\mathbf{x} = (R_1, \ldots, R_k, X_2, \ldots, X_k)' \text{ and } \mathbf{B} = \begin{pmatrix} \text{diag}\,(\beta_1, \beta_2, \ldots, \beta_k) \\ \mathbf{0} \qquad \mathbf{I}_{(k-1) \times (k-1)} \end{pmatrix}.$$

Taking variances of (II.1.30) gives

$$\text{Systematic Variance} = (\mathbf{Bw})'\,\mathbf{\Omega}\,(\mathbf{Bw}), \qquad (\text{II.1.31})$$

where

$$\mathbf{\Omega} = \begin{pmatrix} V(R_1) & \cdots & & \text{Cov}\,(R_1, X_k) \\ \text{Cov}\,(R_1, R_2) & V(R_2) & & \vdots \\ \vdots & & \ddots & \vdots \\ \text{Cov}\,(R_1, X_k) & \cdots & & V(X_k) \end{pmatrix}$$

is the covariance matrix of, the equity and forex risk factor returns.

We may partition the matrix $\mathbf{\Omega}$ as

$$\mathbf{\Omega} = \begin{pmatrix} \mathbf{\Omega}_E & \mathbf{\Omega}_{EX} \\ \mathbf{\Omega}'_{EX} & \mathbf{\Omega}_X \end{pmatrix} \qquad (\text{II.1.32})$$

where $\mathbf{\Omega}_E$ is the $k \times k$ covariance matrix of the equity risk factor returns, $\mathbf{\Omega}_X$ is the $(k-1) \times (k-1)$ covariance matrix of the forex risk factor returns and $\mathbf{\Omega}_{EX}$ is the $k \times (k-1)$ 'quanto' covariance matrix containing the cross covariances between the equity risk factor returns and the forex risk factor returns. Substituting (II.1.32) into (II.1.31) gives the decomposition of systematic variance into equity, forex and equity–forex components as

$$\tilde{\boldsymbol{\beta}}'\,\mathbf{\Omega}_E\,\tilde{\boldsymbol{\beta}} + \tilde{\mathbf{w}}'\,\mathbf{\Omega}_X\,\tilde{\mathbf{w}} + 2\tilde{\boldsymbol{\beta}}'\,\mathbf{\Omega}_{EX}\,\tilde{\mathbf{w}}, \qquad (\text{II.1.33})$$

where $\tilde{\mathbf{w}} = (w_2, \ldots, w_k)'$ and

$$\tilde{\boldsymbol{\beta}} = \text{diag}(\beta_1, \ldots, \beta_k)\mathbf{w} = (w_1\beta_1, \ldots, w_k\beta_k)'.$$

EXAMPLE II.1.6: DECOMPOSITION OF SYSTEMATIC RISK INTO EQUITY AND FOREX FACTORS

A UK investor holds £2.5 million in UK stocks with a FTSE 100 market beta of 1.5, £1 million in US stocks with an S&P 500 market beta of 1.2, and £1.5 million in German stocks with a DAX 30 market beta of 0.8. The volatilities and correlations of the FTSE 100, S&P 500 and DAX 30 indices, and the USD/GBP and EUR/GBP exchange rates, are shown in Table II.1.3. Calculate the systematic risk of the portfolio and decompose it into equity, forex and equity–forex components.

Table II.1.3 Risk factor correlations and volatilities

Correlation	FTSE 100	S&P 500	DAX 30	USD/GBP	EUR/GBP
FTSE 100	1				
S&P 500	0.8	1			
DAX 30	0.7	0.6	1		
USD/GBP	0.2	−0.25	0.05	1	
EUR/GBP	0.3	0.05	−0.15	0.6	1
Volatilities	20%	22%	25%	10%	12%

SOLUTION   The covariance matrix of the risk factor returns is calculated from the information in Table II.1.3 in the spreadsheet, and this is given in Table II.1.4. The upper

Table II.1.4 Risk factor covariance matrix

	FTSE 100	S&P 500	DAX 30	USD/GBP	EUR/GBP
FTSE 100	0.04	0.0352	0.035	0.004	0.0072
S&P 500	0.0352	0.0484	0.033	−0.0055	0.00132
DAX 30	0.035	0.033	0.0625	0.00125	−0.0045
USD/GBP	0.004	−0.0055	0.00125	0.01	0.0072
EUR/GBP	0.0072	0.00132	−0.0045	0.0072	0.0144

left shaded 3×3 matrix is the equity risk factor returns covariance matrix $\boldsymbol{\Omega}_E$, the lower right shaded 2×2 matrix is the forex factor returns covariance matrix $\boldsymbol{\Omega}_X$, and the upper right unshaded 3×2 matrix is the quanto covariance matrix $\boldsymbol{\Omega}_{EX}$. The risk factor beta matrix $\mathbf{B}$, portfolio weights $\mathbf{w}$ and their product $\mathbf{Bw}$ are given as follows:

$$\mathbf{B} = \begin{pmatrix} 1.5 & 0 & 0 \\ 0 & 1.2 & 0 \\ 0 & 0 & 0.8 \\ 0 & 1 & 0 \\ 0 & 0 & 1 \end{pmatrix}, \quad \mathbf{w} = \begin{pmatrix} 0.5 \\ 0.2 \\ 0.3 \end{pmatrix} \Rightarrow \mathbf{Bw} = \begin{pmatrix} 0.75 \\ 0.24 \\ 0.24 \\ 0.2 \\ 0.3 \end{pmatrix}, \quad \tilde{\beta} = \begin{pmatrix} 0.75 \\ 0.24 \\ 0.24 \end{pmatrix}.$$

Hence, the systematic variance is

$$(\mathbf{Bw})' \, \boldsymbol{\Omega} \, (\mathbf{Bw}) = \begin{pmatrix} 0.75 & 0.24 & 0.24 & 0.2 & 0.3 \end{pmatrix} \times$$

$$\begin{pmatrix} 0.04 & 0.0352 & 0.035 & 0.004 & 0.0072 \\ 0.0352 & 0.0484 & 0.033 & -0.0055 & 0.00132 \\ 0.035 & 0.033 & 0.0625 & 0.00125 & -0.0045 \\ 0.004 & -0.0055 & 0.00125 & 0.01 & 0.0072 \\ 0.0072 & 0.00132 & -0.0045 & 0.0072 & 0.0144 \end{pmatrix} \begin{pmatrix} 0.75 \\ 0.24 \\ 0.24 \\ 0.20 \\ 0.30 \end{pmatrix}$$

$$= 0.064096$$

and the systematic risk is $\sqrt{0.064096} = 25.32\%$.

The three terms in (II.1.33) are

$$\text{Equity Variance} = \tilde{\beta}' \boldsymbol{\Omega}_E \tilde{\beta} = \begin{pmatrix} 0.75 & 0.24 & 0.24 \end{pmatrix} \begin{pmatrix} 0.04 & 0.0352 & 0.035 \\ 0.0352 & 0.0484 & 0.033 \\ 0.035 & 0.033 & 0.0625 \end{pmatrix} \begin{pmatrix} 0.75 \\ 0.24 \\ 0.24 \end{pmatrix}$$

$$= 0.05796,$$

so the equity risk component is $\sqrt{0.05796} = 24.08\%$;

$$\text{FX Variance} = \tilde{\mathbf{w}}' \boldsymbol{\Omega}_X \tilde{\mathbf{w}} = \begin{pmatrix} 0.2 & 0.3 \end{pmatrix} \begin{pmatrix} 0.01 & 0.0072 \\ 0.0072 & 0.0144 \end{pmatrix} \begin{pmatrix} 0.2 \\ 0.3 \end{pmatrix} = 0.00256,$$

so the forex risk component is $\sqrt{0.00256} = 5.06\%$;

$$\text{Quanto Covariance} = \tilde{\beta}' \boldsymbol{\Omega}_{EX} \tilde{\mathbf{w}} = \begin{pmatrix} 0.75 & 0.24 & 0.24 \end{pmatrix} \begin{pmatrix} 0.004 & 0.0072 \\ -0.0055 & 0.00132 \\ 0.00125 & -0.0045 \end{pmatrix} \begin{pmatrix} 0.2 \\ 0.3 \end{pmatrix}$$

$$= 0.001787.$$

In accordance with (II.1.33) the three terms sum to the total systematic variance, i.e.

$$0.05796 + 0.00256 + 0.003574 = 0.064096.$$

Taking the square root gives the total systematic risk as 25.32%, which is identical to the result obtained by direct calculation above. The quanto covariance happened to be positive in this example, but it could be negative. In that case the total systematic variance will be less than the sum of the equity variance and the forex variance – and it could even be less than both of them!

When each stock in a portfolio has returns representation (II.1.25), the risk decomposition (II.1.28) shows how the portfolio's systematic risk is represented using the stock's factor betas $\mathbf{B}$ and the risk factor covariance matrix $\boldsymbol{\Omega}$. We can also decompose total risk into systematic risk and specific risk, using techniques that are similar to those used in the simple numerical example above.

II.1.4   CASE STUDY: ESTIMATION OF FUNDAMENTAL FACTOR MODELS

In this section we provide an empirical case study of risk decomposition using historical prices of two stocks (Nokia and Vodafone) and four fundamental risk factors:[16]

(i)   a broad market index, the New York Stock Exchange (NYSE) composite index;
(ii) an industry factor, the Old Mutual communications fund;
(iii) a growth style factor, the Riverside growth fund; and
(iv) a capitalization factor, the AFBA Five Star Large Cap fund.

Figure II.1.4 shows the prices of the two stocks and the four possible risk factors, with each series rebased to be 100 on 31 December 2000.

Figure II.1.4   Two communications stocks and four possible risk factors

---

[16] All data were downloaded from Yahoo! Finance.

Using regression to build a multi-factor model with these four risk factors gives rise to some econometric problems, but these are not insurmountable as will be shown later in this section. The main problem with this factor model is with the selection of the risk factors. In general, the choice of risk factors to include in the regression factor model is based on the user's experience: there is no econometric theory to inform this choice.

II.1.4.1 Estimating Systematic Risk for a Portfolio of US Stocks

The first example in this case study uses a factor model for each stock based on all four risk factors.

EXAMPLE II.1.7: TOTAL RISK AND SYSTEMATIC RISK

On 20 April 2006 a portfolio is currently holding $3 million of Nokia stock and $1 million of Vodafone stock. Using the daily closing prices since 31 December 2000 that are shown in Figure II.1.4:

(a) estimate the total risk of the portfolio volatility based on the historical returns on the two stocks;
(b) estimate the systematic risk of the portfolio using a four-factor regression model for each stock.

SOLUTION

(a) A current weighted daily returns series for the portfolio is constructed by taking $\{0.25 \times$ return on Vodafone $+ 0.75 \times$ return on Nokia$\}$. The standard deviation of these returns (over the whole data period) is 0.0269, hence the estimate of the portfolio volatility is $\sqrt{250} \times 0.0269 = 42.5\%$.[17]
(b) An OLS regression of the daily returns for each stock on the daily returns for the risk factors – again using the whole data period – produces the results shown in Table II.1.5. The t statistics shown in the table are test statistics for the null hypothesis that the true factor beta is 0 against the two-sided alternative hypothesis that it is not equal to 0. The higher the absolute value of the t statistic, the more likely we are to reject the null hypothesis and conclude that the factor does have a significant effect on the stock return. The p value is the probability that the true factor beta is 0, so a high t statistic gives a low probability value.

Table II.1.5 Factor betas from regression model

	Vodafone			Nokia		
	est. beta	t stat.	p value	est. beta	t stat.	p value
Intercept	0.000	−0.467	0.640	0.000	−0.118	0.906
NYSE index	0.857	5.835	0.000	−0.267	−1.545	0.123
Communications	0.137	2.676	0.008	0.271	4.471	0.000
Growth	0.224	1.885	0.060	0.200	1.432	0.152
Large Cap	0.009	0.068	0.946	1.146	7.193	0.000

[17] Nokia and Vodafone are both technology stocks, which were extremely volatile during this sample period.

Leaving aside the problems associated with this regression until the next subsection, we extract from this the sensitivity matrix

$$\mathbf{B} = \begin{pmatrix} 0.857 & -0.267 \\ 0.137 & 0.271 \\ 0.224 & 0.200 \\ 0.009 & 1.146 \end{pmatrix}.$$

Now, given the weights vector

$$\mathbf{w} = \begin{pmatrix} 0.25 \\ 0.75 \end{pmatrix},$$

the net portfolio betas are

$$\beta = \begin{pmatrix} 0.857 & -0.267 \\ 0.137 & 0.271 \\ 0.224 & 0.200 \\ 0.009 & 1.146 \end{pmatrix} \begin{pmatrix} 0.25 \\ 0.75 \end{pmatrix} = \begin{pmatrix} 0.0136 \\ 0.2372 \\ 0.2620 \\ 0.8618 \end{pmatrix}.$$

In the spreadsheet for this example we also calculate the risk factor returns covariance matrix as

$$\Omega = \begin{pmatrix} 10.02 & 17.52 & 10.98 & 11.82 \\ 17.52 & 64.34 & 28.94 & 27.53 \\ 10.98 & 28.94 & 16.86 & 15.06 \\ 11.82 & 27.53 & 15.06 & 16.90 \end{pmatrix} \times 10^{-5}.$$

The portfolio variance attributable to the risk factors is $\beta'\Omega\beta$ and this is calculated in the spreadsheet as 36.78×10^{-5}. The systematic risk, expressed as an annual percentage, is the square root of this. It is calculated in the spreadsheet as 30.3%. The reason why this is much lower than the total risk of the portfolio that is estimated in part (a) is that the factor model does not explain the returns very well. The R^2 of the regression is the squared correlation between the stock return and the explained part of the model (i.e. the sum of the factor returns weighted by their betas). The correlation is 58.9% for the Vodafone regression and 67.9% for the Nokia regression. These are fairly high but not extremely high, so a significant fraction of the variability in each of the stock's returns is unaccounted for by the model. This variability remains in the model's residuals, so the specific risks of these models can be significant.

II.1.4.2   Multicollinearity: A Problem with Fundamental Factor Models

Multicollinearity is defined in Section I.4.4.8. It refers to the correlation between the explanatory variables in a regression model: if one or more explanatory variables are highly correlated then it is difficult to estimate their regression coefficients. We say that a model has a high degree of multicollinearity if two or more explanatory variables are highly (positive or negatively) correlated. Then their regression coefficients cannot be estimated with much precision and, in technical terms, the efficiency of the OLS estimator is reduced. The multicollinearity problem becomes apparent when the estimated coefficients change considerably when adding another (collinear) variable to the regression. There is no statistical test for multicollinearity, but a useful rule of thumb is that a model will suffer from it if the square of the pairwise correlation between two explanatory variables is greater than the multiple R^2 of the regression.

A major problem with estimating fundamental factor models using time series data is that potential factors are very often highly correlated. In this case the factor betas cannot be estimated with precision. To understand the effect that multicollinearity has on the estimated factor betas, let us consider again the factor model of Example II.1.7. Table II.1.6 starts with an OLS estimation of a single factor for each stock (the returns on the NYSE composite index) and then adds one factor at a time. Each time we record the factor beta estimate, its t statistic and probability value as explained in Example II.1.7. We exclude the intercept as it is always insignificantly different from zero in these regressions, but in each case we state the R^2 of the regression.

Table II.1.6   Multicollinearity in time series factor models

Vodafone	1 Factor			2 Factors			3 Factors			4 Factors		
	beta	t stat.	p-value	beta	t stat.	p-value	beta	t stat.	p-value	beta	t stat.	p-value
NYSE index	1.352	25.024	0.000	0.996	13.580	0.000	0.864	8.539	0.000	0.857	5.835	0.000
Communications				0.204	7.042	0.000	0.139	3.103	0.002	0.137	2.676	0.008
Growth							0.224	1.895	0.058	0.224	1.885	0.060
Large Cap										0.009	0.068	0.946
Multiple R		0.566			0.587			0.589			0.589	

Nokia	1 Factor			2 Factors			3 Factors			4 Factors		
	beta	t stat.	p-value	beta	t stat.	p-value	beta	t stat.	p-value	beta	t stat.	p-value
NYSE index	1.777	25.475	0.000	0.795	9.022	0.000	0.635	5.218	0.000	−0.267	−1.545	0.123
Communications				0.561	16.134	0.000	0.483	8.962	0.000	0.271	4.471	0.000
Growth							0.273	1.919	0.055	0.200	1.432	0.152
Large Cap										1.146	7.193	0.000
Multiple R		0.573			0.662			0.663			0.679	

The one-factor model implies that both stocks are high risk, relative to the NYSE index: their estimated betas are 1.352 (Vodafone) and 1.777 (Nokia) and both are significantly greater than 1. The R^2 of 56.6% (Vodafone) and 57.3% (Nokia) indicates a reasonable fit, given there is only one factor. The two-factor model shows that the communications factor is also able to explain the returns on both stocks, and it is especially important for Nokia, with a t statistic of 16.134.

Notice that the addition of this factor has dramatically changed the NYSE beta estimate: it is now below 1, for both stocks. In the three-factor model the NYSE beta estimate becomes even lower, and so does the communications beta. Yet the growth index is only marginally significant: it has a probability value of around 5%. The addition of the final 'large cap' factor in the four-factor model has little effect on Vodafone – except that the NYSE and communications beta estimates become even less precise (their t statistics become smaller) – and the large cap factor does not seem to be important for Vodafone. But it is very important for Nokia: the t statistic is 7.193 so the beta of 1.146 is very highly significantly different from 0. And now the NYSE and communications beta estimates change dramatically. Starting with a NYSE beta of 1.777 in the single factor model, we end up in the four-factor model with a beta estimate of -0.267!

So, what is going on here? Which, if any, of these is the correct beta estimate? Let us see whether multicollinearity could be affecting our results. It certainly seems to be the case, because our betas estimates are changing considerably when we add further factors. Table II.1.7 shows the factor correlation matrix for the sample period. All the factors are very highly correlated. The lowest correlation, of 69%, is between the NYSE Index and the communications factor. The square of this is lower than the multiple R^2 of the regressions. However, the other correlations shown in Table II.1.7 are very high, and their squares are higher than the multiple R^2 of the regressions. Obviously multicollinearity is causing problems in these models. The 'large cap' factor is the most highly correlated with the other factors and this explains why the model really fell apart when we added this factor.

Table II.1.7   Factor correlation matrix

	NYSE Index	Communications	Growth	Large Cap
NYSE index	1			
Communications	0.690	1		
Growth	0.845	0.879	1	
Large Cap	0.909	0.835	0.892	1

Because of the problem with multicollinearity the only reliable factor beta estimate is one where each factor is taken individually in its own single factor model. But no single factor model can explain the returns on a stock very well. A large part of the stock returns variation will be left to the residual and so the systematic risk will be low and the stock specific risk high. We cannot take these individual beta estimates into (II.1.24) with $k = 4$: they need to be estimated simultaneously. So how should we proceed? The next section describes the method that I recommend.

II.1.4.3   Estimating Fundamental Factor Models by Orthogonal Regression

The best solution to a multicollinearity problem is to apply principal component analysis to all the potential factors and then use the principal components as explanatory variables, instead of the original financial or economic factors. Principal component analysis was introduced in Section I.2.6 and we summarize the important learning points about this analysis at the beginning of the next chapter. In the context of the present case study we shall illustrate how principal component analysis may be applied in orthogonal regression to mitigate the multicollinearity problem in our four-factor model.

We shall apply principal component analysis to the risk factor returns covariance matrix. Table II.1.8 displays the eigenvalues of this matrix, and the collinearity of the risk factor returns is evident since the first eigenvalue is relatively large. It indicates that the first principal component explains over 90% of the variation in the risk factors and hence it is capturing a strong common trend in the four risk factors. With just two principal components this proportion rises to 97.68%.[18]

---

[18] But note that the second and higher principal components do not have an intuitive interpretation because the system is not ordered, as it is in a term structure.

Table II.1.8 Eigenvalues and eigenvectors of the risk factor covariance matrix

Eigenvalues	λ_1	λ_2	λ_3	λ_4
Eigenvalue	0.000976	0.000080	0.000017	0.0000078
Variation explained	90.25%	7.44%	1.60%	0.72%
Cumulative variation	90.25%	97.68%	99.28%	100%
Eigenvectors	w_1	w_2	w_3	w_4
NYSE index (RF_1)	0.259987	0.609012	0.103850	0.742110
Communications (RF_2)	0.795271	−0.566012	0.139657	0.166342
Growth (RF_3)	0.391886	0.271074	−0.845368	−0.241448
Large cap (RF_4)	0.382591	0.485030	0.505039	−0.602749

Since the principal components are uncorrelated by design, a regression of the stock's returns on the principal components has no problem with multicollinearity – quite the opposite in fact, because the factors are orthogonal. Then the estimated coefficients in this regression can be used to recover the risk factor betas. To see how this is done, recall from Section I.2.6 that the mth principal component is related to the mth eigenvector $\mathbf{w}_m$ and the risk factor returns as follows:

$$PC_m = w_{1m}RF_1 + \ldots + w_{4m}RF_4, \quad \text{where } \mathbf{w}_m = (w_{1m}, w_{2m}, w_{3m}, w_{4m})'. \quad (II.1.34)$$

Now suppose we estimate a regression of the stock's returns on the principal component factors, using OLS, and the estimated regression model is

$$\text{Vodafone return} = \sum_{i=1}^{k} \hat{\gamma}_i PC_i \quad (k \leq 4). \quad (II.1.35)$$

Substituting (II.1.34) into (II.1.35) gives the representation of the stock's return in terms of the original factors:

$$\text{Vodafone return} = \sum_{i=1}^{4} \hat{\beta}_i RF_i, \quad \text{where } \hat{\beta}_i = \sum_{j=1}^{k} \hat{\gamma}_j w_{ij}. \quad (II.1.36)$$

Hence the net betas will be a weighted sum of the regression coefficients $\hat{\gamma}_i$ in (II.1.35).

Table II.1.9 shows these regression coefficients and their t statistics, first with $k = 4$ and then with $k = 2$, and below this the corresponding risk factor betas obtained using (II.1.36). Note that when all four principal components are used the risk factor betas are identical to those shown in the last column of Table II.1.6, as is the regression R^2.

However, our problem is that the four-factor model estimates were seriously affected by multicollinearity. Of course there is no such problem in the regression of Table II.1.9, so this does not bias the t statistics on the principal components. But we still cannot disentangle the separate effects of the risk factors on the stock returns. The solution is to use only the two main principal components as explanatory variables, as in the right-hand section of Table II.1.9 which corresponds to the results when $k = 2$. Then the regression R^2 is not much less than it is when $k = 4$, but the net betas on each risk factor are quite different from those shown in the right-hand column of Table II.1.6. We conclude that the estimates for the risk factor betas shown in the right-hand column of Table II.1.9 are more reliable than those in the right-hand column of Table II.1.6.

Table II.1.9 Using orthogonal regression to obtain risk factor betas

Vodafone	4-Factor		2-Factor	
	Coefficients	t stat.	Coefficients	t stat.
PC1	0.4230	24.8809	0.4230	24.8044
PC2	0.5090	8.5935	0.5090	8.5670
PC3	−0.0762	−0.5971		
PC4	0.5989	3.1390		
R	58.87%		58.44%	
Net betas				
NYSE index	0.8566		0.4200	
Communications	0.1373		0.0483	
Growth	0.2236		0.3038	
Large Cap	0.0092		0.4087	

Nokia	4-Factor		2-Factor	
	Coefficients	t stat.	Coefficients	t stat.
PC1	0.6626	33.0451	0.6626	32.7808
PC2	0.2942	4.2113	0.2942	4.1776
PC3	0.4194	2.7860		
PC4	−0.8926	−3.9669		
R	67.88%		67.17%	
Net betas				
NYSE index	−0.2674		0.3514	
Communications	0.2705		0.3604	
Growth	0.2003		0.3394	
Large Cap	1.1461		0.3962	

In Example II.1.7 we estimated the systematic risk that is due to the four risk factors as 24.7%. But there the risk factor beta matrix was affected by multicollinearity. Now we use the orthogonal regression estimates given in the right-hand column of Table II.1.9, i.e.

$$\mathbf{B} = \begin{pmatrix} 0.4200 & 0.3514 \\ 0.0483 & 0.3604 \\ 0.3038 & 0.3394 \\ 0.4087 & 0.3962 \end{pmatrix}.$$

This gives the portfolio beta vector as

$$\beta = \begin{pmatrix} 0.3686 \\ 0.2824 \\ 0.3305 \\ 0.3993 \end{pmatrix},$$

and the systematic risk is now calculated as 30.17%, as shown in the spreadsheet for this example.

II.1.5 ANALYSIS OF BARRA MODEL

The Barra model is a fundamental multi-factor regression model where a stock return is modelled using market and industry risk factor returns and certain fundamental factors called the *Barra risk indices*. The risk associated with a stock return is decomposed into the undiversifiable risk due to the market factor and two types of diversifiable risk: (a) the risk due to fundamental factors and industry risk factors, and (b) specific risk.

Barra has developed models for specific equity markets, starting with the US market in 1975, followed by the UK market in 1982, and since then many others. In each market Barra calculates a number of common risk indices and an industry classification to explain the diversifiable risks associated with a given stock. In the UK equity model there are 12 common risk indices and 38 industry indices.

The purpose of the Barra model is to analyse the relationship between a portfolio's return and the return on its benchmark. The difference between these two returns is called the *relative return*, also called the *active return*. A precise definition is given in Section II.1.5.2 below. The Barra model has two parts:

- an optimizer (ACTIVOPS) used to construct benchmark tracking portfolios with a required number of stocks and to design portfolios with maximum expected return given constraints on risk and weightings;
- a risk characterization tool (IPORCH) used to assess the *tracking error* (i.e. the standard deviation of the active returns) given a portfolio and benchmark.

With the help of the risk indices and industry indices, the Barra model explains the active return on a portfolio and the uncertainty about this active return in terms of:

- the *relative alpha* of the portfolio, i.e. the difference between the alpha of the portfolio and the benchmark alpha (note that if the benchmark is the market index then its alpha is 0);
- the *relative betas* of the portfolio, i.e. the difference between the beta of the portfolio and the benchmark beta, with respect to the market, industry factors and Barra risk indices (note that if the benchmark is the market index then its market beta is 1 and its other betas are 0).

II.1.5.1   Risk Indices, Descriptors and Fundamental Betas

The Barra fundamental risk factors are also called *common risk indices* because they reflect common characteristics among different companies. The risk indices and their structure are different for every country. Each risk index is built from a number of subjectively chosen *descriptors*. For instance, the risk index 'Growth' in the UK model is given by the following descriptors:

- earnings growth over 5 years;
- asset growth;
- recent earnings change;
- change in capital structure;
- low yield indicator.

Each descriptor is standardized with respect to the stock universe: in the case of the UK model the universe is the FT All Share index. The standardization is applied so that the FT All Share index has zero sensitivity to each descriptor and so that the variance of descriptor values taken over all stocks in the universe is 1.

The *factor loading* on each descriptor is determined by a cross-sectional regression of all stocks in the universe, updated every month. That is, the factor loading is the estimated regression coefficient on the descriptor from the regression

$$Y_i = \beta_1 D_{i1} + \ldots + \beta_M D_{iM} + \varepsilon_i,$$

where M is the number of descriptors, $D_{i1}, \ldots, D_{iM}$ are the descriptor values for stock i and $i = 1, \ldots, N$ where N is the number of stocks in the universe. Each risk index has a Barra *fundamental beta* which is calculated as the sum of the factor loadings on all the descriptors for that risk index.

The use of these descriptors allows the Barra model to analyse companies with very little history of returns, because the relevant descriptors for a stock can be allocated qualitatively. No history is required because the firm's descriptors may be allocated on the basis of the company profile, but historical data are useful for testing the judgement used. The chosen descriptors are then grouped into risk indices, so that the important determinants of the returns can be analysed. In the UK model the risk indices are:

- *earnings variability*, which also measures cash-flow fluctuations;
- *foreign exposure*, which depends on percentage of sales that are exports, and other descriptors related to tax and world markets;
- *growth*, which indicates the historical growth rate;
- *labour intensity*, which estimates the importance of labour costs, relative to capital;
- *leverage*, which depends on the debt–equity ratio and related descriptors;
- *non-FTA indicator*, which captures the behaviour of small firms not in the FTSE All Share index;
- *size*, which depends on market capitalization;
- *success*, which is related to earnings growth;
- *trading activity*, which is relative turnover as a percentage of total capitalization;
- *value to price*, which is determined by the ratio of book value to market price and other related descriptors;
- *variability*, a measure of the stock's systematic risk; and
- *yield*, a measure of current and historical dividend yield.

The *market portfolio* is the portfolio of all stocks in the universe with weights proportional to their capitalization. In the UK model the market portfolio is taken to be the FT All Share index. Each month descriptors are standardized so that the risk index sensitivities of the market portfolio are 0, and so that each risk index has a variance of 1 when averaged over all stocks in the universe. Hence, the covariance matrix of the descriptors equals the correlation matrix. Each month the risk index correlation matrix is obtained from the correlation matrix of the standardized descriptors for each stock in the universe.

Each stock in the universe is assigned to one or more of the industries. In the UK model this is done according to the Financial Times classification. The Barra handbook is not entirely clear about the method used to estimate the covariances of the industry factors and their factor betas. My own interpretation is that they use cross-sectional analysis, just as they do for the risk indices. Each month there are N data points for each industry factor, where N is the number of stocks in the industry. For instance, the industry 'Breweries' will have a vector such as $(0, 0, 1, 1, 0, \ldots, 1)$ where 1 in the ith place indicates that stock i is included in the brewery industry. This way the industry data will have the same dimension as the descriptor and risk index data, and then the Barra model will be able to estimate, each month, a cross-correlation matrix between the risk indices and the industry factors, as per the results shown in the Barra handbook. The cross-correlation matrix – which is the same as the cross-covariance matrix because of the standardization described above – is important because it is used in the risk decomposition of a portfolio, as explained in the next subsection.

II.1.5.2   Model Specification and Risk Decomposition

Consider a specific portfolio P and its corresponding benchmark B. The multi-factor Barra model applied to this portfolio and its benchmark may be written

$$
\begin{aligned}
R_P &= \alpha_P + \beta_P X + \sum_{k=1}^{12} \beta_P^{F,k} R^{F,k} + \sum_{k=1}^{38} \beta_P^{I,k} R^{I,k} + \varepsilon_P, \\
R_B &= \alpha_B + \beta_B X + \sum_{k=1}^{12} \beta_B^{F,k} R^{F,k} + \sum_{k=1}^{38} \beta_B^{I,k} R^{I,k} + \varepsilon_B,
\end{aligned}
\tag{II.1.37}
$$

with the following notation:

X : return on the market index

$R^{F,k}$: return on the kth (standardized) risk index;

$R^{I,k}$: return on the kth industry index;

α_P : portfolio alpha;

α_B : benchmark alpha ($=0$ if benchmark is market index);

β_P : portfolio market beta;

β_B : benchmark market beta ($=1$ if benchmark is market index);

$\beta_P^{F,k}$: portfolio fundamental beta on the kth (standardized) risk index;

$\beta_B^{F,k}$: benchmark fundamental beta ($=0$ if benchmark is market index);

$\beta_P^{I,i}$: portfolio beta on the ith industry index;

$\beta_B^{F,i}$: benchmark beta on the ith industry index ($=0$ if benchmark is market index);

ε_P : portfolio specific return;

α_B : benchmark specific return ($=0$ if benchmark is market index).

In more concise matrix notation the model (II.1.37) may be written

$$
\begin{aligned}
R_P &= \alpha_P + \beta_P X + \left(\beta_P^F\right)' \mathbf{R}^F + \left(\beta_P^I\right)' \mathbf{R}^I + \varepsilon_P, \\
R_B &= \alpha_B + \beta_B X + \left(\beta_B^F\right)' \mathbf{R}^F + \left(\beta_B^I\right)' \mathbf{R}^I + \varepsilon_B.
\end{aligned}
\tag{II.1.38}
$$

where $\left(\beta_P^F\right)' = \left(\beta_P^{F,1}, \ldots, \beta_P^{F,12}\right)$ and the other vector notation follows analogously.

The active return on the portfolio is then defined as[19]

$$
Y = R_P - R_B = (\alpha_P - \alpha_B) + (\beta_P - \beta_B) X + \left(\beta_P^F - \beta_B^F\right)' \mathbf{R}^F + \left(\beta_P^I - \beta_B^I\right)' \mathbf{R}^I + (\varepsilon_P - \varepsilon_B)
$$

Now defining the *relative alpha* as $\alpha = \alpha_P - \alpha_B$ and the *relative betas* as

$$
\beta = \beta_P - \beta_B, \quad \beta^F = \beta_P^F - \beta_B^F \quad \text{and} \quad \beta^I = \beta_P^I - \beta_B^I
$$

and setting $\varepsilon = \varepsilon_P - \varepsilon_B$ we may write the model in terms of the portfolio's active return as:

$$
Y = \alpha + \beta X + \beta^{F'} \mathbf{R}^F + \beta^{I'} \mathbf{R}^I + \varepsilon.
\tag{II.1.39}
$$

---

[19] This definition is based on the relationship between active, portfolio and benchmark log returns. But ordinary returns are used in the derivation of the factor model for the portfolio (because the portfolio return is the weighted sum of the stock returns, not log returns). Hence, the relationship (II.1.39) is based on the fact that returns and log returns are approximately equal if the return is small, even though this is the case only when returns are measured over a short time interval such as one day.

Taking expectations of the active return and noting that the Barra fundamental risk indices are standardized to have zero expectation gives

$$E(Y) = \alpha + \beta E(X) + \beta^{I'} E(\mathbf{R}^I),$$ (II.1.40)

and taking variances of the active return gives:

$$V(Y) = \beta' \mathbf{\Omega} \beta + V(\varepsilon).$$ (II.1.41)

where β is the column vector of all the betas in the model and $\mathbf{\Omega}$ is the covariance matrix of the market, risk index and industry factor returns.

The user of the Barra model defines a portfolio and a benchmark and then the IPORCH risk characterization tool estimates the portfolio's alpha and the vector of portfolio betas. It also outputs the *ex ante tracking error*, which is defined as the annualized square root of $V(Y)$ in (II.1.41). It is important to note that this ex ante tracking error represents uncertainty about the expected relative return (II.1.40) and not about any other relative return. In particular, the tracking error does *not* represent dispersion about a relative return of zero, unless the portfolio is tracking the benchmark. When a portfolio is designed to track a benchmark, stocks are selected in such a way that the expected relative return is zero. But in actively managed portfolios the alpha should not be zero, otherwise there is no justification for the manager's fees. In this case (II.1.40) will not be zero, unless by chance $\alpha + \beta E(X) + \beta^{I'} E(\mathbf{R}^I) = 0$, which is very highly unlikely.

Further discussion of this very important point about the application of the Barra model to the measurement of active risk is given in the next section. It is important not to lose sight of the fact that the Barra model is essentially a model for *alpha* management, i.e. its primary use is to optimize active returns by designing portfolios with maximum expected return, given constraints on risk and weightings.[20] It is also useful for constructing benchmark tracking portfolios with a required number of stocks. It may also be used for estimating and forecasting portfolio *risk* but only if the user fully understands the risk that the Barra model measures.

Unfortunately, it is a common mistake to estimate the tracking error using the model and then to represent this figure as a measure of active risk when the expected active return is non-zero. In the next section we explain why it is *mathematical nonsense* to use the tracking error to measure active risk when the expected active return is non-zero. Using a series of pedagogical examples, we demonstrate that it is improper practice for active fund managers to represent the tracking error to their clients as a measure of active risk.

II.1.6 TRACKING ERROR AND ACTIVE RISK

In this section we critically examine how the classical methods for estimating and forecasting volatility were applied to fund management during the 1990s. In the 1980s many institutional clients were content with passive fund management that sought merely to track an index or a benchmark. But during the 1990s more clients moved toward active fund management, seeking returns over and above the benchmark return and being willing to accept a small

---

[20] The advantage of using the Barra model as a risk assessment tool is that portfolio returns and risk are measured within the same model. However, its forecasting properties are limited because the parameters are estimated using cross-sectional data. This is especially true for short term risk forecasting over horizons of less than 1 month, because the model is only updated on a monthly basis.

amount of active risk in order to achieve this return. Hence the fund manager's performance was, and still is, assessed relative to a benchmark. This benchmark can be a traded asset itself, but many benchmarks are not necessarily tradable, such as the *London Interbank Offered Rate* (LIBOR).

Whatever the benchmark, it is standard to measure risk relative to the benchmark and to call this risk the *active risk* or the *relative risk* of the fund. We begin this section by demonstrating that the precise definition of active or relative risk is not at all straightforward. In fact, even the fundamental concept of 'measuring risk relative to a benchmark' has led to considerable confusion amongst risk managers of funds. The main aim of this section is to try to dispel this confusion, and so we begin by defining our terminology very carefully.

II.1.6.1   Ex Post versus Ex Ante Measurement of Risk and Return

Ex post is Latin for 'from after', so ex post risk and return are measured directly from historical observations on the past evolution of returns. *Ex ante* is Latin for 'from before'. Ex ante risk and return are forward looking and when they are forecast, these forecasts are usually based on some model. In fund management the ex ante risk model is the same as the ex ante returns model. This is usually a regression-based factor model that portfolio managers use to select assets and allocate capital to these assets in an optimal manner. The model is defined by some prior beliefs about the future evolution of the portfolio and the benchmark. These beliefs may be, but need not be, based on historical data.

II.1.6.2   Definition of Active Returns

Active return is also commonly called the *relative return*. It is the difference between the portfolio's return and the benchmark return. Hence, if a portfolio tracks the benchmark exactly its active returns are zero. In general, we model the active returns using a factor model framework, for instance using the Barra model that was described in the previous section.

The portfolio return is the change in a portfolio's value over a certain period expressed as a percentage of its current value. Thus if V_P and V_B denote the values of the portfolio and the benchmark respectively, then the one-period ex post return on the portfolio, measured at time t, is

$$R_{Pt} = \frac{V_{Pt} - V_{P,t-1}}{V_{P,t-1}} \tag{II.1.42}$$

and the one-period ex post return on the benchmark, measured at time t, is

$$R_{Bt} = \frac{V_{Bt} - V_{B,t-1}}{V_{B,t-1}}. \tag{II.1.43}$$

The one-period ex post active return measured at time t, denoted R_t, is defined by the relationship

$$(1 + R_t)(1 + R_{Bt}) = (1 + R_{Pt}). \tag{II.1.44}$$

A portfolio manager's performance is usually assessed over a period of several months, so for performance measurement it is not really appropriate to use the log approximation to returns. However, in an *ex ante* risk model it may be necessary to assess risks over a short horizon, in which case we may use the log return. The one-period ex post log returns are

$$r_{Pt} = \ln\left(\frac{V_{Pt}}{V_{P,t-1}}\right), \quad r_{Bt} = \ln\left(\frac{V_{Bt}}{V_{B,t-1}}\right), \tag{II.1.45}$$

and the ex ante log returns are

$$r_{Pt} = \ln\left(\frac{V_{P,t+1}}{V_{Pt}}\right), \quad r_{Bt} = \ln\left(\frac{V_{B,t+1}}{V_{Bt}}\right). \tag{II.1.46}$$

Now, either ex post or ex ante,

$$r_t = r_{Pt} - r_{Bt}. \tag{II.1.47}$$

That is, the active log return is the portfolio's log return minus the benchmark's log return.

Note that to measure the ex ante active returns we need a value for both the portfolio and the benchmark at time $t+1$. For this it is necessary to use a model, such as the Barra model, that aims to forecast future values of all the assets in the investment universe.

II.1.6.3 Definition of Active Weights

In Section I.1.4 we proved that

$$R_P = \sum_{i=1}^{k} w_i R_i \tag{II.1.48}$$

where R_P is the return on a portfolio, R_i is the one-period return on asset i, k is the number of assets in the portfolio and w_i is the portfolio weight on asset i at the beginning of the period, defined as the value of the portfolio's holding in asset i at time t divided by the total value of the portfolio at time t.

Log returns are very convenient analytically and, over short time periods the log return is approximately equal to the return, as shown in Section I.1.4. Using this approximation, the log return on the portfolio and the benchmark may also be written as a weighted sum of the asset log returns:

$$r_{Pt} = \sum_{i=1}^{k} w_{Pit} r_{it}, \quad r_{Bt} = \sum_{i=1}^{k} w_{Bit} r_{it}, \tag{II.1.49}$$

where r_{it} is the log return on asset i at time t, w_{Pit} is the portfolio's weight on asset i at time t, and w_{Bit} is the benchmark's weight on asset i at time t. From (II.1.47) and (II.1.49) we have

$$r_t = \sum_{i=1}^{k} (w_{Pit} - w_{Bit}) r_{it} = \sum_{i=1}^{k} w_{it} r_{it}, \tag{II.1.50}$$

and $w_{it} = w_{Pit} - w_{Bit}$ is called the portfolio's *active weight* on asset i at time t.

That is, the active weight on an asset in the benchmark is just the difference between the portfolio's weight and the benchmark's weight on that asset.

II.1.6.4 Ex Post Tracking Error

Suppose that we measure risk ex post, using a time series of T active returns. Denote the active return at time t by R_t and the average active return over the sample by $\bar{R}$. Then the ex post tracking error (TE) is estimated as

$$TE = \sqrt{\frac{1}{T-1} \sum_{t=1}^{T} (R_t - \bar{R})^2}. \tag{II.1.51}$$

Thus the tracking error is the standard deviation of active returns. It is usually quoted in annual terms, like volatility.

EXAMPLE II.1.8: TRACKING ERROR OF AN UNDERPERFORMING FUND

An ex post tracking error is estimated from a sample of monthly returns on the fund and the benchmark. The fund returns exactly 1% less than the benchmark during every month in the sample. More precisely, the active return on the fund is exactly -1% each month. What is the tracking error on this fund?

SOLUTION   Since the active return is constant, it has zero standard deviation. Hence the tracking error is zero.

The above example is extreme, but illustrative. A zero tracking error would also result if we assumed that the active return was exactly $+1\%$ each month. More generally, the tracking error of an underperforming fund – or indeed an overperforming fund – can be very small when the performance is stable. But the fund need not be tracking the benchmark: it may be very far from the benchmark. The following example illustrates this point in a more realistic framework, where the fund does not have a constant active return. Instead we just assume that the fund consistently underperforms the benchmark.

EXAMPLE II.1.9: WHY TRACKING ERROR ONLY APPLIES TO TRACKING FUNDS

A fund's values and its benchmark values between 1990 and 2006 are shown in Table II.1.10. The data cover a period of 16 years and for comparison the value of the benchmark and of the funds are set to 100 at the beginning of the period. What is the ex post tracking error of the fund measured from these data? How risky is this fund?

Table II.1.10   Values of a fund and a benchmark[a]

Date	1990	1991	1992	1993	1994	1995	1996	1997	1998	1999	2000	2001	2002	2003	2004	2005	2006
Benchmark	100	120	138	145	159	159	175	210	200	210	262	249	249	299	284	290	319
Fund	100	115	129	128	135	129	136	155	144	147	178	161	156	179	162	157	164

[a] The prices shown have been rounded – see the spreadsheet for this example for the precise figures.

SOLUTION   The spreadsheet for this example shows how the ex post TE is calculated. In fact the prices of the fund and benchmark were rounded in Table II.1.10 and using their exact values we obtain $TE = 1\%$. But this is not at all representative of the risk of the fund. The fund's value in 2006 was half the value of the benchmark! Figure II.1.5 illustrates the values of the fund and the benchmark to emphasize this point.

We see that the only thing that affects the ex post tracking error is the variability of the active returns. It does not matter what the level of the mean active return is because this mean is taken out of the calculation: only the *mean deviations* of the active returns are used.

   These examples show that there is a real problem with ex post tracking error if risk managers try to apply this metric to active funds, or indeed any fund that has a non-zero mean active return. Tracking error only measures the 'risk of relative returns'. It does not measure the risk of the fund relative to the benchmark. Indeed, the benchmark is *irrelevant* to the calculation of ex post tracking error, as the next example shows.

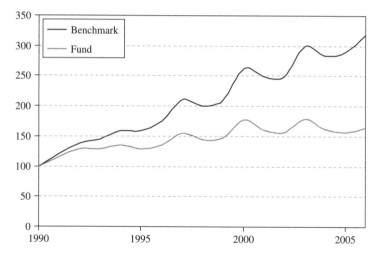

Figure II.1.5   A fund with ex post tracking error of only 1%

EXAMPLE II.1.10: IRRELEVANCE OF THE BENCHMARK FOR TRACKING ERROR

Consider one fund and two possible benchmarks, whose values are shown in Table II.1.11. What is the ex post tracking error of the fund measured relative to each benchmark based on these data?

Table II.1.11   Values of a fund and two benchmarks[a]

Date	1990	1991	1992	1993	1994	1995	1996	1997	1998	1999	2000	2001	2002	2003	2004	2005	2006
Benchmark 1	100	90	104	124	161	186	204	235	258	271	339	254	216	216	238	262	275
Benchmark 2	100	93	110	136	182	216	245	291	330	357	460	355	311	321	364	413	447
Fund	100	91	104	127	167	190	206	234	260	271	346	256	221	223	243	262	273

[a] The prices shown have been rounded – see the spreadsheet for this example for the precise figures.

SOLUTION   The spreadsheet calculates the ex post TE relative to each benchmark and it is 1.38% relative to *both* benchmarks. But the fund is tracking benchmark 1 and substantially underperforming benchmark 2 as we can see from the time series of their values illustrated in Figure II.1.6. The fund has the *same* tracking error relative to both benchmarks. But surely, if the risk is being measured *relative* to the benchmark then the result should be different depending on the benchmark. Indeed, given the past performance shown above, the fund has a very high risk relative to benchmark 2 but a very small risk relative to benchmark 1.

In summary, the name 'tracking error' derives from the fact that *tracking* funds may use (II.1.51) as a risk metric. However, we have demonstrated why ex post tracking error is not a suitable risk metric for actively managed funds. It is only when a fund tracks a benchmark closely that ex post tracking error is a suitable choice of risk metric.

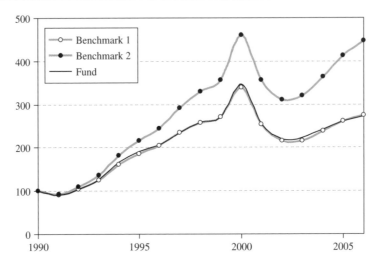

Figure II.1.6 Irrelevance of the benchmark for tracking error

II.1.6.5   Ex Post Mean-Adjusted Tracking Error

We call the square root of the average squared active return the ex post *mean-adjusted tracking error*, i.e.

$$MATE = \sqrt{\frac{1}{T} \sum_{t=1}^{T} R_t^2} \qquad (\text{II.1.52})$$

Straightforward calculations show that

$$(MATE)^2 = \frac{T-1}{T} \left(TE^2\right) + \overline{R}^2 \qquad (\text{II.1.53})$$

Hence, the mean-adjusted tracking error will be larger than the tracking error when the mean active return is quite different from zero:

$$TE \approx MATE \text{ if } \overline{R} \approx 0 \text{ and, for large } T, TE < MATE \text{ when } \overline{R} \neq 0.$$

Earlier we saw that when volatility is estimated from a set of historical *daily* returns it is standard to assume that the mean return is very close to zero. In fact, we have assumed this throughout the chapter. However, in active fund management it should not be assumed that the mean active return is zero for two reasons. Firstly, returns are often measured at the monthly, not the daily frequency, and over a period of 1 month an assumption of zero mean is not usually justified for any market. Secondly, we are dealing with an active return here, not just an ordinary return, and since the fund manager's mandate is to *outperform* the benchmark their client would be very disappointed if $\overline{R} \approx 0$. It is only in a passive fund, which aims merely to track a benchmark, that the average active return should be very close to zero.

EXAMPLE II.1.11: INTERPRETATION OF MEAN-ADJUSTED TRACKING ERROR

Calculate the ex post mean-adjusted tracking error for:

(a) the fund in Example II.1.9 relative to its benchmark; and
(b) the fund in Example II.1.10 relative to both benchmarks.

What can you infer from your results?

SOLUTION   The mean-adjusted tracking error can be calculated directly on the squared active returns using (II.1.52) and this is done in the spreadsheet for this example. Alternatively, since we already know the ex post TE, we may calculate the mean active return and use (II.1.53).

(a) For the fund in Example II.1.9 we have $T = 16$, $TE = 1\%$ and $\bar{R} = -4.06\%$. Hence,

$$MATE = \sqrt{0.01^2 \times \frac{15}{16} + 0.0406^2} = 4.18\%.$$

The $MATE$ is much greater than TE because it captures the fact that the fund deviated considerably from the benchmark.

(b) For the fund in Example II.1.10 we again have $T = 16$, and,

relative to benchmark 1, $TE = 1.38\%$ and $\bar{R} = -0.04\%$;

relative to benchmark 2, $TE = 1.38\%$ and $\bar{R} = -3.04\%$.

Hence, using (II.1.53) we have,

relative to benchmark 1, $MATE = \sqrt{0.0138^2 \times \frac{15}{16} + 0.0004^2} = 1.34\%$;

relative to benchmark 2, $MATE = \sqrt{0.0138^2 \times \frac{15}{16} + 0.0304^2} = 3.32\%$.

Relative to benchmark 1, where the mean active return is very near zero, the mean-adjusted tracking error is approximately the same as the tracking error. In fact $MATE$ is less than TE, which is only possible when both T and $\bar{R}$ are relatively small. Relative to benchmark 2, the mean active return is far from zero and the mean-adjusted tracking error is much larger than the tracking error.

We have already observed that the fund's risk should be much higher relative to benchmark 2, because it substantially underperformed that benchmark, yet the tracking error could not distinguish between the risks relative to either benchmark. However, the mean-adjusted tracking error does capture the difference in mean active returns: it is substantially higher relative to benchmark 2 than benchmark 1.

EXAMPLE II.1.12: COMPARISON OF TE AND $MATE$

Figure II.1.7 shows a benchmark and two funds whose risk is assessed relative to that benchmark. Fund A is a passive fund that tracks the benchmark closely, and fund B is an active fund that has been allowed to deviate substantially from the benchmark allocations. As a result of poor investment decisions it has underperformed the benchmark disastrously. Which fund has more risk relative to the benchmark?

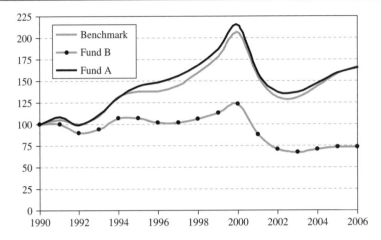

Figure II.1.7   Which fund has an ex post tracking error of zero?

SOLUTION   Fund B has a lower tracking error than fund A. In fact, the tracking error of fund B (the underperforming fund) is zero! So according to *TE* fund A has more risk! However the real difference between the two funds is in their average active return: it is 0 for fund A but −5% for fund B.

Table II.1.12 shows the annual returns on the benchmark and on both of the funds, and the active return on each fund in each year, calculated using (II.1.44). From the active returns, their mean and their squares, formulae (II.1.51) and (II.1.53) have been used to calculate the *TE* and *MATE* for each fund. Only the *MATE* identifies that fund B is more risky than fund A.

Table II.1.12   *TE* and *MATE* for the funds in Figure II.1.7

Year	Benchmark	Fund A	Fund B	Active A	Active B
1990	5%	9%	0%	3.81%	−5.00%
1991	−5%	−9%	−10%	−4.21%	−5.00%
1992	10%	12%	4%	1.82%	−5.00%
1993	20%	18%	14%	−1.67%	−5.00%
1994	5%	10%	0%	4.76%	−5.00%
1995	0%	3%	−5%	3.00%	−5.00%
1996	5%	5%	0%	0.00%	−5.00%
1997	10%	8%	4%	−1.82%	−5.00%
1998	12%	11%	6%	−0.89%	−5.00%
1999	15%	15%	9%	−0.06%	−5.00%
2000	−25%	−26%	−29%	−1.33%	−5.00%
2001	−15%	−14%	−19%	1.18%	−5.00%
2002	0%	0%	−5%	0.00%	−5.00%
2003	10%	8%	4%	−1.82%	−5.00%
2004	10%	8%	4%	−1.82%	−5.00%
2005	5%	4%	0%	−0.95%	−5.00%
		Average		0.00%	−5.00%
		TE		2.38%	0.00%
		MATE		2.30%	5.00%

To summarize the lessons learned from the above examples, the ex post tracking error does not measure the risk of a fund deviating from a benchmark; it only measures the variability of active returns. The level of the benchmark is irrelevant to tracking error – only the variability in benchmark returns and the variability in the fund's returns matter for the tracking error. In short, a fund with a stable active return will always have a low tracking error, irrespective of the level of active returns. However, the mean-adjusted tracking error includes a measure of the fund's deviation from the benchmark as well as a measure of the variability in active returns. Here it is not only the stability of active returns that matters for the risk metric; their general level is also taken into account.

II.1.6.6 Ex Ante Tracking Error

For the definition of an ex ante forecast of TE and of $MATE$ we need to use a model for expected returns, and the most usual type of model to employ for this is regression based on a factor model. In Section II.1.3.1 we wrote the general multi-factor regression model in matrix form as

$$\mathbf{y} = \boldsymbol{\alpha} + \mathbf{X}\boldsymbol{\beta} + \boldsymbol{\varepsilon}, \tag{II.1.54}$$

and hence we derived the following expression for the expected return:

$$E(Y) = \alpha + \boldsymbol{\beta}'E(\mathbf{X}), \tag{II.1.55}$$

where $E(\mathbf{X})$ is the vector of expected returns to each risk factor. Similarly, the variance of the return about this expected value is

$$V(Y) = \boldsymbol{\beta}'\boldsymbol{\Omega}\boldsymbol{\beta} + V(\varepsilon), \tag{II.1.56}$$

where $\boldsymbol{\Omega}$ is the covariance matrix of the factor returns.

To define the ex ante tracking error we suppose that Y represents not the ordinary return but the *active return* on a fund. Likewise, the alpha and betas above are the *relative alpha* and *relative betas* of the fund. These are the difference between the fund's ordinary alpha and factor betas and the benchmark's alpha and factor betas. Now, given the relative alpha and betas in (II.1.54), then (II.1.55) yields the expected active return in terms of the relative alpha and betas and $E(\mathbf{X})$, the vector of expected returns to each risk factor. Similarly, (II.1.56) gives the variance of active returns in terms of β and $\boldsymbol{\Omega}$, the covariance matrix of the factor returns.

The ex ante tracking error is the square root of the variance of active returns given by (II.1.56), quoted in annualized terms. If the covariance matrix $\boldsymbol{\Omega}$ contains forecasts of the volatilities and correlations of the risk factor returns then (II.1.56) represents a *forecast* of the risk of active returns, i.e. the standard deviation of active returns. In other words, the ex ante tracking error measures variance *about the expected active return* (II.1.55).

It is very important to stress that (II.1.56) is a variance about (II.1.55), i.e. the expected active return that is estimated by the factor model and *only* about this expected active return. Thus the square root of (II.1.56), i.e. the tracking error, is a measure of risk relative to the expected active return (II.1.55).

Suppose we target an active return that is different from (II.1.55). For instance, we might target an outperformance of the benchmark by 2% per annum. Then it would be mathematically incorrect to represent the square root of (II.1.56), i.e. the tracking error, as the risk relative to the target active return of 2%. However, during the 1990s it was standard practice, at least by some leading fund managers, to forecast a tracking error in a factor model framework and then, somehow, to interpret this tracking error as representing the potential for a fund to deviate from its *target* active return. Suppose the target active return is 2% per annum and the expected active return based on their risk model is also 2% per annum. Then there is nothing incorrect about this interpretation. But if the expected active return based on their risk model is *not* 2%, then it is misleading to interpret the ex ante tracking error as the potential deviation from the target return.

II.1.6.7   Ex Ante Mean-Adjusted Tracking Error

A forecast active return is a distribution. An expected active return is just one point in this distribution, i.e. its expected value, but the returns model also forecasts the entire distribution, albeit often rather crudely. Indeed, *any* forecast from a statistical model is a distribution. We may choose to focus on a single *point forecast,* usually of the expectation of this distribution, but the model still forecasts an entire distribution and this distribution is specific to the estimated model. If the point forecast of the expected return changes, so does the whole distribution, and usually it does not just 'shift' with a different expected return; the variance of the return about this expectation also changes! In short, there is only *one* distribution of active returns in the future that is forecast by any statistical model and it is inconsistent with the model to change one of its parameters, leaving the other parameters unchanged. One may as well throw away the model and base forecasts entirely on subjective beliefs.

Consider Figure II.1.8, which shows an active return forecast depicted as a normal distribution where the mean of that distribution – the expected active return $E(Y)$ – is assumed to be less than the target active return. Now, if the target active return is *not* equal to $E(Y)$, which is very often the case, then there are *two* sources of risk relative to the benchmark: the risk arising from dispersion about the mean return (i.e. tracking error) and the risk that the mean return differs from the target return. The tracking error *ignores* the second source of active risk.

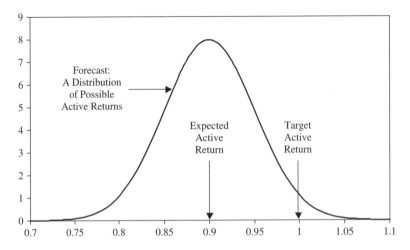

Figure II.1.8   Forecast and target active returns

However, the mean-adjusted ex ante tracking error *does* take account of model predictions for active returns that may differ from the target active return. We define

$$MATE = \sqrt{V(Y) + (E(Y) - Y^*)^2},$$ (II.1.57)

where Y^* is the target active return and $E(Y)$ and $V(Y)$ are forecast by the risk model.

EXAMPLE II.1.13: WHICH FUND IS MORE RISKY (1)?

A risk model is used to forecast the ex ante tracking errors for two funds. Both funds have the same ex ante tracking error of 4%. However, the model gives different predictions for the expected active return on each fund: it is 0% for fund A and 1% for fund B. The target active return is 2%. Which fund is more risky relative to this target?

SOLUTION   Since both funds have the same tracking error (TE), they have the same risk according to the TE metric. But TE does not measure risk relative to the target active return. The mean-adjusted tracking error $(MATE)$ is 4.47% for fund A and 4.12% for fund B. Hence, according to the $MATE$ metric, fund A is more risky. This is intuitive, since the expected active return on fund A is further from the target active return than the expected active return on fund B.

This example has shown that if two index tracking funds have the same tracking error, the fund that has the highest absolute value for expected active return will have the greatest mean-adjusted tracking error.

EXAMPLE II.1.14: WHICH FUND IS MORE RISKY (2)?

A risk model is used to forecast the ex ante tracking error for two funds. The predictions are $TE = 2\%$ for fund A and $TE = 5\%$ for fund B. The funds have the same expected active return. Which fund is more risky?

SOLUTION   Fund B has a larger ex ante tracking error than fund A and so is more risky than fund A according to this risk metric. It does not matter what the target active return is, because this has no effect on the ex ante tracking error. Fund B also has the larger mean-adjusted tracking error, because the funds have the same expected active return. For instance, if the expected active return is either $+1\%$ or -1% then $MATE = 2.24\%$ for fund A and $MATE = 5.10\%$ for fund B.

Hence both the TE and the mean-adjusted TE agree that fund B is more risky. If two funds have the same expected active return then the fund that has the highest tracking error will have the greatest mean-adjusted tracking error.

But this is not the whole story about active risk. Figure II.1.9 depicts the ordinary returns distributions for the two funds considered in Example II.1.14. Now we make the further assumption that the predicted returns are normally distributed, and that the two funds have the same expected return of 1%. Two different target returns, of 0% and 2%, are depicted on the figure using vertical dotted and solid lines, respectively. We note:

- There is a 42% chance that fund B returns less than 0%, but only a 31% chance that fund A returns less than 0%. So, fund B is more risky than fund A relative to a target of 0%.

- There is a 69% chance that fund A returns less than 2% but only a 58% chance that fund B returns less than 2%. So, fund A is more risky than fund B relative to a target of 2%.

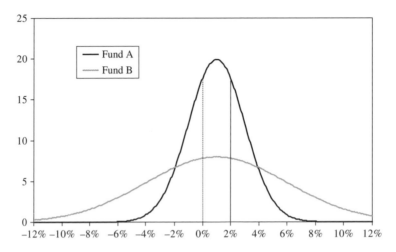

Figure II.1.9   Returns distributions for two funds

However, both TE and $MATE$ rank fund B as the riskier fund relative to *both* benchmarks. Although $MATE$ does capture the risk that the expected return will deviate from the target return, it cannot capture the difference between a good forecast, where the expected return is greater than target, and a bad forecast, where the expected return is less than target.[21] $MATE$ penalizes *any* deviation between the expected return and the target and it does not matter whether the deviation is positive or negative.

This example shows that when the expected active return derived from the risk model is different from the target return Y^* then the potential for the expected return to deviate from the target return usually represents *much* the largest element of active risk as perceived by the clients. Yet this part of the risk is commonly ignored by mathematically inept and ill-informed fund managers.

Another lesson to be learned from the above example is that if $E(Y) < Y^*$, i.e. if the expected active return is less than the target active return, then the worst case occurs when the tracking error is *small*. In other words, if the model predicts an active return that is less than the target it is *better* for the investors if the tracking error is large!

II.1.6.8   Clarification of the Definition of Active Risk

In the 1980s and early 1990s the decisions made by active fund managers were usually controlled through strict imposition of control ranges. That is, the active weights were not allowed to become too great. However, since then some fund managers have dropped control ranges in favour of metrics such as tracking error that could (if used properly) provide

---

[21] This is because their difference is squared in the formula (II.1.57) for this risk metric.

a better description of active risk. Various definitions of active risk can be found in the literature. One of the most complete definitions is given by Wikipedia.[22]

> *Active risk* refers to that segment of risk in an investment portfolio that is due to active management decisions made by the portfolio manager. It does not include any risk (return) that is merely a function of the market's movement. In addition to risk (return) from specific stock selection or industry and factor 'bets', it can also include risk (return) from market timing decisions. *A portfolio's active risk, then, is defined as the annualized standard deviation of the monthly difference between portfolio return and benchmark return.*

The last sentence makes it abundantly clear that, according to this (incorrect) definition, 'active risk' is measured by the tracking error. However, using our series of pedagogical examples above, we have demonstrated that measuring active risk using this metric is mathematically incorrect, except when the expected active return is zero, which is only the case for *passive*, benchmark-tracking funds. The definition of active risk given above is therefore contradictory, because the first sentence states that active risk is the 'risk in an investment portfolio that is due to *active* management decisions'. All risk averse clients and fund managers would agree that the risk 'due to active management decisions' should include the risk that an actively managed portfolio underperforms the benchmark. But we have proved that tracking error, i.e. the annualized standard deviation of the monthly difference between portfolio return and benchmark return, does not include this risk.

The Wikipedia definition is one of numerous other contradictory and confusing definitions of active risk. A myth – that tracking error equates to active risk – is still being perpetuated. In fact, at the time of writing (and I sincerely hope these will be corrected soon) virtually *all* the definitions of active risk available on the internet that also define a way to measure it fall into the trap of assuming tracking error is a suitable metric for active risk. Many simply define active risk as the standard deviation of the active returns, and leave it at that!

Active risk was originally a term applied to *passive* management where the fund manager's objective is to track an index as closely as possible. There is very little scope to deviate from the index because the fund aims for a zero active return. In other words, the *expected* active return is zero for a passive fund and, as shown above, it is only in this case that tracking error *is* synonymous with active risk. But actively managed funds have a mandate to outperform an index, so by definition their expected active return is not zero. Hence the active risk of actively managed funds *cannot* be measured by tracking error.

If nothing else, I hope that this section has made clear to active fund managers that it is extremely important to define one's terms very carefully. The enormously ambiguous phrase *risk of returns relative to the benchmark,* which is often used to define active risk, could be interpreted as the risk [of returns] relative to the benchmark, i.e. the risk of deviating from the benchmark. But it could also be interpreted as the risk of [returns relative to the benchmark], i.e. the standard deviation of active returns, and this is different from the first interpretation! Measuring *returns* relative to a benchmark does not go hand in hand with measuring *risk* relative to a benchmark, unless the expected active return is zero. So the tracking error metric is fine for funds that actually track the benchmark, i.e. for passive funds. Indeed, it is from this that the name derives. But for funds that have a mandate *not*

---

[22] See http://en.wikipedia.org/wiki/Active_risk. This is the definition at the time of going to press, but I shall be adding a discussion to this page with a reference to this chapter when the book is in print.

to track a benchmark, i.e. for actively managed funds, the tracking error cannot be used to measure the active risk. It measures the risk of [returns relative to the benchmark] but says nothing *at all* about the real risk that active managers take, which is the risk that the fund will underperform the benchmark.

II.1.7 SUMMARY AND CONCLUSIONS

In this chapter we have described the use of factor models for analysing the risk and return on portfolios of risky assets. Even though the returns distribution of a portfolio could be modelled without using a factor model, the advantages of factor models include the ability to:

- attribute total risk to different sources, which is useful for performance analysis, benchmark selection and risk capital allocation; and
- evaluate portfolio risk under 'what if' scenarios, i.e. when risk factor values are stressed to extreme levels.

Many factor models are estimated using historical time series data. Such models may be used to forecast the risk and expected returns of portfolios of risky assets. Basic measures of risk may be based purely on a fund's historical returns, but the analyst will gain further insight into the risk characteristics of the portfolio by employing stress tests and scenario analysis. This is the main reason for using factor models to capture portfolio risk. If all that we wanted was a risk measurement, we could just use historical data on stock returns to form a 'current weighted' portfolio and measure its volatility – this is much easier than building a good factor model. But the factor model is a great tool for value-at-risk modelling, especially for the stress tests and scenario analysis that form part of the day-to-day work of a risk analyst.

Factor models are also used for *style analysis*, i.e. to attribute funds' returns to value, growth and other style factors. This helps investors to identify the sources of returns knowing only the funds returns and no details about the fund's strategies. Style analysis can be used to select appropriate benchmarks against which to measure performance and as a guide for portfolio diversification. In one of the empirical examples in this chapter we have implemented a style analysis for a simple portfolio, and the results were based on a constrained quadratic programming problem.

The examples developed in the Excel workbook for this chapter take the reader through many different factor models. In some cases we have decomposed total risk into *systematic risk* and *specific risk* components. We also showed how the total systematic risk of international stock portfolios may be decomposed into *equity risk* and *foreign exchange risk* components. In other examples we estimated *fundamental factor models* whose risk factors are market and style indices, estimating their betas using regression analysis. But there was a very high correlation between the different risk factor returns, as so often happens with these models, and this necessitated the use of *orthogonal regression* techniques to properly identify the factor betas.

We also provided a detailed analysis of the *Barra model*, which employs time series and cross-sectional data to analyse the return (and also the risk) on both active and passive portfolios. For the benefit of users of the Barra model, we have carefully explained the correct way to measure the risk of active portfolios that are optimized using this model. Then we provided a critical discussion of the way that *active risk* has been, and may continue to be, measured by many fund managers. The definition of active risk is fraught with difficulty and ambiguous terms. *Active risk is the risk that an actively managed investment portfolio deviates from the benchmark.* Beware of other definitions, and there are many! In the 1990s many fund managers assessed active risk using the *tracking error*, i.e. the volatility of the active returns. Even nowadays many practitioners regard active risk and tracking error as synonymous. But we have demonstrated that this is a mistake – and potentially a very costly one! It is a common fallacy that tracking error can be used as an active risk metric. Using many pedagogical examples, we have carefully explained why *tracking error says nothing at all about the risk relative to a benchmark*. Tracking error only measures the volatility of relative returns.

Desirable properties for a good active risk metric include:

(a) if the active risk measure falls then the fund moves closer to the benchmark; and
(b) if the fund moves closer to the benchmark then the active risk measure falls.

However, tracking error has neither of these properties. The examples in Section II.1.6 have shown that a reduction in tracking error does not imply that the fund moves closer to the benchmark. It only implies that the active returns have become more stable. Also, moving closer to the benchmark does not imply that tracking error will be reduced and moving away from the benchmark does not imply that tracking error will increase.

Tracking error is *not* a suitable metric for measuring active risk, either ex post or ex ante. It is fine for passive funds, as its name suggests. In passive funds the expected future active return is zero and the ex post mean active return is likely to be very close to zero. Then tracking error measures the volatility around the benchmark. But more generally, tracking error measures volatility around the expected active return in the model – not the volatility around a zero active return, and not the volatility around the target outperformance, nor around any other value! In active fund management the aim is to *outperform* a benchmark by taking positions that may deviate markedly from those in the benchmark. Hence, the expected active return should not be zero; it should be equal to the target outperformance set by the client. The *mean-adjusted* tracking error *is* an active risk metric, but it is not a very good one. It penalizes returns that are greater than the benchmark return as much as it penalizes returns that are less than the benchmark return. That is, it is not a *downside* risk metric.

Principal Component Analysis

II.2.1 INTRODUCTION

This chapter introduces the statistical factor models that are based on principal component analysis (PCA) and that are commonly applied to model the returns on portfolios and the profit and loss (P&L) of cash flows. Such models may also be applied to assess portfolio risks and hence to provide the risk adjusted performance measures that are used to rank investments.[1]

Statistical factor models for portfolios are based on factors that have no economic or financial interpretation. A principal component representation for the percentage return on each asset in the investor's universe is derived from an *eigenvector analysis* of a very large covariance matrix, based on the returns on all the assets in the portfolio. Each principal component represents the percentage return on a *statistical* risk factor and, by choosing the number of principal components in the representation for each asset return, the investor can adjust the asset's *specific risk*. Then optimal portfolios are constructed by adjusting the weights to match the *systematic risk, systematic return* and specific risk characteristics desired by the investor.

Factor models for portfolios of interest rate sensitive instruments such as bonds, floating rate notes, forward rate agreements and swaps assume the portfolio has already been mapped to a fixed set of risk factors which are standard vertices along one or more *yield curves*.[2] In this case a PCA may be based on a covariance or correlation matrix of changes in these risk factors at a certain frequency, i.e. daily, weekly or monthly changes in interest rates. We remark that yield curve factor models differ from the regression-based factor models introduced in the previous chapter in two ways: they capture the portfolio's P&L rather than its percentage return, and the P&L is represented as a linear function of risk factor *changes*, rather than risk factor percentage returns.

These single and multiple *curve* factor models are not only used to model interest rate sensitive portfolios; they also have applications to the risk assessment of *forward currency exposures*, to futures positions in commodities and to implied volatility surfaces. PCA is a very flexible statistical tool. It may be applied to any covariance or correlation matrix based on returns or P&L.[3]

---

[1] Risk adjusted performance measures are introduced in Section I.6.5.
[2] See Section III.4.3 for details on mapping cash flows to a fixed set of interest rate risk factors.
[3] By definition, such a matrix must be positive semi-definite.

The primary aims of the PCA curve factor models are as follows:

- To reduce the number of risk factors to a manageable dimension. For example, instead of *sixty* yields of different maturities as risk factors we might use just *three* principal components.
- To identify the key sources of risk. Typically the most important risk factors are parallel shifts, changes in slope and changes in convexity of the curves.
- To facilitate the measurement of portfolio risk, for instance by introducing scenarios on the movements in the major risk factors.
- To help investors form optimal portfolios which are hedged against the most common types of movements in the curve. For example, using PCA is it easy to derive allocations to bonds so that the portfolio's value is unchanged for 95% (or more) of yield curve variations that have been observed in an historical sample.

PCA has a huge number of financial applications, in particular to term structures of interest rates, forwards, futures or volatility.[4] We shall focus on these applications in this chapter, but PCA also has useful applications to modelling hedge funds, or equity portfolios as described in Alexander and Dimitriu (2004). The outline of this chapter is as follows. Section II.2.2 provides a review of PCA, summarizing the definitions and important properties that we shall be using in this chapter. Here we extract the relevant results of linear algebra from Chapter I.2 in a concise overview of PCA. In Section II.2.3 we present a case study of PCA on UK zero coupon government bond yield curves, comparing the results of using different curves and different matrices in the factor model. For this case study and throughout this chapter we employ the Matrix Excel add-in freeware kindly provided by Leonardo Volpi.[5]

Section II.2.4 describes how PCA is used to derive curve factor models. Here we focus on the application of PCA to fixed income portfolios, forward currency exposures and futures positions in commodities. We also consider multiple curve factor models, where PCA is applied to a large correlation or covariance matrix of two or more curves. In this case the entire system is captured by the factor analysis: not just the volatilities and correlations of each individual curve, but also the correlations *between* two different curves. Empirical examples illustrate several applications to portfolio construction and hedging, risk measurement, risk decomposition and asset and liability management.

Section II.2.5 overviews the application of PCA to equity factor models, and presents an Excel case study based on just 30 stocks in the Dow Jones Industrial Average (DJIA) index. Note that commercial software is available that derives principal component representations for literally thousands of stock returns.[6] Section II.2.6 summarizes and concludes.

II.2.2   REVIEW OF PRINCIPAL COMPONENT ANALYSIS

PCA is based on the eigenvalue–eigenvector decomposition of a returns correlation matrix or a returns covariance matrix. A technical introduction to PCA is provided in Chapter I.2, along with an introduction to the properties of covariance and correlation matrices and their eigenvectors and eigenvalues. In this section we summarize the important definitions and concepts of PCA without much attention to technical details; readers requiring more formal definitions and derivations of mathematical results are referred to Section I.2.6.

---

[4] See Section III.4.4 for further details of its application to volatility surfaces.
[5] The add-in and a tutorial are available on the CD-ROM for *MarketRiskAnalysis* and from the Foxes team website at http://digilander.libero.it/foxes.
[6] See http://www.APT.com. APT provides investors with statistical market risk models, performance and risk analytics, and portfolio optimization and construction tools.

II.2.2.1 Definition of Principal Components

We summarize the concept of principal components by the following definitions and results, all of which are discussed in more detail in Section I.2.6:

1. A matrix is a *linear transformation*: write $\mathbf{Ax} = \mathbf{y}$, then each element of the vector $\mathbf{y}$ is a linear combination of the elements of the vector $\mathbf{x}$.
2. The *eigenvectors* of a square matrix $\mathbf{A}$ are those special vectors $\mathbf{x}$ such that $\mathbf{Ax} = \lambda\mathbf{x}$ for some constant λ which is called the *eigenvalue* belonging to $\mathbf{x}$.
3. Two non-zero vectors are called *orthogonal* if their *dot product is zero*.[7] If each vector represents a time series of returns on a financial asset then the two series of returns are *uncorrelated* if the two vectors are orthogonal.
4. If $\mathbf{A}$ is *symmetric* the eigenvectors are *orthogonal*.
5. Any square non-singular matrix $\mathbf{A}$ of dimension n has n eigenvalues, but they may not be distinct.
6. $\mathbf{A}$ is a real *positive definite* matrix if and only if all its eigenvalues are positive.
7. We find the eigenvalues of a matrix by solving the *characteristic equation*.
8. For each non-zero eigenvalue there are infinitely many eigenvectors. So we choose the eigenvectors to have *unit length*. If $\mathbf{A}$ is symmetric the $n \times n$ matrix $\mathbf{W}$ containing all the eigenvectors in its columns is an *orthogonal matrix* (i.e. its inverse is equal to its transpose).[8]
9. PCA takes as its input the $n \times n$ *covariance matrix* (or *correlation matrix*) of $\mathbf{X}$, which is a $T \times n$ matrix containing data on n correlated time series each containing T observations at contemporaneous points in time. For instance, each column in $\mathbf{X}$ can represent a time series of interest rate changes, or a time series of returns on a financial asset. Let $\mathbf{V}$ be its covariance matrix (or correlation matrix) and let $\mathbf{W}$ be the orthogonal matrix of eigenvectors of $\mathbf{V}$.
10. The linear transformation defined by $\mathbf{W}$ transforms our original data $\mathbf{X}$ on n correlated random variables into a set of *orthogonal* random variables: That is, the columns of the matrix $\mathbf{P} = \mathbf{XW}$ are uncorrelated. These columns are called the *principal components* of $\mathbf{X}$.

II.2.2.2 Principal Component Representation

Consider a set of n returns with time series data summarized in a $T \times n$ matrix $\mathbf{X}$ and let $\mathbf{V}$ be the covariance matrix (or correlation matrix) of $\mathbf{X}$. The principal components of $\mathbf{V}$ are the columns of the $T \times n$ matrix $\mathbf{P}$ defined by

$$\mathbf{P} = \mathbf{XW}, \tag{II.2.1}$$

where $\mathbf{W}$ is the $n \times n$ orthogonal matrix of eigenvectors of $\mathbf{V}$. Thus the original system of correlated returns $\mathbf{X}$ has been transformed into a system of orthogonal returns $\mathbf{P}$, i.e. the system of principal components. We can turn (II.2.1) around into a representation of the original variables in terms of the principal components. Since $\mathbf{W}$ is orthogonal, $\mathbf{W}^{-1} = \mathbf{W}'$ and so

$$\mathbf{X} = \mathbf{PW}'. \tag{II.2.2}$$

---

[7] The dot product is the sum of the products of the elements, for instance,

$$(x_1, x_2, x_3).(y_1, y_2, y_3) = x_1 y_1 + x_2 y_2 + x_3 y_3.$$

[8] A vector has unit length if the sum of the squares of its elements is one.

A major aim of PCA is to use only a *reduced* set of principal components to represent the original variables **X**. For this purpose **W** is ordered so that the first column of **W** is the eigenvector corresponding to the largest eigenvalue of **V**, the second column of **W** is the eigenvector corresponding to the second eigenvalue of **V**, and so on.

The mth principal component is the mth column of **P**, i.e. the column that is derived from the mth column of **W**. When we order the columns of **W** as above then the sum of squares of the elements in the mth principal component is the mth largest eigenvalue of **V**, denoted λ_m. The *total variation* in **X** is the sum of the eigenvalues of **V**, $\lambda_1 + \ldots + \lambda_n$, and the proportion of this total variation that is explained by the mth principal component is

$$\lambda_m (\lambda_1 + \ldots + \lambda_n)^{-1}. \tag{II.2.3}$$

So between them the *first k principal components* of the returns capture a proportion

$$\frac{\lambda_1 + \ldots + \lambda_k}{\lambda_1 + \ldots + \lambda_n} \tag{II.2.4}$$

of the total variation in the system.

Now we can choose k as follows. Either:

- adjust k to capture a certain fixed proportion of the variation, such as 90% or 95%; or
- set the number of principal components, such as $k = 3$ or $k = 5$, and then find how much of the variation is being captured by these components.

When the first k columns of **P** are used as the columns of a $T \times k$ matrix **P*** we adjust (II.2.2) into an *approximation* of the original returns, in terms of the first k principal components only:

$$\mathbf{X} \approx \mathbf{P}^* \mathbf{W}^{*\prime}, \tag{II.2.5}$$

where **W*** is the $n \times k$ matrix whose k columns are given by the first k eigenvectors. This approximation can be made as accurate as we please by increasing k.

The principal component approximation (II.2.5) is a very powerful statistical tool that works best on a highly collinear system, such as a term structure of interest rates or a term structure of commodity futures. This is because there are only a few important sources of information in the data, which are common to all the variables, and the PCA allows one to extract just these key sources of variation from the data.

II.2.2.3 Frequently Asked Questions

In this section we answer some common questions about PCA:

(a) *To which matrix should PCA be applied?*
    Should PCA be performed on the correlation matrix or the covariance matrix? The answer to this question depends on how the results will be used. A principal component representation based on the covariance matrix has the advantage of providing a linear factor model for the returns, and not a linear factor model for the standardized returns, as is the case when we use the correlation matrix.[9] A PCA on the covariance matrix captures all the movements in the variables, which may be dominated by the differing

---

[9] However, if we wish, we can destandardize the principal component representation of standardized returns simply by multiplying each return by its standard deviation, calculated over the same period as the correlation matrix.

volatilities of individual variables. A PCA on the correlation matrix only captures the comovements in returns and ignores their individual volatilities.

It is only when all variables have similar volatilities that the eigenvectors of both matrices will have similar characteristics. Recall from Section I.2.4.3 that the eigenvectors and eigenvalues of covariance and correlation matrices have no simple relationship with each other, so we cannot just apply PCA to one or other of these matrices and then apply some sort of linear transform to the results. In general the eigenvectors of V will be influenced by the differences between the volatilities of the variables, but the eigenvectors of C will not.

The matrix to which PCA is applied need not be an *equally weighted* covariance or correlation matrix, as we assumed in the previous subsection. It could just as well represent an *exponentially* weighted covariance or correlation matrix. We simply have to multiply the return that is observed i periods ago by the ith power of the square root of the smoothing constant, and after this the analysis proceeds unchanged.[10]

We shall see in Section II.4.6 that PCA is a useful technique for generating large covariance matrices based on exponentially weighted moving averages or GARCH models. These large covariance matrices play a very important role in estimating the value at risk for a cash flow portfolio. In this case it makes sense to perform the PCA on the covariance matrix. On the other hand, PCA on the correlation matrix can be useful in the context of stress testing. Recall that the covariance and correlation matrices are related as $V = DCD$, where V, C and D are respectively the covariance matrix, correlation matrix and diagonal matrix of standard deviations of the returns. In the stress testing of fixed income portfolios we perform separate stress tests on the correlations and the standard deviations (i.e. the volatilities, when expressed in annual terms). Stressing the principal components of a correlation matrix makes the calculations much easier and, more importantly, it also ensures that the stressed correlation matrix is positive definite. Moreover, since the principal components capture the variations that are most important historically, we may believe that stressing these components provides a realistic stress test, assuming we also believe that history may repeat itself.

(b) *How many principal components should I use?*
   This depends on how much of the variation you wish to explain. Using all the components explains all the variation, but you may wish to ignore some of the minor variations since these might be viewed as 'noise' from the point of view of making forecasts. For an exact method of determining how many components to use, the eigenvalues of the correlation matrix can be compared with those of a random correlation matrix; see Plerou et al. (2002).

(c) *How can we interpret the first principal component?*
   In a perfectly correlated system of returns on financial assets or changes in interest rates the elements of the first eigenvector are equal. More generally, the more highly correlated the system the more similar the values of the elements of the first eigenvector. Hence, the first principal component captures a *common trend* in assets or interest rates. That is, if the first principal component changes at a time when the other components are fixed, then the returns (or changes in interest rates) all move by roughly the same amount. For this reason we often called the first component the *trend* component.

---

[10] See Section II.3.8 for further details about exponential weighting.

(d) *How can we interpret the other principal components?*

If the system has no natural ordering then the second and higher order principal components have no intuitive interpretation. But if the system is ordered, such as a set of interest rate changes of different maturities or a set of returns on futures of different maturities, then the second principal component usually captures a change in slope of the term structure. Then the elements of the second eigenvector are decreasing (or increasing) in magnitude, so that if the second principal component changes at a time when the other components are fixed then the returns (or changes in interest rates) move up at one end of the term structure and down at the other end. For this reason we often called the second component the *tilt* component. Similarly, the elements of the third eigenvector are usually decreasing (or increasing) and then increasing (or decreasing) in magnitude. Thus if the third principal component changes when the other components are fixed, then the returns (or changes in interest rates) move up (or down) at both ends of the term structure and down (or up) in the middle. For this reason we often called the third component the *curvature* or *convexity* component. Higher order principal components have similar interpretations in terms of movements described by cubic polynomials (fourth component), quartic polynomials (fifth component) and so on.

(e) *What is the effect of normalizing eigenvectors?*

After normalization the eigenvectors are only unique up to a change in the sign. That is, if $\mathbf{w}$ is a normalized eigenvector then so also is $-\mathbf{w}$. The decision whether to normalize eigenvectors to have unit length should have no effect on the final result. It is not necessary to normalize the eigenvectors. The normalization cancels out in the principal component representation (II.2.5) and the only reason we use normalized eigenvectors is to make the analysis easier: when the eigenvectors have unit length $\mathbf{W}$ is orthonormal.

(f) *What frequency of data should be used in X?*

The decision about data frequency depends on the horizon of the model. For instance, when we use the principal component representation to forecast risk over a horizon of a few days then daily data should be used; but if the risk horizon is weeks or months, then weekly or even monthly data suffice.

(g) *What historical period of data should be used in X?*

The length of data period is linked to the decision about data frequency. It is important to use enough data points that the original covariance matrix is estimated with a fair degree of precision and, in this respect, the more data used the better. However, an equally weighted covariance matrix over a very long data period would represent a long term average of variances and covariances, and if we want the model to reflect current market circumstances we should use a shorter period of data. In fact we may prefer to base the PCA on an exponentially weighted moving average covariance matrix as described in Section II.3.8. It is a good idea to perform PCA on a rolling estimation sample, to check how stable the eigenvalues and eigenvectors are. If they are excessively variable then a longer sample period, or a larger smoothing constant, should be used.

(h) *After I calculate the principal components, do I need to take first differences (or returns) on the principal components for subsequent analysis?*

No. The principal components will already be stationary because we perform PCA on a covariance or correlation matrix and that matrix is already based on stationary variables, i.e. the returns on assets or changes in interest rates. See Figure II.2.7 below for an example.

(i) *What statistical packages are available?*

Most statistical and econometric packages, such as *EViews*, *Matlab*, *S-Plus* and *Mathematica*, have eigenvalue and eigenvector routines that can be used for PCA. However, most of the examples in this book have been estimated using the Excel matrix add-in by Leonardo Volpi that is freely downloadable from the internet.[11] This add-in provides several algorithms for computing the eigenvalues and eigenvectors of large matrices.

II.2.3   CASE STUDY: PCA OF UK GOVERNMENT YIELD CURVES

In this case study we consolidate the concepts reviewed in the previous section by analysing a system of 50 key interest rates. We perform a PCA on daily changes in each rate and show that, out of all 50 principal components only the first three will be needed for any subsequent analysis: these three components together explain more than 99% of the total variation in the systems of 50 interest rates.

II.2.3.1   Properties of UK Interest Rates

Daily and monthly data on UK government and commercial liability yield curves for maturities between 6 months and 25 years, and the short curve for monthly maturities from 1 month to 5 years, are available from the Bank of England.[12] Figure II.2.1 illustrates the spot and forward rates of selected maturities for the whole zero coupon curve and for the short rate curve, from January 2000 to December 2007.

Different regimes in interest rates are apparent from these graphs. From January 2000 until early 2001 an inverted yield curve was apparent: short rates were around 5% to 6%, but at the long end the spot rates were around 4% and the long forward rates were even lower. Clearly the market expected interest rates to fall to fuel economic growth, and during this period they were indeed falling. In 2002, 2003 and the first few months of 2004 there was a marked upward sloping spot yield curve. But the long forward rates were mixed and during this time long rates remained relatively stable, between 4.5% and 5%. The period from mid 2005 until mid 2006 was characterized by a very flat spot rate curve and a humped forward rate curve, lower at the long end and with maximum forward rates around maturities of 1 year. From mid 2006 until mid 2007 short rates were higher than forward rates as the Bank of England raised short term interest rates amid inflationary fears. In mid 2007 the 'credit crunch', precipitated by the sub-prime mortgage crisis in the US, forced the monetary policy committee in the UK to lower base rates again.

At the very end of the period the sub-prime mortgage market in the US raised awareness generally that banks have not fully understood their credit risks. Credit risk capital requirements increased as banks were forced to take low grade credits onto their own books. In

---

[11] Be careful about using the Solver when you have a spreadsheet open with the Matrix add-in, and when using the Matrix add-in for very large matrices when a spreadsheet using the Solver is open, as the two add-ins can interfere with each other's performance. In Chapter II.4 we shall see that Solver also finds it difficult to cope when a spreadsheet containing simulations is open, since the simulations are repeated at every iteration!

[12] See http://www.bankofengland.co.uk/statistics/yieldcurve/index.htm.

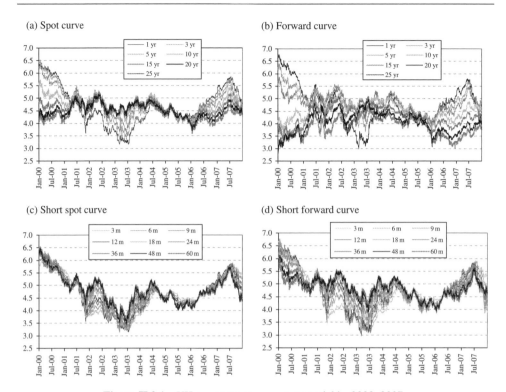

Figure II.2.1 UK government zero coupon yields, 2000–2007

the resulting credit squeeze credit spreads jumped up, having been moving downward for several years, and the Bank was forced to cut base interest rates dramatically.

Given the distinct regimes in UK interest rates over the period 2000–2007, a PCA on daily interest rates over the whole period will not reflect the prevailing market circumstances at the end of the period in December 2007. Therefore, in the following we perform PCA over the period 2005–2007 only. The data for other periods are available in the Excel files for this case study, and the PCA covering different periods is left as an exercise to the reader.

Yield curves form a highly collinear system. In each case the aim of PCA is to extract three or perhaps four uncorrelated time series from the system to use in a subsequent analysis of the risk. This dimension reduction allows sophisticated value-at-risk models to be built with surprising ease. Moreover it simplifies the stress testing of portfolios because it adds clarity to the stress tests that are performed. We shall therefore revisit the results of these PCA models in Volume IV, where they are used to illustrate value-at-risk modelling and stress testing techniques.

The Excel files for this case study contain eight different principal component analyses according to the input data being based on:

- spot rates or forward rates;
- a covariance matrix or a correlation matrix;
- the entire yield curve from 6 months to 25 years (i.e. 50 different yields) or the short curve from 1 month to 60 months (i.e. 60 different yields).

Complete results are in the spreadsheets, but space considerations do not permit us to present and discuss the detailed results of all eight PCA models in the text. So in the following we only present full results for the UK spot rate curve from 6 months to 25 years.

II.2.3.2   Volatility and Correlation of UK Spot Rates

The P&L on fixed income portfolios is mapped to changes in interest rate risk factors, measured in basis points. Hence, the volatilities and correlations of interest rates refer to the absolute changes in interest rates in basis points. Figure II.2.2 shows the volatility of the spot rates in basis points per annum, plotted against the maturity of the spot rate. Volatility is lowest at the short end and highest for rates of between 5 and 10 years' maturity. Rates longer than 5 years have a volatility of around 50 bps per annum. Since the volatility of the shorter rates is so much lower than this, the results of applying PCA to the covariance matrix, which includes the volatilities of the rates, may be quite different from the results of applying PCA to the correlation matrix.

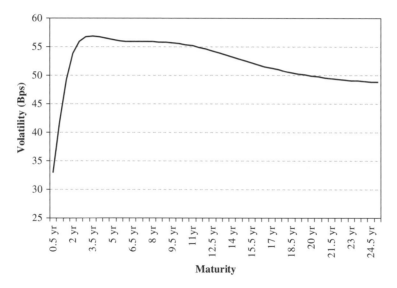

Figure II.2.2   Volatilities of UK spot rates, 2005–2007

The correlation matrix of the changes in UK spot rates is a 50×50 matrix. An extract from this matrix, measured using the equally weighted average methodology on daily data between January 2005 and December 2007, is shown in Table II.2.1. The correlation matrix exhibits the usual structure for correlations in a term structure. Correlations are highest for adjacent maturities and decrease as the maturity difference between the rates increases. Correlations also tend to be higher between longer rates than between shorter rates, as recently the term structure has been more volatile at the short end. In this case the 1-year rate has the lowest correlation with the rest of the system overall, because this is a money market rate that is more influenced by government policies than the longer rates.

Table II.2.1 Correlation matrix of selected UK spot rates

Maturity	1 yr	2 yr	3 yr	4 yr	5 yr	7 yr	10 yr	15 yr	20 yr	25 yr
1 yr	1.000	0.925	0.877	0.843	0.809	0.744	0.674	0.615	0.558	0.501
2 yr	0.925	1.000	0.990	0.972	0.947	0.891	0.827	0.773	0.717	0.657
3 yr	0.877	0.990	1.000	0.994	0.979	0.937	0.883	0.833	0.781	0.723
4 yr	0.843	0.972	0.994	1.000	0.995	0.968	0.924	0.880	0.831	0.776
5 yr	0.809	0.947	0.979	0.995	1.000	0.987	0.955	0.917	0.871	0.819
7 yr	0.744	0.891	0.937	0.968	0.987	1.000	0.989	0.963	0.923	0.877
10 yr	0.674	0.827	0.883	0.924	0.955	0.989	1.000	0.989	0.957	0.918
15 yr	0.615	0.773	0.833	0.880	0.917	0.963	0.989	1.000	0.988	0.962
20 yr	0.558	0.717	0.781	0.831	0.871	0.923	0.957	0.988	1.000	0.992
25 yr	0.501	0.657	0.723	0.776	0.819	0.877	0.918	0.962	0.992	1.000

II.2.3.3   PCA on UK Spot Rates Correlation Matrix

When the PCA is based on correlations, it takes as input a 50×50 matrix containing the correlations between the spot rates of all available maturities. The outputs from PCA are the eigenvalues and eigenvectors of this matrix. Table II.2.2 gives the first six eigenvalues, ordered from largest to smallest, and their corresponding eigenvectors, and Figure II.2.3 plots the first three eigenvectors as a function of the maturity of the rate.

Consider first the eigenvalues shown at the top of Table II.2.2. Since we are dealing with a 50×50 *correlation* matrix, the sum of the eigenvalues is 50. The eigenvalues are all positive because the matrix is positive definite, and they have been ordered in decreasing order of magnitude. The eigenvalues of a correlation matrix determine how much of the covariation in the system of standardized changes in spot rates, over the period used to construct the correlation matrix, is explained by each principal component:[13]

- The first eigenvalue is 45.524, which means that the first principal component explains $45.524/50 = 91.05\%$ of the covariation between changes in UK spot rates.
- The second eigenvalue is 3.424, which means that the second principal component explains $3.424/50 = 6.85\%$ of the variation in the system and that, taken together, the first two principal components explain 97.90% of the covariation between changes in UK spot rates.
- The third eigenvalue is 0.664, which means that the third principal component explains $0.664/50 = 1.33\%$ of the variation in the system and that, taken together, the first three principal components explain 99.22% of the covariation between changes in UK spot rates.
- The fourth eigenvalue is 0.300, which means that the principal component explains $0.300/50 = 0.60\%$ of the variation in the system and that, taken together, the first four principal components explain 98.82% of the covariation between changes in UK spot rates.
- If we add the fifth and sixth principal components to represent the system, as described below, we can explain 99.98% of the covariation using only six principal components.

---

[13] That is, returns are standardized to have variance 1, because we are doing PCA on a correlation matrix.

Table II.2.2 Eigenvalues and eigenvectors of the correlation matrix of UK spot rates

Component	1	2	3	4	5	6
Eigenvalue	45.524	3.424	0.664	0.300	0.062	0.019
% Variation	91.05%	6.85%	1.33%	0.60%	0.12%	0.04%
Cumulative %	91.05%	97.90%	99.22%	99.82%	99.95%	99.98%

Eigenvector	w1	w2	w3	w4	w5	w6
0.5 yr	0.0675	0.3464	0.6878	0.4409	0.3618	0.2458
1 yr	0.1030	0.3536	0.3272	0.0007	−0.4604	−0.4910
1.5 yr	0.1183	0.3136	0.0924	−0.2008	−0.3673	−0.0817
2 yr	0.1248	0.2804	−0.0112	−0.2528	−0.1858	0.1569
2.5 yr	0.1289	0.2541	−0.0602	−0.2490	−0.0422	0.2308
3 yr	0.1323	0.2308	−0.0860	−0.2222	0.0620	0.2184
3.5 yr	0.1352	0.2087	−0.1007	−0.1848	0.1340	0.1643
4 yr	0.1378	0.1870	−0.1096	−0.1426	0.1800	0.0937
4.5 yr	0.1399	0.1657	−0.1150	−0.0992	0.2049	0.0208
5 yr	0.1418	0.1450	−0.1183	−0.0565	0.2125	−0.0454
5.5 yr	0.1432	0.1251	−0.1200	−0.0161	0.2066	−0.1001
6 yr	0.1444	0.1062	−0.1206	0.0209	0.1904	−0.1409
6.5 yr	0.1452	0.0887	−0.1202	0.0540	0.1667	−0.1672
7 yr	0.1459	0.0726	−0.1190	0.0828	0.1381	−0.1798
7.5 yr	0.1463	0.0579	−0.1170	0.1072	0.1069	−0.1804
8 yr	0.1466	0.0446	−0.1143	0.1271	0.0748	−0.1708
8.5 yr	0.1468	0.0326	−0.1110	0.1428	0.0433	−0.1533
9 yr	0.1470	0.0219	−0.1070	0.1545	0.0133	−0.1300
9.5 yr	0.1470	0.0122	−0.1023	0.1625	−0.0142	−0.1028
10 yr	0.1471	0.0034	−0.0970	0.1669	−0.0390	−0.0733
10.5 yr	0.1471	−0.0046	−0.0911	0.1682	−0.0605	−0.0430
11yr	0.1472	−0.0120	−0.0846	0.1666	−0.0786	−0.0129
11.5 yr	0.1472	−0.0189	−0.0774	0.1623	−0.0933	0.0158
12 yr	0.1472	−0.0254	−0.0698	0.1557	−0.1046	0.0424
12.5 yr	0.1472	−0.0317	−0.0616	0.1470	−0.1126	0.0665
13 yr	0.1472	−0.0376	−0.0529	0.1365	−0.1175	0.0875
13.5 yr	0.1472	−0.0435	−0.0438	0.1245	−0.1195	0.1051
14 yr	0.1472	−0.0492	−0.0344	0.1111	−0.1188	0.1192
14.5 yr	0.1471	−0.0548	−0.0246	0.0967	−0.1157	0.1297
15 yr	0.1470	−0.0603	−0.0147	0.0815	−0.1106	0.1367
15.5 yr	0.1469	−0.0659	−0.0045	0.0657	−0.1036	0.1402
16 yr	0.1468	−0.0713	0.0057	0.0496	−0.0950	0.1403
16.5 yr	0.1466	−0.0768	0.0160	0.0332	−0.0852	0.1373
17 yr	0.1464	−0.0822	0.0262	0.0169	−0.0743	0.1312
17.5 yr	0.1461	−0.0875	0.0364	0.0007	−0.0625	0.1225
18 yr	0.1459	−0.0928	0.0464	−0.0152	−0.0502	0.1113
18.5 yr	0.1455	−0.0979	0.0563	−0.0306	−0.0375	0.0979
19 yr	0.1452	−0.1030	0.0658	−0.0455	−0.0246	0.0824
19.5 yr	0.1448	−0.1080	0.0752	−0.0598	−0.0117	0.0652
20 yr	0.1444	−0.1129	0.0842	−0.0734	0.0011	0.0464
20.5 yr	0.1440	−0.1177	0.0928	−0.0862	0.0137	0.0262
21 yr	0.1436	−0.1223	0.1011	−0.0982	0.0259	0.0048
21.5 yr	0.1432	−0.1268	0.1091	−0.1093	0.0376	−0.0176
22 yr	0.1427	−0.1312	0.1166	−0.1196	0.0488	−0.0411
22.5 yr	0.1423	−0.1354	0.1237	−0.1290	0.0594	−0.0654
23 yr	0.1418	−0.1395	0.1305	−0.1376	0.0695	−0.0906
23.5 yr	0.1414	−0.1434	0.1368	−0.1453	0.0789	−0.1164
24 yr	0.1409	−0.1471	0.1428	−0.1521	0.0878	−0.1430
24.5 yr	0.1405	−0.1507	0.1484	−0.1581	0.0960	−0.1701
25 yr	0.1400	−0.1541	0.1535	−0.1633	0.1037	−0.1979

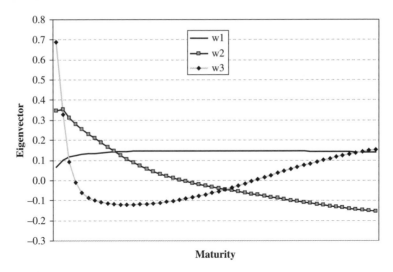

Figure II.2.3 Eigenvectors of the UK daily spot rate correlation matrix

Now consider the eigenvectors and the first three eigenvectors in particular, which are shown in Figure II.2.3. The first eigenvector is almost a horizontal line because the first eigenvector has almost identical values on each maturity, as can be seen from the column labelled 'w1' in Table II.2.2. Note that the eigenvectors are normalized to have unit length, i.e. the sum of the squared elements in each eigenvector is 1. The 6-month rate has a lower correlation with the system than the other rates, and indeed the rates up to about 2 years also have a slightly lower correlation than the others. Hence, at the short maturities the first eigenvector is not as flat as it is for the longer maturities. The second eigenvector is a monotonic decreasing function of maturity. The third eigenvector has shape similar to a quadratic function of maturity, being highest at the short and the long end and lowest for middle maturities, and the fourth eigenvector (not shown) has the shape of a cubic polynomial.[14]

II.2.3.4 Principal Component Representation

Taking just the first three eigenvectors, which together explain over 99% of the system's variation, we read off the principal component representation of the standardized returns in (II.2.6) below. This is a linear risk factor model with three risk factors and with factor weights being given by the eigenvectors in Table II.2.2. Here we use the notation $\Delta \tilde{\mathbf{R}}_m$ to denote the standardized $T \times 1$ vector (i.e. time series) of daily changes in the spot interest rate of maturity m, and the notation $\mathbf{p}_1$, $\mathbf{p}_2$ and $\mathbf{p}_3$ for the time series of principal components. Hence $\mathbf{p}_i = (P_{i1}, \ldots, P_{iT})'$, where P_{it} is the value of the ith principal component at time t and $\mathbf{p}_i$ is the ith column of the matrix of principal components, $\mathbf{P}$.

---

[14] We have not plotted the fifth and sixth eigenvectors but, looking at Table II.2.2, it is evident that they will have the shape of a quartic and a quintic polynomial, respectively.

The principal component representation of the standardized rates is

$$\Delta \tilde{\mathbf{R}}_{6mth} \approx 0.0675\mathbf{p}_1 + 0.3464\mathbf{p}_2 + 0.6878\mathbf{p}_3,$$

$$\Delta \tilde{\mathbf{R}}_{1yr} \approx 0.1030\mathbf{p}_1 + 0.3536\mathbf{p}_2 + 0.3272\mathbf{p}_3,$$

$$\Delta \tilde{\mathbf{R}}_{18mth} \approx 0.1183\mathbf{p}_1 + 0.3136\mathbf{p}_2 + 0.0924\mathbf{p}_3,$$

$$\ldots,$$ (II.2.6)

$$\Delta \tilde{\mathbf{R}}_{24.5yr} \approx 0.1405\mathbf{p}_1 - 0.1507\mathbf{p}_2 + 0.1484\mathbf{p}_3,$$

$$\Delta \tilde{\mathbf{R}}_{25yr} \approx 0.1400\mathbf{p}_1 - 0.1541\mathbf{p}_2 + 0.1535\mathbf{p}_3.$$

On the left-hand side of the above we have 50 time series, one for each (standardized) change in interest rate. On the right-hand side we have a weighted sum of only three time series, the first three principal components. The approximation signs are there because we have only taken the first three principal components in the above. If we had taken enough components to explain 100% of the variation the approximation would be exact.

This principal component representation shows how only three time series, i.e. the first three principal components, can explain over 99% of the daily changes in standardized UK spot interest rates over the period 2005–2007. Furthermore, the principal components are uncorrelated by construction. It is very useful to have a risk factor model with uncorrelated risk factors. For instance, their correlation matrix is just the identity matrix and their covariance matrix is diagonal and the variance of each principal component is equal to the corresponding eigenvalue. So in this example the first principal component has variance 45.524, the second principal component has variance 3.424, and so on.

Table II.2.2 shows that at the longer maturities of 5 years or more, the coefficients on the first principal component are almost identical. This means that if the first principal component shifts upwards, leaving the other principal components fixed, then all the spot rates will move upwards in an approximately parallel shift (although the upward shift is slightly less at the short end, as we can see from the shape of the first eigenvector in Figure II.2.3). We know from the eigenvalue analysis that this type of (almost) parallel shift accounts for 91% of the movements in (standardized) spot rates during 2005–2007.

Since the second eigenvector is very similar to a downward sloping line (again, see Figure II.2.3), an upward shift in the second component, leaving the other components fixed, induces a tilt in the spot curve, with an upward move at the short end and a downward move at the long end. This type of movement accounts for nearly 7% of the variation in standardized spot rates during 2005–2007.

From Figure II.2.3 and Table II.2.2 we know that the third eigenvector is positive at the short end and the long end and negative for middle maturities (between 2.5 and 15.5 years). Since it has the smooth shape of a quadratic function, we know that an upward shift in the third principal component (leaving the other components fixed) will change the convexity of the spot rate curve. It will make a downward sloping curve more convex and an upward sloping curve less convex. This type of movement accounts for only 1.33% of the variation in standardized spot rates during 2005–2007.

Taken together, the first three principal components account for 99.22% of the variation in the term structure of UK forward rates. This finding is typical of any highly correlated term structure, although of course the exact results will depend on the series used, its frequency and the data period chosen. Given the interpretations above, it is common to call the first principal component the *trend component*, or *shift component* of the term structure. The second principal component is commonly referred to as the *tilt component* and the third principal component is called the *convexity or curvature component*.

It is important to note that the above interpretations of the second and third principal components only relate to a term structure, or another highly correlated ordered system such as futures ordered by maturity or implied volatilities ordered by strike. The first principal component is almost flat, provided there is a high degree of correlation in the system, so it will have the same 'trend' interpretation in any highly correlated system – we can 'shuffle up' the order in which variables are taken, without much effect on the shape of the first eigenvector. But if we shuffle up the ordering of the system the second and third principal components will no longer look like a decreasing line, or a quadratic function. Hence, the interpretation of these components does depend on having a natural ordering in the system.

II.2.3.5 PCA on UK Short Spot Rates Covariance Matrix

To illustrate the application of PCA to a covariance matrix, Table II.2.3 summarizes the first six eigenvalues of the short spot rates covariance matrix based on the Bank of England daily data shown in Figure II.2.1 (c), using the period between January 2005 and December 2007. To save space we do not report the eigenvectors in a table this time, but we do plot them as a function of maturity in Figure II.2.4.

Table II.2.3 Eigenvalues of the UK short spot rate covariance matrix

Component	1	2	3	4	5	6
Eigenvalues	589.301	28.911	5.916	2.254	0.981	0.164
% Variation	93.90%	4.61%	0.94%	0.36%	0.16%	0.03%
Cumulative %	93.90%	98.51%	99.45%	99.81%	99.97%	99.99%

When PCA is performed on a covariance matrix the volatility of the variables, as well as their correlations, will influence the output. In this case the volatility graph shown in the spreadsheet for this example demonstrates that the volatility increases quite considerably with maturity at the short end. It is 25 basis points per annum for the 1-month rate and over 55 basis points per annum for the 27-month rate and rates of longer maturity. This affects the shape of the eigenvectors in Figure II.2.4, and particularly the first eigenvector which decreases markedly at the short end. The first principal component has a slope and does not represent an approximately parallel shift in all maturities.

In contrast to (II.2.6) the principal component representation now gives a representation for the changes in interest rates, not the standardized changes. We use the notation $\Delta \mathbf{R}_m$ to denote the time series of daily changes in the spot interest rate of maturity m, and the notation $\mathbf{p}_1$, $\mathbf{p}_2$ and $\mathbf{p}_3$ for the time series of principal components. Of course, these are different from the principal components that were obtained from the correlation matrix. Then, reading the values of the eigenvectors from the spreadsheet for this example, the principal component representation is

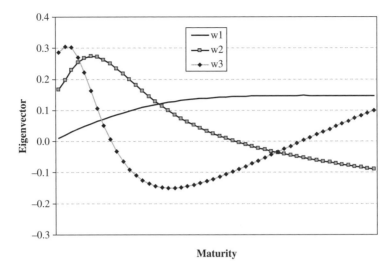

Figure II.2.4 Eigenvectors of the UK daily short spot rate covariance matrix

$$\Delta\mathbf{R}_{1\text{mth}} \approx 0.0099\mathbf{p}_1 + 0.1660\mathbf{p}_2 + 0.2870\mathbf{p}_3,$$

$$\Delta\mathbf{R}_{2\text{mth}} \approx 0.0202\mathbf{p}_1 + 0.1962\mathbf{p}_2 + 0.3055\mathbf{p}_3,$$

$$\Delta\mathbf{R}_{3\text{mth}} \approx 0.0312\mathbf{p}_1 + 0.2286\mathbf{p}_2 + 0.3022\mathbf{p}_3,$$

$$\dots ,$$

$$\Delta\mathbf{R}_{59\text{mth}} \approx 0.1432\mathbf{p}_1 - 0.1117\mathbf{p}_2 + 0.1672\mathbf{p}_3,$$

$$\Delta\mathbf{R}_{60\text{mth}} \approx 0.1429\mathbf{p}_1 - 0.1139\mathbf{p}_2 + 0.1741\mathbf{p}_3.$$

Clearly, using PCA considerably simplifies factor model analysis for interest rates: when we need to model $60 \times 61/2 = 1830$ variances and covariances of 60 different interest rates we reduce the problem to finding only three variances! The factor weights (i.e. the first three eigenvectors of the interest rate covariance matrix) can be used to retrieve the 1830 covariances of the interest rates, as we shall explain in the next section.

II.2.4   TERM STRUCTURE FACTOR MODELS

In this section we explain how PCA can be applied to obtain a factor model for a term structure, such as a single yield curve or a term structure of futures or forwards. In Chapter III.4 we shall apply PCA to model term structures of volatilities, but in this section we only discuss how to build principal component factor models for interest rate sensitive portfolios, or for portfolios with many forward or futures positions. When PCA is applied to model the risk and return on bonds, swaps, notes, futures, forwards or volatility we obtain a linear factor model but we do not use regression to estimate the factor sensitivities. The factors are the principal components, and these and the factor sensitivities are derived directly from the eigenvectors of the covariance or correlation matrix.

II.2.4.1   Interest Rate Sensitive Portfolios

The portfolio may be represented as a series of cash flows at selected maturities along the term structure, such as $\{1 \text{ month}, 2 \text{ months}, \ldots, 60 \text{ months}\}$. Thus the risk factors are these constant maturity interest rates. The *cash-flow mapping* of such portfolios to these risk factors is described in Section III.5.3. After the mapping the P&L on the portfolio is approximated as a weighted sum of the changes in the interest rate risk factors with weights given by the *present value of a basis point* at the maturity corresponding to the interest rate.[15] So we may write

$$P_t - P_{t-1} = -\sum_{i=1}^{n} \text{PV01}_i (R_{i,t} - R_{i,t-1})$$

or, equivalently,

$$\Delta P_t = -\sum_{i=1}^{n} \text{PV01}_i \Delta R_{i,t}$$

or, in matrix notation,

$$\Delta P_t = -\mathbf{p}' \Delta \mathbf{R}_t \qquad (\text{II.2.7})$$

where the $n \times 1$ vectors $\Delta \mathbf{R}_t = (\Delta R_{1t}, \ldots, \Delta R_{nt})'$ and $\mathbf{p} = (\text{PV01}_1, \ldots, \text{PV01}_n)'$ are, respectively, the changes in the fixed maturity zero coupon interest rate risk factors at time t and the *constant* PV01 sensitivities. The PV01 vector $\mathbf{p}$ is held fixed at its current value so that we are measuring the interest rate risk of the *current* portfolio.

Now we perform a PCA on the covariance matrix $\mathbf{V}$ of the changes in the interest rates and obtain a principal component approximation for each interest rate change:

$$\Delta R_{it} \approx w_{i1} P_{1t} + \ldots + w_{ik} P_{kt}, \qquad (\text{II.2.8})$$

where P_{jt} is the value of the jth principal component at time t, w_{ij} is the ith element of the jth eigenvector of $\mathbf{V}$ and k is small compared with n (as mentioned above, k is usually taken to be 3 or 4). The jth principal component risk factor sensitivity is then given by

$$w_j = -\sum_{i=1}^{n} \text{PV01}_i w_{ij}, \qquad (\text{II.2.9})$$

i.e. we obtain the jth principal component risk factor sensitivity from the jth eigenvector of $\mathbf{V}$ by multiplying the ith element of this eigenvector by the PV01 with respect to the ith interest rate, doing this for all i and then summing over all the elements in the eigenvector.

Put another way, we take the dot product of the vector $\mathbf{p}$ and the jth eigenvector $\mathbf{w}_j$ and this gives w_j, the jth principal component risk factor sensitivity. Now substituting (II.2.8) into (II.2.7) and using (II.2.9) yields the *principal component factor model representation* of the portfolio P&L as

$$\Delta P_t \approx \mathbf{w}' \mathbf{p}_t, \qquad (\text{II.2.10})$$

where the $k \times 1$ vectors $\mathbf{p}_t = (P_{1t}, \ldots, P_{kt})'$ and $\mathbf{w} = (w_1, \ldots, w_k)'$ denote the principal component risk factors at time t, and their (constant) factor sensitivities. Comparing (II.2.7) with (II.2.10), the number of risk factors has been reduced from n to k.

---

[15] See Section III.1.5.1 for more detailed definitions and further explanation.

Fixed income portfolios typically have an extremely large number of highly correlated risk factors. But PCA allows us to reduce the dimension of the risk factor space from, for instance, $n = 60$ to $k = 3$ as in the UK short spot rate study above, whilst maintaining a very accurate approximation to the portfolio's P&L. Moreover, the principal component risk factors have an intuitive interpretation: the first component captures an approximately parallel shift in the entire yield curve, and the second and third components capture a change in slope and a change in curvature of the yield curve.

Together, three components often explain over 95% of the variation in interest rates in major currencies such as the US dollar, euro and British pound, but less in emerging currencies where the fixed income markets are less liquid and so the correlation between interest rates is lower. The amount of risk factor variation explained by the first three or four principal components depends on the frequency of the interest changes: weekly and monthly changes are usually more highly correlated than daily changes, so a larger fraction of the total variation can be explained by the first few components.

EXAMPLE II.2.1: PCA FACTOR MODEL FOR A UK BOND PORTFOLIO

A portfolio of UK government bonds has been mapped to interest rates at maturities 1 year, 2 years, . . . , 20 years. The cash flow (in £m) and PV01 sensitivity vectors of the portfolio are shown in Table II.2.4. Use monthly data on these interest rates from 31 December 1994 to 31 December 2007 to build a PCA factor model for this portfolio.

Table II.2.4   Cash flows and PV01 vector for a UK bond portfolio

Maturity (years)	1	2	3	4	5	6	7	8	9	10
Cash flow (£m)	3	2	1	0.5	1	1.25	2	0.5	0.1	0.2
PV01 (£)	273.39	352.15	253.42	161.58	385.86	552.74	985.54	269.08	57.88	123.04

Maturity (years)	11	12	13	14	15	16	17	18	19	20
Cash flow (£m)	0.8	1	0.25	0.1	−0.5	−0.5	−1	−0.75	−0.5	−0.25
PV01 (£)	518.17	676.63	175.58	72.50	−372.50	−381.26	−777.79	−593.25	−401.17	−203.00

SOLUTION   Historical data on UK government yield curves are available from the Bank of England.[16] Monthly rates from 31 December 1994 to 31 December 2007 are shown in Figure II.2.5. Only the *normal run* of interest rates is shown, i.e. the fixed maturity zero coupon rates at maturities 1, 2, 3, 4, 5, 7, 10, 15 and 20 years. Rates were declining in the second half of the 1990s and thereafter the long rates have remained relatively constant. However, the slope of the yield curve has changed considerably during different periods. We observe an upward sloping yield curve in 1995–1996 and 2002–2003, and a downward sloping yield curve in 1999–2000 and 2006–2007.

The five largest eigenvalues of the covariance matrix of all 20 fixed maturity interest rates are shown in Table II.2.5, along with the marginal and cumulative percentage of variation explained by up to five principal components: these are calculated using (II.2.4).

[16] http://213.225.136.206/statistics/yieldcurve/archive.htm.

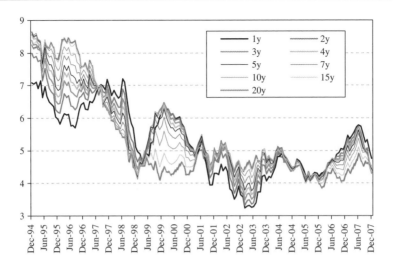

Figure II.2.5   UK government interest rates, monthly, 1995–2007

Clearly the first three principal components are more than adequate for the PCA factor model, since together they explain over 99.5% of the movements in the yield curve over the sample. Recalling the analysis of the Bank of England daily data in the previous section, we remark that three components will explain a greater fraction of the variation in monthly data than in daily data, even when we perform the analysis over a very long period as in this example. The first three eigenvectors are plotted as a function of maturity of interest rate in Figure II.2.6.

Table II.2.5   Eigenvalues of UK yield curve covariance matrix

Component	1	2	3	4	5
Eigenvalues	6855.118	923.747	123.140	30.158	5.191
Percentage variation explained	86.36%	11.64%	1.55%	0.38%	0.07%
Cumulative variation explained	86.36%	97.99%	99.54%	99.92%	99.99%

This figure shows that the principal components have the standard stylized interpretation of trend, tilt and curvature components:

- The *first eigenvector* is almost constant as a function of maturity; hence, if the first principal component increases then the entire yield curve shifts parallel. This component accounts for 86.36% of all the variation in the UK yield curve over the sample.
- The *second eigenvector* is an almost linear decreasing function of maturity moving from positive to negative; hence, if the second component increases the yield curve shifts up at the short end and down at the long end. We remarked above that the slope of the yield curve fluctuated greatly over the data period, and for this reason the second component accounts for a relatively large fraction (11.64%) of all the variation in the UK yield curve over the sample.

- The *third eigenvector* is almost a quadratic function of maturity, positive at the ends but negative in the middle; hence if the third component increases the yield curve shifts up at the ends and down in the middle. This component accounts for only 1.55% of all the variation in the UK yield curve over the sample.

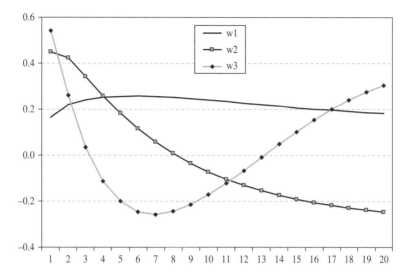

Figure II.2.6   Eigenvectors of the UK monthly spot rate covariance matrix

We know the sensitivities of the portfolio P&L to the annual interest rates – these are the PV01 sensitivities shown in Table II.2.4. For instance, the PV01 of the portfolio with respect to the 1 year interest rate is £273.39, meaning that the portfolio value will increase by approximately £273.39 if the 1 year rate falls by 1 basis point and the other interest rates remain unchanged.

To obtain the sensitivities of the portfolio P&L to the three principal component factors we apply formula (II.2.9). In other words, we take the dot product between the PV01 vector and the respective eigenvector. The calculation is performed in the spreadsheet for this example and the result is the PCA factor model:

$$-\text{P\&L}_t \approx £623.74 \times P_{1t} + £1{,}001.11 \times P_{2t} - £1{,}006.65 \times P_{3t}.$$

Note that the magnitude of coefficients here reflects the magnitude of the principal components, which themselves are based on the eigenvalues of the covariance matrix.

The first principal component is shown in Figure II.2.7. The other two components are calculated in the spreadsheet but not plotted, for reasons of space. Upward (downward) movements in the first component correspond to dates when there was a parallel upward (downward) shift of the yield curve and, unless the second and third components happened to be unchanged on that date, the shift would be accompanied by a change in slope and curvature.

We shall continue this example in Section II.2.4.4, where we show how to immunize the portfolio against common movements in the yield curve, and again in Section II.2.4.6, where we show how the factor model is used for risk assessment.

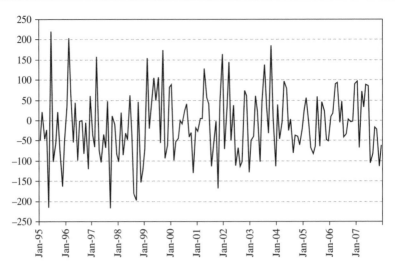

Figure II.2.7 First principal component for UK interest rates

II.2.4.2 Factor Models for Currency Forward Positions

The basis risk of a forward position in a currency depends on the variation of the difference between the spot price and the forward price of the currency in the market.[17] The main component of basis risk in currency forwards is the fluctuation of the forward price about its fair or theoretical price, which is based on the spot price. In liquid currency markets the forward price is normally very close to its fair price so the basis risk is negligible. In this case we can model currency forwards by decomposing each forward exposure into a spot exposure and an exposure to the risk free zero coupon interest rate differential of the same maturity as the forward.

Suppose that at time t we have a sequence of foreign currency payments $\{C_1, \ldots, C_n\}$ at future times $\{T_1, \ldots, T_n\}$. Denote by ΔP_t^d the change in present value of the entire sequence of cash flows in domestic currency when the domestic interest rates change by amounts

$$\Delta \mathbf{R}_t^d = \left(\Delta R_{1t}^d, \ldots, \Delta R_{nt}^d \right)'$$

where ΔR_{it}^d denotes the change at time t in the domestic interest rate of maturity T_i. Then ΔP_t^d is the sum of the present values of all the cash flows, i.e.

$$\Delta P_t^d = -\sum_{i=1}^{n} PV01_i^d \Delta R_{it}^d$$

where $PV01_i^d$ is the PV01 sensitivity of the cash flow in domestic currency at maturity T_i. Similarly, and with the obvious notation

$$\Delta P_t^f = -\sum_{i=1}^{n} PV01_i^f \Delta R_{it}^d \tag{II.2.11}$$

is the change in present value of the sequence of cash flows in foreign currency when the domestic interest rates change by amounts $\Delta \mathbf{R}_t^d$.

---

[17] See Section III.2.4.3 for more details about basis risk.

If S_t denotes the domestic foreign exchange rate at time t, then

$$\Delta P_t^d = S_t \Delta P_t^f. \tag{II.2.12}$$

It can be shown that (II.2.12) implies[18]

$$R_t^d \approx R_t^S + R_t^f, \tag{II.2.13}$$

where R_t^d is the return on the cash flow in domestic currency, R_t^f is the return on the cash flow in foreign currency and R_t^S is the return on the spot exchange rate.

Using the approximation (II.2.13), we may decompose the risk on a sequence of foreign currency forward payments into exchange rate and interest rate risks. Taking variances of (II.2.13) yields the risk decomposition

$$V(R_t^d) \approx V(R_t^S) + V(R_t^f) + 2\,\mathrm{Cov}(R_t^S, R_t^f). \tag{II.2.14}$$

However, although the exchange rate risk is defined in terms of the variance of returns, the interest rate risk from a PCA factor model is defined in terms of the variance of the P&L and not the variance of returns. So we rewrite (II.2.14) in a form that can be applied, i.e.

$$V(\Delta P_t^d) = (\bar{P}^d)^2 V(R_t^S) + (\bar{S})^2 V(\Delta P_t^f) + 2\bar{P}^d\bar{S}\,\mathrm{Cov}(R_t^S, \Delta P_t^f), \tag{II.2.15}$$

where $\bar{P}^d$ is the present value of the cash flows in domestic currency, and $\bar{S}$ is the exchange rate at the time that the risk is measured. Thus $\bar{P}^d$ and $\bar{S}$ are fixed.

On the right-hand side of (II.2.15) we have terms in $V(\Delta P_t^f)$ and $\mathrm{Cov}(R_t^S, \Delta P_t^f)$, where ΔP_t^f is given by (II.2.11). Typically these terms are quadratic forms based on covariance matrices of a very large number of different domestic interest rates. For instance, in the next example we consider a schedule of 60 monthly foreign currency payments so the variance $V(\Delta P_t^f)$ would be calculated from a quadratic form with a 60×60 covariance matrix and the covariance term $\mathrm{Cov}(R_t^S, \Delta P_t^f)$ would have 60 components.

In this situation a PCA factor model of the interest rates allows us to estimate these terms very precisely using only three components. Exactly the same type of PCA factor models that were described earlier in the chapter can be applied to obtain a computationally effective and very accurate approximation to the interest rate and correlation risks of a sequence of forward exposures to a single foreign currency, provided that the currency is liquid so that the forward prices are close to their fair value.

---

[18] To understand this approximation, use the approximation:

$$R_t^d \approx \ln\left(\frac{P_t^d}{P_{t-1}^d}\right).$$

Since $P_t^d = S_t P_t^f$ the above may be written

$$R_t^d \approx \ln\left(\frac{S_t P_t^f}{S_{t-1} P_{t-1}^f}\right) = \ln\left(\frac{S_t}{S_{t-1}}\right) + \ln\left(\frac{P_t^f}{P_{t-1}^f}\right).$$

Hence,

$$R_t^d \approx R_t^S + R_t^f,$$

and this proves (II.2.13).

The next example illustrates the method with a practical problem which could, for instance, relate to a UK oil refinery purchasing crude oil in US dollars, or any other regular UK importer of US commodities. The point to note is that we assume the oil – or the grain or another commodity – has been purchased in a futures contract. So the dollar price of oil or grain has been fixed and there is no commodity price risk. However, the risks remaining are:

- the exchange rate risk, arising from uncertainty about the sterling value of future payments in dollars;
- the interest rate risk, arising from the change in present value of the sterling cash flows; and
- the correlation risk, arising from the correlation between UK interest rates and the sterling–dollar exchange rate.

The following example shows how to decompose the total risk into these three components and how to isolate the key interest rate risk factors.

EXAMPLE II.2.2: PCA FACTOR MODEL FOR FORWARD STERLING EXPOSURES

A UK company has forward payments of $1 million on the 5th of every month over the next 5 years. Using the Bank of England daily interest rate data from 1 month to 60 months between 4 January 2005 and 31 December 2007 and the daily exchange rate data over the same period given in the spreadsheet for this example,[19] apply a PCA factor model to the UK spot rates to describe the interest rate, foreign exchange and correlation risks on 31 December 2007. On this day the dollar–sterling exchange rate was 1.9909 and the US discount curve is given in the spreadsheet.

SOLUTION   A PCA on the 60×60 daily covariance matrix calculated from daily changes in the short spot curve between 4 January 2005 and 31 December 2007 has already been performed in Section II.2.3.5. So the spreadsheet for this example simply copies the PCA results as given in that case study folder. On viewing these results, we see that seven components explain virtually 100% of the variation.

The change in present value of the sequence of foreign currency cash flows when the domestic interest rates change by amounts $\left(\Delta R_{1t}^{£}, \ldots, \Delta R_{nt}^{£}\right)'$ is

$$\Delta P_t^{\$} = -\sum_{i=1}^{n} PV01_i^{\$} \Delta R_{it}^{£}.$$

We shall approximate this using PCA. First we calculate the PV01 for each maturity using the approximation method described in Section III.1.8.2, i.e.

$$PV01_i^{\$} \approx \$N \times 10^{-4} \times (T_i - t) \times \left(1 + R_{it}^{\$}\right)^{-(T_i - t + 1)},$$

where $N = \$1$ million for all i in this example.

We shall use a three-component representation and the first three eigenvalues and the corresponding variation explained are shown in Table II.2.6. We take the dot product between the PV01 vector and the ith eigenvector to get the net weight on the ith principal

[19] Historical daily exchange rate data in numerous currencies are also downloadable free from the Bank of England's interactive statistical database on the www.bankofengland.co.uk CD-ROM.

Table II.2.6 Eigenvalues for UK short spot rates

Component	1	2	3
Eigenvalues	589.301	28.911	5.916
Percentage variation explained	93.90%	4.61%	0.94%
Cumulative variation explained	93.90%	98.51%	99.45%

component, for $i = 1$, 2 and 3, just as we did in the previous example. The result is the factor model

$$\Delta P_t^{\$} \approx 1788.45 \times P_{1t} - 412.71 \times P_{2t} + 331.68 \times P_{3t} \qquad (\text{II.2.16})$$

where P_1, P_2 and P_3 are the first three principal components.

Taking variances of the above is easy because the covariances of the principal components are 0 and their variances are equal to the eigenvalues shown in Table II.2.6. Thus

$$V(\Delta P_t^{\$}) \approx 1788.45^2 \times 589.301 - 412.71^2 \times 28.911 + 331.68^2 \times 5.916 = 1,890,482,830.$$

Using the current £/\$ exchange rate of 1.9909 gives the interest rate risk component of (II.2.15),

$$(\text{£}/\$)^2 V(\Delta P_t^{\$}) = 1.9909^{-2} \times 1,890,482,830.$$

And taking the square root and annualizing using $\sqrt{250}$ gives the P&L volatility due to interest rate uncertainty,

$$\text{IR Risk} = \sqrt{250} \times 1.9909^{-1} \times 43.480 = \text{£}\,345,308. \qquad (\text{II.2.17})$$

Now for the foreign exchange component of (II.2.15) we use the daily historical data on the £/\$ exchange rate given in the spreadsheet. The annual volatility of the daily log returns is calculated there as 7.83%. We also use the UK discount curve given in the spreadsheet to calculate $\overline{P}^{\text{£}}$, the present value of the payments in sterling, obtaining £30,103,503. Multiplying this by the exchange rate volatility gives

$$\text{FX Risk} = \text{£}30,103,503 \times 7.83\% = \text{£}2,355,984. \qquad (\text{II.2.18})$$

The last component of the risk decomposition (II.2.15) is the correlation risk. This is represented by the term corresponding to the covariance between UK interest rates and exchange rates, i.e. $2\overline{P}^{\$}(\text{£}/\$)\,\text{Cov}(R_t^S, \Delta P_t^{\$})$. In the spreadsheet we calculate the present value of the payments in US dollars based on the US discount curve as $\overline{P}^{\$} = \$\,59,937,460$, which is equal to £30,105,711 at the current £/\$ exchange rate, and so

$$2\overline{P}^{\$}(\text{£}/\$) = \text{£}60,211,422.$$

For the other component of the covariance term we use the factor model (II.2.16) to write

$$\text{Cov}(R_t^S, \Delta P_t^{\$}) \approx 1788.45 \times \text{Cov}(R_t^S, PC_{1,t}) - 412.71 \times \text{Cov}(R_t^S, PC_{2t}) + 331.68$$
$$\times \text{Cov}(R_t^S, PC_{3t}).$$

The three covariances are estimated using the historical data on the exchange rate and the principal components. The annualized covariances are

$$\text{Cov}(R_t^S, PC_{1t}) = 3.303, \quad \text{Cov}(R_t^S, PC_{2t}) = 1.516, \quad \text{Cov}(R_t^S, PC_{3t}) = -0.210.$$

Hence,

$$\text{Cov}(R_t^S, \Delta P_t^\$) \approx 1788.45 \times 3.303 - 412.71 \times 1.516 + 331.68 \times 0.210 = 5211.62,$$

and so the correlation risk is

$$\sqrt{2\overline{P}^\$ \, (\pounds/\$) \, \text{Cov}(R_t^S, \Delta P_t^\$)} = \sqrt{\pounds 60,211,422 \times 5211.62} = \pounds 560,178.$$

Finally, the total risk is the square root of the sum of the squared component risks, i.e.

$$\text{Total Risk} = \left(\text{IR Risk}^2 + \text{ FX Risk}^2 + \text{ Correlation Risk}^2 \right)^{1/2}$$

$$= \left(\pounds 345,308^2 + \pounds 2,355,984^2 + \pounds 560,178^2 \right)^{1/2} = \pounds 2,446,160.$$

The result is typical in that the interest rate and correlation risks are negligible compared with the FX risk.

II.2.4.3 Factor Models for Commodity Futures Portfolios

Unlike currency forwards, commodity futures usually have a substantial basis risk due to considerable uncertainties about carry costs, including transportation, storage and insurance costs. It is possible to decompose their risks into the spot price risk, interest rate risks and uncertainties due to carry costs, but carry costs are extremely difficult to quantify. For this reason it is preferable to map exposures to commodity futures to a set of constant maturity futures, as explained in Section III.5.4.2, and to use constant maturity futures as the risk factors. Constant maturity futures are not traded instruments, but it makes sense to use constant maturity futures as risk factors since their prices can be constructed using interpolation between adjacent traded futures and we can thus obtain data over a long sample period for use in our risk analysis.

EXAMPLE II.2.3: PCA ON CRUDE OIL FUTURES

Figure II.2.8 shows daily prices of constant maturity futures on West Texas Intermediate crude oil over the period from February 1992 to February 1999. Only selected maturities

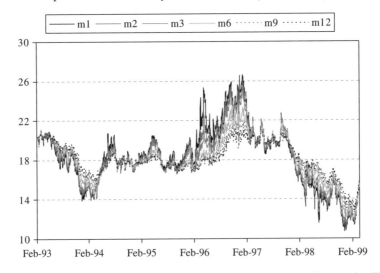

Figure II.2.8 Constant maturity futures on West Texas Intermediate crude oil

are shown, but the spreadsheet contains data on twelve constant maturity futures with maturities between 1 and 12 months. Perform a PCA on the correlation matrix of daily log returns.

SOLUTION   Clearly the returns on constant maturity crude oil futures are so highly correlated that a PCA on these data requires only *two* factors to explain a very large fraction of the variation. In fact, there are only two important risk factors that are driving all the futures: an almost parallel shift in the term structure accounts for nearly 96% of the comovements in the futures, and the other comovements are almost all attributable to a change in the slope of the term structure. Just these two principal components together explain over 99% of the daily covariations. The first three eigenvectors are shown in Figure II.2.9.

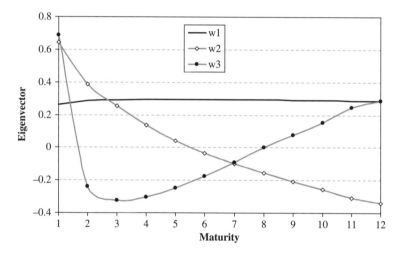

Figure II.2.9   Eigenvectors of crude oil futures correlation matrix

II.2.4.4   Application to Portfolio Immunization

Factor models for a single term structure allow us to isolate the exposure to the most important determinants of risk, i.e. the first few principal components. The principal components do not have the *exact* interpretation of a parallel shift, linear change in slope and quadratic change in curvature. The first three principal components capture the *most commonly occurring* movements in a term structure, i.e. an almost parallel shift, and changes in slope and curvature. In this section we explain how to apply these factor models to hedge a bond portfolio against these risks.[20]

The next example explains how a single interest rate curve factor model may be used to immunize the portfolio against the most commonly occurring movements in the yield curve.

---

[20] And if the fourth component is important, then we can also hedge this type of movement.

EXAMPLE II.2.4: IMMUNIZING A BOND PORTFOLIO USING PCA

In Example II.2.1 we estimated a factor model for the UK bond portfolio that is characterized by the PV01 vector in Table II.2.4. The factor model is

$$-P\&L_t \approx £623.74 \times P_{1t} + £1,001.11 \times P_{2t} - £1,006.65 \times P_{3t}.$$

How much should we add of the 10-year bond so that the new portfolio's P&L is invariant to changes in the first principal component, i.e. an almost parallel shift in interest rates? Having done this, how much should we then add of the 5- and 15-year bonds so that the new portfolio's P&L is also invariant to changes in the second principal component, i.e. a change in slope of the yield curve?

SOLUTION   The spreadsheet for this example uses the Excel Solver twice. The first time we find the cash flow at 10 years that makes the coefficient on the first principal component zero. The Solver setting is shown in the spreadsheet. The result is $-£4,225,242$. Since this is negative, the present value of this cash flow is the face value that we *sell* on the 10-year zero coupon bond, i.e. £2,716,824. Adding this position (or an equivalent exposure) to our portfolio yields the factor model

$$-P\&L_t \approx £1,190.88 \times P_{2t} - £558.54 \times P_{3t}.$$

So the portfolio is immunized against movements in the first principal component.

The second time we apply the solver we find the cash flow at 5 and 15 years that makes the coefficient on the second principal component also zero. Note that we need two bonds to zero the slope sensitivity. The Solver settings are also shown in the spreadsheet, and note that this time we constrain the solution so that the coefficient on the first component remains at 0. The result is a cash flow of $-£7,369,481$ in 5 years and of £4,726,397 in 15 years. The present value of these cash flows give the positions on the two bond, i.e. £5,936,527 is the face value that we *sell* on the 5-year zero coupon bond and £2,452,412 is the face value that we *buy* on the 15-year zero coupon bond. Adding this position (or an equivalent exposure) to our portfolio yields the factor model

$$P\&L_t \approx -£374.04 \times P_{3t}.$$

It is left as an exercise to the reader to find positions on three bonds that also immunize the portfolio from changes in the *curvature* of the yield curve.

II.2.4.5   Application to Asset–Liability Management

A single curve PCA factor model can also be used to balance assets and liabilities. For example, a pension fund may ask how to invest its income from contributors in fixed income securities so that its P&L is insensitive to the most common movements in interest rates, as captured by the first three principal components. Similarly, a firm may have a series of fixed liabilities, such as payments on a fixed rate loan, and seek to finance these payments by issuing fixed coupon bonds or notes. Both these questions can be answered using a PCA factor model representation of spot interest rates. In this section we consider a simplified example of balancing a fixed stream of liabilities with issues of zero coupon bonds.

EXAMPLE II.2.5: ASSET–LIABILITY MANAGEMENT USING PCA

A UK company has a fixed stream of liabilities of £1 million per month over the next 5 years. It seeks to finance these by issuing zero coupon bonds at 1, 3 and 5 years to maturity. How many bonds should it issue (or indeed, purchase) on 31 December 2007 so that its portfolio of assets and liabilities has zero sensitivity to parallel shifts and changes in slope of the UK government spot yield curve?

SOLUTION   Just as in Example II.2.2, we employ the results of the case study of the UK short spot rate curve. These are simply pasted into the spreadsheet for this example.[21] But instead of analysing the factor model for the P&L on a stream of foreign currency payments, this time we assume the payments are fixed in sterling and, using the same process as in Example II.2.2, we derive the factor model

$$-\text{P\&L}_t \approx 31.25 \times P_{1t} + 58.96 \times P_{2t} + 5.20 \times P_{3t}.$$

The present value of the liabilities on 31 December 2007 is calculated using the discount curve on that date, and this is calculated in the spreadsheet as £53,887,892.

   To decide how much of each bond to issue, we need to find cash flows at the 1, 3 and 5 year maturities such that (a) the present value of these cash flows is £53,887,892 and (b) the net position of assets and liabilities has a P&L that has zero sensitivities to the first and second principal components of the UK spot rates. Again we use the Solver for this, and the settings are shown in the spreadsheet. The result is a portfolio that is only sensitive to changes in curvature and not to parallel shifts or changes in the slope of the term structure of UK spot rates. It has the factor model representation

$$\text{P\&L}_t \approx 31.11 \times P_{3t}.$$

The portfolio is achieved by issuing £19,068,087 face value on the 1-year bond, £9,537,960 face value on the 3-year bond and £22,921,686 face value on the 5-year bond.

Just as in Example II.2.4, this example can be extended to the issuance (or indeed, purchase) of further bonds to immunize the net fixed income portfolio against changes in curvature of interest rates. Again, this is left as an exercise to the interested reader.

II.2.4.6   Application to Portfolio Risk Measurement

We have already seen that PCA factor models simplify the measurement of risk. For instance, in Example II.2.2 we used the factor model to decompose the risk from a sequence of forward foreign currency payments into interest rate, exchange rate and correlation components. More generally, PCA factor models help us to assess the risk of all types of 'curve' portfolios, including fixed income portfolios and portfolios containing futures or forwards. There are three reasons why PCA is so successful in this respect:[22]

---

[21] We do this because, as noted above, there is frequently a conflict between the Solver and the Matrix add-in, so whilst both add-ins are always available (once added in) we try not to use them both in the same spreadsheet.
[22] Note that reasons 1 and 2 also apply to equity portfolios and portfolios of spot exchange rates or different commodities. See Section II.4.6 for further details.

- *The principal components are orthogonal.* The orthogonality of principal components means that the PCA factor model provides the basis for highly efficient computations because their (unconditional) correlation matrix is diagonal.
- *We can adjust the level of 'noise' or unwanted variation affecting the volatilities and correlations by taking a reduced set of principal components in the representation.* We know exactly how much variation is being captured by the factor model. The residual variation can be adjusted to reflect the analyst's views on irrelevant variation. Long term volatility and correlation forecasts should be based on representations with fewer components than short term forecasts.
- *The first few components capture the key risk components.* Separate stress tests on each of the first three components identify the worst case portfolio loss resulting from the most commonly occurring movements in the curve. This is illustrated in the next example.

EXAMPLE II.2.6: STRESS TESTING A UK BOND PORTFOLIO

Use the factor model representation for the bond portfolio discussed in Example II.2.1 to estimate the following:

(a) The portfolio's P&L volatility based on a one-, two- and three-component representation. Compare your result with the portfolio's P&L volatility that is calculated without using the factor model.
(b) The 'worst case' loss when the yield curve shifts, tilts and changes convexity and these movements are based on the principal components. How would you evaluate the 'worst case' loss without reference to the factor model?

SOLUTION   The factor model representation with three components was derived in Example II.2.1 as

$$-P\&L_t \approx £623.74 \times P_{1t} + £1,001.11 \times P_{2t} - £1,006.65 \times P_{3t}.$$

The principal components were derived from the 20×20 covariance matrix of the monthly changes in UK interest rates at maturities $1, 2, \ldots, 20$ years.

(a) The 3×3 covariance matrix of the principal components is the diagonal matrix of the first three eigenvalues shown in Table II.2.5. Thus with three components,

$$V(\mathbf{P}) = \begin{pmatrix} 6,855.12 & 0 & 0 \\ 0 & 923.75 & 0 \\ 0 & 0 & 123.14 \end{pmatrix}.$$

The portfolio's P&L volatility is therefore:

(i)   with one component,

$$\sqrt{12 \times V(P\&L)} = £623.74 \times \sqrt{12 \times 6,855.12} = £178,897;$$

(ii) with two components,

$$\sqrt{12 \times V(P\&L)} = \sqrt{12 \times (623.74^2 \times 6,855.12 + 1,001.11^2 \times 923.75)}$$
$$= £207,639;$$

(iii) with three components,

$$\sqrt{12 \times V(P\&L)}$$
$$= \sqrt{12 \times (623.74^2 \times 6{,}855.12 + 1{,}001.11^2 \times 923.75 + 1{,}006.65^2 \times 123.14)}$$
$$= £211{,}214.$$

(iv) Direct calculation: this is performed in the spreadsheet, based on the monthly P&L variance $\mathbf{p'Vp}$, where $\mathbf{p}$ is the PV01 vector and $\mathbf{V}$ is the covariance matrix of the monthly returns. The result is £211,463.

Hence the volatility that is estimated using the principal component representation is less than the directly calculated volatility, but it increases each time we add another component, and even with just three components it is very close to the directly calculated volatility.

(b) We assume a 'worst case' loss occurs when the yield curve moves *six sigma* – i.e. six annualized standard deviations – in the direction that incurs a loss.[23] It is very simple to use the factor model for testing based on six sigma moves in each component, separately and together. Table II.2.7 shows the volatility of each component (the annualized square root of its corresponding eigenvalue), the corresponding six sigma move (which takes account of the sign of the component's factor sensitivity in the factor model) and finally the effect on the P&L (which is the product of the six sigma move and the factor sensitivity).

Table II.2.7   Stress test based on PCA factor model

Stress test	P_1	P_2	P_3
Volatility	286.8125	105.2851	38.4406
Six sigma adverse move	−1720.8751	−631.7108	230.6439
Effect on P&L	−£1,073,384	−£632,415	−£232,178

This simple analysis shows the effect of each type of adverse move: P_1 captures the (almost) parallel shift, P_2 a change in slope and P_3 a change in curvature. The total worst case loss if each of these extreme movements happens simultaneously – which is very unlikely, since the components are uncorrelated – is just the sum of the individual worst case losses, i.e. £1,937,977.

Without the factor model, yield curve stress testing in practice would be more complex computationally and also very *ad hoc*. The entire yield curve would need to be shifted, tilted and changed in convexity and the portfolio re-valued for each of the changes and then again, assuming all changes occurred simultaneously. But the complexity of the computations is not the only problem. An even greater problem is that we do not know how large the shift, tilt and curvature movements should be. The volatilities of interest rates of different maturities can be very different, as we have

---

[23] This is an example of the *factor push* stress testing method that is discussed in full in Chapter IV.7.

seen in Figure II.2.2, so how can we define a six sigma movement in trend? Also, should the shift be parallel or not? How steep should the tilt be? And how convex or flat should we make the curve? Without the PCA factor model these questions are impossible to answer objectively.

II.2.4.7   Multiple Curve Factor Models

When a portfolio contains domestic bonds, swaps, notes and other fixed income instruments with different credit ratings then several zero coupon yield curves of different ratings categories are used as the risk factors. Yield curves of different currencies are very highly correlated. The strength of correlation between the two curves depends on the behaviour of the credit spread, i.e. the difference between a low rated yield of a fixed maturity and the AAA rated yield of the same maturity.

At the time of writing credit spreads have recently increased considerably, after having declined steadily for several years.[24] Figure II.2.10 shows the AAA/A− credit spread on European bonds of different maturities in basis points during 2007.[25] These spreads are of the order of 5–10 basis points only, which is considerably smaller than the spreads that we experience on non-investment grade bonds. Yet the news of the sub-prime mortgage crisis in the USA at the end of July 2007 even affected these spreads. Overnight on 26–27 July the spreads of 5 or more years to maturity increased by over 2 basis points.

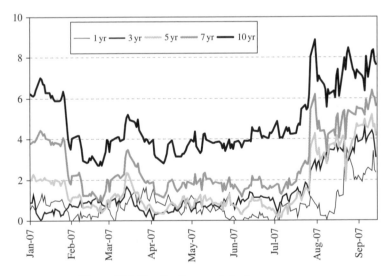

Figure II.2.10   Credit spreads in the euro zone

---

[24] The gradual reduction in the price of credit resulting from increasing securitization in credit markets induced more and more banks to underwrite low grade issues. But the market for these issues dried up with the onset of the sub-prime mortgage crisis in the USA, so banks needed to increase credit risk capital requirements to cover the risks of these credits. As a result they had less money to lend and the price of credit increased dramatically.

[25] Data downloadable from http://sdw.ecb.europa.eu.

Apart from isolated crises such as this, typical movements in interest rates are very often highly correlated across curves as well as within curves. One should account for this correlation when hedging a fixed income portfolio or simply when assessing its risk, and to capture this correlation in a factor model we must perform PCA on two or more curves *simultaneously*.

EXAMPLE II.2.7: PCA ON CURVES WITH DIFFERENT CREDIT RATING

The spreadsheet for this example contains daily data on spot euro interest rate indices based on (a) all euro AAA issuer companies and governments and (b) all euro A– to AA issuer companies and governments.[26] On both curves the spot rates have ten different maturities between 1 and 10 years. Find the eigenvalues and eigenvectors of the 20×20 combined covariance matrix and interpret the first few principal components.

SOLUTION   Since the credit spread between these curves is so small, it comes as no surprise that almost all the variation can be explained by just two components. The first two eigenvectors are shown in Figure II.2.11. The first principal component, which accounts for almost 95% of the variation, represents an almost parallel shift of about the same magnitude in both curves, though slightly less movement of the 1-year rate in each case. The second component together with the first component captures over 99% of the variation, representing an almost identical tilt in both curves.

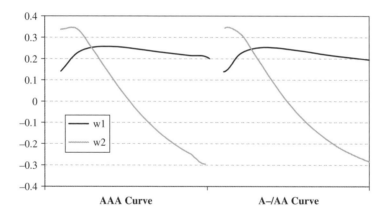

Figure II.2.11   First two eigenvectors on two-curve PCA

The above example considered two extremely highly correlated curves, but in many situations where PCA is applied to derive a factor model for several curves these curves have lower correlation. For instance, when fixed income instruments are in different currencies the risk factors are (at least) one zero coupon yield curve for each currency of exposure. Yield curves in different currencies are sometimes highly correlated, but not always so. However, since any correlation needs to be captured when hedging the

---

[26] Data downloadable from http://sdw.ecb.europa.eu.

portfolio and assessing its risks, a multiple curve PCA factor model is still extremely useful.

Figure II.2.12 show three short spot curves in different currencies: US Treasury bill rates, Euribor rates and the Bank of England short spot rate that we have already analysed in detail above. Data are monthly, covering the period from 31 December 2001 to 31 August 2007. The *between curve* correlations are clearly far lower than the *within curve* correlations. The next example examines the principal components of the combined covariance matrix of all three curves.

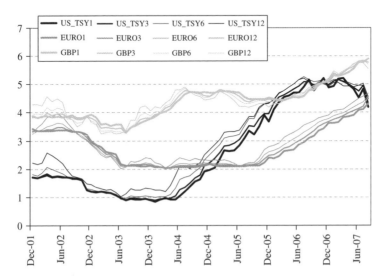

Figure II.2.12   Three short spot curves, December 2001 to August 2007

EXAMPLE II.2.8: PCA ON CURVES IN DIFFERENT CURRENCIES

Perform a combined PCA on the covariance matrix of monthly changes on the USD, EURO and GBP yield curves shown in Figure II.2.12 and interpret the principal components.

SOLUTION   The first six eigenvalues and eigenvectors are shown in Table II.2.8, and the first three eigenvectors are plotted in Figure II.2.13. The first eigenvector accounts for less than 45% of the variation, the second captures nearly 30% of the variation and the third captures over 12%. So the second and third eigenvectors are far more significant than in the single curve case. We also need six eigenvectors to capture almost 99% of the variation. Furthermore, all the eigenvectors have a different interpretation. Figure II.2.13 illustrates the first three of them:

• The first and most important eigenvector corresponds to a shift in the entire USD curve when the EURO and GBP curves only tilt at the longer end.[27]

---

[27] The short rates are very tightly controlled and respond less to the markets.

- The second eigenvector, which also accounts for a lot of the comovements in these curves, is a decrease in USD short rates accompanied by upward moves in EURO and GBP rates, especially at the long end.[28]
- The third eigenvector captures virtually static USD rates when all EURO rates shift but the GBP rates tilt.

Table II.2.8 Eigenvectors and eigenvalues of the three-curve covariance matrix

Components	1	2	3	4	5	6
Eigenvalues	888.81	594.27	250.34	133.87	73.25	38.43
% Variation	44.10%	29.49%	12.42%	6.64%	3.63%	1.91%
Cumulative % variation	44.10%	73.59%	86.01%	92.65%	96.29%	98.19%
Eigenvectors	w1	w2	w3	w4	w5	w6
USD1m	0.5239	0.2914	0.0512	0.6295	0.2463	0.1267
USD3m	0.4621	0.2056	0.0499	0.0872	−0.1114	−0.1515
USD6m	0.4309	0.1017	0.0050	−0.2833	−0.2223	−0.1515
USD12m	0.4606	−0.0313	0.0412	−0.5577	−0.2046	0.0336
EURO1m	0.0361	−0.1406	−0.4619	0.1085	−0.0755	−0.7120
EURO3m	0.0578	−0.1522	−0.4655	0.1202	0.0301	−0.1208
EURO6m	0.1119	−0.1892	−0.4423	0.0438	0.0927	0.1990
EURO12m	0.2018	−0.2712	−0.4123	−0.1501	0.1930	0.5315
GBP1m	-0.0007	−0.2477	0.0045	0.3122	−0.6619	0.2292
GBP3m	0.0605	−0.3391	0.1378	0.2079	−0.3688	0.0288
GBP6m	0.1257	−0.4460	0.2385	0.1147	−0.0140	−0.0751
GBP12m	0.1919	−0.5779	0.3487	−0.0174	0.4570	−0.1853

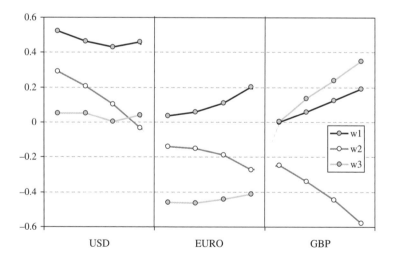

Figure II.2.13 Eigenvectors for multiple curve PCA factor models

---

[28] Or, an increase in USD short rates is accompanied by a decrease in EURO and GBP rates, especially at the long end.

Multiple curve factor models also arise when we analyse positions in commodity futures and options. For instance, in Section III.2.7 we present a case study that applies PCA to three curves simultaneously and hence analyses the risk of a portfolio containing crude oil, heating oil and gasoline futures.

II.2.5 EQUITY PCA FACTOR MODELS

This section explains the application of PCA to develop a statistical factor model for stock returns. After defining the structure of the model we present a case study that illustrates the model's application to the 30 stocks in the DJIA index.

II.2.5.1 Model Structure

Denote by R_{jt} the return on stock j at time t, for $j = 1, \ldots, n$ and $t = 1, \ldots, T$. Here n is the number of stocks in the investor's universe and T is the number of data points on each stock return. Put these returns into the $T \times n$ matrix $\mathbf{X}$ and then perform a PCA on the covariance matrix $\mathbf{V} = V(\mathbf{X})$. Retain k principal components, enough to explain a large faction of the total variation in the system. See the comments in the next subsection about the choice of k.

Note that the covariance matrix could be an equally weighted or an exponentially weighted covariance matrix. For instance, for portfolio allocation decisions we would use an equally weighted covariance matrix based on weekly or monthly data over several years. For risk measurement over a long time horizon we may use the same model as for portfolio allocation, but for the purpose of very short term risk measurement we may choose instead an exponentially weighted matrix based on daily data.

Now estimate a linear regression of each of the stock's returns on the k principal component factors, using ordinary least squares. The regression provides an estimate of the alpha for each stock and the betas with respect to each principal component factor. So the regression model is

$$R_{jt} = \alpha_j + \sum_{i=1}^{k} \beta_{ij} P_{it} + \varepsilon_{jt}, \qquad (\text{II.2.19})$$

and the estimated model provides the return on each stock that is explained by the factor model as

$$\hat{R}_{jt} = \hat{\alpha}_j + \sum_{i=1}^{k} \hat{\beta}_{ij} P_{it}. \qquad (\text{II.2.20})$$

The principal components are based on a covariance (or correlation) matrix, so they have zero mean and $E(P_i) = 0$. Thus the expected return given by the factor model is

$$E(\hat{R}_{ij}) = \hat{\alpha}_j. \qquad (\text{II.2.21})$$

Taking variances and covariance of (II.2.20) gives the systematic covariance matrix of stock returns, i.e. the covariance that is captured by the model, with elements

$$\text{est.} V(R_{jt}) = \sum_{i=1}^{k} \hat{\beta}_{ij}^2 V(P_{it}),$$

$$\text{est.} \text{Cov}(R_{jt}, R_{mt}) = \sum_{i=1}^{k} \hat{\beta}_{ij} \hat{\beta}_{im} V(P_{it}). \qquad (\text{II.2.22})$$

That is, using matrix notation

$$\text{est.} V(\mathbf{X}) = \mathbf{B}' \mathbf{\Omega} \mathbf{B}, \tag{II.2.23}$$

where $\mathbf{B} = \left(\hat{\beta}_{ij} \right)$ is the $k \times n$ matrix of estimated factor betas and $\mathbf{\Omega}$ is the covariance matrix of the principal components

Since the principal components are orthogonal, the covariance between any two principal components is 0 and so their covariance matrix $\mathbf{\Omega}$ is a diagonal matrix. And, since the sum of the squares of the elements in the mth principal component is λ_m, the mth largest eigenvalue of $\mathbf{V}$, the covariance matrix of the principal components is very straightforward to calculate.

Armed with these factor models, one for each stock in our universe, the asset manager can form portfolios with weights $\mathbf{w} = (w_1, \ldots, w_n)'$ and explore their risk and returns characteristics, as captured by the statistical factor model. This helps the manager to match the objectives of their investors, e.g. to find portfolios that are expected to return a given target with the minimum possible risk and that may also be subject to allocation constraints.[29] The portfolio alpha and betas are just the weighted sums of the stock alphas and betas, i.e.

$$\hat{\alpha} = \sum_{j=1}^{n} w_j \hat{\alpha}_j \text{ and } \hat{\beta}_i = \sum_{j=1}^{n} w_j \hat{\beta}_{ij} \quad \text{for } i = 1, \ldots, k.$$

The systematic variance of the portfolio is

$$\sum_{i=1}^{k} \hat{\beta}_i^2 V(P_i) = \hat{\beta}' \mathbf{\Omega} \hat{\beta}, \quad \text{where} \quad \hat{\beta} = \left(\hat{\beta}_1, \ldots, \hat{\beta}_k \right)'.$$

Subtracting this from the total variance of the portfolio, $\mathbf{w}'\mathbf{V}\mathbf{w}$, we derive the specific risk that results from using the factor model, i.e.

$$\text{specific risk} = \left(\mathbf{w}'\mathbf{V}\mathbf{w} - \hat{\beta}' \mathbf{\Omega} \hat{\beta} \right)^{1/2} \tag{II.2.24}$$

when measured as a standard deviation. This can be converted to an annual volatility using the square-root-of-time rule with annualizing factor determined by the frequency of the stock returns, e.g. the annualizing factor is 12 when the model is based on monthly data.

II.2.5.2 Specific Risks and Dimension Reduction

PCA is fairly straightforward to apply to very large systems of stock returns, although considerable computational power is required when finding the eigenvalues. For instance, the APT software applies PCA to 10,000 stocks for the US model and 40,000 stocks for the world model. It will always produce a set of orthogonal factors that explain a known percentage of the system's variation. But in equity PCA factor models the dimensions cannot be reduced as much as they can in systems of interest rates or returns on futures of different maturities. Stock returns are not *very* highly correlated so a large dimension reduction will leave a significant proportion of the variation unexplained by the factor model. For instance,

---

[29] See Section I.6.3 for details of the unconstrained and constrained portfolio allocation problem. Also, in contrast to the Barra model, the risk *is* measured relative to the target return.

in the next subsection we shall apply PCA to the returns on all 30 stocks in the DJIA index. A representation with $k = 5$ principal components captures about 60% of the variation but to explain 95% of the total variation requires 23 components, so there is very little dimension reduction.

The precise number of components required to explain a given percentage of the total variation depends on the correlation between stocks' returns. This will change over time: during periods when all stocks' returns are closely related to systematic factors, fewer components will be needed to achieve a suitable degree of accuracy in the principal component representation. Typically we should try to explain between 70% and 90% of the total variation. If we try to explain more than about 90% of the variation the model may be picking up 'noise' that is not relevant to long term allocation decisions. The components corresponding to the smaller eigenvalues will only reflect some idiosyncratic variation in a few stocks. On the other hand, if we explain less than about 70% of the variation, portfolios that are modelled in this framework will have very large specific risks.

II.2.5.3   Case Study: PCA Factor Model for DJIA Portfolios

In this case study we analyse daily data on the 30 DJIA stocks from 31 December 2004 to 26 April 2006. We build a PCA factor model and use the model to analyse the total, systematic and specific risks of an existing portfolio. The data were downloaded from Yahoo! Finance and the names and symbols for each stock are shown in Table II.2.9.

Table II.2.9   Ticker symbols for DJIA stocks

Symbol	AA	AIG	AXP	BA	C
Name	Alcoa	American International Group	American Express	Boeing	Citigroup
Symbol	CAT	DD	DIS	GE	GM
Name	Caterpillar	Du Pont De Nemours	Walt Disney	General Electric	General Motors
Symbol	HD	HON	HPQ	IBM	INTC
Name	Home Depot	Honeywell	Hewlett Packard	International Business Machines	Intel
Symbol	JNJ	JPM	KO	MCD	MMM
Name	Johnson and Johnson	JP Morgan Chase	Coca Cola	McDonald's	3M Company
Symbol	MO	MRK	MSFT	PFE	PG
Name	Altria Group	Merck	Microsoft	Pfizer	Procter & Gamble
Symbol	ATT	UTX	VZ	WMT	XOM
Name	AT&T	United Tech	Verizon Communications	WalMart Stores	Exxon Mobil

The spreadsheet calculates the eigenvalues and eigenvectors of $\mathbf{V}$, the stock returns covariance matrix. The eigenvectors are ranked in order of magnitude and we calculate the cumulative variation (II.2.4) explained by the first k components. The result is shown in Table II.2.10, for $k = 1, \ldots, 30$. The first five principal components together explain nearly 60% of the variation in the system. As usual the first principal component explains the most variation (27.34%) and the first eigenvector (shown in the spreadsheet) is fairly constant, except for its weight on General Motors (GM). This stock was much more volatile than the others during the data period: its volatility was over 40%, whereas many other stocks had a volatility much less than 20%, and that is why the first eigenvector has a larger than average weight on GM.

Table II.2.10 Cumulative variation explained by the principal components

P1	P2	P3	P4	P5	P6	P7	P8	P9	P10
27.34%	41.12%	47.54%	53.35%	57.45%	61.10%	64.22%	67.27%	70.04%	72.70%
P11	P12	P13	P14	P15	P16	P17	P18	P19	P20
75.24%	77.56%	79.74%	81.74%	83.67%	85.54%	87.27%	88.91%	90.39%	91.75%
P21	P22	P23	P24	P25	P26	P27	P28	P29	P30
93.00%	94.12%	95.14%	96.09%	96.99%	97.81%	98.48%	99.07%	99.61%	100.00%

Since our purpose is simply to illustrate the methodology we shall only use five principal components in the factor model. This allows us to explain only about 60% of the total variation. We estimate a linear regression of each of the stocks' returns on the principal component factors, using ordinary least squares, to obtain each stock's alpha and factor betas. Thus we obtain **B**, the 5×30 matrix of stock betas. The estimated coefficients, t statistics and R^2 of the regressions are reported in Table II.2.11.

The first component is always the most significant variable in these regressions, since it captures a common trend in the stock's returns. This is usually but not always followed by the second component. The regression R^2 ranges from 52.26% for BA (where the intercept is also significantly different from zero, unlike the other stocks) to 99.9% for GM. Using more components in the model would increase the explanatory power of these regressions.

EXAMPLE II.2.9: DECOMPOSITION OF TOTAL RISK USING PCA FACTORS

Consider the following portfolios of DJIA stocks:

(i)   an arbitrary funded portfolio with long or short positions in any of the 30 stocks;
(ii) a portfolio with equal weights in each of the 30 DJIA stocks;
(iii) the DJIA portfolio

In each case, find the portfolio's net beta with respect to each of the five principal components calculated above, in percentage and in dollar terms. Also calculate the total risk, systematic risk and specific risk of the portfolio on 26 April 2006.

Table II.2.11 PCA factor models for DJIA stocks

Stock (R²)	AA (78.74%) Coeffs	t stat.	AIG (63.86%) Coeffs	t stat.	ATT (54.74%) Coeffs	t stat.	AXP (66.73%) Coeffs	t stat.	BA (52.26%) Coeffs	t stat.	CAT (76.05%) Coeffs	t stat.	CITI (64.95%) Coeffs	t stat.	DD (64.15%) Coeffs	t stat.	DIS (59.10%) Coeffs	t stat.	GE (70.39%) Coeffs	t stat.
Intercept	0.000	−0.938	0.000	−0.307	0.000	0.051	0.000	0.119	0.001	2.235	0.001	1.253	0.000	0.385	−0.001	−1.181	0.000	0.068	0.000	−0.718
PC1	0.203	14.921	0.167	10.939	0.124	11.190	0.181	14.995	0.158	9.241	0.255	16.125	0.119	12.881	0.189	13.860	0.152	10.510	0.154	16.268
PC2	0.098	5.109	0.114	5.317	0.039	2.532	0.052	3.042	0.121	5.020	0.125	5.635	0.067	5.181	0.081	4.229	0.071	3.487	0.074	5.528
PC3	0.292	10.412	−0.064	−2.046	−0.022	−0.977	0.063	2.512	0.061	1.738	0.373	11.446	0.033	1.726	0.049	1.742	−0.047	−1.579	0.042	2.174
PC4	0.137	4.635	−0.172	−5.210	−0.049	−2.044	−0.075	−2.877	−0.028	−0.747	−0.052	−1.526	−0.002	−0.085	0.055	1.857	−0.042	−1.347	−0.010	−0.504
PC5	0.425	12.108	−0.256	−6.515	−0.028	−0.982	−0.097	−3.120	−0.116	−2.612	0.167	−4.085	−0.149	−6.265	0.104	2.957	−0.254	−6.772	−0.098	−4.012

Stock (R²)	GM (99.90%) Coeffs	t stat.	HD (69.37%) Coeffs	t stat.	HON (63.14%) Coeffs	t stat.	HP (98.81%) Coeffs	t stat.	IBM (58.23%) Coeffs	t stat.	INT (63.57%) Coeffs	t stat.	JNJ (54.11%) Coeffs	t stat.	JPM (71.54%) Coeffs	t stat.	KO (63.90%) Coeffs	t stat.	MCD (53.28%) Coeffs	t stat.
Intercept	0.000	0.141	0.000	−0.766	0.000	0.529	0.000	1.248	−0.001		0.000	−1.528	0.000	−0.744	0.000	−0.581	0.000	0.827	0.000	0.433
PC1	0.423	219.936	0.218	15.783	0.211	14.159	0.197	47.646	0.155	11.576	0.209	12.295	0.096	8.517	0.154	16.705	0.124	14.370	0.194	11.002
PC2	−0.894	−330.385	0.111	5.721	0.048	2.273	0.023	3.991	0.048	2.520	0.101	4.248	0.096	6.091	0.073	5.625	0.038	3.152	0.020	0.799
PC3	0.019	4.688	0.043	1.521	0.029	0.931	−0.595	−69.605	0.016	0.569	−0.003	−0.085	−0.055	−2.373	0.052	2.725	−0.018	−1.011	−0.027	−0.730
PC4	0.075	18.114	−0.045	−1.517	−0.023	−0.727	−0.626	−69.690	−0.130	−4.470	0.012	0.323	0.035	1.451	−0.032	−1.587	0.008	0.444	0.012	0.303
PC5	−0.017	−3.488	−0.125	−3.500	0.098	2.550	0.384	35.879	−0.073	−2.119	−0.307	−7.005	−0.116	−3.995	−0.098	−4.108	−0.048	−2.131	−0.105	−2.313

Stock (R²)	MMM (55.84%) Coeffs	t stat.	MO (53.57%) Coeffs	t stat.	MRK (91.37%) Coeffs	t stat.	MSFT (58.61%) Coeffs	t stat.	PFE (79.98%) Coeffs	t stat.	PG (57.25%) Coeffs	t stat.	UTX (65.54%) Coeffs	t stat.	VZ (57.37%) Coeffs	t stat.	WM (53.81%) Coeffs	t stat.	XON (76.65%) Coeffs	t stat.
Intercept	0.000	−0.226	0.001	1.030	0.000		0.000	0.944	0.000	−0.199	0.000	−0.354	0.000	0.155	−0.001	0.779	−0.001	−1.407	0.000	−0.627
PC1	0.147	10.884	0.148	10.565	0.169	17.073	0.136	11.822	0.172	13.214	0.126	11.127	0.171	13.824	0.132	10.098	0.123	11.142	0.189	13.716
PC2	0.085	4.460	0.060	3.065	0.115	8.253	0.078	4.782	0.120	6.541	0.068	4.281	0.079	4.540	0.049	2.926	0.067	3.881	0.122	6.292
PC3	0.073	2.617	0.002	0.055	−0.476	−23.283	−0.017	−0.707	−0.304	−11.302	−0.031	−1.329	0.138	5.386	−0.071	−2.906	−0.015	−0.615	0.205	7.205
PC4	−0.024	−0.831	0.000	0.003	0.566	26.312	−0.020	−0.786	0.424	15.012	0.080	3.256	−0.024	−0.890	−0.086	−3.347	−0.012	−0.463	0.017	0.581
PC5	−0.005	−0.152	−0.106	−2.930	0.149	5.835	−0.065	−2.181	0.035	1.027	−0.046	−1.587	0.031	0.958	−0.073	−2.367	−0.116	−3.686	0.475	13.366

SOLUTION

(i) In the spreadsheet for this example the user can change the choice of dollar amounts invested in long or short positions in each stock.[30] For a portfolio that is $100 long in AA, $50 short in AXP and so on (this being the portfolio shown in the original spreadsheet) the portfolio betas are shown in the first column of Table II.2.12.

Table II.2.12 Portfolio betas for the principal component factors, and systematic, total and specific risk

	Arbitrary portfolio	Equal weighted	DJIA
Beta1	0.2140	0.1731	0.1731
Beta2	−0.1617	0.0450	0.0450
Beta3	−0.0965	−0.0086	−0.0086
Beta4	−0.0805	−0.0011	−0.0011
Beta5	0.1972	−0.0144	−0.0144
Systematic risk	15.01%	10.11%	10.05%
Total risk	16.62%	10.11%	10.11%
Specific risk	7.14%	0.00%	1.02%

For this portfolio, the total risk is 16.62%, the systematic risk is 15.01% and the specific risk is 7.14%. We may also express the portfolio betas and portfolio risk in dollar terms, simply by multiplying the betas and the volatility by the total value of the portfolio (or the variance by the square of the dollar value).

(ii) A portfolio with equal dollar amounts invested in each stock has weights

$$\mathbf{w} = \left(\frac{1}{30}, \frac{1}{30}, \ldots, \frac{1}{30}\right)' = \frac{1}{30}(1, 1, \ldots, 1)' = \frac{1}{30} \times \mathbf{1}.$$

Hence the total portfolio variance is $\mathbf{w}'\mathbf{Vw} = (1/30)^2 \times \mathbf{1}'\mathbf{V1}$, where $\mathbf{1}'\mathbf{V1}$ is the sum of all the elements on the stock returns covariance matrix. By the same token, the portfolio betas are just the average of the stock betas. In our example, because we have used all the significant eigenvectors in the factor models, the systematic risk of this portfolio is equal to the total risk and the specific risk is zero. In other words, the equally weighted portfolio is the market portfolio corresponding to a PCA factor model based on stock's returns.

(iii) The DJIA index is a *price-weighted index*, i.e. it is a portfolio holding an equal number of shares in each stock. The portfolio weight on stock i at time t in the DJIA portfolio is

$$w_{it} = \frac{p_{it}}{\sum_{j=1}^{30} p_{jt}},$$

where p_{jt} is the price of stock j at time t. We set the portfolio weights equal to their value on 26 April 2006. That is, we use a *constant* weighted portfolio to measure the risk on the DJIA on 26 April 2006 and to forecast its risk over a short term risk

[30] However, we do not allow fully funded portfolios, i.e. where the sum of the dollar long positions equals the sum of the dollar short positions because in that case the portfolio weights are not defined.

horizon. Of course, the DJIA is not a constant weighted index, it is a price-weighted index, i.e. it has zero rebalancing and the same (constant) holding in each stock. But to measure its risk on 26 April 2006 we need to hold the current weights constant and construct an artificial returns series based on these weights. The results are shown in the last column of Table II.2.4. Note that if we were to regress the actual DJIA returns on the five principal components, the result would differ from those in the table, because the actual DJIA and the reconstructed constant weighted DJIA are different.

II.2.6 SUMMARY AND CONCLUSIONS

This chapter has provided a concise introduction to principal component analysis (PCA) which is based on the *eigenvectors* and *eigenvalues* of a covariance or correlation matrix. We have shown that principal component analysis is a statistical tool with numerous applications to market risk analysis, including portfolio optimization, hedging and asset–liability management as well as to risk assessment, stress testing and risk decomposition.

A principal component factor model represents each of the series of returns (or changes in interest rates) as a linear function of the principal components. It is a linear factor model: the risk factors are the principal components; the factor sensitivities are the elements of the eigenvectors of the original covariance matrix; and the idiosyncratic or specific return is the return defined by the higher principal components that are excluded from the model. The most successful factor models are applied to a highly correlated system of variables. In this case the first component can often explain over 90% of the total variation in the system and a factor model with only the first three or four components as risk factors commonly explains almost 99% of the variation in the system. This ability to reduce the dimension of the risk factor space makes PCA a computationally convenient tool.

There are two types of principal component factor models. For *portfolio optimization* and risk measurement we apply PCA to the returns covariance matrix of all the assets in the investor's universe. Then we use the principal components as the risk factors in a regression factor model. This type of statistical factor model has the same applications as the fundamental factor models that were described in the previous chapter. However, principal component factor models are much easier to estimate than fundamental factor models because there is no possibility for multicollinearity between the explanatory variables. By contrast, principal components are uncorrelated by construction. Statistical factor models are becoming increasingly popular as useful tools for asset managers, and our case study of a factor model for DJIA stocks provides a useful introduction to the area.

The second type of principal component factor model is a *curve factor model*, i.e. when PCA is applied to *term structures* of interest rates, volatilities or forwards or futures of different maturities. In this case the natural ordering of the system imbues the components with meaningful interpretations. The first component, which is constructed so that it explains the largest fraction of the variation, corresponds to a common *trend* in any highly correlated system even if there is no ordering of the variables. That is, when the first component changes all variables shift almost parallel, provided the system is highly correlated. But it is only in an ordered system that the second and higher components also have interpretations – usually as a *tilt* in the term structure and a change in *convexity*. The movement captured by the first component may not correspond to an exact parallel shift and the movement captured by the second component may not correspond to an exact linear tilt. However, these components capture the movements that have been *most commonly observed* in the data. It is often the case that a term structure shifts less (or more) at the short end than at the long end, and if so the first component will capture exactly this type of movement. It therefore makes sense to hedge portfolios against movements in the principal components, rather than a strictly parallel shift or exactly linear tilt.

PCA can also be applied to multiple curves, such as yield curves of different credit ratings or in different currencies. We have here provided simple examples of each application, and in Section III.2.6.3 we present a case study that applies a multi-curve principal component factor model to the futures term structures on three related commodities. In multi-curve factor models the interpretation of the first few components is usually a combination of shifts in some curves and tilts in others, possibly in different directions.

Other empirical examples in this chapter have included: the application of principal component factor models to measure the risk of cash flows in a foreign currency, where the factor model facilitates the decomposition of total risk into foreign exchange, interest rate and correlation components; the immunization of bond portfolios against commonly occurring movements in market interest rates; and the matching of assets with liabilities in such a way that the net position has little or no interest rate risk on a mark-to-market basis.

There are alternative approaches to factor analysis that we do not cover in this chapter. For instance, *common factor analysis* explains only the *common* variation in a system rather than the total variation. It is useful for describing the linear dependencies between variables in a large system but it is not as useful as PCA for financial applications, for two main reasons. Firstly, it is well established that codependencies between financial assets are highly non-linear and are therefore better described by a copula than by analysing common correlation. Secondly, common factors are not observable and so they cannot be extracted from the analysis for use in risk management or other applications. One of the reasons why principal components are so successful is that they are observable, uncorrelated variables that are a simple linear combination of the original variables.

Classical Models of Volatility and Correlation

II.3.1 INTRODUCTION

This chapter introduces the time series models of volatility and correlation that became popular in the industry more than a decade before this book was published. The point of the chapter is to make readers aware of the pitfalls they may encounter when using simple statistical techniques for estimating and forecasting portfolio risk.

We begin with the models of volatility and correlation, made popular by JP Morgan in the 1990s and still employed to construct the *RiskMetrics*™ data. The 1990s were a time when the profession of financial risk management was still in its infancy. Up to this point very few banks, fund managers, corporates or consultants used any sort of time series data to quantify and track the risks they faced. A breakthrough was made in the mid 1990s when JP Morgan released its RiskMetrics data. These are *moving average* estimates of volatility and correlation for major risk factors such as equity indices, exchange rates and interest rates, updated daily, and they used to be freely available to download. The first two versions of RiskMetrics applied incorrect time series analysis and had to be amended, but by the end of the decade a correct if rather simple time series methodology for constructing covariance matrices was made generally available to the industry.

Volatilities and correlations of financial asset returns and changes in interest rates may be summarized in their covariance matrix. There are numerous financial applications for covariance matrices, including but not limited to:

- estimating and forecasting the volatility of a linear portfolio;
- estimating the value at risk of linear portfolios;
- determining optimal portfolio allocations between a set of risky assets;
- simulating correlated returns on a set of assets or interest rates;
- estimating the value at risk of non-linear portfolios;
- pricing multi-asset options;
- hedging the risk of portfolios.

This chapter and the next chapter of this volume describe the ways in which time series models may be applied to estimate and forecast covariance matrices. It is very important to obtain a covariance matrix that is as accurate as possible. But as we progress we shall encounter many sources of *model risk* in the construction of a covariance matrix. Hence, finding a good estimate or forecast of a covariance matrix is not an easy task.

The outline of the chapter is as follows. Sections II.3.2 and II.3.3 introduce the concepts of volatility and correlation and explain how they relate to time series of returns on financial assets or to changes in interest rates. We state their relationship with the covariance matrix and prove the *square root of time* scaling rule that is used for *independent and identically distributed* (i.i.d.) returns. We also discuss the properties of volatility when returns are not i.i.d., deriving a scaling rule that applies when returns are autocorrelated, and the properties of correlation if two returns are not generated by a bivariate normal i.i.d. process.

Sections II.3.4–II.3.6 discuss the properties of the equally weighted average or *historical* method for estimating the unconditional volatility and correlation of time series. We explain the difference between conditional and unconditional volatility and correlation and prove a number of properties for the equally weighted estimators of the unconditional parameters, specifically those concerning the precision of the estimators.

Sections II.3.7 and II.3.8 introduce *moving average models* that are based on the assumption that asset (or risk factor) returns have a multivariate normal distribution and that the returns are generated by an i.i.d. process. This part of the chapter aims to equip the reader with an appreciation of the advantages and limitations of *equally weighted moving average* and *exponentially weighted moving average* models for estimating (and forecasting) covariance matrices. We remark that:

- The 'true' variance and covariance depend on the model. As a result there is a considerable degree of *model risk* inherent in the construction of a covariance or correlation matrix. That is, very different results can be obtained using two different statistical models even when they are based on exactly the same data.
- The estimates of the true covariance matrix are subject to sampling error. Even when two analysts use the same model to estimate a covariance matrix their estimates will differ if they use different data to estimate the matrix. Both changing the sample period and changing the frequency of the observations will affect the covariance matrix estimate.

Section II.3.9 summarizes and concludes.

II.3.2   VARIANCE AND VOLATILITY

This section provides an in-depth understanding of the nature of volatility and of the assumptions that we make when we apply volatility to measure the risk of the returns on an investment. *Volatility* is the annualized standard deviation of the returns on an investment. We focus on the pitfalls that arise when scaling standard deviation into an annualized form. For instance, volatility is much greater when there is positive serial correlation between returns than it is when the returns are i.i.d.

II.3.2.1   Volatility and the Square-Root-of-Time Rule

The precise definition of the *volatility* of an asset is an annualized measure of dispersion in the stochastic process that is used to model the log returns.[1] The most common measure of dispersion about the mean of the distribution is the standard deviation σ. It is a sufficient risk metric for dispersion when returns are normally distributed.[2] The standard deviation of 10-day log returns is not directly comparable with the standard deviation of daily log returns.

---

[1] This definition is consistent with the definition of volatility in continuous time finance, where volatility is the diffusion coefficient in a scale invariant asset price process. The process must be scale invariant if the asset is tradable (see Section III.4.6) so the volatility is based on the log returns. If the process is not scale invariant (for instance we might use an arithmetic Brownian motion for interest rates) then volatility would be based on the changes in interest rates (and therefore quoted in basis points per annum).
[2] Then the distribution is completely determined knowing only the mean and standard deviation. The higher odd order moments such as skewness are zero and the even order moments depend only on σ.

The dispersion will increase as the holding period of returns increases. For this reason we usually transform the standard deviation into annualized terms, and quote the result as a percentage.

Assume that one-period log returns are generated by a stationary i.i.d. process with mean μ and standard deviation σ.[3] Denote by r_{ht} the log return over the next h periods observed at time t, i.e.

$$r_{ht} = \Delta_h \ln(P_t) = \ln(P_{t+h}) - \ln(P_t). \tag{II.3.1}$$

We know from Section I.1.4.6 that the h-period log return is the sum of h consecutive one-period log returns:

$$r_{ht} = \sum_{i=0}^{h-1} r_{t+i}. \tag{II.3.2}$$

Taking means and variances of (II.3.2) and noting that when random variables are independent their covariance is 0, we have

$$E(r_{ht}) = h\mu \quad \text{and} \quad V(r_{ht}) = h\sigma^2. \tag{II.3.3}$$

Hence, the standard deviation of the h-period log return is $\sqrt{h}$ times the standard deviation of the one-period log return. For obvious reasons this is referred to as the *square root of time rule*.

The annualized standard deviation is called the *annual volatility,* or simply the *volatility.* It is often assumed that successive returns are independent of each other so that, as shown above, the variance of h-day log returns will increase with h. In this case we can convert risk and return into annualized terms on multiplying them by a constant which is called the *annualizing factor*, A. For instance, $A = 12$ if returns are i.i.d. and are measured at the monthly frequency.[4] Knowing the annualizing factor, we can convert the mean, variance and standard deviation of i.i.d. returns to annualized terms using:

$$\text{annualized mean} = A\mu,$$
$$\text{annualized variance} = A\sigma^2,$$
$$\text{annualized standard deviation} = \sqrt{A}\sigma.$$

However, the above conversion of variance and standard deviation only applies when returns are i.i.d.

EXAMPLE II.3.1: CALCULATING VOLATILITY FROM STANDARD DEVIATION

Assume returns are generated by an i.i.d. process.

   (a) The variance of daily returns is 0.001. Assuming 250 risk days per year, what is the volatility?

   (b) The volatility is 36%. What is the standard deviation of weekly returns?

SOLUTION

   (a) Volatility $= \sqrt{0.001 \times 250} = \sqrt{0.25} = 0.5 = 50\%$.

   (b) Standard deviation $= \dfrac{0.36}{\sqrt{52}} = 0.05$.

---

[3] See Section I.3.7 for an explanation of this assumption.
[4] In this text we assume the number of trading days (or *risk days*) per year is 250, so if returns are measured daily then $A = 250$. Some other authors assume $A = 252$ for daily returns.

II.3.2.2   Constant Volatility Assumption

The assumption that one-period returns are i.i.d. implies that volatility is constant. This follows on noting that if the annualizing factor for one-period log returns is A then the annualizing factor for h-period log returns is A/h. Let the standard deviation of one-period log returns be σ. Then the volatility of one-period log returns is $\sigma\sqrt{A}$ and, since the i.i.d. assumption implies that the standard deviation of h-period log returns is $\sigma\sqrt{h}$, the volatility of h-period log returns is $\sigma\sqrt{h} \times \sqrt{A/h} = \sigma\sqrt{A}$.

In other words, the i.i.d. returns assumption not only implies the square-root-of-time rule, but also implies that volatility is constant. A constant volatility process is a fundamental assumption for Black–Scholes–Merton type option pricing models, since these are based on geometric Brownian motion price dynamics. In discrete time the constant volatility assumption is a feature of the moving average statistical volatility and correlation models discussed later in this chapter.

But it is not realistic to assume that returns are generated by an i.i.d. process. Many models do not make this assumption, including stochastic volatility option pricing models and GARCH statistical models of volatility. Nevertheless the annualization of standard deviation described above has become the market convention for *quoting* volatility. It is applied to every estimate or forecast of standard deviation, whether or not it is based on an i.i.d. assumption for returns.

II.3.2.3   Volatility when Returns are Autocorrelated

Suppose we drop the assumption that one-period returns are i.i.d. and instead assume they have some positive (or negative) autocorrelation. In particular, we assume they have the stationary AR(1) autoregressive representation introduced in Section I.3.7, i.e.

$$r_t = \alpha + \varrho r_{t-1} + \varepsilon_t, \quad \varepsilon_t \sim \text{i.i.d.} \left(0, \sigma^2\right), \ |\varrho| < 1,$$

where r_t is the daily log return at time t and ϱ is the *autocorrelation*, i.e. the correlation between adjacent returns.[5] In the AR(1) model the correlation between returns two periods apart is ϱ^2 and, more generally, the correlation between returns h periods apart is ϱ^h. Put another way, the hth order autocorrelation coefficient is ϱ^h for $h = 1, 2, \ldots$.

Recall from (II.3.2) that we may write the h-period log return as the sum of h consecutive one-period log returns:

$$r_{ht} = \sum_{i=0}^{h-1} r_{t+i}.$$

Autocorrelation does not affect the *expected* h-period return, but it does affect its standard deviation. Under the AR(1) model the variance of the h-period log return is

$$V(r_{ht}) = \sum_{i=0}^{h-1} V(r_{t+i}) + 2\sum_{i<j} \text{Cov}(r_{t+i}, r_{t+j}) = \sigma^2\left(h + 2\sum_{i=1}^{h-1} (h-i)\varrho^i\right).$$

Now we use the identity

$$\sum_{i=1}^{n} (n-i+1)x^i = \frac{x}{(1-x)^2} \left[n(1-x) - x(1-x^n)\right], \quad |x| < 1. \tag{II.3.4}$$

---

[5] An alternative term for autocorrelation is *serial correlation*.

Setting $x = \varrho$ and $n = h - 1$ in (II.3.4) gives

$$V(r_{ht}) = \sigma^2 \left(h + 2 \frac{\varrho}{(1-\varrho)^2} \left[(h-1)(1-\varrho) - \varrho \left(1 - \varrho^{h-1}\right) \right] \right). \qquad \text{(II.3.5)}$$

Thus we have proved that when returns are autocorrelated with first order autocorrelation coefficient ϱ then the scaling factor for standard deviation, to turn it into a volatility, is not $\sqrt{h}$, but rather

$$\text{AR(1) Scale Factor} = \left(h + 2 \frac{\varrho}{(1-\varrho)^2} \left[(h-1)(1-\varrho) - \varrho \left(1 - \varrho^{h-1}\right) \right] \right)^{1/2}. \qquad \text{(II.3.6)}$$

So if we drop the i.i.d. assumption then (II.3.3) holds only for scaling the mean. The square-root-of-time scaling rule for standard deviation *no longer holds*. Instead we may use (II.3.5) to scale the variance, or (II.3.6) to scale the standard deviation, given an estimate for the autocorrelation of returns. Note that the second term in (II.3.6) is positive if and only if ϱ is positive. In other words, positive serial correlation leads to a larger volatility estimate and negative serial correlation leads to a lower volatility estimate, compared with the i.i.d. case. The following example illustrates this fact.

EXAMPLE II.3.2: ESTIMATING VOLATILITY FOR HEDGE FUNDS

Monthly returns on a hedge fund over the last three years have a standard deviation of 5%. Assume the returns are i.i.d. What is your volatility estimate? Now suppose you discover that the returns have been smoothed before reporting them to the investors. In fact, the returns are *autocorrelated* with autocorrelation 0.25. What is your volatility estimate now?

SOLUTION   If we assume the returns are i.i.d., we do the usual annualization. That is, we take the standard deviations of the monthly returns and multiply by the square root of 12; this gives the volatility estimate

$$\hat{\sigma} = 5\% \times \sqrt{12} = 17.32\%.$$

But if we use our information about autocorrelation our volatility estimate is much higher than this. In fact when $h = 12$ and $\varrho = 0.25$ the scaling factor (II.3.6) is $\sqrt{19.11}$ not $\sqrt{12}$ and our volatility estimate is therefore

$$\hat{\sigma} = 5\% \times \sqrt{19.11} = 21.86\%.$$

The i.i.d. assumption is often made when it is not warranted. For instance, hedge funds usually smooth their reported returns, and the above example shows that ignoring this will lead to a serious under estimation of the true volatility.

II.3.2.4   Remarks about Volatility

Volatility is *unobservable*. We can only ever *estimate* and *forecast* volatility, and this only within the context of an assumed statistical model. So there is no absolute 'true' volatility: what is 'true' depends only on the assumed model. Even if we knew for certain that our model was a correct representation of the data generation process we could never measure the true volatility exactly because pure volatility is not traded in the market.[6] Estimating

---

[6] Futures on volatility indices such as *Vix* and *Vstoxx* are traded and provide an observation for forward volatility under the *market implied* measure, but this chapter deals with spot volatility in the *physical* or *real world* measure.

volatility according to the formulae given by a model gives an estimate of volatility that is 'realized' by the process assumed in our model. But this *realized volatility* is still only ever an estimate of whatever volatility had been during the period used for the estimate.

Moreover, volatility is only a sufficient statistic for the dispersion of the returns distribution when we make a normality assumption. In other words, volatility does not provide a full description of the risks that are taken by the investment unless we assume the investment returns are normally distributed. In general, we need to know more about the distribution of returns than its expected return and its volatility. Volatility tells us the scale and the mean tells us the location, but the dispersion also depends on the *shape* of the distribution. The best dispersion metric would be based on the entire distribution function of returns.

II.3.3   COVARIANCE AND CORRELATION

This section provides an in-depth understanding of the nature of correlation and of the assumptions that we make when we apply correlation to measure portfolio risk. We focus on the pitfalls that arise when using correlation to assess the type of risk we face in financial markets today. For instance, Pearson's correlation is only appropriate when two returns have an *elliptical* joint distribution such as the bivariate normal distribution.[7] Otherwise it gives very misleading indications of the real dependency between returns.

The volatilities and correlations of the assets or risk factors are summarized in a covariance matrix. Under the assumption that all risk factor returns are i.i.d. and that their joint distribution is multivariate normal, the covariance matrix scales with the risk horizon. That is, the h-day covariance matrix is h times the 1-day matrix. Thus the variances and covariances scale with time, the standard deviations scale with the square root of time, and the correlations remain the same.

The assumption of multivariate normal i.i.d. returns is made in the classical theories of Markowitz (1959), Sharpe (1964) and others, but it is not empirically justified. Greater accuracy would be achieved by allowing the marginal distributions of returns to be non-normal and possibly different from each other. For instance, the returns on one asset may have a Student t distribution whilst the returns on the other asset may have a gamma distribution. But then correlation loses its meaning as a measure of dependency. Instead, we need a new measure of dependency called a *copula function*. Copulas are introduced and their applications to finance are discussed in Chapter II.6.

II.3.3.1   Definition of Covariance and Correlation

The covariance between two returns is the first central moment of their joint density function. It is a measure of the *dependency* between the two returns, and it is formally defined in Section I.3.4.3. Since covariance depends on the magnitude of returns it can be any real number: positive, negative or zero. So, just as we standardize the standard deviation into volatility, we also standardize covariance. But now, instead of being related to the scaling of standard deviations over time, the standardization is performed so that the measure of dependency is no longer related to the size of the returns. This measure is called the correlation.

---

[7] Elliptical distributions have contours that are ellipses; see Section I.3.4.6.

Correlation is formally defined in Section I.3.4.4, and its basic properties are also analysed there. Correlation is equal to the covariance of the two returns divided by the product of their standard deviations. It always lies between -1 and $+1$. Perfect negative correlation is a correlation of -1. This implies that when one return increases the other return will always decrease and when one return decreases the other return will always increase. Perfect positive correlation is a correlation of $+1$. This indicates that the returns always move in the same direction. More generally, a positive correlation implies there is a tendency for the returns to move in the same direction and a negative correlation indicates that the returns tend to move in the opposite direction. When the two returns are *independent* and have a *bivariate normal distribution* their covariance is 0 and so also is their correlation. But if returns do *not* have a bivariate normal distribution zero correlation does not necessarily imply independence. The next section describes this, and other pitfalls arising from the use of correlation as a dependency metric.

II.3.3.2   Correlation Pitfalls

The standard correlation metric defined above is more precisely called *Pearson's product moment correlation coefficient*. It has long been known that this dependency metric suffers from the limitation of being only a *linear* measure of association that is not flexible enough to capture non-linear dependencies. For example, if X is a standard normal variable then $Corr(X, X^2) = 0$ even though X and X^2 have perfectly *quadratic* dependence.

Recently a famous paper by Embrechts et al. (2002), which opens with the phrase 'Correlation is a minefield for the unwary', has identified and illustrated several other major problems associated with Pearson's product moment correlation coefficient, including:

- *Correlation is not invariant under transformation of variables.* It is not even invariant under monotonic transforms, such as the natural logarithm. That is, the correlation of X_1 and X_2 is not equal to the correlation of $\ln(X_1)$ and $\ln(X_2)$.
- *Feasible values for correlation depend on the marginal distributions.* For instance, if X_1 and X_2 are lognormal rather than normal variables then certain correlations are *impossible*. For instance, if $\ln(X_1)$ is standard normal and $\ln(X_2)$ has a $N(0, 4)$ distribution then a correlation of more than two-thirds or less than -0.09 is impossible!
- *Perfect positive dependence does not imply a correlation of one.* And neither does perfect negative dependence imply a correlation of -1.[8] With the lognormal variables above, perfect positive dependence implies a correlation of two-thirds and perfect negative dependence implies a correlation of only -0.09, which is very far from -1!
- *Zero correlation does not imply independence.* If $\ln(X)$ is $N(0, \sigma^2)$ then the minimum attainable correlation converges to *zero* as σ increases, even though the minimum attainable correlation is when the variables are perfectly negatively dependent. Also if X_1 and X_2 have a bivariate Student t distribution with infinite kurtosis then a correlation of 0 between X_1 and X_2 would not imply the risks were independent. Also returns may be related through their higher moments, for instance the volatilities could be related even if expected returns are not, but correlation only captures the first moment of their joint density.

---

[8] Variables with perfect positive dependence are called *comonotonic* and variables with perfect negative dependence are called *countermonotonic*. See Section II.6.3.5 for a more precise definition.

Embrechts et al. (2002) warn that unreliable risk management systems are being built using correlation to model dependencies between highly non-normal risks such as credit and operational risks, where distributions are clearly far from normal and correlation may not even be defined,[9] so correlations are very misleading. The only case where Pearson's correlation can be justified as a measure for the dependence between two returns is when the random variables have a multivariate normal or a multivariate t distribution. We shall therefore make this assumption from now on, unless stated otherwise.

II.3.3.3   Covariance Matrices

The covariance matrix of the returns on a set of assets or risk factors is the cornerstone of classical risk and return analysis. It is used to estimate the volatility of a portfolio, to simulate values for its risk factors, to diversify investments and to obtain efficient portfolios that have the optimal trade-off between risk and return. Both risk managers and portfolio managers require covariance matrices that may include very many assets or risk factors. For instance, in a global risk management system of a large international bank all the major yield curves, equity indices, foreign exchange rates and commodity prices will be encompassed in one very large-dimensional covariance matrix.

A covariance matrix $\mathbf{V}$ is an $n \times n$ matrix with the variances of the returns along the diagonal and the covariances of the returns on the off-diagonal. It is shown in Section I.2.4.1 that the covariance matrix may be written in the form $\mathbf{V} = \mathbf{DCD}$, where $\mathbf{D}$ is the $n \times n$ diagonal matrix with standard deviations along its diagonal and $\mathbf{C}$ is the $n \times n$ correlation matrix. Furthermore, it is shown in Section I.2.4.2 that the variance of a portfolio with weights vector $\mathbf{w}$ is given by $\mathbf{w}'\mathbf{Vw}$. Hence, the covariance matrix provides a convenient way to display the information about the volatilities and correlations of a set of returns and it is easy to manipulate formulae using this matrix.

EXAMPLE II.3.3: PORTFOLIO VARIANCE

A portfolio has \$1 million invested in asset 1, \$2 million invested in asset 2 and \$3 million invested in asset 3. The volatilities and correlations of the asset returns are given in Table II.3.1. Find the portfolio volatility.

Table II.3.1   Volatilities and correlations of three assets

Asset 1 volatility	20%	Asset 1 – asset 2 correlation	0.8
Asset 2 volatility	10%	Asset 1 – asset 3 correlation	0.5
Asset 3 volatility	15%	Asset 3 – asset 2 correlation	0.3

SOLUTION   The portfolio weights are

$$\mathbf{w} = \left(\frac{1}{6}, \frac{2}{6}, \frac{3}{6}\right)'$$

---

[9] It is not defined if the variance is infinite.

so the portfolio returns have annual variance

$$V(R) = \mathbf{w}'\mathbf{V}\mathbf{w} = \begin{pmatrix} \dfrac{1}{6}, \dfrac{2}{6}, \dfrac{3}{6} \end{pmatrix} \begin{pmatrix} 0.04 & 0.016 & 0.015 \\ 0.016 & 0.01 & 0.0045 \\ 0.015 & 0.0045 & 0.0225 \end{pmatrix} \begin{pmatrix} 1/6 \\ 2/6 \\ 3/6 \end{pmatrix} = 0.013625.$$

Taking the square root of the annual variance gives the portfolio volatility, 11.67%.

The above example shows that the covariance matrix is all that we need to measure the volatility of the returns on a linear portfolio, assuming we know the amount invested in each asset. In fact, we only need to know the portfolio weights. Of course covariance matrices have many other applications, as we have made clear in the introduction to this chapter.

II.3.3.4 Scaling Covariance Matrices

An h-day covariance matrix is the matrix of variances and covariances of h-day returns. In many applications we need to measure uncertainty over a relatively short risk horizon, for instance 1 day or 10 days. An 1-day covariance matrix $\mathbf{V}_1$ is usually estimated from the variances and covariances of daily log returns. Suppose that daily log returns are i.i.d. and that their joint distribution is multivariate normal. Then the variance and covariance scale with time.[10] So, to perform an analysis over a risk horizon of h days we can use the square-root-of-time rule to estimate the h-day covariance matrix as $h\mathbf{V}_1$, i.e. the matrix where every element of $\mathbf{V}_1$ is multiplied by h.

For instance, suppose we use some data to estimate the standard deviations of daily returns on two assets. These estimates are 0.01 and 0.015, and suppose we measure their correlation to be -0.5. Using the square-root-of-time rule, the 1-day, 10-day and 100-day covariance matrices will be

$$\begin{pmatrix} 1 & -0.75 \\ -0.75 & 2.25 \end{pmatrix} \times 10^{-4}, \quad \begin{pmatrix} 1 & -0.75 \\ -0.75 & 2.25 \end{pmatrix} \times 10^{-3} \text{ and } \begin{pmatrix} 1 & -0.75 \\ -0.75 & 2.25 \end{pmatrix} \times 10^{-2},$$

respectively. Conversely, given an annual covariance matrix, we can obtain the 10-day covariance matrix by dividing each element by 25, assuming there are 250 trading days per year. So volatilities are divided by 5 to obtain 10-day standard deviations, but correlations remain constant. A numerical example is given below.

The next two examples are similar to some that have been given in Volume I, but we include them in this chapter to illustrate the relationships above.

EXAMPLE II.3.4: SCALING AND DECOMPOSITION OF COVARIANCE MATRIX

The volatilities and correlation between returns on three assets are shown in Table II.3.1. As usual, the volatilities are quoted as annualized percentages. Calculate the annual covariance matrix. Then assuming the returns are multivariate normal i.i.d. and assuming 250 trading days per year, derive from this the 10-day covariance matrix, i.e. the matrix of covariances of 10-day returns.

---

[10] When returns are i.i.d. the correlation does not scale with time, the volatility scales with the square root of time, the variance and covariance scale with time so the covariance matrix scales with time.

SOLUTION For the annual covariance matrix we use the decomposition introduced in Section I.2.4.1, i.e.:

$$\mathbf{V} = \mathbf{DCD} = \begin{pmatrix} 0.2 & 0 & 0 \\ 0 & 0.1 & 0 \\ 0 & 0 & 0.15 \end{pmatrix} \begin{pmatrix} 1 & 0.8 & 0.5 \\ 0.8 & 1 & 0.3 \\ 0.5 & 0.3 & 1 \end{pmatrix} \begin{pmatrix} 0.2 & 0 & 0 \\ 0 & 0.1 & 0 \\ 0 & 0 & 0.15 \end{pmatrix} = \begin{pmatrix} 0.04 & 0.016 & 0.015 \\ 0.016 & 0.01 & 0.0045 \\ 0.015 & 0.0045 & 0.0225 \end{pmatrix}.$$

Since there are 25 ten-day periods in 250 days, we obtain the 10-day covariance matrix by dividing each element of $\mathbf{V}$ by 25. The result is

$$\begin{pmatrix} 0.0016 & 0.00064 & 0.0006 \\ 0.00064 & 0.0004 & 0.00018 \\ 0.0006 & 0.00018 & 0.0009 \end{pmatrix} = \begin{pmatrix} 16 & 6.4 & 6 \\ 6.4 & 4 & 1.8 \\ 6 & 1.8 & 9 \end{pmatrix} \times 10^{-4}.$$

Thus the diagonal matrix of 10-day standard deviations is

$$\mathbf{D}_{10} = \begin{pmatrix} 0.04 & 0 & 0 \\ 0 & 0.02 & 0 \\ 0 & 0 & 0.03 \end{pmatrix}.$$

But correlation $\mathbf{C}$ remains unchanged and the 10-day covariance matrix is

$$\begin{pmatrix} 0.04 & 0 & 0 \\ 0 & 0.02 & 0 \\ 0 & 0 & 0.03 \end{pmatrix} \begin{pmatrix} 1 & 0.8 & 0.5 \\ 0.8 & 1 & 0.3 \\ 0.5 & 0.3 & 1 \end{pmatrix} \begin{pmatrix} 0.04 & 0 & 0 \\ 0 & 0.02 & 0 \\ 0 & 0 & 0.03 \end{pmatrix} = \begin{pmatrix} 16 & 6.4 & 6 \\ 6.4 & 4 & 1.8 \\ 6 & 1.8 & 9 \end{pmatrix} \times 10^{-4}.$$

This example shows that we can derive the covariance matrix for any period from knowledge of the volatilities and correlations of return. And conversely, given the covariance matrix for any period, we can derive the volatilities and correlations. But to use the square-root-of-time rule in this way we must assume that returns are driven by i.i.d. processes, and elliptical joint distributions are required to calculate and apply a covariance or correlation matrix to begin with. Unfortunately, this is not a very realistic assumption for most financial asset returns. If we wish to go beyond the standard assumption that returns are jointly normal i.i.d. and if we do not assume their joint distribution is elliptical then covariance and correlation matrices are not appropriate metrics for portfolio risk. Instead, the dependency between returns may be captured by a copula, as explained in Chapter II.6.

II.3.4 EQUALLY WEIGHTED AVERAGES

This section describes how volatility and correlation are estimated and forecast by applying equal weights to certain historical time series data. We outline a number of pitfalls and limitations of this approach and as a result recommend that these models only be used as an indication of the possible *range* for long term volatility and correlation. As we shall see, the estimates from an equally weighted average model are of dubious validity for short term volatility and correlation forecasting.

For simplicity we assume that the mean return is zero and that returns are measured at the daily frequency, unless specifically stated otherwise. A zero mean return is a standard assumption for risk assessments based on time series of daily data, but if returns are measured over longer intervals this assumption may not be very realistic. Under the zero mean assumption the equally weighted estimate of the variance of returns is the average of the squared returns and the corresponding volatility estimate is the square root of this expressed as an annual percentage. The equally weighted estimate of the covariance of two returns is the average of the cross products of returns, and the equally weighted estimate of their correlation is the ratio of the covariance to the square root of the product of the two variances.

Equal weighting of historical data was the first statistical method for forecasting volatility and correlation of financial asset returns to be widely accepted. For many years it was the market standard to forecast average volatility over the next h days by taking an equally weighted average of squared returns over the previous h days. As a result this method was called the *historical volatility* forecast. Nowadays many different statistical forecasting techniques can be applied to historical time series data so it is confusing to call this equally weighted method *the* historical method. However, this rather confusing terminology remains standard.

Perceived changes in volatility and correlation have important consequences for all types of risk management decisions, whether to do with capitalization, resource allocation or hedging strategies. Indeed, it is these parameters of the returns distributions that are the fundamental building blocks of market risk assessment models. It is therefore essential to understand what type of variability in returns the model has measured. The 'historical' model assumes that returns are driven by i.i.d. processes with elliptical joint distributions, so that the square-root-of-time rule applies, as described in the preceding section. The square-root-of-time rule states that the standard deviation of an h-period return is the square root of h times the standard deviation of the one-period return. This in turn implies that both volatility and correlation are constant. So the normal i.i.d. assumption has important ramifications and we shall take care to explain these very carefully in the following.

We first explain the methodology and then derive confidence intervals for the equally weighted average variance and for the corresponding volatility. Then the associated standard errors are shown to decrease as the sample size used to estimate the variance and the volatility increases. After this we put the equally weighted methodology into a time series framework where the *estimation sample*, also called the *data window*, which is the sample that is used to estimate the variance or covariance, is rolled over time. The properties of these so-called *equally weighted moving average* estimates are then investigated and their usefulness for forecasting volatility is critically examined.

II.3.4.1 Unconditional Variance and Volatility

The methodology for constructing a covariance matrix based on equally weighted averages can be described in very simple terms. Denote the time series of *i.i.d.* returns by

$$\{r_{it}\}, \quad i = 1, \ldots, m; \ t = 1, \ldots, T.$$

Here the subscript i denotes the asset or risk factor, and t denotes the time at which each return is measured. We shall assume that each return has zero mean. Then an estimate of the variance of the ith return at time t, based on the T most recent daily returns, is

$$\hat{\sigma}_{it}^2 = T^{-1} \sum_{k=1}^{T} r_{i,t-k}^2. \tag{II.3.7}$$

Since volatility is the annualized standard deviation the equally weighted estimate of volatility is obtained in two stages. First one obtains an unbiased estimate of the variance using an equally weighted average of squared returns, and then these are converted into a volatility estimate by applying the square-root-of-time rule. For instance, if the returns are measured at the daily frequency and we assume there are 250 trading days per year,

$$\text{Equally weighted volatility estimate} = \hat{\sigma}_{it}\sqrt{250}. \tag{II.3.8}$$

EXAMPLE II.3.5: EQUALLY WEIGHTED AVERAGE ESTIMATE OF FTSE 100 VOLATILITY (I)

Daily closing values on the FTSE 100 index between Friday 10 August and Friday 24 August 2007 are shown in Table II.3.2. Use these data to estimate the volatility of the FTSE 100 index at the close of the market on 24 August 2007.

Table II.3.2   Closing prices on the FTSE 100 index

Date	FTSE
10/08/2007	6038.3
13/08/2007	6219.0
14/08/2007	6143.5
15/08/2007	6109.3
16/08/2007	5858.9
17/08/2007	6064.2
20/08/2007	6078.7
21/08/2007	6086.1
22/08/2007	6196.0
23/08/2007	6196.9
24/08/2007	6220.1

SOLUTION   In the spreadsheet for this example we first calculate the daily log returns, then we square them and then we take their average. Since there are ten returns, we divide the sum of the squared returns by 10 to obtain the average. This gives us a daily variance estimate of 0.000433. Then we take the square root of this and multiply it by the annualizing factor, which we assume to be $\sqrt{250}$ since the returns are daily. The result is a volatility estimate of 32.9%.[11]

In the above example there are three reasons why we use the *log* returns, i.e. the difference in the log of the prices, rather than the *ordinary* returns, i.e. the percentage price change:

1. The standard *geometric Brownian motion* assumption for the price process implies that it is log returns and not ordinary returns that are normally distributed. Hence, using log returns conforms to the standard assumptions made for option pricing.[12]
2. The log returns are easier to work with than ordinary returns. For instance, the h-period log return is just the sum of h consecutive one-period returns. This property leads to the square-root-of-time rule that we use for annualization of a standard deviation into a volatility.
3. There is very little difference between the log returns and the ordinary returns when returns are measured at the daily frequency.

---

[11] Recall that the equity markets were unusually volatile during August 2007. The FTSE index lost all the gains it had made since the beginning of the year in the space of a few weeks.
[12] See Section III.3.2 for further details.

However, when returns are measured at the weekly or monthly frequency it is conventional to use ordinary returns rather than log returns in the volatility estimate.

If the expected return is assumed to be zero then (II.3.7) is an *unbiased estimator* of the variance.[13] That is, $E(\hat{\sigma}^2) = \sigma^2$ and so

$$\sqrt{E(\hat{\sigma}^2)} = \sigma. \tag{II.3.9}$$

It is important to note that $E(\hat{\sigma}) \neq \sigma$, i.e. the square root of (II.3.7) is *not* an unbiased estimator of the standard deviation. Only the variance estimate is unbiased.[14]

If the expected return is not assumed to be zero we need to estimate this from the sample, and this places a (linear) constraint on the variance estimated from sample data. In that case, to obtain an unbiased estimate we should use

$$s_{it}^2 = (T-1)^{-1} \sum_{k=1}^{T} \left(r_{i,t-k} - \bar{r}_i \right)^2, \tag{II.3.10}$$

where $\bar{r}_i$ is the arithmetic mean return on the ith series, taken over the whole sample of T data points. This *mean deviation* form of the estimator may be useful for estimating variance using monthly or even weekly data over a period for which average returns are significantly different from zero. However, with daily data the mean return is usually very small. Moreover, the errors induced by other assumptions are huge relative to the error induced by assuming the mean is zero, as we shall see below. Hence, we normally use the form (II.3.7).

EXAMPLE II.3.6: EQUALLY WEIGHTED AVERAGE ESTIMATE OF FTSE 100 VOLATILITY (II)

Re-estimate the FTSE 100 volatility using the same data as in Example II.3.5 but this time do not assume the expected return is zero.

SOLUTION   In the spreadsheet for this example we first calculate the sample mean of the log returns and then we take the mean deviation returns, square them and sum them, and then divide the result by 9, since there are ten returns in the sample. Then we take the square root and annualize the standard deviation estimate using the annualization factor $\sqrt{250}$ as before. The result is an equally weighted volatility estimate of 34.32%. This is quite different from the volatility of 32.9% that we obtained in the previous example, based on the zero mean return assumption, since the sample is small and there is a considerable sampling error. With a large sample the difference would be much smaller.

Formulae (II.3.7) and (II.3.10) are estimators of the *unconditional variance*. In other words, it is the 'overall' or *long term average variance* that we are estimating. Similarly, the volatility estimate (II.3.8) is an *unconditional volatility* estimate. Thus we have an estimate of the long term volatility even when we use only ten days of data as in the above example. Just because we only use a small sample of recent data, this does not imply that our estimate represents a *conditional variance*.[15]

---

[13] The term *unbiased estimator* means that the expected value of the estimator is equal to the true value.
[14] Since we estimate the variance and then take the square root of this estimate for our estimate of standard deviation, really the caret or hat (^) should be written over the whole of σ^2. But it is generally understood that $\hat{\sigma}^2$ is used to denote the estimate or forecast of a variance, and not the square of an estimate of the standard deviation.
[15] A *conditional variance* represents the *instantaneous variance*, and this can change from day to day because it is sensitive to recent events. See Section II.4.1 for further details.

II.3.4.2 Unconditional Covariance and Correlation

An equally weighted estimate of the covariance of two returns at time t, based on the T most recent daily returns, is

$$\hat{\sigma}_{ijt} = T^{-1} \sum_{k=1}^{T} r_{i,t-k} r_{j,t-k}. \qquad (\text{II.3.11})$$

As mentioned above, we would normally ignore the mean deviation adjustment with daily data and formula (II.3.11) is based on the assumption that both returns have zero expectation, in which case it provides an unbiased estimate of the covariance. But with low frequency data we should make the following adjustments to (II.3.11):

1. Base the calculation on ordinary returns rather than log returns.
2. Take the sum of the cross products of the mean deviations of returns.
3. Use $T - 1$ in place of T in the denominator.

Formula (II.3.11) provides an estimate of the *unconditional covariance* which is a long term average covariance, whereas the *conditional covariance* is the instantaneous value of this parameter.

The equally weighted estimate of correlation is obtained as follows. First one obtains three unbiased estimates: of the two variances and of the covariance. We use equally weighted averages of squared returns and cross products of returns, and the same number of data points each time. Then these are converted into correlation estimates by applying the formula

$$\text{Equally weighted correlation estimate} = \hat{\varrho}_{ijt} = \frac{\hat{\sigma}_{ijt}}{\hat{\sigma}_{it}\hat{\sigma}_{jt}}. \qquad (\text{II.3.12})$$

EXAMPLE II.3.7: EQUALLY WEIGHTED CORRELATION OF THE FTSE 100 AND S&P 500

Use the data in Table II.3.3, which is taken over the same period as the FTSE 100 data, to estimate the correlation between the FTSE 100 and S&P 500 index.

Table II.3.3 Closing prices on the S&P 500 index

Date	S&P 500
10/08/2007	1453.64
13/08/2007	1452.92
14/08/2007	1426.54
15/08/2007	1406.70
16/08/2007	1411.27
17/08/2007	1445.94
20/08/2007	1445.55
21/08/2007	1447.12
22/08/2007	1464.07
23/08/2007	1462.50
24/08/2007	1479.37

SOLUTION In the spreadsheet for this example we estimate the variance of the S&P 500 index returns, using the same method as for the FTSE 100 returns in Example II.3.5.[16]

---

[16] The example is based on high frequency data, so we use formula (II.3.11) assuming the mean return is zero.

Incidentally, the volatility estimate for the S&P 500 is only 18.72%. This is typical of the way these two markets operate. The US sneezes and the UK catches a cold! Anyway, we need the two variance estimates for the example, and these are 0.0004329 for the FTSE index and 0.0001401 for the S&P index. We apply formula (II.3.11) to obtain the covariance estimate, which is 0.0001239, and then we divide this estimate by the square root of the product of the variances. This gives a correlation estimate of 0.5032.

However, it is important to remark here that the data on the FTSE 100 and the S&P 500 used in the above example are not contemporaneous. The UK markets close well before the US markets, and hence correlations based on these data will be biased downward. It is likely that our correlation estimate would be larger if the data used were synchronous. Correlations also tend to be large when based on weekly data since there are fewer idiosyncratic movements, which might be viewed as 'noise' for the purposes of estimating long term correlations, than in the daily data.

II.3.4.3   Forecasting with Equally Weighted Averages

The equally weighted unconditional covariance matrix estimate at time t for a set of n returns is denoted $\hat{\mathbf{V}}_t = (\hat{\sigma}_{ijt})$ for $i, j = 1, \ldots, n$, where each $\hat{\sigma}_{ijt}$ is given by (II.3.11). Note that when $i = j$ the formula is equivalent to the variance formula (II.3.7). For instance, the covariance matrix estimate for the FTSE 100 and S&P 500 returns used in the previous example is

$$\hat{\mathbf{V}} = \begin{pmatrix} 4.329 & 1.239 \\ 1.239 & 1.401 \end{pmatrix} \times 10^{-4}. \tag{II.3.13}$$

In the equally weighted model the *covariance matrix forecast* and hence also the associated forecasts of volatilities and correlations are assumed to be *equal* to their estimates. This is the only possibility in the context of an equally weighted model, which assumes returns are i.i.d. Since the volatility and correlation parameters are constant over time, there is nothing in the model to distinguish an estimate from a forecast.

It is usual to take the horizon for the forecast to be determined by the frequency of the data used to estimate the volatilities and correlations. Daily returns data give a 1-day forecast, weekly returns will give the 1-week forecast, and so forth. For instance, the covariance matrix (II.3.13) represents a daily covariance matrix forecast.

Alternatively, since the model assumes that returns are i.i.d. processes, we can use the square-root-of-time rule to convert a one-period forecast into an h-period covariance matrix forecast, just as we did in Section II.3.2.3. This rule implies that we obtain an h-period covariance matrix forecast from a one-period forecast simply by multiplying each element of the one-period covariance matrix by h. For instance, a monthly forecast can be obtained from the weekly forecast by multiplying each element by 4. Thus a forecast of the covariance matrix over the next five days obtained from (II.3.13) is

$$\hat{\mathbf{V}} = \begin{pmatrix} 21.644 & 6.196 \\ 6.196 & 7.006 \end{pmatrix} \times 10^{-4}. \tag{II.3.14}$$

However, the volatility and correlation forecasts are unchanged. When we change from one period to h periods the variance is multiplied by h but the annualizing factor is divided by h and the two adjustments cancel each other. For instance, we multiply the daily variance estimate by 5 to obtain a weekly estimate, but the annualizing factor for 5-day data is 250/5=50, assuming 250 trading days per year. The reason the correlation forecast is unchanged is that the same scaling factor h appears in both the numerator and the denominator in (II.3.12), so they cancel.

II.3.5 PRECISION OF EQUALLY WEIGHTED ESTIMATES

Having explained how to obtain an equally weighted estimate (which is equal to the forecast) of variance, volatility, covariance and correlation, we now address the accuracy of these forecasts. A standard method of gauging the accuracy of any estimate or forecast is to construct a *confidence interval*, i.e. a range within which we are fairly certain that the 'true' parameter will lie. We may also derive a formula for the *standard error* of the estimator and use our data to find an estimated standard error of the estimate. This is the square root of the estimated variance of the estimator.[17] The standard error gives a measure of precision of the estimate and can be used to test hypotheses about the 'true' parameter value.

In the following we explain how to construct confidence intervals and how to estimate standard errors for equally weighted variance and volatility estimators, but before we progress any further there is a very important point to understand. What do we really mean by the 'true' variance, or the 'true' volatility? Variance and volatility are not like market prices of financial assets, which can be observed in the market. In general variance and volatility are not observable in the market because variance and volatility are not traded assets.[18] Hence, we cannot say that the 'true' variance or volatility is the one that is observed in the market. Variance and volatility (and covariance and correlation) only exist in the context of a model! The 'true' parameter – be it variance, volatility, covariance or correlation – is the parameter that is assumed in the model. It is the Greek letter that denotes a parameter of a probability distribution (or, in the case of covariance and correlation, the parameter in a bivariate distribution) which we shall never know. All we can do is to obtain a sample and estimate the parameter (and put a ˆ over it, to denote that the number quoted is an estimate or a forecast). The 'true' parameter will never be known for sure. This is why we calculate confidence intervals – i.e. intervals which we are reasonably sure contain the true parameter of our assumed model for returns (which is the multivariate normal i.i.d. model in this chapter).

II.3.5.1 Confidence Intervals for Variance and Volatility

A confidence interval for the variance σ^2 of an equally weighted average can be derived using a straightforward application of sampling theory. Assume the variance estimate is based on T normally distributed returns with an assumed mean of 0. Then $T\hat{\sigma}^2/\sigma^2$ will have a chi-squared distribution with T degrees of freedom.[19] Thus a $100(1-\alpha)\%$ two-sided confidence interval for $T\hat{\sigma}^2/\sigma^2$ takes the form $\left(\chi^2_{1-\alpha/2,T}, \chi^2_{\alpha/2,T}\right)$ and the associated confidence interval for the variance σ^2 is

$$\left(\frac{T\hat{\sigma}^2}{\chi^2_{\alpha/2,T}}, \frac{T\hat{\sigma}^2}{\chi^2_{1-\alpha/2,T}}\right). \tag{II.3.15}$$

---

[17] We do not call it a standard deviation, although it is one, because the distribution of the estimator arises from differences in samples. So the random variable is a sampling variable.

[18] In fact this statement is not true. It is possible to trade pure variance and volatility using products called variance swaps and volatility swaps. However, these are mostly traded over the counter and, whilst there are some futures on equity index volatility indices, which are a trade on the equity index variance (because their calculation is based on an approximation to the variance swap rate), in general it is not possible to trade variance or volatility in a liquid market. See Section III.5.5 for further details.

[19] See Section I.3.3.8. Note that the usual degrees-of-freedom correction does not apply since we have assumed throughout that returns have zero mean. If the mean return is not assumed to be zero then replace T by $T-1$.

EXAMPLE II.3.8: CONFIDENCE INTERVAL FOR A VARIANCE ESTIMATE

Assuming the daily log returns on the FTSE 100 are normally distributed, use the sample given in Example II.3.5 to construct a 95% confidence interval for the variance of the returns.

SOLUTION   Since we used $T = 10$ returns, the 95% critical values in (II.3.15) are

$$\chi^2_{0.025,10} = 20.483 \text{ and } \chi^2_{0.975,10} = 3.247.$$

Substituting these into (II.3.15) with the variance estimate $\hat{\sigma}^2 = 0.000433$ gives the 95% confidence interval $[0.000211, 0.001333]$.

Figure II.3.1 illustrates the upper and lower bounds for a confidence interval for a variance forecast when the equally weighted variance estimate is 1. We see that as the sample size T increases, the width of the confidence interval decreases, markedly so as T increases from low values. Hence, equally weighted averages become more accurate when they are based on larger samples.

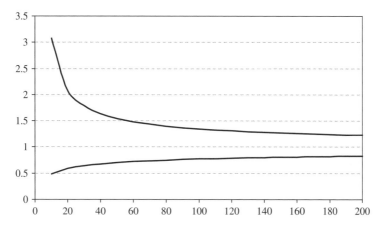

Figure II.3.1   Confidence interval for variance forecasts

We now discuss the confidence intervals that apply to an estimate of *volatility* rather than variance. Recall that volatility, being the square root of the variance, is simply a monotonic increasing transformation of the variance. In Section I.3.2.8 we showed that percentiles are invariant under any strictly monotonic increasing transformation. That is, if f is any monotonic increasing function of a random variable X,[20] then

$$P(c_l < X < c_u) = P(f(c_l) < f(X) < f(c_u)). \tag{II.3.16}$$

Property (II.3.16) allows us to calculate a confidence interval for a historical volatility from the confidence interval for variance (II.3.15). Since $\sqrt{x}$ is a monotonic increasing function of x, one simply annualizes the lower and upper bounds of the variance confidence interval and

---

[20] For instance, f could denote the logarithmic or the exponential function.

takes the square root. This gives the volatility confidence interval.[21] Thus, for instance, the 95% confidence interval for the FTSE 100 volatility based on the result in Example II.3.7 is

$$\left[\sqrt{250 \times 0.000211}, \sqrt{250 \times 0.001333}\right] = [23.0\%, 57.7\%].$$

So we are 95% sure that the true FTSE 100 volatility lies between 23% and 57.7%. This interval is very wide because it is based on a sample with only ten observations. As the sample size increases we obtain narrower confidence intervals.

EXAMPLE II.3.9: CONFIDENCE INTERVALS FOR A VOLATILITY FORECAST

An equally weighted volatility estimate based on 30 observations is 20%. Find a two-sided 95% confidence interval for this estimate.

SOLUTION   The corresponding variance estimate is 0.04 and $T = 30$. The upper and lower chi-squared critical values are

$$\chi^2_{0.025, 30} = 16.791 \text{ and } \chi^2_{0.975, 30} = 46.979.$$

Putting these values into (II.3.15) gives a 95% confidence interval for an equally weighted variance forecast based on 30 observations of [0.02554, 0.07147], and taking the square root gives the confidence interval for the volatility as [16.0%, 26.7%].

II.3.5.2   Standard Error of Variance Estimator

An estimator of any parameter has a distribution. A *point estimate* of volatility is just the expectation of the distribution of the volatility estimator. To measure the accuracy of this point estimate we use an estimate of the *standard error of the estimator*, which is the standard deviation of its distribution. The standard error is measured in the same units as the forecast and its magnitude should be measured relative to the size of the forecast. It indicates how reliable a forecast is considered to be.

Standard errors for equally weighted average variance estimates are based on the assumption that the underlying returns are normally and independently distributed with mean 0 and variance σ^2. Recall that the same assumption was necessary to derive the confidence intervals in the previous section. Note that if X_i are independent random variables for $i = 1, \ldots, T$ then $f(X_i)$ are also independent for any monotonic differentiable function f. Hence, if returns are independent so are the squared returns. It follows that when we apply the variance operator to (II.3.7) we obtain

$$V(\hat{\sigma}_t^2) = T^{-2} \sum_{k=1}^{T} V(r_{t-k}^2). \tag{II.3.17}$$

Since $V(X) = E(X^2) - E(X)^2$ for any random variable X, letting $X = r_t^2$ leads to

$$V(r_t^2) = E(r_t^4) - E(r_t^2)^2.$$

To calculate the right-hand side above we note that

$$E(r_t^2) = \sigma^2,$$

---

[21] And, since x^2 is also monotonic increasing for $x > 0$, the converse also applies. For instance, a 95% confidence interval for the volatility is [4%, 8%] $\Leftrightarrow$ a 95% for the associated variance is [16%, 64%].

since we have assumed that $E(r_t) = 0$ and that, since we have assumed the returns are normally distributed, the kurtosis is 3, so

$$E(r_t^4) = 3\sigma^4.$$

Hence, for every t,

$$V(r_t^2) = 3\sigma^4 - \sigma^4 = 2\sigma^4.$$

Substituting these into (II.3.17) gives

$$V(\hat{\sigma}_t^2) = 2T^{-1}\sigma^4. \tag{II.3.18}$$

Hence the assumption that returns are generated by a zero mean normal i.i.d. process yields a standard error of an equally weighted average variance estimate based on T squared returns of

$$s.e.(\hat{\sigma}^2) = \sqrt{\frac{2}{T}}\,\sigma^2. \tag{II.3.19}$$

When expressed as a percentage of the variance the estimated standard error is

$$\frac{est.s.e.\,(\hat{\sigma}^2)}{\hat{\sigma}^2} = \sqrt{\frac{2}{T}}, \tag{II.3.20}$$

where T is the sample size. For instance, if the sample size is $T = 32$, then the estimated standard error is 25% of the variance estimate.

II.3.5.3 Standard Error of Volatility Estimator

Since volatility is the (annualized) square root of the variance, the density function of the volatility estimator is

$$g(\hat{\sigma}) = 2\hat{\sigma}h(\hat{\sigma}^2), \quad \text{for } \hat{\sigma} > 0, \tag{II.3.21}$$

where $h(\hat{\sigma}^2)$ is the density function of the variance estimator.[22] Hence the distribution function of the equally weighted average volatility estimator is *not* the square root of the distribution function of the corresponding variance estimate. So we cannot simply take the square root of the standard error of the variance and use this as the standard error of the volatility.

In this section we derive an approximate standard error for the volatility estimator. This is based on the approximation

$$V(f(X)) \approx f'(E(X))^2 V(X) \tag{II.3.22}$$

which holds for any continuously differentiable function f and random variable X. To prove (II.3.22), take a second order Taylor expansion of f about the mean of X and then take expectations. This gives

$$E(f(X)) \approx f(E(X)) + \frac{1}{2}f''(E(X))V(X). \tag{II.3.23}$$

Similarly,

$$E\left(f(X)^2\right) \approx f(E(X))^2 + \left(f'(E(X))^2 + f(E(X))f''(E(X))\right)V(X), \tag{II.3.24}$$

---

[22] This follows from the fact that if y is a (monotonic and differentiable) function of x then their probability densities $g(y)$ and $h(x)$ are related as $g(y) = |dx/dy|h(x)$. Note that when $y = x^{1/2}$, $|dx/dy| = 2y$ and so $g(y) = 2yh(x)$.

again ignoring higher order terms. Since

$$V(f(X)) = E(f(X)^2) - E(f(X))^2,$$

the result (II.3.22) follows.

Setting $f(X) = X^{1/2}$ and $X = \hat{\sigma}^2$ in (II.3.22) we have

$$V(\hat{\sigma}) \approx (2\hat{\sigma})^{-2} V(\hat{\sigma}^2). \tag{II.3.25}$$

Now using (II.3.18) in (II.3.25), we obtain the variance of the volatility estimator as

$$V(\hat{\sigma}) \approx \frac{1}{4\sigma^2} \frac{2\sigma^4}{T} = \frac{\sigma^2}{2T}. \tag{II.3.26}$$

Hence, when expressed as a percentage of volatility,

$$\frac{est.s.e.(\hat{\sigma})}{\hat{\sigma}} \approx \sqrt{\frac{1}{2T}}. \tag{II.3.27}$$

Thus the standard error of the volatility estimator expressed as a percentage of volatility is approximately *one-half* the size of the standard error of the variance expressed as a percentage of the variance. For instance, based on a sample of size 32, the estimated standard error of the variance is 25% of the variance estimate (as seen above) and the estimated standard error of the volatility estimate is 12.5% of the volatility estimate.

EXAMPLE II.3.10: STANDARD ERROR FOR VOLATILITY

An equally weighted volatility estimate is 20%, based on a sample of 100 observations. Estimate the standard error of the estimator and find an interval for the estimate based on one-standard-error bounds.

SOLUTION   The percentage standard error is $(2T)^{-1/2}$, which is approximately 7.1% when $T = 100$. Hence, the one-standard-error bounds for volatility are $(1 \pm 0.071) \times 20\%$ in absolute terms, i.e. the interval estimate is

$$[18.59\%, 21.41\%].$$

Note that the one-standard-error bounds for the variance are also calculated in the spreadsheet. If we (erroneously) take the square root of these and express the result as a percentage we obtain $[18.53\%, 21.37\%]$, and these are *not* equal to the volatility standard error bounds.

We have already remarked that

$$E(\hat{\sigma}) \neq \sqrt{E(\hat{\sigma}^2)},$$

and the above example shows that also

$$V(\hat{\sigma}) \neq \sqrt{V(\hat{\sigma}^2)}.$$

Unfortunately much statistical analysis of volatility is actually based on estimating the variance and the distribution of the variance estimate, and then simply taking the square root.[23]

---

[23] For instance, we do this in almost all GARCH volatilities with one notable exception – the exponential GARCH model that is introduced in Section II.4.3.3.

II.3.5.4   Standard Error of Correlation Estimator

It is harder to derive the standard error of an equally weighted average correlation estimator $\hat{\varrho}$. However, we can use the connection between correlation and regression to show that, under our assumption of zero-mean normal i.i.d. returns, the correlation estimate divided by its standard error has a Student t distribution with T degrees of freedom, and that[24]

$$V(\hat{\varrho}) = T^{-1}(1 - \varrho^2).$$ (II.3.28)

Hence,

$$\frac{\hat{\varrho}\sqrt{T}}{\sqrt{1 - \hat{\varrho}^2}} \sim t_T.$$ (II.3.29)

This means that the significance of an equally weighted correlation estimate depends on the number of observations that are used in the sample.

EXAMPLE II.3.11: TESTING THE SIGNIFICANCE OF HISTORICAL CORRELATION

A historical correlation estimate of 0.2 is obtained using 36 observations. Is this significantly greater than 0?

SOLUTION   The null hypothesis is $H_0 : \varrho = 0$, the alternative hypothesis is $H_1 : \varrho > 0$ and the test statistic is (II.3.29). Computing the value of this statistic given our data gives

$$t = \frac{0.2 \times 6}{\sqrt{1 - 0.04}} = \frac{12}{\sqrt{96}} = \frac{3}{\sqrt{6}} = \sqrt{1.5} = 1.225.$$

Even the 10% upper critical value of the t distribution with 36 degrees of freedom is greater than this value (it is in fact 1.3). Hence, we cannot reject the null hypothesis: 0.2 is not significantly greater than 0 when estimated from 36 observations. However, if the same value of 0.2 had been obtained from a sample with, say, 100 observations our t value would have been 2.02, which is significantly greater than 0 at the 2.5% level because the upper 2.5% critical value of the t distribution with 100 degrees of freedom is 1.98.

II.3.6   CASE STUDY: VOLATILITY AND CORRELATION OF US TREASURIES

The interest rate covariance matrix is a very important quantity for market risk analysis. It is used to assess the risk of positions on interest rate sensitive instruments and of futures, forwards and options positions on any type of underlying asset or instrument. For instance, to assess the risk of an international portfolio of futures positions on equity indices we need an estimate of the interest rate covariance matrix in every country where we take a position on an equity index future.

There are very many different methods for estimating a covariance matrix, and different methodologies can give very different results. Put another way, there is a *model risk* that is inherent in covariance matrix estimation. In this section we consider the simplest possible method, the equally weighted estimator of the matrix, and this is obtained using the Excel

---

[24] If the zero mean assumption is dropped, replace T by $T - 2$, because we have to estimate two sample means before we can estimate the correlation so we lose two degrees of freedom.

covariance function. However, even when we fix the methodology as we do here, we can also obtain very different results when the input data are changed. The model we choose is one where volatility and correlation are assumed to be constant, but it is a very well-known fact that our estimates of volatility and correlation will change over time, as the sample data change. This sensitivity to sample data adds further to the model risk of covariance matrix estimation.

In this case study we do not discuss the model risk that arises from the choice of methodology. We fix the methodology to be the equally weighted covariance matrix and we begin by studying the extent of model risk that stems from the choice of the sample data. Then we fix the sample data and show that there are still many subjective decisions that must be made concerning the way the data are handled and that the results can be very different depending on the choices made. This is another major source of model risk in covariance matrix estimation.

II.3.6.1   Choosing the Data

Assuming we know which methodology to use when estimating a covariance matrix – and in this study we use the equally weighted methodology – the first decisions that the analyst faces are about the data to be used. In this section we consider the broad modelling decisions that relate to any type of covariance matrix. Of course there will be specific questions relating to the data generation for the type of asset that is being analysed. For interest rates we may question which instruments we should use to estimate the yield curve and which estimation methodology (e.g. cubic splines) should be applied. But this is a different question. In the following we discuss two general decisions that apply to all covariance matrices.

Decision 1: Which frequency of observations should be used?

This is an important decision, which depends on the end use of the covariance matrix. We could use high frequency data to estimate a short term covariance matrix or low frequency data to estimate a longer term covariance matrix. If we assume returns are joint normal i.i.d. processes we can use the square-root-of-time rule to convert the matrix into matrices with different holding periods.[25] However, we will get inconsistent results. For instance, the five-day covariance matrix that is estimated from weekly data is not the same as the five-day covariance matrix that is estimated from daily data where every element is multiplied by 5.

The problem is that returns become more variable at higher frequencies. With very high frequency data the returns may be regarded as too 'noisy'. For instance, daily variations may not be relevant if we only ever want to measure covariances over a 10-day period. The extra variation in the daily data is not useful, and the crudeness of the square-root-of-time rule will introduce an error. To avoid the use of crude assumptions it is best to use a data frequency that corresponds to the holding period of the covariance matrix, if possible.

---

[25] For instance, a 10-day covariance matrix can be converted into a one-day matrix by dividing each element by 10; and it can be converted into an annual covariance matrix by multiplying each element by 25.

Decision 2: How long an historical data period should be used?

The equally weighted 'historical' method gives an average volatility, or correlation, over the sample period chosen. The longer the data period, the less relevant that average may be today – i.e. at the end of the sample.

Decisions 1 and 2 are linked. For instance, if we take quarterly data because we want to estimate a covariance matrix that will be used over a risk horizon of one quarter, then we would need a data period of 5 or more years, otherwise the standard error of the estimates will be very large (see Section II.3.5). So our quarterly covariance matrix represents an average over many years. This means it will not be very useful for forecasting over short term horizons. A 1-year history is a better representation of today's markets than a history of 5 or more years. A year of data provides plenty of observations to measure the historical model volatilities and correlations accurately if data are daily. But the daily variations that are captured by the matrix may not be relevant information at the quarterly frequency, so it is not sensible to apply the square-root-of-time rule to the daily matrix. In summary, there may be a trade-off between using data at the relevant frequency and using data that are relevant today.

II.3.6.2   Our Data

We take daily data on constant maturity US Treasury rates, between 4 January 1982 and 27 August 2007.[26] The maturity of the interest rates is between 3 months and 10 years, and we do not use all the maturities in the US Treasury term structure, only those that are shown in Figure II.3.2.

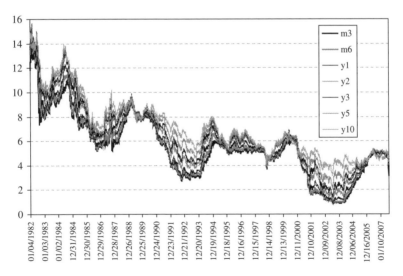

Figure II.3.2   US Treasury rates

---

[26] These data were downloaded from http://www.federalreserve.gov/releases/h15/data.htm.

It is evident that rates followed marked trends over the period. From a high of about 15% in 1982, by the end of 2002 under Alan Greenspan's policies short term interest rates were almost down to 1%. Also periods where the term structure of interest rates was relatively flat are interspersed with periods when the term structure sloped upwards, sometimes with the long term rates being several percent higher than the short term rates. During the upward sloping yield curve regimes, especially the latter one from 2000 to 2005, the medium to long term interest rates are more volatile than the short term rates, in absolute terms. Since term structures usually slope upward the short rates are usually much lower than the medium to long term rates, so it is not clear which rates are the most volatile in relative terms.

II.3.6.3 Effect of Sample Period

A daily matrix based on the entire sample shown in Figure II.3.3 would capture a *very* long term average of volatilities and correlations between daily US Treasury rates; indeed, it is a 25-year average that includes several periods of different regimes in interest rates. A very long term average is useful for long term forecasts and it is probably best to base the estimate on lower frequency data, e.g. monthly.

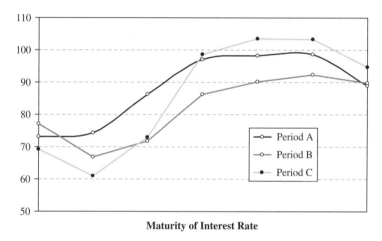

Figure II.3.3   Volatilities of US interest rates (in basis points)

In the following we shall estimate a daily covariance matrix which may be used, for instance, as a 1-day-ahead forecast. We shall use three periods: (A) January 1991 to December 1995; (B) January 1996 to December 1999; and (C) January 2000 to December 2005. Periods A and C are similar in so far as the yield curve had a steep upward slope during most of the period. During period B the shape of the yield curve was generally flatter and it fluctuated between mild upward and downward sloping periods.

Since interest rate sensitivities are usually measured in basis points, the volatilities in an interest rate covariance matrix are usually also expressed in basis points. The volatilities that are estimated over the three different sample periods are shown in Figure II.3.3. These show that the longer maturity interest rates tend to have *higher* volatilities than the short rates. The short rates in the US are very constrained by policy makers when they want to bring down the general level of interest rates. However, during periods A and C the market generally expected interest rates to rise, because the yield curve was upward sloping. The 3-month rate has a volatility of between 70 and 80 basis points and the 10-year rate a volatility of between 90 and 95 basis points. These volatilities are affected by the sample period, but not nearly as much as the rates at the in-between maturities. For instance, the 1-year rate has a volatility estimate of 86 basis points in period A but about 72 basis points in periods B and C. Exact figures for the volatilities are given in the spreadsheet.

The correlations are, of course, independent of the unit of measurement. In Table II.3.5 we report the estimated correlations of the interest rates over the three different periods. All three matrices display the usual characteristics of an interest rate term structure: correlations are higher at the long end than at the short end and they decrease as the difference between the two maturities increases. The short term correlations (i.e. the correlations between the short term rates) are lower and are more dependent on the sample period than the long term correlations. As expected, the short term correlations are lowest in the middle period, when the slope of the yield curve fluctuated considerably.

Table II.3.5   Correlations between US Treasury rates

1991–1995	m3	m6	y1	y2	y3	y5	y10
m3	1	0.8686	0.7170	0.6266	0.5862	0.5427	0.4519
m6	0.8686	1	0.8673	0.7961	0.7614	0.7171	0.6205
y1	0.7170	0.8673	1	0.9111	0.8880	0.8460	0.7447
y2	0.6266	0.7961	0.9111	1	0.9475	0.9221	0.8294
y3	0.5862	0.7614	0.8880	0.9475	1	0.9595	0.8905
y5	0.5427	0.7171	0.8460	0.9221	0.9595	1	0.9414
y10	0.4519	0.6205	0.7447	0.8294	0.8905	0.9414	1

1996–1999	m3	m6	y1	y2	y3	y5	y10
m3	1	0.6798	0.5334	0.4042	0.3779	0.3464	0.3103
m6	0.6798	1	0.7737	0.6713	0.6258	0.5981	0.5532
y1	0.5334	0.7737	1	0.8949	0.8674	0.8434	0.7959
y2	0.4042	0.6713	0.8949	1	0.9561	0.9345	0.8897
y3	0.3779	0.6258	0.8674	0.9561	1	0.9629	0.9273
y5	0.3464	0.5981	0.8434	0.9345	0.9629	1	0.9592
y10	0.3103	0.5532	0.7959	0.8897	0.9273	0.9592	1

2000–2005	m3	m6	y1	y2	y3	y5	y10
m3	1	0.7785	0.5499	0.4040	0.3677	0.3299	0.2646
m6	0.7785	1	0.8200	0.6647	0.6214	0.5697	0.4818
y1	0.5499	0.8200	1	0.8682	0.8279	0.7745	0.6870
y2	0.4040	0.6647	0.8682	1	0.9714	0.9175	0.8349
y3	0.3677	0.6214	0.8279	0.9714	1	0.9542	0.8814
y5	0.3299	0.5697	0.7745	0.9175	0.9542	1	0.9476
y10	0.2646	0.4818	0.6870	0.8349	0.8814	0.9476	1

II.3.6.4 How to Calculate Changes in Interest Rates

In the previous section we estimated volatilities and correlations on the daily changes in interest rates. This is because the daily change in an interest rate, which is not a tradable asset, corresponds to the returns on the tradable asset, i.e. the zero coupon bond with the same maturity as the interest rate.[27] But when using historical data to estimate and forecast interest rate covariance matrices there is another decision to make:

Decision 3: Should the volatilities and correlations be measured directly on absolute changes in interest rates, or should they be measured on relative changes and then converted into absolute terms?

If rates have been trending over the data period the two approaches are likely to give very different results. When applying the equally weighted methodology we assume the volatilities and correlations are constant. So one must ask which is the more stable of the two: relative changes or absolute changes. The decision about how to handle the data depends on which method gives the most stable results over the sample period.

For the data shown in Figure II.3.2 an absolute change of 50 basis points in 1982 was relatively small, but in 2005 it would have represented a very large change. In countries with very high interest rates, or when interest rates have been trending during the sample period, relative changes tend to be more stable than absolute changes.

To inform our choice for Decision 3 we take both the relative daily changes (the difference in the log rates) and the absolute daily changes (the differences in the rates, in basis point terms). Then we obtain the standard deviation, correlation and covariance in each case, and in the case of relative changes we translate the results into absolute terms. We then compare results based on relative changes with results based on absolute changes.[28]

The volatility and correlation estimates are based on the period from 1 January 2006 to 27 August 2007, the most recent data in the sample, and Table II.3.6 compares the results. In August 2007 the US Federal Reserve Bank cut short term interest rates very dramatically due to the credit crisis surrounding sub-prime mortgage lending. For instance, the 3-month rate was a little over 5% on 24 July 2007 but on 20 August 2007 it was only 3.12%! These relatively large cuts in short term rates have a considerable effect on the volatility and correlation estimates shown in Table II.3.6. Notice that the correlation between the 3-month rate and other rates is very low, and the volatility of the 3-month rate is very high.

But there was no significant trend in interest rates over the 2006–2007 sample. The overriding story from these matrices is that they are very much affected by the short term interest rate cuts in August 2007. Interest rates were already fairly low when the cuts were made, so the relative changes in short term interest rates at this time were enormous. Hence, it may be more reasonable to suppose that the volatilities and correlations should be measured on absolute changes during this period.

In summary, there are four crucial decisions to be made when estimating a covariance matrix:

1. Should the data frequency be daily, weekly, monthly or quarterly?
2. Which historical data period should be used?
3. Should we base the matrix on relative or absolute changes?
4. Which statistical model should we employ: equally weighted, exponentially weighted or GARCH?

---

[27] See Section III.1.4 for clarification of this statement.
[28] Using relative changes we multiply the volatility estimate by the level of the interest rate on the last day of the sample, since this is the day that the forecast is made.

Table II.3.6   Volatilities and correlation of US Treasuries, 2006–2007

(a) Based on relative changes

Volatilities (bps)	121.03	63.07	56.70	66.49	66.62	66.26	60.41
Correlations	m3	m6	y1	y2	y3	y5	y10
m3	1	0.5599	0.5124	0.2616	0.2144	0.1862	0.1170
m6	0.5599	1	0.9299	0.5191	0.4906	0.4615	0.3617
y1	0.5124	0.9299	1	0.7775	0.7486	0.7196	0.6149
y2	0.2616	0.5191	0.7775	1	0.9627	0.9443	0.8647
y3	0.2144	0.4906	0.7486	0.9627	1	0.9717	0.9140
y5	0.1862	0.4615	0.7196	0.9443	0.9717	1	0.9497
y10	0.1170	0.3617	0.6149	0.8647	0.9140	0.9497	1

(b) Based on absolute changes

Volatilities (bps)	102.81	63.07	58.65	72.73	72.81	71.05	63.22
Correlations	m3	m6	y1	y2	y3	y5	y10
m3	1	0.6311	0.5623	0.2730	0.2307	0.2056	0.1327
m6	0.6311	1	0.9254	0.5263	0.5013	0.4737	0.3792
y1	0.5623	0.9254	1	0.7884	0.7615	0.7338	0.6350
y2	0.2730	0.5263	0.7884	1	0.9615	0.9437	0.8687
y3	0.2307	0.5013	0.7615	0.9615	1	0.9718	0.9177
y5	0.2056	0.4737	0.7338	0.9437	0.9718	1	0.9518
y10	0.1327	0.3792	0.6350	0.8687	0.9177	0.9518	1

We have shown that the first three decisions give rise to a considerable amount of model risk. But in the remainder of this chapter and in the next chapter we shall see that the greatest model risk arises from the choice of statistical methodology.

II.3.7   EQUALLY WEIGHTED MOVING AVERAGES

A moving average is calculated on a rolling *estimation sample*. In other words, we use a *data window* that has a fixed sample size and is rolled through time, each day adding the new return and taking off the oldest return. In the case of equally weighted moving averages the sample size, also called the *look-back period* or *averaging period*, is the time interval over which we compute the average of the squared returns (for variance) or the average cross products of returns (for covariance). In the past, several large financial institutions have lost a lot of money because they used the equally weighted moving average model inappropriately. I would not be surprised if much more money was lost because of the inexperienced use of this model in the future. The problem is not the model itself – after all, it is a perfectly respectable statistical formula for an unbiased estimator. The problems arise from its inappropriate application within a time series context.

II.3.7.1   Effect of Volatility Clusters

A (fallacious) argument goes as follows: long term predictions should be unaffected by short term phenomena such as *volatility clustering* where the market became turbulent for several weeks before returning to normality. This happens quite frequently in some financial markets and in equity and commodity markets in particular. So for long term forecasts we should use an average over a very long historic period. On the other hand, short term predictions should reflect current market conditions so only the recent data on returns should be used. Some people use a historical averaging period of T days in order to forecast forward T days; others use slightly longer historical periods than the forecast period. For example for a 10-day forecast some practitioners might look back 30 days or more.

But this apparently sensible approach actually induces a major problem. If just one extreme return is included in the averaging period the volatility forecast will be very high. But then it will suddenly jump downward to a much lower level on a day when absolutely nothing happened in the markets. It just happened to be the day when the extreme return dropped out of the moving estimation sample. And all the time that this extreme return stays within the data window the volatility forecast remains high. For instance, suppose the sample size is 100 days of daily data and that an extreme return happened three months ago. Then that return has just as much effect on volatility now as if it happened yesterday.

EXAMPLE II.3.12: HISTORICAL VOLATILITY OF MIB 30

Figure II.3.4 illustrates the daily closing prices of the Italian MIB 30 stock index between the beginning of January 2000 and the end of December 2007 and compares these with the S&P 500 index prices over the same period.[29] Calculate the 30-day, 60-day and 90-day historical volatilities of these two stock indices and compare them graphically.

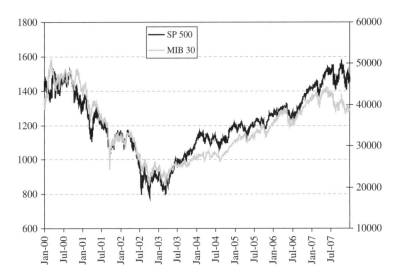

Figure II.3.4   MIB 30 and S&P 500 daily closing prices

SOLUTION   In the spreadsheet for this example we construct three different equally weighted moving average volatility estimates for the MIB 30 index, with $T = 30$ days, 60 days and 90 days respectively. The result is shown in Figure II.3.5. The corresponding graph for the

---

[29] Data were downloaded from Yahoo! Finance: symbols ^GSPC and ^MIB30.

S&P 500 index is shown in the spreadsheet for this example. Let us first focus on the early part of the data period and on the period after the terrorist attacks of 11 September 2001 in particular. The Italian index reacted to the news far more than the S&P 500. The volatility estimate based on 30 days of data jumped from 15% to nearly 50% in 1 day, and then continued to rise further, up to 55%. Once again, the US sneezes and Europe catches a cold! Then suddenly, exactly 30 days after the event, 30-day volatility fell back again to 30%. But nothing special happened in the markets on that day. The drastic fall in volatility was just a 'ghost' of the 9/11 attacks; it was no reflection at all of the underlying market conditions at that time.

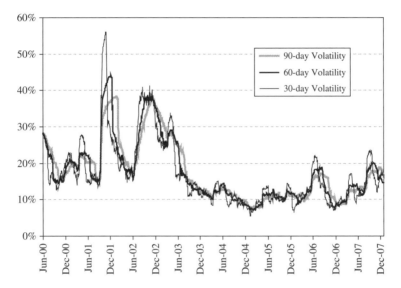

Figure II.3.5   Equally weighted moving average volatility estimates of the MIB 30 index

Similar features are apparent in the 60-day and 90-day volatility series. Each series jumps up immediately after the 9/11 event and then, either 60 or 90 days later, jumps down again. On 9 November 2001 the three different look-back periods gave volatility estimates of 30%, 43% and 36%, but they are all based on the same underlying data and the same i.i.d. assumption for the returns! Other such 'ghost features' are evident later in the period, for instance in March 2001 and March 2003. Later on in the period the choice of look-back period does not make so much difference: the three volatility estimates are all around the 10% level.

II.3.7.2   Pitfalls of the Equally Weighted Moving Average Method

The problems encountered when applying this model stem not from the small jumps that are often encountered in financial asset prices but from the large jumps that are only rarely encountered. When a long averaging period is used the importance of a single extreme event is averaged out within a large sample of returns. Hence, a very long term moving average volatility estimate will not respond very much to a short, sharp shock in the market. In Example II.3.12 above this effect was clearly visible in 2002, where only the 30-day volatility rose significantly over a matter of a few weeks. The longer term volatilities did rise, but it took several months for them to respond to the market falls in the MIB30 during mid 2002. At this point in time there was a volatility cluster and the effect of the cluster was to make the longer term volatilities rise (eventually), and afterwards they took a very long time to return to normal levels. It was not until late 2003 that the three volatility series in Figure II.3.5 moved back into line with each other.

Even when there is just one extreme event in the market this will influence the T-day moving average estimate for exactly T days until that very large squared return falls out of the data window. Hence, volatility will jump up, for exactly T days, and then fall dramatically on day $T+1$, even though nothing happened in the market on that day. This type of 'ghost' feature is simply an artefact of the use of equal weighting. The problem is that extreme events are just as important to current estimates, whether they occurred yesterday or whether they occurred a very long time ago. A single large squared return remains just as important yesterday as it was T days ago. It will affect the T-day volatility or correlation estimate for exactly T days after that return was experienced, and to exactly the same extent. Exactly $T+1$ days after the extreme event the equally weighted moving average volatility estimate mysteriously drops back down to about the correct level – that is, provided that we have not had another extreme return in the interim!

Note that the smaller is T, i.e. the number of data points in the estimation sample, the more variable the historical volatility estimates will be over time. When any estimates are based on a small sample size they will not be very precise. The larger the sample size the more accurate the estimate, because the standard error of the volatility estimate is proportional to $1/\sqrt{T}$. For this reason alone a short moving average will be more variable than a long moving average. Hence, a 30-day historic volatility (or correlation) will always be more variable than a 60-day historic volatility (or correlation) that is based on the same daily return data.[30]

It is important to realize that whatever the length of the estimation sample and whenever the estimate is made, the equally weighted method is always estimating the *same* parameter: the unconditional volatility (or correlation) of the returns. But this is a constant – it does not change over the process. Thus the variation in T-day historic estimates can only be attributed to sampling error: there is nothing else in the model to explain this variation. It is not a time varying volatility model, even though some users try to force it into that framework.

The problem with the equally weighted moving average model is that it tries to make an estimator of a constant volatility into a forecast of a time varying volatility (!). Similarly, it tries to make an estimator of a constant correlation into a forecast of a time varying correlation. This model is really only suitable for long term forecasts of i.i.d. unconditional volatility, or correlation, for instance over a period of between six months and several years. In this case the estimation sample should be long enough to include a variety of price jumps, with a relative frequency that represents the modeller's expectations of the probability of future price jumps of that magnitude during the forecast horizon.

II.3.7.3 Three Ways to Forecast Long Term Volatility

When pricing options it is the long term volatility that is most difficult to forecast. Option trading often concentrates on short maturity options, and long term options are much less

---

[30] Of course, if one really believes in the normal i.i.d. returns assumption and, in particular, in the constant volatility assumption that underlies this approach one should always use a very large estimation sample, so that sampling errors are reduced.

liquid. Hence, it is not easy to forecast a long term implied volatility. Long term volatility holds the greatest uncertainty, yet it is the most important determinant of long term option prices. To forecast a long term average for volatility using the equally weighted model it is standard to use a large estimation sample size T in the variance estimate. The confidence intervals for historical volatility estimators that were derived in Section II.3.5 provide a useful indication of the accuracy of these long term volatility forecasts and the approximate standard errors that we have derived there give an indication of the variability in long term volatility. In Section II.3.5.3 we showed that the variability in estimates decreased as the sample size increased. Hence a long term volatility that is forecast from this model may indeed prove very useful.

Let us now consider three hypothetical historical volatility modellers whom we shall call Tom, Dick and Harry. They are each providing daily forecasts of the FTSE 100 volatility over a 1-year risk horizon. Tom is a classical statistician who believes that historical data are all one needs for predicting the future. He bases his forecast on an equally weighted average of squared returns over the past 12 months of daily data. Imagine that it is January 2008. In August 2007 the FTSE 100 index crashed, falling by 25% in the space of a few days. So some very large jumps occurred during the sample. Tom includes the August 2007 crash returns in his calculation so his volatility forecast will be high. The fact that he uses the crash period in his sample implies that Tom has an implicit belief that another jump of equal magnitude will occur during the forecast horizon.

Time moves on and Tom is still forecasting 1-year volatility using his moving average model. But in August 2008 the data from the previous August will fall out of his sample. Assuming no further crash occurred after August 2007, in August 2008 Tom abruptly changes his implicit belief that another crash will occur during the next 12 months. Suddenly he decides that another crash is very *unlikely*, just because there was no crash during the last 12 months.

Dick is another classical statistician, but he has Bayesian tendencies. Instead of passively adopting beliefs that are totally implied by the historical sample data, he admits an element of subjective choice in forming his beliefs. In January 2008 he does not believe that another market crash could occur in his forecast horizon, and he allows this subjective belief to modify his method of volatility forecasting. He excludes the August crash data from his sample. He still uses historical data to forecast the volatility but he filters out extreme returns in an *ad hoc* way, according to his subjective beliefs, before it is used in the classical model. During a different period Dick is the type of modeller who may also add in some artificial large returns if he feels that the market has not been sufficiently volatile in the recent past.

Harry is a full-blown Bayesian. In the Bayesian framework of uncertain volatility the equally weighted model has an important role to play. He uses equally weighted moving averages only to determine a possible range for long term volatility, which we denote by $[\sigma_{min}, \sigma_{max}]$. He estimates the lower bound σ_{min} using a long period of historical data, but with all the very extreme returns removed. Then he estimates the upper bound σ_{max} using the same historical data but now with the very extreme returns retained – in fact he even adds a few more for good measure! Then Harry formalizes his beliefs about long term volatility with a *subjective probability distribution* over the range $[\sigma_{min}, \sigma_{max}]$. At some times he may have very little objective information about the economy and so forth, and therefore he may feel that each value in the range is equally likely. In that case his beliefs would be represented by a uniform distribution over the range. At other times he may have more news about what analysts believe is likely to happen in the markets. For instance, he may believe that volatility is more likely to be towards the middle of the range, in which case he might consider using a truncated normal distribution to represent his beliefs.

Whatever distribution Harry uses to represent his beliefs, his advantage as a market risk analyst is that he can carry this distribution through for the rest of the analysis. For instance, he could obtain point estimates for long term exposures with option-like structures, such as warrants on a firm's equity or convertible bonds. Using his subjective volatility distribution, these point estimates could be given with a confidence interval, or a standard error, expressing Harry's confidence in the forecast that he is providing. At the time of writing it is my experience that the majority of volatility modellers are like Tom. There are a few like Dick but very few like Harry. However, Bayesians like Harry should be very much appreciated by their traders and managers, so I believe they will become more common in the future.

II.3.8   EXPONENTIALLY WEIGHTED MOVING AVERAGES

An exponentially weighted moving average (EWMA) puts more weight on the more recent observations. That is, as extreme returns move further into the past when the data window moves, they become less important in the average. For this reason EWMA forecasts do not suffer from the 'ghost features' that we find in equally weighted moving averages.

II.3.8.1   Statistical Methodology

An exponentially weighted moving average can be defined on any time series of data. Suppose that on date t we have recorded data up to time $t-1$. The exponentially weighted average of these observations is defined as

$$EWMA(x_{t-1}, \ldots, x_1 \,|\, \lambda) = \frac{x_{t-1} + \lambda x_{t-2} + \lambda^2 x_{t-3} + \ldots + \lambda^{t-2} x_1}{1 + \lambda + \lambda^2 + \ldots + \lambda^{t-2}},$$

where λ is a constant, and $0 < \lambda < 1$, called the *smoothing constant* or, sometimes, the decay parameter. Since $\lambda^n \to 0$ as $n \to \infty$, the exponentially weighted average places negligible weight on observations far in the past. And since

$$1 + \lambda + \lambda^2 + \ldots = (1-\lambda)^{-1}$$

we have, for large t,

$$EWMA(x_{t-1}, \ldots, x_1 \,|\, \lambda) \approx \frac{x_{t-1} + \lambda x_{t-2} + \lambda^2 x_{t-3} + \ldots}{1 + \lambda + \lambda^2 + \ldots} = (1-\lambda) \sum_{i=1}^{\infty} \lambda^{i-1} x_{t-i}. \qquad (II.3.30)$$

This formula is used to calculate EWMA estimates of

- variance, where we take x to be the squared return; and
- covariance, where we take x to be the cross product of the two returns.

As with equally weighted moving averages, it is standard to use squared daily returns and cross products of daily returns, not in mean deviation form, i.e.

$$\hat{\sigma}_t^2 = (1-\lambda) \sum_{i=1}^{\infty} \lambda^{i-1} r_{t-i}^2 \qquad (II.3.31)$$

and

$$\hat{\sigma}_{12t} = (1-\lambda) \sum_{i=1}^{\infty} \lambda^{i-1} r_{1,t-i} r_{2,t-i}. \qquad (II.3.32)$$

The above formulae may be rewritten in the form of recursions that are more easily used in calculations:

$$\hat{\sigma}_t^2 = (1 - \lambda) r_{t-1}^2 + \lambda \hat{\sigma}_{t-1}^2 \qquad (\text{II.3.33})$$

and

$$\hat{\sigma}_{12t} = (1 - \lambda) r_{1,t-1} r_{2,t-1} + \lambda \hat{\sigma}_{12,t-1}. \qquad (\text{II.3.34})$$

An alternative notation, when we want to make explicit the dependence on the smoothing constant, is

$$V_\lambda(r_t) = \hat{\sigma}_t^2 \quad \text{and} \quad \text{Cov}_\lambda(r_{1,t}, r_{2,t}) = \hat{\sigma}_{12t}.$$

The formulae above are applied as follows:

- We convert the EWMA variance (II.3.32) to *EWMA volatility* by taking the annualized square root, the annualizing constant being the number of returns per year.
- To find the *EWMA correlation* the covariance (II.3.34) is divided by the square root of the product of the two EWMA variance estimates, all with the *same* value of λ.

We may also calculate a *EWMA beta*, i.e. a EWMA estimate of the sensitivity of a stock (or portfolio) return to the return on the market index. The covariance between the stock (or portfolio) returns and the market returns is divided by the EWMA estimate for the market variance, both with the same value of λ:

$$\hat{\varrho}_{t\lambda} = \frac{\text{Cov}_\lambda(r_{1t}, r_{2t})}{\sqrt{V_\lambda(r_{1t}) V_\lambda(r_{2t})}} \qquad (\text{II.3.35})$$

and

$$\hat{\beta}_{t\lambda} = \frac{\text{Cov}_\lambda(X_t, Y_t)}{V_\lambda(X_t)}. \qquad (\text{II.3.36})$$

Numerical examples of the calculation of EWMA market correlation, market beta and relative volatility have already been given in Section II.1.2.3.

II.3.8.2 Interpretation of Lambda

There are two terms on the right hand side of (II.3.33). The first term is $(1 - \lambda) r_{t-1}^2$. This determines the *intensity of reaction* of volatility to market events: the smaller is λ the more the volatility reacts to the market information in yesterday's return. The second term is $\lambda \hat{\sigma}_{t-1}^2$. This determines the *persistence in volatility*: irrespective of what happens in the market, if volatility was high yesterday it will be still be high today. The closer λ is to 1, the more persistent is volatility following a market shock.

Thus a high λ gives little reaction to actual market events but great persistence in volatility; and a low λ gives highly reactive volatilities that quickly die away. An unfortunate restriction of EWMA models is they assume that the reaction and persistence parameters are not independent; the strength of reaction to market events is determined by $1 - \lambda$ and the persistence of shocks is determined by λ. But this assumption is, in general, not empirically justified.

The effect of using a different value of λ in EWMA volatility forecasts can be quite substantial. For instance, Figure II.3.6 compares two EWMA volatility estimates/forecasts of the S&P 500 index, with $\lambda = 0.90$ and $\lambda = 0.96$. We can see from the figure that there

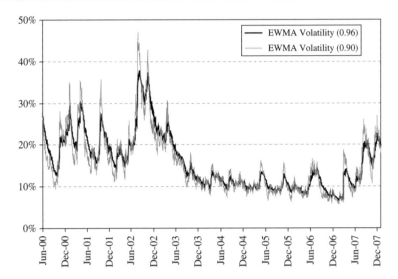

Figure II.3.6   EWMA volatility estimates for S&P 500 with different lambdas

are several instances when the two EWMA estimates differ by as much as 5 percentage points.

So which is the best value to use for the smoothing constant? How should we choose λ? This is not an easy question.[31] Statistical methods may be considered: for example, λ could be chosen to minimize the root mean square error between the EWMA estimate of variance and the squared return. But more often λ is chosen subjectively. This is because the same value of λ has to be used for all elements in a EWMA covariance matrix, otherwise the matrix is not guaranteed to be positive semi-definite. If the value of lambda is chosen subjectively the values usually range between about 0.75 (volatility is highly reactive but has little persistence) and 0.98 (volatility is very persistent but not highly reactive).

II.3.8.3   Properties of EWMA Estimators

A EWMA volatility estimate will react immediately following an unusually large return; then the effect of this return on the EWMA volatility estimate gradually diminishes over time. The reaction of EWMA volatility estimates to market events therefore persists over time and with a strength that is determined by the smoothing constant λ. The larger the value of λ the more weight is placed on observations in the past and so the smoother the series becomes.

Figure II.3.7 compares the EWMA volatility of the MIB index with $\lambda = 0.95$ and the 60-day equally weighted volatility estimate.[32] There is a large difference between the two estimators following an extreme market return. The EWMA estimate gives a higher volatility than the equally weighted estimate but returns to typical levels faster than the equally weighted estimate because it does not suffer from the 'ghost features' discussed above.

---

[31] By contrast, in GARCH models there is no question of 'how' we should estimate parameters, because maximum likelihood estimation is an optimal method that always gives consistent estimators.

[32] This figure is contained in the spreadsheet for Example II.3.12.

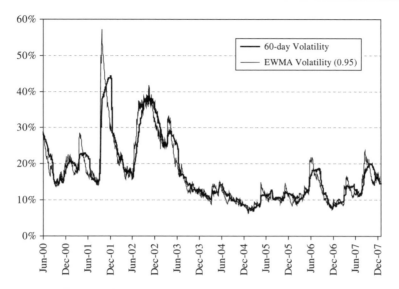

Figure II.3.7   EWMA versus equally weighted volatility

One of the disadvantages of using EWMA to estimate and forecast covariance matrices is that the same value of λ is used for all the variances and covariances in the matrix. For instance, in a large matrix covering several asset classes, the same λ applies to all equity indices, foreign exchange rates, interest rates and/or commodities in the matrix. This constraint is commonly applied merely because it guarantees that the matrix will be positive semi-definite.[33] But why should all these risk factors have similar reaction and persistence to shocks? In fact, more advanced methods give EWMA positive semi-definite matrices without imposing that the same λ generates all the elements in the matrix.[34]

II.3.8.4   Forecasting with EWMA

The exponentially weighted average provides a methodology for calculating an estimate of the variance at any point in time, and we denote this estimate $\hat{\sigma}_t^2$, using the subscript t because the *estimate* changes over time. But the EWMA estimator is based on an i.i.d. returns model. The 'true' variance of returns at every point is constant, it does not change over time. That is, EWMA is not a model for the conditional variance σ_t^2. Without a proper model it is not clear how we should turn our current estimate of variance into a forecast of variance over some future horizon.

However, a EWMA model for the conditional variance could be specified as

$$\sigma_t^2 = (1-\lambda)\, r_{t-1}^2 + \lambda \sigma_{t-1}^2, \quad r_t \,|\, I_{t-1} \sim N\big(0, \sigma_t^2\big). \tag{II.3.37}$$

This is a restricted version of the univariate symmetric normal GARCH model (introduced in the next chapter) but the restrictions are such that the forecast conditional volatility must

---

[33] See Sections I.2.2.8 and I.2.4.3 for the definition of positive semi-definiteness and for reasons why covariance and correlation matrices need to be positive semi-definite.
[34] For further details about these methods, see Section II.3.8.7.

be *constant*,[35] i.e. $\sigma_t^2 = \sigma^2$ for all t. So, after all, even if we specify the model (II.3.37) it reduces to the i.i.d. model for returns. Hence, the returns model for the EWMA estimator is the same as the model for the equally weighted average variance and covariance estimator, i.e. that the returns are generated by multivariate normal i.i.d. processes.[36] The fact that our *estimates* are time varying is merely due to a 'fancy' exponential weighting of sample data. The underlying model for the dynamics of returns is just the same as in the equally weighted average case!

A EWMA volatility forecast must be a constant, in the sense that it is the same for all time horizons. The EWMA model will forecast the *same* average volatility, whether the forecast is over the next 10 days or over the next year. The forecast of average volatility, over any forecast horizon, is set equal to the current estimate of volatility. This is not a very good forecasting model. Similar remarks apply to the EWMA covariance. We can regard EWMA as a simplistic version of bivariate GARCH. But then, using the same reasoning as above, we see that the EWMA correlation forecast, over any risk horizon, is simply set equal to the current EWMA correlation estimate. So again we are reduced to a constant correlation model.

The base horizon for the forecast is given by the frequency of the data – daily returns will give the 1-day covariance matrix forecast, weekly returns will give the 1-week covariance matrix forecast and so forth. Then, since the returns are assumed to be i.i.d. the square-root-of-time rule will apply. So we can convert a 1-day covariance matrix forecast into an h-day forecast by multiplying each element of the 1-day EWMA covariance matrix by h.

Since the choice of λ itself is *ad hoc* some users choose different values of λ for forecasting over different horizons. For instance, in the RiskMetrics™ methodology described below a relatively low value of λ is used for short term forecasts and a higher value of λ is used for long term forecasts. However, this is merely an *ad hoc* rule.

II.3.8.5   Standard Errors for EWMA Forecasts

In this section we use our assumption that the underlying returns are multivariate normally and independently distributed with mean zero to derive a measure of precision for EWMA forecasts. Our assumption implies, for all t and for all $s \neq t$, that

$$E(r_t) = 0, \quad V(r_t) = E(r_t^2) = \sigma^2 \quad \text{and} \quad \text{Cov}(r_t, r_s) = 0,$$

and that

$$V(r_t^2) = E(r_t^4) - E(r_t^2)^2 = 3\sigma^4 - \sigma^4 = 2\sigma^4.$$

We now use these assumptions to derive standard errors for EWMA forecasts. We apply the variance operator to (II.3.31) and hence calculate the variance of the EWMA variance estimator as

$$V(\hat{\sigma}_t^2) = \frac{(1-\lambda)^2}{1-\lambda^2} V(r_t^2) = 2 \left(\frac{1-\lambda}{1+\lambda} \right) \sigma^4. \tag{II.3.38}$$

---

[35] Because $\alpha \equiv 1 - \lambda$ and $\beta \equiv \lambda$ the restrictions are that (a) the GARCH constant ω is 0 and (b) the speed of mean reversion in forecasts, which is given by $1 - (\alpha + \beta)$, is also 0. However the long term volatility is undefined!

[36] The i.i.d. assumption is required for constant volatility and the square-root-of-time scaling rule; the multivariate normality assumption is required so that the covariance matrix is meaningful and so that we can find confidence limits around the forecasts.

Hence,

$$\frac{est.s.e.\left(\hat{\sigma}_t^2\right)}{\hat{\sigma}_t^2} = \sqrt{2\left(\frac{1-\lambda}{1+\lambda}\right)}. \tag{II.3.39}$$

This gives the estimated standard error of the EWMA variance estimator as a percentage of the EWMA variance estimate.

As explained in the previous subsection, the standard model for EWMA is that returns are normal and i.i.d. In Section II.3.5.3 we proved that a normal i.i.d. assumption implies that

$$V(\hat{\sigma}) \approx (2\hat{\sigma})^{-2} V(\hat{\sigma}^2). \tag{II.3.40}$$

So we can use (II.3.40) with (II.3.38) to approximate the standard error of the EWMA estimator for volatility. Substituting (II.3.38) into (II.3.40) gives

$$V(\hat{\sigma}_t) \approx \left(\frac{1-\lambda}{1+\lambda}\right)\frac{\sigma^2}{2}. \tag{II.3.41}$$

So the estimated standard error of the EWMA volatility forecast, expressed as a percentage of that forecast, is

$$\frac{est.s.e.\left(\hat{\sigma}_t\right)}{\hat{\sigma}_t} \approx \sqrt{\frac{1-\lambda}{2\left(1+\lambda\right)}}. \tag{II.3.42}$$

Figure II.3.8 plots the estimated standard error of the EWMA variance forecast, expressed as a percentage of the variance forecast (black line) and the EWMA volatility forecast, expressed as a percentage of the volatility forecast (grey line). Both are plotted as a function of lambda. Higher values of lambda give more precise EWMA estimates. This is logical, since the higher the value of lambda the larger the effective sample of data.

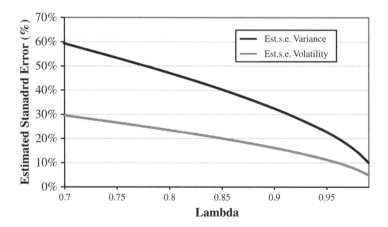

Figure II.3.8   Standard errors of EWMA estimators

A single point forecast of volatility can be very misleading. A complete forecast is a *distribution* that captures our uncertainty over the quantity that is being forecast. And whenever a variance or volatility forecast is applied to price an instrument or measure the risk of a portfolio, the standard error of the forecast can be translated into a standard error for the application. For instance, we may use the EWMA standard error to obtain a standard error for a value-at-risk estimate.[37] This makes one aware of the uncertainty that is introduced into an option price or a value-at-risk estimate by possible errors in the forecast of the covariance matrix.

II.3.8.6 RiskMetrics™ Methodology

Three very large covariance matrices, each based on a different moving average methodology, are available from the RiskMetrics™ website (http://www.riskmetrics.com). These matrices cover all types of assets, including government bonds, money markets, swaps, foreign exchange and equity indices for 31 currencies, and commodities. Subscribers have access to all of these matrices updated on a daily basis – and end-of-year matrices are also available to subscribers wishing to use them in scenario analysis. After a few days the datasets are also made available free for educational use.

The RiskMetrics group is the market leader in market and credit risk data and modelling for banks, corporate asset managers and financial intermediaries. It is highly recommended that readers visit the website, where they will find a surprisingly large amount of information in the form of free publications and data. For instance, at the time of writing the Market Risk publications that anyone can download were as follows:

- The 1996 *RiskMetrics Technical Document*. Prepared while RiskMetrics was still a part of JP Morgan, it remains a much-cited classic in the field and provides a clear introduction to the basics of computing and using value at risk.
- *Return to RiskMetrics: The Evolution of a Standard*. An update and supplement to the 1996 *RiskMetrics Technical Document*, reflecting the wider range of measurement techniques and statistics now part of best practice. It provides comprehensive coverage of Monte Carlo and historical simulation, non-linear exposures, stress testing, and asset management oriented risk reporting.
- *LongRunTechnical Document*. This describes several approaches developed by RiskMetrics for long term forecasting and simulation of financial asset prices.
- *Risk Management: A Practical Guide*. A non-technical introduction to risk management, addressing the basic issues risk managers face when implementing a firm-wide risk management process.
- *CorporateMetrics Technical Document*. This describes the RiskMetrics approach to measuring and managing market risk in the corporate environment. It addresses the particular needs of non-financial corporations, such as the measurement of earnings and cash-flow risk over a horizon of several years and regulatory disclosure of derivatives transactions.

The three covariance matrices provided by the RiskMetrics group are each based on a history of daily returns in all the asset classes mentioned above:

---

[37] Similarly, we could use the standard error of a GARCH forecast that is used to price an option to derive the standard error of the GARCH model option price.

1. *Regulatory matrix*. This takes its name from the (unfortunate) requirement that banks must use at least 250 days of historical data for value-at-risk estimation. Hence, this metric is an equally weighted average matrix with $n = 250$. The volatilities and correlations constructed from this matrix represent forecasts of average volatility (or correlation) over the next 250 days.
2. *Daily matrix*. This is a EWMA covariance matrix with $\lambda = 0.94$ for all elements. It is not dissimilar to an equally weighted average with $n = 25$, except that it does not suffer from the 'ghost features' caused by very extreme market events. The volatilities and correlations constructed from this matrix represent forecasts of average volatility (or correlation) over the next day.
3. *Monthly matrix*. This is a EWMA covariance matrix with $\lambda = 0.97$ for all elements and then multiplied by 25 (i.e. using the square-root-of-time rule and assuming 25 days per month). RiskMetrics use the volatilities and correlations constructed from this matrix to represent forecasts of average volatility (or correlation) over the next 25 days.

The main difference between the three different methods is evident following major market movements: the regulatory forecast will produce a 'ghost' effect of this event, and does not react as much as the daily or monthly forecasts. The forecast that is most reactive to news is the daily forecast, but it also has less persistence than the monthly forecast.

Figure II.3.9 compares the estimates for the FTSE 100 volatility based on each of the three RiskMetrics methodologies and using daily data from 3 January 1995 to 4 January 2008.[38] As mentioned in Section II.3.8.4, these estimates are assumed to be the forecasts over 1 day, 1 month and 1 year. In volatile times the daily and monthly estimates lie well above the regulatory forecast, and the converse is true in more tranquil periods.

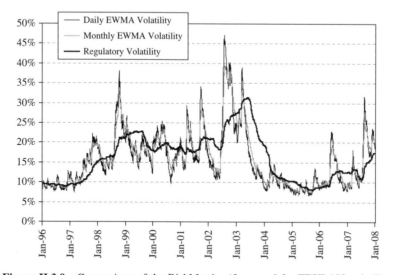

Figure II.3.9   Comparison of the RiskMetrics 'forecasts' for FTSE 100 volatility

---

[38] Data were downloaded from Yahoo! Finance: symbol ^FTSE.

During most of 2003, the regulatory estimate of average volatility over the next year was about 10% higher than both of the shorter term estimates. However, it was falling dramatically during this period and indeed the regulatory forecast between June 2003 and June 2004 was entirely wrong. On the other hand, in August 2007 the daily forecasts were above 30%, the monthly forecasts were 25% but the regulatory forecast over the next year was less than 15%.

When the markets have been tranquil for some time, for instance during the whole of 2005, the three forecasts are similar. But during and directly after a volatile period there are large differences between the regulatory forecasts and the two EWMA forecasts, and these differences are very difficult to justify. Neither the equally weighted average nor the EWMA methodology is based on a proper forecasting model. One simply assumes the current estimate is the volatility forecast. But the current estimate is a backward looking measure based on recent historical data. So both of these moving average models make the assumption that the behaviour of future volatility is the same as its past behaviour, and this is a very simplistic view.

II.3.8.7 Orthogonal EWMA versus RiskMetrics EWMA

The EWMA covariance matrices in RiskMetrics are obtained by applying exponentially weighted moving average models directly to a large set of risk factor returns (i.e. government bonds, money market rates, equity indices, foreign exchange rates and commodities). It was necessary to impose a severe restriction – that the smoothing constant λ is the same for all elements of the matrix – otherwise it may not be positive semi-definite. Thus all factors are assumed to have the same reaction to market shocks. RiskMetrics set λ to be 0.94 in their daily matrix and 0.97 in their monthly matrix. But since there are well over 400 risk factors in the RiskMetrics covariance matrices, there must be many risk factors for which the choice of λ is inappropriate.

An alternative is to use the orthogonal EWMA (O-EWMA) version of the orthogonal GARCH (O-GARCH) model, which is developed in Alexander (2001b).[39] In this approach the EWMA is not applied directly to the returns on the fundamental risk factors themselves, but to the first few principal components of an equally weighted covariance matrix of the risk factor returns. We only need to calculate EWMA variances of the main principal components because their EWMA covariances are assumed to be zero. We do *not* have to use the same smoothing constant λ for each of these EWMA variance estimates. And even if we did, the final O-EWMA matrix would not have the same smoothing constant for all risk factors.

The O-EWMA approach has the following advantages over the RiskMetrics methodology:

- The matrix is always positive semi-definite, even when the smoothing constant is different for each principal component.
- Compared with the RiskMetrics EWMA matrices, relatively few constraints are imposed on the movements in volatility; the reaction in volatility is not the same for all risk factors, and neither is the persistence. Neither are the smoothing constants the same for all series. Instead the parameters in the variance and covariance equations will be determined by the correlations between the different risk factors in the matrix (because these are derived from $\mathbf{W}^*$, the matrix of eigenvectors).

---

[39] The only difference between O-EWMA and O-GARCH is that we use EWMA variances instead of GARCH variances of the principal components. See Section II.4.6 for further details.

- By taking only the first few principal components, enough to represent, say, 90–95% of the variation, the movements that are *not* captured in the O-EWMA covariance matrix can be ascribed to insignificant 'noise' that we would prefer to ignore, especially when computing correlation estimates. By cutting out this noise the covariance matrix is more stable over time than the RiskMetrics EWMA matrices.
- The orthogonal method is computationally efficient because it calculates only k variances instead of the $m(m+1)/2$ variances and covariances of the original system, and typically k will be much less than m.
- Because it is based on PCA, O-EWMA also quantifies how much risk is associated with each statistical factor, which can be a great advantage for risk managers as their attention is directed towards the most important sources of risk.

II.3.9   SUMMARY AND CONCLUSIONS

Volatility and correlation are metrics that are applied to measure the risk of investments in financial assets and in portfolios of financial assets. The standard measure of volatility is obtained by annualizing the standard deviation of monthly, weekly or daily returns using the *square-root-of-time rule*. The correlation is the covariance between two returns divided by the product of their standard deviations. The volatilities and correlations of a set of asset returns are summarized in a *covariance matrix*. This chapter has described the simplest type of covariance matrices, which are generated using *equally weighted moving averages* (also called 'historical' matrices) or *exponentially weighted moving averages* (EWMA matrices).

Some very strong assumptions about the distributions of returns are implicit in the use of these matrices, and if these assumptions are not satisfied then our estimates of portfolio risk that are obtained using these matrices can be very inaccurate. Two important assumptions of moving average covariance matrices are that returns are generated by i.i.d. processes and that the joint distribution of a set of returns is elliptical. What are the consequences if these assumptions do not hold?

- If the returns on an investment are not i.i.d. then the standard measure of volatility can substantially underestimate the risk from the investment. It needs to be adjusted to take account of the autocorrelation in returns. In Section II.3.2.3 we derived a standard deviation scaling rule when returns are autocorrelated.
- If the returns on two investments are not generated by a bivariate normal distribution or a bivariate t distribution, then the correlation between the returns tells us very little about their real dependency. In Section II.3.3.2 we emphasized the pitfalls of using correlation when returns are not i.i.d. with an elliptical distribution.

Moving average models provide an estimate of the current covariance matrix, and this estimate is used as a forecast. The basic time period of the forecast is determined by the frequency of the data. For instance, if the basic returns are measured at the daily frequency we obtain a 1-day covariance matrix and if the returns are weekly we obtain a 5-day covariance matrix. However, we can transform a one-period forecast into a forecast of the covariance matrix over the next h periods using the square-root-of-time rule; that is, we simply multiply each element of the one-period matrix by h.

To forecast portfolio volatility, correlation and covariance matrices we often use historical data alone – without including our personal views about the future – even though there is ample evidence that history is only part of the story. Moreover, we know that the multivariate normal i.i.d. assumption that underlies these simple moving average models is very often violated by the empirical characteristics of returns.[40]

The equally weighted moving average or 'historical' approach to estimating and forecasting volatilities and correlations has been popular amongst practitioners since the 1990s. But the approach suffers from a number of drawbacks, including the following:

- The forecast of volatility/correlation over all future horizons is simply taken to be the current estimate of volatility, because the underlying assumption in the model is that returns are i.i.d.
- The only choice facing the user is on the data points to use in the data window. The forecasts produced depend crucially on this decision, yet there is no statistical procedure to choose the size of data window – it is a purely subjective decision.
- Following an extreme market move, the forecasts of volatility and correlation will exhibit a so-called *ghost feature* of that extreme move which will severely bias the volatility and correlation forecasts upward.
- The extent of this bias and the time for which this bias affects results depends on the size of the data window.

The historical model may provide a useful forecast of the average volatility or correlation over the next several years, but it cannot predict well over the short term. In fact we have argued that the only useful information that one can obtain by using this methodology is an indication of the possible range for a long term average volatility or correlation.

In the mid 1990s JP Morgan launched the RiskMetrics™ data and software suite. Their choice of volatility and correlation forecasting methodology helped to popularize the use of *exponentially weighted moving averages* (EWMA). This approach provides useful forecasts for volatility and correlation over the very short term, such as over the next day or week. However, it is of limited use for long term forecasting. The reasons for this are as follows:

- The forecast of volatility/correlation over all future horizons is simply taken to be the current estimate of volatility, because the underlying assumption in the model is that returns are i.i.d.
- The only choice facing the user is about the value of the smoothing constant, λ. Often an *ad hoc* choice is made, e.g. the same λ is taken for all series and a higher λ is chosen for a longer term forecast. The forecasts will depend crucially on the choice of λ, yet there is no statistical procedure to explain how to choose it.

Both equally and exponentially weighted moving average models assume returns are i.i.d., and under the further assumption that they are multivariate normally distributed we have derived standard errors and confidence intervals for equally and exponentially weighted moving average volatility and correlation forecasts. But empirical observations suggest that returns to financial assets are hardly ever independent and identical, let alone normally distributed. For these reasons more and more practitioners are basing their forecasts on GARCH models, which are introduced in the next chapter.

---

[40] We could also assume a multivariate t distribution, which is more realistic, but then statistical inference (e.g. measuring the precision of forecasts) is more difficult. By contrast, in the multivariate normal case we have derived some nice analytic formulae for the standard errors of moving average forecasts.

II.4
Introduction to GARCH Models

II.4.1 INTRODUCTION

The moving average models described in the previous chapter are based on the assumption that returns are independent and identically distributed (i.i.d.). So the volatility and correlation forecasts that are made from these models are simply equal to the current estimates. But we know that the i.i.d. assumption is very unrealistic. The volatility of financial asset returns changes over time, with periods when volatility is exceptionally high interspersed with periods when volatility is unusually low. This *volatility clustering* behaviour does, of course, depend on the frequency of the data – it would hardly occur in annual data, and may not be very evident in monthly data – but it is normally very obvious in daily data and even more obvious in intraday data.

There is a large body of empirical evidence on volatility clustering in financial markets that dates back to Mandelbrot (1963). Volatility clustering has important implications for risk measurement and for pricing and hedging options. Following a large shock to the market, volatility changes and the probability of another large shock is greatly increased. Portfolio risk measurement and option prices both need to take this into account. Unfortunately the moving average models that we have considered above, though simple, provide only a crude picture of the time variation in volatility. This is because the models assume volatility is constant and the only reason why estimates change over time is because of variations in the estimation sample data.

The *generalized autoregressive conditional heteroscedasticity* (GARCH) models of volatility that were introduced by Engle (1982) and Bollerslev (1986) are specifically designed to capture the volatility clustering of returns. The forecasts that are made from these models are not equal to the current estimate. Instead volatility can be higher or lower than average over the short term but as the forecast horizon increases the GARCH volatility forecasts converge to the long term volatility. Put another way, the GARCH model captures volatility clustering.

Why do we give these models the name *generalized autoregressive conditional heteroscedasticity*?

- The word *generalized* comes from the fact that the approach is based on Bollerslev's (1986) generalization of Engle's (1982) ARCH model;
- the approach is *autoregressive* because GARCH is a time series model with an autoregressive (regression on itself) form;
- and we speak of *conditional heteroscedasticity* because time variation in conditional variance is built into the model.

Clearly, to understand a GARCH model we must clarify the distinction between the unconditional variance and the conditional variance of a time series of returns. The *unconditional variance* is just the variance of the unconditional returns distribution, which is assumed constant over the entire data period considered. It can be thought of as the long term average variance over that period. For instance, if the model is the simple 'returns are i.i.d.' model then we can forget about the ordering of the returns in the sample and just estimate the sample variance using an equally weighted average of squared returns, or mean deviations of returns. This gives an estimate of the unconditional variance of the i.i.d. model. Later we will show how to estimate the unconditional variance of a GARCH model.

The *conditional variance*, on the other hand, will change at every point in time because it depends on the history of returns up to that point. That is, we account for the dynamic properties of returns by regarding their distribution at any point in time as being conditional on all the information up to that point. The distribution of a return at time t regards all the past returns up to and including time $t-1$ as being non-stochastic. We denote the *information set*, which is the set containing all the past returns up to and including time $t-1$, by I_{t-1}. The information set contains all the prices and returns that we can observe, like the *filtration* set in continuous time.

We write σ_t^2 to denote the conditional variance at time t. This is the variance *at time t*, conditional on the information set. That is, we assume that everything in the information set is not random because we have an observation on it.[1] When the conditional distributions of returns at every point in time are all normal we write:

$$r_t \,|I_{t-1} \sim N(0, \sigma_t^2).$$

This chapter provides a pedagogical introduction to the GARCH models that are commonly used by financial institutions to obtain volatility and correlation forecasts of asset and risk factor returns. Section II.4.2 explains the *symmetric normal GARCH* variance process, which is sometimes referred to as the 'plain vanilla' GARCH model. We explain how to estimate the model parameters by maximizing a likelihood function and illustrate this optimization with a simple Excel spreadsheet. Excel parameter estimates for GARCH are not recommended, so the estimates in this example are compared with those obtained using GARCH procedures in the Matlab and EViews software.[2] Then we explain how to use the estimated model to *forecast* the volatility for a financial asset or risk factor, and again we illustrate this in Excel.

The strength of GARCH is that it provides short and medium term volatility forecasts that are based on a proper econometric model. But its use for forecasting *long term volatility* is questionable. Hence, we describe how to use our personal view on the *long term volatility* in conjunction with the GARCH model. Fixing the long term volatility to be a pre-assigned value, such as 20% or 10% or any other value that analysts assume, is very simple to implement in the GARCH framework. We just fix the value of the GARCH constant and then only the GARCH lag and GARCH error parameters are estimated from the data. The lag and error parameters will then determine the short to medium term volatility forecasts that are consistent with our assumption about long term volatility.

The symmetric GARCH model assumes the response of the conditional variance to negative market shocks is exactly the same as its response to positive market shocks of the same magnitude. But then there is no possibility of a *leverage effect* where volatility increases

---

[1] In discrete time, whenever we use the term conditional variance (or conditional volatility or conditional covariance or conditional correlation) it will mean *conditional on the information set* at that time. However, in continuous time we can use the term conditional volatility (or conditional correlation, etc.) to mean that it is conditional on all sorts of things. For instance, *local volatility* is the square root of the conditional expected variance, conditional on the price at a given time in the future being at a given level. See Section III.4.3 for further details.
[2] These software packages, which estimate many different types of univariate and multivariate GARCH models, also provide standard errors for parameter estimates and other useful diagnostics on the goodness of fit of the GARCH model.

more following a negative shock than following a positive shock of the same magnitude. The leverage effect is pronounced in equity markets, where there is usually a strong negative correlation between the equity returns and the change in volatility.[3] The opposite asymmetry, where volatility increases more following a price rise than it does following an equivalent price fall, commonly occurs in commodity markets.

This type of *asymmetric volatility response* is easily captured by adjusting the error term in the GARCH model, as explained in Section II.4.3. Here we define the *asymmetric GARCH* (A-GARCH), *threshold GARCH* (GJR-GARCH) and *exponential GARCH* (E-GARCH) models, specifying their likelihood functions when errors are conditionally normal and deriving analytic formulae for their volatility forecasts. The E-GARCH is an asymmetric GARCH model that specifies not the conditional variance but the logarithm of the conditional volatility. We thus avoid the need for any parameter constraints. It is widely recognized that this model provides a better in-sample fit than other types of GARCH process. We motivate the reason for using exponential GARCH and derive an analytic formula for its volatility forecasts.[4] We explain how to impose the long term volatility in these models and again provide Excel spreadsheets for parameter estimation and volatility forecasting. The conditional variance equation allows yesterday's returns to influence today's volatility, but there is no symmetric feedback from volatility into the returns. We therefore end Section II.4.3 with the specification of the asymmetric GARCH *in mean* model which includes volatility in the conditional mean equation and thus captures a two-way causality between asset returns and changes in volatility.

Section II.4.4 extends the GARCH, A-GARCH, GJR-GARCH and E-GARCH models to the case where the conditional distributions of returns are not normally distributed but have a Student's *t* distribution. This way the GARCH model is better able to explain the heavy tails that we normally encounter in financial asset returns when they are measured at daily or higher frequency. The assumption of Student *t* errors does not alter the formulae used for generating volatility forecasts, but it does change the functional form for the likelihood function. The degrees of freedom (assumed constant) are an additional parameter to be estimated and the maximum likelihood optimization becomes rather more complex. Finding reasonable estimates for Student *t* GARCH processes using Excel Solver is rather optimistic to say the least; nevertheless we do provide a Student *t* GARCH spreadsheet.

Next we discuss a case study on the FTSE 100 index returns that compares the fit of GARCH, GJR-GARCH and E-GARCH with both normal and Student *t* errors. We utilize EViews and Matlab to compare the fit of these six different GARCH models. Not surprisingly, the best fit to the data is the *Student t E-GARCH* model.[5] We compare the volatility forecasts made by all six models for the average volatility over the next h trading days, with $h = 1, 2, \ldots, 250$. The forecasts are made at the end of August 2007, when the FTSE 100 was particularly volatile.

---

[3] For example, see the case study in Section III.4.4 for further details on the relationship between equity indices and their implied volatilities.

[4] In all GARCH models except the E-GARCH, the only way to ensure that the variance is always positive is to constrain the GARCH parameters. That is, we do not allow the GARCH constant, lag or error parameters to take certain values. As a result the maximum likelihood optimization routine often fails to converge to an interior solution (in other words, we can hit a boundary for one of the parameters). If this happens, the estimated GARCH model is useless for volatility forecasting. By contrast, E-GARCH is free of these constraints, it almost always provides the best in-sample fit, and the fact that it is based on volatility and not variance as the basic parameter makes it an extremely attractive model for option pricing. See Section III.4.3 for further details.

[5] However, in Chapter II.8 we introduce more advanced criteria for determining the best volatility forecasts. Just because the Student *t* E-GARCH model usually fits the data best, this does not mean that it provides the most accurate volatility forecasts.

Also in Section II.4.4 we introduce a GARCH model that allows volatility to exhibit regime-specific behaviour. This is *normal mixture GARCH* and it may be extended to *Markov switching GARCH* models. It is important to have a GARCH model that is able to capture regime-specific behaviour of volatility, particularly in equity and commodity markets. In particular, we recommend a two-state Markov switching E-GARCH model for capturing the observed behaviour of financial asset returns.

Whilst GARCH models have been very successful for forecasting statistical volatility, it is a formidable computational task to estimate a very large GARCH covariance matrix. There are a plethora of quite different specifications for multivariate GARCH processes, and it is essential that the analyst chooses the process that is most appropriate for the data being analysed. For instance, the specification of the multivariate GARCH model for interest rates should be different from the specification of the multivariate GARCH model for equities. This is because the dependency characteristics of different asset classes vary enormously. In Section II.4.5 we describe the *factor GARCH* model which may be applied to estimate and forecast very large *equity* covariance matrices using only a single univariate GARCH model on the market index. Then we describe the *dynamic conditional correlation GARCH* model that, in my opinion, is most useful for multivariate GARCH models on different currencies or different commodities.

However, when we require the covariance matrix forecast for a *term structure* of currency forwards, or a *term structure* of futures on a single commodity, then the *orthogonal GARCH* model is recommended. Orthogonal GARCH, which is covered in Section II.4.6, should also be used to forecast covariance matrices for interest rates of different maturities. A simple version of orthogonal GARCH is the *orthogonal exponentially weighted moving average* (O-EWMA) model. A case study in this section compares the forecasts obtained using O-GARCH with the RiskMetrics forecasts for the volatilities and correlation of energy futures.

Section II.4.7 provides many algorithms for simulating returns with different GARCH processes. We implement each algorithm in an Excel spreadsheet. Whilst simple univariate GARCH models allow one to simulate time series for returns that exhibit volatility clustering and heavy tails, *Markov switching GARCH* models allow us to simulate returns that switch between high and low volatility regimes. We demonstrate that only returns that are simulated from Markov switching GARCH models will display properties that reflect the typical characteristics of returns on financial assets. Finally, simulations from multivariate GARCH models are demonstrated, again in Excel. The multivariate GARCH structure allows one to simulate conditionally *correlated* sets of returns with very realistic time series features.

Some financial applications of GARCH models are surveyed in Section II.4.8. There are so many applications that we can provide only an overview here. We explain how to price path-dependent options using GARCH simulations, how to estimate value at risk using correlated GARCH simulations and how to use GARCH covariance matrices in portfolio optimization. Finally, Section II.4.9 summarizes and concludes.

There are so many different GARCH models available, so how do we choose the most appropriate one for our purposes? The answer cannot be determined by examining prediction errors because there is no observable process against which one can measure a prediction of volatility or correlation. The decision about which methodology to apply when constructing a covariance matrix should be related to the asset class, the data frequency and the horizon over which the matrix is to be estimated or forecast. But there are also many statistical tests and operational methodologies for evaluating the accuracy of GARCH models (and other volatility and correlation forecasting models). These are described in Chapter II.8.

The basis of a GARCH model is a simple linear regression. Hence, we assume that readers are already familiar with Chapter I.4. In fact, we shall be drawing quite heavily on material that is introduced in several of the chapters in Volume I. The case studies and almost all the examples in this chapter are implemented in Excel. The parameters for symmetric and asymmetric GARCH models, E-GARCH, Student's t GARCH, factor GARCH, and dynamic conditional correlation models are all estimated using the Excel Solver. This is not because I recommend the Solver as the best optimizer for GARCH. Far from it! The only reason why we estimate GARCH models in Excel is to make all the steps of estimating and forecasting with GARCH models completely transparent. Excel is a great learning tool. We have also used results from EViews and Matlab, which are two of the most powerful statistical packages with purpose-built GARCH optimization procedures. S-Plus also offers an extensive array of in-built GARCH procedures, including orthogonal GARCH in its latest release. Currently the most extensive software for GARCH modelling is that developed by Jurgen Doornik at the University of Oxford, called simply Ox.[6]

II.4.2 THE SYMMETRIC NORMAL GARCH MODEL

This section introduces the *symmetric normal GARCH* model that was developed by Bollerslev (1986). The GARCH model is a generalization of the *autoregressive conditional heteroscedasticity* (ARCH) model that was developed by Engle (1982). Rob Engle's subsequent contributions to research in this area won him the Nobel Prize in 2003.

II.4.2.1 Model Specification

The symmetric normal GARCH is the plain vanilla version of a GARCH model. It assumes that the dynamic behaviour of the conditional variance is given by the following *conditional variance equation*:

$$\sigma_t^2 = \omega + \alpha \varepsilon_{t-1}^2 + \beta \sigma_{t-1}^2, \quad \varepsilon_t \,|\, I_{t-1} \sim N(0, \sigma_t^2). \tag{II.4.1}$$

The GARCH *conditional volatility* is defined as the annualized square root of this conditional variance. The conditional variance and volatility are conditional on the information set.[7] Since the conditional variances at different points in time are related the process is not identically distributed and neither is it independent, because the second conditional moments, i.e. the conditional variances, at different points in time are related.

Conditional Mean Equation

In definition (II.4.1) ε_t denotes the *market shock* or *unexpected return* and is assumed to follow a conditional normal process with zero expected value and time varying conditional variance. The market shock is commonly taken as the mean deviation $(r_t - \bar{r})$ where r_t is the return at time t and $\bar{r} = T^{-1} \sum_{t=1}^{T} r_t$ is the sample mean.[8] More generally, the market shock is the error term from an ordinary simple linear regression.

[6] See http://www.doornik.com.
[7] The information set was defined in the Introduction. It is the discrete time version of the *filtration*. In other words, the information set I_t contains all relevant information up to time t, including all returns on this asset up to and including the return at time t.
[8] We use lower-case r to denote either log or percentage returns here. As the returns are usually daily, or sampled at an even higher frequency, there is not much difference between the log return and the percentage return, so we shall just use the term 'return' until Section II.4.8, where we are more explicit about which returns we are simulating.

In fact a GARCH model really consists of *two* equations: a conditional variance equation such as (II.4.1) and a *conditional mean equation*, which specifies the behaviour of the returns. The GARCH error ε_t is the error process in the conditional mean equation. If we do not bother to specify the conditional mean equation in the model, this implies that we assume it is the simplest conditional mean return equation, i.e.

$$ r_t = c + \varepsilon_t, \tag{II.4.2} $$

where c is a constant.[9] Since the ordinary least squares (OLS) estimate of c is $\bar{r}$ we often assume that $\varepsilon_t = r_t - \bar{r}$, as already mentioned above. However, to include the possibility that returns are autocorrelated the conditional mean equation could be an autoregressive model such as

$$ r_t = c + \varrho r_{t-1} + \varepsilon_t. \tag{II.4.3} $$

Long Term Volatility

In the absence of market shocks the GARCH variance will eventually settle down to a steady state value. This is the value $\bar{\sigma}^2$ such that $\sigma_t^2 = \bar{\sigma}^2$ for all t. We call $\bar{\sigma}^2$ the *unconditional variance* of the GARCH model. It corresponds to a *long term average value* of the conditional variance. The theoretical value of the GARCH long term or unconditional variance is *not* the same as the unconditional variance in a moving average volatility model. The moving average unconditional variance is called the i.i.d. variance because it is based on the i.i.d. returns assumption. The theoretical value of the unconditional variance in a GARCH model is clearly not based on the i.i.d. returns assumption. In fact, the GARCH unconditional variance differs depending on the GARCH model.

The long term or unconditional variance is found by substituting $\sigma_t^2 = \sigma_{t-1}^2 = \bar{\sigma}^2$ into the GARCH conditional variance equation. For instance, for the symmetric normal GARCH we use the fact that $E\left(\varepsilon_{t-1}^2\right) = \sigma_{t-1}^2$ and then put $\sigma_t^2 = \sigma_{t-1}^2 = \bar{\sigma}^2$ into (II.4.1) to obtain

$$ \bar{\sigma}^2 = \frac{\omega}{1 - (\alpha + \beta)}. \tag{II.4.4} $$

The *unconditional volatility* (also called *long term volatility*) of the symmetric GARCH model is the annualized square root of (II.4.4).

Vanilla GARCH Parameters

Clearly the parameter constraints $\omega > 0$, $\alpha + \beta < 1$ are needed to ensure that the unconditional variance is finite and positive. We also need to restrict the possible values of the GARCH parameters so that the conditional variance will always be positive. In fact the parameter constraints for the symmetric normal GARCH model (II.4.1) may be written together as

$$ \omega > 0, \quad \alpha, \beta \geq 0, \quad \alpha + \beta < 1. \tag{II.4.5} $$

Personally, I try to avoid imposing any constraints on the parameter estimation routine. If it is necessary to impose constraints such as (11.4.5) on the optimization then this indicates

---

[9] Note that our treatment of moving average models in the previous chapter assumed the sample mean return is zero. This assumption is only appropriate when returns are measured at the daily, or possibly weekly, frequency. When moving average models are based on monthly returns the mean deviation can be used in place of the return in our analysis. Also, at the daily frequency there may indeed be autocorrelation in returns, in which case the residual from (II.4.3) can be used in place of the return in the moving average model, as well as in the GARCH model.

that the model is inappropriate for the sample data and a different GARCH model should be used. Also, constraints usually result in a boundary value such as $\alpha = 0$ at the solution. In this case the estimated model is useless for simulations or forecasting (or both).

The parameters of the symmetric normal GARCH model have a natural interpretation in terms of the reaction to market shocks and the mean reversion of volatility following a shock:

- The *GARCH error* parameter α measures the reaction of conditional volatility to market shocks. When α is relatively large (e.g. above 0.1) then volatility is very sensitive to market events.
- The *GARCH lag* parameter β measures the persistence in conditional volatility irrespective of anything happening in the market. When β is relatively large (e.g. above 0.9) then volatility takes a long time to die out following a crisis in the market.
- The sum $\alpha + \beta$ determines the *rate of convergence* of the conditional volatility to the long term average level. When $\alpha + \beta$ is relatively large (e.g. above 0.99) then the term structure of volatility forecasts from the GARCH model is relatively flat.[10]
- The *GARCH constant* parameter ω, together with the sum $\alpha + \beta$, determines the level of the long term average volatility, i.e. the *unconditional volatility* in the GARCH model. When $\omega/(1 - \alpha - \beta)$ is relatively large (its magnitude is related to the magnitude of the squared returns) then the long term volatility in the market is relatively high.

II.4.2.2   Parameter Estimation

GARCH models are often estimated on daily or intraday data, sometimes on weekly data and almost never on monthly data. This is because the volatility clustering effects in financial asset returns disappear when returns are measured over long time intervals such as a month. In this section we provide an example of estimating the parameters in (II.4.1) on daily data. Then we transform the resulting conditional variance time series into a time series for GARCH volatility, by annualizing in the usual way.[11]

GARCH parameters are estimated by *maximizing the value of the log likelihood function*. When the conditional distribution of the error process is normal with expectation 0 and variance σ_t^2 we can use the formulation of the normal log likelihood function that was derived in Example I.3.15. But this time we use *time varying* mean and variance. Hence, maximizing the symmetric normal GARCH likelihood reduces to the problem of maximizing[12]

$$\ln L(\theta) = -\frac{1}{2} \sum_{t=1}^{T} \left(\ln(\sigma_t^2) + \left(\frac{\varepsilon_t}{\sigma_t} \right)^2 \right), \qquad (II.4.6)$$

where θ denotes the parameters of the conditional variance equation. Equivalently, we could minimize

$$-2 \ln L(\theta) = \sum_{t=1}^{T} \left(\ln(\sigma_t^2) + \left(\frac{\varepsilon_t}{\sigma_t} \right)^2 \right). \qquad (II.4.7)$$

---

[10] They are linked to the mean reversion parameters and long term variance in the continuous time model described in Section I.3.7.2.
[11] That is, we take the square root of the variance at each point in time, and multiply this by the square root of 250.
[12] We omit the constant in the log likelihood function since this does not affect optimal parameter values.

For the symmetric GARCH model $\theta = (\omega, \alpha, \beta)$. The dependence of the log likelihood on ω, α and β arises because σ_t is given by (II.4.1).

Maximization of the relatively simple log likelihood function (II.4.6) should encounter few convergence problems. The same applies to maximum likelihood estimation of most univariate GARCH models, provided the data are well behaved. Changes in the data will induce some changes in the coefficient estimates, but if the model is 'well tuned' the parameter estimates should not change greatly as new data arrive unless there are real structural breaks in the data generation process.

A certain minimum amount of data is necessary for the likelihood function to be well defined. Often several years of daily data are necessary to ensure proper convergence of the model. If too few observations are used then parameter estimates may lack robustness, so it is a good idea to check the robustness of the parameter estimates by rolling the data period for the estimations and plotting the parameters obtained over time, to ensure that they evolve relatively smoothly.

After estimating the GARCH model parameters standard econometric packages will automatically output the *estimated standard errors* of these estimators. The computational algorithm used normally produces an entire covariance matrix of the estimated variances and covariances of the parameter estimators. This matrix is derived from the *information matrix* of second derivatives of the likelihood function with respect to each of the model parameters.[13] Most packages only automatically quote the square root of the diagonal elements, i.e. the estimated standard errors of the parameter estimates, but it is usually possible to retrieve the entire estimated covariance matrix. The t ratio, which measures the significance of the parameter estimate, is defined in the usual way. That is, it is the ratio of the parameter estimate to the estimated standard error.

The Excel spreadsheet for Example II.4.1 demonstrates how the likelihood function (II.4.6) is calculated, and we use the Excel Solver to maximize the value of (II.4.6) subject to the parameter constraints (II.4.5). In subsequent examples we shall also attempt to use Excel Solver to estimate the parameters of other GARCH models. Our reason for this is that the transparency of an Excel spreadsheet helps readers to understand the process of GARCH parameter estimation. However, it must be stressed that the estimation of GARCH parameters is often too complex to be done using Excel Solver. Convergence problems are common because the log likelihood surface can be very flat.[14] All that one can hope to achieve from using the Solver is a very approximate idea of the optimal parameter estimates. To estimate GARCH parameters in practice readers should use Ox, or one of the purpose-built algorithms for maximizing GARCH likelihood functions that are provided in most econometric software packages. Some are better than others, and a review of various different packages for GARCH optimization is given by Brooks et al. (2003).

---

[13] This is defined in Section I.3.6.3.

[14] Convergence problems with GARCH models can also arise because the gradient algorithm used to maximize the likelihood function has hit a boundary. If there are obvious outliers in the data then it is very likely that the iteration will return the value 0 or 1 for either the alpha or the beta parameter (or both). It may be safe to remove a single outlier if the circumstances that produced the outlier are thought to be unlikely to happen in future. Alternatively, changing the starting values of the parameters or changing the data set so that the likelihood function has a different gradient at the beginning of the search might mitigate the boundary problem. Otherwise the model specification will have to be changed. A sure sign of using the wrong GARCH specification is when the iteration refuses to converge at all, or returns a boundary solution, even after you have checked the data for outliers, changed the starting values or chosen a different data period.

EXAMPLE II.4.1: GARCH ESTIMATES OF FTSE 100 VOLATILITY

Estimate the parameters of a symmetric normal GARCH model for the FTSE 100 using a
sample of daily data from 3 January 1995 to 29 August 2007.

SOLUTION   In the spreadsheet for this example we start with some 'initial values' i.e.
guesses for the values of the parameters, such as $\omega = 0.00001$, $\alpha = 0.09$ and $\beta = 0.89$.[15] The
size of ω is related to the frequency of the data; here we have daily returns, so ω will be
quite small. Given these values, we can calculate the time series for the GARCH conditional
variance using (II.4.1) and then we can find the likelihood of each observation, i.e. each
term in the summation in (II.4.6). Summing these gives the log likelihood function value
shown in cell K7. Now we apply Excel Solver, with the settings shown in Figure II.4.1.[16]
Note that the constraints (II.4.5) have been added.

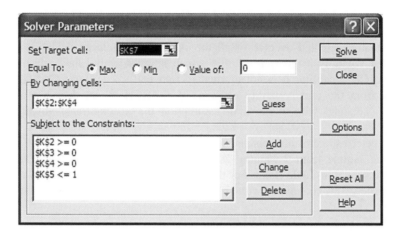

Figure II.4.1   Solver settings for GARCH estimation in Excel

Finally, setting Solver to work produces the following parameter estimates:

$$\hat{\omega} = 9.997 \times 10^{-7}, \quad \hat{\alpha} = 0.0869, \quad \hat{\beta} = 0.9055.$$

The corresponding long term volatility estimate given by (II.4.4) is 18.20% and the maximized log likelihood value is 13,445.95. We compare these results with those obtained,
using identical data, from EViews and Matlab. Both these packages can estimate GARCH
parameters using the *Levenberg–Marquardt* algorithm, which is arguably the best optimization
algorithm for GARCH models.[17]

---

[15] Excel Solver is very sensitive to starting values. Try using the 'Guess' button for setting the initial values. You should try several
starting values and check the value of the optimized log likelihood each time, hopefully converging to the same solution but if not
use the parameter estimates that correspond to the highest value of the log likelihood.
[16] These should be brought up as default settings when you click on Tools and then on Solver. However, you may need to add in
the Solver if it is not already added in.
[17] The Levenberg–Marquardt algorithm is described in Section I.5.4.3.

Table II.4.1 EViews and Matlab estimation of FTSE 100 symmetric normal GARCH

1995–2007	EViews		Matlab	
	Estimate	t ratio	Estimate	t ratio
ω	9.92E-07	3.94428	9.76E-07	3.90029
α	0.08350	9.38145	0.08415	9.39769
β	0.90845	96.02725	0.90798	95.75222
Long term volatility	17.55%		17.61%	
Log likelihood	13445.97		13445.99	

The parameter estimates are shown in Table II.4.1.[18] The estimated parameters, and consequently also the long term volatility estimates, differ slightly depending on the implementation of the optimization algorithm. This is to be expected, given the highly non-linear nature of the problem. Note that the long term volatility estimate from the GARCH models differs markedly from the unconditional volatility that is estimated using an equally weighted average of all the squared return mean deviations. The i.i.d. unconditional volatility estimate is 16.89% which is considerably lower than the unconditional GARCH volatility. It is not unusual to find that a long term GARCH volatility is different from the i.i.d. volatility estimate. A GARCH model does not assume that returns are i.i.d., and without the i.i.d. assumption the unconditional volatility will be different.[19]

The parameter estimates also change when we change the sample data.[20] For instance, based on the sample from 2 January 2003 to 29 August 2007 the GARCH parameter estimates are shown in Table II.4.2. For this period the long term volatility is estimated to be approximately 13%, compared with approximately 17.5% for the period 1995–2007.

Table II.4.2 Estimation of FTSE 100 symmetric normal GARCH, 2003–2007

2003–2007	Excel	EViews		Matlab	
	Estimate	Estimate	t ratio	Estimate	t ratio
ω	1.527E-06	1.63E-06	2.97287	1.63E-06	2.93389
α	0.0952	0.09839	6.18307	0.10052	6.28054
β	0.8824	0.87780	42.49683	0.87624	42.14921
Long term volatility	13.08%	13.08%		13.24%	
Log likelihood	5178.22	5178.26		5178.26	

It is typical that the estimate of the GARCH constant $\hat{\omega}$ is particularly sensitive to the choice of sample data. It is the change in the GARCH constant much more than the change in the reaction and persistence parameters that determines the marked change in the long

---

[18] Roughly speaking, a t ratio in excess of 2 indicates that the explanatory variable is significant. In the table we use the maximized value of the log likelihood according to the formulation (II.4.6) to compute the log likelihood in each case.
[19] We already know this from, for example, Section II.3.2.4.
[20] Readers can change the in-sample data period in the Excel spreadsheets simply by averaging the mean return and summing the log likelihood over a different range.

term volatility. The FTSE 100 volatility was only slightly more reactive and less persistent during the 2003–2007 period than it was during the 1995–2007 period. But the GARCH constant $\hat{\omega}$ for 2003–2007 is much lower because the FTSE 100 market was exceptionally volatile between 2000 and 2002.

II.4.2.3 Volatility Estimates

The time series of estimated GARCH volatilities is given by taking the annualized square root of the GARCH variance estimates. For instance, using the Excel parameter estimates for 2003–2007 from Table II.4.2, we apply the estimated model

$$\hat{\sigma}_t^2 = 1.531 \times 10^{-6} + 0.0952(r_{t-1} - \bar{r})^2 + 0.8824\hat{\sigma}_{t-1}^2$$

to all returns at time t, where t ranges over all the data in the sample. Then we multiply the result by 250 and take the square root. This gives the series labelled *GARCH volatility* in Figure II.4.2.

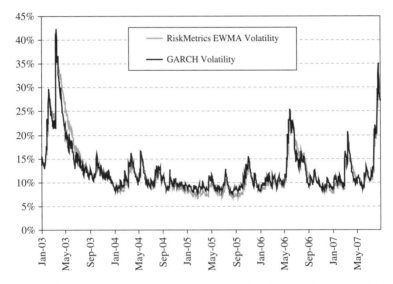

Figure II.4.2 Comparison of GARCH and EWMA volatilities for the FTSE 100

Figure II.4.2 compares the GARCH volatility, based on the symmetric normal GARCH model and estimated using data between 2 January 2003 and 29 August 2007, with the RiskMetrics daily volatility over the same period.[21] The RiskMetrics volatility is calculated using a EWMA with $\lambda = 0.94$. But the GARCH model has a persistence parameter of only 0.8824, which is considerably less than 0.94. Hence, the GARCH volatility is less persistent to market shocks than the RiskMetrics volatility. The extra persistence in the RiskMetrics volatility estimate is very evident during 2003.

---

[21] The RiskMetrics methodology is described in Section II.3.8.6.

II.4.2.4   GARCH Volatility Forecasts

In Figure II.4.2 there was not a huge difference between the GARCH and RiskMetrics volatility *estimates* because the optimal values of the GARCH α and β parameters were not hugely different from the RiskMetrics daily EWMA values for reaction and persistence (these are 0.06 and 0.94, respectively). However, there is a considerable difference between the *forecasts* obtained from these two models. The EWMA volatility forecast at some point in time is the same as the EWMA estimate made at that point in time, and the volatility forecasts are constant for all horizons.[22] But the GARCH forecasts are not only different from the GARCH volatility estimates, they also depend on the horizon of the forecast.

In any GARCH model the estimate of the GARCH volatility at the end of the sample period is the 1-day-ahead volatility forecast on that day. However, the long term volatility in a GARCH model can be very different from this. For instance, in the example above the long term volatility was about 13% but the 1-day-ahead volatility forecast on 29 August 2007 was over 27%. In this subsection we explain how the forecasts for horizons between 1 day and the long term can be obtained from a single estimated GARCH model.[23]

More specifically, we can use the GARCH parameter estimates to generate *forward daily volatility* forecasts and *term structure* volatility forecasts. All forecasts are made on the last day of the sample. To see how these forecasts are generated, let us first write the estimated model as

$$\hat{\sigma}_t^2 = \hat{\omega} + \hat{\alpha}\hat{\varepsilon}_{t-1}^2 + \hat{\beta}\hat{\sigma}_{t-1}^2, \quad t = 1, \dots, T, \tag{II.4.8}$$

where T is the last day in the sample. Assuming the returns data are daily, the 1-day-ahead variance forecast at time T is

$$\hat{\sigma}_{T+1}^2 = \hat{\omega} + \hat{\alpha}\hat{\varepsilon}_T^2 + \hat{\beta}\hat{\sigma}_T^2. \tag{II.4.9}$$

We can observe $\hat{\varepsilon}_T$ because it is the last residual in the GARCH model. But we do not know ε_{T+1} at time T. To forecast the forward variance from day $T+1$ to day $T+2$, i.e. the two-day-ahead forward variance, we use the expectation of ε_{T+1}^2 in the forecast. Since ε_t is an error its conditional expectation is 0, and so $E_T\left(\varepsilon_{T+1}^2\right) = \sigma_{T+1}^2$. Thus,

$$\hat{\sigma}_{T+2}^2 = \hat{\omega} + \hat{\alpha}E_T\left(\varepsilon_{T+1}^2\right) + \hat{\beta}\hat{\sigma}_{T+1}^2 = \hat{\omega} + \left(\hat{\alpha} + \hat{\beta}\right)\hat{\sigma}_{T+1}^2. \tag{II.4.10}$$

In general, the forecast of the forward daily variance from day $T+S$ to day $T+S+1$ is given by

$$\hat{\sigma}_{T+S+1}^2 = \hat{\omega} + \left(\hat{\alpha} + \hat{\beta}\right)\hat{\sigma}_{T+S}^2. \tag{II.4.11}$$

We now use these forward daily variance forecasts to obtain a forecast for the GARCH *term structure* of volatilities, in other words a forecast for the *average* volatility over different periods of time. For instance, suppose we want to forecast average volatility from now (the end of the estimation sample) over the next h days,[24] for $h = 1, 2, \dots$. Having calculated

---

[22] For instance, the average volatility that is forecast over the next year is the same as the average volatility that is forecast over the next week.

[23] In a GARCH model the time taken for the forecasts to converge to a steady state depends on the parameters. For instance, in vanilla GARCH the higher is $\alpha + \beta$ the longer it takes for the forecast to converge. So the long term steady state volatility could be reached in one year, or more or less, depending on the parameters.

[24] Note that if the returns data were weekly we would compute the average volatility over the next h *weeks*, for $h = 1, 2, \dots$.

the forward daily variance forecasts for $S = 0, 1, 2, \ldots$ using (II.4.11), we now need to average them. For instance, to obtain a forecast of the average volatility over the next 10 days we average all the values obtained from (II.4.11) for $S = 0, 1, \ldots, 9$. This is then converted to a volatility using the appropriate annualizing factor, which is 250 since we have assumed the model was estimated using daily data with 250 trading days per year.[25]

For another example, suppose we want to forecast the average volatility over the period $T + 30$ to $T + 60$, such as would be the case when pricing a forward start option which starts 30 days from now and expires in 60 days. Then we average the values obtained from (II.4.11) for $S = 30, 31, \ldots, 60$. This is again converted to volatility by multiplying the result by 250 and taking the square root.

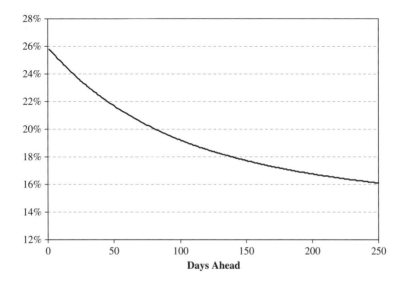

Figure II.4.3 Term structure GARCH volatility forecast for FTSE 100, 29 August 2007

Figure II.4.3 illustrates the GARCH term structure for the FTSE 100 on 29 August 2007, based on the GARCH model used for Figure II.4.2. The average volatility over the next h days for $h = 1, \ldots, 250$ days ahead is shown as the exponentially decreasing function starting at just under 26% for the forecast of volatility on 30 August 2007 and decreasing gradually towards the long term level of 13%. As h increases the GARCH term structure forecasts always converge to the long term average volatility. For instance, the forecast of average volatility over the period from 30 August to 13 September 2007 (i.e. the next 10 trading days) days is 24.88%, over the next 50 trading days it is 21.7%, and so forth.

During relatively volatile periods, such as the period chosen in the example above, the term structure forecasts converge from above: the average volatility decreases as the forecast horizon increases. However, during relatively tranquil periods the GARCH forecasts converge from below. This type of mean reversion in volatility is also evident from implied

---

[25] Be careful with the annualization factor here. If instead of *averaging* the forward variances we had *summed* them to obtain a 10-day variance, then the annualizing factor for converting a 10-day variance into volatility would be 25 and not 250.

volatilities of market prices of options of different maturities but the same strike, which is one of the reasons why GARCH models have become so popular amongst practitioners. Equally and exponentially weighted moving average forecasts have no such term structure: the current volatility estimate is the forecast for all horizons. Another advantage of GARCH is that the parameters can be estimated optimally whereas the value chosen for λ in a EWMA, or the estimation sample size in the equally weighted model, is usually based on an *ad hoc* and subjective criterion.

II.4.2.5   Imposing Long Term Volatility

GARCH volatility term structure forecasts are like implied volatility term structures – they converge to their long term average (i.e. unconditional) volatility. However, the unconditional volatility estimated from a GARCH model is not the same as the implied volatility that is backed out from a long term option. In fact, neither of these long term volatilities is usually very accurate. Forecasting long term volatility is an extremely difficult task.

In Example II.4.1 we saw that the long term volatility forecast is very sensitive to small changes in the estimated values of the GARCH model parameters, and this problem becomes increasingly obvious later when we consider more complex GARCH models. It therefore makes a lot of sense to impose the unconditional volatility on the GARCH model. Thus one can take a *personal view* on long term volatility and then use the GARCH model to fill in the forecasts of volatility over the next day, week, month etc. that are consistent with this view. Another term given to this is *volatility targeting*.

Our main reason for imposing the long term volatility is that any GARCH parameter estimate, but particularly the estimate of the GARCH constant, is sensitive to the historic data used for the model. When the sample covers several years during which there have been some extreme market movements the estimate of the GARCH constant and hence also the long term volatility estimate can be very high. This happens even if the market has been stable for some time. There is a trade-off between having enough data for parameter estimates to be stable, and too much data so that the long term GARCH forecasts do not properly reflect the current market conditions. When choosing the time span of historical data used for estimating a GARCH model the first consideration is whether major market events from several years ago should be influencing forecasts today. For example, we have seen that the standard GARCH unconditional volatility of the FTSE 100 index is about 13% if based on daily data from 2003 to 2007, but about 17.5% if based on daily data from 1995 to 2007. Also, including Black Monday (19 October 1987) in any equity GARCH model will have the effect of raising long term volatility forecasts by several percent.

In short, the choice of historical data period has a significant effect on the long term GARCH volatility estimate. This is not surprising, since it also has a significant effect on the volatility estimated using the equally weighted average method. For this reason we may prefer to impose a personal view for long term volatility. The beauty of GARCH is that it allows one to estimate the mean reversion of volatility to this long term level, whether it is estimated or imposed.

To understand the simple mechanism by which we impose the long term volatility in GARCH, let us formulate the symmetric GARCH model in a slightly different form. We substitute (II.4.4) into (II.4.1) and rearrange. This gives an alternative specification of the symmetric GARCH model in terms of deviations of conditional variance from the long term average variance:

$$\left(\sigma_t^2 - \bar{\sigma}^2\right) = \alpha\left(\varepsilon_{t-1}^2 - \bar{\sigma}^2\right) + \beta\left(\sigma_{t-1}^2 - \bar{\sigma}^2\right) \tag{II.4.12}$$

or, equivalently,

$$\sigma_t^2 = \left[\beta\sigma_{t-1}^2 + (1-\beta)\bar{\sigma}^2\right] + \alpha\left(\varepsilon_{t-1}^2 - \bar{\sigma}^2\right). \tag{II.4.13}$$

The term in square brackets in (II.4.13) gives a point on the line between σ_{t-1}^2 and $\bar{\sigma}^2$, as depicted in Figure II.4.4. Notice that this figure illustrates the *mean reversion of volatility*, the mean being the long term average volatility. In financial data β is much closer to 1 than to 0, therefore the first term in (II.4.13) will be closer to σ_{t-1}^2 than to $\bar{\sigma}^2$ as we have drawn in the diagram. So this first part of the volatility response will increase if $\sigma_{t-1}^2 < \bar{\sigma}^2$ as in Figure II.4.4(a), and decrease if $\sigma_{t-1}^2 > \bar{\sigma}^2$ as in Figure II.4.4(b).

(a) *Current volatility lower than average* ⇒ *volatility increases:*

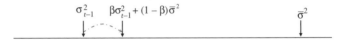

(b) *Current volatility greater than average* ⇒ *volatility decreases:*

Figure II.4.4   The mean reversion effect in GARCH volatility

The second term in (II.4.13) has an effect that depends on how close the market shock ε_{t-1} is to the long term volatility. Suppose we have a large positive or negative market shock, so the size of ε_{t-1} is larger than the size of returns that are normally expected, given the long term volatility level. Then, regardless of the sign of ε_{t-1}, the volatility is likely to increase even if $\sigma_{t-1}^2 > \bar{\sigma}^2$. Hence, if volatility is higher than its long term average a large market shock will make volatility increase away from the long term average. But a market shock will reinforce the mean reversion if volatility is lower than its long term average.

With the formulation (II.4.12) of the symmetric GARCH model we can impose any value we like for the long term average volatility and then estimate, by maximum likelihood, the reaction and mean reversion parameters that are consistent with this value. The spreadsheet for the following example uses Excel Solver to estimate the symmetric normal GARCH parameters α and β given any (sensible) value for long term volatility that you, the reader, may wish to impose.

EXAMPLE II.4.2: IMPOSING A VALUE FOR LONG TERM VOLATILITY IN GARCH

What would the GARCH term structure for the FTSE 100 on 29 August 2007 look like if you believed that the long term average volatility were 10% instead of its estimated value? Estimate the GARCH lag and error parameters that are consistent with this view, using the sample period from 2 January 2003 to 29 August 2007.

SOLUTION   Not surprisingly, when we impose a long term volatility of only 10% we
obtain estimates for the reaction and persistence parameters that are different from those in
Table II.4.2. The maximum value of the likelihood occurs when $\hat{\alpha} = 0.0798$ and $\hat{\beta} = 0.8936$
and the implied value of $\hat{\omega}$ is 1.066×10^{-6}. With these parameters the GARCH term structure
will converge to the long term average level of 10%.

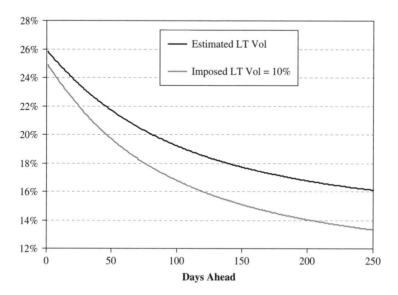

Figure II.4.5   Effect of imposing long term volatility on GARCH term structure

Figure II.4.5 compares this new term structure with the freely estimated term structure of
Figure II.4.3. We know from Table II.4.2 that the estimated long term volatility is 13.08%,
and from Figure II.4.2 we also know that the estimate of FTSE volatility on 29 August 2007
was unusually high. In fact from the spreadsheet for that figure we can see that it is 27.28%.
A substantial difference between these two volatility term structure forecasts is apparent.
For instance, the average volatility over the next 50 days is forecast to be 21.70% according
to the GARCH model that is based on historical data alone. However, when we impose a
personal view that the long term volatility will be 10% then the average volatility over the
next 50 days is forecast to be only 19.71%.

The long term volatility is an important parameter in option pricing models. Most option
pricing models include a mean reversion mechanism in the volatility diffusion, where the
spot volatility, long term volatility, speed of mean reversion and volatility of volatility are
parameters to be calibrated to the current prices of European calls and puts.[26] In this setting
the long term volatility is the most difficult parameter to estimate because the majority of
liquid options are fairly short term and therefore contain little information about long term
volatility.

---

[26] When market data on standard European options are not available because the options are not liquid, the parameters may be
obtained from time series of returns. More recently, calibration models have used a mixture of time series and option market data.
See Section III.4 for further details.

Hence, it makes sense to try several *scenarios* for long term volatility, which could be based on the equally weighted volatility range as explained in Section II.3.6.3. For each value in this range the GARCH model allows us to forecast the short and medium term volatilities that are consistent with this long term volatility forecast. Then if we represent our personal views about long term volatility by a distribution over the range of possible long term forecasts, as Harry does in Section II.3.6.3, the GARCH model allows us to translate these views into a distribution of forecasts for 10-day volatility, or 20-day volatility or indeed volatility over *any* future horizon. These distributions are formed using a combination of personal views and historical data.

II.4.2.6 Comparison of GARCH and EWMA Volatility Models

The exponentially weighted moving average model may be thought of as a simplified version of a symmetric normal GARCH model. But the model has no constant term and the lag and error parameters sum to 1. Hence, the unconditional variance (II.4.4) is not defined and the EWMA forecasts must remain constant at the current variance estimate.

GARCH models have many advantages over EWMA which we summarize as follows:

- Parameters are estimated optimally using maximum likelihood.
- The reaction and persistence coefficients are estimated separately, so a high persistence in volatility following a market shock is not automatically associated with a low reaction to market shocks, as it is in EWMA models.
- The long term average volatility in a GARCH model may be forecast from the estimated parameters. Alternatively, it can be imposed on the model before the reaction and persistence parameters are estimated. However, in the EWMA model the long term average volatility is the same as the volatility over any other period because the volatility term structure is constant.
- GARCH volatility forecasts are not constant as they are in EWMA. Instead the term structure of volatility that is forecast from a GARCH model will mean-revert to the long term average volatility, in a similar fashion to that observed in term structures of implied volatility. For almost all GARCH models these term structures are simple to construct using analytic formulae such as those derived in Section II.4.2.4.

II.4.3 ASYMMETRIC GARCH MODELS

There are many types of GARCH models that modify the conditional variance equation (II.4.1) to include additional features. Typically, the choice of GARCH model will depend on the asset type and the frequency of the data. For instance, a symmetric normal GARCH model might be satisfactory for interest rates and foreign exchange rates at the weekly frequency. However, an *asymmetric* GARCH model is almost always the better fit to daily data, and for equities, equity indices and commodities at any frequency.

The reason why asymmetric GARCH models should be used for equities and commodities is that equity market volatility increases are more pronounced following a large negative return than they are following a positive return of the same size. This so-called *leverage effect* arises because as a stock price falls the debt–equity ratio increases, since debt financing usually takes some time to change, and the firm becomes more highly leveraged.

As a result the future of the firm becomes more uncertain, and consequently the stock price becomes more volatile. However, when the stock price rises by a similar amount we do not experience the same amount of volatility because a price rise is 'good news'. The result is a negative correlation between equity returns and volatility. The opposite asymmetry can occur in commodity markets: a price rise is 'bad news' for the consumers so commodity price rises often have a destabilizing effect. For this reason volatility in commodity markets tends to increase more after a positive return than after a negative return.[27]

Clearly asymmetric GARCH is absolutely necessary for capturing the behaviour of volatility in equity and commodity markets. Even interest rates and foreign exchange rates require asymmetric effects when data are sampled daily or at an intraday frequency. This section introduces three GARCH models that allow volatility to respond asymmetrically to positive and negative returns.

II.4.3.1   A-GARCH

The *asymmetric GARCH* or A-GARCH model simply adds another parameter to the symmetric GARCH model so that it has a mechanism to capture asymmetric volatility response. The asymmetric GARCH model was initially suggested by Engle (1990) and subsequently discussed in Engle and Ng (1993). This model takes the form

$$\sigma_t^2 = \omega + \alpha(\varepsilon_{t-1} - \lambda)^2 + \beta\sigma_{t-1}^2, \tag{II.4.14}$$

where the extra parameter λ captures the leverage effect.

Parameter estimation for the normal A-GARCH is based on maximization of the likelihood function (II.4.6), but note that σ_t now depends on the extra parameter λ. The constraints on the GARCH constant, lag and error parameters are the same as in (II.4.5) and there is no constraint on λ. If $\lambda > 0$, then $(\varepsilon_{t-1} - \lambda)^2$ will be larger when the market shock is negative than when it is positive. The opposite will happen if $\lambda < 0$. Hence, it usually happens that estimating (II.4.14) on equity returns produces a positive value for λ, but on commodity returns a negative value for λ is more common.

To calculate the long term variance in the model (II.4.14) we use the fact that $E(\varepsilon_t^2) = \sigma_t^2$ and then assume $\sigma_t^2 = \bar{\sigma}^2$ for all t. This yields the following formula for the long term variance of the A-GARCH model:

$$\bar{\sigma}^2 = \frac{\omega + \lambda^2\alpha}{1 - (\alpha + \beta)}. \tag{II.4.15}$$

EXAMPLE II.4.3: AN ASYMMETRIC GARCH MODEL FOR THE FTSE 100

Estimate the parameters of the asymmetric normal GARCH model (II.4.14) for the FTSE 100 index, using our sample of daily data from 3 January 1995 to 29 August 2007. Also estimate the long term volatility of the FTSE 100 index based on this model.

---

[27] However, a price rise can be good for the producers, and for the speculators (depending on the sign of their position) so the correlation between commodity returns and volatility can be negative as well as positive.

SOLUTION   The spreadsheet for this example uses Excel Solver to maximize the likelihood.[28] The resulting parameter estimates are compared with those for the symmetric GARCH model, also obtained using Excel Solver, and the results are shown in Table II.4.3. As expected, the leverage parameter estimate is positive. The asymmetric model also appears to be a better fit than the symmetric model because the value of the log likelihood is greater. This is to be expected because it has an extra parameter.

Table II.4.3   Comparison of symmetric and asymmetric GARCH models for the FTSE 100

Model	Symmetric	Asymmetric
ω	9.997×10^{-7}	9.92×10^{-7}
α	0.08691	0.083567
β	0.90554	0.908269
λ	—	0.000242
$\alpha + \beta$	0.99245	0.99184
Long term volatility	18.20%	17.48%
Log likelihood	13445.95	13448.78

Having obtained the parameter estimates, we forecast volatility as follows. The one-step-ahead variance forecast is

$$\hat{\sigma}_{T+1}^2 = \hat{\omega} + \hat{\alpha}\left(\hat{\varepsilon}_T - \hat{\lambda}\right)^2 + \hat{\beta}\hat{\sigma}_T^2. \tag{II.4.16}$$

For the S-step-ahead variance forecasts, $S > 1$, equation (II.4.11) needs to be modified to

$$\hat{\sigma}_{T+S+1}^2 = \left(\hat{\omega} + \hat{\lambda}^2\hat{\alpha}\right) + \left(\hat{\alpha} + \hat{\beta}\right)\hat{\sigma}_{T+S}^2. \tag{II.4.17}$$

Otherwise, the term structure volatility forecasts are calculated as before, i.e. the average variance over the next h periods is the average of the S-step-ahead forward variance forecasts for $S = 1, \ldots, h$. This is then converted to a volatility using the appropriate annualizing factor, e.g. assuming 250 trading days per year. The term structure volatility forecasts will converge to the long term volatility based on the long term variance estimator (II.4.15).

As with the symmetric or any other GARCH model, the forward daily variance forecasts may also be used to forecast *forward average volatilities*, such as the average volatility starting 1 month from now and ending in two months' time. One only needs to start averaging the forward daily variances at some time in the future. This type of forward starting volatility forecast is very useful for pricing forward start options and cliquet options.[29]

It is also possible, and often desirable for reasons already clarified above, to impose long term volatility in the A-GARCH model. Substituting (II.4.15) into (II.4.14) gives

$$\left(\sigma_t^2 - \bar{\sigma}^2\right) = \alpha\left([\varepsilon_{t-1} - \lambda]^2 - \bar{\sigma}^2 - \lambda^2\right) + \beta\left(\sigma_{t-1}^2 - \bar{\sigma}^2\right) \tag{II.4.18}$$

[28] This is not easy because Solver is not a sufficiently powerful optimizer for GARCH models – so see the hints in the spreadsheet on maximizing the likelihood.
[29] Pricing formulae for these and other exotic options are given in Section III.3.8.

or, equivalently,

$$\sigma_t^2 = \left[\beta\sigma_{t-1}^2 + (1-\beta)\,\bar\sigma^2\right] + \alpha\left(\left[\varepsilon_{t-1} - \lambda\right]^2 - \bar\sigma^2 - \lambda^2\right). \tag{II.4.19}$$

The mean reversion effect is the same as in the symmetric GARCH model, but the reaction to market shocks is asymmetric. When the leverage parameter is positive, as is usually the case in equity markets, a positive shock is more likely to reduce the volatility than it is in the symmetric model. Likewise, a negative shock is more likely to increase the volatility in the asymmetric model than in the symmetric model. Whether these effects reinforce or counteract the mean reversion in volatility again depends on whether the current volatility is above or below the long term average level.

II.4.3.2   GJR-GARCH

An alternative version of the asymmetric model of Engle (1990) is the GJR-GARCH model of Glosten *et al.* (1993). Again there is a single extra 'leverage' parameter, but this time the asymmetric response is rewritten to specifically augment the volatility response from only the negative market shocks:

$$\sigma_t^2 = \omega + \alpha\varepsilon_{t-1}^2 + \lambda 1_{\{\varepsilon_{t-1}<0\}}\varepsilon_{t-1}^2 + \beta\sigma_{t-1}^2, \tag{II.4.20}$$

where the indicator function $1_{\{\varepsilon_t<0\}} = 1$ if $\varepsilon_t < 0$, and 0 otherwise. Parameter estimation is based on the usual normal GARCH likelihood function (II.4.6), where again σ_t depends on the extra parameter λ.

GJR-GARCH is really just an alternative formulation to (II.4.14). Both models simply modify the symmetric GARCH equation to capture an effect where negative shocks have a greater volatility impact than positive shocks. Consequently, there is usually very little to choose between the two formulations in practice. Results from either the GJR-GARCH or the A-GARCH model are often very useful, but we do not need to estimate them both.

Often the A-GARCH model is the easiest one to estimate. It is not so easy to optimize a GJR model. For instance, we have difficulties applying Excel Solver to the GJR-GARCH model for the FTSE 100 returns. The optimization hits a boundary for most starting values. In the GJR spreadsheet readers may wish to try changing the sample period – perhaps with different data the likelihood function will be better behaved around its optimum.

Since $E\left(1_{\{\varepsilon_{t-1}<0\}}\varepsilon_{t-1}^2\right) = \frac{1}{2}\sigma_t^2$ and $E\left(\varepsilon_t^2\right) = \sigma_t^2$, setting $\sigma_t^2 = \bar\sigma^2$ for all t yields the following formula for the long term variance of the GJR-GARCH model:

$$\bar\sigma^2 = \frac{\omega}{1 - \left(\alpha + \beta + \frac{1}{2}\lambda\right)}. \tag{II.4.21}$$

The one-step-ahead variance forecast is

$$\hat\sigma_{T+1}^2 = \hat\omega + \hat\alpha\hat\varepsilon_T^2 + \hat\lambda 1_{\{\varepsilon_T<0\}}\hat\varepsilon_T^2 + \hat\beta\hat\sigma_T^2, \tag{II.4.22}$$

and the S-step-ahead variance forecasts, $S > 1$ are

$$\hat\sigma_{T+S+1}^2 = \hat\omega + \left(\hat\alpha + \hat\beta + \frac{1}{2}\hat\lambda\right)\hat\sigma_{T+S}^2. \tag{II.4.23}$$

The term structure volatility forecasts are calculated by averaging the S-step-ahead forward variance forecasts for $S = 1, \ldots, h$ and then converting to a volatility in the usual way.

Table II.4.4 Parameter estimates and standard errors of GJR-GARCH models

Parameter	CAC 40		DAX 30		FTSE 100		Eurostoxx 50	
ω	$5.9E{-}4$	(5.84)	$8.9E{-}4$	(7.83)	$2.4E{-}4$	(5.39)	$4.5E{-}4$	(8.30)
α (reaction)	0.0166	(3.02)	0.0320	(4.93)	0.0155	(2.42)	0.0299	(4.98)
λ (leverage)	0.0664	(7.91)	0.0768	(7.53)	0.0781	(8.96)	0.0630	(6.97)
β (persistence)	0.9348	(141.81)	0.9080	(115.60)	0.9350	(137.35)	0.9230	(147.83)
Long term volatility		19.65%		20.22%		15.05%		17.02%
Log likelihood		901.1		843.1		2021.6		1458.2

Table II.4.4 shows the coefficient estimates and estimated standard errors (in parentheses) derived by applying the GJR-GARCH model in Ox to four major European stock market indices.[30] The daily data used for estimation are from 1 January 1991 to 21 October 2005, and the indices are the CAC 40, DAX 30, FTSE 100 and Dow Jones Eurostoxx 50. As usual, the mean reversion effect is the most significant with a t ratio of more than 100 in each index. The market shock effects, i.e. reaction and leverage, are also very highly significant.

II.4.3.3 Exponential GARCH

The exponential or E-GARCH model introduced by Nelson (1991) addresses the problem of ensuring that the variance is positive not by imposing constraints on the coefficients but by formulating the conditional variance equation in terms of the log of the variance rather than the variance itself. The log may indeed be negative, but the variance will always be positive.

The standard E-GARCH conditional variance specification is defined in terms of an i.i.d. standard normal variable Z_t and an asymmetric response function defined by

$$g(z_t) = \theta z_t + \gamma\left(|z_t| - \sqrt{2/\pi}\right),\tag{II.4.24}$$

where z_t is a realization of Z_t. Since Z_t is a standard normal variable,

$$E(|Z_t|) = \sqrt{2/\pi},\tag{II.4.25}$$

so the term inside brackets on the right-hand side of (II.4.24) is the deviation of a realization of $|Z_t|$ from its expected value.

Figure II.4.6 illustrates the response function $g(z_t)$ for values of z_t between -3 and $+3$ and for different values of θ and γ. Note that when $z_t > 0$ then $g(z_t)$ is linear with slope $\theta + \gamma$, and when $z_t < 0$ then $g(z_t)$ is linear with slope $\theta - \gamma$. Hence, a range of asymmetric responses to unit shocks is possible with E-GARCH. For instance, we may have a response to only positive shocks if $\theta = \gamma$, as in one of the cases shown in Figure II.4.6. Or, if $\theta = -\gamma$, there would be a response only to a negative shock.

Nelson (1991) provides a general framework for E-GARCH models with autoregressive effects in the conditional mean equation, volatility feedback (i.e. the conditional variance also appears in the conditional mean equation) and several lags of the log volatility in

---

[30] These results are abstracted from Alexander and Lazar (2005).

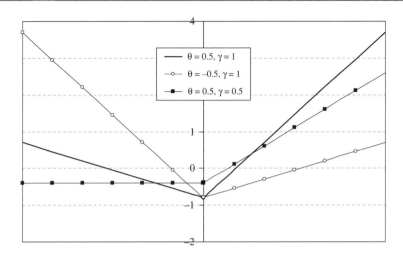

Figure II.4.6   E-GARCH asymmetric response function

the conditional variance equation. In Nelson's framework the random variable Z_t has a *generalized error distribution* of which the standard normal is just a special case. However such models are not easy to estimate.

Here we just describe the simplest specification of E-GARCH, which assumes $Z_t \sim NID(0,1)$ and

$$
\begin{aligned}
r_t &= c + \sigma_t z_t, \\
\ln(\sigma_t^2) &= \omega + g(z_{t-1}) + \beta \ln(\sigma_{t-1}^2).
\end{aligned}
\tag{II.4.26}
$$

Notice that previously we have expressed the conditional mean equation as $r_t = c + \varepsilon_t$. But of course, (II.4.26) is equivalent to this. In fact in every GARCH model we can write

$$
\varepsilon_t = \sigma_t z_t,
\tag{II.4.27}
$$

where z_t is i.i.d. and normalized to have zero mean and unit variance. In the normal GARCH model $\varepsilon_t | I_{t-1} \sim N(0, \sigma_t^2)$.

The long term log variance in the E-GARCH model is[31]

$$
\ln \overline{\sigma}^2 = \frac{\omega}{1 - \beta}.
\tag{II.4.28}
$$

Hence, the β parameter in E-GARCH has some correspondence with $\alpha + \beta$ in symmetric GARCH.

Assuming z_t is standard normal, the log likelihood of the model (II.4.26) is identical to (II.4.6), up to a constant, except that now of course the likelihood is a function of different parameters, $(\omega, \theta, \gamma, \beta)$. That is, the log likelihood of the normal E-GARCH model is, excluding the constant since it has no effect on the maximum likelihood estimates,

$$
\ln L(\omega, \theta, \gamma, \beta) = -\frac{1}{2} \sum_{t=1}^{T} \left(\ln(\sigma_t^2) + \left(\frac{\varepsilon_t}{\sigma_t}\right)^2 \right),
\tag{II.4.29}
$$

---

[31] To prove this, set $\sigma_t^2 = \sigma_{t-1}^2 = \overline{\sigma}^2$ in (II.4.26) and use the fact that $E(g(z_t)) = 0$.

where the dependence of the log likelihood on ω, θ, γ and β arises because σ_t is given by (II.4.24) and (II.4.26). The next example implements the E-GARCH likelihood maximization procedure in Excel.

EXAMPLE II.4.4: AN E-GARCH MODEL FOR THE FTSE 100

Estimate the parameters of the normal E-GARCH model (II.4.26) for the FTSE 100, using our sample of daily data from 3 January 1995 to 29 August 2007.

SOLUTION   In the spreadsheet for this example we set up each part of the likelihood as follows:

1. Start with the following initial values for the parameter estimates:
$$\hat{\omega} = -1, \hat{\theta} = -0.05, \hat{\gamma} = 0.1, \hat{\beta} = 0.9.$$
   These were chosen because they seem reasonable for the FTSE 100 index over the sample period that we have; other starting values would be chosen for other series.
2. Find the daily return r_t at each time t and the sample mean return $\bar{r}$ and put
$$z_t = \left(\frac{r_t - \bar{r}}{\hat{\sigma}_t} \right),$$
   where $\hat{\sigma}_t$ is our initial estimate of the conditional standard deviation obtained by putting the starting values in (II.4.24) and (II.4.26).[32]
3. Use this to obtain the asymmetric response function (II.4.24) and thus also the log conditional variance (II.4.26).
4. Take the exponential of (II.4.26) to obtain the conditional variance and then use this to obtain the log likelihood at time t.
5. Sum the log likelihoods over the sample and use this as the objective function for the Solver optimization. Note that there are *no parameter constraints* in E-GARCH.

The estimates of the parameters, the long term volatility and the maximized value of the log likelihood are shown in Table II.4.5. The maximum value of the log likelihood for the E-GARCH model is considerably higher than either A-GARCH or symmetric GARCH. Hence, the E-GARCH model provides the best fit to this sample of all the models considered so far. For our sample the long term volatility from E-GARCH is also lower than it is in the A-GARCH or symmetric GARCH models (see Table II.4.3).

Table II.4.5 Excel estimates of E-GARCH parameters for the FTSE 100

GARCH	Estimate
ω	−0.1196
θ	−0.0892
γ	0.1131
β	0.9872
Long term volatility	14.83%
Log likelihood	13486.59

---

[32] We also need to choose z_0 (the obvious choice being zero, since this is the mean) and σ_0^2 (the obvious choice is to set $\ln(\sigma_0^2) = \hat{\omega}/(1 - \hat{\beta})$).

Figure II.4.7 compares the E-GARCH volatility estimates for the FTSE 100 index with the symmetric GARCH estimates. The A-GARCH volatility estimates were so close to the symmetric GARCH estimates that there is no point in showing them on this figure. Notice that when volatility spikes, as in March 2003 for instance, the E-GARCH model does not predict such a high short term volatility as the ordinary GARCH. It appears that for the FTSE 100 index E-GARCH volatility is often slightly less than the symmetric GARCH volatility, and E-GARCH is less reactive to market shocks. Also E-GARCH volatilities are not constrained like ordinary GARCH volatilities, so at the lower range of volatility we do not see such a 'floor' as we do with ordinary GARCH estimates. Another point in favour of E-GARCH is that implied volatilities do not usually have such a floor.

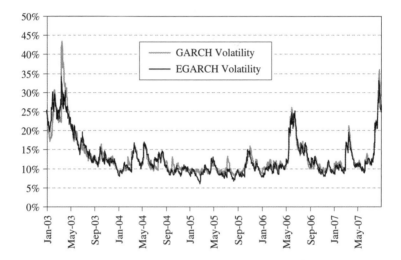

Figure II.4.7   E-GARCH volatility estimates for the FTSE 100

II.4.3.4   Analytic E-GARCH Volatility Term Structure Forecasts[33]

The S-step-ahead forward variance forecast from an E-GARCH model is derived using a recursive formula that is similar to the formula (II.4.11) that we derived for the symmetric GARCH model, only it is a little bit more complex. In fact, the forward 1-day forecast of the variance at the time T that the forecast is made is

$$\hat{\sigma}^2_{T+1} = \exp(\hat{\omega}) \exp(\hat{g}(z_T))\hat{\sigma}_T^{2\hat{\beta}}. \tag{II.4.30}$$

This follows immediately on taking the exponential of (II.4.26) and using the ^ to denote the fact that we are using parameter estimates here. For $S > 1$, the forward 1-day forecast of the variance from day $T + S$ to day $T + S + 1$ is given by

$$\hat{\sigma}^2_{T+S+1} = \hat{C} \exp\left(\hat{\omega} - \hat{\gamma}\sqrt{2/\pi}\right) \hat{\sigma}_{T+S}^{2\hat{\beta}}, \tag{II.4.31}$$

---

[33] An alternative derivation of the formula (II.4.31) is given in Tsay (2005).

where the constant $\hat{C}$ is given by

$$\hat{C} = \exp\left(\tfrac{1}{2}\left(\hat{\gamma}+\hat{\theta}\right)^2\right) \Phi\left(\hat{\gamma}+\hat{\theta}\right) + \exp\left(\tfrac{1}{2}\left(\hat{\gamma}-\hat{\theta}\right)^2\right) \Phi\left(\hat{\gamma}-\hat{\theta}\right). \tag{II.4.32}$$

To see (II.4.32), write

$$\hat{\sigma}^2_{T+S+1} = \exp(\hat{\omega})\, E\left[\exp(\hat{g}\,(z_{T+S}))\,|I_{T+S}\right]\hat{\sigma}^{2\hat{\beta}}_{T+S},$$

and use the fact that

$$E\left[\exp(\hat{g}\,(z_{T+S}))\,|I_{T+S}\right] = \int_{-\infty}^{\infty} \exp\left(\hat{\theta}z + \hat{\gamma}\left(|z| - \sqrt{2/\pi}\right)\right)\varphi(z)dz$$

$$= \exp\left(-\hat{\gamma}\sqrt{2/\pi}\right)\left[\int_0^{\infty} \exp\left(\left(\hat{\theta}+\hat{\gamma}\right)z\right)\varphi(z)dz + \int_{-\infty}^{0} \exp\left(\left(\hat{\theta}-\hat{\gamma}\right)z\right)\varphi(z)dz\right]$$

$$= \exp\left(-\hat{\gamma}\sqrt{2/\pi}\right)\left[\exp\left(\tfrac{1}{2}\left(\hat{\gamma}+\hat{\theta}\right)^2\right)\Phi\left(\hat{\gamma}+\hat{\theta}\right) + \exp\left(\tfrac{1}{2}\left(\hat{\gamma}-\hat{\theta}\right)^2\right)\Phi\left(\hat{\gamma}-\hat{\theta}\right)\right],$$

where φ and Φ denote the standard normal density and distribution functions. Note that the last step above rests on

$$\int_0^{\infty} \exp(ax)\,\varphi(x)dx = (2\pi)^{-1/2}\int_0^{\infty} \exp\left(-\tfrac{1}{2}\left[(x-a)^2 - a^2\right]\right)dx$$

$$= (2\pi)^{-1/2}\exp\left(\tfrac{1}{2}a^2\right)\int_{-a}^{\infty} \exp\left(-\tfrac{1}{2}y^2\right)dy$$

$$= \exp\left(\tfrac{1}{2}a^2\right)\left(1 - \Phi(-a)\right)$$

$$= \exp\left(\tfrac{1}{2}a^2\right)\Phi(a).$$

And similarly,

$$\int_{-\infty}^{0} \exp(ax)\,\varphi(x)dx = \exp\left(\tfrac{1}{2}a^2\right)\Phi(-a).$$

This proves (II.4.31).

Having obtained the S-step-ahead conditional variances for $S = 1, \ldots, h$, term structure volatility forecasts are calculated by averaging the forward variance forecasts and then converting to a volatility in the usual way. This is exactly the same process that we applied to obtain the symmetric, A-GARCH and GJR-GARCH term structure forecasts; the only difference is that we use a different forward variance forecast formula for E-GARCH.

Figure II.4.8 compares the term structure of FTSE 100 volatility forecasts from the E-GARCH model with those from the symmetric GARCH model. Again we have used the Excel parameter estimates based on FTSE 100 returns from January 1995 to August 2007 and the forecasts are made on 29 August 2007. On this particular day the E-GARCH model estimates and forecasts volatility to be considerably lower than the forecasts made using the symmetric GARCH model. As mentioned above, the E-GARCH model is less reactive to market shocks than the symmetric GARCH, at least for the FTSE 100 index.

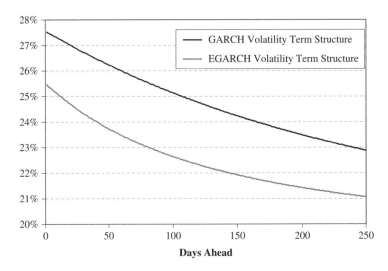

Figure II.4.8   Comparison of GARCH and E-GARCH volatility forecasts

We remark that the rate of mean reversion is rather slow in these GARCH volatility term structures. Even the average volatility over the next year is far from its long term average level. This often happens when the parameters are based on a long data period, and in this case the sample began in 1995. Readers can verify that using a shorter data period, such as one starting in January 2003, yields a more rapid mean reversion in volatility forecasts in this case.

II.4.3.5   Volatility Feedback

The GARCH models that have been introduced up to this point capture an asymmetric *response* in volatility: it increases more following a market move in one direction than it does following a market move of the same size in the opposite direction. Thus market shocks affect volatility. But a high volatility makes it more likely that there will be a large market move in *either* direction. So there is a feedback effect: one large return increases volatility which, in turn, increases returns. This feedback effect of volatility on the return is called, not surprisingly, *volatility feedback.*

Suppose we want to capture an asymmetric price response to volatility whereby prices are more likely to fall than to rise in volatile times. This may be the case in equity markets. The rationale here is that volatile markets make investors nervous. When volatility is very high they may decide to close out positions, thus precipitating further stock price falls.[34] This type of volatility feedback mechanism can be captured by adding the conditional variance to the conditional mean equation, as in the *GARCH in mean* model, introduced by Engle et al. (1987).

Suppose for simplicity that the original conditional mean equation is just $r_t = c + \varepsilon_t$, so that $c = \bar{r}$. Then the GARCH in mean equation becomes

$$r_t = c + \eta \sigma_t^2 + \varepsilon_t, \quad \varepsilon_t \mid I_{t-1} \sim N\left(0, \sigma_t^2\right). \tag{II.4.33}$$

---

[34] See Campbell and Hentschel (1992).

For an equity it seems reasonable to suppose that $\eta < 0$, but in volatile commodity markets prices may be more likely to rise than to fall, in which case it is more likely that $\eta > 0$.

The parameters of both the GARCH in mean equation (II.4.33) and the conditional variance equation must be estimated together, by maximum likelihood. The likelihood function still takes the form (II.4.6) when the errors have conditional normal distributions as in (II.4.33), but the maximization of the likelihood function becomes rather complex because the first derivatives of the likelihood need to be computed recursively or numerically. See Engle et al. (1987) for further details.

Numerous other GARCH models have been developed during the past twenty years, with and without asymmetric effects and volatility feedback. Technically minded readers are referred to Gouriéroux (1997) or Teräsvirta (2006) for a survey. A very readable, less technical but also less up-to-date review of some GARCH models is given in Bollerlsev et al. (1992).

II.4.4   NON-NORMAL GARCH MODELS

Asymmetric normal GARCH models are relatively simple to estimate and much superior to any moving average model, for reasons that have already been outlined. The E-GARCH model is an asymmetric GARCH model that has a better fit than symmetric GARCH for almost all financial assets. However, even this model can be improved by allowing innovations to be drawn from distributions other than the normal. Since daily or even higher frequency data are often used to estimate a GARCH model, non-zero skewness and excess kurtosis in the conditional returns distribution can be pronounced. A normal GARCH model does produce aggregate returns distributions that are non-normal, since they are sums of normal variables with different variances. But the aggregate returns that are generated by a normal GARCH model have only a small skewness and excess kurtosis, by contrast with the extreme non-normality sometimes found in financial asset returns. However, it is fairly straightforward to modify the normal GARCH models that we have considered in the previous section to have non-normal conditional returns distributions. In this section we shall describe two extensions to the normal GARCH framework that allow the innovations to be skewed and leptokurtic, drawn either from a normal mixture or a (skewed or symmetric) Student's t distribution.

II.4.4.1   Student t GARCH Models

The normal GARCH models (II.4.1) and (II.4.14) do not tend to fit financial returns as well as GARCH models in which the market shocks have a non-normal conditional distribution. As mentioned above, if measured at the daily or higher frequency, market returns typically have skewed and leptokurtic conditional (and unconditional) distributions.[35] The Student t GARCH model, introduced by Bollerslev (1987), assumes the conditional distribution of market shocks is t distributed. The *degrees of freedom* in this distribution become an additional parameter that is estimated along with the parameters in the conditional variance equation.

---

[35] Negative skew means that the lower tail is heavier and the centre is shifted to the right. Positive skew means the opposite. *Leptokurtosis* occurs when the distribution has a higher peak and heavier tails than the normal density with the same variance.

The symmetric t GARCH model has also been extended to skewed Student t distributions by Lambert and Laurent (2001).[36]

The specification of the conditional variance does not change: this can be a symmetric GARCH or one of the asymmetric GARCH models introduced in the previous section. But the likelihood function does change. As explained in Section I.3.3.7, the standardized Student t distribution has density function

$$f_\nu(t) = ((\nu - 2)\,\pi)^{-1/2}\,\Gamma\!\left(\frac{\nu}{2}\right)^{-1}\,\Gamma\!\left(\frac{\nu + 1}{2}\right)\left(1 + \frac{t^2}{\nu - 2}\right)^{-(\nu+1)/2}. \qquad (II.4.34)$$

Hence, the log likelihood is not the normal log likelihood (II.4.6) but

$$\ln L(\boldsymbol{\theta}) = -\sum_{t=1}^{T}\left(\ln(\sigma_t) + \left(\frac{\nu + 1}{2}\right)\ln\!\left(1 + (\nu - 2)^{-1}\left(\frac{\varepsilon_t}{\sigma_t}\right)^2\right)\right)$$
$$+ T\ln\left[((\nu - 2)\,\pi)^{-1/2}\,\Gamma\!\left(\frac{\nu}{2}\right)^{-1}\,\Gamma\!\left(\frac{\nu + 1}{2}\right)\right], \qquad (II.4.35)$$

where $\boldsymbol{\theta}$ denotes the parameters of the conditional variance equation. The construction of this likelihood is illustrated by providing the solution to the following example in an Excel spreadsheet.

EXAMPLE II.4.5: SYMMETRIC STUDENT t GARCH

Consider again the 1995–2007 FTSE 100 data set, and set the values for the symmetric GARCH model parameters equal to their values in Example II.4.1. Starting with an initial value of $\nu = 15$ for the degrees of freedom in Student t GARCH, use Excel Solver to find the value of ν that maximizes the likelihood function (II.4.35). Compare the result with the symmetric Student t GARCH parameters that are estimated using Matlab.

SOLUTION   The likelihood function for each returns observation is calculated in column F of this spreadsheet and these are summed to give the value of the function (II.4.35). With the initial value $\nu = 15$ the log likelihood has value 25,563.0 but after optimization, which yields the maximum likelihood estimate $\hat{\nu} = 18.457$, the likelihood has value 25,563.3. So it is already very flat in the region of the initial values.

The (constrained) Excel and Matlab optimal parameter values are compared in Table II.4.6.

Table II.4.6   Student t GARCH parameter estimates from Excel and Matlab

GARCH	Excel	Matlab
ω	9.9973E−07	8.9428E−07
α	0.086910	0.083094
β	0.90554	0.91008
ν	18.457	16.594
Long term volatility	18.20%	18.10%
Log likelihood	25563.33	25569.44

---

[36] Ox programs for Student's t and other GARCH models are provided. See Laurent and Peters (2002) for a review of version 2.x, but note that Ox version 4.x is now available.

Note that the Matlab optimization includes the GARCH conditional variance parameters and it achieves a higher local maximum for the log likelihood. Indeed, it has been obvious since our attempts to apply Solver to A-GARCH models that we have really reached the limit of its ability to estimate GARCH model parameters. This is why we only estimated the degrees-of-freedom parameter in Excel, and we did not add the GARCH conditional variance parameters to the optimization.

II.4.4.2 Case Study: Comparison of GARCH Models for the FTSE 100

In this section we compare the results of estimating six different GARCH models using our FTSE 100 data set.[37] These are:

1. symmetric normal GARCH;
2. normal GJR-GARCH;
3. normal E-GARCH;
4. symmetric Student t GARCH;
5. Student t GJR-GARCH;
6. Student t E-GARCH.

We estimate the models using daily log returns on the FTSE over two different data periods: (a) from 2 January 1995 to 29 August 2007; and (b) from 2 January 2003 to 29 August 2007. Only Matlab, and not EViews, provides results for Student t GARCH, but for the first three models we may also compare the results from using EViews and Matlab.

The results for the three normal GARCH models are shown in Table II.4.7. The parameter estimates are similar, except that the Matlab optimizer has hit a boundary in the GJR model over the 2003–2007 period. For every model the likelihood values are marginally higher using the EViews optimizer. EViews treats the EGARGH constant ω differently – see the EViews manual (User Guide II, page 221). Thus for the specification used here one needs to add 0.08988 to the EViews estimate of ω which yields a result of $\omega = -0.12101$ in line with the other results, and a LT Vol estimate of 15.1%. For both samples the highest likelihood is attained using the E-GARCH model according to both EViews and Matlab.

Notice how different the estimated long term volatilities are when we change the specification of the model, and they are all quite different from the unconditional volatility that is estimated under the i.i.d. assumption (this is 16.89% over the 1995–2007 sample and 13.89% over the 2003–2007 sample). This emphasizes the fact that the true unconditional volatility depends on the model. Never forget that volatility is a parameter of a probability distribution and so it can only be observed in the context of a model.

Table II.4.8 details the Matlab results for the Student t GARCH models. There is again a problem with the GJR model when estimated over the 2003–2007 period, since the reaction parameter hits its lower boundary and the estimated value for α is 0. Otherwise the results are sensible and the maximized values of the log likelihoods are always greater than for the corresponding normal GARCH model. When a leverage effect is allowed for, as in the GJR and E-GARCH models, the effect is always significant. Comparison of the results over the two samples shows that the FTSE 100 index volatility has recently become more reactive

---

[37] I am very grateful to my PhD student Andreza Barbosa for taking time out from writing up her thesis to produce these results.

Table II.4.7 Estimation of symmetric and asymmetric normal GARCH models for the FTSE 100

	Symmetric normal				Normal GJR				Normal E-GARCH			
	EViews		Matlab		EViews		Matlab		EViews		Matlab	
	Estimate	t ratio	Estimate	t ratio	Estimate	t ratio	Estimate	t ratio	Estimate	t ratio	Estimate	t ratio
1995–2007												
ω	9.92E-07	3.94428	9.76E-07	3.90029	1.02E-06	5.45499	1.02E-06	5.37172	−0.21089	−7.84795	−0.12456	−5.80537
α	0.08350	9.38145	0.08415	9.39769	0.00708	0.78824	0.00874	0.95024				
β	0.90845	96.02725	0.90798	95.75222	0.92920	107.18451	0.92762	104.94270	0.98698	449.15022	0.98662	432.84198
λ					0.10503	9.35361	0.10493	9.20600				
γ									0.11265	7.57945	0.11697	7.63462
θ									−0.08991	−11.09727	−0.08977	−10.90927
Long term vol	17.55%		17.61%		15.07%		15.08%		0.48%		15.05%	
Log likelihood	10511.98		10511		10541.663		10540		10549.8		10547	
2003–2007												
ω	1.63E-06	2.97287	1.63E-06	2.93389	1.96E-06	4.58033	1.94E-06	4.04556	−0.27633	−4.54562	−0.19600	−3.70503
α	0.09839	6.18307	0.10052	6.28054	−0.02562	−1.40692	0.00000	0.00000				
β	0.87780	42.49683	0.87624	42.14921	0.89777	46.49008	0.88608	39.65451	0.98007	184.67302	0.97973	180.36931
λ					0.19276	6.37011	0.16496	5.22654				
γ									0.10448	4.23694	0.10674	4.27678
θ									−0.13274	−7.59134	−0.13459	−7.65760
Long term vol	13.08%		13.24%		12.47%		12.41%		1.54%		12.57%	
Log likelihood	4096.6		4096.1		4117.0		4115.5		4118.4		4118	

Table II.4.8 Student t GARCH models for the FTSE 100

	Symmetric t GARCH		t GJR		t E-GARCH	
	Estimate	t ratio	Estimate	t ratio	Estimate	t ratio
1995–2007						
ω	8.94E-07	3.20003	9.36E-07	4.49113	−0.11974	−5.08644
α	0.08309	8.23692	0.00220	0.21142		
β	0.91008	86.44377	0.92957	99.80352	0.98739	394.45110
λ			0.11488	7.94907		
γ					0.11339	6.79674
θ					−0.09754	−8.88199
ν	16.59		17.37		19.00	
Long term vol	18.10%		14.73%		13.71%	
Log likelihood	10521		10551		10556	
2003–2007						
ω	1.6344E-06	2.39585	1.79E-06	3.30673	−0.18127	−3.19064
α	0.09695	5.02124	0.00000	0.00000		
β	0.87909	35.31617	0.88871	37.45091	0.98151	168.17333
λ			0.16182	4.52656		
γ					0.10380	3.78487
θ					−0.13492	−6.85953
ν	12.73		18.19		21.69	
Long term vol	13.06%		12.15%		11.75%	
Log likelihood	4102.5		4118.7		4120.3	

and less persistent, and that the leverage effect has become more pronounced.[38] These are a sign of an increased nervousness in the UK stock market. The highest likelihood is attained using the Student t E-GARCH model over both samples. We conclude that this model fits the sample data best, but that does not necessarily mean that it will outperform the other models for forecasting volatility.[39]

II.4.4.3 Normal Mixture GARCH Models

Time variation in the conditional skewness and conditional kurtosis can explain why equity implied volatility skews are so steep and so persistent into long dated options. Bates (1991), Christoffersen et al. (2006) and many others in between argue that, for a model to capture the empirical characteristics of option implied volatility skews, it is essential to account for time variability in the conditional skewness and kurtosis in the physical (i.e. real-world) measure. Unfortunately, the t GARCH model has constant conditional skewness and conditional kurtosis and the only way to capture time variation in these parameters is to add it exogenously to the GARCH model, as for instance in Harvey and Siddique (1999). However, if we use a normal mixture conditional distribution for the market shocks then

---

[38] That is, in the GJR model the estimated value of λ is higher in the 2003–2007 sample. Also, in the E-GARCH model, recall that for a negative shock the slope of the response function is $\theta - \gamma$, and the estimated value is –0.239 since 2003, compared with –0.211 over the whole period.
[39] See Sections II.8.3 and II.8.5 for details on testing the accuracy of a GARCH model's forecasts.

time variation in the conditional skewness and conditional kurtosis is endogenous to the GARCH model.

Normal mixture distributions were introduced in Section I.3.3.6. They are simple and intuitive distributions for recovering different states or 'regimes' that occur in a financial time series. They have important applications to value-at-risk estimation and to scenario analysis, for instance where one covariance matrix corresponds to ordinary market circumstances and the other corresponds to extreme market circumstances.

In conjunction with GARCH, normal mixtures can also be used to capture different regimes of volatility behaviour where, for instance, mean reversion may be quicker and leverage effects more pronounced in crash markets than they are in normal markets. These models have been extensively studied in the works of Bai et al. (2001, 2003), Klaassen (2002), Haas et al. (2004a) and others. Alexander and Lazar (2006, 2008a) showed that a normal mixture model with just two A-GARCH variance components also provides a closer fit to exchange rate and equity index returns than normal or t GARCH models.

For example, a two-state normal mixture A-GARCH model is specified by two A-GARCH variance components:

$$
\begin{aligned}
\sigma_{1t}^2 &= \omega_1 + \alpha_1(\varepsilon_{t-1} - \lambda_1)^2 + \beta_1\sigma_{1,t-1}^2, \\
\sigma_{2t}^2 &= \omega_2 + \alpha_2(\varepsilon_{t-1} - \lambda_2)^2 + \beta_2\sigma_{2,t-1}^2,
\end{aligned}
\tag{II.4.36}
$$

where $\varepsilon_t \,|I_{t-1} \sim NM(\pi, \sigma_{1t}^2, \sigma_{2t}^2)$. That is, the error process has a conditional distribution that is a zero mean mixture of two normal distributions, with mixing law π.

The general properties of normal mixture GARCH models are derived in extensive appendices in Alexander and Lazar (2006, 2008a). For instance, the unconditional variance for the asymmetric normal mixture GARCH process (II.4.36) is

$$
\bar{\sigma}^2 = \frac{\pi(1-\beta_1)^{-1}\left(\omega_1 + \alpha_1\lambda_1^2\right) + (1-\pi)(1-\beta_2)^{-1}\left(\omega_2 + \alpha_2\lambda_2^2\right)}{1 - \pi(1-\beta_1)^{-1}\alpha_1 - (1-\pi)(1-\beta_2)^{-1}\alpha_2}.
\tag{II.4.37}
$$

Analytic formulae for h-step-ahead forecasts also exist, but are very complex. See Alexander and Lazar (2006, 2008a) for further details.

Table II.4.9, which is adapted from Alexander and Lazar's work mentioned above, shows the parameter estimates for the asymmetric normal mixture model based on the equity index data used in Table II.4.4. The figures in parentheses are the estimated t-ratios of the coefficients. The first component is similar to the one identified in Table II.4.4; indeed, it carries a weight of 95% or more in the mixture. The second component is the 'crash' component because it has much higher long term volatility and occurs less than 5% of the time.

These results show that the response of equities to market shocks is much more extreme during crash periods but after a shock volatility reverts to its long term level much more quickly than it does in normal market circumstances. The long term volatility in the crash regime is more than double that of the normal regime, and the long term volatility level differs markedly according to the market. The CAC and DAX indices are less liquid and

Table II.4.9 Parameter estimates and standard errors of NM(2) A-GARCH models[a]

		CAC 40	DAX 30	FTSE 100	Eurostoxx 50
1st component	ω_1	−1.1E-4 (−0.69)	2.9E-5 (0.27)	−1.6E-4 (−1.65)	5.4E-5 (0.80)
	α_1	0.0524 (8.07)	0.0640 (8.92)	0.0482 (7.26)	0.0642 (8.97)
	λ_1	0.1058 (6.22)	0.0639 (4.89)	0.0899 (6.03)	0.0443 (4.14)
	β_1	0.9311 (122.93)	0.9220 (114.79)	0.9362 (121.85)	0.9206 (112.35)
	$\bar{\sigma}_1$	20.74%	20.59%	14.74%	17.28%
2nd component	ω_2	−0.0018 (−0.12)	0.0335 0.39)	0.0076 (0.78)	0.0084 (0.48)
	α_2	1.5497 (0.85)	0.3729 (0.48)	0.9401 (1.88)	0.2288 (0.64)
	λ_2	−0.0311 (−0.62)	0.0470 (0.19)	−0.0192 (−0.44)	0.0641 (0.39)
	β_2	0.6172 (1.68)	0.7155 (1.04)	0.5821 (2.59)	0.8332 (3.24)
	$\bar{\sigma}_2$	43.71%	42.70%	27.04%	32.09%
$\hat{\pi}$		0.9780	0.9701	0.9583	0.9493
Log likelihood		931.7	957.5	2054.9	1557.2

[a]Figures in parentheses are t-ratios.

contain fewer stocks that the Eurostoxx and FTSE indices, so their volatility is much higher in both normal and crash regimes. The CAC and the FTSE have the most 'jumpy' volatilities in the crash regime, because they have a relatively high α and a relatively low β. In these markets the leverage term actually reinforces a positive shock during the crash regime, perhaps because investors are concerned that a rise in prices will lead to further falls in the future.

II.4.4.4 Markov Switching GARCH

The normal mixture GARCH model is like a powerful magnifying glass through which we can view the behaviour of equity markets. It tells us a lot about the volatility characteristics of equity markets and allows one to characterize its behaviour in two different market regimes.[40] However, normal mixture GARCH is really just a simple version of the Markov Switching GARCH models that were introduced by Hamilton and Susmel (1994), Cai (1994), Gray (1996), Klaassen (2002), Haas et al. (2004b) and others.

In normal mixture GARCH the probability that the volatility is in each regime does not change over time.[41] It is only in Markov switching GARCH that the regime probability varies over time. The conditional probability of being in a given volatility regime varies over time, but there is a constant probability *of switching* from one regime to another. In other words, the *transition probabilities* are constant. And they are usually not symmetric. Thus the probability that the market will switch from low volatility to high volatility is different from the probability that the market will switch from high volatility to low volatility. As with the normal mixture GARCH model, the characteristics of the GARCH volatility process can be very different, depending on the regime.

---

[40] It may also be applied to other markets; see for instance Alexander and Lazar (2006) for an analysis of the normal mixture GARCH model applied to foreign exchange markets. In this paper we also demonstrate that it is extremely difficult to identify normal mixture GARCH models with more than two components.

[41] Thus when we simulate returns from a normal mixture GARCH process in Section II.4.7.2 we choose the ruling regime at any point in time by a random draw on a Bernoulli variable with constant probability π of 'success'.

The advantage of using Markov switching GARCH rather than normal mixture GARCH is that the ruling regime tends to remain unchanged for substantial periods. By contrast, in normal mixture GARCH we switch regime at any point in time, with a constant probability. Hence Markov switching GARCH better captures the volatility clustering that we observe in most financial markets. The disadvantage of using Markov switching GARCH models is that they are much more difficult to estimate than normal mixture GARCH. Even their mathematical specification is rather complex and there are several different versions of Markov switching GARCH models. Interested readers are recommended to consult the paper by Haas et al. (2004b) for one of the most tractable formulations. They should also find the simulations of Markov switching GARCH in Section II.4.7.2 below and the accompanying spreadsheet quite informative.

II.4.5   GARCH COVARIANCE MATRICES

Up to now we have considered only univariate GARCH models, which are used to capture different types of volatility clustering behaviour. Volatility clustering refers to the empirical fact that if volatility rises following a market shock then it tends to stay high for some time, even without further bad news in the market. But clustering is also evident in correlation. During times of crisis correlations also tend to increase as asset prices have a greater tendency to move in the same direction, and we refer to this as *correlation clustering*.

Clustering in correlation can be captured by a multivariate GARCH model. Each asset return has a time varying conditional variance, which is specified using one of the univariate GARCH models described above. In addition, each pair of asset returns has a time varying conditional covariance which is specified by a similar type of equation. For instance, the simplest possible multivariate GARCH model is a bivariate, symmetric normal *diagonal vech GARCH* which has the following specification:

$$\sigma_{1t}^2 = \omega_1 + \alpha_1 \varepsilon_{1,t-1}^2 + \beta_1 \sigma_{1,t-1}^2,$$

$$\sigma_{2t}^2 = \omega_2 + \alpha_2 \varepsilon_{2,t-1}^2 + \beta_2 \sigma_{2,t-1}^2,$$

$$\sigma_{12t} = \omega_3 + \alpha_3 \varepsilon_{1,t-1} \varepsilon_{2,t-1} + \beta_3 \sigma_{12,t-1}, \tag{II.4.38}$$

$$\begin{pmatrix} \varepsilon_{1t} \\ \varepsilon_{2t} \end{pmatrix} \Big| I_{t-1} \sim N\left(\begin{pmatrix} 0 \\ 0 \end{pmatrix}, \begin{pmatrix} \sigma_{1t}^2 & \sigma_{12t} \\ \sigma_{12t} & \sigma_{2t}^2 \end{pmatrix} \right).$$

Equations (II.4.38) may also be written in matrix notation, on setting

$$\boldsymbol{\varepsilon}_t = \begin{pmatrix} \varepsilon_{1t} \\ \varepsilon_{2t} \end{pmatrix} \text{ and } \mathbf{H}_t = \begin{pmatrix} \sigma_{1t}^2 & \sigma_{12t} \\ \sigma_{12t} & \sigma_{2t}^2 \end{pmatrix}$$

for the error vector and the GARCH covariance matrix, respectively. Then (II.4.38) becomes[42]

$$\text{vech}\,(\mathbf{H}_t) = \text{diag}\,(\omega_1, \omega_2, \omega_3) + \text{diag}\,(\alpha_1, \alpha_2, \alpha_3)\,\text{vech}\,(\boldsymbol{\varepsilon}_{t-1}\boldsymbol{\varepsilon}_{t-1}') + \text{diag}\,(\beta_1, \beta_2, \beta_3)$$

$$\text{vech}\,(\mathbf{H}_{t-1}). \tag{II.4.39}$$

---

[42] Here the notation diag(·) refers to the diagonal matrix with the specified elements on the diagonal and zeros elsewhere; and vech(·) refers to the vector that is constructed from a matrix by stacking the columns one on top of each other with the first column at the top without repeating the off-diagonal elements.

Baba, Engle, Kraft and Kroner (BEKK) developed a parameterization of the GARCH equations that ensures positive definiteness of the covariance matrix and allows us to estimate low-dimensional multivariate GARCH systems with some confidence.[43] The BEKK parameterization for symmetric GARCH is

$$\mathbf{H}_t = \mathbf{A}'\mathbf{A} + (\mathbf{B}'\boldsymbol{\varepsilon}_{t-1})(\mathbf{B}'\boldsymbol{\varepsilon}_{t-1})' + \mathbf{C}'\mathbf{H}_{t-1}\mathbf{C}, \qquad (\text{II.4.40})$$

where $\mathbf{A}$, $\mathbf{B}$ and $\mathbf{C}$ are $m \times m$ matrices and $\mathbf{A}$ is triangular where m is the number of assets. This can be extended to a matrix representation for the multivariate version of any of the asymmetric GARCH models that were introduced in Section II.4.3.

However successful the univariate GARCH models, extending GARCH to several dimensions is a challenge. Estimating positive definite GARCH covariance matrices becomes more and more difficult as the dimensions of the matrix increase. Even with the powerful computers of today the optimization of the GARCH likelihood is a complex numerical problem when the dimensions are large, because there are a huge number of parameters to estimate.

Given the number of univariate GARCH models that have been reviewed so far, it will come as no surprise to the reader that the number of different multivariate GARCH specifications is huge. An extensive review of these models is given by Laurent et al. (2006). In this section we propose several alternatives to full multivariate GARCH where only univariate GARCH models or low-dimensional multivariate GARCH models need to be estimated. We consider only the most important multivariate GARCH models and explain how to tailor the model specification to the model application. In several of these approaches it will be necessary to estimate an auxiliary model, such as a factor model for equity returns or a principal component analysis of interest rate changes. We argue that different types of multivariate GARCH models are suitable for different asset classes. In other words, the choice of the best multivariate GARCH specification depends very much on the behaviour of the underlying returns data. I recommend the following:

- constant correlation GARCH (CC-GARCH) or dynamic conditional correlation (DCC) for covariance matrices of foreign exchange rates or of equity indices;
- factor GARCH (F-GARCH) for covariance matrices of equities;
- orthogonal GARCH (O-GARCH) for covariance matrices of interest rates or indeed any term structure, such as commodity futures.

Of course it is possible to forecast foreign exchange covariance matrices using either DCC or O-GARCH, or to forecast equity covariance matrices using either DCC or F-GARCH. The modelling strategy listed above is only a recommendation, albeit based on quite an extensive experience with fitting covariance matrices to different types of financial assets.

II.4.5.1 Estimation of Multivariate GARCH Models

In EWMA matrices we cannot simply estimate all the covariances one by one, using different smoothing constants, because when we put them all together in a matrix it is unlikely to be positive semi-definite. Similarly, in a multivariate GARCH model the parameters of the conditional variance and conditional covariance equations should be estimated simultaneously, by maximizing the log likelihood of the joint distribution over the sample.

---

[43] See Engle and Kroner (1993).

For instance, if the errors have a conditional multivariate normal distribution as in (II.4.38) the log likelihood is based on the multivariate normal density function defined in Section I.3.4.6. Excluding the constant, since it does not affect the optimal value of the GARCH parameters θ, the log likelihood is

$$\ln L(\theta) = -\tfrac{1}{2} \sum_{t=1}^{T} \left(\ln(|\mathbf{H}_t|) + \boldsymbol{\varepsilon}_t' \mathbf{H}_t^{-1} \boldsymbol{\varepsilon}_t \right), \tag{II.4.41}$$

where $\mathbf{H}_t$ is the conditional covariance matrix and $\boldsymbol{\varepsilon}_t$ is the GARCH error vector at time t. This is a multivariate version of (II.4.6). For instance, in a bivariate GARCH model,

$$\mathbf{H}_t = \begin{pmatrix} \sigma_{1t}^2 & \sigma_{12t} \\ \sigma_{12t} & \sigma_{2t}^2 \end{pmatrix} \quad \text{and} \quad \boldsymbol{\varepsilon}_t = \begin{pmatrix} \varepsilon_{1t} \\ \varepsilon_{2t} \end{pmatrix}.$$

Maximizing the log likelihood for multivariate GARCH models is a formidable computational task. Each GARCH variance has three parameters – probably four in fact, since we usually include asymmetric volatility responses. Then, for an $m \times m$ covariance matrix we have to estimate $m(m+1)/2$ covariance equations. Each of these equations has at least three or four parameters. Thus a five-dimensional system of returns has about 80 GARCH parameters and a ten-dimensional system has 260 parameters! Moreover, further parameters might be introduced to capture 'cross-equation' effects, where yesterday's value of one variance can affect today's value of another variance, for instance.

Optimizing a likelihood function with so many parameters is ridiculous. Convergence problems can arise even in univariate models, due to a flat likelihood surface. The more parameters in multivariate GARCH model the flatter the likelihood function becomes and the more difficult it is to maximize. The likelihood function for a multivariate GARCH model is like the surface of the moon, so very often only a local optimum is achieved and we could get different parameter estimates each time we change the starting values.

Hence, even the BEKK parameterization only allows one to estimate multivariate GARCH for relatively low-dimensional systems. With more than about five or six returns in the system the results of BEKK optimization should be viewed with some caution, since the likelihood surface becomes extremely flat and it is very difficult to ensure that a global optimum has been achieved. For this reason the remainder of this chapter deals with multivariate GARCH models that require only univariate GARCH optimization. However, we attempt an estimation of a very simple bivariate GARCH model using Excel(!) in Section II.4.8.3.

II.4.5.2   Constant and Dynamic Conditional Correlation GARCH

Bollerslev (1990) assumes that the covariance matrix at time t is

$$\mathbf{V}_t = \mathbf{D}_t \mathbf{C} \mathbf{D}_t, \tag{II.4.42}$$

where $\mathbf{D}_t$ is a diagonal matrix of time varying GARCH volatilities, and $\mathbf{C}$ is a correlation matrix that is *not* time varying. We know that a covariance matrix is positive definite if and only if the associated correlation matrix is positive definite. Hence, $\mathbf{V}_t$ will be positive definite provided only that $\mathbf{C}$ is positive definite. The correlation matrix $\mathbf{C}$ can contain any correlations, provided that the matrix is positive definite. For instance, $\mathbf{C}$ could be estimated using the equally weighted average method over a long data history. Or we could simply use some 'scenario' values for the correlations in $\mathbf{C}$.

Engle (2002) extends the constant correlation model to the *dynamic conditional correlation* (DCC) model where **C** is time varying but not stochastic. For instance, in the example below it will be estimated using exponentially weighted averages of the cross products of the standardized returns (i.e. the return divided by its time-varying EWMA volatility).

To estimate and forecast the different volatilities in $\mathbf{D}_t$ we may use any type of univariate GARCH model: symmetric or asymmetric, normal or non-normal. The following example uses an asymmetric normal univariate GARCH to illustrate the application of (II.4.42) to a system with just two foreign exchange rates. We compare the results from using (a) equally weighted average correlations (*Constant Correlation GARCH*, or CC model) and (b) exponentially weighted average correlations (DCC model).

EXAMPLE II.4.6: CC AND DCC GARCH APPLIED TO FOREX RATES

Compare the time series of covariances between the daily sterling–dollar and euro–dollar exchange rates between 3 January 2003 and 27 June 2006, using (a) the constant correlation GARCH model (II.4.42) and (b) the DCC model based on EWMA correlations with a smoothing constant of 0.94.

SOLUTION   Figure II.4.9 plots the two exchange rates over the sample period (£/$ on the left-hand scale and €/$ on the right-hand scale). The weakening of the US dollar between 2001 and 2004 has a strong influence over both rates and their average correlation over the whole period is 0.71.

Figure II.4.9   GBP and EUR dollar rates

First we use Excel to fit a univariate A-GARCH model to each exchange rate. The estimated GARCH volatilities between 3 January 2005 and 27 June 2006 are shown in Figure II.4.10.[44] The conditional covariances that are obtained using these volatilities and with a correlation that is (a) constant and (b) exponentially weighted are shown in

---

[44] To view these series over a longer data period, change the horizontal scale of the graphs in the spreadsheet.

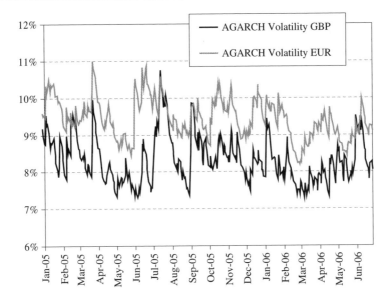

Figure II.4.10   A-GARCH volatilities of GBP/USD and EUR/USD

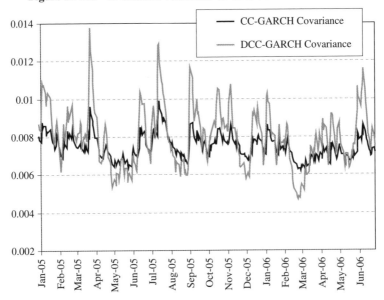

Figure II.4.11   Covariances of GBP/USD and EUR/USD

Figure II.4.11. For comparison both correlations are estimated on the data available only up to the day that the model is estimated. As expected, the DCC covariance estimates are more variable than the constant correlation estimates.

The DCC model with EWMA correlations is a simple form of the general DCC model, where the correlation response to market shocks is symmetric and there is no mean-reversion in correlation. Cappiello et al. (2003) generalize the DCC model to have asymmetric correlation response and mean-reverting effects. Here the conditional correlation matrix is given by

$$\mathbf{C}_t = \mathrm{diag}(\mathbf{Q}_t)^{-1/2}\,\mathbf{Q}_t\,\mathrm{diag}(\mathbf{Q}_t)^{-1/2},$$

where $\mathrm{diag}\,(\mathbf{Q}_t)$ is the diagonal matrix that is formed from the diagonal elements of $\mathbf{Q}_t$ and $\mathbf{Q}_t$ is a positive definite matrix which follows the process

$$\mathbf{Q}_t = \mathbf{\Omega} + \mathbf{A}'\mathbf{\varepsilon}'_{t-1}\mathbf{\varepsilon}_{t-1}\mathbf{A} + \mathbf{G}'\mathbf{\eta}'_{t-1}\mathbf{\eta}_{t-1}\mathbf{G} + \mathbf{B}'\mathbf{Q}_{t-1}\mathbf{B}$$

in which $\mathbf{\eta}_t$ is the vector obtained from $\mathbf{\varepsilon}_t$ by setting its negative elements to zero, $\mathbf{\Omega}$ is positive definite and $\mathbf{A}$ and $\mathbf{B}$ are diagonal matrices. Typically, even more parameter restrictions may need to be imposed to estimate the model in practice.

II.4.5.3 Factor GARCH

In Section II.1.3 we derived a factor model of a system of m stock returns which may be written in the form

$$\mathbf{Y} = \mathbf{A} + \mathbf{X}\mathbf{B} + \mathbf{E}, \tag{II.4.43}$$

where $\mathbf{Y}$ is a $T \times m$ matrix containing the data on the stock returns, $\mathbf{X}$ is a $T \times k$ matrix containing the data on the risk factor returns, $\mathbf{A}$ is the $T \times m$ matrix whose jth column is the vector $\mathbf{\alpha}_j$, $\mathbf{B}$ is the $k \times m$ matrix whose i, jth element is the sensitivity of the jth stock to the ith risk factor, and $\mathbf{E}$ is the $T \times m$ matrix of residuals.

Taking variances of (II.4.43), assuming the risk factor sensitivities are constant and ignoring the specific risk covariance matrix, i.e. the covariance matrix of the residual returns, we obtain

$$\mathbf{V} \approx \mathbf{B}'\mathbf{\Omega}\mathbf{B}, \tag{II.4.44}$$

where $\mathbf{V}$ is the $m \times m$ stock returns systematic covariance matrix and $\mathbf{\Omega}$ is the $k \times k$ covariance matrix of the risk factor returns. Thus the factor model allows one to estimate all the systematic variances and covariances of all stock returns, knowing only their sensitivities to some specified risk factors and the covariance matrix of these risk factors.

A large covariance matrix of equity returns may be estimated using the *factor GARCH*, or F-GARCH model of Engle et al. (1990). In F-GARCH we set

$$\mathbf{V}_t \approx \mathbf{B}'\mathbf{\Omega}_t\mathbf{B}, \tag{II.4.45}$$

where $\mathbf{V}_t$ is the $m \times m$ stock returns systematic covariance matrix at time t and $\mathbf{\Omega}_t$ is a $k \times k$ GARCH covariance matrix of the risk factor returns. But the factor sensitivity matrix $\mathbf{B}$ is still assumed to be constant as in (II.4.44).[45] If k is small enough, say $k < 6$, the $\mathbf{\Omega}_t$ risk factor covariance matrix can be estimated using the BEKK parameterization (II.4.40).

In the next example we estimate the simplest possible asymmetric F-GARCH model, where $k = 1$ and the factor has an asymmetric normal GARCH conditional variance. In this case (II.4.45) takes the form

$$\begin{aligned}
\sigma_{it}^2 &= \beta_i^2 \sigma_t^2, \\
\sigma_{ijt} &= \beta_i \beta_j \sigma_t^2, \\
\sigma_t^2 &= \omega + \alpha(\varepsilon_{t-1} - \lambda)^2 + \beta\sigma_{t-1}^2, \quad \varepsilon_t \,|I_{t-1} \sim N(0, \sigma_t^2),
\end{aligned} \tag{II.4.46}$$

where β_i is the risk factor sensitivity of stock i, σ_{it}^2 is its conditional variance, σ_{ijt} is the conditional covariance between stock i and stock j and σ_t^2 is the conditional variance of the risk factor.

---

[45] As explained in Section II.1.2, for risk management purposes it is often better to use EWMA sensitivity estimates in $\mathbf{B}$ instead of the constant sensitivities based on OLS estimation of the factor model.

Estimating the conditional variance of the factor by univariate GARCH allows time varying volatilities to be estimated for all of the stocks, knowing only their risk factor sensitivities. But whilst the systematic *covariances* in (II.4.46) are time varying, we remark that all the stocks have a systematic correlation equal to 1 because there is only one risk factor in this very simple form of F-GARCH.

EXAMPLE II.4.7: F-GARCH APPLIED TO EQUITY RETURNS

In the case study in Section II.1.4 we estimated several fundamental factor models for Vodafone and Nokia, and in the single-factor model we used the NYSE index as the broad market factor. The equity betas were estimated as 1.325 for Vodafone and 1.777 for Nokia. Using these factor sensitivities and based on historic daily returns on the NYSE from 2 January 2000 to 20 April 2006, estimate the F-GARCH volatilities and covariances for these two stocks, based on the model (II.4.46).

SOLUTION   We know the factor betas for each stock, so we only need to estimate the A-GARCH volatility $\hat{\sigma}_t^2$ of the NYSE index data. This single time series determines the behaviour of the stocks' volatilities: because there is only one factor they are just a constant multiple of $\hat{\sigma}_t$. Similarly, the time varying covariance between the two stocks is just a constant multiple of $\hat{\sigma}_t^2$. Figure II.4.12 illustrates all three series, just for the year 2002 when US stocks were particularly volatile.[46]

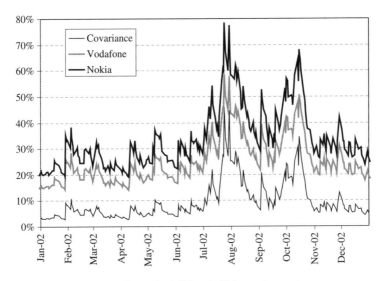

Figure II.4.12   F-GARCH volatilities and covariance

This single-factor GARCH model is rather simplistic because, with only one factor and with constant factor sensitivities, it assumes that all stocks are perfectly correlated. With only one factor the stocks will therefore have identical volatility patterns, as we can see in Figure II.4.12. However, the F-GARCH framework is general enough to include several risk

---

[46] To view these series over a longer data period just change the scale of the horizontal axis for graphs in the spreadsheet.

factors, and even with just two factors the systematic correlations will not be identical for all stocks. It can also be extended to using EWMA risk factor sensitivities, so that systematic correlation estimates can change over time.

The success of this model lies in finding a parsimonious factor model representation of the stock returns that explains a large part of their variation. If we use too many factors then the multivariate GARCH model for $\mathbf{\Omega}_t$ will be difficult to estimate; if there are insufficient factors then the stock's specific returns will be large and variable, so the approximation in (II.4.44) will not be very accurate.

It should be emphasized that F-GARCH only captures the systematic risk and it ignores the specific risk. Thus if capital requirements are based on this approach the bank will still need to add on the specific risk requirement using a standardized rule.

II.4.6 ORTHOGONAL GARCH

Principal component analysis (PCA) is an extremely powerful statistical tool for reducing the dimensions of large, highly correlated systems. In Chapter II.2 we used PCA very effectively to reduce the dimensions of a system of interest rates. For instance, we can obtain a close approximation to the changes in each rate in a system of *sixty* different interest rates using only *three* principal components. Moreover, the principal components are uncorrelated so their covariance matrix is diagonal. Hence, instead of estimating thousands of different variances and covariances we only need to estimate three variances! The computational efficiency of PCA is clearly huge.

I have termed the use of a *reduced* set of principal components with GARCH conditional variance equations *orthogonal GARCH*. In this section we derive the basic properties of this model and illustrate its application in Excel.[47] Then we compare the properties of the RiskMetrics EWMA covariance matrices with the covariance matrices that could be obtained using an alternative approach, based on orthogonal EWMA.

II.4.6.1 Model Specification

O-GARCH was introduced by Alexander and Chibumba (1996) and Alexander (2001b) and later extended by Van der Weide (2002) and others. Consider a set of zero mean returns with data summarized in a $T \times n$ matrix $\mathbf{X}$ and suppose we perform PCA on $\mathbf{V}$, the covariance matrix of $\mathbf{X}$. The *principal components* of $\mathbf{V}$ are the columns of the $T \times n$ matrix $\mathbf{P}$ defined by

$$\mathbf{P} = \mathbf{XW}, \tag{II.4.47}$$

where $\mathbf{W}$ is the $n \times n$ orthogonal matrix of eigenvectors of $\mathbf{V}$ and $\mathbf{W}$ is ordered so that the first column of $\mathbf{W}$ is the eigenvector corresponding to the largest eigenvalue of $\mathbf{V}$, the second column of $\mathbf{W}$ is the eigenvector corresponding to the second largest eigenvalue of $\mathbf{V}$, and so on. We may also perform PCA on the *correlation* matrix of returns instead of $\mathbf{V}$. See Section I.2.6 or Section II.2.2 for further details.

---

[47] O-GARCH estimation is a now standard procedure in the S-Plus package, specifically in S+Finmetrics version 3.0 and above. See http://www.insightful.com/products/finmetrics.

Now we consider using only a reduced set of principal components. The *first k principal components* of the returns are the first k columns of $\mathbf{P}$, and when we put these columns into a $T \times k$ matrix $\mathbf{P}^*$ we have a principal component approximation

$$\mathbf{X} \approx \mathbf{P}^* \mathbf{W}^{*\prime}, \tag{II.4.48}$$

where $\mathbf{W}^*$ is the $n \times k$ matrix whose k columns are given by the first k eigenvectors. This approximation can be made as accurate as we please by increasing k.

Orthogonal GARCH (O-GARCH) is based on the principal component representation (II.4.48) with a small number of components. In a highly correlated system (II.4.48) should be a very accurate approximation even when k is small. For instance, in a single highly correlated term structure of maybe 50 or 60 interest rates it is typical to take $k = 3$. But if the system is not highly correlated then (II.4.48) will not be accurate for small k and the O-GARCH method should not be applied. We recommend O-GARCH only for term structures exactly because they tend to be very highly correlated.

Taking variances of (II.4.48) gives

$$\mathbf{V}_t \approx \mathbf{W}^* \mathbf{\Omega}_t \mathbf{W}^{*\prime}, \tag{II.4.49}$$

where $\mathbf{V}_t$ is the $n \times n$ returns conditional covariance matrix at time t and $\mathbf{\Omega}_t$ is a $k \times k$ *diagonal* covariance matrix of the conditional variances of the principal components.[48] Hence, the full $n \times n$ matrix $\mathbf{V}_t$ with $n(n+1)/2$ different elements is obtained from just k different conditional variance estimates. For instance, in a term structure with $n = 50$ variables we only need to compute *three* GARCH conditional variances to obtain time varying estimates of more than one thousand covariances and variances.

The O-GARCH model requires estimating k separate univariate GARCH models, one for each principal component conditional variance in $\mathbf{\Omega}_t$. Since $\mathbf{\Omega}_t$ will always be positive definite the O-GARCH matrix $\mathbf{V}_t$ is always positive semi-definite. To see this, write

$$\mathbf{x}' \mathbf{V}_t \mathbf{x} = \mathbf{x}' \mathbf{W}^* \mathbf{\Omega}_t \mathbf{W}^{*\prime} \mathbf{x} = \mathbf{y}' \mathbf{\Omega}_t \mathbf{y}, \tag{II.4.50}$$

where $\mathbf{y} = \mathbf{W}^{*\prime} \mathbf{x}$. Since $\mathbf{y}$ can be zero for some non-zero $\mathbf{x}$, $\mathbf{x}' \mathbf{V}_t \mathbf{x}$ need not be strictly positive definite, but it will be positive semi-definite.

Computationally O-GARCH is a very efficient method. There is a huge reduction in the dimension of the problem: often only two or three GARCH variances are computed but from these we can derive hundreds or even thousands of time varying variance and covariance estimates and forecasts. The methodology has many other practical advantages, including the following:

- The number of principal components may be used as a control over the approximation in (II.4.49). This means that we may choose to take fewer components if, for instance, we want to cut down the amount of noise in the conditional correlations.
- Because it is based on PCA, O-GARCH also quantifies how much risk is associated with each systematic factor. In term structures the systematic factors have meaningful interpretations in terms of a shift, tilt and change in curvature in the term structure. This can be a great advantage for risk managers as their attention is directed towards the most important sources of risk.
- The O-GARCH method allows analytic forecasts of the whole covariance matrix to have the nice mean-reverting property of GARCH volatility term structure forecasts.

---

[48] The principal components are only *un*conditionally uncorrelated, but we assume they are also conditionally uncorrelated here.

That is, h-day forecasts for O-GARCH covariance matrices will converge to a long term average covariance matrix as h increases.

II.4.6.2   Case Study: A Comparison of RiskMetrics and O-GARCH

This case study illustrates the application of O-GARCH to term structures of constant maturity energy futures. We shall see in Section III.5.4.2 that constant maturity commodity futures such as these, though not traded assets, are commonly used as risk factors for commodity portfolios. O-GARCH could equally well be applied to any term structure, e.g. of interest rates or implied volatilities. In addition to the O-GARCH analysis, we examine the results of applying the RiskMetrics daily EWMA and regulatory covariance matrix constructions that were described in Section II.3.8.6. The RiskMetrics daily covariance matrix responds to all types of price movements, even those fluctuations that one should ascribe to noise for hedging purposes. So the matrix is very unstable over time.

In energy markets such as crude oil and natural gas, the daily and intraday fluctuations in prices of futures can be considerable. When hedging positions it is neither necessary nor desirable to rebalance the hedged portfolio with every type of movement in the term structure of futures prices. Indeed, some types of variations should be put down to 'noise' rather than systematic variations that need to be hedged. One of the nicest properties of O-GARCH is that it allows one to tailor the amount of noise in the correlation estimates by varying the number of principal components used in (II.4.48).

The case study compares the estimates obtained from the RiskMetrics and the O-GARCH models estimated on the daily returns to constant maturity futures term structures on West Texas Intermediate light sweet crude oil and on natural gas. We used daily closing prices to construct these constant maturity futures for the period from 4 January 1993 to 20 November 2003. The crude oil prices are based on New York Mercantile Exchange (NYMEX) futures prices and these are shown in Figure II.4.13.

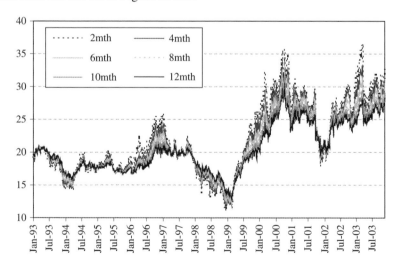

Figure II.4.13   Constant maturity crude oil futures prices

The constant maturity crude oil futures are from 2 to 12 months out. They typically display a downward sloping term structure, i.e. the market is in *backwardation*. However, during periods when prices were trending downwards, e.g. from May 1993 to May 1994 and during the whole of 1998 into early 1999, an upward sloping term structure is apparent, i.e. when the market is in *contango*. Clearly long term futures prices are less volatile than short term futures prices, which respond more to current market demand and are less influenced by expectations. Nevertheless crude oil futures form a very highly correlated system with only a few independent sources of information influencing their movements.

We shall also compare the estimates obtained from the RiskMetrics and the O-GARCH models for constant maturity natural gas futures over the same period. These futures prices are displayed in Figure II.4.14. There is no systemic backwardation or contango in this market and the futures returns display lower and less stable correlations than the crude oil futures. Instead there are significant seasonal effects, with the short term future responding most to fluctuations in demand and supply. Storage also plays an important role and, if filled to capacity, long term futures prices may be little influenced by short term fluctuations in demand.

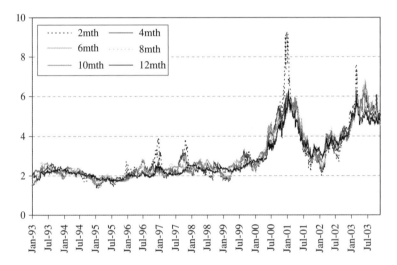

Figure II.4.14   Constant maturity natural gas futures prices

Figures II.4.15 and II.4.16 each illustrate two of the RiskMetrics correlation forecasts. That is, on each figure we compare the daily EWMA forecast (i.e. EWMA correlation on daily returns with $\lambda = 0.94$) and the 250-day 'regulatory' forecast (labelled 'historic' on the figures). The EWMA correlations shown in Figure II.4.15 for crude oil are not as unstable as the natural gas EWMA correlations shown in Figure II.4.16. As expected, the crude oil futures are very highly correlated, with correlations remaining above 0.95 most of the sample period and only falling during times of crisis (e.g. the outbreak of war in Iraq). Following market crises, substantial differences arise between the EWMA short term correlation estimates and the long term 'historic' estimates. The long term correlation is more stable, of course, but it can remain too low for too long. For example, a single outlier in March 1996 induced a low historic correlation estimate for a whole year, miraculously jumping up to the normal level exactly 250 days after the event, even though nothing happened in the markets on that day in March 1997. The single outlier simply fell out of the moving average window.

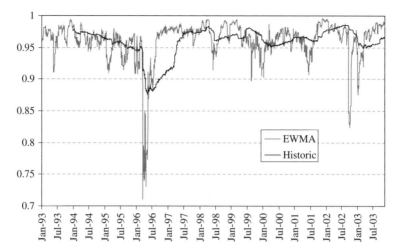

Figure II.4.15 Correlation between 2-month and 6-month crude oil futures forecasted using Risk-Metrics EWMA and 250-day methods

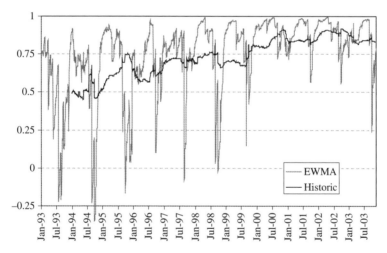

Figure II.4.16 Correlation between 2-month and 6-month natural gas futures forecasted using Risk-Metrics EWMA and 250-day methods

The EWMA method reveals the seasonality of natural gas correlations in Figure II.4.16: when supply is filled to capacity, often between the months of September and November, the 6-month future responds much less than the 2-month future to demand fluctuations, and consequently their correlation can be very low. In the early part of the sample the EWMA correlations even become negative for very short periods. But this type of fluctuation is only very temporary. On the other hand, the historic correlations only capture the trend in correlations and not their seasonal characteristics. Probably as a result of increasing liquidity in the natural gas markets, correlations between 2-month and 6-month futures have been increasing during the sample period.

The O-GARCH model is based on GARCH volatility forecasts of only the first few principal components in the system. It is therefore ideally suited to term structures such as constant maturity energy futures, where PCA is commonly applied to reduce dimensionality. The O-GARCH model is an attractive alternative for generating covariance matrices for energy futures, because it allows one to tailor the amount of noise that is included or excluded from the forecasts. The number of principal components chosen depends on how much of the variation is considered to be unimportant from the perspective of forecasting correlation. Often just the first two or three principal components are required to represent a single term structure. It also allows more realistic forecasts of future covariances because they converge to a long term average value rather than remaining constant, as the EWMA forecasts do.

To generate the O-GARCH correlations, the first step is to perform a PCA of the term structure. Table II.4.10 shows the eigenvalues of the correlation matrix of the returns to crude oil and natural gas. There are 11 variables in each system, being the prices at 11 different future dates. The first few eigenvectors are then given in the columns to the right of the column showing the eigenvalues.

Table II.4.10   PCA of 2mth–12mth crude oil futures and natural gas futures

(a) Crude oil				(b) Natural gas				
Eigenvalues	Eigenvectors			Eigenvalues	Eigenvectors			
	w_1	w_2	w_3		w_1	w_2	w_3	w_4
10.732	0.293	0.537	0.623	8.696	0.292	0.345	0.243	0.306
0.245	0.299	0.412	0.078	0.909	0.298	0.394	0.212	0.310
0.016	0.302	0.280	−0.225	0.584	0.309	0.346	0.139	0.050
0.004	0.304	0.161	−0.348	0.377	0.315	0.239	0.006	−0.292
0.002	0.305	0.054	−0.353	0.242	0.316	0.130	−0.174	−0.462
0.001	0.305	−0.044	−0.276	0.078	0.311	0.026	−0.408	−0.304
0.000	0.304	−0.132	−0.162	0.036	0.306	−0.120	−0.479	0.104
0.000	0.303	−0.211	−0.028	0.029	0.304	−0.266	−0.316	0.392
0.000	0.302	−0.282	0.115	0.023	0.297	−0.393	0.036	0.344
0.000	0.300	−0.350	0.247	0.015	0.289	−0.427	0.370	−0.060
0.000	0.298	−0.411	0.364	0.010	0.277	−0.331	0.461	−0.361

In the crude oil futures term structure the first principal component explains $10.732/11 = 97.6\%$ of the variation. The first eigenvector is almost constant, so the first principal component captures a more or less parallel shift in all maturities. Movements in the second component account for a further 2.2% of the variation and this component captures a 'tilt' in the futures term structure, as can be seen from the downward trending values of the second eigenvector. We only need two principal components for this system: since the higher components together explain only 0.2% of the movements, these can definitely be ascribed to 'noise'.

In the natural gas system the principal components may still be given the standard 'trend–tilt–curvature' interpretation, but the system is less correlated as a whole than the crude oil system so more components are required to capture most of the variation. The trend component explains only $8.696/11 = 79.1\%$ of the variation, the tilt a further 8.3%, and the third and fourth components 5.3% and 3.4% respectively. Hence, with four principal components the remaining 3.9% of the variation would be attributed to 'noise'.

The reduction in dimensionality achieved by a principal component representation can greatly facilitate calculations. Transformations are applied to the principal components and then the factor weights are used to relate these transformations to the original system. Here we have estimated normal symmetric GARCH models for the first two principal components in each system. Then we have used just these two time series of variances, and the 11×2 constant matrix with columns equal to the first two eigenvectors, to generate the full 11×11 covariance matrix of variances and covariances of futures of every maturity. Each covariance matrix contains 11 volatilities and 55 correlations and the model generates term structure covariance matrix forecasts for any risk horizon. So, from univariate GARCH models estimated on just two principal components a remarkably rich structure of correlation forecasts is generated.

Figures II.4.17 and II.4.18 show some of the 1-day forecasts, specifically those relating to just the 2-month, 6-month and 12-month futures, on crude oil. The volatility of the 2-month future in Figure II.4.17 is consistently 2–2.5% higher than that of the 6-month future and 3–3.5% higher than that of the 12-month future. Common peaks in all volatility series corresponding to large upwards shifts in the futures term structure are associated with major political and economic crises and these are accompanied by a general increase in correlation. The O-GARCH 2mth–6mth correlation is relatively stable, and much more stable than the EWMA forecasts, since it is based only on parallel shift and tilt movements in the term structure. However, the stability of the O-GARCH correlation estimates decreases, along with its average level, as the difference in maturity of the futures increases.

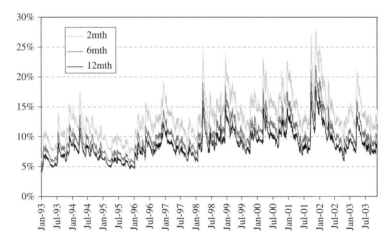

Figure II.4.17   O-GARCH 1-day volatility forecasts for crude oil

Figures II.4.19 and II.4.20 illustrate some of the OGARCH volatilities and correlations for the natural gas futures. Here the 2-month future responds most to variations in supply and demand and is thus more volatile than the longer dated futures. On average its volatility is almost double that of the 6-month future and more than double that of the 12-month future. Peaks in volatility are seasonal and these are common to all futures, though most pronounced in the near term futures. From the year 2000 there has been a general increase in the level of volatility and at the same time the correlation between futures of different maturities also increased. Hence, natural gas has displayed a positive association between volatility and correlation but this is not so obvious in crude oil.

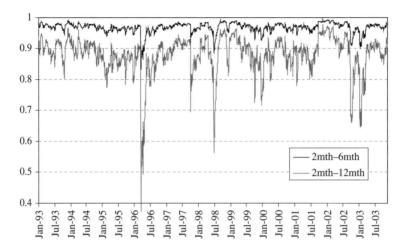

Figure II.4.18   O-GARCH 1-day correlation forecasts for crude oil

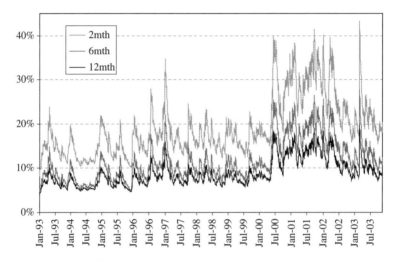

Figure II.4.19   O-GARCH 1-day volatility forecasts for natural gas

Comparing the O-GARCH and EWMA estimates of the natural gas 2mth–6mth correlation, the O-GARCH correlations are much higher and more stable than the EWMA correlations. Being based on only the first two principal components, the O-GARCH correlations only capture the *systematic* trend and tilt movements in futures prices, the other movements being ignored because they are attributed to 'noise'. Ignoring this noise arguably provides a better guide for some risk management decisions such as hedging and portfolio allocation. From the PCA results in Table II.4.10 we know that the O-GARCH model with two components is modelling 99.8% of the variation in the crude oil futures term structure but only 87.3% of the variation in the natural gas futures term structure. The addition of one more principal component to the O-GARCH model is recommended for the natural gas system.

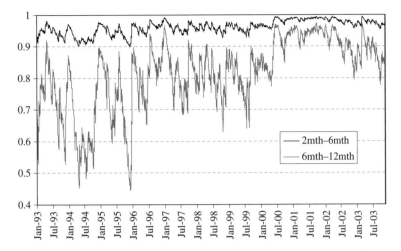

Figure II.4.20   O-GARCH 1-day correlation forecasts for natural gas

II.4.6.3   Splicing Methods for Constructing Large Covariance Matrices

Both O-EWMA and O-GARCH will work very well indeed for any term structure. However, there are problems when one tries to extend these methodologies to different types of asset class. Alexander (2001b) shows how market-specific returns on major equity indices can adversely influence all the other equity market indices in the system that is represented by the PCA. Although some authors have applied the O-GARCH model to equity indices, foreign exchange rates and other assets, in most cases the residual variation from using only a few principal components is too high for the approximation (II.4.48) to be accurate. Using more components in the PCA does *not* help, because the less important principal components pick up idiosyncratic factors that relate only to one or two of the original returns, and in the O-GARCH methodology the variation of every principal component will affect the variation of the original returns.

For this reason the set of returns first need to be 'clustered' into highly correlated subgroups. Then the O-GARCH (or O-EWMA) methodology is applied to each subgroup, each time retaining just the first few principal components, and the final, full-dimensional covariance matrix for the original returns can be obtained using the following 'splicing' method.

The method is explained for just two subgroups; the generalization to a larger number of subgroups is straightforward. Suppose there are m variables in the first category and n variables in the second category. It is not the dimensions that matter. What does matter is that each subgroup of asset or risk factors is suitably co-dependent so that the first few principal components provide an adequate representation of each subgroup. First, compute the principal components of each subgroup, and label these $\{P_1, \ldots, P_r\}$ and $\{Q_1, \ldots, Q_s\}$ where r and s are the number of principal components that are used in the representation of each category. Generally r will be much less than m and s will be much less than n. Denote by $\mathbf{A}$ (dimension $m \times r$) and $\mathbf{B}$ (dimension $n \times s$) the normalized factor weight matrices obtained in the PCA of the first and second categories, respectively. Then the 'within-group' covariances are given by $\mathbf{AD_1A'}$ and $\mathbf{BD_2B'}$ respectively, where $\mathbf{D_1}$ and $\mathbf{D_2}$ are the diagonal matrices of the univariate GARCH or EWMA variances of the principal components of each system.

Denote by $\mathbf{C}$ the $r \times s$ matrix of covariances of principal components across the two systems, i.e. $\mathbf{C} = \text{Cov}(P_i, Q_j)$. This 'cross-group' covariance matrix is computed using O-EWMA or O-GARCH a *second* time, now on a system of the $r + s$ principal components $\{P_1, \ldots, P_r, Q_1, \ldots, Q_s\}$. The cross covariances of the original system will then be $\mathbf{ACB}'$ and the full covariance matrix of the original system will be given by

$$\begin{pmatrix} \mathbf{AD}_1\mathbf{A}' & \mathbf{ACB}' \\ \mathbf{BC'A}' & \mathbf{BD}_2\mathbf{B}' \end{pmatrix}. \qquad (\text{II.4.51})$$

Since $\mathbf{D}_1$ and $\mathbf{D}_2$ are diagonal matrices with positive elements – these are the variances of the principal components – the within-factor covariance matrices $\mathbf{AD}_1\mathbf{A}'$ and $\mathbf{BD}_2\mathbf{B}'$ will always be positive semi-definite. However, it is not always possible to guarantee positive semi-definiteness of the full covariance matrix of the original system. So after splicing together the sub-covariance matrices, the full covariance matrix must be tested for positive definiteness by checking that all its eigenvalues are positive.

II.4.7   MONTE CARLO SIMULATION WITH GARCH MODELS

This section provides empirical examples in interactive Excel spreadsheets where we simulate returns with volatility clustering. This is a main distinguishing feature of simulating with GARCH models. Then in Section II.4.8 we show how GARCH returns simulations can be extended to the simulation of asset prices.

II.4.7.1   Simulation with Volatility Clustering

Section I.5.7 described how to simulate a time series of i.i.d. returns from any distribution. If each return is generated by a continuous distribution function $F(x)$, we simulate a return from this distribution by drawing from the standard uniform distribution (in other words, we simulate a random number u) and then setting $x = F^{-1}(u)$. For instance, to simulate a single time series of 100 standard normal i.i.d. returns in column A of an Excel spreadsheet we simply type = NORMSINV(RAND()) in cells A1:A100. To convert this time series into simulated returns on an i.i.d. process that is normal with mean μ and standard deviation σ we take each standard normal return z_t at time t and apply the transformation $x_t = \mu + z_t\sigma$ for $t = 1, \ldots, T$.[49]

In this section we show how Monte Carlo simulation of standard normal variables is used to simulate a time series of returns that follow a GARCH process. We must first fix the parameters of the GARCH model, either from a personal view or from prior estimation of the model. If the parameters have been estimated from historical *percentage* returns then use the algorithms below to simulate a percentage returns time series with volatility clustering. But if the parameters have been estimated from historical *log* returns, which is the usual case, then we simulate a log returns series with volatility clustering. We first assume the conditional distribution is normal with a constant mean and symmetric or asymmetric GARCH conditional variance.

---

[49] More complete details are given in Section I.5.7.2.

The time series simulation starts with an initial value $\hat{\sigma}_1$. Assuming the parameters are estimated from historical data, then the initial estimate $\hat{\sigma}_1$ is set to either the long term standard deviation or the standard deviation that is estimated by the GARCH model at the time the simulation is made. Under our assumption that the GARCH process is normal, we take a random draw z_1 from a standard normal i.i.d. process and set $\varepsilon_1 = z_1 \hat{\sigma}_1$. Then ε_1 and $\hat{\sigma}_1$ are put into the right-hand side of the GARCH conditional variance equation to estimate $\hat{\sigma}_2$. Thereafter we iterate, by taking further random draws $z_2, \ldots, z_T$ from a standard normal i.i.d. process, and the GARCH model provides an estimate of each $\hat{\sigma}_t$ given ε_{t-1} and $\hat{\sigma}_{t-1}$.

To summarize, when the conditional distribution of the errors is normal then the *normal GARCH simulation algorithm* is as follows:

1. Fix an initial value for $\hat{\sigma}_1$ and set $t = 1$.
2. Take a random draw z_t from a standard normal i.i.d. process.
3. Multiply this by $\hat{\sigma}_t$ to obtain $\hat{\varepsilon}_t = \hat{\sigma}_t z_t$.
4. Find $\hat{\sigma}_{t+1}$ from $\hat{\sigma}_t$ and $\hat{\varepsilon}_t$ using the estimated GARCH model.
5. Return to step 2, replacing t by $t + 1$.

The time series $\{\varepsilon_1, \ldots, \varepsilon_T\}$ is a simulated time series with mean zero that exhibits volatility clustering.

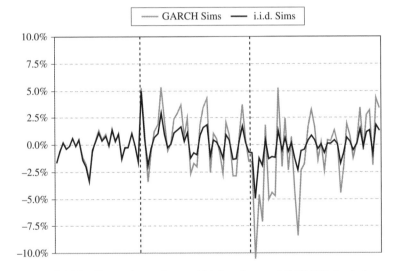

Figure II.4.21   Comparison of normal i.i.d. and normal GARCH simulations

Figure II.4.21 compares simulations from a symmetric normal GARCH model with simulations based on i.i.d. returns with the same unconditional volatility as the GARCH process. The parameters of the GARCH model are assumed to be[50]

$$\hat{\omega} = 1 \times 10^{-6}, \quad \hat{\alpha} = 0.085, \quad \hat{\beta} = 0.905.$$

So the long term standard deviation is 1%. Assuming the simulations are daily and there are 250 trading days per year, the long term volatility is $\sqrt{250} \times 1\% = 15.81\%$. In the figure we

---

[50] These may be changed by the reader.

have simulated a time series of 100 daily returns based on each process. The two simulations shown are based on the same random numbers.[51] These are drawn from a standard uniform distribution except that we have inserted two market shocks, the first one positive and the second one negative. The times that the shocks are inserted are indicated by dotted lines. The point to note about the comparison in the figure is that the GARCH returns exhibit volatility clustering. That is, following a market shock the GARCH returns become more variable than the i.i.d. returns.

The simulation algorithm has a straightforward generalization to Student t GARCH. Now the degrees of freedom are an additional parameter that is fixed for the simulation and we simply replace step 2 with a random draw from the Student t distribution with the required number of degrees of freedom. The spreadsheet for Figure II.4.22 simulates an asymmetric Student t GARCH process and compares this with the symmetric normal GARCH process based on the same basic random numbers. This allows us to examine the effect of (a) asymmetric volatility response and (b) leptokurtosis in the conditional returns distribution.

The parameters used to simulate the returns in Figure II.4.22 are shown in Table II.4.11. These have been chosen so that both symmetric and asymmetric formulations have a long term standard deviation of 1%, which is the same as for the previous figure. In addition, the degrees of freedom for the Student t GARCH process have been set to 15. However, you can change all these values when you use the spreadsheet.

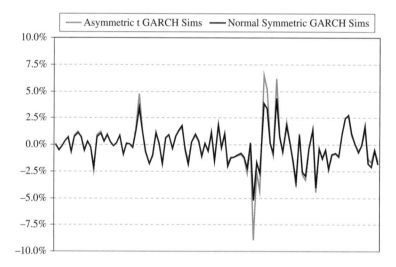

Figure II.4.22 Comparison of symmetric normal GARCH and asymmetric t GARCH simulations

One pair of simulations is compared in Figure II.4.22. Again each series is based on the same random numbers and we have inserted the same positive and negative market shocks to examine the volatility response. We see that the t GARCH process has a more extreme reaction to the second, negative market shock and that the asymmetric volatility response is pronounced. In A-GARCH with positive λ, volatility increases much more following the negative shock than following the positive shock.

---

[51] Press F9 in the spreadsheet to repeat the simulations.

Table II.4.11 Parameter settings for symmetric and asymmetric GARCH simulations

	Symmetric	Asymmetric
ω	1.00E-06	1.00E-06
α	0.085	0.07
β	0.905	0.85
λ	0	0.01
$\alpha + \beta$	0.99	0.92
Long term standard deviation	1.00%	1.00%

II.4.7.2 Simulation with Volatility Clustering Regimes

In this subsection we explain how to simulate from (a) normal mixture GARCH models and (b) Markov switching GARCH models. Recall from Section II.4.4.3 that the normal mixture GARCH process requires two sets of GARCH parameters, one for each volatility regime, and we also need the probability that the ruling regime is regime 1, and we denote this probability by $\hat{\pi}$. That is, at each time step in the normal mixture GARCH simulation the probability that the variance is in regime 1 is $\hat{\pi}$.

The *normal mixture GARCH simulation* algorithm is a straightforward generalization of the standard GARCH simulation algorithm. But at each step we add a preliminary draw of a random number which determines whether we are in the high volatility or the low volatility regime. The algorithm is specified as follows:[52]

1. Set $t = 1$ and fix an initial value for $\hat{\sigma}_{i1}$
2. Draw a random number u in $[0, 1]$.
3. If $u \le \hat{\pi}$ then set $i = 1$, otherwise set $i = 2$.
4. Take a random draw z_t from a standard normal i.i.d. process.
5. Multiply this by $\hat{\sigma}_{it}$ to obtain $\varepsilon_t = \hat{\sigma}_{it} z_t$.
6. Find $\hat{\sigma}_{i,t+1}$ from $\hat{\sigma}_{it}$ and $\hat{\varepsilon}_t$ using the estimated parameters for the ith GARCH component.
7. Return to step 2, replacing t by $t + 1$.

We now show how to simulate returns from an asymmetric normal mixture GARCH process with the parameters shown in Table II.4.12 and where the probability of regime 1 is 0.75. Note that the first component is identical to the asymmetric component used in the previous section, but the second component has greater reaction, less persistence, more leverage and an annual volatility of 70%. This reflects the empirical characteristics of equity markets, as described in Section II.4.4.3.

Figure II.4.23 shows three time series. The series labelled 'high volatility component' and 'low volatility component' are based on the same series of random numbers, one generated by the low volatility GARCH process and the other by the high volatility GARCH process. The third series is the normal mixture GARCH simulation. The spreadsheet is set up so that the probability that the normal mixture GARCH process at any time t is governed by the low volatility component is 0.75 although, as with the other parameters, this can be changed by the user.

---

[52] Notice in the spreadsheet for Markov switching GARCH simulations that both σ_1 and σ_2 will be updated at each iteration.

Table II.4.12   Parameter settings for normal mixture GARCH simulations

	Component 1	Component 2
ω	1.00E-06	4.25E-06
α	0.07	0.15
β	0.85	0.8
λ	0.01	0.025
$\alpha + \beta$	0.92	0.95
Long term standard deviation	1.00%	4.43%

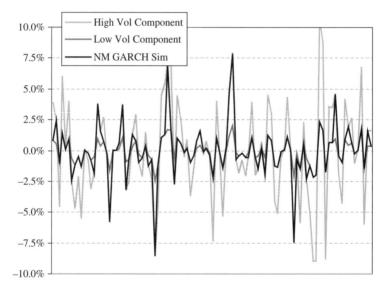

Figure II.4.23   High and low volatility components in normal mixture GARCH

The problem with the normal mixture GARCH model is that the process switches between the two regimes too often. At every time step there is a constant probability that it will be in each regime, and there is no mechanism to prevent the regime switching at each time step. Because of this, the continuous limit of normal mixture GARCH does not exist, as shown by Alexander and Lazar (2008b). Hence, we cannot use the model for option pricing based on continuous time models.

However, a simple extension of the normal mixture simulation algorithm above gives the Markov switching GARCH process, and this is more realistic than any other type of GARCH simulation. Here the probability that the process is in a given volatility regime at any time t is not fixed, but instead there is a fixed probability of *switching* regimes at any time, which is called the *transition probability* of the Markov switching GARCH model, and this is usually different for each regime. The two transition probabilities are estimated by the Markov switching model, and these are denoted $\hat{\pi}_{12}$ for the probability of switching from regime 1 to regime 2 and $\hat{\pi}_{21}$ for the probability of switching from regime 2 to regime 1. Note that the probability of staying in regime 1 is $\hat{\pi}_{11} = 1 - \hat{\pi}_{12}$ and the probability of staying in regime 2 is $\hat{\pi}_{22} = 1 - \hat{\pi}_{21}$. The parameters $\hat{\pi}_{11}$ and $\hat{\pi}_{22}$ are assumed constant and are estimated with the other parameters of the GARCH model. The unconditional probability of being in regime 1 is then given by[53]

$$\hat{\pi} = \frac{\hat{\pi}_{21}}{\hat{\pi}_{12} + \hat{\pi}_{21}}. \qquad (\text{II.4.52})$$

The *Markov switching GARCH simulation* algorithm is a straightforward generalization of the normal mixture GARCH simulation algorithm. But now, in addition to the preliminary draw of a random number to determine where we *start* the simulation (in the high volatility or the low volatility regime), we include a probability of switching regimes at any time in the future. The algorithm is specified as follows:

1. Set $t = 1$ and fix an initial value for $\hat{\sigma}_{i1}$.
2. Draw a random number u in $[0, 1]$.
3. If $u \leq \hat{\pi}$ then set $i = 1$, otherwise set $i = 2$.
4. Take a random draw z_t from a standard normal i.i.d. process.
5. Multiply this by $\hat{\sigma}_{it}$ to obtain $\hat{\varepsilon}_t = \hat{\sigma}_{it} z_t$.
6. Find $\hat{\sigma}_{i,t+1}$ from $\hat{\sigma}_{it}$ and $\hat{\varepsilon}_t$ using the estimated parameters for the ith GARCH component.
7. Draw a random number u in $[0, 1]$.
8. If $u \leq \hat{\pi}_{ii}$ then leave i as it is, otherwise switch i.
9. Return to step 4, replacing t by $t + 1$.

Figure II.4.24 displays two time series resulting from simulations of a Markov switching GARCH process where:

- the two normal GARCH components have the parameters shown in Table II.4.12;
- the unconditional probability of regime 1 – the low volatility regime – is 0.75 as for the normal mixture GARCH process considered above; and
- $\hat{\pi}_{11} = 0.95$ and $\hat{\pi}_{22} = 0.85$. In other words, there is a 5% chance that the low volatility regime switches into a high volatility regime but a 15% chance that the high volatility regime switches into a low volatility regime.[54]

Now if the process switches to the high volatility regime it is more likely to remain in that regime for several periods before switching back to the low volatility regime. Volatility clustering is much more pronounced in these simulations than in other types of GARCH simulations.

II.4.7.3 Simulation with Correlation Clustering

In Section I.5.7.4 we described how the Cholesky matrix of a correlation matrix is used to simulate a set of correlated returns. We applied the method in Section I.5.7.5 to the case where the returns are generated by an i.i.d. multivariate normal process and to the case where the returns are generated by an i.i.d. multivariate Student t distributed process. In this subsection we extend that analysis to generate correlated returns with both volatility and correlation clustering using a simple multivariate GARCH model.

---

[53] But this unconditional probability is the only regime probability parameter in normal mixture GARCH. See Section II.7.5.2 for the proof of (II.4.52).
[54] Note that this choice for transition probabilities and unconditional probability satisfies (II.4.52).

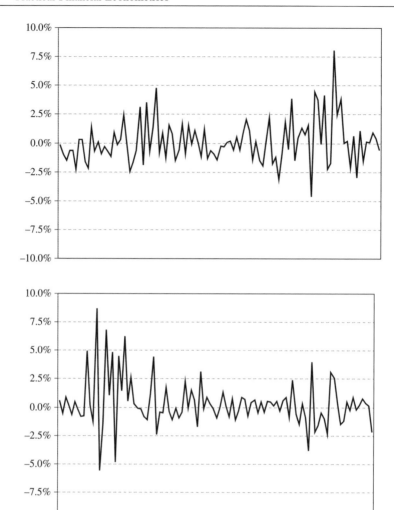

Figure II.4.24   Simulations from a Markov switching GARCH process

To illustrate the basic idea we consider two returns that have a symmetric normal diagonal vech GARCH representation of the form (II.4.39). This is the simplest possible multivariate GARCH model. Moreover, with just two assets we do not need to use an algorithm to find a Cholesky matrix at each stage. Since

$$\begin{pmatrix} 1 & 0 \\ \varrho & \sqrt{1-\varrho^2} \end{pmatrix} \begin{pmatrix} 1 & \varrho \\ 0 & \sqrt{1-\varrho^2} \end{pmatrix} = \begin{pmatrix} 1 & \varrho \\ \varrho & 1 \end{pmatrix},$$

the Cholseky matrix of a 2×2 correlation is just

$$\begin{pmatrix} 1 & 0 \\ \varrho & \sqrt{1-\varrho^2} \end{pmatrix}.$$

This means that we can obtain correlated simulations on standard normal variables using

$$z_{2t} = \varrho_t z_{1t} + \sqrt{1-\varrho_t^2} z_{3t}, \qquad\qquad (\text{II.4.53})$$

where z_{1t} and z_{3t} are independent standard normal variates and ϱ_t is the GARCH correlation simulated at time t. Then the conditional correlation between z_{1t} and z_{2t} will be ϱ_t.

The algorithm for simulating two correlated returns with a diagonal vech parameterization and conditional distributions that are multivariate normal is as follows:

1. Take two independent random draws z_{1t} and z_{3t} from a standard normal i.i.d. process.
2. Set $z_{2t} = \hat{\varrho}_t z_{1t} + \sqrt{1 - \hat{\varrho}_t^2} z_{3t}$, where $\hat{\varrho}_t$ is the GARCH correlation simulated at time t.
3. Set $\hat{\varepsilon}_{1t} = \hat{\sigma}_{1t} z_{1t}$ and $\hat{\varepsilon}_{2t} = \hat{\sigma}_{2t} z_{2t}$.
4. Find $\hat{\sigma}_{1,t+1}$, $\hat{\sigma}_{2,t+1}$ and $\hat{\sigma}_{12,t+1}$ from $\hat{\sigma}_{1t}$, $\hat{\sigma}_{2t}$, $\hat{\sigma}_{12t}$, $\hat{\varepsilon}_{1t}$ and $\hat{\varepsilon}_{2t}$ using the estimated GARCH model.
5. Return to step 1, replacing t by $t + 1$.

Again the algorithm is implemented in Excel. The diagonal vech parameter settings are given in Table II.4.13. Note that the GARCH covariance need not be positive so the reaction parameter in the covariance equation can be negative, as it is in this case. However, the conditional covariance matrix must always be positive definite.

Table II.4.13 Diagonal vech parameters for correlated GARCH simulations

GARCH parameters	Var 1	Var 2	Covar
ω	1.00E-06	1.00E-06	1.00E-05
α	0.085	0.05	−0.05
β	0.905	0.94	0.7
Long term StDev (covariance)	1.00%	1.00%	2.86E-05

One pair of simulations is shown in Figure II.4.25. We also show, in Figure II.4.26, the conditional correlation that corresponds to this simulation.

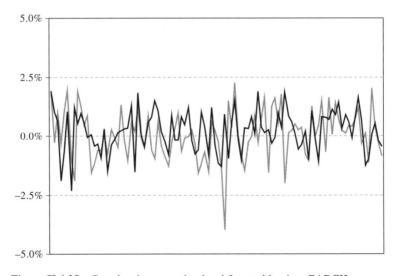

Figure II.4.25 Correlated returns simulated from a bivariate GARCH process

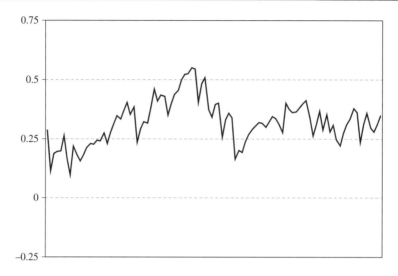

Figure II.4.26   GARCH correlation of the returns shown in Figure II.4.25

Obviously there are numerous extensions of these conditionally correlated Monte Carlo simulations to asymmetric GARCH, Student t, normal mixture or Markov switching multivariate GARCH. They may also have more complex parameterizations based on F-GARCH, CC or DCC, or O-GARCH.

II.4.8   APPLICATIONS OF GARCH MODELS

This section surveys some of the most common financial applications of GARCH models, all of which are based on the ability to simulate returns with volatility and correlation clustering.[55] Using simulations, univariate GARCH models have applications to pricing path-dependent options. And GARCH covariance matrix forecasts provide the centrepiece of advanced risk measurement systems where historical simulation or Monte Carlo value-at-risk (VaR) models can incorporate volatility clustering effects in portfolio returns. GARCH covariance matrices may also be used as a basis for portfolio optimization. The ability to fix scenario values for long term volatility and the mean-reversion property of GARCH forecasts are just three of the properties that increase the attraction of GARCH models as tools for making long term investment decisions.

II.4.8.1   Option Pricing with GARCH Diffusions

Model (II.4.1) is also called a *strong GARCH process* because we make strong assumptions about the conditional distribution of the errors. In the case where they are normally distributed

---

[55] Readers should also consult the excellent survey of GARCH model applications by Andersen et al. (2006).

Nelson (1991) proved that the continuous time limit of the symmetric normal strong GARCH process is a stochastic volatility process where the Brownian motion driving the volatility is uncorrelated with the price process. Unfortunately, stochastic volatility models with zero price–volatility correlation have limited applications and so Nelson's GARCH diffusion has not received very much attention from practitioners. Also to simulate returns based on this process we should be able to discretize the process and obtain model (II.4.1). Unfortunately, no discretization of the strong GARCH diffusion yields (II.4.1). A further problem with strong GARCH is that *ad hoc* assumptions about parameter convergence must be made.

Strong GARCH process are not *time aggregating*, in the following sense. Suppose you simulate a daily time series of returns using strong GARCH and then take a sample from that time series at the weekly frequency. Then your sample will *not* be generated by a strong GARCH process. To have the time aggregation property we need a *weak GARCH* version of (II.4.1) that specifies exactly the same conditional variance equation but weakens our assumptions about the conditional distribution of the error process. The main difference between strong and weak GARCH is that weak GARCH does not impose a functional form on the error distribution, and this is why it can be time aggregating.

Arguing that it makes no sense to derive the continuous limit of a process that is not time aggregating, Alexander and Lazar (2005) derive the continuous limit of weak GARCH and show that it is a stochastic volatility model with *non-zero* price–volatility correlation. Moreover the price–volatility correlation is related to the skewness of the returns and the volatility of volatility depends on the excess kurtosis in the returns, which is very intuitive. Also, when we discretize the process we *do* obtain the weak GARCH process and there is no need to make *ad hoc* assumptions about the convergence of parameters.

The weak GARCH diffusion is therefore a very good model for option pricing. In Section III.4.5.6 we discuss the problems with strong GARCH diffusions and provide Excel examples that simulate price series generated by both strong and weak GARCH processes. We then describe the merits of GARCH diffusions for pricing and hedging with stochastic volatility.

II.4.8.2   Pricing Path-Dependent European Options

In this subsection we show how simulations of log returns based on GARCH processes may be applied to price path-dependent European options. A path-dependent European option is a European option whose pay-off depends on the underlying price at some time prior to expiry. The most common examples of path-dependent European options are barrier options and Asian options.

Often we make the assumption that log returns are i.i.d. normal, in other words that the price process follows a *geometric Brownian motion*. Under this assumption we can derive good analytic approximations to the prices of most path-dependent options.[56] But when log returns are not assumed to follow an i.i.d. process, and it is much more realistic to assume that they follow a GARCH process, we need to use a numerical method to derive the option price.

---

[56] A formula for the approximate price of a barrier option is given in Section III.3.8.9 and a formula for the price of an Asian option is given in Section III.3.8.10. As usual, the formulae are supported using Excel spreadsheets.

Pricing Exotic Options with Asymmetric GARCH

In the previous section we explained how to use a GARCH model to simulate zero mean returns with volatility and correlation clustering. The simulation algorithms applied an estimated GARCH model to i.i.d. standard normal variates z_t, thereby simulating a series $\varepsilon_t = \{z_t \hat{\sigma}_t\}_{t=1}^{T}$ of zero mean conditionally normal log returns with volatility clustering where T is the number of periods until the option expires.

In this section we need to add a *non-zero mean* to these returns in order to simulate asset prices with a non-zero drift. Hence, at each time t in the simulation algorithm we set

$$x_t = z_t \hat{\sigma}_t + r, \qquad (\text{II.4.54})$$

where z_t are i.i.d. standard normal variates, r denotes the risk free rate of return (assuming the asset pays no dividends) and $\hat{\sigma}_t$ is the simulated GARCH standard deviation of log returns at time t as described in the previous section. Then $\{x_t\}_{t=1}^{T}$ is a simulated time series of log returns with volatility clustering.

This is translated into a simulated time series of asset prices, using the standard relationship between prices and log returns that was derived in Section I.5.7.3. That is, we set S_0 to be the current price of the underlying and then set

$$S_{t+1} = \exp(x_t)S_t = \exp(z_t \hat{\sigma}_t + r)S_t. \qquad (\text{II.4.55})$$

So for each simulated time series for log returns, we also have a simulated time series of asset prices.

Typically we would use 10,000 such simulated time series for pricing an option. Then for each simulated time series we calculate the pay-off of the option at maturity and find its present value by discounting at the risk free rate. The option price is the average of the present value of the pay-offs over all simulations. The following examples illustrate the use of Monte Carlo simulation for pricing and hedging options under GARCH processes.

EXAMPLE II.4.8: PRICING AN ASIAN OPTION WITH GARCH[57]

A European average rate call option has pay-off $\max(A_T - K, 0)$, where K is the strike of the option and

$$A_T = n^{-1} \sum_{i=0}^{n-1} S_{T-ik}$$

is an average of the underlying price, taken at n equally spaced dates k days apart, on and before the expiry date of the option, T. Use risk neutral valuation to price a European average rate call option with strike 95 and maturity 360 days when the spot price of the underlying is 100, the spot volatility is 25%, the risk free interest rate is 5%, the underlying pays no dividends and the averaging is over the prices on days 300, 310, 320, 330, 340, 350 and 360. Assume the underlying returns (a) are i.i.d. and (b) follow a symmetric normal GARCH process with parameters[58]

$$\hat{\omega} = 1 \times 10^{-6}, \ \hat{\alpha} = 0.05, \text{ and } \hat{\beta} = 0.94.$$

---

[57] This example and the next may be found in the 'GARCH Simulations' Excel workbook.

[58] These can be changed in the spreadsheet, as can the strike, spot price, spot volatility and risk free rate. A small adjustment also allows the maturity to be changed.

SOLUTION   Since the option expires in 360 days each simulated time series based on (II.4.55) has 360 daily asset prices. For comparison, we also perform the simulations under the assumption of i.i.d. returns. In that case we keep the daily volatility constant at its spot value, which is $25\%/\sqrt{250} = 1.48\%$. In practice we should simulate several thousand time series, but this is not feasible in a demonstration spreadsheet. We leave it to the reader to simulate prices many times, by pressing F9 or by extending the worksheet. On average, taken over a larger number of simulations, the GARCH price is higher than the i.i.d price for the option. It should be the case that the price of an option under stochastic volatility is greater than its price under the i.i.d. assumption,[59] because stochastic volatility increases the leptokurtosis in the returns distribution.

EXAMPLE II.4.9: PRICING A BARRIER OPTION WITH GARCH

A European down and out barrier put option has pay-off $\max(K - S_T, 0)$ provided that $S_t > B$ for all $t = 1, \ldots, T$, otherwise the pay-off is 0. Here K is the strike, B is the barrier and T is the maturity date of the option. Use risk neutral valuation to price a European down and out barrier put with strike 95, barrier 75 and maturity 360 days. As before, assume the spot price of the underlying is 100, the spot volatility is 25%, the risk free interest rate is 5% and the underlying pays no dividends. And, also as in the previous example, assume the underlying returns (a) are i.i.d. and (b) follow a symmetric normal GARCH process with parameters[60]

$$\hat{\omega} = 1 \times 10^{-6}, \quad \hat{\alpha} = 0.05 \quad \text{and} \quad \hat{\beta} = 0.94.$$

SOLUTION   The solution proceeds in exactly the same way as the previous example. The only thing that changes is the pay-off calculation. If a simulated price hits the barrier at any time then the option pay-off based on this simulation is set to 0. Otherwise we use the usual pay-off function for a put option. Again, the reader is left to repeat the simulations many times.

Calibrating GARCH Parameters to Option Prices

When GARCH models are applied to option pricing it is usual to estimate the GARCH parameters by calibration to option prices. We can apply the option price simulation algorithm described above to obtain the GARCH price of liquid standard European calls and puts. Start with some initial value for the GARCH model parameters and simulate the option price and then apply a numerical algorithm (e.g. Excel Solver) to change the parameters in such a way that the GARCH model price equals the market price. The problem is that each calibration to a different option on the same underlying will produce different GARCH parameters, so how do we find a single set of parameter values for a GARCH model?

We start with some initial parameter values and simulate the GARCH price for each of the standard European options on the same underlying for which we have a liquid market price. Then we iterate on the root mean square error between the GARCH prices and the market

---

[59] Except when the option is near to at-the-money, when the two prices should be very close. See Section III.3.6.7 for further explanation.
[60] These can be changed in the spreadsheet, just as for the previous example.

prices. Assuming the iteration converges, the GARCH parameter estimates that minimize the root mean square error provide GARCH option prices for standard European options that are as close as possible to *all* of the market prices.

This approach is computationally complex, because it requires 10,000 simulations to calculate just one GARCH model option price, and the price of each option must be calculated and recalculated many times as we minimize the root mean square error. On the other hand, the Markov switching GARCH model is the best volatility model available in discrete time, so it must surely be worth the effort to apply it also in continuous time.

GARCH Hedge Ratios

The GARCH hedge ratios delta, gamma and vega may be calculated using finite difference approximations. To estimate the delta and gamma we simulate the option price not only starting from the current price of the underlying S_0 but also starting from $S_0 + \eta$ and $S_0 - \eta$, where η is very small compared with S_0. And to estimate vega we simulate the option price not only starting from the current volatility of the underlying σ_0 but also starting from $\sigma_0 + \eta$ and $\sigma_0 - \eta$, where η is very small compared with σ_0. Then we apply first and second order differences as described in Section I.5.5.2. Other Greeks are calculated in a similar fashion. When calculating Greeks in this way the simulation errors can be very large. To reduce simulation errors we can use the *same* random numbers to generate the two option prices, starting from $S_0 + \eta$ and $S_0 - \eta$ respectively (or from $\sigma_0 + \eta$ and $\sigma_0 - \eta$ respectively for the GARCH vega).[61]

II.4.8.3   Value-at-Risk Measurement

GARCH models also allow one to relax the i.i.d. assumption and capture volatility clustering when measuring portfolio VaR. They have applications in the context of historical VaR and Monte Carlo VaR, but applications to analytic linear VaR are questionable.

Historical VaR

Historical simulation has the potential to underestimate historical VaR when markets have been relatively tranquil in the immediate past and to overestimate historical VaR when markets have been relatively volatile in the immediate past. In Section IV.3.3.3 we demonstrate the use of GARCH to adjust historical simulations for volatility clustering. There we estimate the GARCH portfolio returns volatility over the entire historical sample and obtain the *standardized returns* as the historical return at time t divided by its estimated GARCH standard deviation at time t. Then we find the percentile of the standardized returns distribution and multiply this by the current volatility to obtain the *GARCH volatility adjusted VaR* estimate, as a percentage of the portfolio value.

Monte Carlo VaR

Monte Carlo simulation provides an extremely flexible framework for the application of GARCH models for VaR estimation. For instance, utilizing the algorithm described in

---

[61] See Glasserman (2004) for further details.

Section II.4.7.3, we can use the GARCH model to simulate risk factor returns with volatility and correlation clustering, instead of using multivariate normal i.i.d. simulations in the VaR model. Many thousands of simulations for the risk factor returns are obtained, using the multivariate GARCH model to simulate returns with volatility and correlation clustering. Then we use the portfolio's risk factor mapping to translate each set of simulations into a simulated portfolio return, and the percentage VaR is obtained as a percentile of the simulated portfolio returns distribution.[62] Several applications of these *GARCH Monte Carlo VaR* models are described in detail in Chapter IV.4, to which readers are referred for empirical examples.

Analytic Linear VaR

Analytic GARCH variance forecasts are based on the assumption that the squared return in the future is equal to its expected value at the time the forecast is made. Similarly, analytic GARCH covariance forecasts assume the cross product of two future returns is equal to its expected value. So if an analytic GARCH forecast is used in a VaR model there is no room for unexpected returns to influence the VaR estimate. In a sense this ignores the true purpose of GARCH (which is to include correlation and volatility clustering after a market shock) because we assume away the possibility of a shock. Thus simply 'plugging in' the GARCH covariance into a VaR formula without simulating using this matrix makes a very restricting assumption.

Hence, whilst it is possible to apply a GARCH covariance matrix forecast instead of a covariance matrix forecast based on the i.i.d. assumption in the linear VaR model, it is important to understand that this is a fairly crude approximation. Using a GARCH covariance matrix avoids using the square-root-of-time rule to scale a daily VaR estimate up to a 10-day or an even longer-horizon VaR estimate. Since we no longer assume returns are i.i.d. the square root scaling law does not apply. The GARCH covariance matrix forecasts mean-revert to the long term average, but often the mean reversion is rather slow. So while the mean-reversion effect may be noticeable when VaR is measured over long time horizons such as a year, over short horizons such as 10 days there will be little difference between the linear VaR based on an i.i.d. assumption and that based on a GARCH covariance matrix forecast.

There is also a theoretical problem with the use of GARCH in *normal* linear VaR, because in this model the *h*-day portfolio returns distribution is assumed to be normal. But *h*-day returns cannot be normally distributed when daily returns follow a normal GARCH process. Assuming normality in the linear VaR introduces an approximation error and this defeats the purpose of using a GARCH covariance matrix for greater accuracy.

II.4.8.4 Estimation of Time Varying Sensitivities

In Section II.1.2.3 we described how to find a time varying estimate of the market beta of a stock or a portfolio using an exponentially weighted moving average. Denoting the EWMA smoothing constant by λ, the estimate of beta that is made at time t is

$$\hat{\beta}_t^\lambda = \frac{\mathrm{Cov}_\lambda(X_t, Y_t)}{V_\lambda(X_t)}, \qquad (II.4.56)$$

---

[62] When based on the *returns* distribution, rather than the P&L distribution, the VaR is expressed as a percentage of the portfolio value.

where X_t and Y_t denote the returns on the market factor and on the stock (or portfolio) respectively, at time t. The EWMA beta estimates vary over time, but still the model only specifies i.i.d. unconditional variance and covariance.

By contrast, when time varying betas are based on a GARCH model, the variance and covariance in (II.4.56) refer to the conditional variance and conditional covariance in a bivariate GARCH model of the stock (or portfolio) returns and the returns on the market risk factor. The GARCH estimate of the market beta is therefore

$$\hat{\beta}_t = \frac{\hat{\sigma}_{XYt}}{\hat{\sigma}_{Xt}^2}. \tag{II.4.57}$$

In Section II.1.2.3 we estimated a EWMA beta for a portfolio of two stocks in the S&P 500 index, and the result was displayed in Figure II.1.1. Figure II.4.27 compares this EWMA beta with the beta that is estimated using a simple symmetric normal bivariate GARCH model with a diagonal vech specification.[63] Looking at Figure II.4.27, we see that the GARCH model gives a time varying beta estimate that is much more variable over time than the EWMA beta estimate. This is not due our 'rough and ready' optimization of the likelihood using Excel Solver. It also happens when bivariate GARCH models are estimated using all the well-known GARCH software. Conditional covariances are just very unstable over time. A possible reason is that covariance is only a very crude form of dependency measure that is not well suited to financial returns.[64]

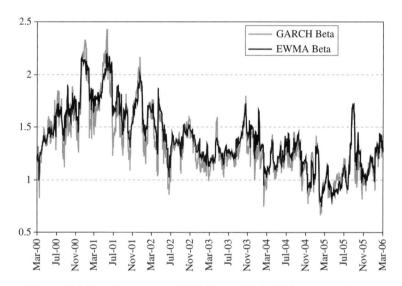

Figure II.4.27   Comparison of EWMA and GARCH time varying betas

Bivariate GARCH models also have applications to the estimation of time varying minimum variance futures hedge ratios. But the excessive variability of GARCH hedge ratio

---

[63] To estimate the model we first set up the log likelihood function (II.4.41) for our data and based on initial parameter estimates. We used starting values 0.00001, 0.08 and 0.9 for the three GARCH parameters. Excel Solver cannot optimize this, so instead we estimate univariate GARCH models for the two conditional variances. Then we use the log likelihood function to optimize the parameters for the conditional covariance equation. But even this is really too much for Solver.

[64] We shall return to this issue when we introduce cointegration in Chapter II.5 and copulas in Chapter II.6.

estimates makes them of less practical use than EWMA estimates. The costs of rebalancing the hedge will be considerable when the hedge ratio varies so much from day to day.
Moreover, there is little evidence that any minimum variance hedge ratio, however it is
estimated, can improve on simple naïve one-to-one hedge ratios. It should be possible to
improve on the naïve hedge for short term proxy hedging, or when basis risk is considerable
as it is in some commodity markets. But there is scant empirical evidence to demonstrate
the superiority of either GARCH or EWMA time varying hedge ratios over the simple OLS
minimum variance hedge ratios. See Section III.2.7 and Alexander and Barbosa (2007) for
further details.

II.4.8.5 Portfolio Optimization

In Section I.6.3 we described how the covariance matrix of the returns on risky assets,
along with the expected returns on the assets, is applied to portfolio allocation. Portfolio weights are chosen to minimize the variance of the portfolio subject to constraints
on the expected portfolio return and possibly also on the permissible weights on certain
assets. For instance, the problem of allocating a portfolio that provides a target return is
called the *Markowitz problem* and is described in detail in Section I.6.3.3. The optimization
problem is

$$\min_{\mathbf{w}} \mathbf{w}'\mathbf{V}\mathbf{w} \quad \text{such that} \quad \sum_{i=1}^{n} w_i = 1 \quad \text{and} \quad \mathbf{w}'E(\mathbf{r}) = \overline{R}, \tag{II.4.58}$$

where $\mathbf{r}$ is the vector of expected returns on each asset and $E(\mathbf{r}) = \overline{R}$ is a target level for the
portfolio return. The solution for the optimal portfolio weights vector $\mathbf{w}*$ is

$$\begin{pmatrix} \mathbf{w}* \\ \lambda_1 \\ \lambda_2 \end{pmatrix} = \begin{pmatrix} 2\mathbf{V} & \mathbf{1} & E(\mathbf{r}) \\ \mathbf{1}' & 0 & 0 \\ E(\mathbf{r})' & 0 & 0 \end{pmatrix}^{-1} \begin{pmatrix} \mathbf{0} \\ 1 \\ \overline{R} \end{pmatrix}, \tag{II.4.59}$$

where λ_1 and λ_2 are Lagrange multipliers.

Portfolio allocation decisions are often taken at a monthly horizon and it is important to
use a good covariance matrix forecast for the returns over the next month. The advantages
of using GARCH covariance matrix forecasts rather than equally or exponentially weighted
covariance matrices for portfolio optimization include the following:

- The responses of volatilities and correlations to market shocks can be asymmetric.
- The GARCH forecasts capture volatility and correlation clustering.
- They converge to the long term covariance matrix and we do not need to apply the
  crude square-root-of-time rule.
- The long term matrix may be set by the portfolio manager according to his views.
  Alternatively it can be estimated from the GARCH parameters.

We end this section with an example that compares the solution to the Markowitz problem
for three risky assets when $\mathbf{V}$ is (a) an equally weighted covariance matrix and (b) a GARCH
covariance matrix.

EXAMPLE II.4.10: PORTFOLIO OPTIMIZATION WITH GARCH

Three assets X, Y and Z have annual volatilities 25%, 20% and 30% respectively when estimated using an equally weighted average of squared monthly returns over a long time period. Their monthly returns correlations are 0.6 for X and Y, -0.5 for X and Z and -0.6 for Y and Z. Their expected returns over the next month are 5%, 4% and -1% respectively. A multivariate normal A-GARCH model is estimated using daily returns on these assets and, when the long term covariance matrix is constrained to take the values above, the GARCH parameter estimates are shown in Table II.4.14. The long term correlations are identical to the correlations given above.

Table II.4.14 Multivariate A-GARCH parameter estimates[a]

	CV X	CV Y	CV Z	CC X $-$ Y	CC X $-$ Z	CC Y $-$ Z
ω	1.16E-05	1.57E-05	1.79E-05	3.59E-07	-5.38E-08	-3.35E-07
α	0.1	0.08	0.07	0.1	0.22	0.15
β	0.85	0.82	0.88	0.8	0.75	0.78
λ	0.003	0.002	0.001	0.0001	0.0005	0.0015

[a]CV stands for conditional variance equation and CC stands for conditional covariance equation. We have used the diagonal vech parameterization.

The current GARCH estimates for the asset's volatilities are, in annualized terms, 32%, 26% and 35% respectively, and the GARCH correlation estimates are 0.75 for X and Y, -0.6 for X and Z and -0.7 for Y and Z. Find a portfolio that is expected to return at least 2.5% over the next month, with the minimum possible variance, based on (a) the equally weighted average covariance matrix and (b) the GARCH model.

SOLUTION   It is easy to calculate (II.4.59) in Excel and we have already provided such an example in Section I.6.3.4. For the problem in hand we want to compare the optimal weights vector $\mathbf{w}^*$ when the covariance matrix $\mathbf{V}$ is given by (a) the equally weighted average covariance matrix and (b) the GARCH model. The equally weighted annual covariance matrix is

$$\mathbf{V}_{EQ}^{Annual} = \begin{pmatrix} 0.25 & 0 & 0 \\ 0 & 0.2 & 0 \\ 0 & 0 & 0.3 \end{pmatrix} \begin{pmatrix} 1 & 0.6 & -0.5 \\ 0.6 & 1 & -0.6 \\ -0.5 & -0.6 & 1 \end{pmatrix} \begin{pmatrix} 0.25 & 0 & 0 \\ 0 & 0.2 & 0 \\ 0 & 0 & 0.3 \end{pmatrix}$$

$$= \begin{pmatrix} 0.0625 & 0.03 & -0.0375 \\ 0.03 & 0.04 & -0.036 \\ -0.0375 & -0.036 & 0.09 \end{pmatrix}.$$

The equally weighted model assumes the returns are i.i.d. normal and hence the monthly covariance matrix is obtained by dividing each element in $\mathbf{V}_{EQ}^{Annual}$ by 12. This gives the equally weighted matrix to use in (II.4.59) as

$$\mathbf{V}_{EQ} = \begin{pmatrix} 0.005208 & 0.0025 & -0.003125 \\ 0.0025 & 0.003333 & -0.003 \\ -0.003125 & -0.003 & 0.0075 \end{pmatrix}.$$

For the GARCH forecasts we apply (II.4.17) and the equivalent formula for the forward daily covariance forecasts for $S = 1, \ldots, 22$ and then sum the results.[65] The calculations are performed in the spreadsheet for this example and we obtain the monthly GARCH covariance matrix forecast:

$$
V_{GARCH} = \begin{pmatrix} 0.00755 & 0.002075 & -0.00424 \\ 0.002075 & 0.004416 & -0.0027 \\ -0.00424 & -0.0027 & 0.00959 \end{pmatrix}.
$$

Note that the GARCH variances are greater than the i.i.d. monthly averages, because the spot volatilities are above their long term average level.[66] Thus we can expect a significant difference between the optimal allocations based on the two covariance matrices.

The results of solving the Markowitz problem based on each matrix are shown in Table II.4.15. The GARCH covariance matrix forecast leads to an optimal allocation with less weight on asset Y and more weight on asset X. The allocations to asset Z are fairly similar. Asset Z, although it has a negative expected return, provides valuable diversification because it is negatively correlated with assets X and Y. By adding this asset to the portfolio we can considerably reduce the portfolio volatility.

Table II.4.15   Optimal allocations under the two covariance matrices

Weight on asset	Under V_{EQ}	Under V_{GARCH}
X	19.51%	26.49%
Y	46.59%	38.21%
Z	33.90%	35.30%
Portfolio volatility	10.26%	12.34%

This example shows that the minimum variance portfolio volatility differs considerably, according to the matrix used. The GARCH matrix recognizes that volatilities are higher than average at the moment, and that correlations are stronger, and this is reflected in the commensurably higher forecast for the portfolio volatility over the next month.

II.4.9   SUMMARY AND CONCLUSIONS

This chapter has reviewed the univariate and multivariate GARCH processes that are commonly used to estimate and forecast volatility and correlation. We have defined and explored the properties of symmetric and asymmetric GARCH processes where the conditional distribution of the errors may be normal or non-normal. Most of these models have been implemented in Excel spreadsheets. Although it is quite a challenge to estimate the parameters using Excel Solver, the transparency of the Excel spreadsheet is a valuable learning aid. In practice, readers should estimate GARCH models using in-built GARCH procedures or specialist econometrics software such as EViews, Matlab, S-Plus or Ox.

There is no doubt that GARCH models produce volatility forecasts superior to those obtained from moving average models. Moving average models have *constant* volatility term

---

[65] We assume this month contains 22 trading days.
[66] The opposite would be the case if the spot volatilities were below their long term average level.

structures, which are inconsistent with the volatility clustering that we observe in almost every liquid market. Moreover, there is only one parameter for a moving average model, the averaging period for the equally weighted model and the smoothing constant for the exponentially weighted model, and the value of this parameter is chosen subjectively. Thus the model risk that results from using moving averages to forecast volatility and correlation is considerable.

By contrast, GARCH parameters are estimated optimally, using maximum likelihood, so they must fit the data better than the parameters of moving average models. Moreover, GARCH volatility models are specifically designed to capture volatility clustering or, put another way, they produce *term structure volatility forecasts* that converge to the long term average volatility. In *volatility targeting* this long term volatility is *imposed* by the modeller, and the GARCH model is used to fill in the short and medium term volatility forecasts that are consistent with this view.

Asymmetric volatility response, e.g. where volatility increases more following a market fall than following a rise in prices, is simple to capture in the *asymmetric GARCH* framework. Several alternative asymmetric GARCH specifications have been developed, notably the *exponential GARCH* model of Nelson (1991) which often provides the best fit of all (single component) GARCH models.

The conditional distribution of GARCH errors is also flexible. 'Vanilla' GARCH uses normal errors but it is easy to extend this to innovations from non-normal distributions such as Student's *t* distribution or a normal mixture. *Student t GARCH models* generally improve the model's fit and forecasting accuracy. The volatility clustering effect can be enhanced by allowing the GARCH process to switch between high and low *volatility regimes* in the *Normal mixture GARCH* and *Markov switching GARCH* processes.

It is a considerable challenge to extend the GARCH framework to forecast a large covariance matrix, which for a large international bank could have more than 400 risk factors. The most successful approaches for very large covariance matrices use a hybrid of methods, for instance mixing univariate GARCH techniques with an equally weighted correlation matrix, or with the principal components of that matrix. We have recommended that the choice of hybrid approach be determined by the type of asset class: *factor GARCH* for equities, *dynamic conditional correlation GARCH* for currencies and *orthogonal GARCH* for term structures of interest rates, futures/forwards, or indeed volatility indices!

GARCH covariance matrices have extensive applications to portfolio allocation. By imposing the long term parameter values on the model the *GARCH covariance matrix* forecast provides an intuitive tool for combining a long term view on volatilities and correlation, which may be set by the portfolio manager if required, and then the GARCH model is applied to construct a covariance matrix that is consistent with the manager's views and with the short term information from the market. An Excel example compares the optimal allocations based on a standard, equally weighted average covariance matrix with the optimal portfolio allocation based on the GARCH model.

Other applications for univariate GARCH models are based on the ability to simulate systems of returns with *volatility clustering*. The most powerful model in this respect is the Markov switching GARCH model, which allows volatility to switch between high and low volatility regimes in a very realistic fashion. The Excel spreadsheet for Markov switching GARCH produces simulations of returns with volatility clusters that accurately reflect the empirical behaviour of returns on many financial assets. We have shown by example how simulations from GARCH models are used to approximate the price of a path-dependent option, such as an average rate or a barrier European option, under the assumption that volatility is stochastic. GARCH models also have numerous applications to market risk measurement and to value-at-risk estimation in particular. In Chapters IV.3 and IV.4 we demonstrate, with several practical examples, how to apply GARCH models to both historical simulation and Monte Carlo VaR models.

Time Series Models and Cointegration

II.5.1 INTRODUCTION

This chapter provides a pedagogical introduction to discrete time series models of stationary and integrated processes. A particular example of an *integrated process* is a random walk. Given enough time, a random walk process could be anywhere, because it has infinite variance, and the best prediction of tomorrow's price is the price today. Hence, there is little point in building a forecasting model of a single random walk. But a *stationary process* is predictable – not perfectly, of course, but there is some degree of predictability based on its mean-reverting behaviour. Individual asset prices are usually integrated processes, but sometimes the spread between two asset prices can be stationary and in this case we say the prices are *cointegrated*. Cointegrated prices are 'tied together' in the long run. Hence, when two asset prices – or interest rates – are cointegrated, we may not know where each price or rate will be in 10 years' time but we do know that wherever one price or rate is, the other one will be along there with it.

Cointegration is a measure of long term dependency between asset prices. This sets it apart from correlation, whose severe limitations as a dependency measure have been discussed in Chapter II.3, and copulas, which are typically used to construct unconditional joint distributions of asset returns that reflect almost any type of dependence. Although copulas have recently been combined with conditional models of returns,[1] our presentation of copulas in Chapter II.6 will only focus on the *unconditional* returns distribution, ignoring any dynamic properties such as autocorrelation in returns.

Whilst both correlation and copulas apply only to returns, cointegration models are constructed in two stages: the first stage examines the association in a *long term equilibrium* between the *prices* of a set of financial assets, and the second stage is a dynamic model of correlation, called an *error correction model*, that is based on linear regression analysis of *returns*. In effect, the first stage of cointegration analysis tests and models the long term dynamics and the second stage models the short term dynamics in a cointegrated system.

When we say that two assets or interest rates are *cointegrated* we are not, initially, referring to any association between their returns. In fact, it is theoretically possible for returns to have low correlation when prices are cointegrated. The presence of cointegration just implies that there is a long term association between their prices. Whenever a spread is found to be mean-reverting the two asset prices or interest rates are 'tied together' in the long term. Each individual price (or interest rate) is a random walk or at least an integrated process, so we have little idea what the price will be many years from now. But when two prices (or interest rates) are cointegrated they can never drift too far apart, because their spread has

---

[1] See Patton (2008).

finite variance. Thus, to say that two prices are cointegrated implies that there is a long term equilibrium relationship between their prices.

The presence of cointegration also implies that there is a statistical *causality* between the *returns*. The returns on one asset tend to lag the returns on the other, so that large price changes in one asset tend to be followed, at some time in the future, by large price changes in the other. This type of statistical causality is called *Granger causality*, after the econometrician Clive Granger who won the Nobel prize in 2006 for his pioneering work on cointegration.

The classic papers on cointegration are by Hendry (1986), Granger (1986) and Engle and Granger (1987). Since then cointegration has become the prevalent statistical tool in applied economics. Every modern econometrics text covers the statistical theory necessary to master the practical application of cointegration.[2] Cointegration has emerged as a powerful technique for investigating long term dependence in *multivariate* time series, not just between two asset prices or interest rates. The main advantage of cointegration is that it provides a sound statistical methodology for modelling both the long term equilibrium and the short term dynamics.

The basic building blocks for time series analysis were first introduced in Section I.3.7, where we defined stationary and integrated processes, and in Chapter I.4 on regression analysis. In this chapter, Section II.5.2 begins by describing the fundamental concepts in stationary discrete time stochastic processes and the univariate time series models that are used to represent such processes. But the main theme of this chapter is the analysis of *non-stationary* processes and the common features that may be shared by several non-stationary processes. We explain why a process that is integrated of order 1 is called a *stochastic trend* and take care to distinguish between stochastic and deterministic trends in price data. We end Section II.5.2 with a description of *unit root* tests for a stochastic trend. Section II.5.3 introduces cointegration, discuses the relationship between cointegration and correlation and surveys the academic literature on cointegration; Section II.5.4 describes how to test for cointegration. Error correction models for the dynamic relationships between returns in cointegrated systems are introduced in Section II.5.5, and the empirical examples from the previous section are extended.

The relationship between the mean and the variance of portfolio returns is a cornerstone of portfolio management. However, returns are *short memory processes* in the sense that the return today is not influenced by the returns that were observed more than a few periods ago. Hence, investments that are based on the characteristics of returns alone cannot model *long term* cointegrating relationships between prices. In Section II.5.4 and II.5.5 we shall discuss some of the numerous new applications of cointegration to portfolio management such as index tracking, enhanced index tracking, statistical arbitrage, pairs trading and calendar spread trading. Section II.5.6 summarizes and concludes.

II.5.2   STATIONARY PROCESSES

This section extends the discussion of stationary processes that began in Section I.3.7.1. Here we categorize the properties of *univariate mean-reverting* time series, discuss how such

---

[2] Among the best sources is Greene (2007), but also see Hamilton (1994).

series arise naturally in financial markets as *spreads*, explain how to model and to predict these series and, finally, how to decide if it is possible to make profitable spread trades.

II.5.2.1   Time Series Models

A discrete time stochastic process $\{X_t\}_{t=1}^{T}$ is *stationary* if

$E(X_t)$ is a finite constant,

$V(X_t)$ is a finite constant,   (II.5.1)

the joint distribution of (X_t, X_s) depends only on $t - s$.

When the third condition is weakened to

$\mathrm{Cov}(X_t, X_s)$ depends only on $|t - s|$,

we call the process *weakly stationary* or *covariance stationary*. If $\{X_t\}_{t=1}^{T}$ is stationary we write, for reasons that will presently become clear,

$$X_t \sim I(0).$$

Stationary processes can be built using *independent and identically distributed* (i.i.d.) processes as building blocks. For instance, we have already encountered a basic model for a stationary process in Section I.3.7.1. This is the *first order autoregressive model*, denoted AR(1) and specified as

$$X_t = \alpha + \varrho X_{t-1} + \varepsilon_t, \quad \text{with } \varepsilon_t \sim \text{i.i.d.} \left(0, \sigma^2\right) \text{ and } |\varrho| < 1, \qquad \text{(II.5.2)}$$

where ϱ is called the *first order autocorrelation coefficient*.

The i.i.d. process, where $\varrho = 0$ in (II.5.2), is the *most* stationary of all processes; in other words, it has the most rapid mean reversion. Figure II.5.1 compares two time series, both with zero mean and the same unconditional variance: one is an i.i.d. process and the other is an AR(1) process with $\varrho = 0.9$.[3] At the tenth observation we introduce a positive shock, making the value of the error term exceptionally high. The figure illustrates that the time taken to mean-revert following this shock increases with ϱ.

Why do we require $|\varrho| < 1$ for the process (II.5.2) to be stationary? Taking unconditional expectations and variances of (II.5.2) and noting that for a stationary process

$$E(X_t) = E(X_{t-1}) \text{ and } V(X_t) = V(X_{t-1}),$$

we have

$$E(X_t) = \frac{\alpha}{1 - \varrho}, \quad V(X_t) = \frac{\sigma^2}{1 - \varrho^2}, \qquad \text{(II.5.3)}$$

and these are only finite constants when $|\varrho| < 1$.

The autocorrelation coefficient ϱ is given by

$$\varrho = \frac{\mathrm{Cov}(X_t, X_{t-1})}{V(X_t)}. \qquad \text{(II.5.4)}$$

---

[3] Whilst the conditional variance is the same for both processes, the unconditional variance differs. The conditional variance is σ^2 in both processes, and in the i.i.d. model this is equal to the unconditional variance. But the unconditional variance formula (II.5.3) implies that the conditional variance in the AR(1) process must be smaller than in the i.i.d. process for both processes to have the same unconditional variance. The reader can change the conditional variance in the spreadsheet for this figure.

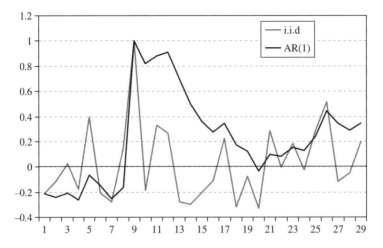

Figure II.5.1   Mean reversion in stationary processes

To verify this, note that, since $\varepsilon_t \sim \text{i.i.d.}(0, \sigma^2)$,

$$E(X_t X_{t-1}) = E\left[(\alpha + \varrho X_{t-1} + \varepsilon_t) X_{t-1}\right] = \alpha E(X_{t-1}) + \varrho E\left(X_{t-1}^2\right)$$

$$= \alpha E(X_{t-1}) + \varrho \left[V(X_{t-1}) + E(X_{t-1})^2\right]$$

$$= \frac{\alpha^2}{1 - \varrho} + \frac{\varrho \sigma^2}{1 - \varrho^2} + \frac{\varrho \alpha^2}{(1 - \varrho)^2} = \frac{\alpha^2}{(1 - \varrho)^2} + \frac{\varrho \sigma^2}{1 - \varrho^2}.$$

Since

$$\text{Cov}(X_t, X_{t-1}) = E(X_t X_{t-1}) - E(X_t) E(X_{t-1}),$$

we have, again using (II.5.3),

$$\text{Cov}(X_t, X_{t-1}) = \frac{\varrho \sigma^2}{1 - \varrho^2},$$

and now (II.5.4) follows from (II.5.3).

A more general model for a stationary process is a generalization of the AR(1) model to a *pth order autoregressive model*, for p an integer greater than 1. This is achieved by adding further lags of X_t to the right-hand side as follows:

$$X_t = \alpha + \varrho_1 X_{t-1} + \varrho_2 X_{t-2} + \ldots + \varrho_p X_{t-p} + \varepsilon_t, \quad \varepsilon_t \sim \text{i.i.d.}(0, \sigma^2). \qquad (\text{II.5.5})$$

It can be shown, for instance in Harvey (1981), that this process is stationary if and only if the roots of its associated *characteristic equation*,

$$x^p - \varrho_1 x^{p-1} - \ldots - \varrho_{p-1} x - \varrho_p = 0,$$

lie *inside the unit circle*.[4] For example, the characteristic equation for the AR(1) process is $x - \varrho = 0$ and the *unit root* condition is therefore simply $|\varrho| < 1$, as we have already seen above.

---

[4] We say 'inside the unit circle' here because one or more of the roots of (II.5.5) could be complex numbers. It is only when all the roots are real that the so-called *unit root* condition reduces to the condition that all roots are less than one in absolute value.

A moving average model is a time series model where the process can be represented as a sum of different lags of an i.i.d. process. For instance, the *first order moving average model*, denoted the MA(1) model, is

$$X_t = \varepsilon_t + \varphi \varepsilon_{t-1}, \quad \varepsilon_t \sim \text{i.i.d.} (0, \sigma^2). \tag{II.5.6}$$

This process is always stationary, provided that φ is finite.

The most general models of stationary time series combine a moving average error process with a stationary autoregressive representation, and we call this model the *autoregressive moving average* (ARMA) representation of a stationary series. The general autoregressive moving average time series model with p autoregressive terms and q moving average terms is denoted ARMA(p, q), and the model is written

$$X_t = \alpha + \varrho_1 X_{t-1} + \ldots + \varrho_p X_{t-p} + \varepsilon_t + \varphi_1 \varepsilon_{t-1} + \ldots + \varphi_q \varepsilon_{t-q}, \quad \varepsilon_t \sim \text{i.i.d.} (0, \sigma^2). \tag{II.5.7}$$

This model represents a stationary process if and only if the moving average coefficients are finite and the roots of the characteristic equation (II.5.5) all lie inside the unit circle. So, in the special case where all the roots are real, they must each be less than 1 in absolute value.

EXAMPLE II.5.1: TESTING AN ARMA PROCESS FOR STATIONARITY

Is the process

$$X_t = 0.03 + 0.75 X_{t-1} - 0.25 X_{t-2} + \varepsilon_t + 0.5 \varepsilon_{t-1} \tag{II.5.8}$$

stationary?

SOLUTION   The process is stationary if and only if the roots of the following characteristic equation lie inside the unit circle:

$$x^2 - 0.75x + 0.25 = 0.$$

The roots are obtained from the usual formula for the roots of a quadratic equation given in Section I.1.2.1, i.e.

$$x = \frac{0.75 \pm \sqrt{0.75^2 - 4 \times 0.25}}{2} = \frac{0.75 \pm i\sqrt{0.4375}}{2} = 0.375 \pm 0.3307i,$$

where $i = \sqrt{-1}$. The modulus of these, i.e. the distance between the origin and the roots (which is the same for both roots) is

$$\sqrt{0.375^2 + 0.3307^2} = 0.5.$$

Since this is less than 1 in absolute value, the process is stationary.

The unconditional mean and variance of a stationary series are constant, and it is straightforward to verify that the mean of the ARMA process (II.5.7) is

$$E(X_t) = \alpha \left(1 - \sum_{i=1}^{p} \varrho_i \right)^{-1}. \tag{II.5.9}$$

However, the *conditional* mean and variance of (II.5.7) assume the lagged values of X are known, because they are in the information set I_{t-1} so

$$E_{t-1}(X_t) = \alpha + \varrho_1 X_{t-1} + \ldots + \varrho_p X_{t-p} \text{ and } V_{t-1}(X_t) = \sigma^2. \tag{II.5.10}$$

To derive the unconditional variances and covariances of (II.5.7), to keep the notation simple first write $y = E(X_t) = \alpha \left(1 - \sum_{i=1}^{p} \varrho_i \right)^{-1}$ and

$$Cov\left(X_i, X_j\right) = E\left(X_i X_j\right) - E\left(X_i\right)E\left(X_j\right) = x_k - y^2$$

where $k = |i - j|$. Let $\mathbf{x} = (x_0, x_1, \ldots, x_p)'$. On multiplying (II.5.7) successively by $X_t, X_{t-1}, \ldots, X_{t-p}$ and each time taking expectations, we obtain $p+1$ linear equations from which we can solve for $\mathbf{x}$. For instance, for the ARMA(3,2) process we have:

$$\begin{pmatrix} x_0 \\ x_1 \\ x_2 \\ x_3 \end{pmatrix} = \begin{pmatrix} 0 & \varrho_1 & \varrho_2 & \varrho_3 \\ \varrho_1 & \varrho_2 & \varrho_3 & 0 \\ \varrho_2 & \varrho_1 + \varrho_3 & 0 & 0 \\ \varrho_3 & \varrho_2 & \varrho_1 & 0 \end{pmatrix} \begin{pmatrix} x_0 \\ x_1 \\ x_2 \\ x_3 \end{pmatrix} + \sigma^2 \begin{pmatrix} 1 \\ \varphi_1 \\ \varphi_2 \\ 0 \end{pmatrix} + \alpha y \begin{pmatrix} 1 \\ 1 \\ 1 \end{pmatrix} \Rightarrow \begin{pmatrix} x_0 \\ x_1 \\ x_2 \\ x_3 \end{pmatrix}$$

$$= \begin{pmatrix} 1 & -\varrho_1 & -\varrho_2 & -\varrho_3 \\ -\varrho_1 & 1 - \varrho_2 & -\varrho_3 & 0 \\ -\varrho_2 & -(\varrho_1 + \varrho_3) & 1 & 0 \\ -\varrho_3 & -\varrho_2 & -\varrho_1 & 1 \end{pmatrix}^{-1} \begin{pmatrix} \sigma^2 + \alpha y \\ \varphi_1 \sigma^2 + \alpha y \\ \varphi_2 \sigma^2 + \alpha y \\ \alpha y \end{pmatrix}$$

Similarly, for the ARMA(2,1) process:

$$\begin{pmatrix} x_0 \\ x_1 \\ x_2 \end{pmatrix} = \begin{pmatrix} 1 & -\varrho_1 & -\varrho_2 \\ -\varrho_1 & 1 - \varrho_2 & 0 \\ -\varrho_2 & -\varrho_1 & 1 \end{pmatrix}^{-1} \begin{pmatrix} \sigma^2 + \alpha y \\ \varphi_1 \sigma^2 + \alpha y \\ \alpha y \end{pmatrix}.$$

In Example II.5.4 we derive the variance of the ARMA(2,1) process using the formula above and setting $V(X_t) = x_0 - y^2$.

II.5.2.2   Inversion and the Lag Operator

ARMA models may be succinctly expressed using the *lag operator*:

$$LX_t = X_{t-1}, \quad L^2 X_t = X_{t-2}, \quad \ldots, \quad L^p X_t = X_{t-p}.$$

For instance, an autoregressive model

$$X_t = \alpha + \varrho_1 X_{t-1} + \ldots + \varrho_p X_{t-p} + \varepsilon_t, \quad \varepsilon_t \sim \text{i.i.d.}\left(0, \sigma^2\right), \tag{II.5.11}$$

may be written as

$$\gamma(L) X_t = \alpha + \varepsilon_t, \quad \text{where} \quad \gamma(L) = 1 - \varrho_1 L - \ldots - \varrho_p L^p. \tag{II.5.12}$$

When the process is stationary we may invert the polynomial in the lag operator to obtain $\gamma(L)^{-1}$, which is an infinite series in L. Then we can represent the process as

$$X_t = \gamma(L)^{-1}\left(\alpha + \varepsilon_t\right). \tag{II.5.13}$$

Thus a stationary autoregressive model has an equivalent representation as an infinite moving average process.

Similarly, a moving average process may be written

$$X_t = \alpha + \delta(L)\varepsilon_t, \quad \text{where} \quad \delta(L) = 1 + \varphi_1 L + \ldots + \varphi_q L^q.$$

The conditions for inversion of the polynomial $\delta(L)$ are similar to the stationarity conditions for the autoregressive process, i.e. the roots of $\delta(L) = 0$ lie *outside* the unit circle.[5] In this case $\delta(L)^{-1}$ exists and will be an infinite series in L. Thus we may also write a moving average process as an infinite autoregressive process:

$$\delta(L)^{-1} X_t = \delta(L)^{-1} \alpha + \varepsilon_t.$$

In general an ARMA(p, q) process may be written

$$\gamma(L) X_t = \alpha + \delta(L) \varepsilon_t. \tag{II.5.14}$$

If it is stationary it has an infinite moving average representation,

$$X_t = \alpha^* + \theta(L) \varepsilon_t, \tag{II.5.15}$$

where $\alpha^* = \gamma(L)^{-1} \alpha$ and $\theta(L) = \gamma(L)^{-1} \delta(L)$. If the moving average part of the process is invertible, (II.5.14) may also be expressed as an infinite autoregressive process,

$$\psi(L) X_t = \tilde{\alpha} + \varepsilon_t, \tag{II.5.16}$$

where $\tilde{\alpha} = \delta(L)^{-1} \alpha$ and $\psi(L) = \delta(L)^{-1} \gamma(L)$.

II.5.2.3 Response to Shocks

Consider a stationary, invertible ARMA process that is written in the infinite autoregressive form (II.5.16) and consider the possibility of an *exogenous shock* Y_t affecting the process at time t. Suppose we have a *unit shock* at time t, i.e.

$$Y_t = \begin{cases} 1, & \text{at time } t, \\ 0, & \text{otherwise.} \end{cases} \tag{II.5.17}$$

Introducing the shock into the process gives

$$\psi(L) X_t = \tilde{\alpha} + Y_t + \varepsilon_t, \tag{II.5.18}$$

where $\tilde{\alpha} = \delta(L)^{-1} \alpha$. Alternatively, writing

$$\psi(L)^{-1} = \gamma(L)^{-1} \delta(L) = \beta(L) = 1 + \beta_1 L + \beta_2 L^2 + \dots,$$

we may express the same process in infinite moving average form:

$$X_t = \psi(L)^{-1} (\tilde{\alpha} + Y_t + \varepsilon_t) = \alpha^* + \beta(L) (Y_t + \varepsilon_t). \tag{II.5.19}$$

Since $\beta(L) = 1 + \beta_1 L + \beta_2 L^2 + \dots$ the shock has a unit effect on X_t and the successive lag coefficients $\beta_1, \beta_2, \dots$ can be interpreted as the effect of the shock on the future values $X_{t+1}, X_{t+2}, \dots$. The sum $1 + \beta_1 + \beta_2 + \dots$ indicates the total or long term effect of the shock on X.

More detailed information about the impact of the shock over time is given by the *impulse response function*. This is simply the function $\beta_s (s = 1, 2, \dots)$ which measures the impact of a unit shock at time t on the process at time $t + s$.[6] In the general stationary ARMA model we can use the impulse response function to identify the time after the shock by which one

---

[5] This is equivalent to the root of the characteristic equation being *inside* the unit circle. For instance, in the ARMA(2,1) model (II.5.8) we have $\delta(L) = 1 + 0.5L = 0$ when $L = -2$, and the characteristic equation for the moving average part is $x + 0.5 = 0$, so it is invertible.

[6] Some authors use the term 'impulse response' to refer to the cumulative effect of a shock over time, i.e. $\iota(s) = \sum_{i=0}^{s} \beta_i$.

half of the total long term impact has been incorporated into X. This is called the *median lag*. An associated measure is the *mean lag*, defined as

$$\text{mean lag} = \frac{\sum_{i=0}^{\infty} i \times \beta_i}{\sum_{i=0}^{\infty} \beta_i} = \beta(1)^{-1} \beta'(1). \tag{II.5.20}$$

EXAMPLE II.5.2: IMPULSE RESPONSE

Calculate the impulse response function for the model considered in the previous example, i.e. the stationary and invertible ARMA(2,1) process

$$X_t = 0.03 + 0.75 X_{t-1} - 0.25 X_{t-2} + \varepsilon_t + 0.5 \varepsilon_{t-1}.$$

How long does it take for one half of the impact to be incorporated into X, and what is the mean lag?

SOLUTION   We have $\gamma(L) = 1 - 0.75L + 0.25L^2$ and $\delta(L) = 1 + 0.5L$, so

$$\beta(L) = \left(1 - 0.75L + 0.25L^2\right)^{-1} (1 + 0.5L).$$

The easiest way to calculate the coefficients in $\beta(L)$ is to write

$$\left(1 - 0.75L + 0.25L^2\right)\left(1 + \beta_1 L + \beta_2 L^2 + \ldots\right) = (1 + 0.5L)$$

and equate coefficients of L. We have

$$\beta_1 - 0.75 = 0.5 \Rightarrow \beta_1 = 1.25.$$

Equating coefficients of L^2, we have

$$\beta_2 - 0.75 \times 1.25 + 0.25 = 0 \Rightarrow \beta_2 = 0.9375 - 0.25 = 0.6875.$$

Similarly, equating coefficients of L^3 gives

$$\beta_3 - 0.75 \times 0.6875 + 0.25 \times 1.25 = 0 \Rightarrow \beta_3 = 0.203125,$$

and for L^4,

$$\beta_4 - 0.75 \times 0.203125 + 0.25 \times 0.6875 = 0 \Rightarrow \beta_4 = -0.0195,$$

and so on.

The impulse response function is computed in the spreadsheet for this example and plotted as the grey curve in Figure II.5.2. The cumulative effect of the shock is shown by the black curve. The total impact of the shock is

$$\iota(\infty) = \sum_{i=0}^{\infty} \beta_i = 3.$$

We see that the effect of the shock lasts for almost ten periods, after which time the shock should produce no further disturbance to the series. By application of the formula (II.5.20)

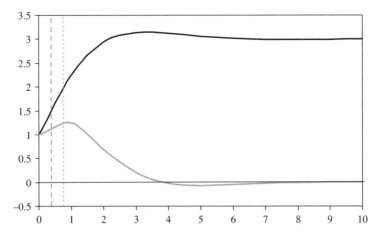

Figure II.5.2   Impulse response for an ARMA(2,1) process

we also calculate a mean lag of 0.833, and this is shown by the dotted black line. The median lag is indicated by the dotted grey line. It is 0.4, so about half the total impact of the shock takes place within one-half of a period.

II.5.2.4   Estimation

In this section we consider an empirical example of estimating an ARMA model for the stationary series shown in Figure II.5.3. Suppose these data are generated by an ARMA process – how should we (a) determine the order of the process and then (b) estimate the parameters? To determine the order of an ARMA process we examine the sample *correlogram*. That is, we graph the sample estimate of the nth order autocorrelation $\text{corr}(X_t, X_{t-n})$ against n. Then we compare its properties with the theoretical autocorrelations derived from an ARMA model and which are derived in Greene (2007), Harvey (1981) and other standard texts on time series analysis.

The AR(1) model (II.5.2) has autocorrelation function

$$\text{corr}(X_t, X_{t-n}) = \varrho^n. \tag{II.5.21}$$

Hence, when $\varrho > 0$ the theoretical correlogram exhibits a smooth exponential decay. It can be also shown that an AR(2) process has a correlogram that has the features of a damped sine wave. The MA(1) model

$$X_t = \alpha + \varepsilon_t + \varphi\varepsilon_{t-1}, \quad \varepsilon_t \sim \text{i.i.d.}\left(0, \sigma^2\right), \tag{II.5.22}$$

has autocorrelation function

$$\text{corr}(X_t, X_{t-n}) = \begin{cases} \varphi, & n = 1, \\ 0, & n > 1, \end{cases} \tag{II.5.23}$$

and, like all autocorrelation functions, it has value 1 at lag 0. Higher order MA processes also have correlograms that are 0 at all lags greater than the order of the process. All stationary ARMA processes have correlograms that tend to 0 as the lag increases.

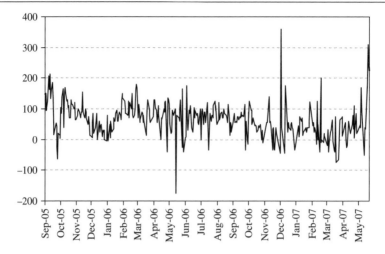

Figure II.5.3   A stationary series

For the spread shown in Figure II.5.3 we compute the correlogram and the result is displayed in Figure II.5.4. The damped sine wave pattern indicates that an AR(2) or higher order autoregressive model, or an ARMA(2,1) model may be appropriate.

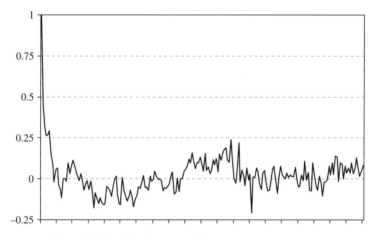

Figure II.5.4   Correlogram of the spread in Figure II.5.3

We estimate the parameters of ARMA models using maximum likelihood estimation (MLE) because these estimators are consistent under fairly general conditions. When the disturbance term ε_t is normally distributed MLE is equivalent to ordinary least squares (OLS) and for simplicity we shall make that assumption here.

It is much easier to estimate an autoregressive model than to estimate a model with moving average terms. Estimation of autoregressive models with normal disturbances is a simple case of OLS where the independent variables are the lags of X. Estimation of moving average models can also be phrased as a least squares minimization problem, but the residuals must be calculated iteratively and minimization of their sum involves a numerical optimization.

EXAMPLE II.5.3: ESTIMATION OF AR(2) MODEL

Estimate the parameters of the model

$$X_t = \alpha + \varrho_1 X_{t-1} + \varrho_2 X_{t-2} + \varepsilon_t, \quad \varepsilon_t \sim \text{NID}\left(0, \sigma^2\right),$$

based on the data shown in Figure II.5.3.

SOLUTION   We apply the regression from the Excel data analysis tools and the result is:

$$\hat{X}_t = \underset{(7.20)}{31.24} + \underset{(6.85)}{0.34} \, \hat{X}_{t-1} + \underset{(3.57)}{0.18} \, \hat{X}_{t-2},$$

with t statistics shown in parentheses. Note that the spreadsheet for this example also reports the result of estimating an AR(3) model, but the third lag is not significant at the 5% level.

II.5.2.5   Prediction

Because of its finite constant unconditional mean and variance, a stationary process is mean-reverting. If the series is very far above the mean it tends to decrease and if it is very far below the mean it tends to increase. We can use the unconditional variance to place 90% or 95% or 99% confidence bands on a stationary series. Then if the process crosses one of these bands we expect that it will soon revert to the usual confidence interval.

EXAMPLE II.5.4: CONFIDENCE LIMITS FOR STATIONARY PROCESSES

Construct a 95% confidence interval for the ARMA(2,1) process (II.5.8) when the process ε_t is normal and identically distributed with variance 0.05.

SOLUTION   We know from Example II.5.1 that this process is stationary. By (II.5.9) the process has expected value

$$E(X_t) = \frac{0.03}{1 - 0.75 + 0.25} = 0.06.$$

Since we have assumed that ε_t is normal with variance 0.05 the ARMA(2,1) process has variance given by the formula derived at the end of Section II.5.2.1. This is calculated in the spreadsheet for this example, as 0.102083. Using the standard normal critical value of 1.96 we obtain a two-sided 95% confidence interval for the process:

$$\left(0.06 - 1.96 \times \sqrt{0.102083}, \, 0.06 + 1.96 \times \sqrt{0.102083}\right) = (-0.566, 0.686).$$

Figure II.5.5 simulates the process, assuming i.i.d. normal errors, and indicates the upper and lower 95% confidence bounds for the process by dotted lines.[7] When the process takes a value outside the confidence interval it reverts to the interval again fairly rapidly. Thus a number of simple trading rules can be placed on this series, and these may make a profit if transactions costs are not too high. For instance, we could sell if the process exceeds its 95% upper bound and buy back when it reverts into the 95% interval. Similarly, we could buy if the process falls below its 95% lower bound and sell back when it reverts into the 95% interval. The profit and loss from such a trading rule would need to be back-tested very thoroughly, factoring in trading costs. See Section II.8.5.1 for a specification of the type of back-testing algorithms that may be used.

---

[7] Press F9 in the spreadsheet to repeat the simulations.

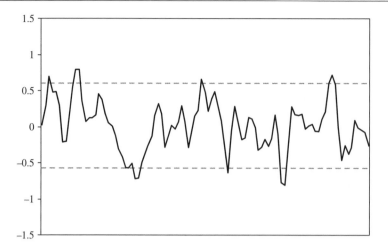

Figure II.5.5   Simulation of stationary process with confidence bounds

If we are to consider trading on a stationary process we may also like to have some idea
of the *time taken for mean reversion* following a shock. We know from Figure II.5.1 and the
discussion following this that the higher the autocorrelation in the process the longer it takes
to mean-revert. More generally, the impulse response function indicates how long it takes for
an exogenous shock to be fully incorporated into the process. For instance, in Example II.5.2
it took almost ten periods for the shock to be fully absorbed. Later, in Section II.5.5.4 we
present a practical application of using impulse response for pairs trading.

II.5.2.6   Multivariate Models for Stationary Processes

So far we have considered only univariate stationary processes. Now consider a set of n
processes $X_1, \ldots, X_n$. We define the *first order vector autoregressive process*, or VAR(1)
process, as

$$
\begin{aligned}
X_{1t} &= \alpha_1 + \beta_{11} X_{1,t-1} + \ldots + \beta_{1n} X_{n,t-1} + \varepsilon_{1t} \\
&\ \vdots \\
X_{nt} &= \alpha_n + \beta_{n1} X_{1,t-1} + \ldots + \beta_{nn} X_{n,t-1} + \varepsilon_{nt}.
\end{aligned}
\tag{II.5.24}
$$

The VAR(1) process is written in matrix form as

$$
\mathbf{X}_t = \boldsymbol{\alpha} + \mathbf{B} \mathbf{X}_{t-1} + \boldsymbol{\varepsilon}_t,
\tag{II.5.25}
$$

where

$$
\mathbf{X}_t = \begin{pmatrix} X_{1t} \\ \vdots \\ X_{nt} \end{pmatrix}, \quad
\boldsymbol{\alpha} = \begin{pmatrix} \alpha_1 \\ \vdots \\ \alpha_n \end{pmatrix}, \quad
\mathbf{B} = \begin{pmatrix} \beta_{11} & \cdots & \beta_{1n} \\ \vdots & \ddots & \vdots \\ \beta_{n1} & \cdots & \beta_{nn} \end{pmatrix}, \quad
\boldsymbol{\varepsilon}_t = \begin{pmatrix} \varepsilon_{1t} \\ \vdots \\ \varepsilon_{nt} \end{pmatrix}.
$$

A *pth order vector autoregressive process*, VAR(p), is a process of the form

$$
\mathbf{X}_t = \boldsymbol{\alpha} + \mathbf{B}_1 \mathbf{X}_{t-1} + \ldots + \mathbf{B}_p \mathbf{X}_{t-p} + \boldsymbol{\varepsilon}_t.
\tag{II.5.26}
$$

It may be written using the lag operator as

$$
\left(\mathbf{I} - \mathbf{B}_1 L - \ldots - \mathbf{B}_p L^p \right) \mathbf{X}_t = \boldsymbol{\alpha} + \boldsymbol{\varepsilon}_t,
$$

where $\mathbf{I}$ is the $n \times n$ identity matrix. The processes $X_1, \ldots, X_n$ are *jointly covariance stationary* if and only if all the roots of the characteristic equation

$$\left| \mathbf{I} x^p - \mathbf{B}_1 x^{p-1} - \ldots - \mathbf{B}_{p-1} x - \mathbf{B}_p \right| = 0 \qquad (\text{II.5.27})$$

lie *inside* the unit circle.[8]

The VAR(p) process is the basic multivariate model that is used to represent a set of dynamically dependent stationary time series. We return to VAR specifications in Section II.5.5, where it will be shown that such a process should, in certain circumstances, be augmented to include an *error correction term* in each equation. We also explain how *Granger causality* testing for a lead–lag relationship between the variables can be done in this framework.

II.5.3   STOCHASTIC TRENDS

Here we categorize the properties of a *random walk* and other non-stationary time series and explain how these properties can be tested. This section provides essential background for understanding the analysis of cointegrated time series.

II.5.3.1   Random Walks and Efficient Markets

Liquid financial markets operate on highly efficient trading platforms. Electronic communications networks, straight-through processing and electronic trading systems all contribute to lower bid–ask spreads and higher trading volumes. Thus new information is very rapidly incorporated into the current market price of a liquid financial instrument. In a stable market the quoted price of a liquid instrument is set so as to equate supply and demand. If a market maker sets his price too high there will be insufficient demand and so he lowers his price. On the other hand, an excess demand will usually prompt an increase in price until supply is balanced with demand.

Traders set orders to buy and sell instruments based on expectations of future movements in their prices. The *efficient market hypothesis* is that the current price of a financial asset or instrument reflects the expectations of all the agents operating in the market. In other words, in an *efficient market* all the public information currently available is instantaneously incorporated into the current price. This means that any new information arriving tomorrow is independent of the price today. And *this* means that best prediction of tomorrow's price – or indeed of any future price – is just the price today. A price process with this property is called a *random walk*.

We now introduce the standard discrete time model for a random walk process. Let ε_t denote the instantaneous price impact of new information arriving into the market, and let X_t denote the price of an asset or instrument at time t. If the market is efficient then the price at time t is the price at the previous time period plus the instantaneous price impact of news, i.e.

$$X_t = X_{t-1} + \varepsilon_t, \qquad (\text{II.5.28})$$

where ε_t is a shock that represents the impact of new information. We often assume that the price impact of news is an i.i.d. process: i.e. $\varepsilon_t \sim \text{i.i.d.}(0, \sigma^2)$.

---

[8] See Hamilton (1994: Chapter 10) for further details.

The discrete time model for a *random walk with drift* is

$$X_t = \alpha + X_{t-1} + \varepsilon_t, \quad \text{with } \varepsilon_t \sim \text{i.i.d.}(0, \sigma^2), \tag{II.5.29}$$

where α is a constant representing the drift in the process and which is 0 in the pure random walk model.

Model (II.5.29) can be thought of as a special case of the AR(1) model with $\varrho = 1$. However, it follows from (II.5.3) that the random walk has *infinite* unconditional mean and variance. Since X_{t-1} is known and therefore not random at time t, the *conditional mean* and *conditional variance*, i.e. the mean and variance taken at every step in the random walk, are finite and are given by

$$E_{t-1}(X_t) = \alpha + X_{t-1} \text{ and } V_{t-1}(X_t) = \sigma^2. \tag{II.5.30}$$

II.5.3.2 Integrated Processes and Stochastic Trends

A time series process is said to be *integrated of order* 1 and denoted $I(1)$ if it is not stationary but its first difference has a stationary ARMA representation. Hence, the random walk model is just one particular type of integrated process, one in which the first difference is i.i.d. More generally, the first difference of an integrated process can have autocorrelated and moving average components. It just needs to be stationary. Hence we have the definition

$$X_t \sim I(1) \quad \Leftrightarrow \quad X_t = \alpha + X_{t-1} + \varepsilon_t \text{ with } \varepsilon_t \sim I(0), \tag{II.5.31}$$

where we use the notation $I(0)$ as before to denote that a series is stationary.

More generally, a process is said to be *integrated of order n* and denoted $I(n)$ if it is not stationary and n is the minimum number of times the process must be differenced in order to achieve a stationary process. Processes with integration of order $n > 1$ are rare but possible; for instance, the retail price index for inflation in some countries may be found to be an $I(2)$ process.

When a process is integrated of order 1 we say that it has a *stochastic trend*. For instance, the random walk model has a stochastic trend as well as a *drift* determined by the sign and magnitude of the constant α. Figure II.5.6 illustrates two random walks, both with conditional volatility 20%. One has drift +5% and the other has drift −5%. But a random walk still has a stochastic trend when the drift is 0.

II.5.3.3 Deterministic Trends

It is important to understand that the trend in a random walk or in any integrated process is not a *deterministic trend*. That is, the $I(1)$ process (II.5.29) is fundamentally different from the deterministic trend, or $I(0) + trend$ process, given by

$$X_t = \alpha + \beta t + \varepsilon_t, \quad \text{with } \varepsilon_t \sim \text{i.i.d.}(0, \sigma^2). \tag{II.5.32}$$

Neither (II.5.29) nor (II.5.32) is a stationary series and the data generated by the two models may seem very similar indeed to the eye. For instance, Figure II.5.7 shows two series: a random walk with drift 5% and volatility 20%, and a deterministic trend process with the same drift, a beta also of 5% and a volatility of 15%. The random realizations of the error used in the simulations are the same in both models.[9]

---

[9] In these graphs we have assumed the errors are normally distributed, but they only have to be i.i.d. in the definition of the process. For instance, the errors could have a Student's t distribution and we would still have a random walk model. The spreadsheet for this figure simulates any number of stochastic trend and deterministic trend processes based on the same random numbers. For a fixed set of parameters (which may be changed by the user) some pairs look very similar, others do not.

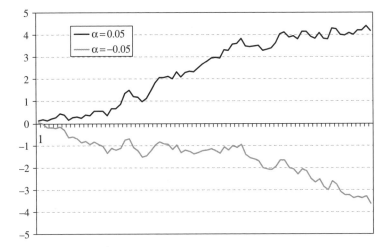

Figure II.5.6   Two random walks with drift

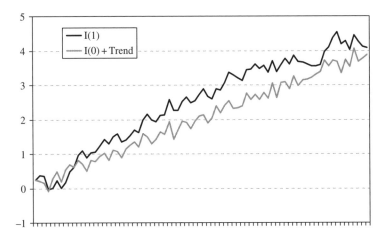

Figure II.5.7   Stochastic trend versus deterministic trend processes

Why is it important to distinguish between $I(1)$ behaviour and $I(0)$ + trend behaviour? Does it really matter which process is generating the prices we observe? The answer is most emphatically yes. This is because the transform required to make each process stationary is *not* the same in both models.

- To transform a random walk, or indeed any $I(1)$ process, into a stationary series we must take the *first difference* of the data. For instance, if the log price is $I(1)$ then log returns are $I(0)$.[10]
- However, the stationarity transform for data generated by the $I(0)$ + trend process (II.5.32) is to take *deviations from a fitted trend line*. That is, we fit a regression model

---

[10] For this reason the $I(1)$ process is also commonly referred to as a *difference stationary process*.

where the independent variable is a time trend and then take the residuals (plus the constant if required, as this will not affect stationarity).[11]

There is considerable empirical evidence to suggest that liquid financial markets are highly efficient. In an efficient market, prices are $I(1)$ processes so they have a stochastic trend and the best prediction of a future price is the price today, plus the drift. So if a trend is fitted to the price all this does is to remove the drift in the random walk. Fitting a trend and taking deviations does not make an $I(1)$ process stationary. The deviations from the fitted trend are *still* a random walk, because all we have done is to remove the drift. Deviations from trend will have no mean reversion and they cannot be predicted using univariate models. Nevertheless some technical analysts do fit deterministic lines and curves to asset price data, assuming that deviations from these trends can somehow be predicted!

By the same token, taking first differences is *not* an appropriate way to detrend an $I(0)$ + trend process. The first difference of a trend stationary process has substantial negative autocorrelation. Indeed, when any stationary process is differenced the result has negative autocorrelation. To detrend an $I(0)$ + trend process we should fit a trend line and take deviations from this line. But trend stationary processes almost never arise in financial markets. When a trend *appears* to be present in a time series plot of the data, such as Figure II.5.7, it is almost certain to be a stochastic and not a deterministic trend.

In summary, if data are not generated by a stationary process but we wish to make them stationary, then it is very important to apply the right sort of stationarity transform. Efficient financial markets generate price, rate or yield data that have a stochastic trend and not a deterministic trend. Hence, it is not appropriate to detrend the data by fitting a trend line and taking deviations. Instead the data should be detrended by taking first differences.

II.5.3.4   Unit Root Tests

Statistical tests of the null hypothesis that a time series is non-stationary versus the alternative that it is stationary are called *unit root tests*. The name derives from the fact that an autoregressive process is stationary if and only if the roots of its characteristic polynomial lie strictly *inside* the unit circle – see Section II.5.3.1 for further details.

A unit root test has stationarity in the *alternative* hypothesis, i.e. the hypotheses for a unit root test are

$$H_0 : X_t \sim I(1) \quad \text{vs} \quad H_1 : X_t \sim I(0). \tag{II.5.33}$$

Thus if the computed value of the test statistic falls into the critical region we conclude that the process is stationary (at the confidence level prescribed by the critical region). But if a null hypothesis cannot be rejected this does not automatically imply that it is true. Hence, if the test statistic for (II.5.33) falls outside the critical region we should then perform *another* unit root test, this time of

$$H_0 : \Delta X_t \sim I(1) \quad \text{vs} \quad H_1 : \Delta X_t \sim I(0), \tag{II.5.34}$$

where Δ denotes the first difference operator. If we reject (II.5.34), only then can we conclude that the series is indeed integrated of order 1, rather than having a higher order of integration.

---

[11] For this reason (II.5.32) is often called a *trend stationary process*.

In Section I.3.7.1 we introduced the most basic – but unfortunately also the least powerful – unit root test. The *Dicky–Fuller test* is based on the *Dicky–Fuller regression*, i.e. a regression of the form

$$\Delta X_t = \alpha + \beta X_{t-1} + \varepsilon_t. \tag{II.5.35}$$

The test statistic is the t ratio on $\hat{\beta}$. It is a one-sided test for

$$H_0 : \beta = 0 \quad \text{vs} \quad H_1 : \beta < 0. \tag{II.5.36}$$

To see why this test applies to the null and alternative hypotheses (II.5.33), assume the data are generated by an AR(1) process of the form

$$X_t = \alpha + \varrho X_{t-1} + \varepsilon_t, \quad \text{with } \varepsilon_t \sim I(0). \tag{II.5.37}$$

Then we must have $\beta = \varrho - 1$ in (II.5.35). Hence, the hypotheses (II.5.36) are equivalent to the hypotheses

$$H_0 : \varrho = 1 \text{ vs } H_1 : \varrho < 1, \tag{II.5.38}$$

which in turn are equivalent to (II.5.33).

If one or more variables in a regression model are non-stationary then the standard diagnostic statistics such as t ratios and regression R^2 are no longer valid. When data have trends, either deterministic or stochastic, the R^2 will always be close to 1 and the t ratios have a severe bias. Hence, the t ratios based on (II.5.35) are biased. Dickey and Fuller (1979) showed that the appropriate critical values for the t ratio on $\hat{\beta}$ are larger than standard t critical values. They have to be increased by an amount that depends on the sample size. Some critical values for the Dickey–Fuller distribution are given in Table II.5.1.

Table II.5.1   Critical values of the Dickey–Fuller distribution[a]

Sample size	Significance level		
	1%	5%	10%
25	−3.75	−3.00	−2.62
50	−3.58	−2.93	−2.60
100	−3.51	−2.89	−2.58
250	−3.46	−2.88	−2.57
500	−3.44	−2.87	−2.57
∞	−3.43	−2.86	−2.57

[a]We only give the critical values for the case where the Dickey–Fuller regression includes a constant but no time trend. As explained in Section II.5.3.3, deterministic trends are rarely present in financial asset returns.

For example, for a sample size of 250 the 5% critical value of the Dickey–Fuller distribution is −2.88 and the 1% critical value is −3.46. Because the test is one-sided with '<' in the alternative hypothesis, the critical values are always negative. If the Dickey–Fuller test statistic, i.e. the t ratio on $\hat{\beta}$ in (II.5.35), is more negative than the critical value at some significance level, then we reject the null hypothesis that the series is integrated in favour of the alternative that it is stationary, at this significance level. For instance, if we obtain a t ratio on $\hat{\beta}$ in (II.5.35) of −4.35 based on a sample of size 250, then we would reject the null hypothesis of integration at the 1% significance level, in favour of the alternative that the series is stationary.

A major problem with ordinary Dickey–Fuller tests is that their critical values are biased if there is autocorrelation in the residuals of the Dickey–Fuller regression. For this reason Dickey and Fuller (1981) suggested augmenting the regression (II.5.35) to include as many lagged dependent variables as necessary to remove any autocorrelation in the residuals.

The *augmented Dickey–Fuller test* of order q, or ADF(q) test, is based on the regression

$$\Delta X_t = \alpha + \beta X_{t-1} + \gamma_1 \Delta X_{t-1} \ldots + \gamma_q \Delta X_{t-q} + \varepsilon_t. \tag{II.5.39}$$

The test proceeds as in the ordinary Dickey–Fuller test above, i.e. the test statistic is still the t ratio on the estimated coefficient $\hat{\beta}$. However, the critical values are not the same as those shown in Table II.5.1. The augmented Dickey–Fuller critical values depend on the number of lags, q. For a sample size of between 500 and 600 these are given in Table II.5.2.[12]

Table II.5.2   Critical values of the augmented Dickey–Fuller distribution[a]

Number of lags	Significance Level		
	1%	5%	10%
1	−3.43	−2.86	−2.57
2	−3.90	−3.34	−3.05
3	−4.30	−3.74	−3.45
4	−4.65	−4.10	−3.81
5	−4.96	−4.42	−4.13

[a]Again we only give the critical values for the case where the augmented Dickey–Fuller regression includes a constant but no time trend.

Augmented Dickey–Fuller tests have very low power to discriminate between alternative hypotheses, and are not valid when the data have jumps or structural breaks in the data generation process.[13] The errors in an augmented Dickey–Fuller regression are also assumed to be i.i.d., but often this is not the case. Less restrictive assumptions on the errors are possible.

For example, the *Phillips–Perron test* allows errors to be dependent with heteroscedastic variance (Phillips and Perron, 1988). Since returns on financial assets often have conditional heteroscedasticity, Phillips–Perron tests are generally favoured for financial data analysis. The Phillips–Perron test statistic is computed by applying a correction to the (augmented) Dickey–Fuller statistic. Several econometrics texts describe the Phillips–Perron test, but it is quite complex and for reasons of space we shall not describe it here.[14] Also many econometrics packages compute the Phillips–Perron statistic automatically.

Finally, we remark that the unit root tests proposed by Durbin and Hausmann are uniformly more powerful than Dickey–Fuller tests in the presence of a deterministic trend (see Choi, 1992). However, it is seldom necessary to test for deterministic trends in financial data. Besides, analytical results of Cochrane (1991) imply that tests for the distinction between deterministic and stochastic trends in the data can have arbitrarily low power.

[12] These were computed by MacKinnon (1991). Now all standard econometric packages include augmented Dickey–Fuller critical values.
[13] See Diebold and Rudebusch (1991).
[14] See Hamilton (1994) p.506.

II.5.3.5   Unit Roots in Asset Prices

In continuous time we model the prices of stocks, stock indices and foreign exchange rates as *geometric Brownian motion*. In Section I.3.7.3 we proved that the equivalent process in discrete time is one in which the logarithm of the price follows a random walk. Hence, if the continuous time and discrete time dynamics are to agree we should find that the log prices of stocks, stock indices and exchange rates have a unit root.[15]

EXAMPLE II.5.5: UNIT ROOTS IN STOCK INDICES AND EXCHANGE RATES

Do the FTSE 100 and S&P 500 indices have unit roots? Does the sterling–US dollar exchange rate have a unit root? Apply augmented Dickey-Fuller tests to daily data on the FTSE 100 and S&P 500 indices and to the sterling–dollar exchange rate between 1996 and 2007, using the daily closing prices shown in Figures II.5.8 and II.5.9.

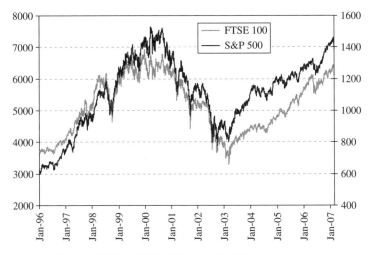

Figure II.5.8   FTSE 100 and S&P 500 stock indices

SOLUTION   We apply ADF(1) regressions since there is little autocorrelation in these series, and apply the test to log prices since then the first difference will be the log returns.[16] The results are reported in the first row of Table II.5.3. Clearly the null hypothesis that the series are integrated cannot be rejected.

Now we repeat the ADF(1) tests but this time using the second difference of the log prices as the dependent variable and the lagged change in log price plus the lagged second difference in log price as dependent variables. That is, we perform an augmented Dickey–Fuller test of (II.5.34), and the results are shown in the second row of Table II.5.3. We can conclude that the logarithm of the stock index prices and the exchange rate are indeed integrated of order 1. We leave it to interested readers to verify that the prices themselves,

---

[15] Note that if the log price has a unit root, then the price usually has a unit root also – and vice versa.

[16] Nevertheless it would be more rigorous to apply more lags in the augmented Dickey–Fuller tests at first, and then 'test down' to obtain the optimal number of lags, i.e. the number of lags that is just sufficient so that there is no autocorrelation in the residuals of the Dickey–Fuller regression. It may be that the result of an ADF(2) test implies a series is integrated, whereas the ADF(1) test indicates stationarity – see the next example, for instance.

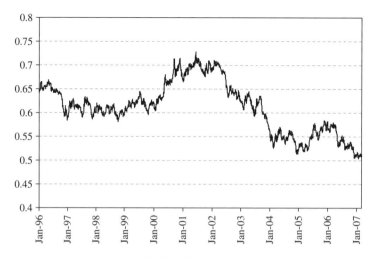

Figure II.5.9   £/$ exchange rate

Table II.5.3   Results of ADF(1) tests

Hypotheses	FTSE 100	S&P 500	USD/GBP
$H_0: X_t \sim I(1)$ vs $H_1: X_t \sim I(0)$	-1.9578	-2.3505	-0.9971
$H_0: \Delta X_t \sim I(1)$ vs $H_1: \Delta X_t \sim I(0)$	-38.8836	-38.1773	-37.2009

not just the log prices, also have a unit root and that this finding applies to most stocks, stock indices and exchange rates.[17]

II.5.3.6   Unit Roots in Interest Rates, Credit Spreads and Implied Volatility

Continuous time models of interest rates, credit spreads and volatility almost always assume that there is a mean-reversion mechanism in the drift term, so that the process is *stationary*. Moreover, it is common to assume that they follow a process of the form (II.5.40) below, which will only be a geometric process when $\alpha = 1$. In the previous section we tested the *logarithm* of a price (or an exchange rate or a commodity price) because these are assumed to follow geometric processes in continuous time. But we usually test the *level* of an interest rate, credit spread or volatility because these are assumed to follow processes in continuous time that need not be geometric. Then the first difference data that we use in the unit root test will correspond to the changes in interest rates, credit spreads or volatility.

EXAMPLE II.5.6: UNIT ROOT TESTS ON INTEREST RATES

Are UK interest rates generated by an integrated process? Base your answer on the Bank of England's 2-year interest rate data shown in Figure II.5.10.

---

[17] The log is just a 'squashed down' version of the price and so has similar time series properties (see Figure I.3.21).

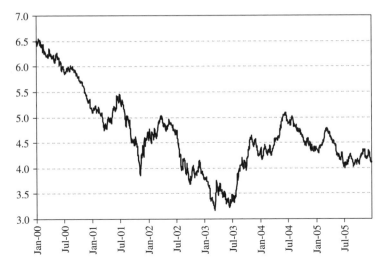

Figure II.5.10   UK 2-year interest rates

SOLUTION   We apply an ADF(2) test. The estimated Dickey–Fuller regression is

$$\Delta 2yr = \underset{(2.087)}{0.014} - \underset{(-2.324)}{0.0033} \times 2yr_{-1} + \underset{(4.386)}{0.112}\,\Delta 2yr_{-1} - \underset{(-0.021)}{0.0005}\,\Delta 2yr_{-2}.$$

Figures in parentheses are t ratios. The Dickey–Fuller statistic is the t ratio on the lagged 2-year interest rate. This is -2.324 and it is not large enough to reject the null hypothesis that the 2-year interest rate has a unit root. But clearly there is no real need for the second lag of the dependent variable, because the t ratio is only -0.021, and an ADF(1) test yields the statistic -2.325. This is still not significant even at the 10% level so the 2-year interest rate is non-stationary.

It is left to the reader to repeat the test using $\Delta 2yr$ in place of $2yr$ (and $\Delta^2 2yr$ in place of $\Delta 2yr$). This time the augmented Dickey–Fuller test statistic will be very large and negative, confirming that the 2-year rate is indeed an integrated process.

EXAMPLE II.5.7: UNIT ROOT TESTS ON CREDIT SPREADS

Are credit spreads stationary? Base your answer on the iTraxx Europe index data shown in Figure II.5.11.

SOLUTION   The ADF(2) regression is

$$\Delta iTraxx = \underset{(0.286)}{0.015} - \underset{(-1.141)}{0.0023} \times iTraxx_{-1} + \underset{(11.409)}{0.4129}\,\Delta iTraxx_{-1} - \underset{(-3.552)}{0.1286}\,\Delta iTraxx_{-2}.$$

With an ADF(2) statistic of only -1.141 we cannot reject the null hypothesis that the series is non-stationary. The interested reader may confirm that $\Delta iTraxx$ is stationary and conclude that the iTraxx data are indeed generated by an $I(1)$ process. Note that the daily changes in iTraxx data have high positive correlation so the iTraxx index is generated by an integrated process, but not by a random walk.

The next example tests whether implied volatility index futures are stationary or integrated. Since these futures are traded on an exchange, one might suppose the market is efficient so

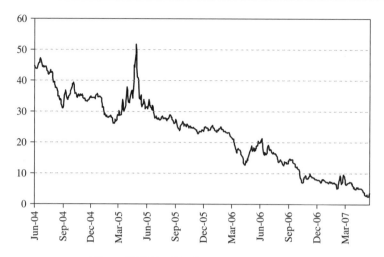

Figure II.5.11   The iTraxx Europe index

their prices are random walks, or at least integrated processes. We shall use this example to illustrate the importance of using the correct number of lagged dependent variables in the augmented Dickey–Fuller test.

EXAMPLE II.5.8: UNIT ROOTS IN IMPLIED VOLATILITY FUTURES

Use a Dickey–Fuller test and an augmented Dickey–Fuller test to test whether the data on volatility index futures' Vdax and Vstoxx[18] shown in Figure II.5.12 are integrated processes.

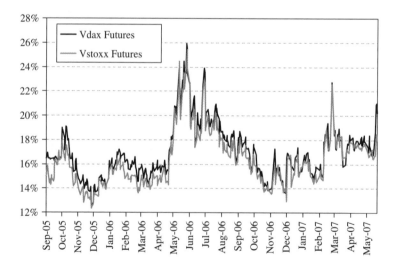

Figure II.5.12   Volatility index futures

---

[18] Vdax and Vstoxx futures contracts are on the implied volatility indices for the DAX 30 stock index and the Dow Jones Eurostoxx index. The contracts are traded on the Eurex exchange.

SOLUTION We first perform a Dickey–Fuller regression for each futures series in the spreadsheet for this example and in each case obtain the Dickey–Fuller statistic as the t ratio on the explanatory variable, i.e. the lagged volatility index future. We obtain the following results (with t ratios in parentheses):

$$\Delta \text{Vdax} = \underset{(3.52)}{0.01} - \underset{(-3.514)}{0.063} \text{ Vdax}_{-1},$$

$$\Delta \text{Vstoxx} = \underset{(3.58)}{0.01} - \underset{(-3.583)}{0.063} \text{ Vstoxx}_{-1}.$$

Hence the Dickey–Fuller statistic is -3.513 for the Vdax and -3.583 for the Vstoxx. These are both larger than the critical values shown in Table II.5.1.[19] Hence, on the basis of these results we should reject the null hypothesis that the series are integrated at the 1% level and conclude that the series are stationary.

However, we must question the conclusion reached above. To the trained eye the series in Figure II.5.8 appear to be *non*-stationary. Indeed, when we apply ADF(2) tests to the Vdax and Vstoxx data the results are:[20]

$$\Delta \text{Vdax} = \underset{(2.99)}{0.01} - \underset{(-2.980)}{0.055} \text{ Vdax}_{-1} - \underset{(-1.447)}{0.074} \Delta \text{Vdax}_{-1} - \underset{(-0.821)}{0.042} \Delta \text{Vdax}_{-2},$$

$$\Delta \text{Vstoxx} = \underset{(2.96)}{0.009} - \underset{(-2.963)}{0.054} \text{ Vstoxx}_{-1} - \underset{(-1.160)}{0.059} \Delta \text{Vstoxx}_{-1} - \underset{(-1.900)}{0.095} \Delta \text{Vstoxx}_{-2}.$$

Hence, the computed values of the ADF(2) statistics are -2.980 for the Vdax and -2.963 for the Vstoxx. Although we have not shown the augmented Dickey–Fuller critical values for a sample size of 400 in Table II.5.2, in fact the null hypothesis cannot even be rejected at the 10% significance level.

Hence, with the ADF(2) test we conclude that the series are *non*-stationary, but only just. Indeed, given the sample from September 2005 to June 2007, the results are marginal. Really we need more data (and to apply the Phillips–Perron test).

We remark that this statistical finding does not preclude continuous time models of implied volatility being (slowly) mean-reverting processes. The next subsection provides a discussion of this point.

II.5.3.7 Reconciliation of Time Series and Continuous Time Models

In the previous subsection our statistical tests confirmed that interest rates, credit spreads and implied volatility index futures in most major currencies are statistically indistinguishable from integrated processes. Nevertheless continuous time models of these variables are often based on a slowly mean-reverting process. Is this a contradiction?

Continuous time models of interest rates, credit spreads and implied volatility are usually based on a mean-reverting diffusion of the form

$$dX(t) = \varphi(\theta - X(t)) \, dt + \sigma X(t)^{\alpha} \, dB(t), \tag{II.5.40}$$

where φ is the *rate of mean reversion* and θ is the long term value of X to which the process would revert in the absence of stochastic moves and the process is only scale invariant if $\alpha = 1$.

---

[19] The size of sample is almost exactly 400, so we interpolate between the values shown in Table II.5.1 for sample sizes 250 and 500 to obtain the required critical value.

[20] We have not tested for the optimal number of lags to use in the augmented Dickey–Fuller test, although this may be done as a matter of course in econometrics software where augmented Dickey–Fuller tests are output as standard diagnostics.

To see that (II.5.40) defines a mean-reverting process, note that if $\sigma = 0$ and so the process is deterministic then[21]

$$X(t) = X(0)\, e^{-\varphi t} + \theta.$$

Provided that $\varphi > 0$ then as time increases from 0 the process decays exponentially at rate φ, eventually reaching the constant value θ.

For interest rates the model parameters are estimated using bond and interest rate option prices, but options on credit spreads and volatility have only recently begun trading, so we may consider estimating the parameters by discretizing (II.5.40) and using time series data.[22] As part of ongoing research at the time of writing I have been investigating the stability of the parameters that are estimated using time series on interest rates, credit spreads and volatility indices, when the estimation window is rolled over time, and the stability of volatility process parameters when these are calibrated to time series of option prices in a stochastic volatility setting. I have found that it is impossible to estimate or calibrate stable values for the α parameter – indeed it fluctuates wildly over time. So its value should be fixed by the modeller. For instance, in the Heston (1993) stochastic volatility model we fix $\alpha = \frac{1}{2}$. Importantly, it is only in GARCH diffusions that $\alpha = 1$ so that volatility is a scale invariant process.

A discrete time version of (II.5.40) is an autoregressive model of order 1 with heteroscedastic errors that is stationary if $\varphi > 0$.[23] To see this, write

$$\Delta X_t = \varphi(\theta - X_t) + \varepsilon_t,$$

with $\varepsilon_t = \sigma X_t^\alpha Z_t$, where $Z_t \sim NID(0, 1)$. That is,

$$(1 + \varphi)\, X_t = \varphi\theta + X_{t-1} + \varepsilon_t$$

or, equivalently,

$$X_t = \tilde{\alpha} + \varrho X_{t-1} + v_t, \quad v_t \sim NID\left(0, \eta_t^2\right),$$

$$\tilde{\alpha} = (1 + \varphi)^{-1}\varphi\theta, \quad \varrho = (1 + \varphi)^{-1} \text{ and } \quad \eta_t = (1 + \varphi)^{-1}\sigma_t, \tag{II.5.41}$$

$$\sigma_t = \sigma X_t^\alpha.$$

Since $\varrho = (1 + \varphi)^{-1}$ we know that $0 < \varrho < 1$ if $\varphi > 0$.

In other words, if the process (II.5.40) mean-reverts then it has a stationary AR(1) representation (II.5.41) as a discrete time equivalent. The parameter φ determines the autocorrelation ϱ in the AR(1) process and if the process is *slowly* mean-reverting then φ will be very near 0 and ϱ will be very near 1.

Our analysis above shows that the null hypothesis of integration versus the stationary alternative can be phrased in two equivalent ways: for discrete time models,

$$H_0 : \varrho = 1 \quad \text{vs} \quad H_1 : \varrho < 1; \tag{II.5.42}$$

and for continuous time models,

$$H_0 : \varphi = 0 \quad \text{vs} \quad H_1 : \varphi > 0. \tag{II.5.43}$$

---

[21] You can verify this solution by differentiating, giving $dX/dt = \varphi(\theta - X)$.

[22] See, for instance, Dotsis et al. (2007).

[23] We say *a* discrete time version, not *the* discrete time version, here because there are several ways that we can discretize a continuous time model.

We make the following remarks:

- In discrete time series analysis models we use historical data to estimate parameters, and to decide whether series are integrated or mean-reverting we apply a statistical test on (II.5.42). We shall see in the next section that it is extremely difficult for unit root tests to distinguish between $\varrho = 1$ and, for instance, $\varrho = 0.99$. This may be why unit root tests on interest rates, credit spreads or implied volatility almost always conclude that these are generated by integrated processes.
- In continuous time option pricing models we usually use the current market prices of options to calibrate parameters and, usually, we do *not* apply a statistical test on (II.5.43) to decide whether series are integrated or mean-reverting. If we *were* able to apply such a test on (II.5.43) it would be based on option price data, not historical time series, so we may or may not reject the null hypothesis. Also it is likely that the test would have very low power to distinguish between $\varphi = 0$ and, for instance, $\varphi = 0.01$.

And now we come to the root of the contradiction between discrete time and continuous time models. In discrete time models we use *historical* data to estimate parameters. But when the parameters of the corresponding continuous process are calibrated from market prices of options these data are based on expectations of the *future* behaviour of the underlying. Interest rates, implied volatilities and credit spreads are usually regarded as mean-reverting processes in continuous time, yet statistical tests on discrete time series data show that they are integrated. We conclude that traders *expect* interest rates, credit spreads and implied volatilities to mean-revert, eventually. However, based on the available historical data, there is no statistical evidence that they do!

II.5.3.8   Unit Roots in Commodity Prices

Testing for a unit root in commodity prices is tricky, due to the propensity for such prices to jump. Spot prices are particularly prone to jumps but futures prices also jump, even for maturities out to 12 months or more. A price jump increases the probability of a type I error, i.e. that a true null hypothesis (of a unit root, in this case) will be rejected. Some papers develop unit root tests that produce reliable results when there is a single endogenous structural break in a series (see, for instance, Zivot and Andrews, 1992). However, no test has yet been developed that applies to price series that have multiple jumps induced by exogenous supply and demand shocks. Whether continuous time models of commodity prices should have mean reversion or not also remains an open question (see Geman, 2005).

II.5.4   LONG TERM EQUILIBRIUM

Although empirical models of cointegrated financial time series are commonplace in the academic literature, the practical implementation of these models into portfolio management systems is still in its early stages. The traditional starting point for both asset allocation and risk management is a correlation matrix, which is based on financial asset *returns*. The price data are detrended before the analysis is even begun, so any long term trend is removed from the data. Hence *a priori* it is impossible to base any decision on *common* trends in prices.

By contrast, the first goal of cointegration analysis is to test whether there are any common stochastic trends in the variables. If there *is* a common trend in a set of prices they must have a long term equilibrium relationship. The second goal of cointegration analysis is to capture this equilibrium in a dynamic correlation analysis. Thus cointegration analysis has two stages:

1. A long term equilibrium relationship between prices is established. A statistical test for cointegration is applied and, if cointegration is present, we identify a stationary linear combination of the prices which best describes the long term equilibrium relationship between them.
2. The long term equilibrium is used in an *error correction model* (ECM) of returns. ECMs are so called because they explain how short term deviations from equilibrium are corrected.

Since it is normally the case that log prices will be cointegrated when the prices are cointegrated it is standard, but not necessary, to perform the cointegration analysis at stage 1 on log prices. ECMs at stage 2 are then based on log returns rather than absolute changes. In the remainder of this section we discuss only stage 1 of cointegration analysis. Stage 2 is covered in Section II.5.5.

II.5.4.1   Cointegration and Correlation Compared

Cointegration and correlation are related but different concepts. High correlation does not imply high cointegration, nor does high cointegration imply high correlation. In fact, cointegrated series can have correlations that are quite low at times. Figure II.5.13 is based on simulated data for the prices of a stock and the stock's index. The prices are very highly cointegrated but the correlation between the returns is only 0.25.[24] Consider a diversified portfolio of 30 S&P 100 stocks with allocations that are proportional to their market cap. This should be cointegrated with the S&P 100, which is a cap-weighted index. So the portfolio should move in line with the index in the long term. However, the portfolio will typically be more volatile than the index and there will be periods when stocks that are not in the portfolio have exceptional price movements. Hence, the empirical correlation between the portfolio returns and the index returns could be low.

The converse also holds: returns may be highly correlated without a high cointegration in prices. Figure II.5.14 is also based on simulated price data, this time where the two returns have a very high correlation – in fact it is a little greater than 0.8. However, the price series are drifting apart so they are clearly not tied together in the long term.[25]

In summary, high correlations can occur when there is cointegration and when there is no cointegration. That is, correlation tells us nothing about the long term behaviour between two markets: they may or may not be moving together over long periods of time, and correlation is not an adequate tool for measuring this.

Correlation reflects comovements in returns, which are liable to great instabilities over time. Returns have no 'memory' of a trend so correlation is intrinsically a short term measure. That is why portfolios that have allocations based on a correlation matrix commonly require frequent rebalancing. Moreover, long-short strategies that are based only on correlations cannot guarantee long term performance because there is no mechanism to ensure the reversion of long and short portfolios. By the same token correlation-based index tracking portfolios require very frequent rebalancing because there is nothing to prevent the tracking error from behaving in the unpredictable manner of a random walk.

---

[24] Press F9 in the spreadsheet for this figure to simulate other price pairs that are highly cointegrated and read off the returns correlation.
[25] Press F9 in the spreadsheet for this figure to simulate other price pairs that are not cointegrated and read off the returns correlation.

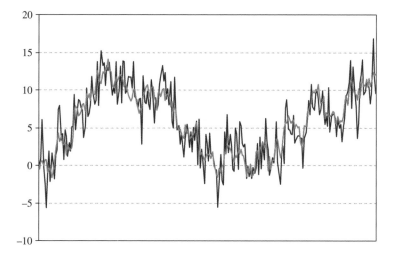

Figure II.5.13   Cointegrated prices, low correlation in returns

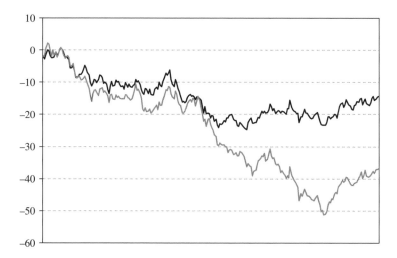

Figure II.5.14   Non-cointegrated prices with highly correlated returns

Since correlation tells us nothing about long term performance there is a need to augment standard risk–return modelling methodologies to take account of common long term trends in prices. This is exactly what cointegration provides. Cointegration measures long term comovements in prices, and these may occur even when correlations are low. Therefore, portfolio management strategies based on cointegrated financial assets should be more effective in the long term. Moreover, stage 2 of cointegration analysis is still based on correlation. In fact, cointegration simply augments correlation analysis to include a first stage in which the price data are analysed and then, in the second stage, it provides a dynamic analysis of correlations which informs us about any lead–lag behaviour between returns.

II.5.4.2 Common Stochastic Trends

The prices (and log prices) of liquid financial assets are integrated, and integrated processes have infinite unconditional variance. Since they can wander virtually anywhere over a period of time there is little point in trying to use past prices to forecast future prices in a univariate time series model. However, when two or more prices are cointegrated a multivariate model *will* be worthwhile. This is because it reveals information about the long term equilibrium in the system. For example, if a spread is found to be mean-reverting we know that, wherever one series is in the future the other series will be right there along with it.

Cointegrated prices have a *common stochastic trend* (Stock and Watson, 1988). They are 'tied together' in the long term even though they might drift apart in the short term, because the spread or some other linear combination of the two prices is mean-reverting.

To understand what it means to have a common stochastic trend consider two prices, X and Y, where

$$X_t = W_t + \varepsilon_t^X, \qquad \varepsilon_t^X \sim \text{i.i.d}(0, \sigma_X^2),$$
$$Y_t = W_t + \varepsilon_t^Y, \qquad \varepsilon_t^Y \sim \text{i.i.d}(0, \sigma_Y^2), \qquad \text{(II.5.44)}$$
$$W_t = W_{t-1} + \varepsilon_t^W, \quad \varepsilon_t^W \sim \text{i.i.d}(0, \sigma_W^2),$$

and the error terms ε_t^Y, ε_t^Y and ε_t^W are independent of each other. Here X and Y are both integrated of order 1 and

$$X_t - Y_t = \varepsilon_t^X - \varepsilon_t^Y$$

is stationary, so X and Y are cointegrated. X and Y have a common stochastic trend given by the random walk component W.[26]

II.5.4.3 Formal Definition of Cointegration

A set of integrated series are *cointegrated* if there is a linear combination of these series that is stationary.[27] Hence, in the case of just two integrated series, X and Y are *cointegrated* if X and Y are both integrated processes but there exists α such that

$$Z = X - \alpha Y \qquad \text{(II.5.45)}$$

is stationary. In (II.5.45) Z is called the *disequilibrium* because it captures deviations from the long term equilibrium. The *expectation* of Z defines a long term equilibrium relationship between X and Y and periods of 'disequilibrium' occur as the observed value of Z varies around its expected value.

The *cointegrating vector* is the vector of constant coefficients in Z. So in the bivariate case the cointegrating vector is $(1, -\alpha)$. When only two integrated processes are considered for cointegration, there can be at most one cointegrating vector, because if there were two cointegrating vectors the original processes would have to be stationary.

More generally, cointegration exists between n integrated processes if there is at least one cointegrating vector. That is, there is at least one linear combination of the integrated

---

[26] Note that the correlation between the changes in X and the changes in Y may be low, especially if the errors have a large variance.
[27] The definition of cointegration given in the seminal paper of Engle and Granger (1987) is more general than this, but the basic definition presented here is sufficient for the purposes of this chapter.

processes that is stationary. Each distinct stationary linear combination acts like 'glue' in the system and so the more cointegrating vectors found the greater the long term association between the series. The maximum number of cointegrating vectors is $n-1$.[28]

For instance, interest rates of different maturities tend to have very high cointegration. In 10 years' time we do not know what the 3-month US Treasury bill rate with be, but whatever the level of the 3-month rate we *do* know that the 6-month rate will be right along there with it. This is because the spread between the 6-month and 3-month rate is mean-reverting. Put another way, the 3-month and 6-month rates are tied together by a common stochastic trend, i.e. they are cointegrated. In a yield curve with 20 different maturity interest rates, each of the 19 independent spreads may be stationary, in which case there will be 19 cointegrating vectors. This is the maximum possible number of cointegrating vectors in a 20-dimensional system of interest rates.

We almost always find a high degree of cointegration between interest rates of different maturities in the same yield curve. Cointegration can also be thought of as a form of factor analysis similar to principal component analysis,[29] so it is not surprising that cointegration analysis often works very well on the term structure data that are so successfully modelled by a principal component analysis.

There are many other cases of cointegrated assets in other financial markets. Cointegration occurs whenever a spread is mean-reverting, or when a basis or tracking error is mean-reverting. But even though a spread, basis or tracking error may be stationary it is not always clear that this will be the *most* stationary linear combination. Put another way, $(1, -1)$ may not be the best cointegrating vector. And if the spread, basis or tracking error is not stationary, that does not preclude the possibility that some other linear combination of the prices (or log prices) *is* stationary.

II.5.4.4   Evidence of Cointegration in Financial Markets

This section reviews some of the academic publications on the existence of cointegration in financial markets. There is a vast body of academic research in this area, dating back two decades, and recently market practitioners have found useful applications for it. Now many hedge funds base statistical arbitrage and pairs trading strategies on cointegration analysis and commodity analysts model the lead–lag relationship between spot and futures returns using ECMs. Even the pricing and hedging of spread options may be based on cointegration.

Term Structures

No financial systems have higher cointegration than term structures, and there is a large academic literature in this area. Cointegration and correlation go together in the yield curve, and we often find strongest cointegration where correlations are highest. See, for example, Bradley and Lumpkin (1992), Hall et al. (1992), Alexander and Johnson (1992, 1994), Davidson et al. (1994), Lee (1994), Brenner et al. (1996).

---

[28] If there are n cointegrating vectors, the variables would have to be stationary.

[29] The more cointegrating vectors there are in the levels variables, the fewer principal components we need to represent the system of first differences. For instance, the system of 12 crude oil futures term structure that we considered in Section II.2.4.3 required only two components to represent over 99% of the covariation in the system, so we expect 10 cointegrating vectors. For a mathematical exposition of the connection between cointegration and principal components, see Gouriéroux et al. (1991).

Stocks Indices and Tracking Portfolios

A stock market index is a weighted sum of stock prices. Hence, a sufficiently large and diversified stock portfolio will be cointegrated with the index, provided that the index weights do not change too much over time. See Alexander (1999), Alexander and Dimitriu (2005a, 2005b) and Dunis and Ho (2005). The sector indices within a given country should also be cointegrated when industrial sectors maintain relatively stable proportions in the economy. By the same token, a basket of equity indices in the Morgan Stanley Country Indices world index, or the Europe, Australasia and Far East index, should be cointegrated with the aggregate index. See Alexander et al. (2002).

Pairs

We shall see later on that the stationary series in Example II.5.3 is a spread. Any two prices with a mean-reverting spread will have some degree of cointegration. Since many spreads are mean-reverting the Granger causality that is inherent in a cointegrated system indicates that one price is leading the other price or, there may be bi-directional causality. This points to a possible inefficiency in the market. It is possible to find pairs of securities, or baskets of securities, that are cointegrated. In this case a pairs trading or statistical arbitrage strategy can be based on an ECM. Such a model provides the most rigorous framework for modelling mean reversion, response to shocks and the lead–lag returns behaviour that must be present when prices are cointegrated. See Section II.5.5.3 for further details.

Spot and Futures

Many financial journals (the *Journal of Futures Markets* in particular) contain papers on cointegration between spot and futures prices. Since spot and futures prices converge at the maturity date of the future, they are tied together and the basis must be mean-reverting. More generally, we can construct non-traded *constant maturity futures* series by concatenating futures prices, and then examine their cointegration with spot prices over a long period of time. Financial futures tend to be very highly cointegrated with their spot prices, but there is less evidence of cointegration between commodity futures and spot prices. This is expected since the commodity basis includes carry costs that can be highly unpredictable, so the commodity basis need not be stationary.[30] When spot and futures prices are cointegrated the error correction mechanism has become the focus of research into the *price discovery* relationship, i.e. the question of whether futures prices lead spot prices.[31] The same framework is also used to derive optimal hedge ratios in minimum variance hedging. See Section III.2.7, and Alexander and Barbosa (2007, 2008) and the many references therein.

Commodities

The prices of commodities derived from the same underlying, such as soya bean crush and soya bean oil, should be cointegrated. Similarly, heating oil, natural gas and light sweet crude

---

[30] But see Beck (1994), Bessler and Covey (1991), Bopp and Sitzer (1987), Khoury and Yourougou (1991), Schroeder and Goodwin (1991), Schwarz and Szakmary (1994) and others for spot-futures cointegration applied to different commodity markets.
[31] See MacDonald and Taylor (1988), Nugent (1990), Bessler and Covey (1991), Bopp and Sitzer (1987), Chowdhury (1991), Khoury and Yourougou (1991), Schroeder and Goodwin (1991), Schwarz and Laatsch (1991), Lee (1994), Schwarz and Szakmary (1994), Brenner and Kroner (1995), Harris et al. (1995), and many others.

oil are all produced when oil is 'cracked' in refineries. The prices may be cointegrated because all three commodities are produced in the same production process. However, in general, the carry costs (which include insurance, storage and transport) on related commodities are difficult to measure and empirically there seems to be little evidence that related commodities such as different types of metals are cointegrated. Brenner and Kroner (1995) present a useful survey of the literature in this area and conclude that the idiosyncratic behaviour of carry costs makes it very difficult to apply cointegration to related commodity prices. High frequency technical traders dominate these markets, and it is unlikely that any cointegration between related commodities is sufficiently robust for trading.

Spread Options

A spread is the difference between two prices, and if the two prices are cointegrated then their spread is usually stationary.[32] Numerous examples of stationary spreads include *calendar spreads*, i.e. the difference between two futures prices on the same underlying but with different maturities, and *crack spreads*, i.e. the difference between heating oil futures prices and crude oil futures prices, or the difference between natural gas futures prices and crude oil futures prices, of identical maturities. These options are traded on NYMEX so how should they be priced to account for the cointegration between the two legs of the spread? Duan and Pliska (2004) derive a theory for option valuation with cointegrated asset prices where the error correction mechanism is incorporated into the correlated Brownian motions that drive the prices. Applied to spread option pricing, their Monte Carlo results show that cointegration can have a substantial influence on spread option prices when volatilities are stochastic. But when volatilities are constant the model simplifies to one of simple bivariate Brownian motion and the standard Black–Scholes–Merton results are recovered.

Market Integration

When $1 can buy exactly the same basket of securities in two different countries, we say that *purchasing power parity* (PPP) holds. We can derive a *PPP exchange rate* by dividing the price of the basket in one country by the price of the same basket in another country. Has the liberalization of capital markets and the increasing globalization of investors led to increasing cointegration between market indices? This would only be the case if market exchange rates are not excessively variable about their PPP value. Under PPP a global investor should allocate funds to securities in international companies regardless of the index they are in. Thus we can compare two country indices, such as the FTSE 100 and the S&P 500 stock market indices,[33] and if PPP holds then their prices measured in the *same* currency units should be cointegrated. But there is very weak evidence of cointegration between international stock market indices; see Taylor and Tonks (1989), and Alexander (2001a).[34] Cointegration is even weaker between international bond markets; see Karfakis and Moschos (1990), Kasa (1992), Smith et al. (1993), Corhay et al. (1993) and Clare et al. (1995).

---

[32] The spread may not be the *most* stationary linear combination of the prices but it is usually stationary when prices are cointegrated.
[33] These are comparable since the average market capitalization of FTSE 100 stocks is similar to that of S&P 500 stocks.
[34] See also Example II.5.9 below, which shows that there is no evidence of cointegration between the FTSE 100 and S&P 500 indices, or even between the DAX 30 and CAC 40 indices.

Foreign Exchange

Two exchange rates are highly unlikely to be cointegrated. If they were, then their logs would also be cointegrated, but the difference between the log rates is the log cross rate and this will be non-stationary if the cross market is efficient. There is, however, some empirical evidence of cointegration between three or more exchange rates: see Goodhart (1988), Hakkio and Rush (1989), Baillie and Bollerslev (1989, 1994), Coleman (1990), Alexander and Johnson (1992, 1994), MacDonald and Taylor (1994) and Nieuwland et al. (1994).

II.5.4.5   Estimation and Testing in Cointegrated Systems

When testing for cointegration it is important that a sufficiently long period of data is used, otherwise no common *long term* trends can be detected. The time span of the data set must be large enough to encompass the 'long term', whatever this means, since 'long term' depends very much on the context. The time span of the data period is more important than the frequency of the observations. For instance, using 260 weekly observations over a period of 5 years is better for testing cointegration than 1 year of daily observations.

In this section we describe and illustrate the two most common cointegration methodologies. Each method consists of a test for cointegration and, should there be cointegration, an estimation of the long run equilibrium. The methodologies we describe are due to Engle and Granger (1987) and Johansen (1988, 1991). The first is based on an OLS linear regression and the second is based on an eigenvalue analysis of a certain matrix. There are many other cointegration tests: for example, Phillips and Ouliaris (1990) propose a two-step cointegration test based on the residuals from a cointegrating regression, and the test of Engle and Yoo (1987) on the significance of the disequilibrium terms in the ECM.[35]

Engle–Granger Methodology

Engle and Granger proposed a simple test for cointegration, which is just to perform OLS regression of one integrated variable on the other integrated variables and then apply a unit root test to the residuals. We remark that OLS estimators are not consistent unless the residuals are stationary, and so it is usually applied only when the dependent and independent variables are themselves stationary. However, when integrated dependent and independent variables are cointegrated then OLS will provide consistent estimates.[36]

Let $X_1, \ldots, X_n$ denote the integrated variables. For instance, these could be a set of (log) prices or a set of interest rates. Choose one of these variables as the dependent variable, say X_1, and then do an OLS regression:

$$X_{1t} = \beta_1 + \beta_2 X_{2t} + \ldots + \beta_n X_{nt} + \varepsilon_t. \qquad (II.5.46)$$

This regression is called the *Engle–Granger regression* and the Engle–Granger test is a *unit root test on the residuals* from this regression. If the unit root test indicates that the error process

---

[35] See Greene (2007), Hamilton (1994) and numerous other econometrics texts for further details.
[36] See Section I.4.3.2 for the definition of a consistent estimator.

in (II.5.46) is stationary then the variables $X_1, \ldots, X_n$ are cointegrated with cointegrating vector $\left(1, -\hat{\beta}_2, \ldots, -\hat{\beta}_n\right)$. In other words,

$$Z = X_1 - \hat{\beta}_2 X_2 - \ldots - \hat{\beta}_n X_n \qquad \text{(II.5.47)}$$

is the stationary linear combination of integrated variables whose mean represents the long run equilibrium.

The Engle–Granger regression is very unusual, because it is the *only* situation where it is legitimate to perform an OLS regression on non-stationary data. If $X_1, \ldots, X_n$ are not cointegrated then the error process in (II.5.46) will be non-stationary and OLS estimators will not be consistent.

There are two problems with Engle–Granger tests. First, when $n > 2$ the result of the test will be influenced by the choice of dependent variable. So if we choose, say, X_2 instead of X_1 to be the dependent variable in the Engle–Granger regression (II.5.46) then the cointegrating vector will be different. The second problem is that the test only allows us to estimate *one* cointegrating vector, yet there may be up to $n - 1$ cointegrating vectors in a system of n integrated series. It is only when $n = 2$ that it does not matter which variable is taken as the dependent variable. There is only one cointegrating vector and this is the same whether estimated by a regression of X_1 on X_2 or of X_2 on X_1.[37]

EXAMPLE II.5.9: ARE INTERNATIONAL STOCK INDICES COINTEGRATED?

(a) Are the S&P 500 and the FTSE 100 indices cointegrated?
(b) Are the DAX 30 and CAC 40 indices cointegrated?

In each case apply the Engle–Granger methodology to daily data on the index values over the period 1996–2007.

SOLUTION   (a) Figure II.5.15 compares the FTSE 100 and S&P 500 indices over the data period. We have rebased both indices to be 100 at the start of the period, simply because this makes them easier to compare graphically. Example II.5.5 has already verified that all series are integrated of order 1 so we can proceed straight to the cointegration analysis.

The spread between the indices in Figure II.5.15 was generally increasing during the periods 1999–2001 and again from 2003–2007. Indeed, there seems little visual evidence that the two series are tied together, and interested readers can verify that an Engle–Granger test leads to the conclusion that the two series are not cointegrated.

If PPP holds then the two indices in the *same currency* units should be cointegrated, as discussed in the previous subsection. For this reason we use the US dollar–sterling exchange rate to convert the S&P 500 index into sterling terms and again rebase both indices to be 100 at the start of the period. The series are shown in Figure II.5.16.

In the spreadsheet for this example we perform an OLS regression of FTSE 100 on S&P 500 in the same currency units and save the residuals. These are shown in Figure II.5.17. There is a high degree of autocorrelation in the residuals. Of course the average value of the residuals is 0 – this is always the case for OLS residuals – but it is not clear to the eye whether the series is very slowly mean-reverting or not mean-reverting at all. The graph in Figure II.5.17 could be generated by a random walk with zero drift. In the spreadsheet an

---

[37] However, the estimate of the cointegrating vector will have a different sampling error when we switch the dependent and independent variable (in effect, the residuals become horizontal differences rather than vertical differences).

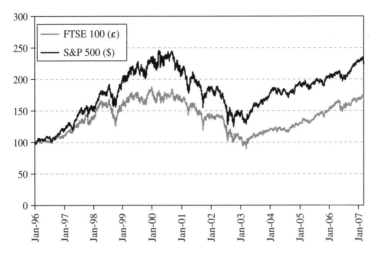

Figure II.5.15 FTSE 100 and S&P 500 indices, 1996–2007

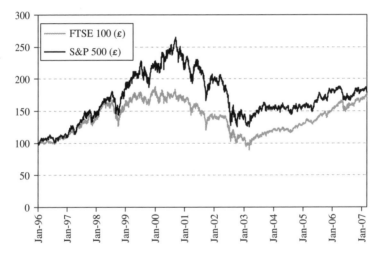

Figure II.5.16 FTSE 100 and S&P 500 indices in common currency, 1996–2007

ADF(2) test on the residuals gives an estimated ADF(2) statistic of -1.86 which is not large enough to reject the null hypothesis that the residuals are non-stationary. Hence, the FTSE 100 and S&P 500 indices are *not* cointegrated.

(b) Turning now to the DAX 30 and CAC 40 indices, these are already in the same currency units. Daily data on the two indices, rebased to be 100 at the beginning of the period, are displayed in Figure II.5.18 and the residuals from the Engle–Granger regression are shown in Figure II.5.19. Again we reach the conclusion that the series are not cointegrated. The spreadsheet shows that an ADF(3) test gives a value of -1.47, which is well below any critical value and the results of any other unit root test would lead to a similar conclusion.

The Engle–Granger methodology for estimating and testing for cointegration is intuitive, theoretically simple and very easy to apply. But when there are more than two

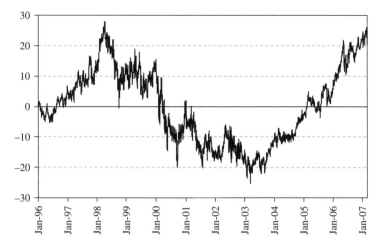

Figure II.5.17   Residuals from Engle–Granger regression of FTSE 100 on S&P 500

Figure II.5.18   DAX 30 and CAC 40 indices, 1996–2007

series the procedure is both limited and biased. Nevertheless in special circumstances the Engle–Granger procedure can still be the preferred approach to estimating and testing high-dimensional systems. See also the remarks made at the end of this section.

Johansen Methodology

Johansen's methodology investigates cointegration in general multivariate systems where there are at least two integrated series. The standard references are Johansen (1988, 1991) and Johansen and Juselius (1990), the last of these papers being the easiest to read. It is more powerful than the Engle–Granger method, but it is important to recognize that the two tests have different objectives. The Johansen tests seek the linear combination which is *most stationary* whereas the Engle–Granger tests, being based on OLS, seek the stationary linear combination that has the *minimum variance*.

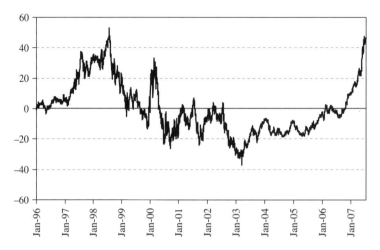

Figure II.5.19　Residuals from Engle–Granger regression of DAX 30 on CAC40

Johansen tests can be thought of as a multivariate generalization of the unit root tests that were described in Section II.5.3. There it was shown that an AR(1) process may be rewritten in the form (II.5.35) where the first difference is regressed on the lagged level variable, and that the test for a stochastic trend is based on the fact that the coefficient on the lagged level should be 0 if the process has a unit root.

We now generalize this argument for a system of n integrated variables. Suppose the variables $\{X_1, \ldots, X_n\}$ have a first order vector autoregressive representation of the form (II.5.24). Using the matrix form (II.5.25), the VAR(1) is written

$$\mathbf{X}_t = \boldsymbol{\alpha} + \mathbf{B}\mathbf{X}_{t-1} + \boldsymbol{\varepsilon}_t \tag{II.5.48}$$

or, equivalently, subtracting $\mathbf{X}_{t-1}$ from both sides,

$$\Delta \mathbf{X}_t = \boldsymbol{\alpha} + \mathbf{\Pi}\mathbf{X}_{t-1} + \boldsymbol{\varepsilon}_t \tag{II.5.49}$$

where $\mathbf{\Pi} = \mathbf{B} - \mathbf{I}$ and $\mathbf{I}$ is the $n \times n$ identity matrix. But a VAR(1) may not be the most appropriate representation of the data. Returning to the univariate analogy, recall that the Dickey–Fuller regression may be augmented with sufficient lagged dependent variables to remove autocorrelation in residuals. Similarly, for the Johansen test the general model is

$$\Delta \mathbf{X}_t = \boldsymbol{\alpha} + \mathbf{\Pi}\mathbf{X}_{t-1} + \mathbf{\Gamma}_1 \Delta \mathbf{X}_{t-1} + \ldots + \mathbf{\Gamma}_q \Delta \mathbf{X}_{t-q} + \boldsymbol{\varepsilon}_t, \tag{II.5.50}$$

where the number of lagged first differences is chosen so that residuals are not autocorrelated. Since each of the variables $\{X_1, \ldots, X_n\}$ is integrated, each equation in (II.5.50) has a stationary dependent variable so the right-hand side must also represent a stationary process. Thus $\mathbf{\Pi}\mathbf{X}_{t-1}$ must be stationary.

The condition that $\mathbf{\Pi}\mathbf{X}_{t-1}$ must be stationary implies nothing at all about the relationships between $\{X_1, \ldots, X_n\}$ if the rank of the matrix $\mathbf{\Pi}$ is 0. However, if the rank of $\mathbf{\Pi}$ is r, with $r > 0$, then when $\mathbf{\Pi}\mathbf{X}_{t-1}$ is stationary there will be r independent linear relations between $\{X_1, \ldots, X_n\}$ that must be stationary. In other words, the variables will be cointegrated. Thus the test for cointegration is a test on the *rank* of $\mathbf{\Pi}$, and the rank of $\mathbf{\Pi}$ is the number of cointegrating vectors.

If there are r cointegrating vectors in the system $\{X_1, \ldots, X_n\}$, i.e. if the matrix $\mathbf{\Pi}$ has rank r, then $\mathbf{\Pi}$ can be expressed in the equivalent form

$$\begin{pmatrix} 1 & \alpha_{12} & \cdots & \cdots & \alpha_{1n} \\ 0 & 1 & \alpha_{23} & \cdots & \alpha_{2n} \\ 0 & 0 & 1 & \cdots & \alpha_{3n} \\ \vdots & \vdots & \vdots & \vdots & \vdots \\ 0 & 0 & 0 & 0 & 0 \end{pmatrix}, \tag{II.5.51}$$

where there are r non-zero rows in the matrix.[38] The elements of these rows define the disequilibrium terms as follows:

$$Z_1 = X_1 + \alpha_{12}X_2 + \ldots + \alpha_{1n}X_n$$

$$Z_2 = X_2 + \alpha_{23}X_3 + \ldots + \alpha_{2n}X_n$$

$$Z_3 = X_3 + \alpha_{34}X_4 + \ldots + \alpha_{3n}X_n$$

$$\vdots$$

$$Z_n = X_n.$$

Put another way, the Johansen procedure is a test for the number of non-zero eigenvalues of $\mathbf{\Pi}$.[39] Johansen and Juselius (1990) recommend using the *trace test* for the number r of non-zero eigenvalues in $\mathbf{\Pi}$.[40] The test statistic for

$$H_0 : r \leq R \quad \text{vs} \quad H_1 : r > R \tag{II.5.52}$$

is

$$Tr = -T \sum_{i=R+1}^{n} \ln(1 - \lambda_i), \tag{II.5.53}$$

where T is the sample size, n is the number of variables in the system and the eigenvalues of $\mathbf{\Pi}$ are real numbers such that $1 > \lambda_1 > \ldots > \lambda_n \geq 0$.[41]

The Johansen procedure for testing cointegration is standard in virtually every econometrics package. Critical values of the maximum eigenvalue and trace statistics are provided with the results of the procedure, and they are also given in Johansen and Juselius (1990). They depend on the number of lags in (II.5.50) and whether the model includes a constant and/or a trend.[42]

EXAMPLE II.5.10: JOHANSEN TESTS FOR COINTEGRATION IN UK INTEREST RATES

How many cointegrating vectors are there in UK short spot rates of maturities 1 month, 2 months, 3 months, 6 months, 9 months and 12 months? What are the cointegrating vectors?

---

[38] This is called the *row reduced Echelon form*.

[39] The rank of a matrix is equal to the number of non-zero eigenvalues (see Section I.2.2).

[40] Another test, the *maximal eigenvalue test*, is described in their paper and some packages offer this as well as the trace test as standard output from a cointegration procedure. However the maximal eigenvalue test does not have nested hypotheses and in some (isolated) cases the maximal eigenvalue and trace tests imply different conclusions. In that case the results of the trace test should be preferred.

[41] Ordering and normalizing the eigenvalues in this way ensures that the size of Tr increases with the number of non-zero eigenvalues.

[42] The presence of the constant term is necessary for variables that exhibit a drift in the stochastic trend. Likewise if one or more variables are thought to contain a deterministic trend, i.e. they are $I(1)$ + trend, then a time trend may be included also. However, it is very unlikely that a time trend would be necessary for most financial markets.

SOLUTION   We use daily data from 2000–2007, downloaded from the Bank of England website and shown in Figure II.5.20.[43] Clearly there is a very high degree of cointegration, as expected since each independent spread over the 1-month rate should be stationary. The Johansen trace test is performed using the EViews software, and the results are shown in Table II.5.4.[44]

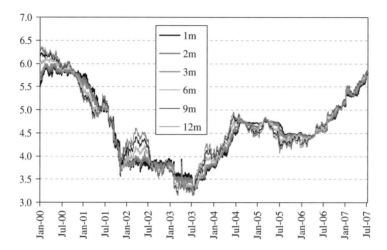

Figure II.5.20   UK short spot rates, 2000–2007

Table II.5.4   Johansen trace tests on UK short rates

No. of cointegrating vectors	Eigenvalue	Tr	5% critical value
None	0.0924	372.22	103.85
At most 1	0.0439	188.57	76.97
At most 2	0.0296	103.42	54.08
At most 3	0.0191	46.47	35.19
At most 4	0.0037	9.96	20.26
At most 5	0.0016	2.99	9.16

The test for the null hypothesis (II.5.52) is rejected at the 1% level (although only the 5% critical values are shown in the table) for $R = 1$, 2 and 3. Thus there are four cointegrating vectors. Since there are six variables in the system the maximum possible number of cointegrating vectors is five. Hence, there is a very high degree of cointegration in the system.

---

[43] See http://www.bankofengland.co.uk/statistics/yieldcurve/index.htm.
[44] Maximal eigenvalue tests are also output automatically. In this case they provide the same conclusion of four cointegrating vectors.

The cointegrating vectors are also estimated in EViews. They may be written in normalized form as:

$$Z_1 = m1 - 3.126m2 + 2.814m3 - 1.270m6 + 0.889m9 - 0.309m12 - 0.014,$$

$$Z_2 = m2 + 26.475m3 - 60.821m6 + 43.909m9 - 10.185m12 - 1.880,$$

$$Z_3 = m3 - 2.209m6 + 1.596m9 - 0.374m12 - 0.066,$$

$$Z_4 = m6 - 2.042m9 + 1.055m12 - 0.064,$$

where constants are included so that $E(Z_i) = 0$ for $i = 1, \ldots, 4$. For instance, the first cointegrating vector indicates that one long term equilibrium between UK short rates is

$$m1 = 0.014 + 3.126\ m2 - 2.814\ m3 + 1.270\ m6 - 0.889\ m9 + 0.309\ m12.$$

Comparison of Engle–Granger and Johansen Procedures

The Johansen procedure is more informative than the Engle–Granger procedure because it finds all possible cointegrating relationships. It is commonly employed for economic problems because there are usually many variables in the system and often there is no clear indication of which should be the dependent variable in an Engle–Granger regression.

However, there can be good reasons for choosing Engle–Granger as the preferred methodology for some financial applications of cointegration:

- From a risk management point of view, the Engle–Granger criterion of minimum variance is often more important than the Johansen criterion of maximum stationarity.
- There is often a natural choice of dependent variable in the cointegrating regressions (e.g. in equity index tracking – see the next subsection).
- The Engle–Granger small sample bias may not be a problem since sample sizes are generally quite large in financial analysis and the OLS estimator of the cointegrating vector is *superconsistent*.[45]

II.5.4.6   Application to Benchmark Tracking

The traditional benchmark tracking optimization problem is to *minimize the variance of the tracking error*.[46] We call this the tracking error variance minimization (TEVM) approach. Here ordinary least squares is applied to estimate a linear regression of benchmark returns on asset returns. The estimates of the regression betas determine the portfolio weights and the residual is the tracking error. However, there is nothing in this objective to ensure that the tracking error is a mean-reverting process. By contrast, in the cointegration-based tracking model we apply OLS to estimate a regression of the log index price on the log prices of

---

[45] A consistent estimator is one whose distribution converges to the true value of the parameter as the sample size increases to infinity. See Section I.4.3.2 for further details. A *superconsistent* estimator is a consistent estimator with a very fast convergence.
[46] Note that we use the term *tracking error* to denote deviations from the benchmark here, and *not* the volatility of deviations from the benchmark. Hence, this terminology differs from that is used in Section II.1.6.

the assets. If the basket of assets is cointegrated with the index, then the residual will be stationary. This objective ensures the tracking error is a mean-reverting process, i.e. that the portfolio remains tied to the index in the long run. To illustrate this point, Figure II.5.21 compares the in-sample tracking error from the tracking error variance minimization (TEVM) model with the tracking error from the cointegration-based tracking model.

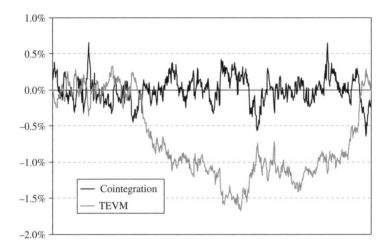

Figure II.5.21   Comparison of TEVM and cointegration tracking error[a]
[a]Reproduced with kind permission of the *Journal of Portfolio Management*.

Since the TEVM model may yield a non-stationary tracking error the replicating portfolio could, theoretically, drift arbitrarily far from the benchmark unless it is frequently rebalanced. But when the tracking portfolio is cointegrated with the benchmark the tracking error will be stationary. Indeed, any strategy that guarantees stationary tracking errors must be based on cointegration.

The optimization criterion used in Johansen cointegration analysis is to *maximize the stationarity of the tracking error*. Hence, deviations from the benchmark may be greater than they are under the minimum variance objective, but when tracking errors are highly stationary the portfolio will be more closely tied to the index than it is under the traditional approach. The optimization criterion used in Engle–Granger cointegration analysis is to *minimize the variance of the tracking error* whilst also ensuring the tracking error is stationary. Hence, deviations of the portfolio from the index will be stationary processes with minimum variance. Also, in the context of benchmark tracking there is no doubt about the choice of dependent variable in the Engle–Granger procedure. Hence this criterion is a better choice than the Johansen criterion for the benchmark tracking problem.

The cointegration-based index tracker introduced by Alexander (1999) and further developed by Alexander and Dimitriu (2005a, 2005b, 2005c) and by Dunis and Ho (2005), employs the Engle–Granger methodology where the log of the current weighted index price is the dependent variable and the log of the stock prices are the independent variables. Thus we perform a regression of the form

$$\ln(I_t) = \alpha + \sum_{k=1}^{n} \beta_k \ln(P_{kt}) + \varepsilon_t, \qquad (\text{II.5.54})$$

where I_t is the price of the reconstructed index, i.e. the index based on the current (cap or price) weights, and P_{kt} is the price of the kth stock at time t. Provided the number of stocks in the portfolio is sufficiently large, the error term will be stationary and the cointegration optimal portfolio has weights

$$\beta^* = \left(\sum_{k=1}^{n}\hat\beta_k\right)^{-1}\left(\hat\beta_1, \ldots, \hat\beta_n\right)'. \tag{II.5.55}$$

Also, since OLS regression is applied to (II.5.54), the coefficients are estimated in such a way as to minimize the variance of the residuals. In other words, the tracking error has a minimum variance property, as well as being mean reverting.

Of the two stages in portfolio optimization, i.e. selecting the stocks to be included in the portfolio and then determining the optimal portfolio holdings in each stock, cointegration optimality is primarily a property of allocation rather than selection. Nevertheless the selection process can have a dramatic effect on the results of the optimization and consequently the tracking performance of the portfolio. It is easy to find strong and stable cointegrating relationships for some stock selections but more difficult for others. An important consideration is the number of stocks selected. For instance, the portfolio containing all stocks is trivially cointegrated with the reconstructed index (i.e. the index based on current weights). As the number of stocks included in the portfolio decreases, cointegration relationships between the tracking portfolio and the benchmark become less stable. Below some critical number of stocks, cointegration may be impossible to find.

When there are a large number of potential assets in the universe the method used for stock selection is not trivial. One needs to test all possible portfolios to find those that have highly stationary tracking error relative to the benchmark. If there are N assets in total and n assets in the portfolio the possible number of cointegrating portfolios is

$$\frac{N!}{n!\,(N-n)!}$$

and this may be a very large number indeed. Taking account of investors' preferences helps to reduce the number of portfolios considered for cointegration with the benchmark.

II.5.4.7   Case Study: Cointegration Index Tracking in the Dow Jones Index

We use the data on the Dow Jones 30 stocks and the index provided in the spreadsheet to find a tracking portfolio based on (II.5.54) and (II.5.55). Whilst readers may like to experiment with using many different stocks, our study will use only the first 16 stocks in the spreadsheet to track the index. The reason for this is that Excel regression is limited to no more than 16 independent variables. It also highlights the fact that it is very easy to use cointegration to track an index with relatively few stocks.

We take the first 16 stocks and perform an Engle–Granger regression of the form (II.5.54), saving the residuals, which are shown in Figure II.5.22. Then we test the residuals for stationarity, and if they are stationary then we normalize the coefficient estimates as in (II.5.55) so that they sum to 1. These are the optimal weights on the cointegration tracking portfolio.

An augmented Dickey–Fuller test on these residuals indicates that they are indeed stationary; the ADF(1) statistic is -7.49. Hence, the portfolio is cointegrated with the index. The optimal portfolio weights are now obtained using (II.5.55) and the results are shown in Table II.5.5.

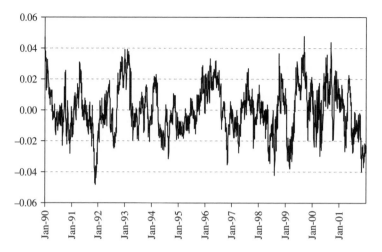

Figure II.5.22   Residuals from Engle–Granger regression of log DJIA on log stock prices

Table II.5.5   Optimal weights on 16 stocks tracking the Dow Jones
Industrial Average

IBM	10.24%	CAT	−2.37%
MMM	8.60%	HD	2.82%
PG	−0.02%	C	16.02%
MSFT	3.42%	GM	13.70%
UTX	18.15%	KO	8.31%
JNJ	3.78%	MO	−5.80%
MRK	6.97%	DD	12.21%
WMT	−1.75%	IP	5.74%

Alexander and Dimitriu (2005a) provide a detailed comparison between cointegration-based index tracking and tracking error variance minimization. They find that both strategies provide effective index tracking and that the properties of the tracking error under each strategy have different properties in different market circumstances. Taken from this paper, Figure II.5.23 shows the *post-sample performance* of the cointegration tracker and the TEVM model for the Dow Jones index. It is based on the following values of the model parameters:[47]

(a) number of stocks in portfolio, 30;
(b) calibration period, 3 years;
(c) rebalancing period, 2 weeks.

The series shown in the figure is constructed using the following steps:[48]

1. Take three years of data from 2 January 1990 to 31 December 1992.
2. Compute the optimal portfolio of 30 stocks based on cointegration tracking and on TEVM.

---

[47] These parameters can be changed. Indeed, the purpose of backtesting in this model is to determine which choice of these parameters is optimal.
[48] This is a specific implementation of the general backtesting methodology described in Section II.8.5.1.

3. Keep the portfolio holdings constant for 2 weeks and at the end of the period record the returns on both portfolios.
4. Roll the data set forward by 2 weeks, so that it now starts in the middle of January 1990 and ends in the middle of January 1993.
5. Return to step 2 and repeat, rebalancing the portfolio at each repetition (and including transaction costs in the portfolio value) until all the data are exhausted.

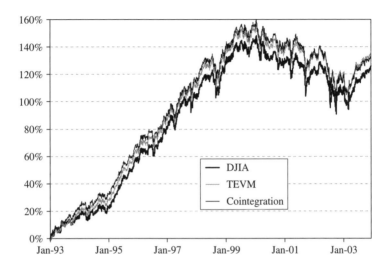

Figure II.5.23   Comparison of cointegration and TEVM tracking[a]
[a]Reproduced with kind permission of the *Journal of Portfolio Management*.

Alexander and Dimitriu (2005a) vary the choices made in (a)–(c) above and compare the performance of both cointegration-based and TEVM tracking portfolios. Provided that both models use a sufficiently long calibration period both tracking error variance minimization and cointegration-based index tracking are capable of producing optimal portfolios that outperform the index in post-sample performance measurement, and they are both robust to reducing the rebalancing frequency and to introducing no short sales constraints.

However, when the tracking task becomes more difficult, ensuring a cointegration relationship becomes a clear advantage. In *enhanced indexation*, e.g. when the objective is to outperform an index by 2% or 5% per annum, cointegration optimal portfolios clearly dominate the TEVM equivalents.

Alexander and Dimitriu (2005b) explain why cointegration-based index tracking provides a form of *crash insurance* where the cointegration-based tracker will outperform the index quite spectacularly if the index declines sharply after a period of stability. A natural development of cointegration-based tracking that is explored in Alexander et al. (2002), Alexander and Dimitriu (2005a) and Dunis and Ho (2005) is that of *statistical arbitrage strategies* which take a long position on an enhanced indexation portfolio and a short position on the index futures. Other recent research on applications of cointegration to portfolio management includes that of Füss and Kaiser (2007), who demonstrate the presence of cointegration between hedge fund strategies and indices of traditional asset classes.

II.5.5   MODELLING SHORT TERM DYNAMICS

Cointegrated series are tied together in the long term. In the short term they can drift apart, but over a period of time they must drift back together. This is because the spread – or some weighted difference of prices – has a finite, constant mean and variance.

In this section we examine the mechanisms that tie cointegrated series together. We derive a model for their short term dynamics, which is called an *error correction model*, and explain how the error correction mechanism works. Then we show that there must be at least one *causal flow* in a cointegrated system. Here we use the term 'causality' in the sense that turning points in one series precede turning points in the other, i.e. there is a *lead–lag* relationship between some of the variables. It does not mean that if we make a structural change to one series the other series will change too. We examine causality only in a statistical sense, and we call this *Granger causality*. The important point to note is that when time series are cointegrated there must be at least one Granger causal flow in the system.[49]

II.5.5.1   Error Correction Models

The *Granger representation theorem* states that when integrated variables are cointegrated a vector autoregressive model on differences will be misspecified (Granger, 1986). The disequilibrium term is missing from the vector autoregressive representation (II.5.25), but when lagged disequilibrium terms are included as explanatory variables the model becomes well specified. Such a model is called an *error correction model* because it has a self-regulating mechanism whereby deviations from the long term equilibrium are automatically corrected.

Following the process outlined in Section II.5.4, building an ECM is the second stage of the cointegration analysis. It is a dynamic model on *first differences* of the integrated variables that were used in the cointegrating regression. Thus if log prices are cointegrated the corresponding ECM is a dynamic model of correlation in the log returns.

The ECM provides a short term analysis of dynamic correlations, quite distinct from the first stage of cointegration analysis, where we seek cointegrating relationships between integrated variables, each one corresponding to a different long term equilibrium. The connection between the two stages is that the disequilibrium term Z that is used in the ECM is determined during the first stage by (II.5.47).[50]

The reason for the name *error correction* stems from the fact that the model is structured so that short term deviations from the long term equilibrium will be corrected. We illustrate this in the case where there are two cointegrated log price series X and Y. Here an ECM takes the form

$$\Delta X_t = \alpha_1 + \sum_{i=1}^{m} \beta_{11}^i \Delta X_{t-i} + \sum_{i=1}^{m} \beta_{12}^i \Delta Y_{t-i} + \gamma_1 Z_{t-1} + \varepsilon_{1t},$$

$$\Delta Y_t = \alpha_2 + \sum_{i=1}^{m} \beta_{21}^i \Delta X_{t-i} + \sum_{i=1}^{m} \beta_{22}^i \Delta Y_{t-i} + \gamma_2 Z_{t-1} + \varepsilon_{2t},$$

$$(\text{II.5.56})$$

---

[49] But the converse is not true, i.e. Granger causality does not imply cointegration. It may be that causal flows exist between time series because they have some other common feature such as a common GARCH volatility process. See Engle and Kozicki (1993) for further information on common volatility.

[50] And if several long term equilibriums exist each has its own disequilibrium term, and lagged values of all of these are used as explanatory variables in the ECM.

where Z is the disequilibrium term given by (II.5.45) and the lag lengths and coefficients are determined by OLS regression. Note that more lags of the disequilibrium term may be added if significant, as in the general ECM (II.5.58) defined below.

In what sense does (II.5.56) define an error correction mechanism? Recall from (II.5.45) that $Z = X - \alpha Y$. Suppose $\alpha > 0$. Then the model (II.5.56) only has an error correction mechanism if $\gamma_1 < 0$ and $\gamma_2 > 0$, because only in that case will the last term in each equation *constrain* deviations from the long term equilibrium in such a way that errors will be corrected. To see this, suppose Z is large and positive: then X will decrease because $\gamma_1 < 0$ and Y will increase because $\gamma_2 > 0$; both have the effect of reducing Z, and in this way errors are corrected. Now suppose that Z is large and negative: then X will increase because $\gamma_1 < 0$ and Y will decrease because $\gamma_2 > 0$; both have the effect of increasing Z, and in this way errors are corrected. Similarly, if $\alpha < 0$ we must have $\gamma_1 < 0$ and $\gamma_2 < 0$ for (II.5.56) to capture an error correction mechanism.

Hence, the reason why (II.5.56) defines an error correction mechanism is that, when we estimate the model we will find that our estimates of γ_1 and γ_2 have the appropriate signs, i.e.

$$\hat{\gamma}_1 < 0 \text{ and } \hat{\alpha}\hat{\gamma}_2 > 0.$$

The magnitudes of the coefficient estimates $\hat{\gamma}_1$ and $\hat{\gamma}_2$ determine the speed of adjustment back to the long term equilibrium following an exogenous shock. When these coefficients are large, adjustment is quick so Z will be highly stationary and reversion to the long term equilibrium determined by $E(Z)$ will be rapid. In fact, a test for cointegration proposed by Engle and Yoo (1987) is based on the significance of the coefficients γ_1 and γ_2.

We illustrate the construction of an ECM in Example II.5.11 below by applying the simplest possible such model, i.e.

$$\Delta X_t = \alpha_1 + \beta_{11}\Delta X_{t-1} + \beta_{12}\Delta Y_{t-1} + \gamma_1 Z_{t-1} + \varepsilon_{1t},$$
$$\Delta Y_t = \alpha_2 + \beta_{21}\Delta X_{t-1} + \beta_{22}\Delta Y_{t-1} + \gamma_2 Z_{t-1} + \varepsilon_{2t}, \tag{II.5.57}$$

where X is the log of a spot index price and Y is the log of the index futures price. Hence, the variables ΔX and ΔY are the log returns on the spot and the futures, respectively. We therefore write $\Delta X = R^S$ and $\Delta Y = R^F$. And in this case

$$Z = X - \alpha Y = \ln(S) - \alpha \ln(F).$$

For simplicity we skip the first stage of the cointegration analysis and simply *assume* that the cointegrating vector is $(1, -1)$, i.e. that $\alpha = 1$ and Z is just the difference between the two log prices. Spot index and index futures prices are very highly cointegrated, since the basis on liquid market indices exhibits very rapid mean reversion. Hence, this choice of Z is sure to be stationary, even if it is not the most stationary linear combination of spot and futures prices.

EXAMPLE II.5.11: AN ECM OF SPOT AND FUTURES ON THE HANG SENG INDEX

Build a simple ECM of the form (II.5.57) for the log returns on the spot and futures on the Hang Seng index based on daily data over the period from April 1991 to April 2006.

SOLUTION   A continuous futures price series is obtained by concatenating the near term futures contract prices and then adjusting the futures for the deterministic component of the basis.[51] Figure II.5.24 depicts Z, i.e. the difference between the log spot price and the log futures price. Clearly it is very highly stationary.

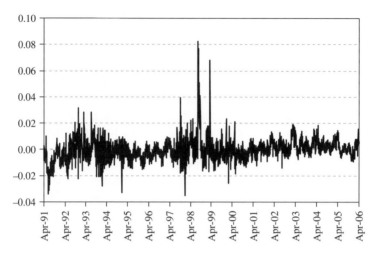

Figure II.5.24   Difference between log spot price and log futures price

Each equation in the model (II.5.57) is estimated separately by OLS and the results are, with t statistics in parentheses:

$$R_t^S = \underset{(1.555)}{0.0004} - \underset{(-7.069)}{0.3389} R_{t-1}^S + \underset{(7.810)}{0.3385} R_{t-1}^F - \underset{(-0.566)}{0.0193} Z_{t-1},$$

$$R_t^F = \underset{(1.628)}{0.0005} - \underset{(-1.752)}{0.0964} R_{t-1}^S + \underset{(1.003)}{0.0499} R_{t-1}^F + \underset{(4.615)}{0.181} Z_{t-1}.$$

Notice that the estimated values of the coefficients γ_1 and γ_2 have the correct sign for an error correction mechanism. Since $\alpha = 1$ we must have $\gamma_1 < 0$ and $\gamma_2 > 0$ in order that deviations from the long run equilibrium are corrected. Also note that the disequilibrium term in the second equation is highly significant, so the Engle and Yoo (1987) procedure indicates that two variables are cointegrated, as already assumed.

The generalization of an error correction model to more than two variables is straightforward. There is one equation in the model for each integrated variable $X_1, \ldots, X_n$ in the cointegrated system, and each cointegrating vector gives a disequilibrium term to be added to the vector autoregression on first difference. If there are r cointegrating vectors we can write the general ECM in matrix form as

$$\Delta \mathbf{X}_t = \boldsymbol{\alpha} + \sum_{i=1}^{p} \mathbf{B}_i \Delta \mathbf{X}_{t-i} + \sum_{j=1}^{q} \boldsymbol{\Gamma}_j \mathbf{Z}_{t-j} + \boldsymbol{\varepsilon}_t, \tag{II.5.58}$$

where

$$\mathbf{Z}_t = \begin{pmatrix} Z_{1t} \\ \vdots \\ Z_{rt} \end{pmatrix} \tag{II.5.59}$$

---

[51] See Alexander and Barbosa (2007) for further details.

is a vector of disequilibrium terms, one for each cointegrating vector, and

$$
\mathbf{X}_t = \begin{pmatrix} X_{1t} \\ \vdots \\ X_{nt} \end{pmatrix}, \quad
\boldsymbol{\alpha} = \begin{pmatrix} \alpha_1 \\ \vdots \\ \alpha_n \end{pmatrix}, \quad
\mathbf{B}_i = \begin{pmatrix} \beta_{11}^i & \cdots & \beta_{1n}^i \\ \vdots & \ddots & \vdots \\ \beta_{n1}^i & \cdots & \beta_{nn}^i \end{pmatrix}, \quad
\boldsymbol{\Gamma}_j = \begin{pmatrix} \gamma_{11}^j & \cdots & \gamma_{1r}^j \\ \vdots & \ddots & \vdots \\ \gamma_{n1}^j & \cdots & \gamma_{nr}^j \end{pmatrix}, \quad
\boldsymbol{\varepsilon}_t = \begin{pmatrix} \varepsilon_{1t} \\ \vdots \\ \varepsilon_{nt} \end{pmatrix}.
$$

To estimate the ECM we can apply OLS to each equation separately. Note that in large systems (II.5.58) has a huge number of potential regressors and it is unlikely that they would all be significant in every equation. More details on estimating short term dynamics in cointegrated systems may be found in Proietti (1997) and in many of the texts already cited in this chapter.

II.5.5.2 Granger Causality

We say that X *Granger causes* Y if lagged values of X help to predict current and future values of Y better than just lagged values of Y alone. Hence Granger causality merely refers to a *lead–lag relationship* between the variables, and it may be that both variables are actually 'caused' by a third variable that is not in the model.

Once an ECM has been specified it may be used to model the lead–lag behaviour between returns in a system of cointegrated log prices or rates, and hence to test the Granger causal flows in the system. Consider the two-dimensional ECM (II.5.56). The test for Granger causality from Y to X is a test for the joint significance of all the variables containing lagged Y in the first equation, and a test for Granger causality from X to Y is a test for the joint significance of all the variables containing lagged X in the second equation. That is:

$$
\begin{aligned}
& Y \text{ Granger causes } X \Leftrightarrow H_0 : \beta_{12}^1 = \beta_{12}^2 = \ldots = \beta_{12}^m = \gamma_1 = 0 \text{ is rejected,} \\
& X \text{ Granger causes } Y \Leftrightarrow H_0 : \beta_{21}^1 = \beta_{21}^2 = \ldots = \beta_{21}^m = \gamma_2 = 0 \text{ is rejected.}
\end{aligned}
\tag{II.5.60}
$$

Note that at least one of the coefficients γ_1 or γ_2 must be significant, otherwise the variables would not be cointegrated. That is why there must be at least one Granger causal flow in a cointegrated system.

EXAMPLE II.5.12: PRICE DISCOVERY IN THE HANG SENG INDEX[52]

Use the ECM of the previous example, i.e.

$$
R_t^S = \underset{(1.555)}{0.0004} - \underset{(-7.069)}{0.3389}\, R_{t-1}^S + \underset{(7.810)}{0.3385}\, R_{t-1}^F - \underset{(-0.566)}{0.0193}\, Z_{t-1},
$$

$$
R_t^F = \underset{(1.628)}{0.0005} - \underset{(-1.752)}{0.0964}\, R_{t-1}^S + \underset{(1.003)}{0.0499}\, R_{t-1}^F + \underset{(4.615)}{0.181}\, Z_{t-1},
$$

to investigate whether Hang Seng futures prices lead spot prices, or conversely or indeed both, because there may be bivariate causality.

SOLUTION   Examine the t ratios in the estimated model. The t ratio on the lagged futures return in the spot return equation is 7.810, which is very highly significant. Hence, futures prices lead spot prices. However, the only t ratio that is significant in the futures return

---

[52] We remark that this example uses daily closing prices and we have only estimated the model (II.5.57). However, the price discovery relationship, which is well documented in the academic literature (see Section II.5.4.4), is best investigated using high frequency data (e.g. hourly). Also we should start with many lags in the ECM, testing the model down until we obtain the best formulation.

equation is that on the lagged disequilibrium term. This indicates that the error correction mechanism is operating primarily through the adjustment of the futures price F_t rather than the spot price S_t.[53] To see why, note that the coefficient on Z_{t-1} is positive and highly significant in the future returns regression. So when Z is above its equilibrium value the futures return increases, thus raising the futures price. Since $Z_t = \ln(S_t) - \ln(F_t)$, when F_t increases Z_t decreases and Z moves closer to its equilibrium value. Similarly, when Z is below its equilibrium value the futures price adjusts downward and Z increases. We conclude that futures prices tend to move before index prices. Of course, this result is entirely expected since there is a much higher volume of trading on the futures than on the stocks in the index.

II.5.5.3   Case Study: Pairs Trading Volatility Index Futures

Another application of cointegration that has recently received considerable attention from hedge funds is pairs trading.[54] When the prices of two assets or two baskets of assets are cointegrated the spread will be stationary and so it can be traded. We illustrate the application of a pairs trading strategy using two cointegrated volatility futures contracts: Vdax and Vstoxx. Time series on the two volatility index futures are shown in Figure II.5.12 and they are highly cointegrated. In fact, we now reveal that it was *their* spread that was shown in Figure II.5.3 and used as an example of a stationary process throughout Section II.5.2.

In this case study we estimate a bivariate ECM on the two volatility futures and use this model to (a) identify the Granger causal flows between the two futures and (b) estimate the impulse response function following an exogenous shock. Using the spread itself as the disequilibrium term, the ECM is estimated in the spreadsheet. Finding that third lags of each dependent variable are significant in neither equation, we begin the analysis with two lags of each dependent variable, and the estimated models are shown in Table II.5.6. Note that the spread is here measured as a percentage rather than in basis points, so that all variables are measured on the same scale.

Table II.5.6   ECMs of volatility index futures

	ΔVdax		ΔVstoxx	
	Coefficients	t stat.	Coefficients	t stat.
Intercept	0.0016	2.1650	−0.0012	−1.6809
Spread (−1)	−0.2352	−2.3963	0.1946	2.0633
ΔVstoxx (−1)	0.0012	0.0117	−0.2241	−2.2799
ΔVstoxx (−2)	−0.0856	−0.9984	−0.1830	−2.2227
ΔVdax (−1)	−0.0559	−0.5465	0.2007	2.0434
ΔVdax (−2)	−0.0002	−0.0024	0.0833	0.9989

We now test down the models by removing variables that are not significant at 10%, and the resulting estimations are shown in Table II.5.7. These indicate that the Vstoxx futures have significant autocorrelation. Notice that the first lag of changes in Vdax futures was significant at 5% in the Vstoxx equation before testing down, but that after testing down this

---

[53] Because the lagged disequilibrium term has an insignificant effect in the spot equation.
[54] See the book by Vidyamurthy (2004).

becomes significant only at 7%.[55] Equilibrium adjustments are made through both indices via the significant lagged spread, but the Granger causal flows run from the Vdax to Vstoxx futures.[56]

Table II.5.7 ECMs of volatility index futures (tested down)

	ΔVdax		ΔVstoxx	
	Coefficients	t stat.	Coefficients	t stat.
Intercept	0.0016	2.7752	−0.0015	−2.1946
Spread (−1)	−0.2513	−3.4767	0.2359	2.7844
ΔVstoxx (−1)			−0.1691	−2.0768
ΔVstoxx (−2)			−0.1171	−2.3788
ΔVdax (-1)			0.1465	1.7893

Now we examine the impulse response functions of the two volatility futures. Starting with the Vdax we rewrite its error correction mechanism in levels form as[57]

$$\text{Vdax}_t = 0.0016 + 0.7487\text{Vdax}_{t-1} + 0.2513\text{Vstoxx}_{t-1} + e_{1t}, \qquad (\text{II.5.61})$$

where e_1 denotes the OLS residual from the ECM. Shocking this residual has an immediate and equivalent effect on the Vdax index, i.e. if the residual is 0 in one period but 10% in the next, the Vdax will increase by 10% in absolute terms. Similarly, the Vstoxx equation in levels form is[58]

$$\text{Vstoxx}_t = -0.0015 + 0.5950\text{Vstoxx}_{t-1} + 0.0520\text{Vstoxx}_{t-2} + 0.1171\text{Vstoxx}_{t-3}$$
$$+ 0.3824\text{Vdax}_{t-1} - 0.1465\text{Vdax}_{t-2} + e_{2t}, \qquad (\text{II.5.62})$$

where e_2 denotes the OLS residual. Shocking this residual has an immediate and equivalent effect on the Vstoxx index.

Let us suppose that both volatility futures are stable at the level of 15% so that the spread begins at zero. First we investigate the response of the futures and the spread to a 2% shock on the Vdax futures at the same time as a 1% shock on the Vstoxx futures. We know from Figure II.5.12 that this magnitude of increase in volatility index futures is not that unusual. For instance, between 10 May 2006 and 8 June 2006 the Vdax futures increased from 15.5% to 24.5%. We assume therefore that $e_{1t} = 0.02$ and $e_{1t} = 0.01$ and the initial shock to the spread is 100 basis points.

Figure II.5.25 uses models (II.5.61) and (II.5.62) to track the effect of these shocks on both futures and on the spread over time. The horizontal axis refers to days, since the data used in this model were daily. We assume there are no further shocks to either index and the figure shows the expected path of the futures contracts (on the left-hand scale) and on the spread (on the right-hand scale) over the next 25 days. By this time, in the absence of any further (upward or downward) shocks to the futures, they reach a new level of almost

---

[55] This is an example of multicollinearity – for further details on this see Section I.4.4.8.

[56] The reason for this is that whilst futures on both volatility indices were launched at the same time (in September 2005) at the time of writing the trading volume is higher on Vdax futures than on Vstoxx futures, probably because the exchange has quoted the Vdax index for many more years than the Vstoxx index.

[57] The models $\Delta X_t = \hat{\alpha} + \hat{\beta}(X - Y)_{t-1} + e_t$ and $X_t = \hat{\alpha} + \left(1 + \hat{\beta}\right)X_{t-1} - \hat{\beta}Y_{t-1} + e_t$ are equivalent.

[58] The model $\Delta Y_t = \hat{\alpha} + \hat{\beta}_1(X - Y)_{t-1} + \hat{\beta}_2 \Delta Y_{t-1} + \hat{\beta}_3 \Delta Y_{t-2} + \hat{\beta}_4 \Delta X_{t-1} + e_t$ is equivalent to the model

$Y_t = \hat{\alpha} + \left(1 - \hat{\beta}_1 + \hat{\beta}_2\right)Y_{t-1} + \left(\hat{\beta}_3 - \hat{\beta}_2\right)Y_{t-2} - \hat{\beta}_3 Y_{t-3} + \left(\hat{\beta}_1 + \hat{\beta}_4\right)X_{t-1} - \hat{\beta}_4 X_{t-2} + e_t.$

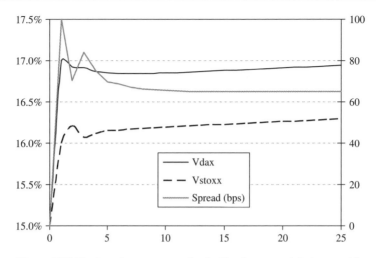

Figure II.5.25 Impulse response of volatility futures and their spread I

16.94% for the Vdax futures and 16.3% for the Vstoxx futures. The spread settles down at almost 65 basis points.

Whilst the long term effects of a shock are interesting, pairs traders will be more interested in the short term adjustment mechanism. On day 1 the spread jumps immediately to 100 basis points, because the two indices have different size shocks, and then oscillates over the next few days, at 70.41, 84.16, 74.85, 69.70 and so on.

In the spreadsheet for this case study the reader can change the assumed size of the initial shocks and the initial values of the volatility futures. For instance, Figure II.5.26 shows the impulse response when both futures are rising from 18% two days before an exceptionally large shock, 19% the day before the shock, 20% on the day of the shock and then both

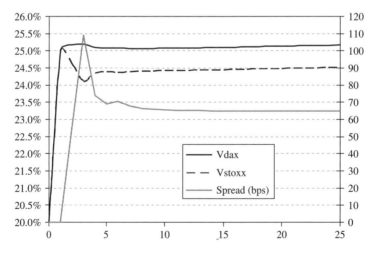

Figure II.5.26 Impulse response of volatility futures and their spread II

futures increase by 5%. Notice that, in the absence of any further shock, the spread always returns to its equilibrium level of 65 basis points.

This case study has explained how to forecast the adjustment paths of two cointegrated assets and their spread over the course of the next few days, following a shock to each asset price. This information can be used to formulate pairs trading strategies that could be profitable, provided trading costs are not excessive and in the absence of any further unexpected large shocks in the market.

II.5.6   SUMMARY AND CONCLUSIONS

This chapter has introduced time series models with a particular emphasis on cointegration. We have covered all the econometric theory necessary for applying cointegration to portfolio management, deliberately using a less formal presentational style than the majority of econometrics texts. For once the constraints of Excel for illustrating every concept have proven too great; we have resorted to EViews for the Johansen tests. However, many other examples and case studies have been used to illustrate each concept and these were implemented in Excel.

Starting with the theory of stationary or *mean-reverting processes*, we have introduced the standard *autoregressive moving average models* of such processes and stated conditions for stationarity of both univariate and vector autoregressive processes. We have explained how to estimate such models, how to trade on a stationary series and how to estimate the *impulse response function* following an exogenous shock.

The next section introduced the *integrated process* of which the random walk process is a special case. We have defined the basic *unit root tests* for integration and have illustrated these concepts with empirical examples using data from various financial markets. Continuous time option pricing models regard interest rates, credit spreads and implied volatility (or implied variance) as *stationary* processes, yet in discrete time series analysis we usually model these variables as *integrated* processes. This apparent contradiction can be reconciled. Traders and investors may believe that these processes are mean reverting, and hence the option prices that are used to calibrate the parameters of continuous time models would reflect this, even though there is no solid statistical evidence in historical data that this is so.

All the above was laying the foundations for the introduction of cointegration. Financial asset prices are integrated, but if the spread between prices is mean-reverting then the prices are *cointegrated*. The same applies to log prices, interest rates, volatilities and credit spreads: these series are integrated, but if the spread between two such series is mean-reverting then the series are *cointegrated*. This is an intuitive definition of cointegration. The precise definition of cointegration in an n-dimensional system of prices (or log prices, or interest rates, etc.) is far more general than this.

We have explained the difference between cointegration and correlation, and simulated examples have shown how cointegration can be present without high correlation, and vice versa. We have also explained why correlation fails as a tool for measuring long term dependency. For this we must use cointegration.

Cointegration analysis is a two-stage process: at the first stage we estimate a long term equilibrium relationship between levels variables (e.g. log prices) and at the second stage we estimate a dynamic model of their differences (e.g. log returns). Testing for cointegration can be done using either *Engle–Granger tests* or *Johansen tests*, the latter being more powerful and less biased in large systems.

- The objective of the Engle–Granger methodology is to find a stationary linear combination of integrated processes that has the minimum possible variance. It employs ordinary least squares regression and is so simple that it can easily be implemented in Excel. In fact the minimum variance criterion also has many advantages for portfolio management, and we have illustrated the procedure by showing that international equity indices are not cointegrated, even when measured in the same currency. We also used the Engle-Granger procedure to find a basket of DJIA stocks that is cointegrated with the index.
- The Johansen procedure aims to find the most stationary linear combination of many integrated processes, and we have illustrated this with an application to a set of UK market interest rates of different maturities. Here we find there are many cointegrating vectors, i.e. there are many linear combinations of interest rates that are stationary. Each distinct cointegrating vector acts like 'glue' in the system, hence UK interest rates move together very closely indeed over time.

In the second stage of cointegration analysis we build an *error correction model*, so called because the model has a self-correcting mechanism whereby deviations from the long term equilibrium will revert back to the equilibrium. The error correction model, which is based on returns rather than prices, may be used to investigate any lead–lag relationships or *Granger causal flows* between returns. When log asset prices are cointegrated their log returns must have such a lead–lag relationship. We have illustrated this using Hang Seng spot and futures prices, revealing the usual *price discovery* relationship where futures prices move before the spot.

The error correction model may also be used to investigate the response of cointegrated variables to an exogenous shock to one or more of the variables. This model may be used to build an impulse response function that shows how each variable adjusts to the shock over a period of time. In particular, we can examine the mean reversion mechanism in a stationary spread. We have illustrated this by estimating the impulse response function for futures on volatility indices. Pairs of related volatility futures, such as the Vdax and Vstoxx in our example, are highly cointegrated, and we have demonstrated how the impulse response function can identify *pairs trading* strategies.

Cointegration is a powerful tool for portfolio management and so, not surprisingly, it has recently come to the attention of many hedge funds and other investors able to take short positions. Cointegration can also be a useful basis for allocations to long-only positions, and for long term allocations. It makes sense to base long term investments on the common long term trends in asset prices as the portfolio will require minimal rebalancing. By contrast, it makes no sense to base long term investments on returns correlations since returns have no 'memory' of the trend, let alone any common trend. Moreover, correlations are very unstable over time, so such portfolios require frequent rebalancing.

By the same token it is difficult to construct tracking portfolios on the basis of returns correlations. The tracking error may not be stationary because there is nothing in the correlation model to guarantee this, and in this case the tracking portfolio could deviate very far from the index unless it is frequently rebalanced. If the allocations in a portfolio are designed so that the portfolio tracks an index then the portfolio should be cointegrated with the index. The portfolio and the index may deviate in the short term, but in the long term they will be tied together through their cointegration.

II.6
Introduction to Copulas

II.6.1 INTRODUCTION

Portfolio risk is a measure of the uncertainty in the portfolio returns distribution. We use some measure of the dispersion about the mean of this distribution as the risk metric. But if we depart from the classical assumption that mean deviations are independent and symmetric with identical elliptical distributions, it is not possible to summarize uncertainty by a simple figure such as portfolio volatility.[1] Similarly, correlation is a measure of dependence that is very commonly applied in financial risk management, but it can only represent a certain type of risk. Each asset return must follow an i.i.d. process and the joint distribution of the variables must be elliptical. In practice very few assets or portfolios satisfy these assumptions, so we can use neither portfolio volatility as a measure of risk, nor the correlation of returns as a measure of association.[2] Instead we must work with the entire joint distribution of returns.

Classical theories of portfolio management and risk management have been built on the assumption of multivariate normal i.i.d. returns distributions. It is important to include classical theories in a text of this type, but financial markets do not behave according to these idealized assumptions. Assuming multivariate normal i.i.d. returns distributions is convenient not only because it allows one to use correlation as a measure of dependence, but also because linear value at risk (VaR) is a coherent risk metric in this framework and because modelling linear VaR is equivalent to modelling volatility. [3] This chapter explains how to base portfolio risk assessment on more realistic assumptions about the behaviour of returns on financial assets.

The joint distribution of two i.i.d. random variables X and Y is the bivariate distribution function that gives the probabilities of both X and Y taking certain values at the same time. In this chapter we build the joint distribution of two or more asset returns by first specifying the *marginals*, i.e. the 'stand-alone' distributions, and then using a *copula* to represent the association between these returns. One of the advantages of using copulas is that they isolate the dependence structure from the structure of the marginal distributions. So copulas can be applied with *any* marginal distributions, and the marginals can be different for each return. For instance, we could assume that the marginal distribution of one variable is a Student t distribution with 10 degrees of freedom, the marginal distribution of another variable is a chi-squared distribution with 15 degrees of freedom, and another variable has a gamma distribution and so on. Since the copula imposes a dependence structure on the marginals that can be quite different from the distribution of the marginals, the marginals may be specified separately from the copula.

---

[1] Elliptical distributions are those that, in their bivariate form, have elliptical contours. These include the normal distribution and the Student t distribution.

[2] For this reason we were careful to point out the pitfalls of using correlation as a measure of association in Section II.3.3.

[3] Also, the linear portfolio that minimizes VaR is the Markowitz minimum variance portfolio. See Embrechts et al. (2002).

To summarize, we use copulas to specify a joint distribution in a two-stage process: first we specify the type of the marginal distributions and then we specify the copula distribution. The construction of a joint distribution entails estimating the parameters of both the marginal distributions and the copula. Often the estimation of the parameters for the marginal distributions is performed separately from the copula calibration.

Because copulas only specify the dependence structure, different copulas produce different joint distributions when applied to the same marginals. Consider two random variables and assume that we have calibrated their marginal distributions. Now suppose we apply two different copulas and so we obtain two different joint distributions. So if only one joint distribution exhibits strong lower tail dependence then this distribution should be regarded as more risky than one with a weaker, symmetric dependence, at least according to a downside risk metric. Now suppose that we 'back out' the Pearson correlation from each joint distribution.[4] It is possible to choose the parameters of each copula so that the Pearson correlation estimate is the *same* for both joint distributions, even though they have different dependency structures. Hence, the standard Pearson correlation cannot capture the different risk characteristics of the two distributions, and this is because it is only a symmetric, linear dependence metric. One of the main aims of this chapter is to introduce some copulas designed specifically to capture asymmetric tail dependence.

The outline of this chapter is as follows. Section II.6.2 introduces different measures of association between two random variables. We define *concordance* as the most basic criterion for association and introduce Spearman's and Kendall's *rank correlations* as concordance metrics that are closely related to copulas. In Sections II.6.3 and II.6.4 we define the concept of a copula, introduce some standard copula functions that have recently become very popular in all branches of empirical finance and then implement these in Excel spreadsheets. The reader may change the parameters in these spreadsheets, and watch how the copula changes.

The *copula quantile curves* depict the conditional copula distribution. In Section II.6.5 we derive and interpret quantile curves of the bivariate copulas that were described in Section II.6.4. These will be used in Section II.6.7 for simulations from copulas and in Sections II.7.2 and II.7.3 for copula quantile regressions.

Section II.6.6 explains how to estimate copula parameters. For certain one-parameter copulas there is an analytic expression for the copula parameter in terms of the rank correlation. Such copulas are thus very easy to calibrate to a sample. However, it is often necessary and usually desirable to apply some form of maximum likelihood method to estimate the copula parameters. We explain how to construct an *empirical copula*, and how the empirical copula can be used to help choose the 'best' copula, given a sample.

Section II.6.7 explains how to simulate returns when the joint distribution is specified by marginals and a copula, and we use some standard copulas for the empirical examples. Section II.6.8 explains how copulas are applied to compute the Monte Carlo VaR of a portfolio. Many other applications of copulas to market risk analysis are based on simulations under a copula. Two other market risk applications are described in this section: how to use *convolution* over the copula to aggregate returns; and how copulas can play an important role in portfolio optimization. Section II.6.9 summarizes and concludes.

The empirical examples for this chapter are based on several Excel spreadsheets in which common types of bivariate copulas are illustrated, calibrated and then applied to

---

[4] For instance, simulate a sample scatter plot from each joint distribution and then estimate Pearson's correlation on each simulated sample.

risk management problems. As usual, the spreadsheets involving simulation have to be in a different workbook from those requiring the use of Solver.

Our presentation is selective and focuses on the main definitions and properties of copulas that are important for market risk management. I have learned from many research papers in this field, frequently referring to results in Embrechts et al. (2002, 2003), Demarta and McNeil (2005) and many others. Readers seeking a more detailed and advanced treatment of copulas are referred to two specialist texts on copulas, by Nelsen (2006) and by Cherubini et al. (2004) and to Chapter 5 of the excellent text on risk management by McNeil et al. (2005). I would like to express my thanks to Alexander McNeil for extremely useful comments on the first draft of this chapter. Many thanks also to my PhD student Joydeep Lahiri for turning my Excel charts of copula densities into attractive colour MatLab^{TM} graphs.

II.6.2   CONCORDANCE METRICS

This section begins by specifying the basic properties that should be exhibited by any good measure of association between two random variables. We introduce the concept of concordance and two fundamental concordance metrics that have an important link with copulas.

II.6.2.1   Concordance

When returns are not assumed to have elliptical distributions Pearson's linear correlation is an inaccurate and misleading measure of association between two returns series, as we have explained in Section III.3.3. So what metric should we use instead? To answer this question requires a tighter definition of *association* between two random variables. That 'one tends to increase when the other increases' is too loose.

Consider two pairs of observations on continuous random variables X and Y, denoted (x_1, y_1) and (x_2, y_2). We say that the pairs are *concordant* if $x_1 - x_2$ has the same sign as $y_1 - y_2$ and *discordant* if $x_1 - x_2$ has the opposite sign to $y_1 - y_2$. That is, the pairs are concordant if $(x_1 - x_2)(y_1 - y_2) > 0$ and discordant if $(x_1 - x_2)(y_1 - y_2) < 0$. For instance:

- (2, 5) is concordant with any pair (x, y) with $5x + 2y - xy < 10$
- (2, 2) is neither concordant nor discordant with any pair where $x \neq y$.

A basic measure of association between X and Y is the *proportion of concordant pairs* in the sample. As the proportion of concordant pairs in a sample increases, so does the probability that large values of X are paired with large values of Y, and small values of X are paired with small values of Y. Similarly, as the proportion of concordant pairs in a sample decreases, the probability that large values of X are paired with small values of Y, and small values of X are paired with large values of Y increases.

Formally, a *concordance metric* $m(X, Y)$ is a numerical measure of association between two continuous random variables X and Y such that:

1. $m(X, Y) \in [-1, 1]$ and its value within this range depends on $F(X, Y)$, the joint distribution of X and Y.
2. $m(X, X) = 1$ and $m(X, -X) = -1$.
3. $m(X, Y) = m(Y, X)$ and $m(X, -Y) = -m(X, Y)$.
4. If X and Y are independent then $m(X, Y) = 0$.

5. Given two possible joint distributions $F(X, Y)$ and $G(X, Y)$, let $m_F(X, Y)$ and $m_G(X, Y)$ denote the concordance measures under the two distributions. Then if $F(X, Y) \geq G(X, Y)$ we must have $m_F(X, Y) \geq m_G(X, Y)$.

It follows that $m(X, Y) = m(h(X), h(Y))$ for any continuous monotonic increasing function h.

The problem with the ordinary Pearson 'linear' correlation is that it is *not* a concordance metric, except when the returns have an elliptical distribution.[5] We now provide examples of two concordance metrics that play a fundamental role in copulas.

II.6.2.2   Rank Correlations

Rank correlations are non-parametric measures of dependence based on *ranked data.* If the data are on continuous variables such as asset returns we convert the data to ranked form by marking the *smallest* return with the rank 1, the second smallest return with the rank 2, and so forth.[6] Thereafter we retain only the ranks of the observations.

To estimate *Spearman's rank correlation*, we rank the data for each of the two returns series individually and then sum the squared differences between the ranks. Suppose a sample contains n paired observations (x_i, y_i) and denote the difference between the rank of x_i and the rank of y_i by d_i. Let

$$D = \sum_{i=1}^{n} d_i^2$$

be the sum of the squared differences between the ranks. Then the sample estimate of *Spearman's rank correlation* is given by[7]

$$\rho = 1 - \frac{6D}{n(n^2 - 1)}. \tag{II.6.1}$$

EXAMPLE II.6.1: SPEARMAN'S RHO

Calculate Spearman's rank correlation for the sample on X and Y shown in the first two columns of Table II.6.1. How does the result compare with Pearson's correlation estimate?

SOLUTION   Table II.6.1 shows the rank of each observation, adjusting for ties.[8] The sum of the squared differences between the ranks, adjusted for ties, is 69, as shown in the table. The result of applying formula (II.6.1) with $n = 10$ is a Spearman's rho estimate of 0.5818, which is less than the Pearson correlation estimate. This is computed in the spreadsheet as 0.6811.

Another rank correlation is *Kendall's tau.* Given a sample with n observations (x_i, y_i) for $i = 1, \ldots, n$, Kendall's tau is calculated by comparing all possible pairs of observations $\{(x_i, y_i), (x_j, y_j)\}$ for $i \neq j$. Ordering does not matter, so the total number of pairs is

$$\binom{n}{2} = \frac{1}{2}n(n - 1).$$

---

[5] And even then, a linear correlation of zero does not imply that the returns are independent when they have a bivariate Student t distribution. See Section II.6.5.
[6] If two or more returns are equal then each gets the average rank – see Example II.6.1 for illustration.
[7] Another way is to apply Pearson's correlation on the ranked paired data.
[8] This means that tied places are ranked equally but at the average rank, not at the highest possible ranking: i.e. the adjusted ranking of 1, 2, 2, 2, 5, ... would be 1, 3, 3, 3, 5. Note that the Excel RANK function gives unadjusted rankings for ties. As a check you always want your ranks to sum, for n observations, to $n(n + 1)/2$.

Table II.6.1   Calculation of Spearman's rho

X	Y	X rank	Y rank	X rank with ties	Y rank with ties	Squared difference
50	40	6	7	7	7.5	0.25
10	−10	3	2	3.5	2	2.25
50	20	6	5	7	5	4
−20	−80	1	1	1	1	0
20	50	5	9	5	9	16
60	10	9	3	9	3.5	30.25
10	10	3	3	3.5	3.5	0
0	30	2	6	2	6	16
90	60	10	10	10	10	0
50	40	6	7	7	7.5	0.25
Sum		51	53	55	55	69

Count the number N_C of concordant pairs and the number N_D of discordant pairs. Then the sample estimate of Kendall's tau is given by

$$\tau = \frac{N_C - N_D}{\frac{1}{2}n(n-1)}. \tag{II.6.2}$$

EXAMPLE II.6.2: KENDALL'S TAU

Calculate Kendall's rank correlation for the same sample as in the previous example.

SOLUTION   Table II.6.2 sets out the calculation. There are 22 concordant pairs and 14 discordant pairs. So the estimate of Kendall's tau is

$$\tau = \frac{29 - 11}{\frac{1}{2} \times 10 \times 9} = 0.4 \tag{II.6.3}$$

Table II.6.2   Calculation of Kendall's tau[a]

X	Y	N_C	N_D
50	40	5	2
10	−10	7	1
50	20	4	3
−20	−80	9	0
20	50	5	4
60	10	3	5
10	10	6	1
0	30	5	4
90	60	9	0
50	40	5	2
Total Pairs		29	11

[a] The totals in the last two columns are divided by 2 to avoid double counting.

This is much less than the other two measures of dependence. Indeed, Kendall's tau and Spearman's rho will only agree for very special joint distributions – see Nelsen (2006: Section 5.1.3) for further details.

So far we have only considered *sample estimates* of Spearman's rho and Kendall's tau. To define the corresponding population parameters requires a specification of the joint distribution, and for this we need to define the copula. In Section II.6.6.1 we shall return to our discussion of rank correlations and explain the correspondence between population rank correlations and copula functions.

II.6.3 COPULAS AND ASSOCIATED THEORETICAL CONCEPTS

It is very often the case in practice that either marginal returns distributions are asymmetric, or the dependence is non-linear, or both. This means that correlation makes no sense as a dependence metric, because it only applies when the random variables have an elliptical multivariate distribution. The alternative is to use a copula, which is a very flexible tool for constructing joint distributions. Typically, using a copula to construct a joint distribution gives a functional form that captures the observed behaviour of financial asset returns far better than an elliptical distribution.

II.6.3.1 Simulation of a Single Random Variable

To understand the concept of a copula it will help us to fix ideas and notation by reconsidering the method we used to simulate values from a given distribution function. But first, let us refresh our memory of some of the basic definitions and properties of univariate continuous distribution functions that were introduced in Chapter I.3.

Let X be a continuous random variable with domain D.[9]

- A *distribution function* F for X is a continuous, monotonic increasing function from D to $[0, 1]$ such that[10]

$$F(x) = P(X < x).\tag{II.6.4}$$

  Thus, for any $x \in D$, the probability that X is less than x is given by the value of its distribution function at x.[11]

- Assuming it exists, the *inverse distribution function* $F^{-1} : [0, 1] \to D$ is defined just like any other inverse function, i.e.

$$F^{-1}(F(x)) = x \quad \text{for all } x \in D.\tag{II.6.5}$$

- Assuming F is differentiable on the whole of D, its *density* function is defined as the derivative of the distribution function, i.e. $f(x) = F'(x)$. Since F is monotonic increasing, $f(x) \geq 0$.

Another important concept is that of a *quantile*. In Sections I.3.2.8 and I.3.5.1 we defined a quantile of a continuous random variable X associated with some probability $\alpha \in [0, 1]$. The α quantile of X is the value x_α of X such that $P(X < x_\alpha) = \alpha$.

---

[9] Typically D will be $(-\infty, \infty)$, $[0, \infty)$ or $[0, 1]$.
[10] A strictly *monotonic increasing* function is one whose first derivative is always positive. An ordinary monotonic increasing function may have a zero derivative, but it is never negative, i.e. the function never decreases.
[11] Recall that when X is continuous, $F(x) = P(X < x) = P(X \leq x)$.

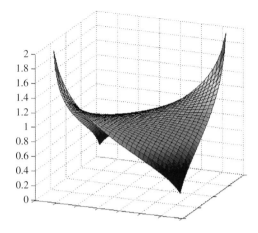

Plate 1 Bivariate normal copula density with $\varrho = -0.25$. (See Figure II.6.6)

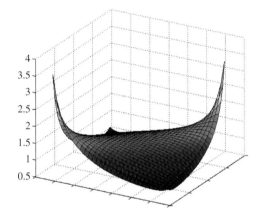

Plate 2 Bivariate Student t copula density with $\varrho = -0.25$ and seven degrees of fredom.
(See Figure II.6.7)

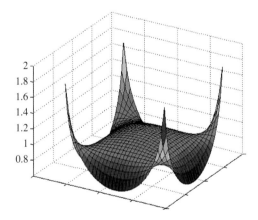

Plate 3 Bivariate normal mixture copula density with $\pi = 0.25$, $\varrho_1 = 0.5$ and $\varrho_2 = -0.5$.
(See Figure II.6.8)

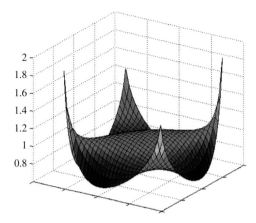

Plate 4   Bivariate normal mixture copula density with $\pi = 0.75$, $\varrho_1 = 0.25$ and $\varrho_2 = -0.75$.
(See   Figure II.6.9)

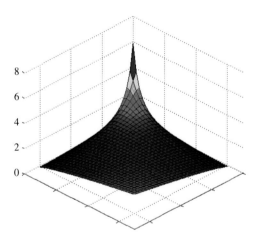

Plate 5   Bivariate Clayton copula density with $\alpha = 0.75$. (See Figure II.6.10)

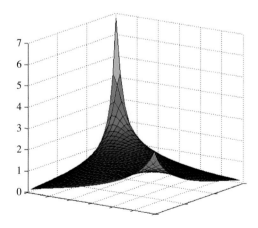

Plate 6   Bivariate Gumbel copula density with $\delta = 1.5$. (See Figure II.6.11)

Quantiles are used in simulation as follows. First simulate a random number u to represent a probability. We denote this by u because it is a random draw from a standard uniform distribution. Now use the inverse distribution function to find the corresponding quantile. That is, set

$$x = F^{-1}(u),\tag{II.6.6}$$

and then x is the u quantile of X.

Recall from Section I.3.3.2 that uniform variables have linear distribution functions. In particular, the standard uniform variable $U \sim U[0, 1]$ has the property that

$$P(U < u) = u.\tag{II.6.7}$$

Now for all $u \in [0, 1]$,

$$P(F(X) < u) = P\big(X < F^{-1}(u)\big) = F\big(F^{-1}(u)\big) = u.$$

Hence,

$$F(X) \sim U(0, 1).\tag{II.6.8}$$

This shows that when we apply the distribution function to X we obtain a new random variable $F(X)$, one that has a standard uniform distribution. The technical term given to this is the *probability integral transform*. It is the transform of a continuously distributed random variable to a uniform variable.

Now, putting $u = F(x)$ in (II.6.7), we have

$$P(U < F(x)) = F(x).$$

In other words,

$$F(x) = P\big(F^{-1}(U) < x\big).\tag{II.6.9}$$

This shows that we can simulate from the distribution of X by *applying the inverse distribution to a standard uniform variable*. Each time we take a random number u we apply the inverse distribution function to obtain the corresponding quantile for X and in this way a set of independent random numbers is transformed into a set of independent simulations from the distribution of X.

In other words, to simulate values of a *single* random variable we take some random numbers (i.e. independent observations from a $U(0, 1)$ variable) and apply the inverse distribution function to them. In fact, this is exactly how we introduced simulation, in Section I.5.7, without going through the formal definitions above. Since many Excel spreadsheets with empirical examples of univariate simulations were given in Chapter I.5, we do not repeat these here. Instead, Section II.6.7 below will focus on multivariate simulations, using copulas. When we simulate values of *several* random variables we have to take into account their co-dependence. As soon as we depart from the assumption that random variables have a multivariate elliptical distribution, correlation becomes an inadequate measure of dependence and we must use a more general dependence measure (of which correlation is a special case) called a *copula*.

II.6.3.2   Definition of a Copula

Consider two random variables X_1 and X_2 with continuous marginal distribution functions $F_1(x_1)$ and $F_2(x_2)$ and set $u_i = F_i(x_i)$, $i = 1, 2$. The following class of functions are eligible to be two-dimensional copulas:

(i) $C:[0, 1] \times [0, 1] \rightarrow [0, 1]$;
(ii) $C(u_1, 0) = C(0, u_2) = 0$;
(iii) $C(u_1, 1) = u_1$ and $C(1, u_2) = u_2$;
(iv) $C(v_1, v_2) - C(u_1, v_2) \geq C(v_1, u_2) - C(u_1, u_2)$ for every $u_1, u_2, v_1, v_2 \in [0, 1]$ with $u_1 \leq v_1$ and $u_2 \leq v_2$.

Condition (i) implies that the copula acts on the values of the two distribution functions. We know from the previous subsection that the value of any distribution function is a standard uniform variable, so we can set $U_i = F_i(X_i)$, $i = 1, 2$. The other three conditions specify a copula as a joint distribution function for U_1 and U_2. But there are very many possible joint distribution functions on standard uniform variables. Hence many functions fulfil conditions (i)–(iv) above. In other words, there are a very large number of copulas.

However, a famous result due to Sklar (1959) shows that copulas are unique in a very precise sense. The bivariate form of *Sklar's theorem* is as follows: given *any* joint distribution function $F(x_1, x_2)$ there is a *unique* copula function $C:[0, 1] \times [0, 1] \rightarrow [0, 1]$ such that:

$$F(x_1, x_2) = C(F_1(x_1), F_2(x_2)). \tag{II.6.10}$$

Conversely, if C is a copula and $F_1(x_1)$ and $F_2(x_2)$ are distribution functions then (II.6.10) defines a bivariate distribution function with marginal distributions $F_1(x_1)$ and $F_2(x_2)$.

For instance, suppose X_1 and X_2 are independent. Then their joint distribution is just the product of the marginals, so the unique copula is

$$C(F_1(x_1), F_2(x_2)) = F_1(x_1) F_2(x_2). \tag{II.6.11}$$

Differentiating (II.6.10) with respect to x_1 and x_2 yields a simple expression for the joint density function, $f(x_1, x_2)$ in terms of the marginal density functions $f_1(x_1)$ and $f_2(x_2)$. We have

$$f(x_1, x_2) = f_1(x_1) f_2(x_2) c(F_1(x_1), F_2(x_2)), \tag{II.6.12}$$

where

$$c(F_1(x_1), F_2(x_2)) = \frac{\partial^2 C(F_1(x_1), F_2(x_2))}{\partial F_1(x_1) \partial F_2(x_2)}. \tag{II.6.13}$$

Now, by (II.6.8) the marginals $F_i(x_i)$ are uniformly distributed. Substituting in the above $F_i(x_i) = u_i$, for $i = 1, 2$, with each u_i being an observation on a standard uniform variable, the function defined by (II.6.13) may be written $c(u_1, u_2)$. When regarded as a function of (u_1, u_2) rather than a function of (x_1, x_2), (II.6.13) is called the *copula density* of (II.6.10).

Figures II.6.1–II.6.5 below illustrate the densities for some common types of copula. Readers may generate similar graphs for many other values of the copula parameters, using the spreadsheet labelled 'copula densities'.

We can generalize these concepts to the multivariate case. Consider n random variables $X_1, X_2, \ldots, X_n$ with known (and continuous) marginal distributions $F_1(x_1), \ldots, F_n(x_n)$. A *copula* is a monotonic increasing function from $[0, 1] \times [0, 1] \times \ldots \times [0, 1] \rightarrow [0, 1]$ that satisfies conditions that are generalizations of (i)–(iii) above. There are, therefore, very many different types of copulas.[12]

---

[12] In fact, in Section II.6.4.4 we shall see that any convex, monotonic decreasing function can be used to generate an Archimedean copula.

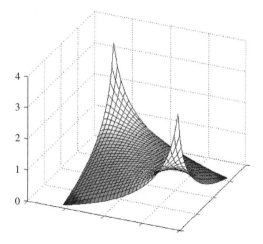

Figure II.6.1   Bivariate normal copula density with correlation 0.5

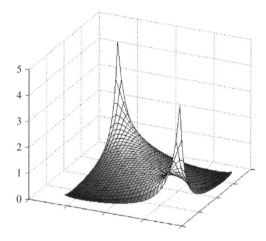

Figure II.6.2   Bivariate Student t copula density with correlation 0.5 and 5 degrees of freedom

Sklar's (1959) theorem tells us that, given a fixed set of continuous marginal distributions, distinct copulas define distinct joint densities. Thus given any joint density $F(x_1, x_2, \ldots, x_n)$ with continuous marginals, we can back out a *unique* copula function C such that[13]

$$F(x_1, \ldots, x_n) = C(F_1(x_1), \ldots, F_n(x_n)).$$ (II.6.14)

If it exists, the associated *copula density* is the function

$$c(F_1(x_1), \ldots, F_n(x_n)) = \frac{\partial^n C(F_1(x_1), \ldots, F_n(x_n))}{\partial F_1(x_1) \ldots \ldots \partial F_n(x_n)}$$ (II.6.15)

regarded as a function of $u_i = F_i(x_i)$.

---

[13] This result is part of *Sklar's theorem*. It is formalized for a bivariate copula in (II.6.10) and for a general copula in (II.6.17).

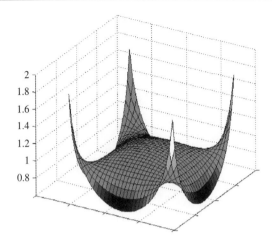

Figure II.6.3   A bivariate normal mixture copula density

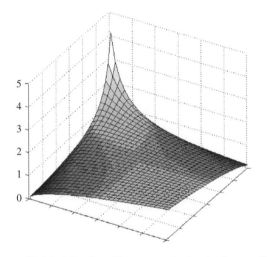

Figure II.6.4   Bivariate Clayton copula density for $\alpha = 0.5$

Given the copula density and, if they exist, the marginal densities $f_i(x) = F_i'(x)$, we can obtain the joint density of the original variables using

$$f(x_1, \ldots, x_n) = f_1(x_1) \ldots f_n(x_n) c(F_1(x_1), \ldots, F_n(x_n)). \qquad (\text{II.6.16})$$

The values $F_i(x_i)$ of the distribution functions of the marginals are uniformly distributed. Hence, an alternative notation is possible for the copula distribution, using uniformly distributed variables $u_i \in [0, 1]$ in place of $F_i(x_i)$ to represent the values of the marginal distributions at the realizations x_i.

Setting $F_i(x_i) = u_i$, each joint distribution function F defines an *implicit copula* of the form

$$C(u_1, \ldots, u_n) = F\big(F_1^{-1}(u_1), \ldots, F_n^{-1}(u_n)\big), \qquad (\text{II.6.17})$$

where the u_i are the quantiles of the marginals, i.e. realizations of variables on $[0, 1]$ representing the values of the marginal distributions at the realizations x_i. Thus there is an implicit copula corresponding to every multivariate distribution, the most important of which

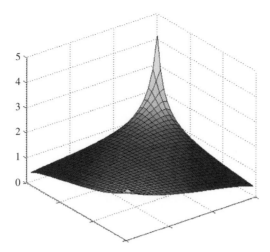

Figure II.6.5 Bivariate Gumbel copula density for $\delta = 1.25$

are the *normal or Gaussian copulas* and the *Student t copulas*. Standard versions of both of these copulas are examined in detail in the following sections.

With the notation $u_i = F_i(x_i)$, the copula density may be written

$$c(u_1, \ldots, u_n) = \frac{\partial^n C(u_1, \ldots, u_n)}{\partial u_1 \ldots \partial u_n}. \tag{II.6.18}$$

Sometimes (e.g. for the normal and Student t copulas) only the copula density has closed form, not the copula distribution, and we express the distribution as an integral. There are no problems with this, because most calculations are actually based on the copula density rather than the copula distribution.

II.6.3.3   Conditional Copula Distributions and their Quantile Curves

Like any joint distribution function, copulas have conditional distributions. A conditional distribution is the distribution of one variable given that the others take some specified fixed values. The only difference between a conditional copula distribution and an ordinary distribution is that the marginals of *every* copula are uniformly distributed by definition. However, the conditional copula distributions can be quite different for different copulas, and we will demonstrate this, using empirical examples, in Section II.6.5. The conditional copula distributions, usually expressed in terms of their density functions, are one of the most useful parts of the copula for many financial applications. For instance, in Section II.6.6 we apply them to simulations, and in Sections II.7.2 and II.7.3 we use them for quantile regression.

To define the conditional copula distribution we shall again consider, for simplicity, a bivariate $C(u_1, u_2)$. Then there are two conditional distributions of the copula and these are defined by functions

$$C_{1|2}(u_1 \,|\, u_2) = P(U_1 < u_1 \,|\, U_2 = u_2) \tag{II.6.19}$$

and

$$C_{2|1}(u_2 \,|\, u_1) = P(U_2 < u_2 \,|\, U_1 = u_1). \tag{II.6.20}$$

The conditional distributions are obtained by taking first derivatives of the copula with respect to each variable, i.e.

$$C_{1|2}(u_1 \,|u_2) = \frac{\partial C(u_1, u_2)}{\partial u_2} \quad \text{and} \quad C_{2|1}(u_2 \,|u_1) = \frac{\partial C(u_1, u_2)}{\partial u_1}. \tag{II.6.21}$$

We can depict the conditional distributions by their associated quantiles. For some fixed probability q, set

$$C_{2|1}(u_2 \,|u_1) = q. \tag{II.6.22}$$

This defines u_2 as a function of q and u_1 (but it need not be an *explicit* function of q and u_1). So we may write

$$u_2 = g_q(u_1), \tag{II.6.23}$$

where g_q is some implicit or explicit function called the q *quantile curve* of the copula. Plotting the q *quantile curve* provides a means of visualizing the conditional distribution of the copula. The quantile curves for some standard copulas are shown in Figures II.6.12 and II.6.13 below (see Section II.6.5.5).

II.6.3.4 Tail Dependence

Tail dependence examines the concordance in the *tails* (i.e. the extreme values) of the joint distribution. For independent variables the copula density is one everywhere. Otherwise, a bivariate copula density will look something like the copula densities shown in Figures II.6.1 to II.6.5 above. Copula densities do not look like an ordinary density function, which is always positive and has greater values in the centre. Indeed, it is quite the reverse: the copula densities that we use in finance often have higher values in the corners, indicating the importance of the dependence in the tails.

Define the i,jth *lower tail dependence coefficient* as

$$\lambda_{ij}^l = \lim_{q \downarrow 0} P\left(X_i < F_i^{-1}(q) \,\middle|\, X_j < F_j^{-1}(q) \right), \tag{II.6.24}$$

provided the limit exists. Loosely speaking, it represents the conditional probability that one variable takes a value in its lower tail, given that the other variable takes a value in its lower tail. Since the coefficient is a conditional probability, $\lambda_{ij}^l \in [0, 1]$. The copula is said to have lower tail dependence for X_i and X_j when $\lambda_{ij}^l > 0$, and the higher the value of the dependence coefficient, the stronger the lower tail dependence.

Similarly the i,jth *upper tail dependence coefficient* is defined by the following limit, if it exists:

$$\lambda_{ij}^u = \lim_{q \uparrow 1} P\left(X_i > F_i^{-1}(q) \,\middle|\, X_j > F_j^{-1}(q) \right). \tag{II.6.25}$$

Loosely speaking, it represents the conditional probability that one variable takes a value in its upper tail, given that the other variable takes a value in its upper tail. Since the coefficient is a conditional probability, $\lambda_{ij}^u \in [0, 1]$. The copula is said to have upper tail dependence for X_i and X_j when $\lambda_{ij}^u > 0$, and the higher the value of the dependence coefficient, the stronger the upper tail dependence.

A copula has *symmetric tail dependence* if $\lambda_{ij}^u = \lambda_{ij}^l$ for all i, j, and *asymmetric tail dependence* if the upper or lower tail dependence coefficients are different. All the copulas we examine below are *exchangeable copulas*. In other words, they are fixed under permutations of the variables because this is a basic and intuitive property for market risk applications. For an exchangeable copula

$$\lambda_{ij}^u = \lambda_{ji}^u \quad \text{and} \quad \lambda_{ij}^l = \lambda_{ji}^l, \quad \text{for all } i, j.$$

In the empirical sections of this chapter we shall examine some copulas with symmetric tail dependence, such as the normal and Student t copulas, and others with asymmetric tail dependence, such as the Clayton and Gumbel copulas. Notice that asymmetric tail dependence is very easy to see from the graph of the copula density. Compare, for instance, the normal and Student t copula densities shown in Figures II.6.1 and II.6.2, which have symmetric tail dependence, with the Clayton and Gumbel copula densities shown in Figures II.6.4 and II.6.5 which have asymmetric tail dependence.

Finally, we derive an alternative expression for the tail dependence coefficients, considering only the bivariate case, for simplicity.[14] Since

$$P\left(X_1 < F_1^{-1}(q) \big| X_2 < F_2^{-1}(q)\right) = \frac{P\left(X_1 < F_1^{-1}(q), X_2 < F_2^{-1}(q)\right)}{P\left(X_2 < F_2^{-1}(q)\right)} = \frac{F\left(F_1^{-1}(q), F_2^{-1}(q)\right)}{q} = \frac{C(q, q)}{q},$$

the lower tail dependence coefficient may be expressed as

$$\lambda^l = \lim_{q \downarrow 0} q^{-1} C(q, q). \tag{II.6.26}$$

We know that this limit must lie in the interval $[0, 1]$, and if (II.6.26) is positive the copula has lower tail dependence. Similarly, it can be shown that[15]

$$\lambda^u = \lim_{q \uparrow 1} \left[(1-q)^{-1} \overline{C}(1-q, 1-q)\right], \tag{II.6.27}$$

where $\overline{C}(u_1, u_2) = u_1 + u_2 - 1 + C(1 - u_1, 1 - u_2)$ is called the *survival copula* associated with $C(u_1, u_2)$.[16] Again (II.6.27) lies in the interval $[0,1]$ and, if it is positive, the copula has upper tail dependence.

II.6.3.5 Bounds for Dependence

We introduce some special copulas which may be thought of as the copula 'analogues' of zero correlation and of correlations of -1 and 1. The multivariate version of (II.6.11) is the *independence copula* that applies whenever the random variables are independent. This may be written

$$C(u_1, u_2, \ldots, u_n) = u_1 u_2 \ldots u_n. \tag{II.6.28}$$

Hence, the joint distribution is just the product of the marginal distributions.

The *Fréchet upper bound copula* is given by

$$C(u_1, u_2, \ldots, u_n) = \min(u_1, u_2, \ldots, u_n). \tag{II.6.29}$$

This is the upper bound of all possible copulas in the sense that no other copula can take a value that is greater than the value of this copula, and when the random variables have the Fréchet upper bound copula we say they have *perfect positive dependence*.

---

[14] The generalization to multivariate copulas should be obvious.
[15] See McNeil et al. (2005: Chapter 5).
[16] The name follows from the fact that $\overline{C}(1 - u_1, 1 - u_2) = P(U_1 > u_1, U_2 > u_2)$. We call $\overline{C}(1 - u_1, 1 - u_2)$ the *joint survival function* associated with $C(u_1, u_2)$.

The *Fréchet lower bound* is actually only a copula for $n = 2$. It is defined as

$$C(u_1, u_2, \ldots, u_n) = \max(u_1 + u_2 + \ldots + u_n - n + 1, 0). \qquad (\text{II.6.30})$$

No copula can take a value that is less than this value, and it corresponds to the case where the random variables have *perfect negative dependence*.

Less than perfect (positive or negative) dependence is linked to certain parametric copulas. We say that a copula captures positive or negative dependence between the variables if it tends to one of the Fréchet bounds as its parameter values change. But the Gaussian copula does not tend to the Fréchet upper bound as the correlation increases to 1, and neither does it tend to the Fréchet lower bound as the correlation decreases to -1. In the case of bivariate normal variables comonotonic dependence corresponds to perfect positive correlation and countermonotonic dependence corresponds to perfect negative correlation. Two random variables X and Y are *countermonotonic* if there is another random variable Z such that X is a monotonic decreasing transformation of Z and Y is a monotonic increasing transformation of Z. If they are both increasing (or decreasing) transformations of Z then X and Y are called *comonotonic*.

II.6.4 EXAMPLES OF COPULAS

This section illustrates the theoretical concepts introduced in the previous section by defining some families of copulas that are very commonly used in market risk analysis. In each case we derive the appropriate copula density function and discuss the properties of the copula. All the copula density graphs shown below are contained in the Excel workbook 'Copula Densities'.

As above, there are n random variables $\{X_1, \ldots, X_n\}$ with marginal distributions $\{F_1, \ldots, F_n\}$ and we use the notation $u_i = F_i(x_i)$. That is, each u_i is in the interval $[0, 1]$ and it represents the value of the ith marginal distribution at the realization x_i for $i = 1, \ldots, n$. So we use $C(u_1, \ldots, u_n)$ to denote the copula and $c(u_1, \ldots, u_n)$ to denote the associated copula density function, if it exists.

II.6.4.1 Normal or Gaussian Copulas

Since $C(u_1, \ldots, u_n)$ takes a value between 0 and 1 for every $(u_1, \ldots, u_n)$, it is possible to derive a copula from any standard multivariate distribution. In other words, we isolate only the *dependence* part of the joint distribution and this is the *implicit copula* of that distribution. Then we can apply the copula to other types of marginals, as explained above. Perhaps the most important of these implicit copulas is the *normal copula*, also called the *Gaussian copula*. The multivariate normal copula function has a correlation matrix Σ for parameters. Since correlation matrices have always played a central role in financial analysis, normal copulas are very frequently applied in finance. However, they are used for convenience rather than accuracy, as we have already remarked.

A normal (or Gaussian) copula is derived from the n-dimensional multivariate and univariate standard normal distribution functions, denoted $\mathbf{\Phi}$ and Φ, respectively. It is defined by

$$C(u_1, \ldots, u_n; \mathbf{\Sigma}) = \mathbf{\Phi}\big(\Phi^{-1}(u_1), \ldots, \Phi^{-1}(u_n)\big). \qquad (\text{II.6.31})$$

The copula distribution cannot be written in a simple closed form. It can only be expressed as an integral and therefore it is easier to work with the copula density rather than its distribution. Differentiating (II.6.31) yields the *normal* or *Gaussian copula density* which is given by

$$c(u_1, \ldots, u_n; \boldsymbol{\Sigma}) = |\boldsymbol{\Sigma}|^{-1/2} \exp\left(-\tfrac{1}{2}\boldsymbol{\xi}'\left(\boldsymbol{\Sigma}^{-1} - \mathbf{I}\right)\boldsymbol{\xi}\right), \qquad (\text{II.6.32})$$

where $\boldsymbol{\Sigma}$ denotes the correlation matrix, $|\boldsymbol{\Sigma}|$ is its determinant and $\boldsymbol{\xi} = (\xi_1, \ldots, \xi_n)'$ where ξ_i is the u_i quantile of the standard normal random variable X_i, i.e.

$$u_i = P(X_i < \xi_i), \quad X_i \sim N(0, 1), \quad i = 1, \ldots, n. \qquad (\text{II.6.33})$$

We emphasize that the normal copula is a function of $(u_1, \ldots, u_n)$ and *not* a function of $(\xi_1, \ldots, \xi_n)$, since $\boldsymbol{\xi} = \left(\Phi^{-1}(u_1), \ldots, \Phi^{-1}(u_n)\right)$ in (II.6.32).

Given a correlation matrix $\boldsymbol{\Sigma}$, how do we find a joint distribution when the copula is normal but one or more of the marginals is a *non*-normal distribution function? To express the normal copula density as a function of $(x_1, \ldots, x_n)$ we must proceed as follows:

1. For the (not necessarily normal) marginals, set $u_i = F_i(x_i)$ for $i = 1, \ldots, n$;
2. Apply the inverse Gaussian distribution, $\xi_i = \Phi^{-1}(u_i)$ for $i = 1, \ldots, n$;
3. Use the correlation matrix $\boldsymbol{\Sigma}$ and the vector $\boldsymbol{\xi}$ in the copula density (II.6.32).

In the case $n = 2$ the normal copula distribution is

$$C(u_1, u_2; \varrho) = \boldsymbol{\Phi}\left(\Phi^{-1}(u_1), \Phi^{-1}(u_2)\right), \qquad (\text{II.6.34})$$

where $\boldsymbol{\Phi}$ is the bivariate standard normal distribution function and Φ is the univariate standard normal distribution function. Alternatively,

$$C(u_1, u_2; \varrho) = \int_0^{\Phi^{-1}(u_2)} \int_0^{\Phi^{-1}(u_1)} (2\pi)^{-1}\left(1 - \varrho^2\right)^{-1/2} \exp\left(-\frac{\left[x_1^2 - 2\varrho x_1 x_2 + x_2^2\right]}{2(1 - \varrho^2)}\right) dx_1 dx_2. \qquad (\text{II.6.35})$$

The *bivariate normal copula density* is the two-dimensional version of (II.6.32), i.e.

$$c(u_1, u_2; \varrho) = \left(1 - \varrho^2\right)^{-1/2} \exp\left(-\frac{\varrho^2\xi_1^2 - 2\varrho\xi_1\xi_2 + \varrho^2\xi_2^2}{2(1 - \varrho^2)}\right), \qquad (\text{II.6.36})$$

where $\xi_1 = \Phi^{-1}(u_1)$ and $\xi_2 = \Phi^{-1}(u_2)$ are quantiles of standard normal variables. Since the correlation is the only parameter the bivariate normal copula is easy to calibrate (see Section II.6.6).

Figure II.6.6, which may be replicated by setting the appropriate value for the correlation in the 'Copula Densities' Excel workbook, shows the bivariate normal copula density with $\varrho = -0.25$. As always, the copula density is drawn as a function of u_1 and u_2 each of which ranges from 0 to 1. The reader may change the correlation in the spreadsheet to see the effect on the copula density. Note that when correlation is zero the copula takes the value 1 everywhere.

The normal family are *symmetric copulas*, i.e. $C(u_1, u_2) = C(u_2, u_1)$. They also have zero or very weak tail dependence unless the correlation is 1.[17] This is not usually appropriate for modelling dependencies between financial assets. For example, stock returns appear to

---

[17] With a normal copula the coefficient of tail dependence is one *if and only if* the correlation is one. See the general formula in McNeil et al. (2005: Section 5.3). When the marginals are normal there is zero tail dependency but otherwise there can be very weak tail dependency – see Figure II.6.13(b) for example.

become more related when they are large and negative than when they are large and positive. In other words, when two stock prices fall by large amounts their dependence is greater than when their prices rise. This means that there is *asymmetric tail dependence* in stock returns, but asymmetric tail dependence cannot be captured by a normal copula.

II.6.4.2 Student t Copulas

The n-dimensional symmetric Student t copula is another copula that is derived implicitly from a multivariate distribution function. It is defined by

$$C_\nu(u_1,\ldots,u_n;\Sigma)=\mathbf{t}_\nu\!\left(t_\nu^{-1}(u_1),\ldots,t_\nu^{-1}(u_n)\right),\qquad(\text{II.6.37})$$

where $\mathbf{t}_\nu$ and t_ν are multivariate and univariate Student t distribution functions with ν degrees of freedom and Σ denotes the correlation matrix (see Section I.3.4.8).

Like the normal copula, the Student t copula distribution cannot be written in a simple closed form. We use the definition of multivariate Student t density function given in Section I.3.4.8, i.e.

$$f(\mathbf{x})=k\,|\Sigma|^{-1/2}\!\left(1+\nu^{-1}\mathbf{x}'\Sigma^{-1}\mathbf{x}\right)^{-(\nu+n)/2},\qquad(\text{II.6.38})$$

where $|\Sigma|$ denotes the determinant of the correlation matrix and

$$k=\Gamma\!\left(\frac{\nu}{2}\right)^{-1}\Gamma\!\left(\frac{\nu+n}{2}\right)(\nu\pi)^{-n/2}.$$

Then the multivariate *Student t copula distribution* may be written

$$C_\nu(u_1,\ldots,u_n;\Sigma)=\int_0^{t_\nu^{-1}(u_n)}\!\!\!\cdots\int_0^{t_\nu^{-1}(u_1)}k\,|\Sigma|^{-1/2}\!\left(1+\nu^{-1}\mathbf{x}'\Sigma^{-1}\mathbf{x}\right)^{-(\nu+n)/2}dx_1\ldots dx_n.\qquad(\text{II.6.39})$$

Differentiation of (II.6.39) yields the corresponding *Student t copula density* as[18]

$$c_\nu(u_1,\ldots,u_n;\Sigma)=K\,|\Sigma|^{-1/2}\!\left(1+\nu^{-1}\,\boldsymbol{\xi}'\Sigma^{-1}\boldsymbol{\xi}\right)^{-(\nu+n)/2}\prod_{i=1}^{n}\left(1+\nu^{-1}\xi_i^2\right)^{(\nu+1)/2},\qquad(\text{II.6.40})$$

where $\boldsymbol{\xi}=\left(t_\nu^{-1}(u_1),\ldots,t_\nu^{-1}(u_n)\right)$ is a vector of realizations of Student t variables, and

$$K=\Gamma\!\left(\frac{\nu}{2}\right)^{n-1}\Gamma\!\left(\frac{\nu+1}{2}\right)^{-n}\Gamma\!\left(\frac{\nu+n}{2}\right).\qquad(\text{II.6.41})$$

In the case $n=2$ we have the *symmetric bivariate t copula* distribution

$$C_\nu(u_1,u_2;\varrho)=\int_0^{t^{-1}(u_2)}\int^{t^{-1}(u_1)}(2\pi)^{-1}\!\left(1-\varrho^2\right)^{-1/2}\left[1+\nu^{-1}\!\left(x_1^2-2\varrho x_1x_2+x_2^2\right)\right]^{-(\nu+2)/2}dx_1dx_2,$$

and the corresponding *bivariate t copula density* is

$$c_\nu(u_1,u_2;\varrho)=K\!\left(1-\varrho^2\right)^{-1/2}\left[1+\nu^{-1}\!\left(1-\varrho^2\right)^{-1}\!\left(\xi_1^2-2\varrho\xi_1\xi_2+\xi_2^2\right)\right]^{-(\nu+2)/2}\times$$
$$\left[\left(1+\nu^{-1}\xi_1^2\right)\left(1+\nu^{-1}\xi_2^2\right)\right]^{(\nu+1)/2},\qquad(\text{II.6.42})$$

---

[18] See also Bouyé et al. (2000).

where $\xi_1 = t_\nu^{-1}(u_1)$ and $\xi_2 = t_\nu^{-1}(u_2)$. The constant K in (II.6.42) is defined by setting $n = 2$ in (II.6.41).

Figure II.6.7 shows the bivariate t copula density with seven degrees of freedom and with $\varrho = -0.25$ drawn, as usual, as a function of u_1 and u_2 each of which ranges from 0 to 1. Note that the peaks in the tails are symmetric, because the copula has symmetric tail dependency, and they are *higher* than those in the normal copula with $\varrho = -0.25$ (shown in Figure II.6.6) because the t copula has relatively strong tail dependence.[19] However, not all of the t copula family are symmetric copulas. Demarta and McNeil (2005) develop a wide variety of Student t copulas, many of them with asymmetric tail dependence.

We emphasize that $\xi = \left(t_\nu^{-1}(u_1), \ldots, t_\nu^{-1}(u_n) \right)$, where ν is the degrees of freedom in the copula. So if we want to build a joint density $f(x_1, \ldots, x_n) = c(x_1, \ldots, x_n) f_1(x_1) \ldots f_n(x_n)$ where the copula is a Student t with ν degrees of freedom but one or more of the marginals are *not* Student t with ν degrees of freedom then, in order to apply (II.6.16), we must first express the Student t copula as a function of $(x_1, \ldots, x_n)$. As with the normal copula, this entails three steps: first use the marginal distributions to obtain standard uniform variables; then apply the inverse Student t distribution with ν degrees of freedom to the uniform variables; then apply (II.6.40).

II.6.4.3 Normal Mixture Copulas

Some very interesting types of association can be captured using a *normal mixture* copula. This is a mixture of two or more normal copulas. The parameters are the correlation matrices (one for each normal copula) and a mixing law (i.e. a probability vector governing the mixture). Other mixture copulas may be built using similar principles. For instance, we could use a mixture of Student t copulas if we want stronger tail dependence.

If there are just two variables and a mixture of just two normal copulas, the normal mixture copula density may be written

$$c(u_1, u_2; \pi, \varrho_1, \varrho_2) = \pi c_N(u_1, u_2; \varrho_1) + (1 - \pi) c_N(u_1, u_2; \varrho_2),$$

where c_N is the bivariate normal copula density and the mixing law is $(\pi, 1 - \pi)$. That is,

$$\begin{aligned} c(u_1, u_2; \pi, \varrho_1, \varrho_2) = {} & \pi \left(1 - \varrho_1^2\right)^{-1/2} \exp\left(-\frac{\varrho_1^2 \xi_1^2 - 2\varrho_1 \xi_1 \xi_2 + \varrho_1^2 \xi_2^2}{2\left(1 - \varrho_1^2\right)} \right) \\ & + (1 - \pi) \left(1 - \varrho_2^2\right)^{-1/2} \exp\left(-\frac{\varrho_2^2 \xi_1^2 - 2\varrho_2 \xi_1 \xi_2 + \varrho_2^2 \xi_2^2}{2\left(1 - \varrho_2^2\right)} \right). \end{aligned} \tag{II.6.43}$$

Normal mixture copulas are attractive because they capture complex association patterns yet still allow for a very tractable analysis. For instance, the use of a positive correlation in one normal copula and a negative correlation in the other normal copula will produce an association between the variables in all four tails of their joint density function. To illustrate this, the two-dimensional normal mixture copula density for $\pi = 0.5$, $\varrho_1 = 0.5$ and $\varrho_2 = -0.5$ is shown in Figure II.6.8 As usual, the copula parameters can be changed in the spreadsheet. Figure II.6.9 depicts another normal mixture copula density, this one with $\pi = 0.75$, $\varrho_1 = 0.25$, $\varrho_2 = -0.75$.

---

[19] See the general formula in Demarta and McNeil (2005), Section 3.5.1. Both the Gaussian copula and the symmetric t copula have a tail dependence of one when the correlation is one, but when the correlation is less than one the Gaussian copula has zero tail dependence.

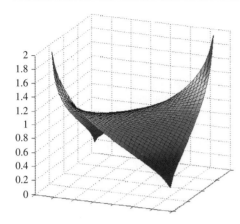

Figure II.6.6 Bivariate normal copula density with $\varrho = -0.25$. (See Plate 1)

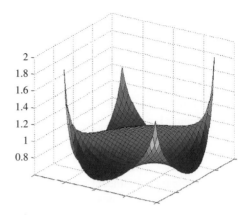

Figure II.6.9   Bivariate normal mixture copula density with $\pi = 0.75$, $\varrho_1 = 0.25$ and $\varrho_2 = -0.75$. (See Plate 4)

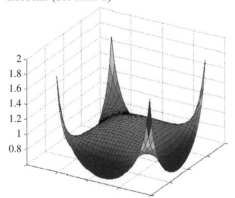

Figure II.6.7   Bivariate Student t copula density with $\varrho = -0.25$ and seven degrees of freedom. (See Plate 2)

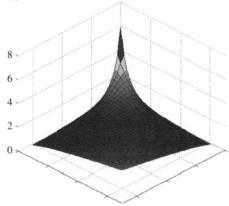

Figure II.6.10   Bivariate Clayton copula density with $\alpha = 0.75$. (See Plate 5)

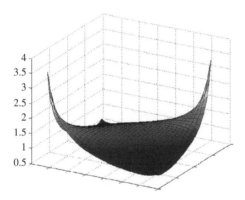

Figure II.6.8 Bivariate normal mixture copula density with $\pi = 0.25$, $\varrho_1 = 0.5$ and $\varrho_2 = -0.5$. (See Plate 3)

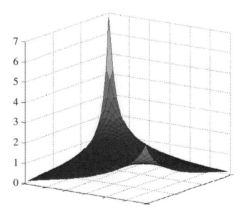

Figure II.6.11   Bivariate Gumbel copula density with $\delta = 1.5$. (See Plate 6)

II.6.4.4   Archimedean Copulas

Elliptical copulas such as the normal and Student t are implicit copulas, so they are built using an *inversion method*, i.e. they are derived from a multivariate distribution such as in (II.6.31). An alternative method for building copulas is based on a *generator function* which will be denoted in the following by $\Psi(u)$.[20] Given any generator function Ψ, we define the corresponding *Archimedean copula* as

$$C(u_1,\ldots,u_n) = \Psi^{-1}(\Psi(u_1)+\ldots+\Psi(u_n)).\tag{II.6.44}$$

Its associated density function is

$$c(u_1,\ldots,u_n) = \Psi_{(n)}^{-1}(\Psi(u_1)+\ldots+\Psi(u_n))\prod_{i=1}^{n}\Psi'(u_i),\tag{II.6.45}$$

where $\Psi_{(n)}^{-1}$ is the nth derivative of the inverse generator function.

Note that when the generator function $\Psi(u) = -\ln u$ the Archimedean copula becomes the independent copula. More generally, the generator function can be *any* strictly convex and monotonic decreasing function with $\Psi(1) = 0$ and $\Psi(u) \to \infty$ as $u \to 0$. Hence, a very large number of different Archimedean copulas can be constructed. Just using one parameter to specify the generator function generates a great variety of Archimedean copulas. Nelsen (2006) lists no less than 22 different one-parameter Archimedean copulas!

Two simple Archimedean copulas that are commonly used in market risk analysis are described below. These are the Clayton and Gumbel copulas, and they are useful because they capture an asymmetric tail dependence that we know to be important for modelling many relationships between financial asset returns. The Clayton copula captures lower tail dependence and the Gumbel copula captures upper tail dependence.

Clayton Copulas

A popular choice of generator function in finance is

$$\Psi(u) = \alpha^{-1}(u^{-\alpha}-1),\quad \alpha \neq 0,\tag{II.6.46}$$

so the inverse generator function is

$$\Psi^{-1}(x) = (\alpha x + 1)^{-1/\alpha}.\tag{II.6.47}$$

This gives an Archimedean copula of the form

$$C(u_1,\ldots,u_n;\alpha) = (u_1^{-\alpha}+\ldots+u_n^{-\alpha}-n+1)^{-1/\alpha}.\tag{II.6.48}$$

This was introduced by Clayton (1978) and so is commonly called the *Clayton copula*.[21]

Differentiating (II.6.48) yields the *Clayton copula density function*,

$$c(u_1,\ldots,u_n) = \left(1-n+\sum_{i=1}^{n}u_i^{-\alpha}\right)^{-n-(1/\alpha)}\prod_{j=1}^{n}\left(u_j^{-\alpha-1}((j-1)\alpha+1)\right).\tag{II.6.49}$$

---

[20] Whilst it is common to use the notation $\varphi(u)$ for the generator function, we prefer the notation $\Psi(u)$ because φ is standard notation for the normal density function.
[21] Other names for this copula are in use: see Nelsen (2006).

So when $n = 2$,

$$c(u_1, u_2) = (\alpha + 1)\,(u_1^{-\alpha} + u_2^{-\alpha} - 1)^{-2-(1/\alpha)}\,u_1^{-\alpha-1}u_2^{-\alpha-1}. \tag{II.6.50}$$

A Clayton copula has asymmetric tail dependence. In fact it has zero upper tail dependence but a positive lower tail dependence coefficient, when $\alpha > 0$, with[22]

$$\lambda^l = \begin{cases} 2^{-1/\alpha}, & \text{if } \alpha > 0, \\ 0, & \text{otherwise.} \end{cases} \tag{II.6.51}$$

As the parameter α varies, the Clayton copulas capture a range of dependence, with *perfect positive dependence* as $\alpha \to \infty$. That is, as α increases the Clayton copulas converge to the Fréchet upper bound copula (II.6.29). The lower tail dependence for any finite $\alpha > 0$ is clear from Figure II.6.10, which plots the Clayton copula density on the unit square with $\alpha = 0.75$.

Gumbel Copulas

A Gumbel copula is an Archimedean copula with generating function

$$\Psi(u) = -(\ln u)^\delta, \quad \delta \geq 1. \tag{II.6.52}$$

Thus the inverse generator function is

$$\Psi^{-1}(x) = \exp\left((-x)^{1/\delta}\right). \tag{II.6.53}$$

The Gumbel copula distribution may therefore be written

$$C(u_1, \ldots, u_n; \delta) = \exp\left(-\left[(-\ln u_1)^\delta + \ldots + (-\ln u_n)^\delta\right]^{1/\delta}\right) \tag{II.6.54}$$

or, setting

$$A(u_1, .., u_n; \delta) = \left(\sum_{i=1}^{n}(-\ln u_i)^\delta\right)^{1/\delta},$$

as

$$C(u_1, \ldots, u_n; \delta) = \exp\left(-A(u_1, \ldots, u_n; \delta)\right). \tag{II.6.55}$$

Differentiating and applying (II.6.45) to derive the Gumbel copula density is tedious. When $n = 2$ we obtain the *bivariate Gumbel copula density*,

$$c(u_1, u_2; \delta) = (A + \delta - 1)\,A^{1-2\delta}\exp(-A)\,(u_1 u_2)^{-1}(-\ln u_1)^{\delta-1}(-\ln u_2)^{\delta-1}, \tag{II.6.56}$$

where

$$A = \left((-\ln u_1)^\delta + (-\ln u_2)^\delta\right)^{1/\delta}.$$

The Gumbel copula has positive upper tail dependence if $\delta > 1$. This is evident from Figure II.6.11 which plots the Gumbel copula density on the unit square for $\delta = 1.5$. In fact, $\lambda^l = 0$ and $\lambda^u = 2 - 2^{1/\delta}$. As the parameter δ varies Gumbel copulas capture a range of dependence between *independence* ($\delta = 1$) and *perfect positive dependence*: i.e. as $\delta \to \infty$ the Gumbel copulas converge to the maximum copula (II.6.30).

---

[22] See Cuvelier and Noirhomme-Fraiture (2005).

II.6.5   CONDITIONAL COPULA DISTRIBUTIONS AND QUANTILE CURVES

To apply copulas in simulation and regression we generally require a combination of the conditional copula distribution and the marginal distributions of the random variables. Quantile curves are a means of depicting these. In other words, the points (ξ_1, ξ_2) shown by the *q quantile curve* are such that

$$P(X_2 < \xi_2 \mid X_1 = \xi_1) = q. \tag{II.6.57}$$

In this section we first derive expressions for the conditional distributions and q quantile curves for the bivariate copulas introduced above. Then, in Section II.6.5.5, we illustrate the formulae that we have derived with empirical examples (these are contained in the Excel workbook 'Copula Quantiles').

II.6.5.1   Normal or Gaussian Copulas

The conditional distributions of the bivariate normal copula (also called the Gaussian copula) are derived by differentiating (II.6.34), i.e.

$$C_{1|2}(u_1 \mid u_2) = \frac{\partial}{\partial u_2} \Phi\big(\Phi^{-1}(u_1), \Phi^{-1}(u_2)\big), \tag{II.6.58}$$

and the other conditional distribution follows by symmetry.

Recall from Section I.3.4.6 that the conditional distributions of a bivariate standard normal distribution Φ given that $X = x$ are univariate normal distributions with expectation and variance given by

$$E(Y \mid X = x) = \varrho x, \quad V(Y \mid X = x) = 1 - \varrho^2. \tag{II.6.59}$$

Hence, the following variable has a standard normal distribution:

$$Z = \frac{Y - \varrho x}{\sqrt{1 - \varrho^2}}. \tag{II.6.60}$$

It follows that differentiating (II.6.58) yields the bivariate normal copula's *conditional* distribution as

$$C_{1|2}(u_1 \mid u_2) = \frac{\partial}{\partial u_2} \Phi\big(\Phi^{-1}(u_1), \Phi^{-1}(u_2)\big) = \Phi\left(\frac{\Phi^{-1}(u_1) - \varrho\Phi^{-1}(u_2)}{\sqrt{1 - \varrho^2}}\right). \tag{II.6.61}$$

Similarly,

$$C_{2|1}(u_2 \mid u_1) = \Phi\left(\frac{\Phi^{-1}(u_2) - \varrho\Phi^{-1}(u_1)}{\sqrt{1 - \varrho^2}}\right).$$

The q quantile curve (II.6.23) of the normal copula with standard normal marginals may thus be written in explicit form, setting (II.6.61) equal to the fixed probability q. That is,

$$q = \Phi\left(\frac{\Phi^{-1}(u_2) - \varrho\Phi^{-1}(u_1)}{\sqrt{1 - \varrho^2}}\right).$$

And solving for u_2 gives the *q quantile curve of the normal copula with standard normal marginals* as

$$u_2 = \Phi\big(\varrho\Phi^{-1}(u_1) + \sqrt{1 - \varrho^2}\,\Phi^{-1}(q)\big). \tag{II.6.62}$$

The marginal densities translate the q quantile curve of the normal copula into (ξ_1, ξ_2) coordinates. When the marginals are standard normal $\xi_1 = \Phi^{-1}(u_1)$ and $\xi_2 = \Phi^{-1}(u_2)$ so the q quantile curve in (ξ_1, ξ_2) coordinates is

$$\xi_2 = \varrho\xi_1 + \sqrt{1-\varrho^2}\,\Phi^{-1}(q). \tag{II.6.63}$$

This is a straight line with slope ϱ and intercept $\sqrt{1-\varrho^2}\,\Phi^{-1}(q)$ as is evident in Figure II.6.13(a) in Section II.6.5.5.

More generally, if the marginals are normal but with means μ_1, μ_2 and standard deviations σ_1, σ_2, then the q quantile curve is still a straight line in (ξ_1, ξ_2) coordinates but with modified slope and intercept:

$$\frac{\xi_2}{\sigma_2} = \varrho\left(\frac{\xi_1}{\sigma_1}\right) + \frac{\mu_2}{\sigma_2} - \varrho\left(\frac{\mu_1}{\sigma_1}\right) + \sqrt{1-\varrho^2}\,\Phi^{-1}(q). \tag{II.6.64}$$

Even more generally, when the marginals are arbitrary distributions F_1 and F_2 then substituting $u_1 = F_1(\xi_1)$ and $u_2 = F_2(\xi_2)$ into (II.6.62) gives a *non*-linear q quantile curve in (ξ_1, ξ_2) coordinates as

$$\xi_2 = F_2^{-1}\left[\Phi\left(\varrho\Phi^{-1}(F_1(\xi_1)) + \sqrt{1-\varrho^2}\,\Phi^{-1}(q)\right)\right]. \tag{II.6.65}$$

For example, the q quantile curves of the normal copula with t marginals are shown in Figure II.6.13(b) in Section II.6.5.5.

II.6.5.2   Student t Copulas

The conditional distributions of the t copula derived from the bivariate Student t distribution are derived by partial differentiation of (II.6.37). Thus with $n = 2$ we have

$$C_{1|2}(u_1 \,|\, u_2) = \frac{\partial}{\partial u_2} \mathbf{t}_\nu\!\left(t_\nu^{-1}(u_1), t_\nu^{-1}(u_2)\right). \tag{II.6.66}$$

To derive the explicit form of the above we use an analysis similar to that applied to the bivariate normal copula. The conditional distribution of a standard bivariate t distribution with ν degrees of freedom, given that $X = x$, is a univariate t distribution with $\nu + 1$ degrees of freedom. In fact the following variable has a standard univariate t distribution with $\nu + 1$ degrees of freedom:[23]

$$t = \sqrt{\frac{\nu+1}{\nu+x^2}} \times \frac{Y - \varrho x}{\sqrt{1-\varrho^2}}. \tag{II.6.67}$$

Hence, the conditional distribution of a bivariate Student t copula derived from the bivariate Student t distribution is

$$C_{1|2}(u_1 \,|\, u_2) = t_{\nu+1}\!\left(\sqrt{\frac{\nu+1}{\nu+t_\nu^{-1}(u_1)^2}} \times \frac{t_\nu^{-1}(u_2) - \varrho t_\nu^{-1}(u_1)}{\sqrt{1-\varrho^2}}\right); \tag{II.6.68}$$

the other conditional distribution follows by symmetry.

The q quantile curve (II.6.23) of the Student t copula may thus be written in explicit form, setting (II.6.61) equal to the fixed probability q. That is, for $n = 2$ we set

$$q = t_{\nu+1}\!\left(\sqrt{\frac{\nu+1}{\nu+t_\nu^{-1}(u_1)^2}} \times \frac{t_\nu^{-1}(u_2) - \varrho t_\nu^{-1}(u_1)}{\sqrt{1-\varrho^2}}\right)$$

---

[23] See Cherubini et al. (2004, Section 3.2.2).

and solve for u_2, giving the q quantile curve

$$u_2 = t_\nu \left(\varrho t_\nu^{-1}(u_1) + \sqrt{(1 - \varrho^2)(\nu + 1)^{-1} \left(\nu + t_\nu^{-1}(u_1)^2 \right)} \, t_{\nu+1}^{-1}(q) \right). \qquad (\text{II.6.69})$$

Unlike the bivariate normal case, the q quantile curve in (ξ_1, ξ_2) coordinates is *not* a straight line. For example, see Figures II.6.12 and II.6.13 in Section II.6.5.5 where the bivariate t copula quantile curves are shown, for zero and non-zero correlation, with both standard normal and student t distributed marginals.

The q quantile curve corresponding to Student t marginals is most easily expressed by setting $\xi_1 = t_\nu^{-1}(u_1)$ and $\xi_2 = t_\nu^{-1}(u_2)$ and writing ξ_2 as a function of ξ_1, as:

$$\xi_2 = \varrho \xi_1 + \sqrt{(1 - \varrho^2)(\nu + 1)^{-1} \left(\nu + \xi_1^2 \right)} \, t_{\nu+1}^{-1}(q). \qquad (\text{II.6.70})$$

With arbitrary marginals the q quantile curves are obtained by setting $u_1 = F_1(\xi_1)$ and $u_2 = F_2(\xi_2)$ in (II.6.69). This gives a rather formidable expression for the q quantile curve in (ξ_1, ξ_2) coordinates:

$$\xi_2 = F_2^{-1} \left[t_\nu \left(\varrho t_\nu^{-1}(F_1(\xi_1)) + \sqrt{(1 - \varrho^2)(\nu + 1)^{-1} \left(\nu + t_\nu^{-1}(F_1(\xi_1))^2 \right)} \, t_{\nu+1}^{-1}(q) \right) \right]. \qquad (\text{II.6.71})$$

II.6.5.3   Normal Mixture Copulas

The conditional copula distributions for a normal mixture copula are easy to derive from those of the normal copula:

$$C_{1|2}(u_1 | u_2) = \pi \Phi \left(\frac{\Phi^{-1}(u_1) - \varrho_1 \Phi^{-1}(u_2)}{\sqrt{1 - \varrho_1^2}} \right) + (1 - \pi) \Phi \left(\frac{\Phi^{-1}(u_1) - \varrho_2 \Phi^{-1}(u_2)}{\sqrt{1 - \varrho_2^2}} \right).$$

However, this time we cannot express the quantile curves as an explicit function of the form (II.6.23) and numerical methods need to be used to 'back out' a value of u_2 from

$$q = \pi \Phi \left(\frac{\Phi^{-1}(u_1) - \varrho_1 \Phi^{-1}(u_2)}{\sqrt{1 - \varrho_1^2}} \right) + (1 - \pi) \Phi \left(\frac{\Phi^{-1}(u_1) - \varrho_2 \Phi^{-1}(u_2)}{\sqrt{1 - \varrho_2^2}} \right), \qquad (\text{II.6.72})$$

for each u_1 and q.

II.6.5.4   Archimedean Copulas

The conditional distributions for the Clayton copula are also easy to derive. For instance, in the bivariate Clayton copula the conditional distribution of u_2 given u_1 is

$$C_{2|1}(u_2 | u_1; \alpha) = \frac{\partial}{\partial u_1} (u_1^{-\alpha} + u_2^{-\alpha} - 1)^{-1/\alpha} = u_1^{-(1+\alpha)} (u_1^{-\alpha} + u_2^{-\alpha} - 1)^{-(1+\alpha)/\alpha}, \qquad (\text{II.6.73})$$

and similarly for $C_{1|2}(u_1 | u_2; \alpha)$ by symmetry. The q quantile curve (II.6.23) of the Clayton copula may thus be written in explicit form, setting (II.6.73) equal to the fixed probability q. That is, we set

$$q = u_1^{-(1+\alpha)} (u_1^{-\alpha} + u_2^{-\alpha} - 1)^{-(1+\alpha)/\alpha}$$

and solve for u_2, giving the q quantile curve of the Clayton copula as

$$u_2 = C_{2|1}^{-1}(u_2 | u_1) = \left(1 + u_1^{-\alpha} \left(q^{-\alpha/(1+\alpha)} - 1 \right) \right)^{-1/\alpha}. \qquad (\text{II.6.74})$$

An equivalent expression in terms of $\xi_i = F_i^{-1}(u_i)$ for $i = 1, 2$ is

$$\xi_2 = F_2^{-1}\left[\left(1 + F_1(\xi_1)^{-\alpha}\left(q^{-\alpha/(1+\alpha)} - 1\right)\right)^{-1/\alpha}\right]. \tag{II.6.75}$$

These quantile curves will be used in the case study in Section II.7.2, when we consider regression models where the variables have bivariate distributions based on the Clayton copula. Also, in Section II.6.7 we shall use the inverse conditional copula to simulate returns with uniform marginals that have dependence defined by a Clayton copula. Then we can impose any marginals we like upon these simulations to obtain simulated returns on financial assets that have these marginals and dependence defined by the Clayton copula.

The conditional distributions of the bivariate Gumbel copula are given by

$$C_{2|1}(u_2 | u_1;\ \delta) = \frac{\partial}{\partial u_1} \exp\left(-\left[(-\ln u_1)^\delta + (-\ln u_2)^\delta\right]^{1/\delta}\right)$$

$$= u_1^{-1}(-\ln u_1)^{\delta-1}\left[(-\ln u_1)^\delta + (-\ln u_2)^\delta\right]^{(1-\delta)/\delta} \tag{II.6.76}$$

$$\exp\left(-\left[(-\ln u_1)^\delta + (-\ln u_2)^\delta\right]^{1/\delta}\right),$$

and similarly for $C_{1|2}(u_1 | u_2;\ \delta)$ by symmetry. The q quantile curve (II.6.23) of the Gumbel copula cannot be written in explicit form, so for the examples in the next subsection we have used Excel Solver to derive the curves.

II.6.5.5   Examples

Figure II.6.12 depicts the 5%, 25%, 50%, 75% and 95% quantile curves (II.6.57) of four bivariate distributions on two random variables, X_1 and X_2. We have used standard normal or Student t marginals, so the mean is equal to the median, because these distributions are symmetric, and in the graphs we combine these marginals with either normal or symmetric Student t copulas, assuming the correlation is 0.[24]

All graphs are shown on the same scale, with ξ_1 (i.e. realizations of X_1) along the horizontal axis and ξ_2 (i.e. realizations of X_2) on the vertical axis. The values of ξ_1 and ξ_2 range from -5 to 5, with $\xi_i = 0$ corresponding to the mean.

The quantile curves in Figures II.6.12(a) and II.6.12(d) correspond to the case where both the copula and the marginals are derived from the same bivariate distribution: the bivariate normal in (a) and the bivariate Student t with five degrees of freedom in (d). The quantile curves in Figure II.6.12(b) are for a normal copula with Student t marginals with five degrees of freedom, and Figure II.6.12(c) illustrates the quantile curves of the Student t copula with five degrees of freedom when the marginals are standard normal.

To interpret the lines shown in these graphs, consider the light grey line labelled 0.05 in graph (c). Fix the value of X_1, for instance take $\xi_1 = 3$. Then the line labelled 0.05 has the value -2.79. Thus

$$P(X_2 < -2.79 | X_1 = 3) = 0.05.$$

In other words, in these q quantile graphs we are plotting (ξ_1, ξ_2) such that

$$P(X_2 < \xi_2 | X_1 = \xi_1) = q$$

for $q = 0.05, 0.25, 0.5, 0.75$ and 0.95.

---

[24] In each graph in Figure II.6.12 the degrees of freedom for the Student t copula and/or marginals are set at 5, but this can be changed by the reader.

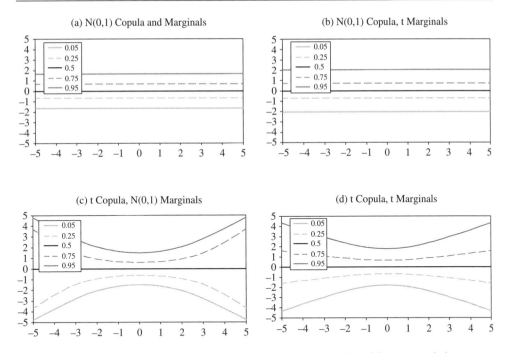

Figure II.6.12   Quantile curves of normal and Student t copulas with zero correlation

Figures II.6.12(a) and II.6.12(b) show that the quantile curves under the normal copula are straight horizontal lines. This is because zero correlation implies independence under the normal copula. The *interquartile range* (i.e. the distance between the 75% curve and the 25% curve) when the marginals are t distributed (Figure II.6.12(b)) is wider than when the marginals are normally distributed (Figure II.6.12(a)) and all four quantile curves in the figure are symmetric about the median curve shown in black.

In Section III.2.3.3 it was noted that zero correlation does *not* imply independence under the Student t copula. Thus the quantile curves in Figures II.6.12(c) and II.6.12(d) are not straight lines. The leptokurtosis of the Student t copula leads to positive tail dependence. Thus when X_1 is near its mean value the interquartile range for X_2 is smaller than that depicted in Figures II.6.12(a) and II.6.12(b), but it is wider when X_1 takes values that are substantially above or below its mean.

Figures II.6.13(a)–(d) show the quantile curves for the same four distributions shown in Figure II.6.12, but now the correlation is assumed to be $\frac{1}{2}$. Figure II.6.13(a) corresponds to the bivariate normal distribution. Note that here the quantile curves are straight lines because there is no tail dependence. But when the marginals are Student t the normal copula quantile curves shown in Figure II.6.13(b) display weak symmetric tail dependence.[25] The quantile curves in Figure II.6.13(c) are derived from the t copula with standard normal marginals. These are very dispersed at extreme values of (ξ_1, ξ_2) and are not symmetric about the median quantile curve. By contrast, those in Figure II.6.13(d), which corresponds to the

---

[25] See Cherubini et al. (2004: 116).

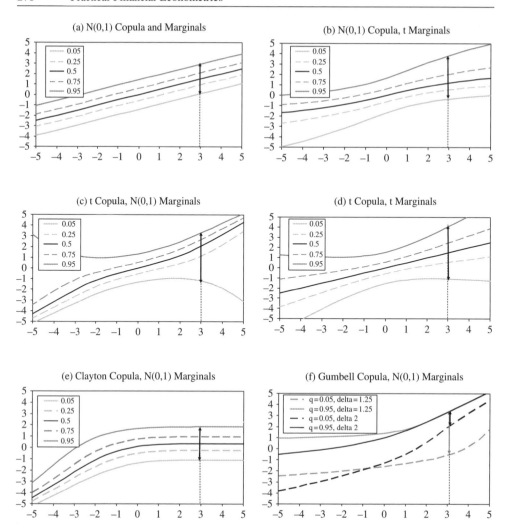

Figure II.6.13   Quantile curves for different copulas and marginals

bivariate Student t distribution, are symmetrically distributed about the median because of the symmetry in the distribution.

We also show the quantile curves for the Clayton copula when $\alpha = 0.5$ and for the Gumbel copula when $\delta = 1.25$ and $\delta = 2$. Figure II.6.13(e) depicts the quantile curves of the Clayton copula when $\alpha = 0.5$ and both the marginals are standard normal. Notice that the dependence between X_1 and X_2 is concentrated only in the lower tails of X_1 and X_2, because the Clayton copula has lower tail dependence. Finally, Figure II.6.13(f) shows the 5% and 95% quantile curves of the Gumbel copula when $\delta = 1.25$ and again when $\delta = 2$, with both marginals being standard normal. Now the dependence between X_1 and X_2 is concentrated only in the upper tails of X_1 and X_2, because the Gumbel copula has upper tail dependence, and the figure shows that the dependence becomes more pronounced as the parameter δ increases.

Table II.6.3 Ninety per cent confidence limits for X_2 given that $X_1 = 3$

Graph	Copula	Parameter	Marginal	Lower (l)	Upper (u)	Width
(a)	$N(0,1)$	$\varrho = 0.5$	$N(0,1)$	0.08	2.92	2.85
(b)	$N(0,1)$	$\varrho = 0.5$	$t(5)$	−0.36	3.84	4.20
(c)	$t(5)$	$\varrho = 0.5$	$N(0,1)$	−1.17	3.28	4.46
(d)	$t(5)$	$\varrho = 0.5$	$t(5)$	−1.07	4.07	5.14
(e)	Clayton	$\alpha = 0.5$	$N(0,1)$	−1.10	1.83	2.93
(f)(i)	Gumbel	$\delta = 1.25$	$N(0,1)$	−0.59	3.29	3.88
(f)(ii)	Gumbel	$\delta = 2$	$N(0,1)$	1.94	3.32	1.38

To see why the quantile curves in Figure II.6.13 have the shape that they do, we have marked a 90% confidence interval for X_2 given that $X_1 = 3$ on each graph. That is, we have taken the 5% and 95% quantile curves to construct, for each graph, a 90% confidence limit $[l, u]$ such that

$$P(l < X_2 < u \,|\, X_1 = 3) = 90\%.$$

Other confidence limits may be generated in the spreadsheet, corresponding to different percentiles, and also to different copula parameters.

The width of the confidence intervals decreases as dependence increases, as expected for conditional confidence intervals. The exact confidence bounds can be seen in the spreadsheet and they are summarized for convenience in Table II.6.3. To interpret the table, first compare cases (a) and (b). Conditional on $X_1 = 3$, the 90% confidence interval for X_2 has width 2.85 in case (a) but 4.20 in case (b). This is because the application of a Student t marginal leads to heavier tails for the conditional distributions of X_2. On the other hand, comparing (c) and (d) shows that with a t copula the 90% conditional confidence intervals for X_2 are much wider, even when normal marginals are applied as in case (c).

The Clayton confidence interval for X_2 conditional on a fixed positive value for X_1 has similar width to the bivariate normal confidence interval. Indeed, knowing only that X_1 is positive is sufficient – the confidence interval for X_2 is virtually the same whatever the value X_1, because there is no dependence in the upper tail. However, when X_1 is negative the Clayton copula predicts a very narrow, positive range for X_2. This illustrates the lower tail dependence induced by the Clayton copula. The Gumbel confidence intervals range from being wider than the normal when $\delta = 1.25$ to being narrower than the normal when $\delta = 2$. For high values of delta we become very highly confident about X_2 if we know that X_1 takes a relatively high value, due to the upper tail dependence in the Gumbel copula.

II.6.6   CALIBRATING COPULAS

This section begins by describing the connection between rank correlations and certain one-parameter bivariate copulas. This correspondence allows for easy calibration of the parameter. Then we describe more general numerical calibration techniques that are based on maximum likelihood estimation (MLE).

II.6.6.1   Correspondence between Copulas and Rank Correlations

It can be shown that Kendall's tau, τ, has a direct relationship with a bivariate copula function $C(u, v)$ as follows:[26]

$$\tau = 4 \int_0^1 \int_0^1 C(u_1, u_2) dC(u_1, u_2) - 1. \tag{II.6.77}$$

Hence if the copula depends on one parameter then (II.6.77) provides a means of calibrating this parameter using a sample estimate of the rank correlation. And the right-hand side of (II.6.77) sometimes has a simple solution. For instance, the bivariate normal copula has one parameter, the correlation ϱ, and here the identity (II.6.77) yields

$$\varrho = \sin\left(\frac{\pi}{2}\tau\right). \tag{II.6.78}$$

We remark that (II.6.78) also applies to the *Student t copula* and any other *elliptical copula*, i.e. the copula implicit in an elliptical distribution; see Lindskog et al. (2003). These authors also show that for the normal copula there is a relationship between the correlation parameter and Spearman's rho, ρ. Using

$$\rho = 12 \int_0^1 \int_0^1 u_1 u_2 dC(u_1, u_2) - 3,$$

they prove that

$$\varrho = 2 \sin\left(\frac{\pi}{6}\rho\right). \tag{II.6.79}$$

Finally, for the Archimedean copulas we have

$$\tau = 1 + 4 \int_0^1 \left(\frac{\Psi(x)}{\Psi'(x)}\right) dx. \tag{II.6.80}$$

Applying (II.6.80) to the Gumbel copula gives

$$\tau = 1 - \delta^{-1} \Rightarrow \delta = (1 - \tau)^{-1}, \tag{II.6.81}$$

and for a Clayton copula

$$\tau = \frac{\alpha}{\alpha + 2} \Rightarrow \alpha = 2\tau (1 - \tau)^{-1}. \tag{II.6.82}$$

EXAMPLE II.6.3: CALIBRATING COPULAS USING RANK CORRELATIONS

Suppose a sample produces an estimate of Kendall's tau of 0.2. What parameter should we use for (a) the normal copula; (b) the Gumbel copula; and (c) the Clayton copula?

SOLUTION

(a) The correlation in the normal – and, indeed, in any elliptical – copula should be set equal to $\varrho = \sin(0.1\pi) = 0.309$.
(b) In the Gumbel copula we set $\delta = (1 - 0.2)^{-1} = 1.25$.
(c) In the Clayton copula we set $\alpha = 0.4 (1 - 0.2)^{-1} = 0.5$.

---

[26] For instance, see McNeil et al. (2005: Proposition 5.29).

II.6.6.2   Maximum Likelihood Estimation

It is possible to calibrate the copula parameters by making the copula density as close as possible to the *empirical copula density*.[27] However, the empirical copula density can be so 'spiky' that small changes in the sample lead to great changes in the calibrated parameters. Thus the empirical copula density is better used to judge the goodness of fit of the estimated copula, as explained in the next subsection.

We estimate the copula parameters using MLE applied to the theoretical joint distribution function. Usually we either estimate the marginal parameters first, an approach that is called the *inference on margins* (IFM) calibration method, or we do not specify a functional form for the marginals at all, an approach that is called *canonical maximum likelihood* estimation.[28] These methods may lead to potential misspecification problems, and may provide less efficient estimators than full MLE, i.e. calibrating all parameters of copula and marginals at the same time. But they are considerably easier and more transparent than full MLE and they do lead to consistent estimators.

First we describe the calibration algorithm in general terms, and then we provide an empirical example in Excel. Suppose the joint density is defined by (II.6.16) and let us specify the parameters of both the marginals and the copula. For simplicity we suppose that each marginal has only one parameter α_i, but the following can easily be generalized to the case where each marginal has a vector of parameters. So we write the marginal densities and distributions as $f_i(x_i; \alpha_i)$ and $F_i(x_i; \alpha_i)$ and then we can rewrite (II.6.16) as

$$f(x_1, \ldots, x_n; \boldsymbol{\alpha}, \boldsymbol{\theta}) = c(F_1(x_1; \alpha_1), \ldots, F_n(x_n; \alpha_n); \boldsymbol{\theta}) \prod_{i=1}^{n} f_i(x_i; \alpha_i), \tag{II.6.83}$$

where $\boldsymbol{\alpha} = (\alpha_1, \ldots, \alpha_n)$ is the vector of marginals parameters and $\boldsymbol{\theta}$ is the vector of copula parameters.

From (II.6.83) we obtain the log likelihood function

$$\ln L(\boldsymbol{\alpha}, \boldsymbol{\theta}; \mathbf{x}_1, \ldots, \mathbf{x}_T) = \sum_{t=1}^{T} \left(\ln c(F_1(x_{1t}; \alpha_1), \ldots, F_n(x_{nt}; \alpha_n); \boldsymbol{\theta}) + \sum_{i=1}^{n} \ln f_i(x_{it}; \alpha_i) \right),$$
$$\tag{II.6.84}$$

where $\mathbf{x}_t = (x_{1t}, \ldots, x_{nt})$ is the row vector of observations on the n random variables at time t in a sample of time series on the variables. We can write (II.6.84) in the form

$$\ln L(\boldsymbol{\alpha}, \boldsymbol{\theta}; \mathbf{x}_1, \ldots, \mathbf{x}_T) = \sum_{t=1}^{T} \ln c(F_1(x_{1t}; \alpha_1), \ldots, F_n(x_{nt}; \alpha_n); \boldsymbol{\theta}) + \sum_{i=1}^{n} \sum_{t=1}^{T} \ln f_i(x_{it}; \alpha_i),$$
$$\tag{II.6.85}$$

and this shows that it is possible to maximize the log likelihood (II.6.84) in two *separate* steps as follows:

1. Calibrate the parameters for each marginal density, individually, using MLE in the usual way.[29] That is, find each $\hat{\alpha}_i$ in the vector of maximum likelihood estimates $\hat{\boldsymbol{\alpha}}$ by solving

$$\max_{\alpha_i} \sum_{t=1}^{T} \ln f_i(x_{it}; \alpha_i), \quad \text{for } i = 1, \ldots, n. \tag{II.6.86}$$

---

[27] This is defined in the next subsection, following Nelsen (2006: Section 5.5).
[28] See Bouyé et al. (2000).
[29] See Section I.3.6 for further details.

2. Calibrate the copula parameters by solving

$$\max_{\boldsymbol{\theta}} \sum_{t=1}^{T} \ln c\left(F_1(x_{1t}; \hat{\alpha}_1), \ldots, F_n(x_{nt}; \hat{\alpha}_n); \boldsymbol{\theta}\right). \qquad (\text{II.6.87})$$

EXAMPLE II.6.4: CALIBRATION OF COPULAS

Figure II.6.14 shows a scatter plot of daily percentage returns on the Vftse 30-day volatility index on the vertical axis and the daily percentage returns on the FTSE 100 index along the horizontal axis.[30] The data period is from 2 January 2004 to 29 December 2006, so 765 data points are shown. Use these data to calibrate (a) the Student t copula and (b) the Clayton copula. In each case assume the marginals are Student t distributed.

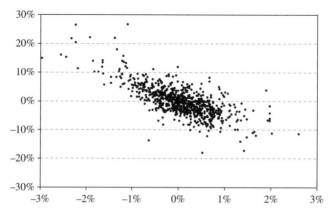

Figure II.6.14   Scatter plot of FTSE 100 index and Vftse index returns, 2004–2006

SOLUTION   The spreadsheet for this example first calibrates the marginals by:

(i)   finding the sample mean and standard deviation of the two returns series;
(ii) standardizing the returns to have zero mean and unit variance and then using maximum likelihood to fit a standardized t distribution to each standardized returns series.

We find that the calibrated parameters for the marginals are as shown in Table II.6.4.

Table II.6.4   Calibrated parameters for Student t marginals

Series	Mean	Standard deviation	Degrees of freedom
FTSE 100	0.04%	0.68%	6.18
Vftse	−0.02%	5.26%	5.02

Now we calibrate the copula parameters. First consider the Student t copula, case (a). The bivariate Student t copula has two parameters: the correlation ϱ and the degrees of freedom v. We could calibrate ϱ by using its relationship with a rank correlation, but we

---

[30] See Section III.4.7 for more details on volatility indices, their construction and futures and options on volatility indices.

must use MLE at least for calibrating the degrees of freedom. Hence, in this example we compare the calibration of the copula parameters under two different approaches:

(i) full MLE – calibrate both ϱ and v simultaneously using MLE;
(ii) calibrate ϱ first using the relationship (II.6.79) with Spearman's rho and then use MLE to calibrate v.

In the spreadsheet the reader can see that:

- under approach (i) we obtain $\hat{\varrho} = -0.723$ and $\hat{v} = 5.836$ with a log likelihood of 296.08;
- under approach (ii) we obtain $\hat{\varrho} = -0.706$, since Spearman's rho is estimated as -0.689, and $\hat{v} = 5.325$ with a log likelihood of $295.62;$[31]

Of course full MLE gives the highest likelihood because it is maximized by changing two parameters, whilst only one parameter is allowed to change in the other optimizations. In fact, for the bivariate case it is usually fairly robust to perform the MLE on both steps simultaneously. It is only when we move to higher dimensions that the computational complexity of simultaneous parameter calibration becomes a problem. In particular, maximum likelihood optimization algorithms on multivariate elliptical copulas of high dimension can become difficult to manage as the number of correlation parameters grows. The likelihood surface can become quite flat and then the location of a global optimum is not so easy. In this case it may be better to fix each pairwise correlation using either (II.6.78) or (II.6.79) and then calibrate only the degrees of freedom using MLE.

For the Clayton copula the optimization yields $\hat{\alpha} = 1.579$ with a log likelihood of only 272.51. (In the spreadsheet we can use -1 times the Vftse return, to obtain positive lower tail dependency as required in the Clayton copula.)

Finally, we remark that it is possible to calibrate a copula without specifying the marginals at all. We simply transform the returns into observations on uniform variables using the *empirical* marginal returns distributions and then base the MLE of the copula parameters on the copula density (II.6.18). This is the *canonical maximum likelihood* approach referred to above. It has the distinct advantage that the choice of best-fitting copula will not be influenced by the choice of parametric form for the marginals.

II.6.6.3 How to Choose the Best Copula

A straightforward way to determine which copula provides the best fit to the data is to compare the values of the optimized likelihood function, as we have done in the previous subsection. But the more parameters in the copula, the higher the likelihood tends to be. So to reward parsimony in the copula specification the *Akaike information criterion* (AIC) or the *Bayesian information criterion* (BIC) can be applied. The AIC is defined as

$$AIC = 2k - 2\ln L, \tag{II.6.88}$$

where $\ln L$ is the optimized value of the log likelihood function and k is the number of parameters to be estimated; and the BIC is defined as

$$BIC = T^{-1}(k\ln T - 2\ln L), \tag{II.6.89}$$

where T is the number of data points.[32] Then the copula that yields the lowest value of the AIC or the BIC is considered to be the best fit.

---

[31] You need to apply the solver again as shown in the spreadsheet.
[32] See Section II.8.3.1 for further details.

Alternatively, we could measure the goodness of fit between the fitted copula and the *empirical copula*. To define the empirical copula consider a sample of size T on two random variables X and Y. Denote the paired observations by (x_t, y_t) for $t = 1, \ldots, T$. Now individually order the observations on X and Y in increasing order of magnitude. That is, set $x^{(1)} = \min(x_1, \ldots, x_T)$, then $x^{(2)}$ is the second smallest observation in the sample on X, and so on until $x^{(T)} = \max(x_1, \ldots, x_T)$. These are called the sample *order statistics*; the order statistics for the sample on Y are defined analogously.

Now the *empirical copula distribution function* is defined as

$$\hat{C}\left(\frac{i}{T}, \frac{j}{T}\right) = \frac{\text{Number of pairs } (x, y) \text{ such that } x \le x^{(i)} \text{ and } y \le y^{(j)}}{T}, \tag{II.6.90}$$

where $x^{(i)}$ and $y^{(j)}$ are the order statistics from the sample. When there are ties it is often easier to compute the empirical copula distribution by cumulating the *empirical copula density*, which is defined as

$$\hat{c}\left(\frac{i}{T}, \frac{j}{T}\right) = \begin{cases} T^{-1}, & \text{if } \{x^{(i)}, y^{(j)}\} \text{ is an element of the sample,} \\ 0, & \text{otherwise.} \end{cases} \tag{II.6.91}$$

Table II.6.5 illustrates the calculation of first the density and then the distribution of the empirical copula of the sample used in Examples II.6.1 and II.6.2. The observations on

Table II.6.5   Empirical copula density and distribution

		Empirical copula density									
		−20	0	10	10	20	50	50	50	60	90
		0.1	0.2	0.3	0.4	0.5	0.6	0.7	0.8	0.9	1
−80	0.1	0.1	0	0	0	0	0	0	0	0	0
−10	0.2	0	0	0.1	0	0	0	0	0	0	0
10	0.3	0	0	0.1	0	0	0	0	0	0.1	0
10	0.4	0	0	0	0	0	0	0	0	0	0
20	0.5	0	0	0	0	0	0.1	0	0	0	0
30	0.6	0	0.1	0	0	0	0	0	0	0	0
40	0.7	0	0	0	0	0	0.1	0.1	0	0	0
40	0.8	0	0	0	0	0	0	0	0	0	0
50	0.9	0	0	0	0	0.1	0	0	0	0	0
60	1	0	0	0	0	0	0	0	0	0	0.1

		Empirical copula distribution									
		−20	0	10	10	20	50	50	50	60	90
		0.1	0.2	0.3	0.4	0.5	0.6	0.7	0.8	0.9	1
−80	0.1	0.1	0.1	0.1	0.1	0.1	0.1	0.1	0.1	0.1	0.1
−10	0.2	0.1	0.1	0.2	0.2	0.2	0.2	0.2	0.2	0.2	0.2
10	0.3	0.1	0.1	0.3	0.3	0.3	0.3	0.3	0.3	0.4	0.4
10	0.4	0.1	0.1	0.3	0.3	0.3	0.3	0.3	0.3	0.4	0.4
20	0.5	0.1	0.1	0.3	0.3	0.3	0.4	0.4	0.4	0.5	0.5
30	0.6	0.1	0.2	0.4	0.4	0.4	0.5	0.5	0.5	0.6	0.6
40	0.7	0.1	0.2	0.4	0.4	0.4	0.6	0.7	0.7	0.8	0.8
40	0.8	0.1	0.2	0.4	0.4	0.4	0.6	0.7	0.7	0.8	0.8
50	0.9	0.1	0.2	0.4	0.4	0.5	0.7	0.8	0.8	0.9	0.9
60	1	0.1	0.2	0.4	0.4	0.5	0.7	0.8	0.8	0.9	1

X and Y are listed in increasing order. Then each cell in the empirical copula density in Table II.6.5 is either 0, if there is no observation in the sample corresponding to the order statistics in the row and column, or, since there are 10 observations in the sample, 0.1 if there is such an observation. Note that exactly 10 pairs in the copula density have the value 0.1, since they must sum to 1 over the sample, and when there are tied pairs we insert 0.1 only for the first pair listed.

The empirical copula distribution is just the sum of all the copula density values up to and including that element. For instance, at the point 0.4 for X and 0.6 for Y, the copula distribution takes the value 0.4, indicated in the table by underlining. This is because the sum of the copula density elements up to and including that point (indicated by the dotted line in the copula density table) is 0.4.

To select a parametric copula based on goodness of fit to the empirical copula we compute the *root mean square error*, i.e. the square root of the sum of the squared differences between the empirical copula distribution and the fitted copula. Then the best-fit copula is the one that has the smallest root mean square error. But this criterion is not a statistical test, nor does it offer the possibility to emphasize the fit of the copula in the tails of the multivariate distribution. However, Malevergne and Sornette (2003) and Kole et al. (2007) explain how to extend the Kolmogorov–Smirnoff and Anderson–Darling distance metrics that were introduced in Section I.3.5.7 to test the goodness of fit of copulas.

II.6.7   SIMULATION WITH COPULAS

We have seen above that when calibrating copulas it is common to calibrate the marginals first, and then calibrate the copula. In simulation it is usually the other way around: generally speaking, first we simulate the dependence and then we simulate the marginals. And the wonderful thing about copulas is that the distributions of the marginals can all be different, and different from the copula. Hence, the random variables do not need to be themselves normally distributed for their dependence to be modelled using the normal copula; and similar remarks apply to any other distribution family. For instance, in Examples II.6.6 and II.6.7 below the two random variables have gamma marginal distributions, but we still apply the normal copula to them. This technique of simulation in two steps, separately imposing the copula and then the marginals, will be used in Section II.6.8.1 and in Chapter IV.4 to simulate returns for use in Monte Carlo VaR models.

In this section we describe two simulation algorithms, the first for simulation based on a copula with arbitrary marginals and the second for simulating from multivariate normal or Student t distributions. The empirical examples are in the workbook labelled 'Copula Simulations'.

II.6.7.1   Using Conditional Copulas for Simulation

Suppose the joint distribution of $X_1, \ldots, X_n$ is represented by n marginal distributions $F_i(x_i)$ and a copula $C(u_1, \ldots, u_n)$ where $x_i = F_i^{-1}(u_i)$. The following algorithm will generate simulations from such a joint distribution:

Alogrithm 1

1. Generate simulations $\{u_1, \ldots, u_n\}$ from independent uniform random variables.[33]
2. Fix $u_1^* = u_1$ and then apply the *inverse conditional copula* $C_{2|1}^{-1}$ to translate u_2 into u_2^*. That is, set

$$u_2^* = C_{2|1}^{-1}(u_2 | u_1^*).$$

   Repeat with u_1^* and u_2^* fixed, setting

$$u_3^* = C_{3|1,2}^{-1}(u_3 | u_1^*, u_2^*).$$

   Then repeat for the other variables. The simulations $\{u_1^*, \ldots, u_n^*\}$ are simulations on the copula with uniform marginals such as those shown in Figure II.6.15 below.
3. Feed the simulations $\{u_1^*, \ldots, u_n^*\}$ into the inverse marginal distributions to obtain a corresponding simulation $\{F_1^{-1}(u_1^*), \ldots, F_n^{-1}(u_n^*)\}$ on the random variables themselves, such as the simulations shown in Figure II.6.16 below.[34]

In this algorithm the Monte Carlo simulation process has been split into two separate parts. Step 2 concerns only the copula and step 3 concerns only the marginals. Hence, we can use this algorithm to simulate returns with any marginals we like, and with any copula we like.

This algorithm is used, for instance, to generate simulations from Archimedean copulas. However, it becomes rather inefficient as the dimensions increase. So how do we simulate from higher-dimensional distributions? Simulation from standard multivariate normal and Student t distributions is simple, as explained in the next subsection. Simulation from higher-dimensional Archimedean copulas is best performed using the *Marshall and Olkin* algorithm.[35]

II.6.7.2   Simulation from Elliptical Copulas

When the marginals and the copula are derived from the *same* joint elliptical density we can very easily achieve the result of step 3 above directly from step 1. There is no need for step 2 to precede step 3. To illustrate, let us assume the joint distribution is either multivariate standard normal or multivariate Student t so that we have marginals

$$F_i(x_i) = \begin{cases} \Phi(x_i), & \text{for the multivariate standard normal distribution,} \\ t_\nu(x_i), & \text{for the multivariate Student's } t \text{ distribution.} \end{cases}$$

Now we use the *Cholesky matrix* of the covariance matrix (which is defined in Section I.2.5.2) in the following algorithm to simulate a set of correlated multivariate normal or multivariate Student t returns.

Alogrithm 2

1. Generate simulations $\{u_1, \ldots, u_n\}$ from independent uniform random variables.
2. Set $x_i = F_i^{-1}(u_i)$ and apply the Cholesky matrix of the covariance matrix to $\{x_1, \ldots, x_n\}$, , to obtain a simulation $\{x_1^*, \ldots, x_n^*\}$.[36]

---

[33] For example, in Excel, use the RAND() function.
[34] From Section II.6.3.1 we know that for any set $\{x_1, \ldots, x_n\}$ of independent random variables with marginal distributions $F_i(x_i)$, the marginals are uniformly distributed.
[35] See algorithm 5.48 of McNeil et al. (2005).
[36] The application of the Cholesky matrix to generate correlated simulations is explained, with empirical examples, in Section I.5.7.4.

3. If required, set $u_i^* = F_i(x_i^*)$ to obtain a simulation $\{u_1^*, \ldots, u_n^*\}$ from the copula alone, with uniform marginals.

We remark that if we choose, we may also use the inverse conditional copula as outlined in Algorithm 1: the result will be the same. This fact is illustrated for the case $n = 2$ in the spreadsheet used to generate Figure II.6.15. Figures II.6.15(a) and II.6.15(b) depict simulations from the bivariate normal and bivariate Student t copula with seven degrees of freedom when the correlation is 0.7. The calculations are performed using steps 1 and 2 of Algorithm 1, then again using steps 1, 2 and 3 of Algorithm 2. Readers can verify by looking at the spreadsheet that the results are identical.[37] The advantage of using the conditional copula algorithm 1 is that we have the freedom to specify different types of distributions for the marginals than for the copula. For instance, we could use a normal copula with Student t marginals.

Whilst this relatively simple simulation approach produces accurate normal copula simulations, there are some problems with the Student t copula samples simulated in this way. If we try to re-calibrate a Student t copula to such a sample it is not possible to recover the degrees of freedom of the copula, or indeed of the second marginal, accurately. However, the Marshall-Olkin algorithm does produce accurate simulations. Hence, it should be used even for the Student t copula. The spreadsheet labelled 'T (Marshall-Olkin)' in the Copula Simulations Excel workbook kindly provided by a reader, Peter Hoadley, implements this algorithm for the Student t copula.

II.6.7.3   Simulation with Normal and Student t Copulas

It is all very well simulating from the copula with uniform marginals as we have done in Figure II.6.15, but the usual aim of risk analysis is to simulate the returns on financial assets, not uniformly distributed random variables. This will be done in the following subsection.

Figure II.6.16 depicts simulations from (a) bivariate standard normal variables; (b) standard normal marginals with a Student t copula; (c) normal copula with Student t marginals; (d) Student t copula with Student t marginals; and (e) Clayton copula with normal marginals. These are based on the same random numbers and the same copula parameters as those used to generate Figure II.6.15. That is, we have drawn 1000 uniform simulations and applied the copula using a correlation of 0.7 for the normal and t copulas, seven degrees of freedom in the t copula and $\alpha = 2$ for the Clayton copula. This produces the results shown in Figure II.6.15, and then we apply the appropriate inverse marginal distributions to translate the scatter plots in Figure II.6.15 into those shown in Figure II.6.16.

In the spreadsheet for Figure II.6.16, changing the parameters will change the shape of the simulations from the bivariate normal and Student t copulas.[38] In Figure II.6.16(d) the degrees of freedom in the copula and the marginals are different.[39] Thus whilst case (a) is easiest to generate using Algorithm 2, for the other cases Algorithm 1 must be used. As expected, the Student t copula produces a sample that has heavier tails than the simulated sample from the normal copula. Also the Student t marginals have a great influence on the dispersion and leptokurtosis in the sample. Note that case (e) will be discussed in detail in the next subsection.

---

[37] Identical random numbers are used to draw all scatter plots in Figure II.6.15. Figure II.6.15(c) is a simulation from a Clayton copula with $\alpha = 2$. See Section II.6.7.4 for a discussion of this figure.

[38] The spreadsheet also reports the empirical correlations derived from the scatter plots. This is for comparison: for example it helps us to choose a Clayton parameter roughly corresponding to the chosen level of correlation in the other copulas.

[39] We have used 7 degrees of freedom for the copula and 5 degrees of freedom for the marginals in these figures.

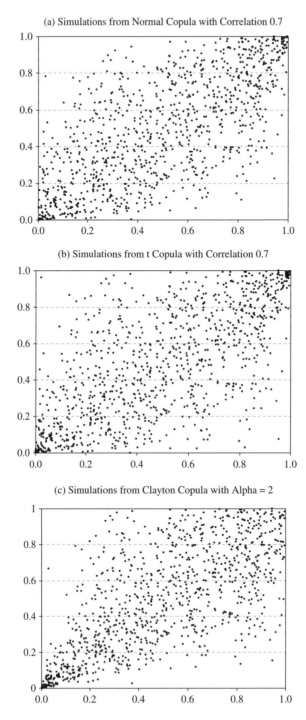

Figure II.6.15   Uniform simulations from three bivariate copulas

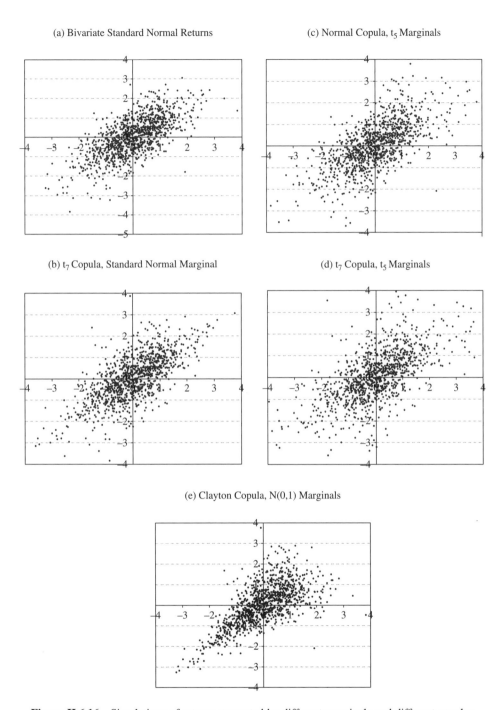

Figure II.6.16 Simulations of returns generated by different marginals and different copulas

II.6.7.4   Simulation from Archimedean Copulas

For a bivariate Archimedean copula we use the following simulation algorithm, which is equivalent to the bivariate case of Algorithm 1:

1. Generate independent random numbers $\{u_1, v\}$.
2. Set $u_2 = C_{2|1}^{-1}(v|u_1)$, so that $\{u_1, u_2\}$ are simulations on the copula with uniform marginals.
3. Find the corresponding simulations on the random variables using the marginals, as $\{F_1^{-1}(u_1), F_2^{-1}(u_2)\}$.

Hence, to simulate from an Archimedean copula we must specify the inverse conditional distributions of the copula. From (II.6.73) the inverse of the Clayton copula conditional distribution is

$$u_2 = C_{2|1}^{-1}(v|u_1) = \left(1 + u_1^{-\alpha}\left(v^{-\alpha/(1+\alpha)} - 1\right)\right)^{-1/\alpha}. \tag{II.6.92}$$

There is no explicit form for the inverse of the Gumbel copula conditional distribution. Instead we use the implicit relationship for u_2 in terms of the independent random numbers $\{u_1, v\}$:

$$v = C_{2|1}(u_2|u_1)$$

$$= u_1^{-1}(-\ln u_1)^{\delta-1}\left[(-\ln u_1)^\delta + (-\ln u_2)^\delta\right]^{(1-\delta)/\delta} \exp\left(-\left[(-\ln u_1)^\delta + (-\ln u_2)^\delta\right]^{1/\delta}\right).$$

Figures II.6.15(c) and II.6.16(e) illustrate simulations from the bivariate Clayton copulas, first with uniform marginals and then with standard normal marginals. We assumed a Pearson's correlation of 0.7 for the other scatter plots so to draw comparisons we set $\alpha = 2$ in (II.6.92).[40] The lower tail dependence is clearly apparent in the Clayton simulations.

To generate Figure II.6.16(e) we have translated the simulations on the Clayton copula with uniform marginals, shown in Figure II.6.15(c), into simulations on variables with standard normal marginals. Of course, these variables will not have a bivariate normal distribution. The Clayton copula imbues the standard normal marginal returns with strong lower tail dependence, as is evident from the scatter plot in Figure II.6.16(e).

II.6.8   MARKET RISK APPLICATIONS

In this section we describe three applications of copulas to market risk analysis. Section II.6.8.1 shows how copulas are used in Monte Carlo models to capture more realistic value-at-risk estimates than those obtained under the assumption that the returns on risk factors (or assets) have multivariate normal distributions. Section II.6.8.2 describes how copulas are used to aggregate distributions of portfolio returns (or P&L). This way we can obtain an aggregate VaR that is more precise than simply summing the individual VaRs. Then Section II.6.8.3 explains how copulas are applied to portfolio optimization to derive asset allocations based on returns distributions that are more general than the multivariate normal.

---

[40] By the correspondence given in Section II.6.4.1, $\alpha = 2$ corresponds to a Kendall's tau of 0.5. Note that Kendall's tau is often lower than Pearson's correlation.

II.6.8.1   Value-at-Risk Estimation

In Chapter IV.4 we describe how Monte Carlo simulation is used to estimate the VaR of a portfolio. In the Monte Carlo (MC) VaR model we simulate a large number of returns (or P&L) on all the risk factors of the portfolio over the risk horizon of the model. Then we apply the risk factor mapping to each set of simulations to derive the return (or P&L) on the portfolio. Finally we estimate the VaR as a lower percentile of the simulated distribution of portfolio returns (or P&L).

In this subsection we show how the simulations from bivariate copulas that were derived in Section II.6.7 can be extended to simulate the MC VaR of a simple portfolio with two assets or risk factors. The Student t copula allows the returns to have a tail dependence that is not captured by the multivariate normal distribution. And by using a Clayton or Gumbel copula instead of a correlation matrix to represent the dependence between returns, the simulated portfolio distribution can reflect asymmetric tail dependence.

EXAMPLE II.6.5: VaR WITH SYMMETRIC AND ASYMMETRIC TAIL DEPENDENCE

Consider a portfolio containing two assets with returns that have zero mean normal distributions with volatilities 20% and 15%, respectively. Use Monte Carlo simulation to estimate the 1% 10-day VaR of a portfolio with 75% of capital invested in asset 1 and 25% in asset 2. Assume that the returns dependence is represented by:

(a) a normal copula with correlation 0.7;
(b) a Student t copula with seven degrees of freedom and a correlation of 0.7;
(c) a Clayton copula with $\alpha = 2$.

SOLUTION   Figures II.6.16(a), II.6.16(b) and II.6.16(e) depict simulations from the required distributions. Hence, to find the portfolio VaR we apply the portfolio weights to these simulations and estimate the empirical 1% quantile of the simulated portfolio return distribution. This gives the 1% daily VaR as a percentage of the portfolio value.

The calculations are performed in the spreadsheet labelled VaR in the 'Copula Simulations' workbook, and the results shown in Table II.6.6 are based on 1000 simulations only. Of course, more simulations should be used in practice, but we restrict our result to just 1000 simulations so that the workbook does not become too large. In every simulation the Student t copula gives the largest VaR and the normal copula the smallest VaR.[41] For the specific simulations shown in the table, the Student t VaR is approximately 8% greater than the normal VaR.

Table II.6.6   1% 10-day VaR based on different dependence assumptions

Normal dependence	9.03%
Student t dependence	9.78%
Clayton	9.25%

---

[41] The VaR estimates shown in the table are based on one particular set of simulations, but the corresponding figures in the spreadsheets change each time the simulations are repeated, for instance by pressing F9.

Chapter IV.4 presents further empirical examples of the use of copulas in Monte Carlo VaR, applied to different types of portfolios, and the interested reader is referred there for more specific details of the MC VaR methodology.

II.6.8.2   Aggregation and Portfolio Diversification

In Section I.6.3 we introduced the portfolio diversification effect as the ability to reduce portfolio variance whenever asset returns have less than perfect correlation. More generally, diversification effects are present whenever portfolio returns have less than perfect dependence. In this subsection we assume the dependence between the returns distributions on two portfolios has been captured using a copula and show how this allows us to account for diversification effects when aggregating returns distributions.

Aggregating distributions is not only important for portfolio management; it is also one of the basic problems in regulatory or economic risk capital analysis. For instance, to obtain a figure for their total risk capital banks often simply *add up* the market, credit and operational VaRs from different activities, since this total provides an upper bound to the total VaR. More generally, when VaR is estimated within one of these broad classes, we take account of the diversification effects between different portfolios when aggregating their VaR. Then the total VaR, which accounts for the dependence between the returns distributions, may be calculated from a percentile of this aggregate distribution.

For instance, consider a bank that has positions in German stocks and bonds. Suppose we know the VaR, or another risk estimate, for German bonds because we have calculated a returns distribution based on our exposures to German bonds; and suppose we also have a returns distribution and therefore a risk estimate corresponding to the German stock positions. Now we want to know what is the risk arising from *both* these exposures in Germany, i.e. what is the aggregate risk, taking account of any diversification effects between stock and bond returns.

To answer this we phrase the problem as follows. Suppose we know the distributions of two random variables X_1 and X_2. Then what is the *distribution of the sum* $X_1 + X_2$? If the variables are jointly normal the answer is easy: the sum of two normal variables is another normal variable. Thus we know the whole distribution if we know the mean and variance of $X_1 + X_2$, and we know the variance of $X_1 + X_2$ if we know the correlation of X_1 and X_2.

The sum of normal variables is another normal variable. So the assumption of multivariate normal returns is very convenient. We can describe the entire distribution of the aggregate return on a portfolio: we only need to use the rules for expectation and variance of a sum of random variables to obtain its mean and variance. There is also a unique dependence measure, i.e. Pearson's correlation. But if we depart from the assumption of multivariate normality the process of aggregating returns into portfolio returns, and aggregating portfolio returns into larger portfolio returns, becomes more complex. In this subsection we describe how copulas can be used to aggregate returns, providing empirical comparisons of the distribution of aggregate returns based on different copulas.

First we need to introduce some mathematics. For two continuous random variables X_1 and X_2 the distribution of their sum may be derived from only their joint density function $f(x_1, x_2)$, using the *convolution integral* (II.6.93). Specifically, write $Y = X_1 + X_2$ and denote the density of Y by $g(y)$. Then

$$g(y) = \int_{x_1} f(x_1, y - x_1)\, dx_1 = \int_{x_2} f(y - x_2, x_2)\, dx_2. \qquad \text{(II.6.93)}$$

Thus in order to derive the distribution of the sum of two random variables, we need to know their joint density function, assuming this exists.

If we know the marginal distributions of two returns X_1 and X_2 and a copula function then we can obtain the joint density $f(x_1, x_2)$ using (II.6.12). Then we apply (II.6.93) to obtain the density of their sum.[42]

The density of a sum $X_1 + \ldots + X_n$ of n random variables is obtained by generalizing (II.6.93) to more than two variables. For instance, if $f(x_1, x_2, x_3)$ denotes the joint density of X_1, X_2 and X_3, then

$$g(y) = \int_{x_2} \int_{x_1} f(x_1, x_2, y - x_1 - x_2) dx_1 dx_2 \qquad \text{(II.6.94)}$$

gives the density of $Y = X_1 + X_2 + X_3$, and if $f(x_1, x_2, x_3, x_4)$ denotes the joint density of X_1, X_2, X_3 and X_4 then

$$g(y) = \int_{x_3} \int_{x_2} \int_{x_1} f(x_1, x_2, x_3, y - x_1 - x_2 - x_3) dx_1 dx_2 dx_3 \qquad \text{(II.6.95)}$$

gives the density of $Y = X_1 + X_2 + X_3 + X_4$. For example, if

$$f(x_1, x_2, x_3) = \exp(-(x_1 + x_2 + x_3)), \quad x_1 > 0, x_2 > 0, x_3 > 0,$$

then[43]

$$g(y) = \int_0^y \int_0^{y - x_3} \exp(-y) \, dx_2 dx_3 = \tfrac{1}{2} y^2 \exp(-y), \quad y > 0.$$

In the next example we apply the convolution integral (II.6.93) to find the density of the sum of two random variables when their marginals have (different) gamma distributions and their copula is a normal copula. Later we shall extend this example to assume the dependence is represented by a normal mixture copula.

EXAMPLE II.6.6: AGGREGATION UNDER THE NORMAL COPULA

Consider two random variables X_1 and X_2 with the marginal densities shown in Figure II.6.17. Use the normal copula, with (a) correlation 0.5 and (b) correlation -0.5, to find their joint density. Hence, find the density of X_1 and X_2 and compare the two densities that are obtained under the two assumptions for correlation.

SOLUTION   The spreadsheet for this example calculates the normal copula density (II.6.36), applies it in (II.6.12) to obtain the joint density function and then uses convolution to obtain the density of the sum. As expected, since the variance of a sum of two random variables increases with their correlation, the effect of increasing the correlation is to increase the variance of this density. The density of the sum is shown in Figure II.6.18 for the two different values of correlation.

---

[42] In the empirical examples in the next subsection we apply a discrete version of the convolution integral (II.6.93). That is, for some increasing sequence $0 < x_1 < \ldots < x_N < m$ and for each m covering the range of Y we compute $P(Y = m) = P(X_1 = m - x_1 \text{ and } X_2 = x_1) + P(X_1 = m - x_2 \text{ and } X_2 = x_2) + \ldots + P(X_1 = m - x_N \text{ and } X_2 = x_N)$.
[43] The limits here follow from the fact that the integrand is 0 when $x_3 > y$ or $x_2 > y - x_3$.

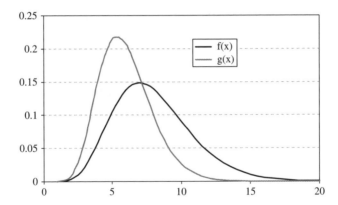

Figure II.6.17   Marginal densities of two gamma distributed random variables

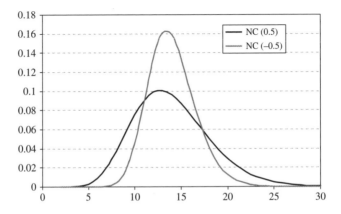

Figure II.6.18   Distribution of the sum for different correlation assumptions

EXAMPLE II.6.7: AGGREGATION UNDER THE NORMAL MIXTURE COPULA

Calculate the density of $X_1 + X_2$ when the marginal densities are as in the previous example but now use a normal mixture copula (II.6.43) for the aggregation. Assume the parameters of the normal mixture copula are $\pi = 0.3$, $\varrho_1 = 0.5$ and $\varrho_2 = -0.5$.

SOLUTION   The spreadsheet for this example produces the three densities of $X_1 + X_2$ depicted in Figure II.6.19. These are obtained using different assumptions about dependencies between X and Y – specifically:

- NC(ϱ) assumes a normal copula with parameter ϱ;
- NMC($\pi, \varrho_1, \varrho_2$) assume a normal mixture copula with parameters ($\pi, \varrho_1, \varrho_2$)

The spreadsheet demonstrates that the density of the sum labelled NMC can be obtained in two equivalent ways: either we find the normal mixture copula and then apply convolution to the joint density based on this copula, or we take the mixture of the two densities that are obtained using the two normal copulas. The result is the same either way. Readers may

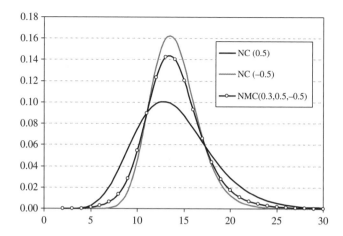

Figure II.6.19 Density of the sum of the random variables in Figure II.6.17 under different dependence assumptions

change the parameters in this example to see the effect on the copula, the joint density and the density of the sum.

Having obtained the aggregate distribution, i.e. the distribution of the sum of several random variables, as illustrated in the two previous examples, it is a straightforward matter to estimate the risk of the aggregate position. For instance, we could find the standard deviation to estimate the volatility, or we could find a lower percentile of the aggregate distribution to estimate the VaR, or we could apply any other downside risk metric.

Finally, we remark that the aggregation of returns distributions using copulas has applications to performance measurement as well as risk measurement, simply by applying one of the risk adjusted performance measures described in Section I.6.5 to the aggregate distribution. An empirical example of this is provided in the next subsection.

II.6.8.3   Using Copulas for Portfolio Optimization

To find the optimal mix of risky assets in a portfolio, portfolio optimizers can apply any one of the performance measures described in Section I.6.5 to a distribution of portfolio returns. As explained in Chapter II.1, this distribution can be generated using either

- simulation of a current weighted time series of portfolio returns, or
- an assumption that the asset returns have a multivariate normal distribution, in which case we only need to know the returns covariance matrix.

The advantage of the first approach is that the portfolio returns distribution, and hence the performance measure for the optimal portfolio, is based on experienced rather than assumed behaviour of the asset returns. The disadvantage of the first approach is that we need to have long time series of returns on each asset, which may not be available. The second approach requires only the asset returns covariance matrix, and this may be estimated using only recent historical data – or indeed, it could be set without using historical data at all – it could be based on the personal view of the portfolio manager. However, the assumption of multivariate normal asset returns is not very realistic, and the second approach can lead to portfolio allocations that are very unstable over time. Consequently, considerable rebalancing costs can arise when following allocations recommended by such optimizers.

In this subsection we outline how a multivariate copula can be used in portfolio optimization with the aim of increasing the stability of optimal allocations. Note that if the normal or t copula is used, the optimization will still be based on a correlation matrix. But the importance difference here is that we are now free to specify the marginals to have their empirical distribution, or any parametric distribution that fits the sample data well. The normality constraint for the marginals is no longer necessary.

Suppose $X_1, \ldots, X_n$ are returns on n financial assets that may be included in a portfolio, and let $w_1, \ldots, w_n$ denote the portfolio weights, i.e. the proportion of capital invested in each asset. The density function of cX, where c is a constant, is just c^{-1} times the density function of X.[44] Hence the marginal density of X_i can be translated into a marginal density of $w_i X_i$ by multiplying the density of X_i by w_i^{-1}, for $i = 1, \ldots, n$. Hence the convolution integral introduced in Section II.6.8.2 can be applied to construct the density of a portfolio return $w_1 X_1 + \ldots + w_n X_n$. Such a density will also depend on the copula and the marginals that are used to model the joint distribution of $X_1, \ldots, X_n$.

Suppose we are given the marginal densities of the asset returns and a copula. For some fixed set of portfolio weights we construct the density of $w_1 X_1 + \ldots + w_n X_n$, as defined above. From this density we can derive a risk adjusted performance measure such as the Sharpe or Sortino ratios, a 'generalized' form of these, omega or kappa indices (see Section I.6.5 for a full description). Now we can change the portfolio weights, each time using the marginals and the copula to derive the portfolio returns density. Hence, we can find the optimal portfolio weights, i.e. those that maximize our performance metric.

We end this section with a simple empirical example, illustrating the method outlined above, based on the problem of an equity hedge fund that seeks improved risk adjusted performance by adding volatility as an asset. Equity implied volatility has a strong negative dependence with the underlying stock price, i.e. when the stock price decreases the volatility increases. Hence, the diversification effect of including volatility in the portfolio is attractive to many equity hedge funds.

EXAMPLE II.6.8: PORTFOLIO OPTIMIZATION WITH COPULAS

Student t marginals for the FTSE and Vftse indices were calibrated in Example II.6.4. Use these marginals and a normal copula with correlation -0.795, as in Example II.6.4, to find the portfolio of FTSE and Vftse that maximizes the Sharpe ratio. Assume the risk free rate of return is 5%. How does the correlation affect the result?

SOLUTION   The spreadsheet for this example performs the following calculations:

1. Compute the normal copula with correlation -0.795.
2. Use the copula and the marginals to compute the joint density of standardized returns, i.e. returns with zero mean and unit standard deviation.
3. For a fixed set of portfolio weights, compute the portfolio return.

---

[44] Since the distribution function of cX is $F(c^{-1}X)$, where $F(X)$ is the distribution of X.

4. Estimate the Sharpe ratio using the formula

$$\hat{\lambda} = \frac{\overline{R} - R_f}{s},$$
(II.6.96)

where $\overline{R}$ is the annualized sample mean return, s is the annualized sample standard deviation of returns and R_f is the risk free rate.

5. Use Excel Solver to find the portfolio weights that maximize the Sharpe ratio.

The result, when the correlation is −0.795, is that 91.4% of capital should be invested in the FTSE and 8.6% of capital invested in the Vftse.[45] The allocation to the Vftse is positive even though the mean–variance characteristics of the FTSE are far more favourable than the Vftse, as shown in Table II.6.4. Over the sample the FTSE index had an average annualized mean return of 10.52% with a volatility of 10.68%, whereas the Vftse had an average annualized mean return of –4.11% with volatility of 83.10%. So why should we include the Vftse in the portfolio at all? The reason is that even though returns on volatility are often negative, they have a very high negative correlation with equity. Thus adding volatility to the portfolio considerably reduces the portfolio volatility and the risk adjusted performance improves.

Finally, repeating the above for different values of the correlation produces the data used to construct Figure II.6.20. This illustrates how the optimal portfolio weight on the FTSE index and the optimal Sharpe ratio (SR) change as the correlation ranges between −0.95 and −0.05.[46] The more negative the correlation, the greater the potential gain from diversification into the Vftse. Thus the more weight is placed on the Vftse index and the higher the Sharpe ratio.

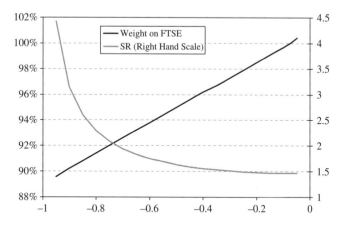

Figure II.6.20 Optimal weight on FTSE and Sharpe ratio vs FTSE–Vftse returns correlation

---

[45] At the time of writing this would necessitate over-the-counter trades, as no exchange traded fund on the Vftse exists and Vftse futures behave quite differently from the Vftse index – see Section III.5.5 for further explanation.
[46] We do not consider positive correlation, as this is empirically highly unlikely.

II.6.9   SUMMARY AND CONCLUSIONS

Since the seminal works of Embrechts et al. (2002, 2003) a large academic literature on copulas has been directed towards problems in financial risk management. All the major academic players in the field agree that copulas are essential for accurate modelling of financial risks. But, as is typical, the industry has been cautious to incorporate these new ideas into market risk models. This may be partly due to the level of difficulty usually associated with using copulas. Indeed, most academic papers require a pretty high level of abstract statistical knowledge.

The aim of this chapter is to bring copulas to the attention of a wider audience, to quantitative finance academics, postgraduate finance students and most of all to the practitioners who really do need copulas for accurate models of the behaviour of asset returns. Of course a considerable amount of theory is necessary, but I have tried to adopt a pedagogical approach, and so have provided numerous examples in Excel. My hope is that practitioners and students with a reasonable knowledge of statistics will gain confidence in using copulas and, through their application, progress in their theoretical understanding.

A good starting point for this chapter is actually Section II.3.3, with the summary of the 'pitfalls of correlation' described by Embrechts et al. (2002). The poor properties of linear correlation as a measure of association provide tremendous motivation for the reader to learn about copulas. The present chapter begins by introducing a general measure of association called *concordance* which is a more general concept of dependence than linear correlation. Empirical examples illustrate how to calculate two concordance metrics: *Spearman's rho* and *Kendall's tau*. These are introduced here because they play a useful role in calibrating copulas.

Then we follow with the formal definition of a copula distribution, its associated copula density and the fundamental theorem of Sklar (1959). This theorem allows us to 'build' joint distributions by first specifying the marginals and then specifying the copula. The presentation here focuses on the *conditional copula distribution*, showing how to derive it and providing several empirical examples. The conditional copula density is (usually) required for simulating random variables and for copula *quantile regression* analysis, which is discussed in detail in the next chapter.

The copulas that are implemented in the Excel spreadsheets are bivariate versions of the *normal copula* (which is also called the Gaussian copula), *Student t*, *normal mixture*, *Clayton* and *Gumbel* copulas. The first two are *implicit copulas* because they are derived from a known bivariate distribution. The last two are *Archimedean copulas*, which are constructed from a generator function. Any convex, monotonic decreasing function can be used to generate an Archimedean copula. Hence, there are a vast number of copulas that could be applied to a fixed pair of marginal distributions to generate a different joint distribution each time! The big question is: which is the 'best' copula? This is the subject of a considerable amount of ongoing research.

After explaining how to calibrate copulas and assess their goodness of fit to sample data we move on to the main risk management applications. The first application is *Monte Carlo simulation*, where we simulate returns that have a joint distribution characterized by any marginal distributions and any copula. Monte Carlo simulations are very widely used in risk management, from pricing and hedging options to portfolio risk assessment. Simulation is computationally burdensome, yet practitioners commonly view it as worthwhile because it is based on a realistic model of returns behaviour. In particular, we do not need to assume normality in Monte Carlo simulations. Structured Monte Carlo simulation may still be based on a correlation matrix if we assume the returns have an elliptical distribution, and if the joint distribution is a Student t then the returns will display symmetric tail dependence. However, most realistic models of returns behaviour have asymmetric tail dependence. For instance, the dependence between stock returns is greater during stressful periods, when many extreme negative returns are observed. We have provided empirical examples that show how the Clayton and Gumbel copulas capture asymmetric tail dependence. We chose these copulas because they are particularly simple one-parameter Archimedean copulas, but there are numerous other copulas with asymmetric tail dependence.

An immediate application of Monte Carlo simulation is of course to estimate *portfolio value at risk*. Instead of assuming that risk factor or asset returns have elliptical joint distributions, the use of copulas in simulations allows one to estimate portfolio VaR under virtually any assumptions about the marginal returns distributions and about the symmetric or asymmetric tail dependence in asset returns. Aggregation of distributions is based on a *convolution integral* whereby we derive the distribution of a sum of random variables from the marginal distributions of the variables and a copula. An immediate application of convolution on the joint distribution specified by a copula is risk aggregation. By successively deriving returns distributions of larger and larger portfolios and applying a risk metric (such as VaR) to each distribution, market risk analysts may provide senior managers with *aggregate risk assessments* of the various activities in a firm, and of the firm as a whole.

Many commercial *portfolio optimization* packages base allocations to risky assets on an empirical returns joint distribution, using historical data on all the assets in the investor's universe. The 'best' allocation is the one that produces a portfolio returns distribution that has the best performance metric, e.g. the highest Sharpe ratio. There are advantages in using an empirical returns joint distribution, because then we are not limited to the multivariate normality assumption of standard mean–variance analysis. Using an empirical distribution, all the characteristics of the joint distribution of returns on risky assets can influence the optimal allocation, not just the asset volatilities and correlations. However, a problem arises when no parametric form of joint distribution is fitted to the historical data, because the optimization can produce very unstable allocations over time. We have shown how copulas provide a very flexible tool for modelling this joint distribution. We do not need to assume that asset returns are multivariate normal, or even elliptical, to derive optimal allocations. Parametric portfolio optimization can take account of asymmetric tail dependence, for instance, if we use the simple Clayton copula.

During the last decade financial statisticians have developed copula theory in the directions that are useful for financial applications. Recognizing the fact that credit loss distributions are highly non-normal, it has now become a market standard to use copulas in credit risk analysis, for instance to price and hedge collateralized debt obligations. But copulas also have a wide variety of applications to market risk analysis, perhaps even more than they do in credit risk. Several of these applications have been described in this chapter. Yet the industry has been slow to change its established practice for market risk, where risk and performance metrics are still usually based on the assumption that asset returns have multivariate normal distributions.

II.7
Advanced Econometric Models

II.7.1 INTRODUCTION

A regression model is a tool that is rather like a pair of spectacles. Like spectacles, regression models allow you to see more clearly. Characteristics of the data that cannot be seen from simple graphs or by calculating basic sample statistics *can* be seen when we apply a regression model. Spectacles come in all shapes and sizes, and some are specifically designed to be worn for certain purposes. Likewise regression models come in many varieties and some models should only be applied to certain types of data. A standard multiple linear regression estimated using ordinary least squares (OLS) is like an ordinary pair of spectacles. It is fine when the data are in the right form and you do not want to see too much. But for special types of data we need to use a different type of model; for instance, when data are discrete we may use a probit or logit model. Also, like spectacles, some regression models are more powerful than others. For instance, non-linear regression, quantile regression, copula quantile regression or Markov switching regression models allow one to see far more than is possible using a simple linear regression.

We should *always* plot data before estimating a regression model. This is a golden rule that should never be overlooked. Forgetting to plot the data before prescribing and fitting the regression model is like an optician forgetting to do an eye test before prescribing the lenses and fitting the frames. A visual inspection of the data allows us to see details about the individual data and about the relationships between variables that will help us formulate the model, and to choose appropriate parameter estimation methods. For instance, we may notice a structural break or jump in the data and a simple tool for dealing with this is to include a dummy. A basic *dummy variable* takes the value 0 except during the unusual period, where it takes the value 1. Adding such a dummy to the regression is like having two constant terms. It gives the model the freedom to shift up during the unusual period and therefore it improves the fit. You may also, for any explanatory variable, add another explanatory variable equal to the product of the dummy and the variable. In other words, include all the values of the explanatory variable X *and* include another variable which is zero everywhere except during the unusual period when it takes the X values. This has the effect of allowing the slope coefficients to be different during the unusual period and will improve the fit further still.

Like the prior plotting of data, running an OLS linear regression is another elementary principle that we should adhere to. This is the first stage of building any regression model, except for probit and logit models where linear regression cannot be applied. Running an OLS regression is like putting on your ordinary spectacles. It allows you to gain some idea about the relationship between the variables. Then we may decide to use a more powerful model that allows us to see the relationship more clearly, but only if a relationship is already obvious from OLS.

The optimization of a standard linear regression by OLS is straightforward. We only need a very simple sort of engine to drive the model, like the engine of an old Citroën 2CV car. In fact, we do not even need to use a numerical method to estimate the coefficients because analytic solutions exist, i.e. the OLS formulae. But the optimization of more advanced regression models is not simple. Most use a form of maximum likelihood for parameter estimation and in some models, for instance in Markov switching models, the optimization engine for maximum likelihood estimation is extremely complex. A 2CV engine will no longer do the job.

We should only use a more advanced model *if* OLS has already indicated that there is a relationship there to model. Otherwise we are in danger of detecting spurious relationships that are merely an artefact of running a Ferrari rather than a 2CV engine on the model. To use yet another simile, when baking a cake there is no point in putting beautiful decorations on the icing unless you have ensured that the basic cake underneath is good . . . but enough! Let me move on to outline the ingredients of this chapter.

The next section provides a detailed introduction to quantile regression. *Linear quantile regression* is a natural extension of OLS regression where the optimization objective of minimizing the residual sum of squares is replaced by an asymmetric objective. Thus we estimate the regression lines that, rather than passing through the mean of the sample, divide the sample into two unequal parts. For instance, in the 0.1 quantile regression 10% of the data lie above the regression line. OLS regression only provides a prediction of the conditional mean, but finding several quantile regression lines gives a more complete picture of the joint distribution of the data. With linear quantile regression we can obtain predictions of all the quantiles of the conditional joint distribution. *Non-linear quantile regression* is harder, since it is based on a copula. A good understanding of Chapter II.6 on copulas is essential for understanding the subsections on *copula quantile regression*. Once this is understood the rest is plain sailing, and in Section II.7.3 we have provided several detailed Excel spreadsheets that implement all the standard copula quantile regressions in two separate case studies.

Section II.7.4 covers some advanced regression models, including *discrete choice models* which qualify as regression models only because they can be expressed in this form. But they cannot be estimated as a linear regression, because the dependent variable is a *latent variable*, i.e. an unobservable variable. The input data that are relevant to the dependent variable are just a series of flags, or zeros and ones. The actual dependent variable is a non-linear transformation of an unobservable probability, such as the probability of default. This may sound complicated, but these models are actually very simple to implement. We provide an Excel spreadsheet for estimating probit, logit and Weibull models in the context of credit default and hence compare the default probabilities that are estimated using different functional forms.

Section II.7.5 introduces *Markov switching models*. These models provide a very powerful pair of spectacles since they allow the data generation process for returns to switch as the market changes between regimes. They are incredibly useful for modelling financial data and may be applied to capture regime-specific behaviour in all financial markets. Equity, commodity and credit markets tend to have two very distinct regimes, one with high volatility that rules during a crisis or turbulent market and the other with a lower volatility that rules during typical market circumstances. Foreign exchange markets have less regime-specific behaviour and interest rates tend to have three regimes, one when interest rates are declining and the yield curve slopes downwards, one stable regime with a flat curve, and a third when interest rates are increasing and the yield curve slopes upwards. Since Markov switching models are rather complex, this section focuses on presenting an easy-to-read description of the model structure. But the engine that is used to optimize these models cannot be presented in Excel. Instead my PhD student Andreas Kaeck has allowed his EViews code to be made available on the CD. Many thanks, Andreas!

Section II.7.6 surveys the vast academic literature on the use of ultra high frequency data in regression analysis. After describing some useful sources of tic by tic data and how to deal with the errors that are often found in these data sets, we survey the *autoregressive conditional duration* models that attempt to capture the time between trades using an autoregressive framework that is similar to that of a GARCH volatility process. Much of the recent econometric research on the use of ultra high frequency data concerns the prediction of *realized volatility*. This is because the volume of trading on variance swaps has increased very rapidly over the last few years, and the ability to forecast realized volatility is important for pricing these instruments.[1] We do not survey the literature on point forecasts of high frequency returns since Neural networks, genetic algorithms and chaotic dynamics rather than econometric models are the statistical tools that are usually implemented in this case.[2] Section II.7.7 summarizes and concludes.

II.7.2 QUANTILE REGRESSION

Standard regression provides a prediction of the mean and variance of the dependent variable, Y, conditional on some given value of an associated independent variable X. Recall that when simple linear regression was introduced in Chapter I.4 we assumed that X and Y had a *bivariate normal* distribution. In that case we can infer everything about the conditional distribution of the dependent variable from the standard linear regression. That is, knowing only the conditional mean and variance, we know the whole conditional distribution. But more generally, when X and Y have an *arbitrary* joint distribution, the conditional mean and variance do not provide all the information we need to describe the conditional distribution of the dependent variable. The goal of quantile regression is to compute a family of regression curves, each corresponding to a different quantile of the conditional distribution of the dependent variable. This way we can build up a much more complete picture of the conditional distribution of Y given X.

The aims of this section are:[3]

- to explain the concept of quantile regression, introduced by Koenker and Basset (1978);
- following Bouyé and Salmon (2002) to describe the crucial role that conditional copula distributions play in non-linear quantile regression analysis; and
- to provide simple examples in Excel that focus on the useful risk management applications of quantile regression.

Two case studies are provided to illustrate the main concepts.

---

[1] See Section III.4.7 for further details on variance swaps.
[2] However, see Alexander (2001a: Chapter 13) for further details.
[3] Readers who wish to delve into this subject in more detail, though not with reference to copulas, are referred to the excellent text book by Koenker (2005).

II.7.2.1   Review of Standard Regression

For convenience we first summarize some basic facts about simple linear regression from Chapter I.4. Using the notation defined in Section I.4.2, the simple linear regression model may be written

$$Y = \alpha + \beta X + \varepsilon, \tag{II.7.1}$$

where the parameters α and β are constants, Y is the dependent variable, X is the independent variable and ε is an independent and identically distributed (i.i.d.) error term that is also independent of X. Since ε is an error we expect it to be zero – otherwise it would represent a systematic bias. So we assume that $E(\varepsilon) = 0$ and indeed, since ε is assumed to be independent of X, all conditional expectations of ε are also assumed to be zero. This means that taking conditional expectations of (II.7.1) gives

$$E(Y \mid X) = \alpha + \beta X. \tag{II.7.2}$$

In standard regression we assume that X and Y have a bivariate normal distribution. Then the conditional expectation of Y given some value for X is

$$E(Y \mid X) = E(Y) + \varrho \sqrt{\frac{V(Y)}{V(X)}} (X - E(X)), \tag{II.7.3}$$

where ϱ is the correlation between X and Y.[4] It is easy to show the conditional distribution $F(Y \mid X)$ is normal when X and Y are bivariate normal and also that

$$V(Y \mid X) = V(Y) \left(1 - \varrho^2\right).$$

Hence the simple linear regression model specifies the entire conditional distribution in this case.

Equating (II.7.2) and (II.7.3) gives

$$\beta = \varrho \sqrt{\frac{V(Y)}{V(X)}} = \frac{\mathrm{Cov}(X, Y)}{V(X)} \quad \text{and} \quad \alpha = E(Y) - \beta E(X). \tag{II.7.4}$$

Replacing (II.7.4) with sample estimates of the means and standard deviations and correlation of X and Y, based on some sample of size T, yields the familiar *ordinary least squares estimators* for the coefficients, i.e.

$$\hat{\beta} = \frac{s_{XY}}{s_X^2} \quad \text{and} \quad \hat{\alpha} = \overline{Y} - \hat{\beta}\overline{X}, \tag{II.7.5}$$

where $\overline{X}$ and $\overline{Y}$ denote the sample means, s_X^2 is the sample variance of X and s_{XY} is the sample covariance. Finally, in Section I.4.2 we showed that the OLS estimators $\hat{\alpha}$ and $\hat{\beta}$ are the solutions to the optimization problem

$$\min_{\alpha, \beta} \sum_{t=1}^{T} (Y_t - (\alpha + \beta X_t))^2. \tag{II.7.6}$$

In other words, we obtain the OLS estimators by *minimizing the residual sum of squares*.

---

[4] See Section I.3.4.6 for further details.

II.7.2.2   What is Quantile Regression?

In the simple linear regression model reviewed above we derived the conditional expectation and conditional variance of Y and, assuming the variables were bivariate normal, we completely specified the conditional distribution of the dependent variable. But if X and Y do not have a bivariate normal distribution then we need more than the conditional expectation and conditional variance to describe the conditional distribution $F(Y|X)$. Indeed, the most convenient way to describe the conditional distribution of the dependent variable is using its quantiles.

As a prelude to introducing the quantile regression equation, we now derive an expression for the *conditional quantiles* of Y given X, based on an arbitrary joint distribution. For the moment we still assume that X and Y are related by the simple linear model (II.7.1), although quantile regression has a straightforward extension to non-linear relationships between X and Y, as we shall see in Section II.7.2.5 below.

In quantile regression we still assume that the error is i.i.d. But now we must introduce a specific error distribution function denoted F_ε. Now consider the conditional quantiles of the simple linear regression model (II.7.1). Whilst the expectation of ε is still assumed to be zero because it is an error, its quantiles are not zero in general. Hence, when we take *quantiles* instead of expectations of the simple linear model (II.7.1), the error term no longer disappears.

Let $q \in (0, 1)$ and denote the q quantile of the error by $F_\varepsilon^{-1}(q)$. Also denote the conditional q quantile of the dependent variable, which is found from the inverse of $F(Y|X)$, by $F^{-1}(q|X)$. Now, taking conditional q quantiles of (II.7.1) yields

$$F^{-1}(q|X) = \alpha + \beta X + F_\varepsilon^{-1}(q|X). \qquad \text{(II.7.7)}$$

This is the simple linear *quantile regression model.*

In simple linear quantile regression we still aim to estimate a regression line through a scatter plot. In other words, we shall estimate the parameters α and β based on a paired sample on X and Y. But the difference between quantile regression and standard regression is that with standard regression coefficient estimates the regression line passes through the average or 'centre of gravity' of the points, whereas a quantile regression line will pass through a quantile of the points. For instance, when q is small, say $q = 0.1$, then the majority of points would lie *above* the q quantile regression line.

In Figure II.7.1 the black line is the median regression line, the solid grey line is the 0.1 quantile line and the dashed grey line is the 0.9 quantile line. Note that the quantile regression lines are not parallel. This fact is verified empirically in the case studies later in this chapter.

II.7.2.3   Parameter Estimation in Quantile Regression

We now explain how to estimate the coefficients α and β in the simple linear quantile regression model, given a sample on X and Y. Again we shall draw analogies with standard regression, where using OLS estimators for the coefficients yields an estimate $\hat{\alpha} + \hat{\beta} X$ of the conditional mean of Y. We show how to find the q quantile *regression coefficient estimates*, which we shall denote $\hat{\alpha}_q$ and $\hat{\beta}_q$, and hence obtain an estimate $\hat{\alpha}_q + \hat{\beta}_q X$ of the conditional q quantile of Y. By letting q vary throughout its range from 0 to 1 we can obtain all the information we want about the conditional distribution of Y.

In standard regression we find the OLS estimates as a solution to an optimization problem. That is, we minimize the sum of the squared residuals as in (II.7.6) above. In quantile

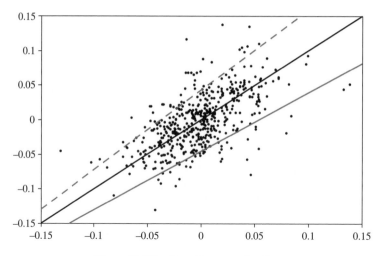

Figure II.7.1   Quantile regression lines

regression we also find the q quantile regression coefficient estimates as a solution to an optimization problem. In fact, we find $\hat{\alpha}_q$ and $\hat{\beta}_q$ as the solution to

$$\min_{\alpha,\beta} \sum_{t=1}^{T} \left(q - \mathbf{1}_{Y_t \le \alpha + \beta X_t}\right)(Y_t - (\alpha + \beta X_t)),\qquad\text{(II.7.8)}$$

where

$$\mathbf{1}_{Y_t \le \alpha + \beta X_t} = \begin{cases} 1 & \text{if } Y_t \le \alpha + \beta X_t, \\ 0 & \text{otherwise.} \end{cases}$$

To understand why this is the case, recall that in standard regression we express the 'loss' associated with a large residual by the square of the residual. It does not matter whether the residual is positive or negative. In quantile regression we express the 'loss' associated with a large residual by the function $q - \mathbf{1}_{Y_t \le \alpha + \beta X_t}$, which is shown in Figure II.7.2. Along the horizontal axis we show the residual, and the OLS loss function (the square of the residual)

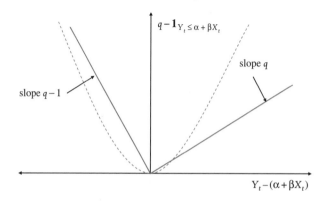

Figure II.7.2   Loss function for q quantile regression objective

is depicted by the dotted quadratic curve. The loss function for the q quantile regression objective is depicted by the bold grey lines.

In quantile regression we choose $\hat{\alpha}_q$ and $\hat{\beta}_q$ to minimize expected loss, just as in OLS we choose $\hat{\alpha}$ and $\hat{\beta}$ to minimize expected loss. The only difference between standard and quantile regression is the form of the loss function. The solution $(\hat{\alpha}, \hat{\beta})$ to minimizing the OLS loss function satisfies

$$\hat{\alpha} + \hat{\beta}X = \hat{E}(Y|X), \tag{II.7.9}$$

where $\hat{E}(Y|X)$ is the sample estimate of the conditional mean. Similarly, the solution $(\hat{\alpha}_q, \hat{\beta}_q)$ to minimizing the quantile loss function shown in Figure III.4.13 satisfies[5]

$$\hat{F}^{-1}(q|X) = \hat{\alpha}_q + \hat{\beta}_q X + F_\varepsilon^{-1}(q|X), \tag{II.7.10}$$

where $\hat{F}_q^{-1}(Y|X)$ is the sample estimate of the conditional q quantile.

Unlike OLS regression, where simple formulae can be used to find values of $\hat{\alpha}$ and $\hat{\beta}$ given a sample on X and Y, there are generally no analytic formulae for the solutions $\hat{\alpha}_q$ and $\hat{\beta}_q$ to (II.7.8). Therefore, we need to use a numerical algorithm. In the case study of Section II.7.2.6 below we shall use Excel Solver. However, Koenker and Hallock (2001) emphasize that specialized numerical algorithms are necessary to obtain reliable results. We remark that free software for many regression models, including linear quantile regression and inference on these models, is available from Bierens (2007).[6]

II.7.2.4   Inference in Linear Quantile Regression

Inference in linear quantile regression is based on a remarkable 'model free' result that *the confidence intervals for quantiles are independent of the distribution*. In fact, the distribution of a quantile estimator is based on the fact that the number of observations in a random sample (from any population) that are less than the q quantile has a binomial distribution. Confidence intervals for a quantile estimator are derived in Section II.8.4.1, and a numerical example is given there.

The binomial distribution for the quantile estimator is simple enough to extend to the linear quantile regression framework. In fact confidence intervals and standard errors of linear quantile regression estimators are now being included in some econometrics packages, including the EasyReg package referred to above. Koenker (2005) provides a useful chapter on inference in linear quantile regression, but the theory of inference in non-linear quantile regression has yet to be fully developed.

II.7.2.5   Using Copulas for Non-linear Quantile Regression

Following Bouyé and Salmon (2002), a tractable approach to non-linear quantile regression is to replace the linear model in (II.7.7) by the q quantile curve of a copula. This is an extremely useful tool, because returns on financial assets very often have highly non-linear relationships.

---

[5] See Koenker (2005: Section 1.3) for the proof.
[6] See http://econ.la.psu.edu/~hbierens/EASYREG.HTM for free software for many regression models, including linear quantile regression.

Recall from Section II.6.5 that every copula has a q quantile curve which may sometimes be expressed as an explicit function. For instance, when the marginals are both standard normal the normal (i.e. Gaussian) copula quantile curves are given by

$$Y = \varrho X + \sqrt{1 - \varrho^2} \Phi^{-1}(q). \tag{II.7.11}$$

Now suppose we know the marginal distributions $F(X)$ and $G(Y)$ of X and Y have been specified and their parameters have already been estimated using maximum likelihood. We then specify some functional form for a bivariate copula, and this will depend on certain parameters θ. For instance, the normal bivariate copula has one parameter, the correlation ϱ, the Clayton copula has one parameter, α, and the bivariate Student t copula has two parameters, the degrees of freedom ν and the correlation, ϱ.

The normal copula quantile curves may be written

$$Y = G^{-1}\left[\Phi\left(\varrho\Phi^{-1}(F(X)) + \sqrt{1 - \varrho^2}\Phi^{-1}(q)\right)\right]. \tag{II.7.12}$$

Similarly, from (II.6.69) we derive the Student t copula quantile curves as

$$Y = G^{-1}\left[t_\nu\left(\varrho t_\nu^{-1}(F(X)) + \sqrt{(1 - \varrho^2)(\nu + 1)^{-1}\left(\nu + t_\nu^{-1}(F(X))^2\right)}\, t_{\nu+1}^{-1}(q)\right)\right], \tag{II.7.13}$$

and from (II.6.75) the Clayton copula quantile curves take the form

$$Y = G^{-1}\left[\left(1 + F(X)^{-\alpha}\left(q^{-\alpha/(1+\alpha)} - 1\right)\right)^{-1/\alpha}\right]. \tag{II.7.14}$$

There is no closed form for the Gumbel copula quantile curves, but there are many other types of copula in addition to normal, t and Clayton copulas for which the q quantile curve can be expressed as an *explicit* function: $Y = Q_q(X, q; \theta)$.

We aim to estimate a different set of copula parameters $\hat{\theta}_q$ for each quantile regression. Using the quantile function in place of the linear function, we perform a special type of non-linear quantile regression that Bouyé and Salmon (2002) call *copula quantile regression*. To be more precise, given a sample $\{(X_t, Y_t)\}_{t=1}^T$, we define the q quantile *regression curve* as the curve $Y_t = Q_q\left(X_t, q; \hat{\theta}_q\right)$ where the parameters $\hat{\theta}_q$ are found by solving the optimization problem

$$\min_{\theta} \sum_{t=1}^T \left(q - \mathbf{1}_{Y_t \le Q_q(X_t, q; \theta)}\right)\left(Y_t - Q_q(X_t, q; \theta)\right). \tag{II.7.15}$$

Empirical examples are given in the case study of the next section.

Finally, we remark that it is not essential to calibrate the marginals separately from the quantile regression. Set $F(X; \alpha_X)$ and $G(Y; \alpha_Y)$ so that $\alpha = \{\alpha_X, \alpha_Y\}$ are the marginal parameters.[7] Then the q quantile regression curve is $Y_t = Q_q\left(X_t, q; \hat{\alpha}_q, \hat{\theta}_q\right)$, where $\left\{\hat{\alpha}_q, \hat{\theta}_q\right\}$ are the solutions to the optimization problem

$$\min_{\alpha, \theta} \sum_{t=1}^T \left(q - \mathbf{1}_{Y_t \le Q_q(X_t, q; \alpha, \theta)}\right)\left(Y_t - Q_q(X_t, q; \alpha, \theta)\right). \tag{II.7.16}$$

However, it is already a difficult problem to calibrate copula parameters in quantile regression. Adding marginal parameters to the problem requires sophisticated optimization routines, and since the case study in the next section is based on Excel we shall use either empirical marginals or pre-calibrated marginals in our copula quantile regression examples.

---

[7] Note that we assume the marginals are constant over time.

II.7.3   CASE STUDIES ON QUANTILE REGRESSION

We now present two case studies: the first shows how to implement linear and non-linear quantile regression in Excel and the second covers an empirical application to hedging futures positions.[8]

II.7.3.1   Case Study 1: Quantile Regression of Vftse on FTSE 100 Index

In this case study we use the data on the FTSE 100 index and Vftse index returns shown in Figure II.6.14 and analysed in Example II.6.4 to perform a set of simple linear and quantile regressions where Y is the daily log return on the Vftse index and X is the daily log return on the FTSE 100 index.[9] The data period is from 2 January 2004 to 29 December 2006, so there are 765 data points.

Simple Linear Regression

The first spreadsheet of the workbook for this case study estimates the following linear regression by OLS:[10]

$$\text{Vftse Rtn} = \underset{(1.701)}{0.0022} - \underset{(-29.35)}{5.6683}\,\text{FTSE Rtn} \qquad R^2 = 53\%, s = 3.6\%.$$

To be precise, this simple linear regression model estimates the *expected value* of the Vftse return conditional on a given value for the FTSE return. For instance, if the FTSE index falls by 10% then we expect the Vftse to rise by 56.68%. In other words, supposing the FTSE index is currently at 7000 and the Vftse is at 15%, if the index were to fall by 10% (i.e. by 700 points) then the expected value of the Vftse would increase to 23.5% (since this is a 56.68% increase on 15%).

Assuming the variables have a bivariate normal distribution, we can use further output from the simple linear regression to find a confidence interval, and indeed the entire conditional distribution for Vftse returns, given some value for the change in FTSE index. But this distribution will be not only symmetric but also normal, which is very unrealistic for the variables in question. Clearly, there are many problems with this model, including the following:

- Price and implied volatility returns certainly do not have a bivariate normal distribution.
- It cannot capture asymmetric dependence between price and implied volatility, i.e. that volatility increases much more following a large price fall than it decreases following a large price rise.
- It cannot capture tail dependence, i.e. that volatility reacts strongly to extreme moves in price but changes very little when price moves are within the ordinary daily variations seen in the market.

---

[8] Although we do not cover this here, linear and non-linear regression quantile techniques may also be applied to value-at-risk estimation, as in Taylor (1999), Chernozhukov and Umantsev (2001) and Engle and Manganelli (2004). Instead of modelling the entire distribution of returns, the *CAViaR* approach introduced by Engle and Manganelli models a time varying value at risk directly, via autoregression, and the parameters of these models are estimated using non-linear quantile regression. A few specifications of the generic process are tested empirically in the paper.

[9] See Section III.4.7 for more details on volatility indices, their construction and futures and options on volatility indices.

[10] Standard t ratios are shown in parentheses. For simplicity, in our discussion we assume the log return is equal to the return.

Linear Quantile Regressions

In the second spreadsheet of the workbook, we use Excel Solver to perform a series of quantile regressions. That is, we repeatedly solve the minimization problem (II.7.8), setting $q = 0.1, 0.2, \ldots, 0.9$ in turn.

The application of Excel Solver to the minimization (II.7.8) produces results that are dependent on the starting values for α and β, and the estimate of β is particularly sensitive to this choice. Also the algorithm chosen in the Solver options (Newton–Raphson or conjugate gradient) leads to different results, again especially for the estimate of β. Therefore the results shown in Table II.7.1 compare the Excel Solver estimates with those obtained using the quantile regression software in the *EasyReg* package developed by Bierens (2007).[11]

Table II.7.1 Quantile regression coefficient estimates of Vftse–FTSE model

q	0.1	0.2	0.3	0.4	0.5	0.6	0.7	0.8	0.9
$\alpha^{(1)}$	−0.039	−0.025	−0.016	−0.006	0.001	0.008	0.016	0.027	0.045
$\alpha^{(2)}$	−0.040	−0.025	−0.016	−0.006	0.001	0.008	0.016	0.027	0.045
t stat. α	−21.815	−15.661	−9.716	−4.278	0.681	5.920	10.366	14.952	16.957
$\beta^{(1)}$	−6.010	−5.784	−5.609	−5.653	−5.525	−5.381	−5.388	−5.434	−5.403
$\beta^{(2)}$	−6.032	−5.791	−5.581	−5.667	−5.534	−5.371	−5.368	−5.429	−5.386
t stat. β	−22.465	−24.525	−23.263	−26.729	−27.687	−26.475	−23.975	−20.592	−13.622

The two sets of coefficient estimates are very similar, especially for the alpha estimates, and this gives us at least some confidence that when we apply Excel Solver to copula quantile regressions in the remainder of this section the results will be satisfactory. The most important feature of Table II.7.1 is that the sensitivity of implied volatility to the underlying (beta) is always negative – and of course we expect negative dependence between implied volatility and equity index returns. Notice that as the quantile increases the intercept increases and the implied volatility sensitivity lessens. This indicates a type of tail dependency between price and implied volatility that was *not* captured by the simple linear regression estimated above.

Conditional Quantiles Based on Linear Quantile Regression

Table II.7.2 shows the quantiles of the conditional distribution of Vftse log returns given that the FTSE index log returns are (a) 1% and (b) −1%.[12] In the top row we again state the quantile, in the second row we have the conditional quantiles for the given percentage change in implied volatility, and in the third row we have the resulting new value of the Vftse index when the current value is 12.8% (as it is on the last day of our sample). The fourth and fifth rows are repeats of rows 2 and 3, but now corresponding to a 1% fall instead of a 1% rise in the FTSE index.

Figure II.7.3 depicts the conditional distribution function for Vftse returns – given that the FTSE index falls by 1% – that is estimated by the quantile regression lines. Hence, when the Vftse starts at 12.8% and then the FTSE index falls 1% there is probability of 0.1 that

---

[11] The Excel results are indexed (1) and the EasyReg results are indexed (2). The t statistics refer to the EasyReg estimates.
[12] These results are obtained using the Excel parameter estimates of Table II.7.1, not the EasyReg parameter estimates.

Table II.7.2   Conditional quantiles of Vftse

FTSE rtn	q	0.1	0.2	0.3	0.4	0.5	0.6	0.7	0.8	0.9
1%	Vftse rtn	−9.9%	−8.3%	−7.2%	−6.3%	−5.4%	−4.6%	−3.8%	−2.8%	−0.9%
	New Vftse	11.53	11.74	11.88	12.00	12.10	12.21	12.31	12.45	12.69
−1%	Vftse rtn	2.1%	3.3%	4.0%	5.0%	5.6%	6.2%	7.0%	8.1%	10.0%
	New Vftse	13.07	13.22	13.32	13.44	13.52	13.59	13.69	13.84	14.07

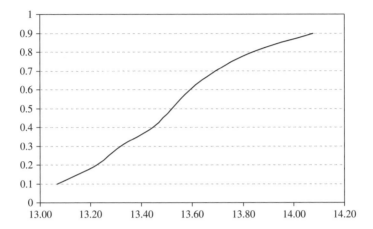

Figure II.7.3   Distribution of Vftse conditional on FTSE falling by 1% (linear quantile regression)

the Vftse has a new value of less than 13.07%, a probability of 0.2 that the Vftse has a new value of less than 13.22%, ... , a probability of 0.9 that the Vftse has a new value of less than 14.07%.

Unfortunately, there remains a major problem with this model because it assumes there is a *linear* relationship between price changes and implied volatility changes and we know that this assumption is not empirically justified.[13] Readers can verify, using the linear quantile regression spreadsheet, that an assumed linear relationship between price and volatility predicts totally unreasonable changes in volatility conditional on very large index returns. There is no facility in the linear model to capture an asymmetric relationship between price and volatility changes, and such linear behaviour is very far from that observed in the market.

Non-linear Quantile Regressions

Now we estimate a non-linear quantile regression using copulas. We assume the marginals are Student t distributions, with degrees of freedom 5.02 for the Vftse and 6.18 for the FTSE. (Recall that the degrees of freedom were calibrated in Example II.6.4.) Now we compare the results of quantile regression based on the normal copula, the Student

---

[13] The implied volatility sensitivity to stock price is larger for price falls than it is for price rises. Also the sensitivity of implied volatility to commodity prices is usually, but not always, larger for price rises than for price falls, and even in currency markets the implied volatility sensitivity to exchange rate moves is not identical for rate increases and rate decreases. See Chapter III.5 for further details.

t copula and the Clayton copula, using their quantile regression models as described in Section II.7.2.5. In the spreadsheet labelled with each copula quantile regression we calibrate the copula parameters for each of the quantiles $q = 0.1, 0.2, \ldots, 0.9$ in turn. In other words, the copula parameter estimates will depend on q, just as the estimates in Table II.7.1 for the linear quantile regressions changed with q. The results are displayed in Figure II.7.4.[14]

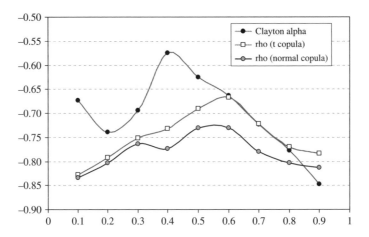

Figure II.7.4   Calibration of copula quantile regressions of Vftse on FTSE

The strong tail dependence between the FTSE index and Vftse returns is clear from the fact that the quantile regression estimates of the correlation in the Student t and the normal copulas is more negative for the very low and very high quantiles than it is for the quantiles around the median. In other words, the graphs have an approximate inverted U shape. Also, dependence in the lower tail is marginally greater than it is in the upper tail. For instance, at the 10% quantile the correlation is estimated at approximately -0.83 by both the normal and the t copula quantile regressions, but at the 90% quantile the correlation is estimated at approximately -0.81 for the normal and -0.78 for the t copula quantile regressions.

For completeness we have added the Clayton copula quantile regression estimates. We remark that even though the Clayton alpha estimates lie between -1 and 0, these are permissible values for alpha.[15]

Conditional Quantiles Based on Non-Linear Quantile Regression

Figure II.7.5 compares the conditional distribution of the Vftse, given that the FTSE index falls by 1%, based on the three different quantile regressions. For comparison we also show the linear quantile regression conditional distribution already displayed in Figure II.7.3. It is clear that whilst linear quantile regression may provide a fairly accurate prediction of the conditional distribution of Vftse at low quantiles, it underestimates the change in the Vftse at high percentiles, compared with the normal and t copula quantile regressions.

---

[14] Note that Excel Solver struggles a bit with the optimization, and for this reason the degrees-of-freedom parameter for the Student t copula has been fixed at 6.66, this being the value calibrated in Example II.6.4. With a more sophisticated optimizer than Excel Solver we could calibrate both the degrees of freedom and the correlation to be different for each quantile regression curve.

[15] See Remark 5.44 in McNeil et al (2005) for further details.

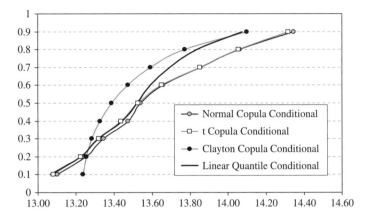

Figure II.7.5 Distribution of Vftse conditional on FTSE falling by 1%

Figure II.7.6 depicts the results when we repeat the exercise, this time assuming that the FTSE index falls by 3%. For instance, from Figure II.7.6 and from column J of the quantile regression results spreadsheet, if the FTSE were to fall by 3% then we would be 90% confident that the Vftse would be less than:

(a) 16.74% according to a t copula quantile regression;
(b) 16.62% according to a normal copula quantile regression;
(c) 15.59% according to a Clayton copula quantile regression;
(d) 15.46% according to a linear quantile regression.

Other conditional confidence intervals may easily be constructed from the spreadsheet: this is left as an exercise for the interested reader.[16]

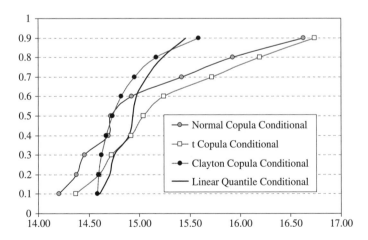

Figure II.7.6 Distribution of Vftse conditional on FTSE falling by 3%

---

[16] Readers can input different values for the FTSE returns and the current value of the Vftse in the spreadsheet labelled 'Graphs' to generate other conditional distributions for the Vftse.

Conclusion

This case study shows that the information we obtain from returns to financial assets depends very much on the model we use. We know that an idealized model where only linear relationships between bivariate normal variables are possible is not a good model for market risk analysis. Such a model would produce very inaccurate results, not only for conditional confidence intervals discussed in this section but also for standard market risk management activities, such as hedging and portfolio diversification.

II.7.3.2   Case Study 2: Hedging with Copula Quantile Regression

Alpha traders hedge their systematic risk. That is, they attempt to zero the beta of their portfolio so that their return is not influenced by the market factor. Market makers also hedge their positions, using futures, so that the variance of the hedged portfolio P&L is minimized. They aim to make enough money on the bid–ask spread to cover the hedging costs and still make a profit.

It is standard to estimate a portfolio beta by minimizing the variance of the hedged portfolio returns. In other words, it is standard to employ the OLS criterion, since minimizing the sum of the squared residuals will also minimize the unconditional variance of the hedged portfolio returns over the sample. More sophisticated time varying hedge ratios, based on exponentially weighted moving average (EWMA) or GARCH models, can also be applied to minimize the conditional variance of the hedged portfolio returns in this context. These are defined and their properties are discussed in Section III.2.7.

Yet the minimum variance criterion that underlies OLS regression is only one possible criterion for estimating a hedge ratio, and it is not necessarily the best. It is based on a quadratic loss function, such as that shown by the dashed curve in Figure II.7.2. Since the objective is simply to make hedged portfolio returns as small as possible, regardless of their sign, a positive return on the hedged portfolio is just as 'bad' as a negative return on the portfolio. The is because the OLS loss function is symmetric.

By contrast, when $q < 0.5$ the quantile regression loss function shown in Figure II.7.2 attributes a greater penalty to negative returns than to positive returns on the hedged portfolio. Quantile regression beta estimates thus provide an *asymmetric hedge*, and when q is small the hedged portfolio will be specifically designed to hedge downside risk.

A typical situation where quantile regression should be applied to derive hedge ratios is when traders, operating under daily risk limits, require a partial hedge of systematic risk in order to reduce but not eliminate exposure to the market factor. Such a hedge ratio is legitimately based on regression analysis of daily returns since the partial hedge is placed for only a short period, often overnight. Although a little more complex than linear quantile regression, copula quantile regressions have a very useful application here, because daily returns on the portfolio and the market factor are very unlikely to have a bivariate normal distribution. We illustrate the approach with a case study.

Statement of Hedging Problem and Data

An equity trader calculates that he has exceeded his limits with three very large positions, holding an equal value in each of Vodafone, British Petroleum and HSBC. Thus he decides to reduce his risk overnight by taking a partial hedge of the portfolio with the FTSE index future. Compare the hedge ratios that he would obtain using:

(a) simple linear regression based on OLS;
(b) linear quantile regression at the median;
(c) linear quantile regression at the 20% quantile.

What are the advantages and limitations of each hedge ratio?

For the case study we use the stocks' daily closing price data from 31 July 2006 to 8 July 2007, displayed in Figure II.7.7. For comparison, prices are rebased to be equal to 100 at the beginning of the period. Note that in July 2006 Vodafone stock fell almost 20% following rationalization of its operations, but the price recovered significantly during the data period chosen for the study.

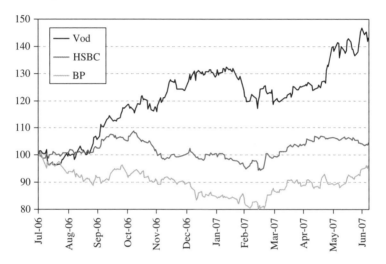

Figure II.7.7   Vodafone, HSBC and BP stock prices (rebased)

Figure II.7.8 compares the prices of the trader's portfolio, which has an equal value in each stock, with the FTSE 100 index over the data period. Again, prices are rebased to be 100 at the beginning of the period.

OLS Hedge Ratio

We use the portfolio's prices shown in Figure II.7.8 to compute daily log returns on the portfolio and we estimate the hedge ratio β using OLS on a simple linear regression model,

$$R_t = \alpha + \beta X_t + \varepsilon_t, \qquad (II.7.17)$$

where the error term is assumed to be i.i.d. and the joint density of the portfolio returns R and the index returns X is assumed to be bivariate normal.[17]

---

[17] The portfolio to be hedged is a long-only portfolio and so it is acceptable to use its returns in the hedge ratio regression. But with a long-short portfolio we cannot measure its return R if the price is zero so we would, in general, use P&L instead of returns for both variables in (II.7.17).

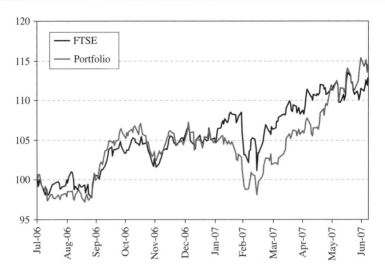

Figure II.7.8   Comparison of FTSE index and portfolio price

The spreadsheet labelled (a) in this case study reports the results of this regression. We obtain an OLS estimate of the hedge ratio of 0.547. This hedge ratio is based on minimizing the sum of the squared hedged portfolio returns. Negative returns are treated the same as positive returns, so it is not hedging downside risk. How does this compare with the hedge ratios (b) and (c) that are based on quantile linear regressions?

Hedge Ratios Based on Linear Quantile Regressions

The OLS hedge ratio is based on a quadratic loss function where positive and negative returns of the same magnitude contribute equally to the loss. But the quantile regressions are based on the loss function shown in Figure II.7.2. The median quantile regression loss function is obtained by setting $q = 0.5$ in (II.7.8). In other words, the median quantile regression loss function is to minimize the sum of the *absolute values* of the hedged portfolio returns. More significance is placed on the potential for large losses compared with OLS, but it has no direct relationship with the variance of hedged portfolio returns. The median quantile regression hedge ratio is calculated by setting $q = 0.5$ in spreadsheet '(b) and (c)' and following the instructions shown. We obtain a value of 0.496, which is less than the OLS hedge ratio.

Still, neither (a) nor (b) is a downside hedge ratio. So in part (c) we ask how much of the hedge should be sold to minimize the sum of the absolute values of the hedged portfolio returns when negative returns have a greater penalty than positive returns. Setting $q = 0.2$ in spreadsheet '(b) and (c)' gives a quantile regression-based hedge ratio of 0.479. Hence, a smaller short position in the hedge provides a better protection against the downside in this case. This is not a general rule. In general it can be either more or less of the hedge that needs be taken to increase the downside protection; it depends on the characteristics of the data.

Hedge Ratios Based on Non-linear Quantile Regressions

All the hedge ratios derived above are based on the assumption that the returns have a bivariate normal distribution. They also assume there is a linear dependence between the portfolio and the index returns. The next two hedge ratios make more realistic assumptions about the joint distribution of portfolio returns and compute downside hedge ratios that also allow for a non-linear relationship in the regression. These are based on:

(d) normal copula quantile regression at the 20% quantile with Student t marginals;
(e) Student t copula quantile regression at the 20% quantile with Student t marginals.

To estimate these hedge ratios we first estimate the marginal densities of the returns, and we shall assume they both have Student t marginal distributions. Applying maximum likelihood to estimate the degrees of freedom, as in Example II.6.4, we obtain 9.99 degrees of freedom for the FTSE index returns and 13.10 for the portfolio returns.

The normal copula 20% quantile regression hedge ratio estimate is computed in spreadsheet (d) and that for the Student t copula is computed in spreadsheet (e). These use the methodology described in Section II.7.2.5 which has already been illustrated in the case study of the previous section. Once the copula parameters have been calibrated using Excel Solver,[18] we estimate the hedge ratio using the relationship

$$\hat{\beta} = \hat{\varrho}\left(\frac{s_R}{s_X}\right), \qquad (\text{II.7.18})$$

where s_R and s_X are the standard deviations of the portfolio returns and the index returns over the sample. The results are hedge ratios of 0.557 for the normal copula quantile regression and 0.555 for the t copula (which is calibrated to have 7 degrees of freedom). These are similar, and both are substantially greater than the linear quantile regression hedge ratio of 0.482. We conclude that the assumption of normal marginals leads to substantial underestimation of the downside hedge ratio but that the normal copula is similar to the t copula as a dependence model.

Time Varying Hedge Ratios

All the hedge ratios estimated above represent an average hedge ratio over the whole sample of 231 observations – almost 1 year of data. This does not necessarily reflect current market conditions, which can be important for an overnight hedge. For this reason the spreadsheet labelled (f) recalculates the hedge ratio based on EWMA estimates of the covariance between the portfolio return and the index return, and the variance of the index return. The EWMA beta estimate at time t is given in Section II.1.2.3 as

$$\hat{\beta}_t = \frac{\text{Cov}_\lambda(R_t, X_t)}{V_\lambda(X_t)}, \qquad (\text{II.7.19})$$

where λ is the smoothing constant. With a value $\lambda = 0.95$ we obtain the hedge ratio estimates shown in Figure II.7.9. Note that the spreadsheet allows one to change the value of the smoothing constant.

---

[18] We remark that the Excel Solver is not sufficiently accurate to calibrate the correlation and degrees of freedom of the t copula simultaneously. Hence, we iterate by fixing the degrees of freedom and optimizing on the correlation, then fixing the correlation and optimizing on the degrees of freedom, and continue alternating like this until there is no further improvement in the objective.

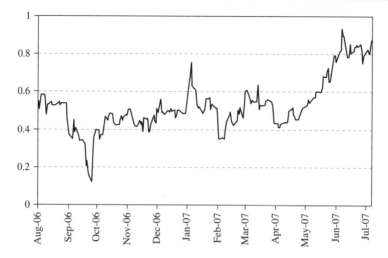

Figure II.7.9   EWMA hedge ratio

Whilst the average value of the EWMA beta is close to the OLS hedge ratio estimate it
varies considerably over time, reflecting the time varying systematic risk of the portfolio.
At the time the hedge is placed, on 6 July 2007, the value of the hedge ratio is 0.875.
This far exceeds the hedge ratio based on OLS. Readers may verify that the EWMA
hedge ratio exceeds the OLS ratio significantly for any reasonable choice of smoothing
constant.

Obviously this portfolio had a greater systematic risk during recent months than during
2006. Since May 2007, when stock market volatility increased following fears over the
Chinese economy, this particular portfolio has been unusually volatile. Thus the higher
hedge ratio that is estimated using EWMA better reflects the trader's current risk exposure.
Nevertheless, the trader may view this as an over-hedge if he only seeks a partial hedge of
his position to bring it back within his trading limits.

Conclusions

The important learning point of this case study is that there is a very significant model
risk in the estimation of hedge ratios. Different hedging criteria and different assumptions
about the behaviour of returns lead to different hedge ratios. In our case study we found that
hedge ratios should be slightly lower if they are to account for downside risk but slightly
higher if they are to account for non-linear dependency with returns that are not bivariate
normal; and that time varying hedge ratios that better reflect current market conditions are
considerably higher than hedge ratios that are estimated using sample averages. But there is
no general rule here. A sophisticated model would simultaneously capture all three of the
properties that are important for short term hedging. That is, its short term hedge ratios would
capture:

- downside risk;
- non-normal conditional distributions;
- time variation.

Such hedge ratios may be obtained using conditional copula quantile regressions.[19]

But a single estimation such as that discussed above is not a sufficient basis for trading. The sample period, sample size and data frequency will have a great influence on the resulting hedge ratio estimate. The only way that a trader can properly assess which is the best hedge ratio according to his chosen criteria is to backtest the various hedge ratios derived from different assumptions on returns behaviour, and then decide which ratio performs the best in out-of-sample diagnostics tests. See Section II.8.5.3 for further details.

II.7.4   OTHER NON-LINEAR REGRESSION MODELS

This section explains how to estimate regression models that have non-linear functional forms, i.e. where the dependent variable is assumed to be a non-linear function of the explanatory variables. We also introduce the probit and logit models that are commonly used for regressions where the dependent variable can only take two values. These values may be labelled 0 or 1, default or no default, success or failure, and so on. Most financial applications of probit and logit models are to modelling credit default, so we provide a brief introduction to these below.

II.7.4.1   Non-linear Least Squares

The general form of a non-linear regression is

$$Y_t = h(\mathbf{x}_t; \boldsymbol{\beta}) + \varepsilon_t,$$ (II.7.20)

where Y_t is the value of the dependent variable, h is a non-linear function of the explanatory variables $\mathbf{x}_t = (X_{1t}, \ldots, X_{kt})'$, $\boldsymbol{\beta}$ is a vector of constant parameters, often including an intercept term, and ε_t denotes the residual at time t. As usual, we assume that the data are time series, noting that the main results generalize to the case of cross-sectional data.

The function h can be non-linear in $\mathbf{x}_t$ with linearity in the coefficient, as in the case of the *logarithmic regression*,

$$Y_t = \alpha + \beta \ln X_t + \varepsilon_t,$$ (II.7.21)

which is one simple example of a non-linear regression model. Another simple but useful example of a non-linear regression model is the *quadratic regression*,

$$Y_t = \alpha + \beta_1 X_t + \beta_2 X_t^2 + \varepsilon_t.$$ (II.7.22)

A more general response for the dependent variable to changes in an explanatory variable is captured by a *polynomial regression*,

$$Y_t = \alpha + \beta_1 X_t + \beta_2 X_t^2 + \ldots + \beta_k X_t^k + \varepsilon_t,$$ (II.7.23)

where k is some integer greater than 2.

A quadratic regression curve is depicted in Figure II.7.10 for the case $\beta_1 < 0, \beta_2 > 0$. It is clear that the model (II.7.22) captures the possibility that Y has an asymmetric response to X. If $\beta_2 > 0$ then, when $X > -\frac{1}{2}\beta_1\beta_2^{-1}$ an increase in X is associated with an increase in Y, but when $X < -\frac{1}{2}\beta_1\beta_2^{-1}$ an increase in X is associated with a decrease in Y. The opposite is the case when $\beta_2 < 0$.

---

[19] See Patton (2008) for an introduction to copula-based models for time series analysis. The copula quantile regressions for short term futures hedging are the subject of forthcoming research by the author.

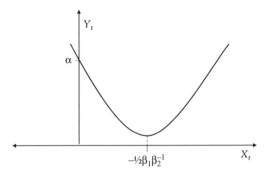

Figure II.7.10   Quadratic regression curve

To estimate the parameters of a non-linear regression we may obtain the *non-linear least squares estimators* as the solution to the optimization problem

$$\min_{\beta} \sum_{t=1}^{T} (Y_t - h(\mathbf{x}_t; \beta))^2. \tag{II.7.24}$$

Unlike the linear case, there is no general analytical solution for the non-linear least squares estimators, except in some special cases such as polynomial regression where the function h is linear in β. However it is straightforward to apply a numerical algorithm to find non-linear least square estimates, and we illustrate this using Excel Solver in the following empirical example.

EXAMPLE II.7.1: NON-LINEAR REGRESSIONS FOR THE FTSE 100 AND VFTSE

Estimate a quadratic regression of the form (II.7.22), where Y is the daily log return on the Vftse index and X is the daily log return on the FTSE 100 index based on data used in the case study of Section II.7.2.6.

SOLUTION   The spreadsheet shows the Solver setting and calculates the least square estimates as follows:[20]

$$\text{Vftse Rtn} = -0.2549 - 5.5289\,\text{FTSE Rtn} + 1.0301\,\text{FTSE Rtn}^2, \quad R^2 = 55.9\%, \quad s = 3.5\%.$$

This quadratic regression provides a slightly better fit to the data than the linear model estimated at the beginning of the case study, i.e.

$$\text{Vftse Rtn} = 0.2221 - 5.6683\,\text{FTSE Rtn}, \quad R^2 = 53\%, s = 3.6\%.$$

The quadratic regression captures the asymmetric response of implied volatility to changes in the FTSE index. Since $-\frac{1}{2}\hat{\beta}_1\hat{\beta}_2^{-1} = 2.68\%$, which is large and positive, in most circumstances a reduction in the FTSE return is associated with an increase in the return on implied volatility. But on days when the FTSE index jumps up considerably, a subsequent reduction in FTSE index return is associated with a *decrease* in its implied volatility. This agrees with

---

[20] So that all coefficient estimates are of similar orders of magnitude, in the following we measure returns in *percentage points*, i.e. a 1% return is 1 not 0.01. Compared with the case study results, where returns were represented as proportions (i.e. a 1% return is 0.01 not 1), the effect is to multiply the constant by 100 and divide the coefficient of X^2 by 100. The slope coefficient remains unchanged because *both* X and Y have been scaled up by a factor of 100.

the intuition that two consecutive large returns may increase uncertainty in the market, since traders believe the correction has not yet been completed.

We have not estimated the standard errors of the coefficient estimators in the above example, but it can be shown that the least squares estimators are consistent and asymptotically normal when the error term is normally distributed, and their asymptotic covariance matrix takes the usual form for least squares regression.[21]

II.7.4.2   Discrete Choice Models

In this section we provide a brief introduction to *binary choice* models, i.e. models that are applied when a variable can take only two states. We shall call these states *default* and *no default* since binary choice models are commonly applied to model cross-sectional data on company defaults.[22] Denote the factors that contribute to a company's default by variables $X_1, X_2, \ldots, X_k$ and summarize the model parameters in a vector β. As usual, we represent the data on the explanatory variables by a matrix,

$$\mathbf{X} = (X_{ij}), \quad i = 1, \ldots, n; j = 1, \ldots, k,$$

where n is the number of firms and k is the number of factors influencing default including a constant.[23] Also denote the ith row of $\mathbf{X}$, i.e. the data for the ith firm, by $\mathbf{x}_i$.

The default probability for firm i is represented as a function

$$p_i = P(\text{firm } i \text{ defaults}) = h(\mathbf{x}_i; \beta), \quad i = 1, \ldots, n, \tag{II.7.25}$$

and so P (firm i does not default) $= 1 - h(\mathbf{x}_i; \beta)$. We assume the function $h(\mathbf{x}_i; \beta)$ has the form of a continuous probability distribution function.

The *probit model* assumes the function $h(\mathbf{x}_i; \beta)$ is the standard normal distribution function of a linear function of the explanatory variables, i.e. $h(\mathbf{x}_i; \beta) = \Phi(\beta'\mathbf{x}_i)$, and this yields the *probit regression* as a linear model of the form

$$\Phi^{-1}(p_i) = \beta'\mathbf{x}_i + \varepsilon_i \tag{II.7.26}$$

or, written out in full as a linear regression,[24]

$$Y_i = \alpha + \beta_1 X_{1i} + \ldots + \beta_k X_{ki} + \varepsilon_i, \quad i = 1, \ldots, n, \tag{II.7.27}$$

where $Y_i = \Phi^{-1}(p_i)$ and p_i is the probability that the ith firm defaults.

The *logit model* assumes $h(\mathbf{x}_i; \beta)$ has a logistic form, i.e.

$$h(\mathbf{x}_i; \beta) = \frac{\exp(\beta'\mathbf{x}_i)}{1 + \exp(\beta'\mathbf{x}_i)}. \tag{II.7.28}$$

This yields the *logistic regression*

$$\ln\left(\frac{p_i}{1 - p_i}\right) = \beta'\mathbf{x}_i + \varepsilon_i, \quad i = 1, \ldots, n. \tag{II.7.29}$$

---

[21] See Section I.4.4.2.

[22] These models are more generally applied to model the probability of credit downgrading. In that case simply substitute *downgrade* for *default* in the following.

[23] So the first column of $\mathbf{X}$ is all 1s.

[24] We use cross sectional notation here since these models are most often applied to such data but they may also be applied to time series.

Equivalently, we have the identical form of linear regression (II.7.27) but now with

$$Y_i = \ln p_i - \ln(1 - p_i).$$

The *Weibull model* assumes $h(x_i; \beta) = 1 - \exp(-\exp(\beta' x_i))$ and so the *Weibull regression* takes the form (II.7.27) with dependent variable $Y_i = \ln(-\ln(1 - p_i))$.

To summarize, we have

$$p_i = h(x_i; \beta) = \begin{cases} \Phi(\beta' x_i), & \text{in the probit model,} \\[2mm] \dfrac{\exp(\beta' x_i)}{1 + \exp(\beta' x_i)}, & \text{in the logit model,} \\[2mm] 1 - \exp(-\exp(\beta' x_i)), & \text{in the Weibull model.} \end{cases} \qquad \text{(II.7.30)}$$

But we cannot estimate a discrete choice model as a standard linear regression. The dependent variable Y_i is a continuous non-linear function of a *latent variable* p_i, i.e. the probability that the ith firm defaults. That is, p_i is unobservable. The input data consists of a string of indicators that flag whether each company in the data set has defaulted. In other words, the input data are

$$\mathbf{1}_i = \begin{cases} 1, & \text{if company } i \text{ defaults,} \\ 0, & \text{otherwise,} \end{cases} \qquad \text{(II.7.31)}$$

The values for the explanatory variables are summarized in the matrix $\mathbf{X}$.

Although we cannot perform a least squares regression we *can* find maximum likelihood estimates of the model parameters β. In fact maximum likelihood estimation turns out to be very simple in this case. We can treat each observation as a draw from a *Bernoulli distribution*, where the outcomes are default with probability p_i and no default with probability $1 - p_i$. The log likelihood function is therefore

$$\ln L(\mathbf{X}; \beta) = \sum_{i=1}^{n} \left[\mathbf{1}_i \ln(h(x_i; \beta)) + (1 - \mathbf{1}_i) \ln (1 - h(x_i; \beta)) \right]. \qquad \text{(II.7.32)}$$

And it is simple to find the value of β that maximizes this using a numerical algorithm.

The best way to illustrate the simplicity of the implementation of discrete choice models is to provide some empirical examples in an Excel spreadsheet. In the following example we consider only one explanatory variable, i.e. the debt–equity ratio of a firm. However, it is straightforward for the reader to extend the example to include further explanatory variables, as explained in a comment on the spreadsheet.

EXAMPLE II.7.2: SIMPLE DISCRETE CHOICE MODELS FOR CREDIT DEFAULT

The spreadsheet for this example contains cross-sectional data on the debt–equity ratio of 500 non-investment grade companies on 31 December 2006. The companies are ordered by increasing debt–equity ratio. Beside this is shown an indicator variable that takes the value 1 if the company had defaulted on its debt by 31 December 2007, and the value 0 otherwise. Estimate the probit, logit and Weibull models for the default probability using these data.

SOLUTION   The spreadsheet for this example calculates the probabilities (II.7.30) and then evaluates the log likelihood (II.7.32) for each firm and under each of the three models. Summing the log likelihoods over all firms gives the objective function to be maximized by changing the values of the model parameters. The parameters for each model are a constant

α and a parameter β for the debt–equity ratio. Excel Solver is then applied to each log likelihood as indicated in the spreadsheet, and the results are displayed in the first three rows of Table II.7.3.

Table II.7.3 Estimation of discrete choice models

Model	Probit	Logit	Weibull
α	−2.340	−4.154	−3.999
β	0.761	1.367	1.200
Log likelihood	−133.49	−134.44	−134.65
Default probability (at mean)	6.64%	6.60%	6.63%
Sensitivity to debt–equity ratio (at mean)	9.81%	8.42%	7.69%

Error terms have zero expectation, hence the conditional expectation of the default probability, or *default probability* for short, given a value $\mathbf{x}$ for the explanatory variables, is

$$E(p \,|\, \mathbf{x}) = \begin{cases} \Phi(\hat{\beta}'\mathbf{x}), & \text{in the probit model,} \\ \dfrac{\exp(\hat{\beta}'\mathbf{x})}{1 + \exp(\hat{\beta}'\mathbf{x})}, & \text{in the logit model,} \\ 1 - \exp(-\exp(\hat{\beta}'\mathbf{x})), & \text{in the Weibull model.} \end{cases} \tag{II.7.33}$$

We can also derive the sensitivity of the default probability to changes in the explanatory variables by differentiating (II.7.33). This gives

$$\frac{\partial E(p \,|\, \mathbf{x})}{\partial X_j} = \begin{cases} \varphi(\hat{\beta}'\mathbf{x})\hat{\beta}_j, & \text{in the probit model,} \\ \exp(\hat{\beta}'\mathbf{x})(1 + \exp(\hat{\beta}'\mathbf{x}))^{-2}\hat{\beta}_j, & \text{in the logit model,} \\ \exp(\hat{\beta}'\mathbf{x} - \exp(\hat{\beta}'\mathbf{x}))\hat{\beta}_j, & \text{in the Weibull model,} \end{cases} \tag{II.7.34}$$

where φ denotes the standard normal density function.

We remark that, unlike the standard linear regression case where the sensitivities are given by the constant regression coefficients, in discrete choice models each sensitivity depends on the values of *all* the explanatory variables! In the following we estimate the default probability and its sensitivity to the debt–equity ratio when this ratio is at its sample mean value. We also plot the default probability and its sensitivity to the debt–equity ratio as a function of the debt–equity ratio.

EXAMPLE II.7.3: ESTIMATING THE DEFAULT PROBABILITY AND ITS SENSITIVITY

Continue Example II.7.2, estimating for each model, at the average debt–equity ratio, the default probability and its sensitivity to changes in the debt–equity ratio. Also plot the default probability and its sensitivity to changes in the debt–equity ratio as a function of this ratio.

SOLUTION   The sample mean debt–equity ratio is 1.100 and the default probability at this value is shown in the fourth row of Table II.7.3. It is approximately the same for each model, i.e. 6.64% for the probit model, 6.60% for the logit model and 6.63% for the Weibull model. All these are considerably less than the proportion of defaults in the sample: since 50 of the firms defaulted, the sample proportion of defaults is 10%. The sensitivity of the default probability to a unit change in the debt–equity ratio, when the current debt–equity ratio is 1.100, is 9.81% in the probit model, 8.42% in the logit model and 7.69% in the Weibull model. Thus if the debt–equity ratio of the average firm rises from 1.100 to 2.100 then the default probability would be $6.64\% + 9.81\% = 16.45\%$ according to the probit model, 15.02% according to the logit model and 14.32% according to the Weibull model.

Figure II.7.11 shows the default probability estimated by each model and Figure II.7.12 shows the sensitivity of the default probability as a function of the debt–equity ratio. The three models do not differ greatly when the debt–equity ratio is near its sample average of 1.100. However, for firms having unusually high debt–equity ratios, for instance with debt–equity ratios of 3 or greater, there is a significant difference between the models' default probabilities and their sensitivities.

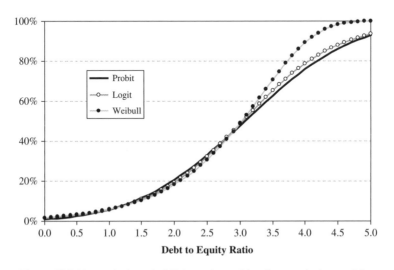

Figure II.7.11   Default probabilities estimated by discrete choice models

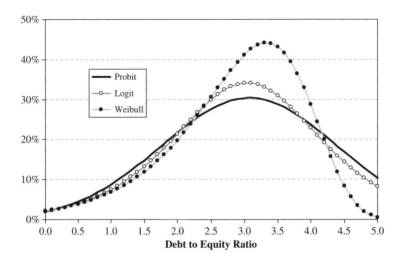

Figure II.7.12   Sensitivity of default probabilities to debt–equity ratio

II.7.5 MARKOV SWITCHING MODELS

Hamilton (1989) provided the first formal statistical representation of the idea that economic recession and expansion can influence the behaviour of economic variables. He demonstrated that real output growth may follow one of two different autoregressions, depending on whether the economy is expanding or contracting, with the shift between the two states generated by the outcome of an unobserved Markov chain. The pioneering research of Hamilton has precipitated a huge research literature on the theory of Markov switching models.[25]

In this section we first explain how simple but arbitrary structural break tests can be used to investigate whether there may be regime shifts in the dependent variable of a linear regression. Then we formally define the Markov switching regression model and briefly survey some of its empirical applications.

II.7.5.1 Testing for Structural Breaks

A regression model is said to undergo a structural break in parameters at time t^* if

$$\mathbf{y}_1 = \mathbf{X}_1\boldsymbol{\beta}_1 + \boldsymbol{\varepsilon}_1, \quad \text{for } t = 1, \ldots, t^*,$$
$$\mathbf{y}_2 = \mathbf{X}_2\boldsymbol{\beta}_2 + \boldsymbol{\varepsilon}_2, \quad \text{for } t = t^* + 1, \ldots, T, \tag{II.7.35}$$

where

$$\mathbf{y}_1 = (Y_1, \ldots, Y_{t^*})', \quad \mathbf{y}_2 = (Y_{t^*+1}, \ldots, Y_T)',$$
$$\boldsymbol{\varepsilon}_1 = (\varepsilon_1, \ldots, \varepsilon_{t^*})', \quad \boldsymbol{\varepsilon}_2 = (\varepsilon_{t^*+1}, \ldots, \varepsilon_T)',$$

$$\mathbf{X}_1 = \begin{pmatrix} X_{11} & X_{21} & \cdots & X_{k1} \\ \vdots & \vdots & & \vdots \\ X_{1t^*} & X_{12t^*} & \cdots & X_{kt^*} \end{pmatrix} \quad \text{and} \quad \mathbf{X}_2 = \begin{pmatrix} X_{1,t^*+1} & X_{2,t^*+1} & \cdots & X_{k,t^*+1} \\ \vdots & \vdots & & \vdots \\ X_{1T} & X_{2T} & \cdots & X_{kT} \end{pmatrix}.$$

and the first column of each $\mathbf{X}$ matrix has all elements equal to 1, assuming there is a constant term in the model.

We can test for the presence of a structural break using a *Chow test*, as follows:

1. Calculate the residual sum of squares on each model in (II.7.35), i.e. by estimating the model first on the data up to time t^* and then on the remaining data.
2. Add the two residual sums of squares to obtain RSS_U, the unrestricted residual sum of squares.
3. Estimate the model over all the data, which assumes the restriction that the model parameters are identical in both periods, and hence obtain RSS_R, the restricted residual sum of squares. Note that the vector of restrictions is $\boldsymbol{\beta}_1 = \boldsymbol{\beta}_2$, so there are k linear restrictions.
4. Use any of the tests for multiple linear restrictions described in Section I.4.4.6. For instance, we use the simple F test below, with test statistic

$$\frac{(k-1)^{-1}(RSS_R - RSS_U)}{(T-k)^{-1}RSS_U} \sim F_{k-1,T-k}.$$

[25] See, for instance, Hansen (1992, 1996), Kim (1994), Diebold et al. (1994), Garcia (1998), Psaradakis and Sola (1998) and Clarida et al. (2003).

EXAMPLE II.7.4: CHOW TEST

Consider the simple linear regression model

$$Y_t = \alpha + \beta X_t + \varepsilon_t,$$

where Y denotes the daily log return on the Vftse index and X denotes the daily log return on the FTSE 100 index and where the error process is assumed to be normally distributed. Using data between 5 January 2004 and 26 December 2006, as in the previous example in this chapter, the Vftse index and FTSE 100 index are shown in Figure II.7.13. We want to test whether there was a structural break in their relationship on 19 May 2006, after which the FTSE index fell about 500 points and the Vftse index jumped from about 12% to over 20% in the space of a few days. Was the correlation between the FTSE and the Vftse different after this date? Use a Chow test to answer this question.

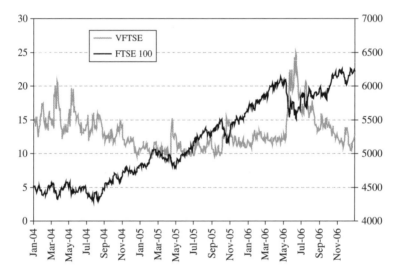

Figure II.7.13   Vftse and FTSE 100 indices

SOLUTION   We estimate the simple linear model three times: using only data up to the break point, only data after the break point, and finally all data. The sum of the residual sums of squares from the first two regressions gives the unrestricted residual sum of squares as 9891.5, and the residual sum of squares from the overall regression gives the restricted sum of squares as 9893.5. We use the F test statistic introduced in Section I.4.4.6, i.e.

$$\frac{(RSS_R - RSS_U)}{RSS_U/762} \sim F_{1,762},$$

since there are 764 observations and only two coefficients in the model. The 5% critical value of this statistic is 3.85 but our value is only 0.153, so we cannot reject the null hypothesis that there is no structural break and conclude that the relationship between the FTSE and its implied volatility index was stable over the period.

II.7.5.2   Model Specification

Evidence of multiple structural breaks in a regression model indicates that the dependent variable is subject to *regime shifts* where one or more of the model parameters jump between two or more values. In a regime-switching regression model we assume the parameter values switch between constant values, each value being conditional on a *state variable* which is a latent variable that indicates the regime prevailing at the time. By using a latent variable approach instead of a binary indicator, Markov switching regressions produce estimates of the conditional probability of being in a particular state at a particular point in time. These *conditional state probabilities* contain more precise information about the process than a simple binary indicator. The switching process is captured by time varying estimates of the conditional probability of each state and an estimate of a constant matrix of *state transition probabilities*.

In the Markov switching model the regression coefficients and the variance of the error terms are all assumed to be state-dependent. In the following we suppose there are only two possible states, only one explanatory variable and that the error process is normally distributed and homoscedastic in each state.[26] Now the Markov switching model may be written

$$Y_t = \begin{cases} \alpha_1 + \beta_1 X_t + \varepsilon_{1t}, & \varepsilon_{1t} \sim N\left(0, \sigma_1^2\right), & \text{in state 1,} \\ \alpha_2 + \beta_2 X_t + \varepsilon_{2t}, & \varepsilon_{2t} \sim N\left(0, \sigma_2^2\right), & \text{in state 2.} \end{cases} \tag{II.7.36}$$

Alternatively, denote by s_t the latent state variable which can take one of two possible values:

$$s_t = \begin{cases} 1, & \text{if state 1 governs at time } t, \\ 2, & \text{if state 2 governs at time } t. \end{cases} \tag{II.7.37}$$

Then the regression model with normally distributed homoscedastic errors can be written more succinctly as

$$Y_t = \alpha_{s_t} + \beta_{s_t} X_t + \varepsilon_{s_t t}. \quad \varepsilon_{s_t t} \sim N\left(0, \sigma_{s_t}^2\right). \tag{II.7.38}$$

The state variable is assumed to follow a first-order Markov chain where the *transition probabilities* for the two states are assumed to be constant.[27] Denoting by π_{ij} the probability of switching from state i to state j, the matrix of transition probabilities can be written as

$$\mathbf{\Pi} = \begin{pmatrix} \pi_{11} & \pi_{21} \\ \pi_{12} & \pi_{22} \end{pmatrix} = \begin{pmatrix} \pi_{11} & 1 - \pi_{22} \\ 1 - \pi_{11} & \pi_{22} \end{pmatrix} = \left(\pi_{ij}\right).$$

Note that the unconditional probability of regime 1 is given by[28]

$$\pi = \frac{\pi_{21}}{\pi_{12} + \pi_{21}}. \tag{II.7.39}$$

---

[26] The notation is difficult enough even with these simplifying assumptions. However, the theory generalizes to Markov switching models with more than two states and with more than one explanatory variable, provided the error process is normal and homoscedastic in each state.

[27] The *Markov property* means that the probability of being in the ith state at time t depends only on the state at time $t - 1$ and not on the states that occurred at any times $t - 2, t - 3, \ldots$. The *transition probabilities* determine the probability of being in a certain state at time t given a certain state at time $t - 1$. By the Markov property the states at times $t - 2, t - 3, \ldots$ are irrelevant for this transition probability. For simplicity here we also assume the transition probabilities do not depend on the time that they are measured, i.e. that they are constant throughout the Markov chain.

[28] This follows on assuming the system is in equilibrium and writing

$$P(\text{state } 1) = P(\text{state } 1 \,|\text{previously state } 1)\, P(\text{state } 1) + P(\text{state } 1 \,|\text{previously state } 2)\, P(\text{state } 2).$$

In other words $\pi = \pi_{11} \pi + \pi_{21}(1 - \pi)$, from which (II.7.39) can be derived.

The complete set of model parameters can be summarized in a vector,

$$\boldsymbol{\theta} = (\alpha_1, \alpha_2, \beta_1, \beta_2, \sigma_1, \sigma_2, \pi_{11}, \pi_{22})'. \tag{II.7.40}$$

The Markov chain is represented by a random *state indicator* vector $\boldsymbol{\xi}_t$ whose ith element equals 1 if $s_t = i$ and 0 otherwise. Thus, in a two-state Markov chain the state indicator vector is

$$\boldsymbol{\xi}_t = \begin{pmatrix} \xi_t^1 \\ \xi_t^2 \end{pmatrix} = \begin{cases} \begin{pmatrix} 1 \\ 0 \end{pmatrix}, & \text{if state 1 rules at time } t, \\[2mm] \begin{pmatrix} 0 \\ 1 \end{pmatrix}, & \text{if state 2 rules at time } t. \end{cases} \tag{II.7.41}$$

However the states are assumed to be *unobservable*, i.e. we do not know which value is taken by $\boldsymbol{\xi}_t$ at any time. We can never be sure about the ruling regime at time t, we can only assign *conditional probabilities* of being in one regime or another. The conditional expectation of the state indicator $\boldsymbol{\xi}_t$ at time t, given all information up to time $t-1$, is denoted $\boldsymbol{\xi}_{t|t-1}$ and, by the definition of the transition matrix $\boldsymbol{\Pi}$, this conditional expectation is the product of the transition matrix and the state indicator at time $t-1$:

$$\boldsymbol{\xi}_{t|t-1} = E_{t-1}(\boldsymbol{\xi}_t) = \boldsymbol{\Pi}\boldsymbol{\xi}_{t-1}. \tag{II.7.42}$$

The model is estimated using maximum likelihood, so we need to construct the likelihood function based on a sample $(X_t, Y_t)_{t=1}^T$ and the model. Maximum likelihood estimation is complicated by the fact that we also estimate conditional regime probabilities during the estimation and this requires a sub-iteration at every step of the numerical algorithm used to maximize the log likelihood function. This numerical algorithm is simplified considerably when the errors are assumed to be normally distributed in each state.

Denote by $\varphi(x; \mu, \sigma^2)$ the normal density function with expectation μ and standard deviation σ:

$$\varphi(x; \mu, \sigma^2) = \frac{1}{\sqrt{2\pi}\,\sigma} \exp\left[-\frac{1}{2}\left(\frac{x-\mu}{\sigma} \right)^2 \right].$$

Now set the starting value

$$\hat{\boldsymbol{\xi}}_{1|0} = \begin{pmatrix} \hat{\xi}_{1|0}^1 \\ \hat{\xi}_{1|0}^2 \end{pmatrix} = \begin{pmatrix} 1 \\ 0 \end{pmatrix} \quad \text{or} \quad \begin{pmatrix} 0 \\ 1 \end{pmatrix},$$

and also set starting values for the model parameters. Usually we set the regression coefficients and error standard deviations to be equal to their values from a standard linear regression, thus $\hat{\alpha}_1 = \hat{\alpha}_2, \hat{\beta}_1 = \hat{\beta}_2, \hat{\sigma}_1 = \hat{\sigma}_2$ at their starting values. Also we usually set $\hat{\pi}_{11} = \hat{\pi}_{22} = 0.5$.

Now starting at $t = 1$ we iterate as follows:

1. Set $f_t\left(Y_t \,\middle|\, X_t; \hat{\boldsymbol{\theta}} \right) = \hat{\xi}_{t|t-1}^1\, \varphi\left(Y_t; \hat{\alpha}_1 + \hat{\beta}_1 X_t, \hat{\sigma}_1 \right) + \hat{\xi}_{t|t-1}^2\, \varphi\left(Y_t; \hat{\alpha}_2 + \hat{\beta}_2 X_t, \hat{\sigma}_2 \right).$
2. Set

$$\hat{\boldsymbol{\xi}}_{t|t} = \begin{pmatrix} \hat{\xi}_{t|t}^1 \\ \hat{\xi}_{t|t}^2 \end{pmatrix} = \begin{pmatrix} \dfrac{\hat{\xi}_{t|t-1}^1\, \varphi\left(Y_t; \hat{\alpha}_1 + \hat{\beta}_1 X_t, \hat{\sigma}_1 \right)}{f_t\left(Y_t \,\middle|\, X_t; \hat{\boldsymbol{\theta}} \right)} \\[6mm] \dfrac{\hat{\xi}_{t|t-1}^2\, \varphi\left(Y_t; \hat{\alpha}_2 + \hat{\beta}_2 X_t, \hat{\sigma}_2 \right)}{f_t\left(Y_t \,\middle|\, X_t; \hat{\boldsymbol{\theta}} \right)} \end{pmatrix}.$$

3. Set $\hat{\xi}_{t+1|t} = \hat{\Pi}\hat{\xi}_{t|t}$.

4. Set $t = t+1$ and return to step 1 and repeat until $t = T$.

This iteration gives us two things:

- a set of conditional densities $\left\{f_t\left(Y_t \,\middle|\, X_t; \hat{\theta}\right)\right\}_{t=1}^{T}$; and

- a set of *conditional state probabilities* $\left\{\hat{\xi}_{t|t}\right\}_{t=1}^{T}$.

Initially, both of the above are based only on the *starting* values of the model parameters for the maximum likelihood estimation described below. Note that the conditional state probability vector is a 2×1 vector with elements that sum to one at each point in time. The first element gives the conditional probability of state 1 being the ruling regime and the second element is the conditional probability that state 2 is the ruling regime at time t.

The model parameters θ are now estimated by maximizing the value of the log likelihood function,

$$\ln L(\theta) = \sum_{t=1}^{T} \ln f_t(Y_t \,|\, X_t; \theta). \tag{II.7.43}$$

At each step of the optimization algorithm we return to the iteration for the conditional state probabilities and conditional densities described above, with the current iterated values of the model parameters. Considering the complexity of the log likelihood function and the relatively high number of parameters to be estimated, the selection of starting values can be critical for the convergence of the likelihood estimation. Also a number of restrictions need to be imposed on the coefficient values, specifically

$$\hat{\sigma}_1, \hat{\sigma}_2 > 0 \text{ and } 0 < \hat{\pi}_{11}, \hat{\pi}_{22} < 1.$$

Finally, we remark that it is essential to use a sufficiently large sample to correctly identify the parameters.

II.7.5.3   Financial Applications and Software

Markov switching regression models provide a powerful and systematic approach to modelling multiple breaks and regime shifts in financial asset returns. There are many diverse applications of Markov switching regressions in finance, including models of:[29]

- volatility regimes (Hamilton and Lin, 1996);
- state dependent returns (Perez-Quiros and Timmermann, 2000);
- bull and bear markets (Maheu and McCurdy, 2000);
- financial crises (Coe, 2002);
- periodically collapsing bubbles (Hall et al., 1999);
- equity trading rules (Alexander and Dimitriu, 2005b, 2005e);
- determinants of credit spreads (Alexander and Kaeck, 2008).

---

[29] The literature is so vast in this area that for each topic we quote only one reference where readers can find further references to related literature.

Markov switching model estimation is not standard in all econometric packages. Some EViews code and data for illustration are provided on the CD-ROM.[30] Matlab Markov switching code is also available to download.[31]

II.7.6   MODELLING ULTRA HIGH FREQUENCY DATA

High frequency data provide a rich source of information on the microstructure of financial markets. Empirical research focusing on the characteristics of high frequency data has demonstrated that high frequency data have pronounced 'seasonal' patterns,[32] and that there is a strong relationship between trading volume and volatility.[33] Several studies investigate the effect of news arrival and other public information on market activity.[34] The effect of new information is to increase the volatility of returns and the volatility of the bid–ask spread but this is often very short lived, lasting little more than a few hours in most cases. Other studies investigate the mechanisms by which news is carried around the world and the 'spillover' of volume and volatility between international markets.[35] In addition to the references cited so far there are several useful surveys of high frequency data analysis in financial markets.[36]

In this section we list some popular high frequency commercial databases and describe the errors that commonly occur in high frequency data. Then we discuss the application of econometric models to forecast the time between trades and to forecast realized volatility. Forecasting realized volatility is an especially 'hot topic' at present, since the price one is prepared to pay for a variance swap, i.e. a swap of realized variance with a fixed variance, depends on one's forecast of realized volatility. Whilst there is much to be said for using *subjective* views to inform forecasts of realized volatility over the next month or so, econometric analysis considerably aids our understanding of, and ability to forecast, realized variance over the very short term.

II.7.6.1   Data Sources and Filtering

We begin by listing some commercial high frequency databases.[37] High frequency data on all trades and quotes on stocks and bonds are available from the New York Stock Exchange (NYSE).[38] Their *ABS data* provide individual quotes and transactions for all their bond issues and their *Trade and Quote Detail* (TAQ) database gives access to all trades and quotes on listed and non-listed stocks. Tic by tic data on stocks are also available from the London Stock Exchange, which has provided data on trade and best prices for all UK securities traded on the exchange since September 1996.[39]

---

[30] Many thanks indeed to my PhD student Andreas Kaeck for providing these.
[31] From http://www.mathworks.com/matlabcentral/fileexchange/loadFile.do?objectId=15324&objectType=FILE you can download Matlab code for Markov switching written by Marcelo Perlin, also an ICMA Centre PhD student.
[32] See, for instance, Admati and Pfeiderer (1988), Bollerslev and Domowitz (1993) and Andersen and Bollerslev (1997, 1998b).
[33] See Tauchen and Pitts (1983), Low and Muthuswamy (1996), Andersen (1996), Jones et al. (1994) and many others.
[34] See, for instance, Almeida et al. (1998), Goodhart et al. (1993), Andersen and Bollerslev (1998b) and Andersen et al. (2003b).
[35] See Engle and Susmel (1993), Ng (2000) and many others.
[36] Such as Goodhart and O'Hara (1997), Engle (2000), Madhavan (2000), Bauwens and Giot (2001) and Andersen et al. (2005).
[37] Many thanks to my colleague at the ICMA Centre, Dr Alfonso Dufour, for advice on these databases.
[38] See http://www.nysedata.com/nysedata/InformationProducts/tabid/73/Default.aspx.
[39] See http://www.londonstockexchange.com/en-gb/products/informationproducts/historic/tickbest.htm.

High frequency bond data may be obtained from the MTS group.[40] *MTS data* contain daily cash and repo information and high frequency trade and quote data for European sovereign bond markets. Another main source of high frequency data is the electronic inter-dealer broker ICAP. Its *GovPX data* include trade information for all US Treasury issues from 1991 onward.[41] Also from ICAP, the *Electronic Broking System (EBS) Data Mine* provides historical trading activity in electronic spot foreign exchange transactions and daily electronic trades in gold and silver.

A huge amount of information can be filtered out of tic data. These data may be used to analyse market microstructure effects such as the *bid–ask bounce*,[42] the volume of trading activity at various times in the day and the behaviour of intraday prices at open, close and in-between times throughout the trading day. We can measure the times between trades, and change the time scale to this *transaction time* as explained in the next subsection. But if we want to construct equally spaced time series, the data are usually sorted into equal length consecutive time buckets. Within each n-minute interval the open, close, high, and low of the transaction prices and the volume of trades may be recorded.

High frequency data require 'cleaning' for a number of errors, including obvious errors, such as those that arise from misplaced decimal points and less obvious errors, such as reporting a trade out of sequence or discrepancies between two markets simultaneously trading the same security. Errors commonly arise from human intervention between the point of trade and data capture. Data from electronic platforms are therefore usually more reliable than data from open outcry or auction markets, where trades are recorded by pit reporters located on the floor. These reporters are trained to understand the signs that confirm trade, bid and ask prices and enter these prices by hand. Software reduces but does not eliminate the possibility of multiple reports from the same signals. Electronic trading avoids these human errors but when trading volumes are very high errors can nevertheless arise.

The removal of obvious outliers is a relatively easy problem to solve. For example, a cleaned price series $\tilde{p}_t$ can be constructed from a series p_t by defining a suitably large price increment C. If the price changes more than this amount, but the next price does not verify this change then the price is ignored. So $\tilde{p}_t$ is defined recursively by setting $\tilde{p}_1 = p_1$, and then

$$\tilde{p}_t = \begin{cases} \tilde{p}_{t-1}, & \text{if } p_t - \tilde{p}_{t-1} > C \text{ but } p_{t+1} - \tilde{p}_{t-1} < C. \\ p_t, & \text{otherwise.} \end{cases}$$

Continuous tic data may also cover periods such as weekends and public holidays where little or no activity is recorded. Long series of zero returns will distort the statistical properties of prices and returns and make volatility and correlation modelling extremely difficult, so it is normal to remove these periods before examining the data.

When data are only bid and ask quotes and not the actual transaction prices, some preliminary filters should be applied in order that they can be analysed as if they were price series. An equally spaced price series is normally obtained by taking an average of the latest bid and ask quotes during the interval. Error filters may be applied so that price data are not recorded from impossible or erroneous quotes, as described for example in Guillaume et al.

---

[40] The database is compiled by the ICMA centre. See http://www.mtsgroup.org/newcontent/timeseries/ and http://www.icmacentre.ac.uk/research_and_consultancy_services/mts_time_series for further details.

[41] See http://www.icap.com/market-commentary/market-information/historical/multi-asset-class-data.aspx.

[42] When markets are not trending there is a roughly equal proportion of buyers and sellers so the traded price tends to flip between the bid and the ask prices. Thus we commonly observe a negative serial correlation in ultra high frequency data on traded prices, but this may be purely due to the bid–ask bounce effect.

(1997). Of course it is not possible to remove all quotes that are made simply by players attempting to bid the market up or down. However, simple rules may be applied to filter out obvious bad quotes. It is more difficult to filter out marginal errors from the data because if the filter is too tight then the statistical properties of the data could be changed.

II.7.6.2   Modelling the Time between Trades

The strong relationship between volume and volatility has motivated the analysis of high frequency data that are not sampled at regular intervals. Suppose transactions arrive at irregular times $\{t_0, t_1, t_2, \ldots \}$ and let

$$x_i = t_i - t_{i-1}, \quad i = 1, 2, \ldots, \tag{II.7.44}$$

denote the *time between transactions*, also called the *trading interval* or the trade *durations*. Transaction time can flow very rapidly during busy periods and very slowly at others. Zhou (1996) and Ghysels et al. (1998) explain how time may be translated by mapping calendar time to transaction time. Andersen and Bollerslev (1998a) and Ané and Geman (2000) show that when high frequency data are transformed in this way they become more amenable to standard modelling techniques (for instance, volatility clustering is less apparent).

An alternative approach to time transformation of data is to model the trading intervals themselves, i.e. to estimate the conditional distribution of the series determined by (II.7.44). To this end Engle and Russell (1997) developed the *autoregressive conditional duration* (ACD) model and applied it to high frequency exchange rate data. Engle and Russell (1998) later applied the model to high frequency stock market data, and the model was further developed by Ghysels and Jasiak (1998).

The ACD model uses a parametric model for the duration (i.e. the time between trades) that has much in common with a GARCH model. In the ACD model the expected duration depends on past durations. Specifically, the model assumes that the conditional distribution of the durations, given past durations, is exponential. We denote by

$$\psi_i \equiv \psi_i(x_{i-1}, x_{i-2}, \ldots, x_1 \,|\, \boldsymbol{\theta}) = E(x_i \,|\, x_{i-1}, x_{i-2}, \ldots, x_1)$$

the conditional expectation of the duration and write

$$x_i = \psi_i \varepsilon_i, \tag{II.7.45}$$

where the error process $\{\varepsilon_i\}$ is i.i.d.

Many different ACD models are possible, depending on the error distribution and on the specification of the conditional expectation of the duration, ψ_i. Here we consider only the simplest case, where the error process is exponential with parameter $\lambda = 1$. Thus $E(\varepsilon_i) = 1$ for all i and x_i has an exponential distribution with parameter ψ_i^{-1}. From our discussion in Section I.3.3.2, we know that the exponential duration distribution is equivalent to assuming that the time between the $(i-1)$th trade and the ith trade is governed by a Poisson process with intensity ψ_i^{-1}. Hence, we can model the clustering of trading times by specifying an autoregressive process for the conditional expectations of the duration, ψ_i.

Just like GARCH models, different specifications of the process for ψ_i lead to different specifications of ACD model. For instance, the symmetric ACD(1, 1) process is given by[43]

$$\psi_i = \omega + \alpha x_{i-1} + \beta \psi_{i-1}. \tag{II.7.46}$$

---

[43] Note that Engle and Russell (1998) find that a better fit to IBM stock trading data can be obtained by adding further lags of both ψ_i and x_i to the right hand side of (II.7.46).

This ACD model captures the *clustering in durations*, where trades are more frequent during volatile markets, especially during the busy opening and closing times of the exchange, but less frequent during 'off peak' periods and during tranquil markets. Dufour and Engle (2000) have applied this ACD model to model liquidity risk and measure the price impact of trades. Since then a number of different ACD models have been developed, notably by Bauwens and Giot (2000). Grammig and Fernandes (2006) formulate a generic ACD model that encompasses most ACD specifications in the literature.

In (II.7.46) we use the same parameter notation as we did for the symmetric GARCH model, and this is no coincidence. Many of the properties that we developed in Chapter 4 for the symmetric GARCH model also carry over to the ACD model. For instance, we must have $\alpha, \beta \geq 0$, $\omega > 0$ so that the durations are positive. The interpretations of the parameters should be clear from the model specification:

- A relatively high value for α indicates that active trading can rapidly die out.
- A relatively high value for β indicates that the market is slow to change between periods of sluggish and active trading.
- A relatively low value for ω indicates that trading on this market is quite active in general.

The unconditional expected duration is easily calculated as

$$E(x_i) = \frac{\omega}{1 - \alpha - \beta} \tag{II.7.47}$$

In the case where the errors are exponentially distributed, a few calculations give

$$V(x_i) = \left(\frac{1 - \beta^2 - 2\alpha\beta}{1 - \beta^2 - 2\alpha\beta - 2\alpha^2} \right) E(x_i)^2 . \tag{II.7.48}$$

Parameters are estimated using maximum likelihood, in much the same way as the parameters of a GARCH model are estimated. In fact, the standard GARCH maximum likelihood estimation packages can easily be adapted for use on the ACD model. Since this is not easy to do using the Excel Solver, we simply illustrate the model by simulating a duration series using some ad hoc values for the parameters.

In the spreadsheet used to generate Figure II.7.14 we suppose that time between trades is measured in minutes and have have set[44]

$$\omega = 0.01, \ \alpha = 0.04 \text{ and } \beta = 0.95,$$

so that the expected duration (II.7.47) is 1 minute. We have simulated 500 durations, which is expected to cover at least one trading day, and we assume that the error process is exponential. Although trading always tends to be more active at certain times of day (generally, soon after the market opens and just before the market closes) no seasonal pattern is included in the simulation.[45] Nevertheless, by chance, the simulation we have chosen to depict in the figure does display more active trading at the beginning of the day. The first 250 trades take place over approximately 3 hours, whereas the second 250 trades take place over approximately 6 hours.

---

[44] But these values can be changed by the reader in the spreadsheet.
[45] But see Engle and Russell (1998) for further details on how to incorporate these effects in the ACD model.

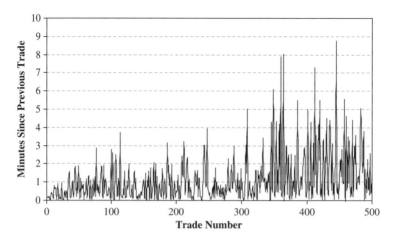

Figure II.7.14   A simulation from the exponential symmetric ACD(1,1) model

II.7.6.3   Forecasting Volatility

The h-period *realized volatility* of a stochastic process is its *forward looking* average volatility over a period of time in the future.[46] Assuming that the return at time t is not already observed when making the calculation, the h-period *realized variance* at time t is calculated from returns observed at times $t, t + 1, \ldots, t + h - 1$, often as an equally weighted average of squared log returns under the assumption that these are i.i.d. Then the realized volatility is the annualized square root of this realized variance. Realized volatility (or variance) may be estimated only ex post, and it must be forecast ex ante. It is very difficult to forecast because the realization of a process will be influenced by events that happen in the future. If there is a large market movement at any time before the risk horizon then the forecast that is made now will need to take this into account.

The h-period *historical volatility* of a stochastic process is its *backward looking* average volatility over a period of time in the past. At time t the historical volatility is calculated from log returns observed at times $t - 1, t - 2, \ldots, t - h$, so the h-period realized volatility is just a *lag* of h-period historical volatility, as shown in Figure II.7.15. Like realized variance, the term *historical variance* is usually applied to an equally weighted average of the squared log returns, which is based on a zero mean i.i.d. process assumption for log returns, and the historical volatility is the annualized square root of the historical variance.

Figure II.7.15 illustrates the relationship between realized and historical volatility, assuming that the log returns are generated by an i.i.d. process. The figure compares the historical and realized volatilities based on an equally weighted moving average of the S&P 500 squared log returns, using a rolling estimation sample of 60 days. Between 17 and 23 July 2002 the S&P 500 fell over 100 points, from over 900 to less than 800, a return of -12%. This negative return was already reflected in the realized volatility series at the end of May, with realized volatility eventually exceeding 35%. An identical feature is evident in the historical volatility series, but it happens *after* the market events. Notice

---

[46] This is different from the *forward volatility*, which is an instantaneous volatility, not an average volatility, at some time point in the future.

that very often historical volatility catches up with realized volatility just when the latter jumps down again to normal levels. On average there is about a 10% difference between them, with historical being sometimes lower and sometimes higher than realized volatility. However, during the period 2004–2006, when the market was less volatile than it generally is, there is much less difference between the historical and the realized volatility.

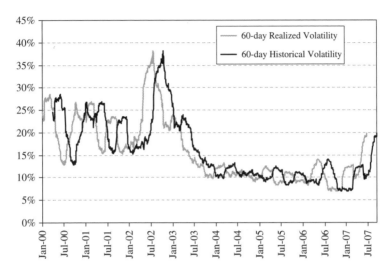

Figure II.7.15   Historical versus realized volatility of S&P 500

As these quantities are usually defined, the historical volatility has the advantage of being based on the same assumptions about the price process as the realized volatility. But since realized volatility is a lag of historical volatility, historical volatility is unlikely to be a good forecast of realized volatility. Obviously, trying to predict the lag of a time series by its current value will not usually give good results!

There is a large and growing literature on the best way to forecast realized volatility using high frequency data. A naïve approach is to apply the equally weighted volatility estimator defined above, but even within this simple framework we must make several important modelling decisions. We discuss these decisions below, as we survey some recent research on using ultra high frequency data to forecast volatility.

1. How should we sample from the high frequency data set?

Until recently it was standard practice for practitioners to drop most of the data and sample every 5 minutes at most.[47] More recently, Oomen (2006) demonstrates how the methods used to sample from high frequency data affect the statistical properties of the realized variance estimator in the presence of microstructure noise. Assuming a Lévy process for asset prices, he shows that the usual calendar time sampling is not as efficient as business time or transaction time sampling.

---

[47] Following the recommendation from Andersen et al. (2001).

From a purely statistical viewpoint the observation frequency should be as high as possible, to fully exploit the information it contains. But if data are sampled every few seconds the historical volatility forecast will be biased by microstructure effects such as the *bid–ask bounce*. Aït-Sahalia et al. (2005) compute realized volatility estimators based on two data sets, sampled at different frequencies, and combine them in such a way as to remove the effect of the noise. This way they can extract as much information as possible about volatility from the high frequency data without the forecast being biased by microstructure noise.

2. Which realized volatility are we forecasting and how do we estimate this ex post?

Variance and volatility are unobservable. They only exist in the context of a model. So how do we find a suitable ex post estimate of realized variance against which to evaluate the accuracy of a forecast? If log returns are generated by an i.i.d. process then the sum of squared returns is an unbiased estimator of realized variance. But in the presence of the negative serial correlation that often appears in the presence of microstructure noise, and under other assumptions about the data generation process, such as volatility clustering, new unbiased estimators need to be derived.

Gatheral and Oomen (2007) provide a useful survey of the many different realized variance estimators that are unbiased in the presence of microstructure noise. We can compare the *theoretical* properties of the realized variance estimators, but most of these are linked to their asymptotic distributions and infinitely large samples are not available in practice. Thus, instead of a theoretical comparison, Gatheral and Oomen compare a comprehensive set of 20 estimators by examining their performance on *simulated data* from an artificial 'zero-intelligence' market that mimics some key properties of actual markets. They conclude that the best approach is to fit a kernel to the realized returns distribution using the *realized kernel estimator* of Barndorff-Nielsen et al. (2006). We remark that Barndorff-Nielsen and Shephard (2002), as well as providing a thorough analysis of the properties of realized volatility, demonstrate its application to the calibration of stochastic volatility models.[48]

Realized variance depends on our assumptions about the price process. In the Black–Scholes–Merton model this process is assumed to be a geometric Brownian motion with constant volatility. But the market prices of options are not consistent with the Black-Scholes–Merton model so if a forecast of realized volatility is used to forecast option prices then we do *not* want to forecast the i.i.d. realized volatility. Rather we should forecast realized volatility under the assumption that the price process has stochastic volatility and jumps. A recent series of papers by Andersen, Bollerslev, Diebold and Labys (or a subset of these authors) thoroughly explores the properties of density forecasts when the price process can have stochastic volatility and jumps. Andersen et al. (2003a) provide a general framework for using high frequency data to forecast daily and weekly return distributions. They also show how the realized volatility constructed from high frequency intraday returns permits the use of traditional time series forecasting models for returns distributions. Other papers from these authors focus on the characteristics of realized volatility, and of the returns standardized by realized volatility, in stock and in currency markets.[49]

---

[48] See Neil Shephard's workpage on http://www.nuff.ox.ac.uk/users/shephard/.
[49] See Frank Diebold's home page on http://www.ssc.upenn.edu/~fdiebold/ for a full list of these papers and pdf copies.

3. Which is the best volatility model?

With so many models to choose from, how do we choose the best realized volatility forecast? Moreover, the criteria used to assess the 'best' realized volatility or realized variance forecasting model have values that depend on (a) the data sampling frequency and (b) the realized variance estimator chosen. That is, your answers to questions 1 and 2 above will influence your view on which is the best forecasting model. Therefore it is important to study the empirical performance of models for forecasting different realized variances in finite samples of different frequencies. In addition to the sampling scheme and the realized variance estimator, empirical results depend on the market studied and the forest horizon.[50]

For instance, Pong et al. (2004) compare various high frequency forecasts of the realized volatility of some major foreign exchange rates over horizons ranging from 1 day to 3 months. They fit three types of time series models to high frequency squared returns: the short memory ARMA, the long memory ARFIMA and the GARCH. Then they show that the econometric models provide better forecasts of realized volatility than daily implied volatilities alone, but only over the short forecasting horizons. In a similar study, this time based on stock market data, Oomen (2001) remarks that the marginal improvement of the ARMA and ARFIMA models over the GARCH models may not justify their additional complexity.

High frequency data may also improve the accuracy of other forecasts. For instance, recognizing the complexity of using high frequency data due to microstructure noise in intraday data, and in the absence of a single 'best' or 'true' volatility measure, Engle and Gallo (2006) propose using a set of positive indicators extracted from high frequency price series. They develop a forecasting model for monthly *implied* volatility, measured by the Vix volatility index,[51] based on the conditional dynamics of the daily high–low range, absolute daily returns and daily realized volatility.

Barndorff-Nielsen and Shephard (2004) show how to estimate and forecast the *realized covariance* and the *realized correlation* between two log returns series. Just as forecasts of realized variance and realized volatility are used to price variance swaps and volatility swaps, accurate forecasts of realized covariance and realized correlation are required to price the equity *correlation swaps* and *covariance swaps* that are actively traded in over-the-counter markets.

II.7.7 SUMMARY AND CONCLUSIONS

This chapter has provided a brief introduction to some of the advanced econometric models that are used in financial data analysis. A more complete introduction to *quantile regression* was given since this is an extremely useful tool that will surely become more popular as its importance is understood. Several Excel spreadsheets show how to implement both linear and non-linear quantile regression models, the latter being most easily estimated via copula conditional distributions.

Two case studies have implemented linear and non-linear quantile regression models using daily data. The first analysed the relationship between the FTSE 100 index and its implied

---

[50] A survey of the literature in this area is provided in Andersen et al. (2005).
[51] See Section III.4.7 for further details on volatility indices.

volatility index, the Vftse. We found a very strong tail dependency here and concluded that the returns do not have a linear relationship. Copula quantile regression provides a neat way to derive the conditional distribution of one variable given a hypothesized value for the other. For each copula considered (we used the normal, Student t and Clayton copulas) we derived a conditional confidence interval for the Vftse, given that the FTSE index falls by a fixed percentage.

The second case study examined the problem of overnight hedging of a stock portfolio, such as would be faced by a trader who has exceeded his risk limit for the day. Quantile regressions allow hedge ratios to be based on an asymmetric, downside risk optimization criteria. The case study examined six different constant and time varying hedge ratios derived from ordinary regression, EWMA, linear quantile regressions and non-linear copula quantile regressions, for a small portfolio of major stocks in the FTSE 100 index.

The next section provided a brief introduction to non-linear regression and discrete choice models. Non-linear regression and the *probit, logit* and *Weibull* discrete choice models that we considered here are easy enough to implement in Excel. We provided a simple illustration of the application of discrete choice models to estimate conditional *default probabilities*, and to estimate their sensitivities to changes in the explanatory variables (although we considered only one explanatory variable here, the debt–equity ratio). Given a sample of continuous data on the explanatory variables and a set of indicator variables which flagged whether the firm has defaulted by the end of the year, we applied three different default probability distributions (the probit, logit and Weibull) to obtain estimates for conditional default probabilities. At the sample mean of the debt–equity ratio, all three models estimated the default probability of this 'average' firm to be about 6.6%. This should be compared with the proportion of defaulting firms in the sample, which was 10%. However, these models provide quite different distributions for the default probability, conditional on any value for the debt–equity ratio.

Next we described the structure of *Markov switching regression models* using the simplest possible mathematical notation. Even with a single explanatory variable and only two states the notation for Markov switching is difficult. Yet the concept is very intuitive and these models are extremely useful tools for capturing the behaviour of financial assets returns. Our treatment of Markov switching was restricted to a careful, and hopefully tractable, exposition of the econometric structure of these models. The estimation of these models is beyond the capacity of Excel Solver and so we have included EViews code for Markov switching on the CD-ROM. There is considerable evidence of regime switching in financial markets, particularly in equity markets. The long, stable trending market regime with a low volatility is commonly broken by a high volatility crash and recovery regime, or a sideways market regime where traders appear undecided, the volatility is high and the index is bounded within a fixed range, sometimes for many months at a time. We shall return to this topic later with some case studies on volatility regimes in Section III.4.4.

Finally, this chapter surveyed the burgeoning literature on the use of high frequency data in econometric analysis. Several good commercial tic data sets are now available to the public, and consequently two major strands of econometric research on high frequency data have developed. The first uses the tic data themselves to model the durations between trades, using the *autoregressive conditional duration* framework. This framework can be extended to predict not only the time of the next trade, but also the direction in which the price is expected to move. The second main strand of research usually uses filtered tic data so that they are equally spaced in time, and then attempts to forecast *realized volatility* and *realized correlation*. These forecasts are extremely useful to traders of variance swaps and covariance swaps. At least three important questions are being addressed in this branch of the econometric literature on ultra high frequency data. How should the data be sampled so as to retain the maximum information whilst minimizing microstructure noise? How should we estimate realized volatility in order to assess the accuracy of a volatility forecasting model? And which model provides the most accurate forecasts?

More and more econometricians are moving into the finance arena, creating a vast body of research published in academic journals that is not always read, understood or even required by practitioners. Therefore the concepts and models introduced in this chapter have been selected to highlight the areas of financial econometric research that are likely to prove the most useful for practitioners.

II.8

Forecasting and Model Evaluation

II.8.1 INTRODUCTION

Previous chapters in this volume have described econometric models for estimating and forecasting expected returns, volatility, correlation and multivariate distributions. This chapter describes how to select the best model when several models are available. We introduce the *model specification criteria* and *model evaluation tests* that are designed to help us choose between competing models, dividing them into two groups:

- *Goodness-of-fit* criteria and tests, which measure the success of a model to capture the empirical characteristics of the estimation sample. Goodness-of-fit tests are a form of *in-sample specification* tests.
- *Post-sample prediction* criteria and tests, which judge the ability of the model to provide accurate forecasts. Testing whether a forecast is accurate is a form of *out-of-sample specification* testing.

The second type of criterion or test is the most important. It is often possible to obtain an excellent fit within the estimation sample by adding more parameters to the model, but sometimes a tight fit on the estimation sample can lead to worse predictions than a loose fit. And it is the predictions of the model that really matter for market risk analysis. Analysing the risk and the performance in the past, when fitting a model to the estimation sample data, may provide some indication of the risk and the performance in the future. But we should never lose sight of the fact that portfolio risk is *forward looking*: it is a metric based on the distribution of portfolio returns that are forecast over the future risk horizon. Similarly, to optimize a portfolio is to allocate resources so that the *future* risk adjusted performance is optimized.

We have already described a rudimentary goodness-of-fit test in Chapter I.4. The R^2 criterion from a standard multivariate linear regression may be transformed into a goodness-of-fit test statistic that has an F distribution.[1] But more advanced regression models require more advanced goodness-of-fit criteria, and in this chapter we shall describe several approaches to *in-sample* specification that are common to most classes of models. For instance, several in-sample specification criteria for expected returns models can equally well be applied to volatility models.

By contrast, most *forecasting* criteria and tests are specific to the class of models being considered. In particular, post-sample statistical tests on expected returns models tend to be different from post-sample statistical tests on volatility models. This is because returns are observable ex post, but volatility is not. Different volatility models have different 'true' volatilities, so any estimate or forecast of volatility is model-specific. In many cases, for

---

[1] See Sections I.4.2.4 and I.4.4.5.

instance when we are forecasting a forward conditional volatility as we do in GARCH models, there is only *one* market observation against which to measure the success of a forecast, i.e. the return that is observed on the market price at a particular point in time. Somehow we must derive criteria for conditional volatility forecasts (and, more generally, for conditional distribution forecasts) using only the observed returns.

The distributions of financial asset returns can change considerably over time. Hence, the results of a forecast evaluation will depend on the data period chosen for the assessment. Furthermore, the assessment of forecasting accuracy also depends on the criterion that is employed. It is unlikely that the same model will be the most accurate according to all possible statistical and operational criteria and over every possible data period. A forecasting model may perform well according to some criteria but not so well according to others. In short, usually no definitive answer can be given to the questions:

- Which model best captures the data characteristics?
- Which model produces the most accurate forecasts?

The rest of this chapter is structured as follows. Section II.8.2 covers the evaluation of econometric models designed to capture the characteristics of expected returns, and not the volatility or the distribution of returns. These include the regression factor models that were introduced and described in Chapter II.1 and the Markov switching models that were introduced in Chapter II.7. We focus on the statistical criteria only, since operational criteria are covered later on in the chapter, in Section II.8.5.

Section II.8.3 describes the statistical criteria that we apply to the evaluation of time varying volatility and correlation forecasts obtained from univariate and multivariate GARCH models. We also provide an empirical example of the application of model selection criteria to EWMA models, where the estimates of volatility and correlation are time varying even though the models assume they are constant. Section II.8.4 focuses on the methods used to evaluate models that are designed to capture the *tails* of a distribution. These include the quantile regression models introduced in the previous chapter as well as volatility forecasting models, since a forecast of volatility also allows the tail of a distribution to be forecast when the conditional returns distribution is either normal or Student t distributed.

Section II.8.5 covers the main types of operational criteria that are used to evaluate econometric models in *backtesting*. These are based on subjective performance criteria that are derived from the particular use of the forecast. The general procedure for backtesting is common to all models, but in the backtest different criteria and tests apply to trading models, hedging models, portfolio optimization and value-at-risk (VaR) estimation. Section II.8.6 summarizes and concludes.

II.8.2   RETURNS MODELS

This section describes the model evaluation criteria and model specification tests that may be used to assess the accuracy of regression models for expected returns. Some of these criteria and tests are specific to time series regression models for expected returns, and others have wider applications. For instance, two of the in-sample fit criteria described below may also be applied to evaluate volatility models, as we shall see in Section II.8.3.1. Others are more specific to the return model. Many of the test statistics have non-standard distributions. Hence, at the end of this section we explain how their critical values may be obtained by simulating the distribution of the test statistic under the null hypothesis.

II.8.2.1   Goodness of Fit

After reviewing the basic goodness-of-fit tests for regression models, we describe two standard methods for in-sample specification testing of returns models. These methods both involve a comparison, but of different statistical objects:

- comparison of the empirical returns distribution with the distribution that is simulated using the fitted model;
- comparison of the empirical returns autocorrelation function with the autocorrelation function that is estimated from the fitted model.

Standard Goodness-of-fit Tests for Regression Models

The *regression* R^2 is the square of the multiple correlation between the dependent variable and the explanatory variables. In other words, it is the square of the correlation between the fitted value $\hat{Y}$ and Y. It is calculated as the ratio of the explained sum of squares to the total sum of squares of the regression:[2]

$$R^2 = \frac{ESS}{TSS}. \tag{II.8.1}$$

The regression R^2 takes a value between 0 and 1 and a large value indicates a good fit for the model. We can perform a statistical test of the significance of the R^2 using the F statistic,

$$F = \frac{R^2/(k-1)}{(1-R^2)/(T-k)} \sim F_{k-1, T-k}, \tag{II.8.2}$$

where T is the number of data points used to estimate the model and k is the number of coefficients in the model, including the constant. Several examples of the F test for goodness of fit were given in Chapter I.4, so there is no need to provide examples here.

When comparing several competing models for expected returns, the model that gives the highest R^2 is not necessarily regarded as the best model. The problem is that R^2 always increases as we add more explanatory variables. When comparing models it is important to reward parsimony, and this will be a recurring theme in several specification tests that we describe below. A *parsimonious model* is one that captures the characteristics of the distribution of a random variable effectively with the fewest possible parameters.

We can adjust R^2 to account for the number of parameters used in the model. Indeed, this *adjusted* R^2 is automatically output in the set of model diagnostics in most statistical packages, including Excel. Recall from Section I.4.2.4 that

$$R^2 = \frac{ESS}{TSS} = 1 - \frac{RSS}{TSS}. \tag{II.8.3}$$

Hence, the greater the residual sum of squares the lower the R^2 and the worse the model fits the sample data.

The problem with this definition is that it takes no account of the number of coefficient parameters k in the model. But if we adjust (II.8.3) to account for the degrees of freedom of RSS and TSS, so that the right-hand side contains terms in the variance of the residuals and the total variance (rather than just the sum of squares) we obtain the *adjusted* R^2 statistic,

$$\overline{R}^2 = 1 - \frac{RSS/(T-k)}{TSS/(T-1)}. \tag{II.8.4}$$

---

[2] These concepts are defined in Section I.4.4.1.

This statistic rewards parsimonious models and it is preferable to compare the fit of models with different numbers of explanatory variables using the adjusted R^2 rather than the ordinary R^2. It is related to the ordinary R^2 as

$$\overline{R}^2 = \frac{T-1}{T-k}R^2 - \frac{k-1}{T-k}. \tag{II.8.5}$$

EXAMPLE II.8.1: STANDARD GOODNESS-OF-FIT TESTS FOR REGRESSION MODELS

Two regression models for the same dependent variable have the analysis of variance shown in Table II.8.1. Compare the goodness of fit of the two models.

Table II.8.1   Analysis of variance for two models

Model	TSS	ESS	RSS	T	k
1	50	40	10	26	4
2	50	42.5	7.5	26	11

SOLUTION   Without adjustment for the fact that model 2 has ten explanatory variables but model 1 has only three, the higher ESS from model 2 would indicate that model 2 has a better fit. The R^2 is 0.85, compared with 0.8 in model 1, and the F goodness-of-fit statistic has a p value of only 0.078%, compared with 0.42% in model 1. Both these indicate that model 2 provides a better fit. But when we consider that model 1 is a lot more parsimonious than model 2, our view changes. The adjusted values of R^2 of the two models are calculated using (II.8.4) and these are shown, with the other diagnostics for goodness of fit, in Table II.8.2. Model 1 has an adjusted R^2 of 0.77 but that for model 2 is only 0.75. From this we would conclude that model 1 is the better model.

Table II.8.2   Comparison of goodness of fit

Model	R^2	$\overline{R}^2$	F	p value
1	0.80	0.77	22	0.0042
2	0.85	0.75	7.73	0.00078

The above example highlights the fact that different model selection criteria may lead to different recommendations. If we use several criteria to evaluate two different models it is not uncommon for some criteria to favour one model and other criteria to favour the other. Very often an econometrician must have a personal ranking of different model selection criteria, viewing some criteria as more important than others, in order to select the 'best' model.

Likelihood-Based Criteria and Tests

When models are estimated using maximum likelihood, the maximized value of the likelihood based on the estimation sample provides an immediate indication of the goodness of fit of different models. It is also possible to compare the quality of fit of a simple model with a more complex model by computing the *likelihood ratio* (LR) of the maximized log likelihoods based on two fitted models. The numerator of the LR statistic is the maximized likelihood of the simpler model and the denominator is the maximized likelihood of the more complex model, which we suppose has q additional parameters. The test statistic $-2\ln(LR)$ is asymptotically chi-squared distributed with q degrees of freedom.

The maximized value of the likelihood tends to increase as more parameters are added to the model, just because there is more flexibility in the optimization. For this reason we usually prefer to quote either the *Akaike information criterion* (AIC) or the *Bayesian information criterion* (BIC), which penalize models for additional parameters. The AIC is defined as

$$AIC = 2k - 2\ln L \tag{II.8.6}$$

where $\ln L$ is the optimized value of the log likelihood function and k is the number of parameters to be estimated; and the BIC is defined as

$$BIC = T^{-1}(k \ln T - 2 \ln L), \tag{II.8.7}$$

where T is the number of data points in the estimation sample. Then the model that yields the lowest value of the AIC or the BIC is considered to be the best fit.

The reliability of likelihood-based tests and criteria depends on one's ability to specify the return distributions accurately. If we assume the returns have a normal distribution then the likelihood function will be normal, but if we assume returns are t distributed then the likelihood function will be that of the t distribution. Naturally, the two assumptions may lead to different conclusions. Hence, if likelihood criteria are to be used it is advisable to accompany results with a test for the assumed distribution of returns.

Unconditional Distribution Tests

These tests are based on a comparison of the empirical returns distribution with a simulated returns distribution generated by the estimated model. We simulate a very large number of returns based on the estimated parameters: typically 50,000 replications are used. To avoid any influence of the starting values on the results the model-based returns are simulated dynamically over many periods but only the returns simulated over the last period are used. Taking all these 50,000 simulated returns, we may fit a kernel to the model-based returns distribution, labelling this $F_1(x)$; similarly, the empirical returns distribution may also be fitted using a kernel, and the resulting distribution is denoted $F_2(x)$.[3] Now a statistic such as the *Kolmogorov–Smirnoff* (KS) statistic for the equality of two distributions is applied.[4] The statistic is

$$KS = \max_x |F_1(x) - F_2(x)|. \tag{II.8.8}$$

That is, KS is the maximum of the vertical differences between two cumulative distribution functions. The model that minimizes the value of this statistic is the preferred choice.[5]

For instance, suppose we wish to compare two models: model 1 is an autoregressive model of order 2, so the only explanatory variables are two lags of the dependent variable;

---

[3] The kernel allows one to smooth the empirical density and also to extend the tails beyond the sample range. See Section I.3.3.12 for details about kernel fitting.

[4] More details on the KS test and an associated non-parametric distribution test called the *Andersen–Darling* test are given in Section I.3.5.8. We remark that Aït-Sahalia (1996) suggests using a test statistic based on the sum of the squared differences between the two densities.

[5] This uses the KS statistic as a model selection criterion; it is not a statistical test, but it can be extended to a test by simulating critical values for KS, as explained in Section II.8.2.3.

model 2 has one exogenous explanatory variable and one lagged dependent variable. The fitted models are

$$\text{(model 1)} \quad Y_t = \hat{\alpha}_1 + \hat{\beta}_1 Y_{t-1} + \hat{\gamma}_1 Y_{t-2} + e_{1t},$$

$$\text{(model 2)} \quad Y_t = \hat{\alpha}_2 + \hat{\beta}_2 Y_{t-1} + \hat{\gamma}_2 X_t + e_{2t},$$

$$(II.8.9)$$

where e_1 and e_2 are the residuals which are distributed according to the model assumptions.

To implement the unconditional distribution test we must first find the empirical distribution of Y and, for model 2, we also need to use the empirical distribution of X. So we form a histogram based on their values over the entire sample and then if we choose, fit a kernel to this histogram. To generate the simulated distribution of the values of Y under the hypothesis that model 1 is the true model we proceed as follows:

1. Take two random draws from the empirical distribution of Y and use these as *starting values* Y_0 and Y_1 in the iteration defined by the fitted model 1.
2. At each time t we draw randomly from the distribution of the model 1 residuals to obtain Y_t given Y_{t-1} and Y_{t-2}.
3. Generate a time series of about 1000 points for Y_t under model 1.
4. Take the very last value for Y_t in this time series.
5. Return to step 1 and repeat about 50,000 times.
6. Build a distribution for Y under model 1, using these 50,000 values.

To generate the simulated distribution of the values of Y under the hypothesis that model 2 is the true model we proceed as follows:

1. Take a random draw from the empirical distribution of Y and use this as a starting value Y_0 in the iteration defined by the fitted model 2.
2. At each time t we draw randomly from the distribution of the model 2 residuals to obtain Y_t given Y_{t-1} and X_t. Here X_t is drawn randomly from the empirical distribution of X.
3. Steps 3–6 are identical to those for model 1 above.

Now we have three distributions for Y: the empirical distribution and the two distributions generated by the simulations as described above. The better model is the one that has a distribution that is closer to the empirical distribution according to a statistic such as the KS statistic (II.8.8) or one of its modifications.

EXAMPLE II.8.2: GENERATING UNCONDITIONAL DISTRIBUTIONS

Using the data given in the spreadsheet for this example, estimate the two models (II.8.9) by OLS where Y denotes the daily return on the Bank of America Corporation (BAC) stock and X denotes the return on the S&P 500 index. Compare their goodness of fit using the methodology described above.

SOLUTION   The daily returns data in the spreadsheet covers the period 31 December 2003 to 18 September 2007. First we estimate the two models using the Excel regression data analysis tool and then we use the estimated model parameters to simulate 1000 model-based returns for each model. Taking the two last returns in these two simulations gives the simulated return for BAC under the two models – these are shown in cells K2 and L2. To repeat the simulations press F9. We need to repeat the simulations about 50,000 times, each time recording the result shown in K2 and L2, which is not feasible in this Excel work-sheet. However, the method used to generate each simulation should be clear. Taking 50,000 simulated returns for each model, we can build two distributions of model-based returns and each should be compared with the empirical distribution shown in column W, using a KS test or a modified version of this.[6]

II.8.2.2   Forecasting

So far we have considered how well a model for predicting returns fits *within* the data period used to estimate the model parameters. But in many cases we plan to use a model to forecast future returns. In this section we describe statistical criteria and tests to assess the forecasting accuracy, or 'post-sample predictive ability' of an econometric model. These criteria are distinguished from the goodness-of-fit or *in-sample* criteria that were described in Section II.8.2.1 by referring to them as *post-sample* or *out-of-sample* criteria.[7] These tests and criteria are difficult to illustrate in Excel because we need to estimate models many times, each time rolling the estimation sample forward.

The following procedure is used to generate a long time series of predictions on which to base our model selection criteria:

1. Take a fixed size *estimation window*, i.e. a subsample of historic data.
2. Use this as the sample to estimate the model parameters.
3. Take a fixed size *test period* of returns, usually a short period immediately after the data window. This could be just one period if *one-step-ahead* predictions are the only predictions required by the model, but often we require forecasts over longer horizons than this.
4. Compute the model predictions for the test period.
5. Roll the estimation window forward to the end of the test period, keeping the number of observations fixed, return to step 2 and repeat the above until the entire historical sample is exhausted.
6. Combine the model predictions over all the test periods joined together, to obtain a continuous *out-of-sample* prediction set.
7. Evaluate the model predictions by computing the values of any of the criteria and test statistics that are described below.

The following model evaluation criteria and tests are designed to compare the forecasting power of a returns model by comparing two time series of returns. These time series cover the entire post-sample period, which we assume runs from time 1 until time T. They are:

- the model's post-sample predictions for returns, $\{\hat{r}_t\}_{t=1}^{T}$; and
- the observed or *realized* returns $\{r_t\}_{t=1}^{T}$ over the post-sample period.

---

[6] Since the R^2 of model 2 is 0.5123 but the R^2 of model 1 is only 0.0026, we expect that the distribution of simulated returns based on model 2 will be much closer to the empirical distribution.

[7] Post-sample tests lie in the class of out-of-sample specification tests, where the out-of-sample data set is immediately after the in-sample data set.

Common criteria for forecasting accuracy are based on a measure of proximity, i.e. a *distance metric* between these two time series. Common distance metrics include:

- *root mean square error* (RMSE), given by

$$RMSE = \sqrt{T^{-1} \sum_{t=1}^{T} (r_t - \hat{r}_t)^2};$$

- *mean absolute error* (MAE), given by

$$MAE = T^{-1} \sum_{t=1}^{T} |r_t - \hat{r}_t|;$$

- *sample correlation*,

$$\text{Corr}(r, \hat{r}) = \frac{\sum_{t=1}^{T} (r_t - \bar{r}_t)(\hat{r}_t - \bar{\hat{r}}_t)}{\sqrt{\sum_{t=1}^{T} (r_t - \bar{r}_t)^2} \sqrt{\sum_{t=1}^{T} (\hat{r}_t - \bar{\hat{r}}_t)^2}}.$$

The model giving the lowest prediction error (as measured by the RMSE or MAE) or the highest correlation is the preferred model.

Another criterion is based on the *autocorrelation function*. This is one of the most stringent criteria for model selection. The autocorrelation function of a time series of returns is the set of autocorrelations $\text{Corr}(r_t, r_{t-j})$ at lags $j = 1, 2, 3, \ldots$.[8] A model's ability to capture the *dynamic* properties of the returns can be assessed by comparing two autocorrelation functions: the autocorrelation function based on the returns that are predicted by the model and the empirical autocorrelation of the returns. We can apply an RMSE or MAE criterion to judge the proximity between the two autocorrelation functions.

II.8.2.3 Simulating Critical Values for Test Statistics

Whilst a goodness-of-fit criterion or a distance metric can be used to compare the in-sample fit or the forecasting accuracy of two different models, a formal statistical test is more conclusive. Standard tests of the null hypothesis that two models give identical forecasts are difficult to derive. A well-known non-parametric test is the Kolmogorov–Smirnoff test and its extensions.[9] Diebold and Mariano (1995) develop several other formal tests for the null hypothesis that there is no difference in the accuracy of two competing forecasts. In this framework forecast errors do not have to be i.i.d. normally distributed and a wide variety of accuracy measures can be used. A useful survey of other methods used to evaluate the accuracy of returns forecasts is given in Diebold and Lopez (1996).

More often than not we can define a test statistic but we cannot derive a standard parametric form for its distribution even asymptotically. In this section we explain how to simulate the critical values of an arbitrary test statistic. We introduce the method via a simple but illustrative example and then explain the general procedure.

---

[8] See Section II.5.2.4.
[9] The standard distribution of the *KS* statistic (or its modified forms) assumes the theoretical distribution is specified. But when we simulate a distribution under a model we use an estimated and not a predefined set of parameters. Then the distribution of the *KS* statistic must be simulated to estimate the critical values, as explained below and in Section I.5.7.2.

Suppose we wish to find the critical values of the test statistic

$$Q = \frac{\overline{X} - \mu_0}{s/\sqrt{n}}, \qquad (\text{II.8.10})$$

where $\overline{X}$ is the sample mean, based on a sample of size n, s is the sample standard deviation and the null hypothesis is that the population mean μ takes the value μ_0. We know from Section I.3.3.8 that if the population is normally distributed then Q has a Student t distribution with $n-1$ degrees of freedom. But what is the distribution of Q when the population is not normally distributed?

We may use the *statistical bootstrap* on the sample $\{x_1, \ldots, x_n\}$ to simulate a distribution for Q as follows:

1. Take a random sample (with replacement) of size n from the original sample. Thus some observations may be excluded and others repeated.[10]
2. Compute the value of Q and call this value Q_1.
3. Return to step 1 and repeat N times, where N is a very large number, thus obtaining N different values for Q, which we label $\{Q_1, \ldots, Q_N\}$.

Now the empirical distribution of $\{Q_1, \ldots, Q_N\}$ is the required distribution. We estimate the critical values for Q from the percentiles of this distribution. Under fairly general conditions the simulated distribution gives accurate critical values for the test statistic, provided N is sufficiently large.

EXAMPLE II.8.3: BOOTSTRAP ESTIMATION OF THE DISTRIBUTION OF A TEST STATISTIC

Use the sample of S&P 500 returns given in the spreadsheet for Example II.8.2 to simulate a distribution for (II.8.10) under the null hypothesis that the mean is 0.

SOLUTION The spreadsheet for this example goes only part of the way toward the solution. For reasons of space we simulate only two values of the test statistic using the bootstrap. Press F9 to repeat the simulations as usual. In practice we need to simulate several thousand values to estimate the distribution of the test statistic.

In the above example the model was very simple because we assumed an unconditional returns distribution with zero mean. But the bootstrap procedure has a straightforward extension to more general models. For instance, when testing a regression model we proceed as follows:

1. Apply the bootstrap to resample many *vectors* $\left\{Y_{t_i}, X_{1t_i}, \ldots, X_{k-1,t_i}\right\}$ for $i = 1, \ldots, T$, where T is the number of observations on each variable. That is, when a date is selected for inclusion in the bootstrapped sample we take the values of all the variables on that date and we do not 'shuffle up' the data.
2. Estimate the regression model based on the bootstrapped sample, noting the value of the statistic of interest. As before, we denote this by Q. This statistic could be an estimated parameter, a residual diagnostic or any other statistic associated with the estimated model.
3. Return to step 1 and repeat N times, where N is a very large number.
4. The empirical distribution of $\{Q_1, \ldots, Q_N\}$ is the required distribution, and the critical values are the percentiles of this distribution.

---

[10] For instance, in Excel use the INDIRECT function as described in Section I.5.7.2.

The bootstrap procedure just described may also be applied to simulate distributions of non-parametric test statistics such as Kolmogorov–Smirnoff and Anderson–Darling statistics.[11] Simulation may also be applied to estimate critical values of test statistics of complex parametric models. For instance, in the next section we summarize a test for the specification of Markov switching models where the distribution of a likelihood ratio test statistic is simulated by this method. The statistical bootstrap is a very flexible tool for estimating critical values for test statistics. Its only disadvantage is that we must use a very large number of simulations, and this can be extremely computationally intensive in complex models.

II.8.2.4 Specification Tests for Regime Switching Models

Statistical tests of a *Markov switching model* against its non-switching alternative face the problem of unidentified parameters under the null hypothesis of no switching. For this reason standard test statistics do not converge to their usual distribution. For example, the asymptotic distribution for a likelihood ratio test statistic does not have a chi-squared distribution. Alternative tests have been suggested by Engel and Hamilton (1990), Hansen (1992, 1996), Rydén et al. (1998), Garcia (1998), Breunig et al. (2003) and many others.

Engel and Hamilton (1990) describe how to perform likelihood ratio, Lagrange multiplier and Wald tests for the null hypothesis that the coefficients do not switch (i.e. their values are the same in both regimes) but the residual volatility is different in the two regimes.[12] This hypothesis is more conservative than the hypothesis that the coefficients and residual volatility are identical. It is also possible to refine these tests to determine whether specific coefficients exhibit switching behaviour. Breunig et al. (2003) modifies the unconditional distribution tests described in Section II.8.2.1 to the case of Markov switching models. However, most of the research in this area seeks a generalization of the likelihood ratio model specification test to the case of Markov switching.

The likelihood ratio statistic is obtained by dividing the maximized value of the log likelihood function obtained when estimating the Markov switching model by the maximized value obtained using the non-switching alternative. But how do we estimate the critical region for this test? An intuitive procedure suggested by Rydén et al. (1998) is to estimate the critical region using bootstrap simulation, as explained in the previous subsection. The empirical distribution of the likelihood ratio test statistic is simulated by estimating a Markov switching model and its non-switching alternative for a very large number of simulations. Naturally, this is very computationally intensive when the model has many switching parameters. A similar, but even more computationally intensive procedure can be used to test the null hypothesis that there are three regimes against the alternative that there are two regimes.

II.8.3   VOLATILITY MODELS

This section provides an overview of the statistical methods used to evaluate volatility models. Most of the academic literature in this area concerns the comparison of different GARCH models. For instance, Alexander and Lazar (2006) apply several of the tests described below to decide which is the best of 15 different GARCH models, for modelling the volatility

---

[11] The simulation of these critical values was described in detail in Section I.3.5.8.
[12] Likelihood ratio, Wald and Lagrange multiplier model specification tests were defined in Section I.4.4.6.

of major foreign exchange rates. Readers seeking a thorough survey of GARCH model evaluation tests are recommended to consult Lundbergh and Teräsvirta (2002).

We have seen in Chapters II.3 and II.4 that different volatility models can produce very different forecasts especially during volatile periods, which is when accurate volatility forecasting matters most. It is only when markets have been steady for some time that different models usually agree, broadly, about the forecasts. Why do such different forecasts arise when the models are estimated using the same data? Unlike prices, volatility is unobservable. It is a parameter of a returns distribution that measures the dispersion of that distribution.[13] It governs how much of the weight in the distribution is around the centre and at the same time how much weight is in the tails.

Tests of volatility forecasts include those that consider the entire returns distribution and those that concentrate only on the forecasts of the tails. It may be that some volatility models give better forecasts of the centre section of the return distribution, whilst others forecast the tails better. For instance, Alexander and Leigh (1997) perform a statistical evaluation of econometric volatility models using data from the major equity indices and foreign exchange rates. They find that whilst exponentially weighted moving average (EWMA) methods perform well for predicting the centre of a normal distribution, GARCH models are more accurate for the tail predictions required by VaR models.

II.8.3.1   Goodness of Fit of GARCH Models

The vast majority of sophisticated time varying volatility models fall into the category of GARCH models. Recall that the EWMA model can be thought of as a restricted version of a GARCH model. The main categories of GARCH models were introduced in Chapter II.4. These include symmetric and asymmetric, normal and t distributed, mixture and switching GARCH models. However, we have demonstrated via simulations in Section II.4.7 that the GARCH model really does need to have Markov switching between two asymmetric GARCH processes to be able to replicate the type of volatility clustering that is commonly observed in most financial markets.

This subsection describes the moment specification tests that were introduced by Harvey and Siddique (1999) to assess the in-sample fit of GARCH models, and other in-sample diagnostic tests.

Moment Specification Tests

The *volatility adjusted return* at time t is the observed return divided by the estimated conditional volatility at time t,

$$\tilde{r}_t = \hat{\sigma}_t^{-1} r_t. \qquad (\text{II.8.11})$$

If a model for conditional volatility is able to capture all the time variation in volatility over a sample then the time series of volatility adjusted returns should be independent and have volatility 1. The volatility adjusted return will have the same functional form of distribution as specified in the model. Denote this distribution function by F.

The volatility adjusted returns are transformed into a series that has a standard normal distribution under the null hypothesis that the estimated model is valid. For each volatility

---

[13] Time varying volatility is a parameter of the conditional distribution of returns, and constant volatility is a parameter of the unconditional returns distribution.

adjusted return $\tilde{r}_t$ we take the value of the cumulative distribution $u_t = F(\tilde{r}_t)$. Under the null hypothesis u_t will be independently and uniformly distributed. In that case

$$z_t = \Phi^{-1}(u_t), \quad t = 1, \ldots, T, \tag{II.8.12}$$

gives a time series that is independent and standard normally distributed under the null hypothesis.

If indeed (II.8.12) is a standard normal i.i.d. series then the first and third moments are 0, the second moment is 1 and the fourth moment is 3. These moment restrictions can be tested using the Jarque–Bera normality test.[14] Additionally, the time series (II.8.12) and its powers should not exhibit any autocorrelation. Specifically, we should have that, for $j = 1, 2, \ldots$,

$$E(z_t z_{t-j}) = E(z_t^2 z_{t-j}^2) = E(z_t^3 z_{t-j}^3) = E(z_t^4 z_{t-j}^4) = 0. \tag{II.8.13}$$

It is also possible to perform a *joint* test of all the moment restrictions using a Wald test.[15]

Other Goodness-of-Fit Tests for GARCH Models

The likelihood-based criteria that were defined in Section II.8.2.3 may also be applied to assess the goodness-of-fit of volatility models that are estimated using maximum likelihood. For instance, in the case study of Section II.4.4.2 we evaluated different GARCH models based on the in-sample likelihood.

We can also simulate unconditional distributions of returns based on the fitted GARCH model following the procedure outlined in Section II.8.2.1, and compare the simulated histogram with the empirical histogram. If the *KS* test (or a modification of the *KS* test) concludes that there is no significant difference between the two distributions then the GARCH model provides a good in-sample fit.

Another in-sample specification criterion examines whether the volatility model properly captures the dynamic properties of the returns by comparing the empirical autocorrelations of the squared returns with the autocorrelation function of the squared returns based on the fitted model, as described in Section II.8.2.2. We can apply an RMSE or MAE criterion to judge the proximity between the empirical autocorrelation function and the autocorrelation function generated by an arbitrary fitted model. The model having the smallest error is judged to be the best.

II.8.3.2   Forecasting with GARCH Volatility Models

We begin by pointing out the pitfalls of the tests that are based on comparison of the squared returns with the volatility forecast. These tests are seldom used nowadays, but were commonly used in the older volatility forecasting literature. Then we explain how to assess a volatility model's predictions based on the out-of-sample likelihood. Amongst the most effective of the out-of-sample tests are the conditional and unconditional coverage tests developed by Christoffersen (1998). These tests focus on the model's ability to forecast the *tails* of a distribution so we shall describe them later, in Section II.8.4.

---

[14] See Section I.4.3.5.
[15] See Section I.4.4.6 and Greene (2007).

Regression R²

This test is based on a regression of the squared out-of-sample returns on the squared volatility forecast. If the volatility is correctly specified the constant from this regression should be 0 and the slope coefficient should be 1. The R^2 from this regression will assess the amount of variation in squared returns that is explained by the variance forecasts. However, since the values for the explanatory variable are only estimates, the standard *errors in variables* problem of regression produces a downwards bias on the estimate of the slope coefficient. For instance, Andersen and Bollerslev (1998a) showed that if the true data generation process for returns is a symmetric normal GARCH model then the true R^2 from a regression of the squared returns on the squared volatility forecast will be very small indeed. In fact, its maximum value is

$$\max R^2 = \frac{\alpha^2}{1 - \beta - 2\alpha\beta}. \tag{II.8.14}$$

Table II.8.3 computes (II.8.14) based on different representative values for the GARCH coefficients. The largest value of (II.8.14) is only 0.3606. Hence, we are likely to obtain a very small R^2 in this test. Similar upper bounds for R^2 may be derived for other standard forecasting models. We conclude that the regression R^2 has a non-standard distribution and the usual F test based on this statistic will not provide a good indicator of a model's forecasting performance.

Table II.8.3   Maximum R^2 from regression of squared returns on GARCH variance forecast

α	β	max R^2	α	β	max R^2	α	β	max R^2
0.05	0.85	0.0130	0.075	0.83	0.0301	0.1	0.8	0.0500
0.05	0.86	0.0143	0.075	0.84	0.0334	0.1	0.81	0.0550
0.05	0.87	0.0160	0.075	0.85	0.0375	0.1	0.82	0.0611
0.05	0.88	0.0182	0.075	0.86	0.0428	0.1	0.83	0.0689
0.05	0.89	0.0210	0.075	0.87	0.0500	0.1	0.84	0.0791
0.05	0.9	0.0250	0.075	0.88	0.0601	0.1	0.85	0.0930
0.05	0.91	0.0309	0.075	0.89	0.0756	0.1	0.86	0.1131
0.05	0.92	0.0406	0.075	0.9	0.1023	0.1	0.87	0.1447
0.05	0.93	0.0594	0.075	0.91	0.1589	0.1	0.88	0.2016
0.05	0.94	0.1116	0.075	0.92	0.3606	0.1	0.89	0.3344

There is a similar problem with much of the older literature on volatility forecasting, which used an RMSE criterion to measure the distance between the squared h-period returns and the h-period variance forecasts. The difference between the variance forecast and the squared return is taken as the forecast error. These errors are squared and summed over a long out-of-sample period, and then the square root is taken, to give the RMSE between the variance forecast and the squared returns. Although the expectation of the squared return is the variance, there is typically a very large standard error around this expectation, as we have seen in Sections II.2.2.3 and II.2.3.5. Hence, these RMSE tests also have very low power.

Out-of-Sample Likelihood

A common statistical measure of volatility forecasting accuracy is the likelihood of the out-of-sample returns series. Figure II.8.1 depicts an out-of-sample return r that has a higher

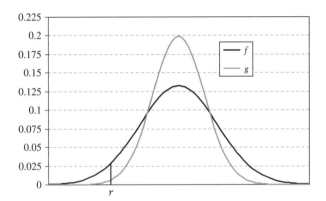

Figure II.8.1   Likelihood comparison

likelihood under the normal conditional density f than under the normal conditional density g. Since density f has a higher volatility than density g, we could conclude from this that the higher volatility forecast was more accurate on the day that the return was observed. Formally, if a density function $f(r \,|\, \mu, \sigma, \dots)$ has a functional form with fixed parameters except for the volatility, then volatility forecast $\hat{\sigma}_A$ is better than volatility forecast $\hat{\sigma}_B$ for predicting a given return r if

$$f(r \,|\, \mu, \hat{\sigma}_A, \dots) > f(r \,|\, \mu, \hat{\sigma}_B, \dots).$$

More generally, if two volatility models A and B generate a sequence of out-of-sample forecasts $\{\hat{\sigma}_{A1}, \hat{\sigma}_{A2}, \dots, \hat{\sigma}_{AT}\}$ and $\{\hat{\sigma}_{B1}, \hat{\sigma}_{B2}, \dots, \hat{\sigma}_{BT}\}$, then A is the better model according to the likelihood criterion, if and only if

$$L(r_1, r_2, \dots, r_T \,|\, \hat{\sigma}_{A1}, \hat{\sigma}_{A2}, \dots, \hat{\sigma}_{AT}) > L(r_1, r_2, \dots, r_T \,|\, \hat{\sigma}_{B1}, \hat{\sigma}_{B2}, \dots, \hat{\sigma}_{BT}), \qquad \text{(II.8.15)}$$

where L denotes the likelihood function associated with the models and $\{r_1, r_2, \dots, r_T\}$ are the out-of-sample returns.[16]

II.8.3.3   Moving Average Models

Equally or exponentially weighted moving average models of volatility and correlation are commonly used to estimate and forecast the volatility of a portfolio.[17] Suppose the volatility and correlation forecasts are for a set of financial assets or instruments (which can be stocks, stock indices, interest rates, foreign exchange rates, commodity futures, etc.) and denote the h-period covariance matrix forecast from the model by $\hat{\mathbf{V}}_h$.[18] If the portfolio weights are summarized in a vector $\mathbf{w}$ then the forecast of portfolio variance over the next h time periods is $\mathbf{w}' \hat{\mathbf{V}}_h \mathbf{w}$, and taking the square root of this and annualising gives the forecast of the average volatility of the portfolio over the next h days.

---

[16] We may also penalize the likelihood for lack of parsimony; thus we could just as well employ the AIC and BIC on post-sample predictions as on the estimation sample.

[17] The post-sample prediction test described in this section may also be applied to a multivariate GARCH model for conditional volatility and correlation, but see the discussion in Section II.8.4.3 below.

[18] Recall that these models set the covariance matrix forecast to be equal to the current estimate.

By comparing these portfolio volatility forecasts with the realized volatility of the same portfolio we can evaluate the accuracy of the moving average model. The evaluation procedure is as follows:

1. Take a long period of historical data on the returns on the constituents of the portfolio.[19] Typically these data will be daily when the covariance matrix is being tested for use in risk management systems, but weekly or monthly when the covariance matrix is being tested for use in asset management systems.[20]
2. Choose an estimation sample size T and, for the EWMA model, a value for the smoothing constant.
3. Set a value for the risk horizon h such as 1 day, 10 days, 1 month or longer. This value depends on the application. Typically h will be small for risk management but larger for portfolio optimization.
4. Estimate the covariance matrix $\hat{\mathbf{V}}_h$ using data from $t = 1$ to $t = T$ and obtain a forecast of the portfolio volatility over the next h periods as the annualized square root of the quadratic form $\mathbf{w}' \hat{\mathbf{V}}_h \mathbf{w}$.
5. Compute the realized portfolio volatility between T and $T + h$ as the volatility computed from the equally weighted average covariance matrix based on these h returns. If $h = 1$ then we have only one observation on each asset, so the variance of each asset is the squared return and the covariance is just the cross product of two returns.[21]
6. Record the prediction error, i.e. the difference between the model forecast of portfolio volatility and the realized value of the portfolio volatility.
7. Roll the estimation sample forward h periods and return to step 4, this time using the estimation sample from $t = 1 + h$ to $t = T + h$. Again record the prediction error.
8. Continue to roll the estimation sample forward, each time recording the prediction error between the portfolio volatility forecast and its realized value, until all the data are exhausted.

Now the forecasting accuracy may be assessed using an RMSE criterion, for instance.[22]

The result will depend upon our choice of portfolio weights $\mathbf{w}$, which are kept constant throughout the test. The value of $\mathbf{w}$ should reflect a particular portfolio, such as an equally weighted portfolio. The result will also depend on the choice made at step 2. Hence we should repeat the test, this time choosing a different size for the estimation window, which will have a significant effect on the equally weighted moving average prediction errors, and choosing a different value for the smoothing constant, which has a significant effect on the EWMA prediction errors.

---

[19] We may also use data on risk factors rather than assets, but this does not really simplify matters since it has the added complication of requiring an estimate of the betas of each asset at each iteration in the backtest. Assuming the betas are constant at their current value introduces a considerable model risk into the backtest. However, if a historical series of asset betas is available or can be estimated without too much difficulty then this is a viable option.

[20] A problem with monthly data is that they seriously limit the scope of the backtest because the total number of observations for use in the backtest is rather small.

[21] Or, if data are weekly or monthly we may use mean deviations in the models and the backtest, i.e. we do not necessarily assume the mean return is zero.

[22] For other criteria, as well as for more sophisticated models for forecasting realized volatility and in particular those based on ultra high frequency data, see Gatheral and Oomen (2007).

II.8.4   FORECASTING THE TAILS OF A DISTRIBUTION

This section describes statistical inference on the accuracy in the tails of a forecasted univariate distribution. Section II.8.4.1 derives confidence intervals for the quantiles of an empirical distribution and Section II.8.4.2 explains how interval coverage tests can be applied to assess the accuracy of volatility forecasts. In both sections we use statistics that are derived from the fact that the number of observations from *any* random sample that fall into a given interval has a binomial distribution. This holds irrespective of the population distribution – in other words, the statistics we introduce here are *non-parametric*.

The most common application of tail forecasts to market risk analysis is to estimate the *value at risk* of a portfolio. The VaR may be estimated as a lower quantile of either:

- a portfolio returns distribution, when expressed as a percentage of portfolio value; or
- a distribution of the profit and loss (P&L) of the portfolio, when expressed in value terms.

If the returns are assumed to have a normal, Student t or normal mixture distribution then this quantile may be expressed as a simple function of the mean and variance of the distribution (or means and variances in the case of normal mixture). More generally, we can simulate the distribution of portfolio returns or P&L, using either historical data on asset returns or via Monte Carlo simulation, and then estimate VaR as the quantile of this distribution.

II.8.4.1   Confidence Intervals for Quantiles

Conover (1999) explains how to construct confidence intervals for quantile estimates based on large samples.[23] In a random sample of size n, denote by $X(n, q)$ the number of observations less than the q quantile. This has a binomial distribution with parameters n and q, so the expectation and variance of $X(n, q)$ are nq and $nq(1 - q)$, respectively.[24] As the sample size increases the distribution of

$$\frac{X(n, q) - nq}{\sqrt{nq(1 - q)}}.$$

converges to a standard normal distribution. Hence, the lower and upper bounds of a $100(1 - \alpha)\%$ confidence interval for $X(n, q)$ are, approximately,

$$\tilde{l} \approx nq + \Phi^{-1}\left(\frac{\alpha}{2}\right)\sqrt{nq(1 - q)},$$

$$\tilde{u} \approx nq - \Phi^{-1}\left(\frac{\alpha}{2}\right)\sqrt{nq(1 - q)},$$

(II.8.16)

where Φ denotes the standard normal distribution function.[25]

We can apply (II.8.16) to find an approximate confidence interval for the quantiles of an empirical distribution by rounding $\tilde{l}$ down and $\tilde{u}$ up to the nearest integers, l and u. Then the $100(1 - \alpha)\%$ confidence interval has approximate lower bound equal to the lth observation and approximate upper bound equal to the uth observation in the *ordered* sample data.

---

[23] There is no analytic formula for the quantile confidence interval in small samples. For instance, Butler and Schachter (1998) derive confidence intervals using numerical integration techniques.

[24] See Section I.3.3.1.

[25] For instance, if $\alpha = 0.05$ then $\Phi^{-1}(\alpha/2) = -1.96$.

EXAMPLE II.8.4: QUANTILE CONFIDENCE INTERVALS FOR THE S&P 500

Based on the S&P 500 returns used in Example II.8.2 and II.8.3, approximate the following confidence intervals:

  (a) 95% confidence interval for the lower 1% percentile;
  (b) 99% confidence interval for the lower 5% percentile.

SOLUTION   We have a sample of size $n = 935$ on the S&P 500 returns and column A of the spreadsheet lists these in ascending order.[26] Then we apply formula (II.8.16) with α and q given in Table II.8.4, and round (down and up) to the nearest integer to find the row numbers for the lower and upper bounds. Finally, using the Excel INDIRECT function as in the previous example, we read off the returns that mark the lower and upper confidence bounds from column A. The results are shown in Table II.8.4.

Table II.8.4   Confidence intervals for empirical quantiles of S&P 500

Parameters	95%	99%
α	5%	1%
q	1%	5%
l	3	29
u	16	65
Lower bound	-2.69%	-1.40%
Upper bound	-1.61%	-1.05%

Thus if we were to use these data to estimate VaR over the 1-day horizon, we would be:

  • 95% sure that the 1% daily VaR would be between 1.61% and 2.69% of the portfolio value; and
  • 99% sure that the 5% daily VaR would be between 1.05% and 1.40% of the portfolio value.

By changing the parameters in the spreadsheet readers can find 90%, 99.9% and indeed any other confidence intervals for daily VaR at different significance levels.

II.8.4.2   Coverage Tests

The *coverage probability* is the probability associated with a given interval of a distribution. For instance, the coverage probability of a 5% tail of a distribution is 5%; and the coverage probability of the interval lying between the median and the upper 10% tail is 40%. In this subsection we describe the *unconditional coverage* and *conditional coverage* tests that are designed to evaluate the accuracy of a forecast for a specific interval of the distribution.

---

[26] Paste the returns values into column A and then click on Data and then on Sort.

The test for unconditional coverage is a likelihood ratio test based on the hypothesis that the forecast is accurate. The test statistic is

$$LR_{uc} = \frac{\left(1 - \pi_{exp}\right)^{n_0} \pi_{exp}^{n_1}}{\left(1 - \pi_{obs}\right)^{n_0} \pi_{obs}^{n_1}},$$

(II.8.17)

where π_{exp} is the expected proportion of returns that lie in the prescribed interval of the distribution, π_{obs} is the observed proportion of returns that lie in the prescribed interval, n_1 is the number of returns that lie inside the interval, and n_0 is the number of returns that lie outside the interval. Hence $n_1 + n_0 = n$, the total number of returns in the out-of-sample testing period and

$$\pi_{obs} = \frac{n_1}{n}.$$

The asymptotic distribution of $-2 \ln LR_{uc}$ is chi-squared with one degree of freedom.

VaR modelling requires accuracy in forecasting the tails of a returns density rather than accuracy in the main body of the returns distribution. We therefore focus on the ability of a forecast to predict returns in the lower tail, i.e. the extreme losses in a portfolio. If we assume that the portfolio returns have a normal distribution with known mean or a Student t distribution, where both the degrees of freedom and the mean are known, then these tests may also be applied to assess the accuracy of a volatility forecast when it is used to predict the tails of the returns distribution. The next example provides a simple illustration. See also Example II.8.7 for a practical implementation of unconditional and conditional coverage tests in Excel.

EXAMPLE II.8.5: UNCONDITIONAL COVERAGE TEST FOR VOLATILITY FORECAST

We are testing a volatility model for forecasting accuracy in the lower 1% tail of a returns distribution. In a post-sample test we generate 1000 forecasts for the 0.01 quantile of the returns distribution from the model. Then we count one for every *exceedance*, i.e. when the return was less than the 0.01 quantile. We observed 15 exceedances.[27] How accurate is this model?

SOLUTION   We expect 1% of the returns to lie in the lower 1% tail if the forecasts are accurate, i.e. $\pi_{exp} = 1\%$, but we have 15 exceedances out of 1000 observations, so we observe $\pi_{obs} = 1.5\%$. We calculate the value of the likelihood ratio in (II.8.17) with $n_1 = 15$ and $n_0 = 985$:

$$LR_{uc} = \frac{0.01^{15} (0.99)^{985}}{0.015^{15} (0.985)^{985}} = 0.335.$$

Now $-2 \ln(0.335) = 2.19$, but the 10% critical value of the chi-squared distribution is 2.71. Since our value for the test statistic does not even exceed this, we cannot reject the hypothesis that the model is accurate.

A feature that is important for forecasting accuracy in the tails is whether several exceedances occur in rapid succession, or whether they tend to be isolated. It is far worse for a bank if its VaR model fails to predict well for several days in a row. If the conditional volatility is properly modelled, as one hopes will be the case in the GARCH framework, the model will respond appropriately to volatility clusters. That is, the model will increase the volatility forecast during a cluster and reduce its forecast after the cluster. But this is not a feature

---

[27] We assume the first and last observations are not exceedances.

of an equally weighted moving average model based on a long averaging period, and Example II.8.7 below provides empirical verification of this fact.

Christoffersen (1998) developed the following *conditional coverage* test for whether a model's forecasts produce clusters of exceedances. To define the test statistic, first let us formalize the counting of exceedances, following Example II.8.5, by introducing the indicator function

$$I_t = \begin{cases} 1, & \text{if } r_t \text{ lies in the tail,} \\ 0, & \text{otherwise.} \end{cases} \tag{II.8.18}$$

As before, let n_1 be the number of returns that lie inside the tail of the forecasted distribution (i.e. the number of exceedances) and let n_0 be the number of returns that do not fall into the tail of the forecasted distribution (i.e. the number of returns with indicator 0: we can call these returns the 'good' returns). Further, define n_{ij} to be the number of returns with indicator value i followed by indicator value j, i.e. n_{00} is the number of times a good return is followed by another good return, n_{01} the number of times a good return is followed by an exceedance, n_{10} the number of times an exceedance is followed by a good return, and n_{11} the number of times an exceedance is followed by another exceedance. So $n_1 = n_{11} + n_{01}$ and $n_0 = n_{10} + n_{00}$. Also let

$$\pi_{01} = \frac{n_{01}}{n_{00} + n_{01}} \quad \text{and} \quad \pi_{11} = \frac{n_{11}}{n_{10} + n_{11}},$$

i.e. π_{01} is the proportion of exceedances, given that the last return was a 'good' return, and π_{11} is the proportion of exceedances, given that the last return was an exceedance.

The conditional coverage test statistic, based on the hypothesis that the forecast is accurate *and* that there is no clustering in exceedances, is

$$LR_{cc} = \frac{\pi_{exp}^{n_1}(1 - \pi_{exp})^{n_0}}{\pi_{01}^{n_{01}}(1 - \pi_{01})^{n_{00}} \pi_{11}^{n_{11}}(1 - \pi_{11})^{n_{10}}} \tag{II.8.19}$$

The asymptotic distribution of $-2 \ln LR_{cc}$ is chi-squared with two degrees of freedom.

To minimize rounding errors it is preferable to calculate the log likelihood ratio directly. Hence, we write the unconditional coverage test statistic (II.8.17) in the form

$$-2\ln(LR_{uc}) = -2 \left[n_0 \ln(1 - \pi_{exp}) + n_1 \ln(\pi_{exp}) - n_0 \ln(1 - \pi_{obs}) - n_1 \ln(\pi_{obs}) \right] \sim \chi_1^2.$$

Similarly we use the following form for the conditional coverage test statistic (II.8.19):

$$-2\ln(LR_{cc}) = -2 \left[n_0 \ln(1 - \pi_{exp}) + n_1 \ln(\pi_{exp}) - n_{00} \ln(1 - \pi_{01}) \right.$$
$$\left. - n_{01} \ln(\pi_{01}) - n_{10} \ln(1 - \pi_{11}) - n_{11} \ln(\pi_{11}) \right] \sim \chi_2^2.$$

EXAMPLE II.8.6: CONDITIONAL COVERAGE TEST

Continuing on from Example II.8.5, suppose that the 15 exceedances occur in a cluster of 3 and then in clusters of 4, 5 and 3, in between which all the returns are 'good'. Can we still accept that this model is accurate?

SOLUTION   We have $n_1 = 15$ and $n_0 = 985$ as before, and further $n_{10} = n_{01} = 4$ because there are four clusters, so $n_{11} = 11$, and $n_{00} = 981$. Furthermore, we have $\pi_{01} = 4/985$ and $\pi_{11} = 11/15$. Substituting all these values into (II.8.19) gives $-2\ln LR_{cc} = 88.52$! Clearly this far exceeds even the 0.1% critical value of the chi-squared distribution with two degrees of freedom. Hence, we can reject the hypothesis that this is a good model – not because of the number of exceedances but because they are autocorrelated.

Christoffersen (1998) shows that the conditional coverage test encompasses unconditional coverage and an *independence test* that focuses only on whether the exceedences are independent or autocorrelated. We have

$$LR_{cc} = LR_{uc} \times LR_{ind}, \tag{II.8.20}$$

so the likelihood ratio statistic for the null hypothesis that the exceedances are independent can be derived from the conditional and unconditional coverage test statistics, and $-2 \ln LR_{ind}$ is chi-squared distributed with one degree of freedom.

The above examples illustrate a common case: where the conditional coverage test fails because the independence test fails even though the unconditional coverage test passes. We have $-2 \ln LR_{cc} = 88.52$ and $-2 \ln LR_{uc} = 2.19$, so $-2 \ln LR_{ind} = 88.52 - 2.19 = 86.33$.

II.8.4.3   Application of Coverage Tests to GARCH Models

When GARCH models are applied to estimate VaR we shall *simulate* the GARCH model's returns over the risk horizon and then assess the accuracy of the model using coverage tests for the tail. The simulation of GARCH volatility based on a fitted GARCH model has been described in considerable detail in Section II.4.7.

For post-sample prediction testing and, in particular, to assess the accuracy of tail predictions, we proceed as follows:

1. Fix an estimation sample and estimate the GARCH model on daily log returns.
2. Use the fitted GARCH model to simulate the log returns over the next h days.
3. Sum these returns over the h-day period to obtain the h-day log return.
4. Return to step 2 and repeat a very large number of times (e.g. 10,000 times).
5. Estimate the required quantile(s) of the simulated distribution of h-day log returns.
6. Roll the estimation sample forward h days.
7. Return to step 1 and repeat until the entire sample of available data is exhausted.
8. Compare the actual h-day returns with the quantiles that have been simulated using the GARCH model and record the exceedances.
9. Use the time series of exceedances in the coverage tests described in the previous subsection.

I am often asked the question: why simulate? Is it not equivalent, and much easier, to use the *analytic* forecast for the h-day GARCH standard deviation $\hat{\sigma}_{t,t+h}$ in a quantile formula? For instance, in the normal linear VaR model described in Chapter IV.2 we set

$$\text{VaR}_{h\alpha t} = -\Phi^{-1}(\alpha)\,\hat{\sigma}_{t,t+h}. \tag{II.8.21}$$

Can we not use the h-day GARCH standard deviation forecast for $\hat{\sigma}_{t,t+h}$ in the above? After all, this is much quicker than simulating the quantiles!

There are two reasons why we cannot just plug the GARCH h-day forecast into a quantile formula such as (II.8.21). Firstly, this approach assumes that all the innovations during the risk horizon are 'typical', i.e. that the square of each innovation is equal to its expected value. In other words, there is no extreme return which could precipitate an increase in volatility under the assumptions of the model. Secondly, when daily returns have a conditional normal distribution with time varying volatility then the h-day return is no longer normally distributed. Hence, it is incorrect to use normal critical values $\Phi^{-1}(\alpha)$ in (II.8.21).

Nevertheless, in the academic literature you will find papers where a GARCH covariance matrix forecast is applied directly in predicting the quantiles of a portfolio returns distribution, for instance when backtesting a VaR model. The problem with this approach is that it assumes away the real power of a GARCH model, which is to capture volatility and correlation clustering following an abnormally large return in the market. Using a single GARCH covariance matrix forecast makes the assumption that all market returns during the forecasting period are at their expected value.

The quantile prediction approach described above, which relates to a univariate GARCH model, may be extended to multivariate GARCH models. But it is extremely demanding computationally except for very simple portfolios. In this approach we use the multivariate GARCH model to generate correlated simulations of h-day returns on each asset in a portfolio, as described in Section II.4.7.3. Then we use these to compute the portfolio h-day return, based on some fixed portfolio weights vector $\mathbf{w}$, and repeat many times. Then it is the returns distribution on this portfolio that we use to estimate the quantiles at step 5 of the algorithm above, and that we use to generate the actual h-day returns at step 8.

II.8.4.4 Forecasting Conditional Correlations

Like volatility, correlation is unobservable. There is no single 'true' correlation because the 'true' correlation depends on the model. Hence, the assessment of correlation forecasts becomes a problem of multivariate GARCH model specification testing.

Goodness of Fit

The in-sample fit of a multivariate GARCH model is difficult to evaluate directly using the autocorrelation function tests described in Section II.8.3.2 because the theoretical autocorrelation functions for multivariate GARCH models are not easy to derive.[28] On the other hand, it is straightforward to assess the in-sample fit of a multivariate GARCH model by examining the in-sample likelihood and the penalized likelihoods given by the AIC (II.8.6) or the BIC (II.8.7).

Adapting Moment Specification Tests to Multivariate GARCH

There are too many constraints in the moment specification tests suggested by Harvey and Siddique (1999) for these to be applied directly to the multivariate GARCH time varying variances and covariances. A multivariate GARCH model for n returns gives an estimate of an $n \times n$ covariance matrix $\mathbf{H}_t$ at every point in time! However, we can summarize the time varying covariance matrix into a *single* time series by applying it to a standard portfolio, such as a portfolio with equal weights i.e. $\mathbf{w}' = (n^{-1}, \ldots, n^{-1})$.

Denote by $\mathbf{r}_t$ the returns time series in the multivariate GARCH model. Then the equally weighted portfolio's return at time t is $r_t = \mathbf{w}'\mathbf{r}_t$ and its estimated variance at time t is $\hat{V}_t = \mathbf{w}'\hat{\mathbf{H}}_t\mathbf{w}$. If the GARCH model is capturing the time variation in the covariance matrix properly then it will also capture the time varying volatility of the equally weighted

---

[28] For the autocorrelation functions of univariate normal and normal mixture symmetric and asymmetric GARCH models, see the appendices to Alexander and Lazar (2005, 2008a).

portfolio.[29] Hence, we calculate the time series of volatility adjusted portfolio returns, $e_t \hat{V}_t^{-1/2}$, and this is the series on which we perform the moment specification tests.

Post-sample Prediction

The coverage criteria described in Sections II.8.4.2 and II.8.4.3 may be applied to evaluate a multivariate GARCH model by applying the model to forecast the volatility of an equally weighted portfolio. Alternatively, we may wish to evaluate the model based on a different portfolio, perhaps one with weights $\mathbf{w}$ that represent the 'typical' distribution of funds into different types of assets.[30] We proceed as follows:

1. Fix the estimation sample size, calculate the daily log returns for each asset and use these to estimate the parameters of the multivariate GARCH model.[31]
2. Use the fitted GARCH model to simulate the log returns on each asset over the next h days.
3. Sum these returns over the h-day period to obtain the h-day log return on each asset.
4. Apply the portfolio weights vector $\mathbf{w}$ to obtain a GARCH simulation for the h-day portfolio return.[32]
5. Return to step 2 and repeat a very large number of times (e.g. 10,000 times).
6. Hence simulate a distribution of h-day portfolio returns.
7. Estimate the required quantile(s) from this distribution.
8. Roll the estimation sample forward h days, compute the log returns and again fit the GARCH model.
9. Return to step 2 and repeat until the entire period of historical data is exhausted.
10. Now form a current weighted portfolio returns series, i.e. apply the weights $\mathbf{w}$ to all the historical data on the constituent assets' returns.
11. Compare the empirical h-day portfolio returns with the quantiles that have been simulated using the multivariate GARCH model.
12. Record the exceedances, i.e. the times when the empirical h-day return exceeds the GARCH forecast.
13. Use the time series of exceedances in the coverage tests described in Section II.8.4.2.

The *out-of-sample likelihood* can also be used to assess the predictions from a multivariate GARCH model. In this case at step 6 we forecast the conditional distribution of h-day portfolio returns, to compare the empirical h-day portfolio return with the simulated distribution and record the log likelihood; then we sum the values of the log likelihood over the entire set of post-sample predictions. The best model is the one with the highest value of the log likelihood, or the highest penalized log likelihood based on Akaike or Bayesian information criteria.

---

[29] But the converse is not true. Just because the equally weighted portfolio passes these tests, other portfolios may not. Hence to test the multivariate GARCH model properly many different portfolio weights should be used.
[30] These weights are set at the time of the test and are kept constant throughout.
[31] We need log returns so that we can aggregate at step 3, but at step 4 we assume these are ordinary (percentage) returns. However, the log returns are approximately equal to the ordinary returns provided the returns are daily. If the data are at a lower frequency then take care to use the percentage return in steps 1 and 2 and set $h = 1$ at step 3.
[32] The portfolio return is the weighted sum of the percentage returns, not the log returns on the assets. See Section I.1.4.7. Hence, the approximation worsens as the holding period h increases.

II.8.5 OPERATIONAL EVALUATION

An operational evaluation of an econometric model is based on a specific application. For instance, if a returns model is used to derive optimal portfolio allocations then we test the model by forming portfolios according to its recommendations and by assessing the performance of these portfolios. Practitioners often refer to this type of evaluation as the *backtesting* of the model because we pretend that we are at some time in the past, we estimate the model and then use the subsequent historical data to evaluate the outcome. We must not *data snoop*. That is, we must not cheat by using data that we are not supposed to know at the time when we estimate the model.

Operational evaluation is based on a long time series of post-sample observations. The best strategy is the one that produces the 'best' performance according to this time series. The method for constructing a time series of post-sample observations and the criteria for determining the best performance depend on the type of application. That is, alpha trading, volatility trading, hedging and risk measurement models each use slightly different forms of backtests and different performance metrics.

The advantage of operational evaluation is that the model is being assessed in the actual context in which it will be used. The disadvantage is that the best model is likely to be specific to the application. For instance, we might find that an asymmetric Student t GARCH model is best for trading implied volatility but an asymmetric normal GARCH model with implied volatility in the conditional variance equation is best for trading realized volatility.

In the following we focus on several of the most common financial applications of econometric forecasting models, describe how the backtests are performed in each case and suggest some of the performance metrics that may be applied. We start by describing the backtest procedure in general terms, and then explain how backtests are applied in several specific applications of econometric models.

II.8.5.1 General Backtesting Algorithm

The idea of a backtest is to use an econometric model to determine the weights in a portfolio, and to generate a long time series of post-sample profit and loss (P&L) on this portfolio (or returns, but only if the portfolio has no short positions). Then we apply a performance criterion to this time series, to determine whether it has desirable properties.

In order to perform a backtest we need a long, concurrent time series of prices or returns for every asset, factor or instrument in the investment universe and on the benchmark, if there is one. Denote the total number of observations in these time series by T. There are five stages to every backtest, and the first, third and fifth stages are common to all backtests. The second and fourth stages are model-specific, so we shall describe these in more detail in the following subsections. The general algorithm is as follows:

Stage 1: Choose the backtest parameters. A backtest has two basic parameters, which are the number of observations

- in the estimation sample, denoted N,
- until rebalancing of the portfolio, denoted h.

The results will depend on the choice made for these parameters, so backtests should be repeated for many different choices of N and h. If our data are sampled at the rebalancing frequency then $h = 1$, but often the series are sampled at a higher frequency (e.g. we may take daily data but only rebalance weekly, then $h = 5$). The first estimation sample contains data from $t = 1$ until $t = N$.

Stage 2: Model estimation and application. Estimate the model using the observations in the estimation sample. Then determine the optimal portfolio allocations that are recommended by the model. Buy or sell the assets or instruments in the quantities that are as close as possible to the recommended allocations, factoring in the trading costs.

Stage 3: Recording, rolling and repeating. Hold the portfolio that has been recommended at stage 2 for h periods and record the profit or loss made on the portfolio, i.e. the difference between the value of the portfolio at the end of the period and its value when the hypothetical trades were made.[33] Roll the estimation sample forward h periods, keeping the number of observations N constant.[34] Return to stage 2 and repeat, each time rebalancing the portfolio and factoring in the rebalancing costs to the value of the portfolio, until the entire sample of T observations is exhausted.

Stage 4: Performance measurement. Now we have a single time series of P&L, or returns, running from $t = N$ until $t = T$ and having the same frequency as the rebalancing period. These observations are generated *post sample* so there is no possibility of data snooping. Now we can apply a risk adjusted performance metric, such as the Sharpe ratio (SR) or any one of the other metrics described in Section I.6.5, to this series.[35] Alternatively, we apply a performance criterion that accounts for the risk tolerance of the investor, via an assumed utility function.[36] Note that when the operational evaluation is on value-at-risk estimation, it is standard to use the conditional coverage statistics described in Section II.8.4.2.

Stage 5: Summarize results. The algorithm just described is for one particular model, based on one particular choice of backtest parameters. The analyst now needs to change two things:

- the model parameters, N and h, to investigate how his choice of parameters influenced results; and
- the econometric model, since the whole purpose of backtesting is to compare the performance of several possible models.

Finally, the results of a backtest can be summarized in a table, such as Table II.8.5 below, which allows the analyst to rank the models in order of the value that each model gives for the chosen performance criterion.[37]

We conclude this subsection by making two further remarks on backtesting methodology. Firstly, the results are specific to the evaluation criterion that is applied at stage 4. For example, we might use a Sharpe ratio, or a metric that penalizes negative skewness and positive excess kurtosis in the P&L distribution. The ranking of the models may be different

---

[33] Alternatively, if the portfolio can only ever have long positions, you may record the portfolio return over this period.

[34] For instance, if the data are daily, the estimation sample size is 500 and the rebalancing period is 10 trading days, the second estimation window runs from $t = 11$ until $t = 510$, the next runs from $t = 21$ until $t = 520$, and so forth.

[35] The Sharpe ratio can be applied to a series of P&L simply by multiplying the risk free return by the nominal value invested, and this becomes the second term in the numerator. The mean and standard deviation terms in the SR are the mean and standard deviation of P&L, not of returns.

[36] Further details are given in Section I.6.2.

[37] Most performance metrics will favour a positive average return in excess of the benchmark return with a low volatility and a near-normal distribution. We may need a time series on the benchmark at stage 2 is so that we can determine the values of these risk adjusted performance metrics which may be measured relative to a benchmark.

under these two metrics. Secondly, the longer the total period covered by the backtest, the more information we can derive from the results. For instance, if the sample period covers both ordinary and stressful market circumstances, then we could distinguish between the backtest performances during different market regimes. This way we might consider adopting one model during stressful markets and another model during ordinary market circumstances.

II.8.5.2 Alpha Models

The managers of funds, hedge funds and funds of funds often use *factor models* to attempt to identify profitable investment opportunities. Factor models for expected returns are commonly based on a linear regression, and they are given the name *alpha models* because the constant term in a regression model is usually denoted α. Applying the factor model to each asset in the investor's universe provides an estimate of both the alpha and the systematic risk of each asset, and the skill of the analyst lies in determining allocations to these assets to construct a portfolio with a significant positive α. This is thought to indicate that the portfolio provides abnormal returns.[38] The only problem is that there is a huge *model risk* when estimating alpha. That is, the estimates of alpha vary enormously depending on the explanatory variables used in the factor model.[39]

Another area where regression models are applied in fund management is in the development of indexation and enhanced indexation products, pairs trading and statistical arbitrage strategies. These models can be based on standard regressions (of returns on returns) or cointegrating regressions (of prices on prices, or log prices on log prices).[40] Whenever regression models are used to determine portfolio allocations the analyst must make several subjective decisions concerning the data and the variables used, and again the potential for model risk to influence results is considerable.

The backtesting of regression models is an essential part of the portfolio analyst's job. The particular choices he made about the model specification can only be justified by demonstrating that the model performs well in backtesting. In stage 2 of the general backtesting algorithm we must determine the optimal portfolio allocations to each asset and use all the capital that is available. Note that some long-short strategies could be specifically designed to be self-financing. Just how we determine the optimal allocations depends on the model. For instance, a cointegration-based statistical arbitrage strategy would:

- use OLS to estimate the parameters of a linear regression, where the dependent variable is the log of the index plus α per annum, and the explanatory variables are the log asset prices;
- translate the OLS estimates of the coefficients into portfolio weights, simply by normalizing them to sum to 1;
- also take an equal short position on the index futures.

---

[38] *Abnormal returns* are returns that are consistently above the security market line, so the portfolio is expected to outperform the market portfolio. See Section I.6.4 for further details.

[39] Nevertheless there is useful information in the *ranking* of alphas according to different factor models. Given any factor model, we can estimate a distribution for alpha over all securities in the universe. If the alpha of security X is in a specified upper quantile (e.g. the top 10%) of the distribution of alpha according to every factor model then it is likely that security X does provide a profitable investment. Further details of applications of ranking alphas are given in Alexander and Dimitriu (2005d).

[40] Indexation models in general, plus a case study on indexation of the Dow Jones Industrial Average, were described in Section II.5.4, and a cointegration-based pairs trading model was developed and tested in Section II.5.5.

At the end of the backtest we produce a table of results, such as that shown in Table II.8.5. The results should help fund managers determine both the preferred model and the optimal choice of parameters (the size of the estimation window and the rebalancing frequency). For instance, given the results shown in Table II.8.5, we can immediately identify model D as being the worst model. The best model for small samples is model B and the best model for larger samples is model A. The highest Sharpe ratio is obtained when model A is estimated on a sample of 500 observations.

Table II.8.5 Hypothetical Sharpe ratios from alpha model backtest results

Model	A		B		C		D	
Estimation sample size	SR	Rank	SR	Rank	SR	Rank	SR	Rank
50	0.88	2	1.02	1	0.75	3	−0.34	4
100	0.54	3	1.31	1	0.64	2	−0.22	4
250	1.36	1	1.27	2	1.24	3	0.45	4
500	1.44	1	0.89	3	1.39	2	0.42	4
1000	1.02	1	0.75	3	0.97	2	0.51	4

II.8.5.3 Portfolio Optimization

In standard portfolio optimization, optimal allocations are based on the Markowitz criterion that the portfolio should have the minimum possible risk whist providing a target level of return. These are easy to derive because there is an analytic solution to the problem. More generally, we can always apply a numerical algorithm to determine optimal portfolio allocations, even when there are many constraints on allocations.[41] Without constraints, the optimal allocations are often too extreme, and lack robustness as the portfolio is rebalanced.

Over the years various statistical techniques have been designed to cope with the difficulty of forecasting expected returns. Notably, Black and Litterman (1992) raised the general issue of whether the analyst should use *personal views* when making forecasts, wherever these views may come from. An excellent survey of the literature in this area, a critique and an extension of the Black–Litterman model, is given by Pézier (2007).

Sheedy et al. (1999) develop a backtesting methodology for assessing the accuracy of moving average covariance matrices when they are used to inform portfolio allocation decisions. At stage 2 of the backtest we use the N observations in the estimation sample to construct an h-period covariance matrix $\hat{V}_h$. This matrix is then used to derive the optimal portfolio weights according to the classical approach, which is described in Section I.6.3 or, if used in conjunction with the analyst's, personal views, according to the Black–Litterman model.

II.8.5.4 Hedging with Futures

When two asset returns are highly correlated, but not perfectly correlated, it is possible to use an econometric model to derive a short term minimum variance hedge ratio for hedging one asset with the other. If the two returns are perfectly correlated the optimal hedge ratio

---

[41] As described in Section I.6.3.4.

will be to match a long position in one asset with an equal short position in the other, i.e. to use the one-to-one or 'naïve' hedge ratio. But when they are highly but not perfectly correlated then the hedge ratio that minimizes the variance of the hedged portfolio may be different from 1.

We remark that a common example where minimum variance has been employed (in the academic literature if not in practice) is the hedging of a spot exposure with a futures contract. But in Section III.2.7 we explain that minimum variance hedging is only relevant for short term hedging and show that, in many futures markets, the spot–futures returns correlation is so high that there is no need for minimum variance hedging in this context: the naïve hedge ratio performs just as well, even over very short intervals such as 1 day. But if an econometric model *is* used to derive minimum variance hedge ratios in practice, then we should test the model in this context.

Consider two portfolios with h-period returns X_1 and X_2. Then the minimum variance hedge ratio, for hedging a position in asset 1 with $\hat{\beta}_t$ units of asset 2, over the time interval t to $t+h$ is

$$\hat{\beta}_t = \frac{\hat{\sigma}_{12t}}{\hat{\sigma}_{2t}^2},\qquad\qquad (\text{II.8.22})$$

where $\hat{\sigma}_{12t}$ denotes the time varying estimate of the covariance between the returns of asset 1 and asset 2, and $\hat{\sigma}_{2t}^2$ denotes the time varying estimate of the variance of the returns on asset 2. This is proved in Section III.2.7.1. The variance and covariance in (II.8.22) can be estimated via equal weighting or exponential weighting of cross products and squares of returns, or via bivariate GARCH models. Note that even when the equal weighting or exponential weighting models are used, i.e. when the theoretical hedge ratios are constant over time, their estimates will vary as the sample changes.

A backtest of a model that is used for minimum variance hedging determines at stage 2 the quantity of the hedge to buy (if short the underlying) or sell (if long the underlying). We may use any hedging effectiveness criterion in stage 4. Possible effectiveness criteria range from the very basic *Ederington effectiveness*, which measures the reduction in variance as a percentage of the unhedged portfolio's variance, to the more complex *certain equivalent* criterion which depends on the utility function and risk tolerance of the hedger. These criteria are defined and discussed in Section III.2.5.7. Then Section III.2.7 surveys the vast academic literature on backtesting models for minimum variance hedging, and presents some empirical results.

II.8.5.5 Value-at-Risk Measurement

Econometric models of volatility and correlation may also be used to estimate the value at risk of a portfolio. The volatility and correlation forecasts are summarized in an h-period covariance matrix forecast $\hat{\mathbf{V}}_h$, which is commonly based on a moving average model for unconditional volatility and correlation. If the portfolio weights are summarized in a vector $\mathbf{w}$ then the forecast of portfolio variance over the next h time periods is $\mathbf{w}'\hat{\mathbf{V}}_h\mathbf{w}$.

In the following we describe a backtest based on the normal linear VaR formula (II.8.21), where

$$\hat{\sigma}_{t,t+h} = \sqrt{\mathbf{w}'\hat{\mathbf{V}}_{ht}\mathbf{w}}.\qquad\qquad (\text{II.8.23})$$

and $\hat{\mathbf{V}}_{ht}$ denotes the h-period covariance matrix forecast made at time t, which is the last day of the estimation sample. But the test can be modified to accommodate other types of

VaR estimates. For instance, when a GARCH covariance matrix is used we need to apply simulation, following our discussion in Section II.8.4.3. A more complete discussion of backtests of VaR models, including Monte Carlo simulation and historical simulation, is given in Chapter IV.6.

The backtest requires us to fix the significance level α for the VaR estimate and to keep the portfolio weights $\mathbf{w}$ constant throughout. Thus the results depend on these parameters, in addition to h and N. We set a value for h such as 1 day, 10 days, 1 month or longer. This value depends on the application of the VaR estimate.

At stage 2 of the backtest we estimate the equally weighted covariance matrix $\hat{\mathbf{V}}_{ht}$ on the estimation sample ending at time t, or we use the estimation sample to determine the EWMA covariance matrix for some fixed smoothing constant.[42] Then we calculate the portfolio variance $\mathbf{w}' \hat{\mathbf{V}}_{ht} \mathbf{w}$, and take its square root to obtain the h-period standard deviation forecast $\hat{\sigma}_{t,t+h}$ starting at the end of the estimation window. Finally, we set

$$\mathrm{VaR}_{h\alpha t} = -\Phi^{-1}(\alpha)\,\hat{\sigma}_{t,t+h}.$$

At stage 4 of the backtest we apply the *coverage tests* that are described in Section II.8.4.2. At each time t we must compare the VaR estimate with the realized h-period portfolio return, $\mathbf{w}'\mathbf{r}_{t,t+h}$, where $\mathbf{r}_{t,t+h}$ denotes the vector of asset returns between time t and $t+h$. If there is a negative portfolio return that exceeds the VaR estimate in magnitude, then the indicator (II.8.18) takes the value 1, to flag this exceedance of the VaR. The result of rolling the estimation sample and repeating the above is a time series of exceedances on which we can perform the unconditional and conditional coverage tests.

To illustrate this procedure, the next example performs a backtest for VaR estimation assuming a simple portfolio that has a fixed point position on the S&P 500 index shown in Figure II.8.2.

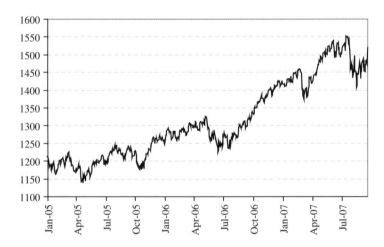

Figure II.8.2   S&P 500 Index January 2000–September 2007

---

[42] The smoothing constant is a parameter of the model rather than a parameter of the backtest.

EXAMPLE II.8.7: BACKTESTING A SIMPLE VaR MODEL

Use the daily returns on the S&P 500 index shown in Figure II.8.2 to backtest (a) the equally weighted volatility forecast based on the past 60 daily returns and (b) the EWMA volatility forecast with a smoothing constant of 0.95.[43] Roll over the backtest daily, each time forecasting the S&P 500 volatility and hence the 5% 1-day VaR of the portfolio. Then apply unconditional and conditional coverage tests to test the performance of each model.

SOLUTION   The tests are implemented in the spreadsheet, and the results are displayed in Table II.8.6. Neither model fails the unconditional coverage test for 5% VaR. The 10% critical value of the chi-squared distribution with one degree of freedom is 2.71 and both the unconditional coverage statistics are less than this. The EWMA model also passes the conditional coverage test but the equally weighted model fails this test at 5%, though not at 1%: the test statistic is 8.74 and its 1% critical value is 9.21. We conclude that the EWMA model is able to estimate 5% VaR adequately but the equally weighted model is less able to capture the volatility clustering feature of the S&P 500 index, at least at the 5% VaR level.

Table II.8.6   Coverage tails for VaR prediction on the S&P 500 index

	Equally weighed	Exponentially weighted
n	1875	1875
n_1	107	97
n_0	1768	1778
π_{obs}	5.71%	5.17%
π_{exp}	5%	5%
Unconditional	1.89	0.12
π_{01}	5.32%	4.95%
π_{11}	12.15%	9.28%
Conditional	8.74	3.03

Chi-squared critical values			
	1%	5%	10%
1 df	6.63	3.84	2.71
2 df	9.21	5.99	4.61

Readers can change the significance level of the VaR in the spreadsheet simply by changing the percentile in π_{exp}. You will find that both models pass unconditional and conditional coverage tests for 10% VaR but both models fail even the unconditional coverage test for the accurate estimation of 1% VaR. The accurate estimation of VaR at very high confidence levels is very difficult and it is not easy to find a model that can pass the coverage tests. However, some VaR models *are* able to pass the tests at very high confidence levels for the VaR, as shown by Alexander and Sheedy (2008).

[43] The smoothing constant can be changed in the spreadsheet, as can the look-back period for the equally weighted moving average volatility, although this requires a little more work.

II.8.5.6   Trading Implied Volatility

Implied volatility is the forecast of realized volatility that is implied from the current market price of a standard European call or put option. Implied volatility is 'backed out' from the market price using the Black–Scholes–Merton formula, as described in Section III.4.2. The price of a standard call or put option increases with implied volatility and if the volatility were 0 the option would have the same value as a futures contract. Hence, we can trade implied volatility by trading standard call or put options: buying a call or put option is a long position on volatility, and selling a call or put option is a short position on volatility.

Accurate predictions of implied volatility give an option trader an edge over the market. If his forecast of implied volatility is significantly greater than the current market implied volatility then he believes that the market prices of European call and put options are too low and he should buy them, and if his forecast of implied volatility is significantly less than market implied volatility then the market prices of European call and put options are too high and he should sell them.

However, options are trades on implied volatility *and* the direction on the underlying. If we want to trade implied volatility alone, we can trade an options strategy, such as an at-the-money (ATM) straddle, that has a pay-off which depends *only* on implied volatility.[44] The operational evaluation of a statistical forecast of volatility based on its use for trading implied volatility is illustrated with the following example.

EXAMPLE II.8.8: USING VOLATILITY FORECASTS TO TRADE IMPLIED VOLATILITY

Every day an option trader uses an asymmetric GARCH model to forecast FTSE 100 volatility over the next 30 days, and according to his forecast he may buy or sell a 30-day ATM straddle on the FTSE100 index options, or make no trade.[45] He has an historical series of 30-day

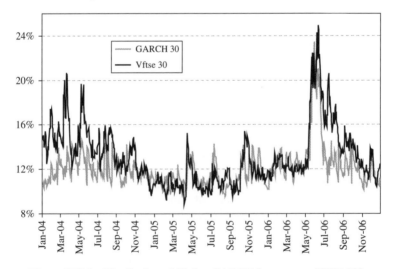

Figure II.8.3   Distribution of 30-day GARCH forecasts on FTSE 100

---

[44] Straddles, strangles and other options trading strategies are defined in Section III.3.5.
[45] FTSE 100 European call and put options are at fixed maturity dates, so to buy a 30-day straddle he will usually need to make four trades, buying calls and puts of the nearest expiry date and the next nearest expiry date in proportion to their time to expiry.

GARCH volatility forecasts that has been estimated by rolling the GARCH model forward daily, each time re-estimating the parameters and making the 30-day volatility forecast. He also has daily historical data on an implied volatility index for the FTSE 100 index, and both series are shown in Figure II.8.3. Denote the 30-day GARCH volatility forecast by $\hat{\sigma}_t^{30}$ and the 30-day implied volatility on the FTSE 100 index by θ_t^{30}, both estimated on day t.[46] Both volatilities are measured in annualized terms. Which of the following simple trading metrics is more appropriate?

1. If $\theta_t^{30} > \hat{\sigma}_t^{30}$ sell a 30-day ATM straddle, and if $\theta_t^{30} < \hat{\sigma}_t^{30}$ buy a 30-day ATM straddle, otherwise make no trade.
2. If $\theta_t^{30} - \hat{\sigma}_t^{30} > 1\%$ sell a 30-day ATM straddle, if $\theta_t^{30} - \hat{\sigma}_t^{30} < -1\%$ buy a 30-day ATM straddle, otherwise make no trade.
3. If $\theta_t^{30} - \hat{\sigma}_t^{30} > 3\%$ sell a 30-day ATM straddle, if $\theta_t^{30} - \hat{\sigma}_t^{30} < -1\%$ buy a 30-day ATM straddle, otherwise make no trade.

SOLUTION   Figure II.8.4 shows the empirical distribution of the spread between the 30-day implied volatility and the 30-day GARCH forecast based on this sample. A strong positive skewness is evident from Figure II.8.4, and on this figure we have also marked the mean, which is approximately 1% and plus and minus one standard error bounds. These are at approximately -1% and $+3\%$ since the standard deviation of the spread is approximately 2%.[47]

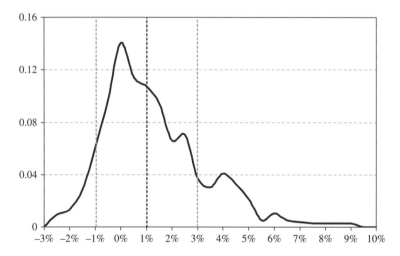

Figure II.8.4   Distribution of spread between implied and GARCH volatilities

The reason for the positive mean and positive skew is that implied volatility tends to be too persistent following a severe market shock. In other words, option traders have a lot of uncertainty about volatility, and because of this the market remains 'nervous' for too long. Following a market crisis it is quite common that the market prices of options are too

---

[46] The trades are determined on every day t for some undefined nominal exposure.
[47] The sample statistics are: mean, 1.04%; standard deviation, 1.97%; skewness, 0.940; excess kurtosis, 1.06.

high compared with the price we would obtain by plugging the GARCH forecast into the Black–Scholes–Merton formula.

Since the standard error of the spread between the two volatilities is almost twice the mean spread, there is a good deal of uncertainty in this distribution, which is also highly non-normal. Strategy 1 recommends selling straddles whenever the spread is negative and buying them whenever the spread is positive. Clearly, this will result in very frequent trading and the trading costs would quickly erode any profit that is made. Strategy 2 is to trade at the mean and the lower one standard error bound, but this may still lead to too much trading. Trading strategy 3 is likely to be the most profitable, since it trades on a mean reversion of the spread between the two forecasts. To investigate exactly how profitable it is would require a model for the stationary process.[48]

It is impossible to say which volatility forecast provides the best prediction of implied volatility without fixing the trading strategy. Hence, any backtesting methodology based on implied volatility trading is complicated by the fact that there are *two* things to test: the volatility forecasting model *and* the trading strategy. For a fixed trading strategy we can test which model provides the best implied volatility forecasts by using the strategy at stage 2 of the backtest. Alternatively, for a fixed volatility forecasting model we can test which is the best trading strategy by using different strategies at stage 2 of the backtest. What we cannot do is test both the model and the trading strategy simultaneously.

II.8.5.7   Trading Realized Volatility

During the past few years realized volatility has become a traded asset. Variance swaps, which are described in detail in Section III.4.7, allow investors to buy or sell realized volatility. The two parties swap a variable volatility, defined by the annualized square root of the realized variance over the time between inception and maturity of the swap, for a fixed rate volatility called the *variance swap rate*. The pay-off to the buyer of a variance swap is the difference between the realized variance and the square of the variance swap rate. Variance swap contracts are only traded over the counter, and in most contracts the realized variance is based on the constant volatility geometric Brownian motion assumption. In fact most contracts define the realized volatility as a zero mean i.i.d. realized volatility, i.e. as the annualized square root of the equally weighted average of squared daily returns over the period between inception of the swap and its maturity.

Since implied volatility is based on a market option price, which in turn is based on the expectations of all the traders in the market, implied volatility should provide a good forecast of the i.i.d. realized volatility. A fundamental assumption of the Black–Scholes–Merton model is that log returns follow an i.i.d. normal process and this assumption is also implicit in an implied volatility, because it is obtained via the Black–Scholes–Merton formula. If the assumptions made by the Black–Scholes–Merton model were accurate the implied volatility that is backed out from all options on the same underlying would be the same, since they all represent the same realized volatility. However, traders do not appear to believe the Black–Scholes–Merton assumption since the implied volatilities that are backed out from different options on the same underlying can be very different. This is what is commonly referred

---

[48] Following the methodology outlined in Section II.5.5, for instance.

to as the volatility *smile effect*.[49] Also the way that option traders respond to information is very unpredictable. For both these reasons an implied volatility is usually found to be a biased predictor of realized volatility. In particular, ATM implied volatility (i.e. the implied volatility of the ATM option) is usually much higher than realized volatility during and immediately after market crises.

We can assess the accuracy of a model for forecasting realized volatility in an operational backtest based on trading variance swaps. At stage 2 of the backtest we only need to compute the prediction error, i.e. the difference between the h-day realized volatility and the forecast of the average volatility over the next h days. Then at stage 4 we analyse the time series of prediction errors generated by each of the volatility forecasting models. The performance metric could be very simple, such as taking the preferred model to be the one that minimizes the root mean square prediction error, or the mean absolute prediction error.

Poon and Granger (2003) provide an excellent review of a vast body of academic research comparing the ability of implied volatility, historical, EMWA and GARCH models to forecast realized volatility, and similar reviews are given in Christensen and Hansen (2002), Giot (2003), Mayhew and Stivers (2003) and Szakmary at al. (2003).[50] The general consensus is that, when based on daily data, ATM implied volatility contains the most useful information for predicting realized volatility, but that GARCH volatility forecasts also contain significant information about realized volatility that may not be contained in implied volatility.[51] We conclude by remarking that ATM implied volatilities contain only part of the information available in option prices. To capture more information about traders' expectations we could instead use an *implied volatility index*, which represents an average of implied volatilities across different strike options.[52] In comparison to the rest of the literature in this area, there is relatively little empirical research on the forecasting accuracy of implied volatility indices at the time of writing, notable exceptions being Giot (2005), Becker et al. (2006) and Nishina et al. (2006).

II.8.5.8 Pricing and Hedging Options

GARCH volatility forecasts are based on the assumption that the price process has stochastic volatility,[53] hence these forecasts can be used to price options consistently with observed market prices. But few GARCH models give closed form options prices even for standard European options, a notable exception being the model proposed by Heston and Nandi (2000).

Given a GARCH process with some fixed parameters, and leaving aside for the moment the question of how these parameters are calibrated, we derive the GARCH option price using the risk neutral valuation principle.[54] This entails simulating the underlying price process using the GARCH model, as explained in Section II.4.7, from now until the expiry

---

[49] Many more details about the characteristics of volatility smiles are given in Section III.4.2.
[50] See Section II.7.7.4 for a review of more recent research on using statistical models estimated on *high frequency* data to forecast realized volatility.
[51] We remark that GARCH models also have the ability to include the implied volatility index in the conditional variance equation, thus combining the informational content from both forecasts. See Day and Lewis (1992).
[52] It is constructed to be equal to the square root of the risk neutral expectation of the realized variance, i.e. the variance swap rate. Full details are given in Section III.4.7.4.
[53] This is explained in Section III.4.5.6.
[54] See Section III.3.2.

date of the option. We repeat this simulation a very large number of times, thus obtaining a distribution for the underlying price on every day from now until the option's expiry.[55] Then we apply the option's pay off function to the simulated prices, find the average pay-off, and discount the average pay-off to today using the risk free rate. This gives the risk neutral GARCH option price. GARCH hedge ratios are based on finite difference approximations, and are also calculated using simulation. See Section II.4.8.1 for further details and some practical examples.

When using a GARCH model for option pricing, it is appropriate to calibrate the GARCH model parameters to the liquid market prices of standard European call and put options, in just the same way as we would calibrate a continuous time option pricing model.[56] Thus we fix some starting values for the GARCH model parameters, compute the GARCH option prices for all the options in the calibration set and calculate the root mean square error between the GARCH option prices and the market prices. Then we apply an optimization algorithm, for instance a gradient method, to change the model parameters in such a way as to minimize the root mean square error. This requires simulating thousands of underlying prices at each step of the iteration, so it is rather computationally intensive.

If the GARCH model is calibrated to market prices of options then an operational evaluation of the model consists in backtesting its hedging performance. Option market makers set prices, at least those for liquid options, according to supply and demand in the market and not according to any model. For each option they set a premium that is expected to cover the cost of hedging the position, and it is in the hedging of the position that substantial losses could be made. Hence, the real test of any option pricing model is in its hedging performance. Following Engle and Rosenberg (1995) several research papers address this issue.[57]

However, recent advances in the option pricing literature have cut through a considerable amount of academic research in this area, rendering it redundant. This is because we now know that virtually all option pricing models for tradable assets should have the *same* price hedge ratios, for virtually every traded option! The only differences that are observed in practice are due to different models having differing quality of fit to market prices of options. Alexander and Nogueira (2007) have shown that:[58]

- Price processes for tradable assets must be *scale invariant*.
- The class of scale invariant processes includes virtually all stochastic volatility models, with or without jumps in the price and volatility, continuous time GARCH processes and most Lévy price processes.[59]
- All scale invariant models have the *same price hedge ratios* for virtually all contingent claims. Any differences between the estimated hedge ratios from different models is simply due to the models' better or worse fits to the market data!

[55] Note that if we are pricing a standard European option all we need to save here is the distribution of the terminal prices, i.e. the price distribution at the expiry of the option. Otherwise the option may have path-dependent or early exercise features, so we need to know the price distribution at every day until expiry.
[56] In fact, for this purpose we prefer to use the continuous version of the GARCH model. The continuous limit of GARCH models is an interesting theoretical problem in econometrics that has provoked a good deal of controversy. A full discussion – and resolution – of this issue is provided in Section III.4.5.6.
[57] For instance, see Duan et al. (2006).
[58] See Section III.4.6 for further information.
[59] It excludes the CEV (constant elasticity of variance) and SABR (stochastic alpha–beta–rho) models, and all models for interest rates and credit spreads which are typically based on *arithmetic* Brownian motion.

So the price hedge ratios for all GARCH models, including those with jumps, are theoretically equal to the *model free* hedge ratios that are derived directly from market prices. If differences are observed between these two hedge ratios then this is only due to calibration errors.

II.8.6 SUMMARY AND CONCLUSIONS

Econometric time series models are used to estimate and forecast the conditional distributions of financial asset returns. The selection criteria that we have introduced in the chapter are based on the model's goodness-of-fit to sample data and on the model's ability to make accurate forecasts. Where possible we have described parametric and non-parametric statistical tests based on both in-sample and post-sample criteria. We remark that the goodness-of-fit of copulas, which model the *un*conditional multivariate distribution, was discussed in Section II.6.6.3 and is not covered in this chapter.

The non-linear regression models and the Markov switching models that we have considered in Section II.8.2 fall into the class of *returns* models because their focus is on estimating and forecasting the expected return. These models still estimate and forecast a conditional *distribution* about this expected return but we make simplifying assumptions about this distribution, for instance that it is normal and has constant volatility, so that only the expected value varies over time. This is because the primary object of interest is the conditional *expectation* of the returns distribution.

Section II.8.3 focuses on the evaluation of conditional volatility models, where the focus is on the time varying variance of a univariate conditional distribution for the returns; and conditional correlation models, where the focus is on the time varying covariance of a conditional multivariate distribution for returns. This time we make simplifying assumptions about the conditional expectation of the distribution, for instance that it is constant over time or that it follows a simple autoregressive process, because the primary objects of interest are the conditional *variance* of the marginal distributions and the conditional *covariance* of the joint distribution.

Statistical tests and criteria compare the model's predictions with the empirical returns, or with measures such as realized volatility that are based on these returns. One of the most stringent, but also very relevant, tests for the forecasting accuracy of a volatility model is its ability to forecast the tails of the returns distribution. *Unconditional coverage* tests are based on a comparison of the quantiles predicted by the model with the empirical returns. For instance, 5% of the empirical returns should be less than the lower 5% percentile of the forecast returns distribution, if the model is accurate. Also if a volatility model is able to capture the volatility clustering that is commonly observed in financial asset returns, then the empirical returns that fall into the tails of the forecasted distribution should not be autocorrelated. This is what *conditional coverage* tests are designed to investigate. Coverage tests and likelihood-based criteria for forecasting accuracy may also be applied to conditional correlation models, and to multivariate GARCH models in particular. In this case we apply the conditional covariance matrix that is forecast by the model to a portfolio with constant weights, such as an equally weighted portfolio.

The assessment of forecasting accuracy can be based on operational as well as statistical criteria. These criteria are based on a set of post-sample returns or P&L that are generated by rolling a fixed sized estimation sample forward over the forecasting horizon, each time recording the model's predictions, and comparing these predictions with empirical returns or

P&L. This type of evaluation is often called a *backtest* of the model. The form of post-sample prediction in the backtest and the metrics used to assess the results depend on the particular application of the model. We have discussed how to backtest several econometric models, including: the factor models that are used in portfolio management; covariance matrices that are used for portfolio optimization and VaR estimation; and the GARCH (and EWMA) volatility models that are used for short term hedging with futures, trading implied volatility, trading variance swaps and hedging options.

References

Admati, A. and Pfeiderer, P. (1988) A theory of intraday patterns: Volume and price variability. *Review of Financial Studies* 1, 3–40.

Aït-Sahalia, Y. (1996) Testing continuous-time models of the spot interest rate. *Review of Financial Studies* 9(2), 385–426.

Aït-Sahalia, Y., Mykland, P. and Zhang, L. (2005) A tale of two time scales: Determining integrated volatility with noisy high-frequency data. *Journal of the American Statistical Association* 100, 1394–1411.

Alexander, C. (1999) Optimal hedging using cointegration. *Philosophical Transactions of the Royal Society Series A* 357, 2039–2058.

Alexander, C. (2001a) *Market Models: A Guide to Financial Data Analysis.* John Wiley & Sons, Ltd, Chichester.

Alexander, C. (2001b) Orthogonal GARCH. In C. Alexander (ed.), *Mastering Risk*, Volume 2, pp. 21–38. Financial Times Prentice Hall, Harlow.

Alexander, C. and Barbosa, A. (2007) Effectiveness of minimum variance hedging. *Journal of Portfolio Management* 33(2), 46–59.

Alexander, C. and Barbosa, A. (2008) Hedging exchange traded funds. *Journal of Banking and Finance* 32(2), 326–337.

Alexander, C. and Chibumba, A. (1996) Multivariate orthogonal factor GARCH. Working paper, Mathematics Department, University of Sussex.

Alexander, C. and Dimitriu, A. (2004) Sources of out-performance in equity markets: Common trends, mean reversion and herding. *Journal of Portfolio Management* 30(4), 170–185.

Alexander, C. and Dimitriu, A. (2005a) Indexing and statistical arbitrage: Tracking error or cointegration? *Journal of Portfolio Management* 31(2), 50–63.

Alexander, C. and Dimitriu, A. (2005b) Indexing, cointegration and equity market regimes. *International Journal of Finance and Economics* 10, 213–231.

Alexander, C. and Dimitriu, A. (2005c) Hedge fund index tracking. In G.N. Gregoriou, G. Hübner, N. Papageorgiou, and F. Rouah (eds), *Hedge Funds: Insights in Performance Measurement, Risk Analysis, and Portfolio Allocation*, pp. 165–179. John Wiley & Sons, Inc., Hoboken, NJ.

Alexander, C. and Dimitriu, A. (2005d) Rank alpha funds of hedge funds. *Journal of Alternative Investments* 8(2), 48–61.

Alexander, C. and Dimitriu, A. (2005e) Detecting switching strategies in equity hedge funds returns. *Journal of Alternative Investments* 8(1), 7–13.

Alexander, C. and Johnson, A. (1992) Are foreign exchange markets really efficient? *Economics Letters* 40, 449–453.

Alexander, C. and Johnson, A. (1994) Dynamic Links. *Risk* 7(2), 56–61.

Alexander, C. and Kaeck, A. (2008) Regime dependent determinants of credit default swap spreads. *Journal of Banking and Finance* 32. In press. http://dx.doi.org/10.1016/j.jbankfin.2007.08.002.

Alexander, C. and Lazar, E. (2005) The continuous limit of GARCH. ICMA Centre Discussion Papers in Finance DP2005-13.

Alexander, C. and Lazar, E. (2006) Normal mixture GARCH(1,1): Applications to foreign exchange markets. *Journal of Applied Econometrics* 21(3), 307–336.

Alexander, C. and Lazar, E. (2008a) Modelling regime specific stock volatility behaviour. Revised version of ICMA Centre Discussion Papers in Finance DP2005-14.

Alexander, C. and Lazar, E. (2008b) Markov switching GARCH diffusion ICMA Centre Discussion Papers in Finance DP2008–01.

Alexander, C. and Leigh, C. (1997) On the covariance matrices used in VaR models. *Journal of Derivatives* 4(3), 50–62.

Alexander, C. and Nogueira, L. (2007) Model-free hedge ratios and scale-invariant models. *Journal of Banking and Finance* 31(6), 1839–1861.

Alexander, C. and Sheedy, E. (2008) Developing a stress testing framework based on market risk models. *Journal of Banking and Finance*. In Press. http://dx.doi.org/10.1016/j.jbankfin.2007.08.041.

Alexander, C., Giblin, I. and Weddington, W. (2002) Cointegration and asset allocation: A new active hedge fund strategy. *Research in International Business and Finance* 16, 65–90.

Almeida, A., Goodhart, C. and Payne, R. (1998) The effect of macroeconomic news on high frequency exchange rate behaviour. *Journal of Financial and Quantitative Analysis* 33(3), 383–408.

Andersen, T.G. (1996) Return volatility and trading volume: An information flow interpretation of stochastic volatility. *Journal of Finance* 51, 169–204.

Andersen, T.G. and Bollerslev, T. (1997) Intraday periodicity and volatility persistence in financial markets. *Journal of Empirical Finance* 4, 115–158.

Andersen, T.G. and Bollerslev, T. (1998a) Answering the skeptics: Yes, standard volatility models do provide accurate forecasts. *International Economic Review* 39, 885–905.

Andersen, T.G. and Bollerslev, T. (1998b) Deutschemark-dollar volatility: Intraday activity patterns, macroeconomic announcements, and longer-run dependencies. *Journal of Finance* 53, 219–265.

Andersen, T.G., Bollerslev, T., Diebold, F.X. and Ebens, H. (2001) The distribution of realized stock return volatility. *Journal of Financial Economics* 61, 43–76

Andersen, T.G., Bollerslev, T., Diebold, F.X. and Labys, P. (2003a) Modeling and forecasting realized volatility. *Econometrica* 71, 579–625.

Andersen, T.G., Bollerslev, T., Diebold, F.X. and Vega, C. (2003b) Micro effects of macro announcements: Real-time price discovery in foreign exchange. *American Economic Review* 93, 38–62.

Andersen, T.G., Bollerslev, T. and Diebold, F.X. (2005) Parametric and nonparametric volatility measurement. In L.P. Hansen and Y. Aït-Sahalia (eds), *Handbook of Financial Econometrics*. North-Holland, Amsterdam.

Andersen, T.G., Bollerslev, T., Christoffersen, P.F. and Diebold, F.X. (2006) Volatility and correlation forecasting. In G. Elliott, C.W.J. Granger, and A. Timmermann (eds), *Handbook of Economic Forecasting*, pp. 778–878. North-Holland, Amsterdam.

Ané, T. and Geman, H. (2000) Order flow, transaction clock, and normality of asset returns. *Journal of Finance* 55, 2259–2284.

Bai, X., Russell, J.R. and Tiao, G.C. (2001) Beyond Merton's utopia, I: Effects of non-normality and dependence on the precision of variance using high-frequency financial data. GSB Working Paper, University of Chicago.

Bai, X., Russell, J.R. and Tiao, G.C. (2003) Kurtosis of GARCH and stochastic volatility models with non-normal innovations. *Journal of Econometrics* 114(2), 349–360.

Baillie, R.T. and Bollerslev, T. (1989) Common stochastic trends in a system of exchange rates. *Journal of Finance* 44(1), 167–181.

Baillie, R.T. and Bollerslev, T. (1994) Cointegration, fractional cointegration, and exchange rate dynamics. *Journal of Finance* 49(2), 737–745.

Barndorff-Nielsen, O.E. and Shephard, N. (2002) Econometric analysis of realized volatility and its use in estimating stochastic volatility models. *Journal of the Royal Statistical Society Series B* 64, 253–280.

Barndorff-Nielsen, O.E. and Shephard, N. (2004) Econometric analysis of realised covariation: High Frequency based covariance, regression and correlation in financial economics. *Econometrica* 72, 885–925.

Barndorff-Nielsen, O.E., Hansen, P.R., Lunde, A. and Shephard, N. (2006) Designing realised kernels to measure the ex-post variation of equity prices in the presence of noise. Manuscript, Nuffield College, University of Oxford.

Bates, D.S. (1991) The crash of '87: Was it expected? The evidence from options markets. *Journal of Finance* 46, 1009–1044.

Bauwens, L. and Giot, P. (2000) The logarithmic ACD model: An application to the bid-ask quotes process of three NYSE stocks. *Annales d'Economie et de Statistique* 60, 117–149.

Bauwens, L. and Giot, P. (2001) *Econometric Modelling of Stock Market Intraday Activity*. Kluwer Academic, Boston.

Beck, S.E. (1994) Cointegration and market efficiency in commodities futures markets. *Applied Economics* 26(3), 249–257.

Becker, R., Clements, A. and White, S. (2006) On the informational efficiency of S&P500 implied volatility. *North American Journal of Economics and Finance* 17, 139–153.

Bessler, D.A. and T. Covey. (1991) Cointegration – some results on cattle prices. *Journal of Futures Markets* 11(4), 461–474.

Bierens, H.J. (2007) *Easyreg International*. Department of Economics, Pennsylvania State University, University Park, PA. http://grizzly.la.psu.edu/~Hbierens/EASYREG.HTM.

Black, F. and Litterman, R. (1992) Global portfolio optimization. *Financial Analysts Journal*, 48(5), 28–43.

Bollerslev, T. (1986) Generalised autoregressive conditional heteroscedasticity. *Journal of Econometrics* 31, 307–327.

Bollerslev, T. (1987) A conditionally heteroskedastic time series model for speculative prices and rates of return. *Review of Economics and Statistics* 69, 542–547.

Bollerslev, T. (1990) Modelling the coherence in short-run nominal exchange rates: A multivariate generalized ARCH model. *Review of Economics and Statistics* 72(3), 498–505.

Bollerslev, T. and Domowitz, I. (1993) Trading patterns and prices in the interbank foreign exchange market. *Journal of Finance* 48, 1421–1443.

Bollerslev, T., Chou, R.Y. and Kroner, K.F. (1992) ARCH modeling in finance: A review of the theory and empirical evidence. *Journal of Econometrics* 52, 5–59.

Bopp A.E. and Sitzer, S. (1987) Are petroleum prices good predictors of cash value? *Journal of Futures Markets* 7, 705–719.

Bouyé, E. and Salmon, M. (2002) Dynamic copula quantile regressions and tail area dynamic dependence in forex markets. Working Paper WP03-01, Financial Econometrics Research Centre, Warwick University. Available from http://www2.warwick.ac.uk/fac/soc/wbs/research/wfri/rsrchcentres/ferc/wrkingpaprseries (accessed November 2007).

Bouyé, E., Durrleman, V., Nikeghbali, A., Riboulet, G. and Roncalli, T. (2000) Copulas for finance – A reading guide and some applications. Working Paper, Groupe de Recherche Opérationnelle, Crédit Lyonnais.

Bradley, M. and Lumpkin, S. (1992) The Treasury yield curve as a cointegrated system. *Journal of Financial and Quantitative Analysis* 27, 449–463.

Brenner, R.J. and Kroner, K.F. (1995) Arbitrage, cointegration, and testing the unbiasedness hypothesis in financial markets. *Journal of Financial and Quantitative Analysis* 30(1), 23–42

Brenner, R.J., Harjes, R.H. and Kroner, K.F. (1996) Another look at alternative models of the short term interest rate. *Journal of Financial and Quantitative Analysis* 31(1), 85–108.

Breunig, R., Najarian, S. and. Pagan, A (2003) Specification testing of Markov switching models. *Oxford Bulletin of Economics and Statistics* 65(1), 703–725.

Brooks, C. (2008) *Introductory Econometrics for Finance*, 2nd edition. Cambridge University Press, Cambridge.

Brooks, C., Burke, S.P. and Persand, G. (2003) Multivariate GARCH models: Software choice and estimation issues. *Journal of Applied Econometrics* 18, 725–734.

Butler J.S. and Schachter, B. (1998) Estimating value-at-risk with a precision measure by combining kernel estimation with historical simulation. *Review of Derivatives Research* 1(4), 371–390.

Cai, J. (1994) A Markov model of switching-regime ARCH. *Journal of Business and Economic Statistics* 12(3), 309–316.

Campbell, J.Y. and Hentschel, L. (1992) No news is good news: An asymmetric model of changing volatility in stock returns. *Journal of Financial Economics* 31, 281–318.

Cappiello, L., Engle, R.F. and Sheppard, K. (2003) Asymmetric dynamics in the correlations of global equity and bond returns. ECB Working Paper No. 204, January.

Chernozhukov, V. and Umantsev, L. (2001) Conditional value-at-risk: Aspects of modelling and estimation. *Empirical Economics* 26, 271–293.

Cherubini, U., Luciano, E. and Vecchiato, W. (2004) *Copula Methods in Finance*. John Wiley & Sons, Ltd, Chichester.

Choi, I. (1992) Durbin-Hausman tests for a unit root. *Oxford Bulletin of Economics and Statistics* 54(3), 289–304.

Chowdhury, A.R. (1991) Futures market efficiency: Evidence from cointegration tests. *Journal of Futures Markets* 11(5), 577–589.

Christensen, B.J. and Hansen, C.S. (2002) New evidence on the implied realized volatility relation. *European Journal of Finance* 7, 187–205.

Christoffersen, P. (1998) Evaluating interval forecasts. *International Economic Review* 39(4), 817–840.

Christoffersen, P., Heston, S. and Jacobs. K. (2006) Option valuation with conditional skewness. *Journal of Econometrics* 131, 253–284.

Clare, A.D., Maras, M. and Thomas, S.H. (1995) The integration and efficiency of international bond markets. *Journal of Business Finance and Accounting* 22(2), 313–322.

Clarida, R.H., Sarno, L., Taylor, M.P. and Valente, G. (2003) The out-of-sample success of term structure models as exchange rate predictors: A step beyond. *Journal of International Economics* 60, 61–83.

Clayton, D. (1978) A model for association in bivariate life tables and its application in epidemiological studies of familial tendency in chronic disease incidence. *Biometrika* 65, 141–151.

Cochrane, J.H. (1991) A critique of the application of unit root tests. *Journal of Economic Dynamics and Control* 15, 275–284.

Coe, P. (2002) Financial crisis and the Great Depression: A regime switching approach. *Journal of Money, Credit and Banking* 34, 76–93.

Coleman, M. (1990) Cointegration-based tests of daily foreign exchange market efficiency. *Economics Letters* 32, 53–59.

Conover W.J. (1999) *Practical Nonparametric Statistics*, 3rd edition. John Wiley & Sons, Inc., New York.

Corhay, A., Tourani Rad, A. and Urbain, J.-P. (1993) Common stochastic trends in European stock markets. *Economics Letters* 42, 385–390.

Cuvelier, E. and Noirhomme-Fraiture, M. (2005) Clayton copula and mixture decomposition. In J. Janssen and P. Lenca (eds), *Applied Stochastic Models and Data Analysis*, pp. 699–708. ENST Bretagne, Brest.

Davidson, J., Madonia, G. and Westaway, P. (1994) Modelling the UK gilt-edged market. *Journal of Applied Econometrics* 9(3), 231–253.

Day, T. and Lewis, C. (1992) Stock market volatility and the information content of stock index options. *Journal of Econometrics* 52, 267–287.

Demarta, S. and McNeil, A.J. (2005) The *t* copula and related copulas. *International Statistical Review* 73(1), 111–129.

Dickey, D.A. and Fuller, W.A. (1979) Distribution of the estimators for autoregressive time series with a unit root. *Journal of the American Statistical Association* 74, 427–431.

Dickey, D.A. and Fuller, W.A. (1981) Likelihood ratio statistics for autoregressive time series with a unit root. *Econometrica* 49, 1057–1079.

Diebold, F.X. and Lopez, J.A. (1996) Forecast evaluation and combination. In G.S. Maddala and C.R. Rao (eds), *Handbook of Statistics*, Vol. 14: *Statistical Methods in Finance*, pp. 241–268. North-Holland, Amsterdam.

Diebold, F.X. and Mariano, R.S. (1995) Comparing predictive accuracy. *Journal of Business and Economic Statistics* 13, 253–265.

Diebold, F.X. and Rudebusch, G.D. (1991) Forecasting output with the composite leading index: A real time analysis. *Journal of the American Statistical Association* 86, 603–610.

Diebold, F.X., Lee, J.H. and Weinbach, G.C. (1994) Regime switching with time-varying transition probabilities. In C. Hargreaves (ed.) *Nonstationary Time Series Analysis and Cointegration*, pp. 283–302. Oxford University Press, Oxford.

Dotsis, G., Psychoyios, D. and Skiadopoulos, G. (2007) An empirical comparison of continuous-time models of implied volatility indices. *Journal of Banking and Finance* 31, 3584–3603.

Duan, J.-C. and Pliska, S. (2004) Option valuation with cointegrated asset prices. *Journal of Economic Dynamics and Control* 28(4), 727–754.

Duan, J.-C., Ritchken, P. and Zhiqiang, S. (2006) Jump starting GARCH: Pricing and hedging options with jumps in returns and volatilities. FRB of Cleveland Working Paper No. 06–19.

Dufour, A. and Engle, R.F. (2000) Time and the price impact of a trade. *Journal of Finance* 55, 2467–2498.

Dunis, C. and Ho, R. (2005) Cointegration portfolios of European equities for index tracking and market neutral strategies. *Journal of Asset Management* 6, 33–52.

Embrechts. P., McNeil, A.J. and Straumann, D. (2002) Correlation and dependence in risk management: Properties and pitfalls. In M. Dempster (ed.), *Risk Management: Value at Risk and Beyond*. Cambridge University Press, Cambridge.

Embrechts. P., Lindskog, F. and McNeil, A.J. (2003) Modelling dependence with copulas and applications to risk management. In S.T. Rachev (ed.), *Handbook of Heavy Tailed Distributions in Finance*. Elsevier/North-Holland, Amsterdam.

Engel, C. and Hamilton, J.D. (1990) Long swings in the dollar: Are they in the data and do markets know it? *American Economic Review* 80(4), 689–713.

Engle, R.F. (1982). Autoregressive conditional heteroscedasticity with estimates of the variance of UK inflation. *Econometrica* 50, 987–1007.

Engle, R.F. (1990) Stock volatility and the crash of '87: Discussion. *Review of Financial Studies* 3(1), 103–106.

Engle, R.F. (2000) The econometrics of ultra-high frequency data. *Econometrica* 68, 1–22.

Engle, R.F. (2002) Dynamic conditional correlation – a simple class of multivariate GARCH models. *Journal of Business and Economic Statistics* 20(3), 339–350.

Engle, R.F. and Gallo, G. (2006) A multiple indicators model for volatility using intra-daily data. *Journal of Econometrics* 131, 3–27.

Engle, R.F. and Granger, C.W.J. (1987) Co-integration and error correction: Representation, estimation and testing. *Econometrica* 55(2), 251–276.

Engle, R.F. and Kozicki, S. (1993) Testing for common features. *Journal of Business and Economic Statistics* 11, 369–395.

Engle, R.F. and Kroner, K.F. (1993) Multivariate simultaneous generalized ARCH. *Econometric Theory* 11, 122–150.

Engle, R.F. and Manganelli, S. (2004) Caviar: Conditional autoregressive value at risk by regression quantile. *Journal of Business and Economic Statistics* 22(4), 367–381.

Engle, R.F. and Ng, V.K. (1993) Measuring and testing the impact of news on volatility. *Journal of Finance* 48, 1749–1778.

Engle, R.F. and Rosenberg, J. (1995) GARCH gammas. *Journal of Derivatives* 2, 47–59.

Engle, R.F. and Russell, J.R. (1997) Forecasting the frequency of changes in the quoted foreign exchange prices with the autoregressive conditional duration model. *Journal of Empirical Finance* 4, 187–212.

Engle, R. F., and Russell, J.R. (1998) Autoregressive conditional duration: A new model for irregularly spaced transaction data. *Econometrica* 66, 1127–1162.

Engle, R.F. and Susmel, R. (1993) Common volatility in international equity markets. *Journal of Business and Economic Statistics* 11, 167–176.

Engle, R.F. and Yoo, B.S. (1987) Forecasting and testing in cointegrated systems. *Journal of Econometrics* 35, 143–159.

Engle, R.F., Lilien, D.M. and Robins, R.P. (1987) Estimating time varying risk premia in the term structure: The ARCH-M model. *Econometrica* 55(2), 391–407.

Engle, R.F., Ng, V. and Rothschild, M. (1990) Asset pricing with a factor ARCH covariance structure: Empirical estimates for Treasury bills. *Journal of Econometrics* 45, 213–238.

Füss, R. and Kaiser, D.G. (2007) The tactical and strategic value of hedge fund strategies: A cointegration approach. *Financial Markets and Portfolio Management*. To appear. doi: 10.1007/s11408-007-0060-8.

Garcia, R. (1998) Asymptotic null distribution of the likelihood ratio test in Markov switching models. *International Economic Review* 39(3), 763–788.

Gatheral, J. and Oomen, R. (2007) Zero-intelligence realized variance estimation. Working paper available from SSRN. http://ssrn.com/abstract=970358 (accessed November 2007).

Geman, G. (2005) Energy commodity prices: Is mean-reversion dead? *Journal of Alternative Investments* 8(1).

Ghysels, E. and Jasiak, J. (1998) GARCH for irregularly spaced financial data: The ACD-GARCH model. *Studies in Nonlinear Dynamics and Econometrics* 2, 133–149.

Ghysels, E., Gouriéroux, C. and Jasiak, J. (1998) High frequency financial time series data: Some stylised facts and models of stochastic volatility. In C. Dunis and B. Zhou. (eds) *Non-linear Modelling of High Frequency Financial Time Series*. John Wiley & Sons, Ltd, Chichester.

Giot, P. (2003) The information content of implied volatility in agricultural commodity markets. *Journal of Futures Markets* 23(5), 441–454.

Giot, P. (2005) Implied volatility indexes and daily value at risk models. *Journal of Derivatives* 12, 54–64.

Glasserman, P. (2004) *Monte Carlo Methods in Financial Engineering*. Springer, New York.

Glosten, L.R., Jagannathan, R. and Runkle, D.E. (1993) On the relation between the expected value of the volatility of the nominal excess return on stocks. *Journal of Finance* 48, 1779–1801.

Goodhart, C. (1988) The foreign exchange market: A random walk with a dragging anchor. *Economica* 55, 437–460.

Goodhart, C.A.E. and O'Hara, M. (1997) High frequency data in financial markets: Issues and applications. *Journal of Empirical Finance* 4, 73–114.

Goodhart, C.A.E., Hall, S.G., Henry, S.G.B. and Pesaran, B. (1993) News effects in a high-frequency model of the sterling–dollar exchange rate. *Journal of Applied Econometrics* 8, 1–13.

Gouriéroux, C., (1997) *ARCH Models and Financial Applications*. Springer, New York.

Gouriéroux, C., Monfort, A. and Renault, E. (1991) A general framework for factor models. Institut National de la Statistique et des Etudes Economiques No. 9107.

Grammig, J. and Fernandes, M. (2006) A family of autoregressive conditional duration models. *Journal of Econometrics* 130, 1–23.

Granger, C.W.J. (1986) Developments in the study of cointegrated economic variables. *Oxford Bulletin of Economics and Statistics* 42(3), 213–227.

Gray, S.F. (1996) Modeling the conditional distribution of interest rates as a regime-switching process. *Journal of Financial Economics* 42, 27–62.

Greene, W. (2007) *Econometric Analysis*, 6th edition. Prentice Hall, Upper Saddle River, NJ.

Gross, J. (2003) *Linear Regression*. Lecture Notes in Statistics, Springer, 2003.

Guillaume, D.M., Dacorogna, M. and Pictet, O.V. (1997) From the bird's eye to the microscope: A survey of new stylised facts of the intra-daily foreign exchange markets. *Finance and Stochastics* 1, 95–129.

Haas, M., Mittnik, S. and Paolella, M.S. (2004a) Mixed normal conditional heteroskedasticity. *Journal of Financial Econometrics* 2(2), 211–250.

Haas, M., Mittnik, S. and Paolella, M.S. (2004b) A new approach to Markov-switching GARCH models. *Journal of Financial Econometrics* 2(4), 493–530.

Hakkio, C.S. and Rush, M. (1989) Market efficiency and cointegration: An application to the sterling and Deutschmark exchange markets. *Journal of International Money and Finance* 8, 75–88.

Hall, A.D., Anderson, H.M. and Granger, C.W.J. (1992) A cointegration analysis of Treasury bill yields. *Review of Economics and Statistics* 74(1), 116–126.

Hall, S.G., Psaradakis, Z. and Sola, M. (1999) Detecting periodically collapsing bubbles: A Markov switching unit root test. *Journal of Applied Econometrics* 14, 143–154.

Hamilton, J.D. (1989) A new approach to the economic analysis of nonstationary time series and the business cycle. *Econometrica* 57, 357–384.

Hamilton, J.D. (1994) *Time Series Analysis*. Princeton University Press, Princeton, NJ.

Hamilton, J.D. and Lin, G. (1996) Stock market volatility and the business cycle. *Journal of Applied Econometrics* 11(5), 573–593.

Hamilton, J.D. and Susmel, R. (1994) Autoregressive conditional heteroscedasticity and changes in regime. *Journal of Econometrics* 64, 307–333.

Hansen, B. (1992) The likelihood ratio test under non-standard conditions: Testing the Markov switching model of GNP. *Journal of Applied Econometrics* 7, S61–S82.

Hansen, B. (1996) Erratum: The likelihood ratio test under non-standard conditions: Testing the Markov switching model of GNP. *Journal of Applied Econometrics* 11, 195–198.

Harris, F.H.deB., McInish, T.H., Shoesmith, G.L. and Wood, R.A. (1995) Cointegration, error correction, and price discovery on informationally linked security markets. *Journal of Financial and Quantitative Analysis* 30(4), 563–579.

Harvey, A. (1981) *The Econometric Analysis of Time Series*. Phillip Allan, Oxford.

Harvey, C.R. and Siddique, A. (1999) Autoregressive conditional skewness. *Journal of Financial and Quantitative Analysis* 34, 465–487.

Hendry, D.F. (1986) Econometric modelling with cointegrated variables: An overview. *Oxford Bulletin of Economics and Statistics* 48(3), 201–212.

Heston, S. (1993) A closed form solution for options with stochastic volatility with applications to bond and currency options. *Review of Financial Studies* 6(2), 327–343.

Heston, S. and Nandi, S. (2000) A closed form GARCH option pricing model. *Review of Financial Studies* 13, 585–625.

Johansen, S. (1988) Statistical analysis of cointegration vectors. *Journal of Economic Dynamics and Control* 12, 231–254.

Johansen, S. (1991) Estimation and hypothesis testing of cointegration vectors in Gaussian vector autoregressive models. *Econometrica* 59(6), 1551–1580.

Johansen, S. and Juselius, K. (1990) Maximum likelihood estimation and inference on cointegration – with applications to the demand for money. *Oxford Bulletin of Economics and Statistics* 52(2), 169–210.

Jones, C.M., Kaul, G. and Lipton, M.L. (1994) Transactions, volume and volatility. *Review of Financial Studies* 7, 631–651.

Karfakis, C.J. and Moschos, D.M. (1990) Interest rate linkages within the European Monetary System: A time series analysis. *Journal of Money, Credit, and Banking* 22(3), 388–394.

Kasa, K. (1992) Common stochastic trends in international stock markets. *Journal of Monetary Economics* 29, 95–124.

Khoury N.T. and Yourougou, P. (1991) The informational content of the basis: Evidence from Canadian barley, oats and canola futures markets. *Journal of Futures Markets* 11(1), 69–80.

Kim, C.J. (1994) Dynamic linear models with Markov switching. *Journal of Econometrics* 60, 1–22.

Kim T.-H., Stone, D. and White, H. (2005) Asymptotic and Bayesian confidence intervals for Sharpe style weights. *Journal of Financial Econometrics* 3(3), 315–343.

Klaassen, F. (2002) Improving GARCH volatility forecasts with regime-switching GARCH. *Empirical Economics* 27, 363–394.

Koenker, R. (2005) *Quantile Regression*. Cambridge University Press, Cambridge.

Koenker, R. and Bassett, G., Jr (1978) Regression quantiles. *Econometrica* 46(1), 33–50.

Koenker, R. and Hallock, K. (2001) Quantile regression. *Journal of Economic Perspectives* 15, 143–156.

Kole, E., Koedijk, K. and M. Verbeek, M. (2007) Selecting copulas for risk management. *Journal of Banking and Finance* 31(8), 2405–2423.

Lambert, P. and Laurent, S. (2001) Modelling financial time series using GARCH-type models with a skewed Student distribution for the innovations. Discussion Paper 0125, Institut de Statistique, Louvain-la-Neuve, Belgium.

Laurent, S. and Peters, J.-P. (2002) G@RCH 2.2: An Ox package for estimating and forecasting various ARCH models. *Journal of Economic Surveys*, 16(3), 447–485.

Laurent, S., Bauwens, L. and Rombouts, J. (2006) Multivariate GARCH models: A survey. *Journal of Applied Econometrics* 21(1), 79–109.

Lee, T.-H. (1994) Spread and volatility in spot and forward exchange rates. *Journal of International Money and Finance* 13(3), 375–383.

Lindskog, F., McNeil, A. and Schmock, U. (2003) Kendall's tau for elliptical distributions. In G. Bol, G. Nakhaeizadeh, S.T. Rachev, T. Ridder and K.-H. Vollmer (eds), *Credit Risk: Measurement, Evaluation and Management*. Physica-Verlag, Heidelberg.

Low, A. and Muthuswamy, J. (1996) Information flows in high-frequency exchange rates. In C. Dunis (ed.), *Forecasting Financial Markets*. John Wiley & Sons, Ltd, Chichester.

Lundbergh, S. and Teräsvirta, T. (2002) Evaluating GARCH models. *Journal of Econometrics* 110, 417–435.

MacDonald, R. and Taylor, M. (1988) Metals prices, efficiency and cointegration: Some evidence from the London Metal Exchange. *Bulletin of Economic Research* 40, 235–239.

MacDonald, R. and Taylor, M. (1994) The monetary model of the exchange rate: Long-run relationships, short-run dynamics and how to beat a random walk. *Journal of International Money and Finance* 13(3), 276–290.

MacKinnon, J. (1991) Critical values for the cointegration tests. In R.F. Engle and C.W.J. Granger (eds), *Long-Run Economic Relationships*, pp. 267–276. Oxford University Press, Oxford.

Madhavan, A.N. (2000) Market microstructure: A survey. *Journal of Financial Markets* 3, 205–258.

Maheu, J.M. and McCurdy, T.H. (2000) Identifying bull and bear markets in stock returns. *Journal of Business and Economic Statistics* 18(1), 100–112.

Malevergne, Y. and Sornette, D. (2003) Testing the Gaussian copula hypothesis for financial assets dependences. *Quantitative Finance* 3(4), 231–250.

Mandelbrot, B. (1963) The variation of certain speculative prices. *Journal of Business* 36, 394–419.

Markowitz, H. (1959) *Portfolio Selection*. John Wiley & Sons, Inc, New York.

Mayhew, S. and Stivers, C. (2003) Stock return dynamics, options, and the information content of implied volatility. *Journal of Futures Markets* 23, 615–646.

McNeil A.J., Frey, R. and Embrechts, P. (2005) *Quantitative Risk Management: Concepts, Techniques and Tools*. Princeton University Press, Princeton, NJ.

Nelsen, R.B. (2006) *An Introduction to Copulas*, 2nd edition. Springer, New York.

Nelson, D.B. (1991) Conditional heteroskedasticity in asset returns: A new approach. *Econometrica* 59, 347–370.

Ng, A. (2000) Volatility spillover effects from Japan and the US to the Pacific-Basin. *Journal of International Money and Finance* 19, 207–233.

Nieuwland, F.G.M., Verschoor, W., Willen, F.C. and Wolff, C.C.P. (1994) Stochastic trends and jumps in EMS exchange rates. *Journal of International Money and Finance* 13(6), 669–727.

Nishina. K., Maghrebi, N. and Kim, M.-S. (2006) Stock market volatility and the forecasting accuracy of implied volatility indices. Osaka University Discussion Papers in Economics and Business No. 06–09.

Nugent, J. (1990) Further evidence of forward exchange market efficiency: An application of cointegration using German and U.K. data. *Economic and Social Reviews* 22, 35–42.

Oomen, R. (2001) Using high frequency stock market index data to calculate, model & forecast realized return variance. Unpublished manuscript, revised version, available from SSRN.

Oomen, R.C. (2006) Properties of realized variance under alternative sampling schemes. *Journal of Business and Economic Statistics* 24(2), 219–237.

Patton, A. (2008) Copula-based models for financial time series. In T.G. Andersen, R.A. Davis, J.-P. Kreiss and T. Mikosch (eds), *Handbook of Financial Time Series*. Springer, Berlin. To appear.

Perez-Quiros, G. and Timmermann, A. (2000) Firm size and cyclical variation in stock returns. *Journal of Finance* 50, 1229–1262.

Pézier, J. (2007) Global portfolio optimization revisited: A least discrimination alternative to Black-Litterman. ICMA Centre Discussion Papers in Finance, DP2007-07.

Phillips, P.C.B. and Perron, P. (1988) Testing for a unit root in time series regressions. *Biometrika* 75, 335–346.

Phillips, P.C.B. and Ouliaris, S. (1990) Asymptotic properties of residual based tests for cointegration. *Econometrica* 58, 165–193.

Plerou, V., Gopikrishnan, P., Rosenow, B., Amaral, N., Guhr, T. and Stanley, E. (2002) Random matrix approach to cross correlations in financial data. *Physical Review E* 65, 1–18.

Pong, S., Shackleton, M., Taylor, S. and Xu, X. (2004) Forecasting currency volatility: A comparison of implied volatilities and AR(FI)MA models. *Journal of Banking and Finance* 28, 2541–2563.

Poon, S. and Granger, C.W.J. (2003) Forecasting volatility in financial markets: A review. *Journal of Economic Literature* 41, 478–539.

Proietti, T. (1997) Short-run dynamics in cointegrated systems. *Oxford Bulletin of Economics and Statistics* 59, 405–422.

Psaradakis, Z. and Sola, M. (1998) Finite-sample properties of the maximum likelihood estimator in autoregressive models with Markov switching. *Journal of Econometrics* 86, 369–386.

Ross, S. (1976) The arbitrage theory of capital asset pricing. *Journal of Economic Theory* 8, 343–362.

Rydén, T., Teräsvirta, T. and Asbrink, S. (1998) Stylized facts of daily return series and the hidden Markov model. *Journal of Applied Econometrics* 13, 217–244.

Schroeder, T.C. and Goodwin, B.K. (1991) Price discovery and cointegration for live hogs. *Journal of Futures Markets* 11(6), 685–696.

Schwarz, T.V. and Laatsch, F.E. (1991) Dynamic efficiency and price discovery leadership in stock index cash and futures market. *Journal of Futures Markets* 11(6), 669–684.

Schwarz, T.V. and Szakmary, A.C. (1994) Price discovery in petroleum markets: Arbitrage, cointegration, and the time interval of analysis. *Journal of Futures Markets* 14(2), 147–167.

Sharpe, W. (1964) Capital asset prices: A theory of market equilibrium under conditions of risk. *Journal of Finance* 19, 425–442.

Sharpe, W. (1988) Determining the fund's effective asset mix. *Investment Management Review*, November–December, 59–69.

Sharpe, W. (1992) Asset allocation: Management style and performance measurement. *Journal of Portfolio Management* 18, 7–19.

Sheedy, E., Trevor, R. and Wood, J. (1999) Asset allocation decisions when risk is changing. *Journal of Financial Research* 22(3), 301–315.

Sklar, A. (1959) Fonctions de répartition à *n* dimensions et leurs marges. *Publications de l'Institut de Statistique de l'Université de Paris*, 8, 229–231.

Smith, K.L., Brocato, J. and Rogers, J.E. (1993) Regularities in the data between major equity markets: Evidence from Granger causality tests. *Applied Financial Economics* 3, 55–60.

Stock, J.H. and Watson, M.W. (1988) Testing for common trends. *Journal of the American Statistical Association* 83, 1097–1107.

Szakmary, A., Ors, E., Kim, J.K. and Davidson, W.N. (2003) The predictive power of implied volatility: Evidence from 35 futures markets. *Journal of Banking and Finance* 27, 2151–2175.

Tauchen, G.E. and Pitts, M. (1983) The price variability–volume relationship on speculative markets. *Econometrica* 51, 485–505.

Taylor, J. (1999) A quantile regression approach to estimating the distribution of multi-period returns. *Journal of Derivatives* 7, 64–78.

Taylor, M.P. and Tonks, I. (1989) The internationalisation of stock markets and the abolition of UK exchange control. *Review of Economics and Statistics* 2, 332–336.

Teräsvirta, T. (2006) An introduction to univariate GARCH models. SSE/EFI Working Papers in Economics and Finance No. 646.

Tsay, R. (2005) *Analysis of Financial Time Series*, 2nd edition. John Wiley & Sons, Inc., Hoboken, NJ.

Van der Weide, R. (2002) GO-GARCH: A multivariate generalized orthogonal GARCH model. *Journal of Applied Econometrics* 17, 549–564.

Vidyamurthy, G. (2004) *Pairs Trading: Quantitative Methods and Analysis*. John Wiley & Sons, Ltd, Chichester.

Zhou, B. (1996) High frequency data and volatility in foreign exchange markets. *Journal of Business and Economic Statistics* 14, 45–52.

Zivot, E. and Andrews, D.W.K. (1992) Further evidence on the great crash, the oil-price shock and the unit root hypothesis. *Journal of Business and Economic Statistics* 10, 251–270.

Index